Merrill Algebra One

Foster • Rath • Winters

Charles E. Merrill Publishing Co.
Columbus, Ohio

Authors

Alan G. Foster is chairman of the Mathematics Department at Addison Trail High School, Addison, Illinois. He has taught mathematics courses at every level of the high school curriculum. Mr. Foster obtained his B.S. from Illinois State University and his M.A. in mathematics from the University of Illinois, with additional work at Northern Illinois University, Purdue, Northwestern, and Princeton. Mr. Foster is active in professional organizations at local, state, and national levels, frequently speaking and conducting workshops. He is a past president of the Illinois Council of Teachers of Mathematics. Mr. Foster is a co-author of *Merrill Geometry*.

James N. Rath has 25 years of classroom experience in teaching mathematics at every level of the high school curriculum. He has also taught calculus at the college level. Mr. Rath is a former head of the Mathematics Department at Darien High School, Darien, Connecticut. He earned his B.A. in Philosophy from the Catholic University of America. He obtained both his M.Ed. and his M.A. in mathematics from Boston College. He developed a minicourse in BASIC for the Darien Public Schools. Mr. Rath is a member of various professional organizations in which he is active at local, state, and national levels. He is a co-author of *Merrill Pre-Algebra*.

Leslie J. Winters is chairperson of the Mathematics Department at John F. Kennedy High School, Granada Hills, California. He has taught mathematics at every level from junior high to college. He received his B.A. in mathematics from Pepperdine University, his B.S. in secondary education from the University of Dayton, his M.S. in secondary education from the University of Southern California, and his M.A. in mathematics from Boston College. Mr. Winters is a frequent speaker at local, state, and national conferences. He is a past president of the California Mathematics Council–Southern Section. Mr. Winters was one of two recipients of the 1983 Presidential Award for Excellence in Mathematics Teaching in the state of California.

ISBN 0-675-05476-1
Published by
Charles E. Merrill Publishing Co.
Columbus, Ohio

Printed in the United States of America

12 13 14 15 VH 00 99 98 97 96 95 94 93

Consultants

Jack Price
Superintendent of Schools
Palos Verdes, California

Margaret J. Kenney
Assistant to the Director
Mathematics Institute
Boston College
Chestnut Hill, Massachusetts

Reviewers

Ronald L. Ashby
Secondary Math Chairperson
Terre Haute North Vigo High School
Terre Haute, Indiana

Carl Blair
Mathematics and
    Computer Science Teacher
Mustang Public Schools
Mustang, Oklahoma

Dorothy Coleman
Mathematics Teacher
John C. Fremont High School
Los Angeles, California

Diane M. Fite
Mathematics Teacher
Temple High School
Temple, Texas

Mary Hines
Mathematics Department Chairperson
Manzano High School
Albuquerque, New Mexico

Charles E. Loyet
Coordinator of Mathematics/Testing
Carman/Ainsworth Community Schools
Flint, Michigan

Eileen McGinty
Mathematics Teacher
Robert E. Lee High School
Baton Rouge, Louisiana

Harry J. Needham
Mathematics Teacher
Yuma High School
Yuma, Arizona

Winston J. Rose
Mathematics Department Chairperson
Masconomet Regional School
Topsfield, Massachusetts

Sylvia Shugart
Mathematics Teacher and
    Department Chairperson
Clovis High School
Clovis, New Mexico

Staff

Editorial

Series Editor: Evangeline Seltzer; *Project Editor:* Susan Danko;
Editor: Jane Seliga; *Photo Editor:* Lindsay Gerard;
Production Editor: Joy Dickerson

Art:

Book Designer and Project Artist: Larry W. Collins; *Artist:* Jeffrey A. Clark

Photo Credits

Preface

This third edition of *Merrill Algebra One* is designed for use by students in first-year high school algebra courses. The text, which was developed in the classroom by experienced high school teachers, is based on the successful prior editions of *Merrill Algebra One*. The goals of the text are to develop proficiency with mathematical skills, to expand understanding of mathematical concepts, to improve logical thinking, and to promote success. To achieve these goals, the following strategies are used.

Build upon a Solid Foundation. This program develops and utilizes the learning spiral. Students first review those concepts basic to the understanding of algebra. Students' understanding is thus solidified before the introduction of more difficult concepts.

Utilize Sound Pedagogy. *Merrill Algebra One* covers in logical sequence all topics generally presented at this level. Concepts are introduced when they are needed. Each concept presented is then used within that lesson and in later lessons.

Gear Presentation for Learning. An appropriate reading level has been maintained throughout the text. Furthermore, many photographs, illustrations, charts, graphs, and tables provide visual aids for the concepts and skills presented. Hence, students are able to read and learn with increased understanding.

Use Relevant Real-Life Applications. Applications are provided not only for practice but also to aid understanding of how concepts are used.

The text offers a variety of aids for the students.

Student Annotations	Help students identify important concepts as they study.
Selected Answers	Allow students to check their progress as they work. These answers are provided at the back of the text.
Mini-Review	Provides students with a quick review of skills and concepts taught previously.
Vocabulary	Enables students to focus on increasing their mathematical vocabulary.
Chapter Summary	Provides students with a compact listing of major concepts presented within each chapter.
Chapter Review	Permits students to review each chapter by working sample problems from each lesson.
Chapter Test	Enables students to check their own progress.
Cumulative Review	Helps students to maintain their skills in applying algebraic concepts.
Standardized Test Practice Questions	Help students to become familiar with types of questions that appear on standardized tests.

The following special features, which appear periodically throughout the text, provide interesting and useful extra topics.

Using Calculators	Instructs students in using a calculator. The use of the calculator is related to concepts taught within the chapter.
Reading Algebra	Provides students with the instruction needed to read and interpret mathematical symbolism.
Problem Solving	Illustrates several helpful strategies for solving mathematical problems.
Applications	Provide insights into the uses of mathematics in everyday life, from a variety of disciplines.
Using Computers	Provides a computer program and exercises related to the objectives of the chapter.
Excursions in Algebra	Enliven and help maintain student interest by providing interesting side trips. Topics are varied and include history, glimpses into development of algebra, enrichment concepts, and puzzles.

The textbook contains an appendix on **BASIC** which provides instruction in writing programs using the BASIC computer language.

The **Algebraic Skills Review** at the back of the text provides review exercises to help students maintain algebraic skills. These exercises can be used for remediation, to supplement exercises in the lessons, and as review material at the end of the school year.

Teacher and students familiar with the prior editions of this text will be pleased to see that the clarity of explanations and careful sequencing of topics have been retained in this new edition of *Merrill Algebra One*.

Table of Contents

3 Multiplying and Dividing Rational Numbers _____ 74

4 Inequalities _____ 110

5 Powers _____ 144

6 Polynomials _____ 174

7 Factoring ——————————————— 210

8 Applications of Factoring —————————— 244

9 Functions and Graphs 270

10 Lines and Slopes 304

11 Systems of Open Sentences _____ 336

12 Radical Expressions _____ 370

13 Quadratics ———————— 404

14 Rational Expressions ———————— 436

15 Applications of Rational Expressions —————— 468

16 Trigonometry ————————————— 498

Appendix: BASIC ————————————————

To the Student

When you read this book, you should look for special features. These features will help you in studying algebra. Consider the following features when studying section.

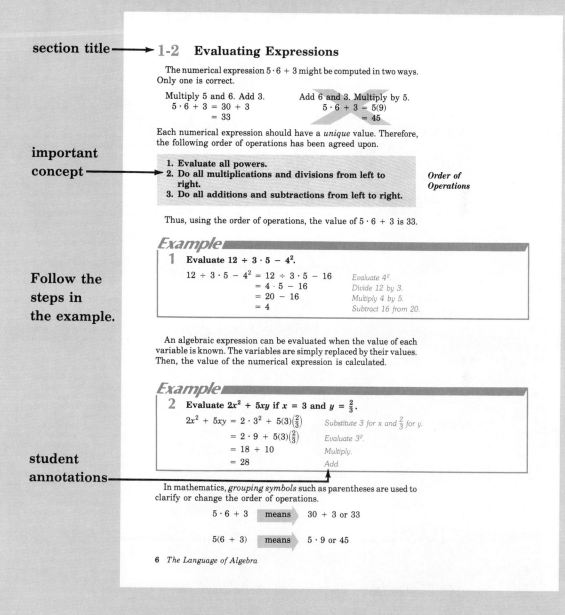

section title →

1-2 Evaluating Expressions

The numerical expression $5 \cdot 6 + 3$ might be computed in two ways. Only one is correct.

Multiply 5 and 6. Add 3.
$$5 \cdot 6 + 3 = 30 + 3$$
$$= 33$$

Add 6 and 3. Multiply by 5.
$$5 \cdot 6 + 3 = 5(9)$$
$$= 45$$

Each numerical expression should have a *unique* value. Therefore, the following order of operations has been agreed upon.

important concept →

1. **Evaluate all powers.**
2. **Do all multiplications and divisions from left to right.**
3. **Do all additions and subtractions from left to right.**

Order of Operations

Thus, using the order of operations, the value of $5 \cdot 6 + 3$ is 33.

Example

Follow the steps in the example.

1 Evaluate $12 \div 3 \cdot 5 - 4^2$.

$$12 \div 3 \cdot 5 - 4^2 = 12 \div 3 \cdot 5 - 16 \qquad \textit{Evaluate } 4^2.$$
$$= 4 \cdot 5 - 16 \qquad \textit{Divide 12 by 3.}$$
$$= 20 - 16 \qquad \textit{Multiply 4 by 5.}$$
$$= 4 \qquad \textit{Subtract 16 from 20.}$$

An algebraic expression can be evaluated when the value of each variable is known. The variables are simply replaced by their values. Then, the value of the numerical expression is calculated.

Example

2 Evaluate $2x^2 + 5xy$ if $x = 3$ and $y = \frac{2}{3}$.

$$2x^2 + 5xy = 2 \cdot 3^2 + 5(3)\left(\frac{2}{3}\right) \qquad \textit{Substitute 3 for x and } \tfrac{2}{3} \textit{ for y.}$$
$$= 2 \cdot 9 + 5(3)\left(\frac{2}{3}\right) \qquad \textit{Evaluate } 3^2.$$
$$= 18 + 10 \qquad \textit{Multiply.}$$
$$= 28 \qquad \textit{Add.}$$

student annotations →

In mathematics, *grouping symbols* such as parentheses are used to clarify or change the order of operations.

$$5 \cdot 6 + 3 \quad \boxed{means} \quad 30 + 3 \text{ or } 33$$

$$5(6 + 3) \quad \boxed{means} \quad 5 \cdot 9 \text{ or } 45$$

6 *The Language of Algebra*

At the end of each chapter, use the **Vocabulary** and **Chapter Summary** to review the key ideas. Then use the problems in the **Chapter Review** to review methods of working problems. If you follow these steps, your study of algebra should be interesting and enjoyable.

CHAPTER 1

The Language of Algebra

Many deaf people use sign language to express thoughts and ideas. Each hand signal that they use has a meaning. In mathematics, numbers and math symbols have meanings. In this chapter, you will learn about symbols used in algebra.

1-1 Variables and Expressions

In algebra, verbal expressions are often translated into mathematical expressions. Consider the following sentence.

Kathy has three more dollars than Nick.

From the information given, you do not know exactly how much money Nick has or how much Kathy has. However, you can find the amount Kathy has if you know the amount Nick has.

If Nick has 6 dollars, then Kathy has 6 + 3 dollars.
If Nick has 10 dollars, then Kathy has 10 + 3 dollars.
If Nick has n dollars, then Kathy has n + 3 dollars.

The letter n is a **variable**, and $n + 3$ is an algebraic **expression**. In algebra, variables are symbols that are used to represent unspecified numbers. Any letter may be used as a variable.

6 + 3 and 10 + 3 are numerical expressions.

An algebraic expression consists of one or more numbers and variables with the operations of addition, subtraction, multiplication, and/or division. Some algebraic expressions are shown below.

$$ab + 4 \qquad \frac{s}{t} - 1 \qquad 6a(4n) \qquad 8rs \cdot 3k$$

In a multiplication expression, the quantities being multiplied are called **factors** and the result is called the **product**. In a division expression, the **dividend** is divided by the **divisor**. The result is called the **quotient**.

$$4 \times 5 \times 8 = 160 \qquad\qquad 12 \div 3 = 4$$

factors   product   dividend divisor quotient

In algebraic expressions, a dot or parentheses are often used instead of × to indicate multiplication. When variables are used to represent factors, the multiplication sign is usually omitted. Each of the following expressions represents the product of a and b.

$$ab \qquad\qquad a \cdot b \qquad\qquad a(b)$$

A fraction bar is often used to indicate division.

$$\frac{x}{3} \qquad \text{means} \qquad x \div 3$$

To solve verbal problems in mathematics, words must be translated into mathematical symbols. Thus, "the product of 3 and 4" becomes "3 · 4." The following chart shows some of the words that are used to indicate mathematical operations.

ADDITION	SUBTRACTION	MULTIPLICATION	DIVISION
the sum of	the difference of	the product of	the quotient of
increased by	decreased by	multiplied by	divided by
plus	minus	times	the ratio of
more than	less than		
the total of	subtracted from		
added to			

Example

1 **Write an algebraic expression for each verbal expression.**

a. x decreased by 9
The algebraic expression is $x - 9$.

b. the sum of a and b
The algebraic expression is $a + b$.

c. a number k divided by a number n
The algebraic expression is $\frac{k}{n}$.

In an expression like 10^3, the 10 names the **base** and the 3 names the **exponent**. An exponent indicates the number of times the base is used as a factor.

3^4 **means** $3 \cdot 3 \cdot 3 \cdot 3$ a^2 **means** $a \cdot a$ *An expression in the form x^n is called a* power.

Study the following chart.

Symbols	Words	Meaning
8^1	8 to the first power	8
8^2	8 to the second power or 8 squared	$8 \cdot 8$
8^3	8 to the third power or 8 cubed	$8 \cdot 8 \cdot 8$
8^4	8 to the fourth power	$8 \cdot 8 \cdot 8 \cdot 8$
$6n^5$	6 times n to the fifth power	$6 \cdot n \cdot n \cdot n \cdot n \cdot n$

Examples

2 Evaluate 2^5.

$2^5 = 2 \cdot 2 \cdot 2 \cdot 2 \cdot 2$
$\quad = 32$

3 Evaluate 29^2.

$29^2 = 29 \cdot 29$
$\quad\ \ = 841$

4 Write an algebraic expression for the following verbal expression:
the cube of a number y decreased by nine.

The algebraic expression is $y^3 - 9$.

Exploratory Exercises

Write an algebraic expression for each verbal expression.

1. the product of x and 7
2. the quotient of r and s
3. the total of a and 19
4. a number c increased by 10
5. a number b to the third power
6. 7 less than w
7. 2 divided by a number k
8. a number h cubed
9. 25 squared
10. 16 multiplied by m
11. a number n decreased by 4
12. 9 to the fifth power

State a verbal expression for each of the following.

13. x^2
14. n^4
15. 5^3
16. y^5
17. n^1
18. z^7

Written Exercises

Write each of the following as an expression using exponents.

1. $5 \cdot 5 \cdot 5$
2. $4 \cdot 4 \cdot 4 \cdot 4$
3. $7 \cdot a \cdot a \cdot a \cdot a$
4. $2(m)(m)(m)$
5. $\frac{1}{2} \cdot a \cdot a \cdot b \cdot b \cdot b$
6. $\frac{3}{4} \cdot x \cdot y \cdot y \cdot y \cdot y \cdot y$
7. $5 \cdot 5 \cdot 5 \cdot x \cdot x \cdot y$
8. $3 \cdot 3 \cdot a \cdot a \cdot a$

Write an algebraic expression for each verbal expression. Use x as the variable.

9. a number increased by 17
10. seven times a number
11. the cube of a number
12. a number to the sixth power
13. twice the square of a number
14. one-half the square of a number
15. 8 times a number decreased by 17
16. twice a number decreased by 25
17. 94 increased by twice a number
18. twice the cube of a number
19. three-fourths of the square of a number
20. the product of 7 and the cube of a number
21. the cube of a number increased by seven
22. 29 increased by the square of a number

Evaluate each expression.

23. 2^4
24. 6^2
25. 5^3
26. 10^4
27. 4^5
28. 3^6

1-2 Evaluating Expressions

The numerical expression $5 \cdot 6 + 3$ might be computed in two ways. Only one is correct.

Multiply 5 and 6. Add 3.
$$5 \cdot 6 + 3 = 30 + 3$$
$$= 33$$

Add 6 and 3. Multiply by 5.
$$5 \cdot 6 + 3 = 5(9)$$
$$= 45$$

Each numerical expression should have a *unique* value. Therefore, the following order of operations has been agreed upon.

> 1. Evaluate all powers.
> 2. Do all multiplications and divisions from left to right.
> 3. Do all additions and subtractions from left to right.

Order of Operations

Thus, using the order of operations, the value of $5 \cdot 6 + 3$ is 33.

Example 1

Evaluate $12 \div 3 \cdot 5 - 4^2$.

$$\begin{aligned} 12 \div 3 \cdot 5 - 4^2 &= 12 \div 3 \cdot 5 - 16 & \text{\textit{Evaluate } } 4^2. \\ &= 4 \cdot 5 - 16 & \text{\textit{Divide 12 by 3.}} \\ &= 20 - 16 & \text{\textit{Multiply 4 by 5.}} \\ &= 4 & \text{\textit{Subtract 16 from 20.}} \end{aligned}$$

An algebraic expression can be evaluated when the value of each variable is known. The variables are simply replaced by their values. Then, the value of the numerical expression is calculated.

Example 2

Evaluate $2x^2 + 5xy$ if $x = 3$ and $y = \frac{2}{3}$.

$$\begin{aligned} 2x^2 + 5xy &= 2 \cdot 3^2 + 5(3)\left(\tfrac{2}{3}\right) & \text{\textit{Substitute 3 for x and } } \tfrac{2}{3} \text{ \textit{for y.}} \\ &= 2 \cdot 9 + 5(3)\left(\tfrac{2}{3}\right) & \text{\textit{Evaluate } } 3^2. \\ &= 18 + 10 & \text{\textit{Multiply.}} \\ &= 28 & \text{\textit{Add.}} \end{aligned}$$

In mathematics, *grouping symbols* such as parentheses are used to clarify or change the order of operations.

$5 \cdot 6 + 3$ means $30 + 3$ or 33

$5(6 + 3)$ means $5 \cdot 9$ or 45

The basic grouping symbols used are parentheses, ( ), brackets, [ ], and the fraction bar. Parentheses and brackets indicate that the expression within is to be treated as a single value and should be evaluated first. A fraction bar indicates that the numerator and denominator should each be treated as a single value.

When more than one grouping symbol is used, start evaluating expressions within the innermost grouping symbols.

Examples

3 **Evaluate $3(2 + 5)^2 \div 7$.**

$$
\begin{aligned}
3(2 + 5)^2 \div 7 &= 3(7)^2 \div 7 & \textit{Add 2 and 5.} \\
&= 3(49) \div 7 & \textit{Evaluate } 7^2. \\
&= 147 \div 7 & \textit{Multiply 3 by 49.} \\
&= 21 & \textit{Divide 147 by 7.}
\end{aligned}
$$

4 **Evaluate $\frac{2}{3}[8(a - b)^2 + 3b]$ if $a = 5$ and $b = 2$.**

$$
\begin{aligned}
\frac{2}{3}[8(a - b)^2 + 3b] &= \frac{2}{3}[8(5 - 2)^2 + 3 \cdot 2] & \textit{Substitute 5 for a and 2 for b.} \\
&= \frac{2}{3}[8(3)^2 + 3 \cdot 2] & \textit{Subtract 2 from 5.} \\
&= \frac{2}{3}[8 \cdot 9 + 3 \cdot 2] & \textit{Evaluate } 3^2. \\
&= \frac{2}{3}[72 + 6] & \textit{Multiply 8 by 9 and 3 by 2.} \\
&= \frac{2}{3}[78] & \textit{Add 72 and 6.} \\
&= 52 & \textit{Multiply } \tfrac{2}{3} \textit{ by 78.}
\end{aligned}
$$

5 **Evaluate $\dfrac{b^2 - 2}{b + x^3}$ if $b = 5$ and $x = 3$.**

$$
\begin{aligned}
\frac{b^2 - 2}{b + x^3} &= \frac{5^2 - 2}{5 + 3^3} & \textit{Substitute 5 for b and 3 for x.} \\
&= \frac{25 - 2}{5 + 27} & \textit{Simplify the numerator and the denominator.} \\
&= \frac{23}{32}
\end{aligned}
$$

Exploratory Exercises

State how to evaluate each expression. Do *not* evaluate.

1. $3 + 2 \cdot 4$
2. $2 \cdot 4 + 3$
3. $8 \div 4 \cdot 2$
4. $8 \cdot 2 \div 4$
5. $12 - 6 \cdot 2$
6. $(12 - 6) \cdot 2$
7. $(9 - 3)^2$
8. $9 - 3^2$
9. $9^2 - 3^2$
10. $3(3^2 - 3)$
11. $7 \cdot 3^2$
12. $7^2 \cdot 2$
13. $4(5 - 3)^2$
14. $8 \div 2 + 6 \cdot 2$
15. $(8 + 6) \div 2 + 2$
16. $8 + 6 \div (2 + 1)$

Written Exercises

Evaluate each expression.

1. $3 + 8 \div 2 - 5$
2. $4 + 7 \cdot 2 + 8$
3. $12 \div 4 + 15 \cdot 3$
4. $3 \cdot 6 - 12 \div 4$
5. $5(9 + 3) - 3 \cdot 4$
6. $7(8 - 4) + 11$
7. $29 - 3(9 - 4)$
8. $4(11 + 7) - 9 \cdot 8$
9. $12 \cdot 6 \div 3 \cdot 2 \div 8$
10. $16 \div 2 \cdot 5 \cdot 3 \div 6$
11. $288 \div [3(9 + 3)]$
12. $196 \div [4(11 - 4)]$
13. $5^3 + 6^3 - 5^2$
14. $6(4^3 + 2^2)$
15. $\dfrac{38 - 12}{2 \cdot 13}$
16. $\dfrac{9 \cdot 4 + 2 \cdot 6}{7 \cdot 7}$
17. $\dfrac{9 \cdot 3 - 4^2}{3^2 + 2^2}$
18. $\dfrac{2 \cdot 8^2 - 2^2 \cdot 8}{2 \cdot 8}$
19. $\frac{2}{3}(16) - \frac{1}{3}(6)$
20. $\frac{3}{4}(6) + \frac{1}{3}(12)$
21. $\frac{1}{2}(8 + 30) - 4$
22. $25 - \frac{1}{3}(18 + 9)$
23. $0.2(0.6) + 3(0.4)$
24. $7(0.2 + 0.5) - 0.6$

Evaluate if $a = 6$, $b = 4$, $c = 3$, $d = \frac{1}{2}$, $e = \frac{2}{3}$, $x = 0.2$, and $y = 1.3$.

25. $a + b^2 + c^2$
26. $3ab - c^2$
27. $8(a - c)^2 + 3$
28. $\dfrac{a^2 - b^2}{2}$
29. $\dfrac{2ab - c^3}{7}$
30. $12d + bc$
31. $d(a + b) - c$
32. $a(8 - 3e) + 4d$
33. $ax + bc$
34. $5y + 3$
35. $x^2 + 6d$
36. $c^2 + y^2$
37. $(100x)^2 + 10y$
38. $(15x)^3 - y$
39. $\dfrac{a + b^2}{3bc}$
40. $\dfrac{4d^2}{4ce}$
41. $\dfrac{8b^2c}{x}$
42. $\dfrac{6ab^2}{x + y}$

Write an algebraic expression for each verbal expression. Then, evaluate the expression if $a = 3$, $b = \frac{1}{2}$, and $c = 0$.

43. twice the sum of a and b
44. twice the product of a and b
45. the square of b increased by c
46. the cube of a decreased by b

Using Calculators _____ Order of Operations

What is the result if you enter the following on your calculator?

ENTER: 25 ⊟ 6 ⊠ 3 ⊟

If the display shows 7, the calculator followed the correct order of operations. It multiplied 6 and 3 first, then subtracted the result from 25.

If the display shows 57, the calculator performed the operations in the order that the keys were pressed. This result is incorrect. How can you get the correct value?

ENTER: 6 ⊠ 3 ⊟   *The display should show 18.*
Then ENTER: 25 ⊟ 18 ⊟

The display should show 7, the correct value of the expression $25 - 6 \times 3$.

Exercises   Evaluate each expression.

1. $70 - 6 \times 8 + 10$
2. $300 - 4 \times 32$
3. $61 \times 4 + 3 \times 47$

1-3   Open Sentences and Equations

Which of the following sentences are true?
Which are false?

A dog has three ears.

California is larger than Rhode Island.

$3 \times 7 = 21$

27 divided by 3 is less than 7.

$\frac{3}{4} + \frac{1}{2} = 1\frac{1}{4}$

Note that each of the previous sentences are either true or false. However, it is not possible to say whether the following sentences are true or false.

Words	Open Sentences
A number x plus six is equal to 8.	$x + 6 = 8$
A number n is less than 10.	$n < 10$
Seven is greater than twice a number c.	$7 > 2c$

Before you can determine whether these sentences are true or false, you must know what numbers will replace the variables x, n, and c. Mathematical sentences such as $x + 6 = 8$ are called **open sentences**. In an open sentence such as $x + 6 = 8$, the variable must be replaced in order to determine if the sentence is true or false.

Open sentences are neither true nor false.

> **Finding the replacements for the variable that make a sentence true is called solving the open sentence. Each replacement is called a solution of the open sentence.**

Solving an
Open Sentence

Is 11 a solution of the open sentence $n < 10$?
Is 3 a solution of the open sentence $x + 6 = 8$?
Try naming some solutions of the three open sentences listed above.

A mathematical sentence that contains an **equals sign**, =, is called an **equation**. Sometimes you can solve an equation by simply performing the indicated operations.

Examples

1 Solve: $a = 9.4 - 3.06$

$$a = 9.4 - 3.06$$
$$= 9.40 - 3.06$$
$$= 6.34$$

The solution is 6.34.

2 Solve: $\frac{5 \cdot 3 + 3}{4 \cdot 2 - 2} = t$

$$\frac{5 \cdot 3 + 3}{4 \cdot 2 - 2} = t$$
$$\frac{15 + 3}{8 - 2} = t$$
$$\frac{18}{6} = t$$
$$3 = t$$

The solution is 3.

Exploratory Exercises

State whether each sentence is true or false.

1. The capital of the U.S. is Houston.
2. Birds have wings.
3. $3(11 - 5) > 18$
4. $15 \div 3 + 7 < 13$
5. $0.01 + 0.01 = 0.0002$
6. $\frac{2}{3}(6) = 9 - 5$
7. $\frac{3 + 15}{6} = \frac{1}{2}(6)$
8. $\frac{1}{2} + \frac{3}{4} = \frac{3}{2} + \frac{1}{4}$
9. $3 - 1\frac{1}{2} = \frac{1}{2}$
10. $21 - 12 > 9$
11. $17 + 3 < 100 \div 4$
12. $0.11 + 1.1 > 1.2$
13. $10\left(\frac{2}{5}\right) = \frac{1}{5} \cdot 2 \cdot 10$
14. $0.101 > 0.110$
15. $7 = 7(0)$
16. $0 + 7 = 7$

Replace the variable to make each open sentence true.

17. x is President of the U.S.
18. There are y states in the U.S.
19. $18 + y = 20$
20. $3 \cdot a = 24$
21. t is an author of this book.
22. $\frac{1}{2}(m) = 10$

Written Exercises

Solve each equation.

1. $x = 8 + 3$
2. $y = 7 - 4$
3. $x = 12 - 0.03$
4. $x = 6 + 0.28$
5. $a = \frac{3}{4} \cdot 12$
6. $\frac{5}{6} \cdot 18 = m$
7. $8.2 - 6.75 = a$
8. $9.6 + 4.53 = b$
9. $a = \frac{12 + 8}{4}$
10. $m = \frac{64 + 4}{17}$
11. $\frac{21 - 3}{12 - 3} = x$
12. $\frac{14 + 28}{4 + 3} = y$
13. $14.8 - 3.75 = a$
14. $29.7 - 5.86 = t$
15. $x = \frac{84 \div 7}{18 \div 9}$
16. $x = \frac{96 \div 6}{8 \div 2}$
17. $\frac{2}{13} + \frac{5}{13} = x$
18. $\frac{3}{7} + \frac{2}{7} = y$
19. $\frac{5}{8} + \frac{1}{4} = x$
20. $\frac{7}{12} + \frac{1}{3} = x$
21. $a = 3\frac{1}{2} \div 2$
22. $m = 3\frac{1}{3} \div 3$
23. $r = 5\frac{1}{2} + \frac{1}{3}$
24. $s = 6\frac{3}{4} + \frac{1}{6}$

The set of numbers that a variable may represent is called a *replacement set*. Find all numbers from the replacement set $\{4, 5, 6, 7, 8\}$ that are solutions to each open sentence.

25. $x + 2 > 7$

26. $10 - x < 7$

27. $\dfrac{x + 3}{2} < 5$

28. $x - 3 > \dfrac{x + 1}{2}$

29. $\dfrac{2(x - 2)}{3} = \dfrac{4}{7 - 5}$

30. $9x - 20 = x^2$

31. $0.3(x + 4) \leq 0.4(2x + 3)$

32. $1.3x - 12 < 0.9x + 4$

33. $\dfrac{2x + 1}{7} \geq \dfrac{x + 4}{5}$

Excursions in Algebra _____ Sets

A collection of objects or numbers is often called a **set**. A set can be shown by using braces.

$\{1, 2, 3\}$ is *the set of numbers 1, 2, 3.*

Each object or number in a set is called an **element**.

1 *is an element of* $\{1, 2, 3\}$.
1 $\quad\in\quad$ $\{1, 2, 3\}$

Sets are often named by capital letters.

Set A is $\{1, 2, 3\}$.
A = $\{1, 2, 3\}$

If every element of set A is also an element of set B, then set A is a **subset** of set B.

$\{1, 2\}$ *is a subset of* $\{1, 2, 3\}$. $\qquad$ $\{1\}$ *is a subset of* $\{1, 2, 3\}$.
$\{1, 2\}$ $\quad\subset\quad$ $\{1, 2, 3\}$. $\qquad$ $\{1\}$ $\quad\subset\quad$ $\{1, 2, 3\}$

The set with no elements is the **null** or **empty set**. It is shown by $\{\ \}$ or $\emptyset$. The empty set is a subset of every set.

Exercises

Write in symbols.

1. the set of numbers 3, 4, 5, 6

2. the set of numbers 6, 7, 8, 9, 10, 11

3. 3 is an element of the set of numbers 3, 4, 5, 6.

4. 6 is an element of the set of integers between and including 5 and 10.

Find all subsets of each set to show that the following are true.

5. $\{1, 2, 4\}$ has 8 subsets.

6. $\{5, 6, 7, 8\}$ has 16 subsets.

1-4 Identity and Equality Properties

Solve each equation.

$$6 + a = 6 \qquad b + 15 = 15 \qquad 4780 + c = 4780$$

The solution of each equation is 0. The sum of any given number and 0 is the given number. The **additive identity** of any number is 0.

For any number a, $\quad a + 0 = 0 + a = a.$

Additive Identity Property

Solve each equation.

$$5x = 5 \qquad 18y = 18 \qquad z \cdot 655 = 655$$

The solution of each equation is 1. The product of any given number and 1 is the given number. The **multiplicative identity** of any number is 1.

For any number a, $\quad a \cdot 1 = 1 \cdot a = a.$

Multiplicative Identity Property

What role does 0 play in multiplication?

$$0(11) = 0 \qquad 5 \cdot 0 = 0 \qquad 8 \cdot 3 \cdot 0 = 0 \qquad 4 \cdot 0 \cdot 27 \cdot 8 = 0$$

When a factor is 0, the product is 0.

For any number a, $\quad a \cdot 0 = 0 \cdot a = 0.$

Multiplicative Property of Zero

Think about the following statements.

1. $5 = 5$
2. If $7 + 3 = 10$, then $10 = 7 + 3$.
3. If $10 - 2 = 8$ and $8 = 5 + 3$, then $10 - 2 = 5 + 3$.

You have assumed statements like these to be true from your experiences in arithmetic. Actually, these are examples of the properties of equality.

The following properties are true for any numbers a, b, and c.   Reflexive Property: $\quad a = a$ Symmetric Property: $\quad$ If $a = b$, then $b = a$,   Transitive Property: $\quad$ If $a = b$ and $b = c$, then $a = c$.

Properties of Equality

Which property corresponds to each of the three numbered statements given above?

Another property of equality is the substitution property. This property permits substitution of a quantity for its equal. You use this property regularly. For example, you would simplify the expression $8 + (3 + 9)$ as follows.

$$8 + (3 + 9) = 8 + 12 \qquad \text{Substitute 12 for } (3 + 9).$$
$$= 20 \qquad \text{Substitute 20 for } 8 + 12.$$

For any numbers a and b, if $a = b$ then a may be replaced by b.	**Substitution Property of Equality**

Exploratory Exercises

State the property shown in each of the following.

1. $3 = 3$
2. $7 + 6 = 7 + 6$
3. If $7 = 2 + 5$, then $2 + 5 = 7$.
4. If $6 = 3 + 3$, then $3 + 3 = 6$.
5. If $8 = 6 + 2$ and $6 + 2 = 5 + 3$, then $8 = 5 + 3$.
6. If $8 + 1 = 9$ and $9 = 3 + 6$, then $8 + 1 = 3 + 6$.
7. $3 + (2 + 1) = 3 + 3$
8. $9 + 5 = (6 + 3) + 5$

Solve each equation.

9. $0 + x = 7$
10. $a \cdot 1 = 5$
11. $7b = 7$
12. $0(18) = n$

Written Exercises

State the property shown in each of the following.

1. If $8 + 1 = 9$, then $9 = 8 + 1$.
2. $0 \cdot 36 = 0$
3. If $5 + 1 = 6$ and $6 = 4 + 2$, then $5 + 1 = 4 + 2$.
4. $9 + (2 + 10) = 9 + 12$
5. $1(87) = 87$
6. $0 + 17 = 17$
7. $14 + 16 = 14 + 16$
8. $6 \cdot 1 = 6$
9. $14 \cdot 0 = 0$
10. If $3 = 4 - 1$, then $4 - 1 = 3$.
11. $6 + 8 = 6 + 8$
12. If $9 + 1 = 10$ and $10 = 5(2)$, then $9 + 1 = 5(2)$.
13. $(9 - 7)(5) = 2(5)$
14. $62 = 62$
15. If $11 - 5 = 4 + 2$, then $4 + 2 = 11 - 5$.
16. If $a = 6 + 1$ and $6 + 1 = b$, then $a = b$.
17. $7(0) = 0$
18. $3 + 5 + 7 = 3 + 5 + 7$
19. $abc = 1abc$
20. If $a + b = c + d$, then $c + d = a + b$.

mini-review

Evaluate each expression.

1. 4^3
2. $5(7 + 4) - 3$
3. $\frac{16 + 8}{4 - 2}$

Solve.

4. $\frac{1}{2} + \frac{1}{6} = m$
5. $r = 2.3 + 12$

During the 1790's, a group of French scientists developed a new system of measurement called the **metric system**. The basic unit of length is the **meter**.

The metric system is a *decimal* system. That is, units increase or decrease in size by multiples of ten. A prefix is attached to the word *meter* to define larger and smaller units. The table shows some metric prefixes and their meanings.

Prefix	Symbol	Increase or decrease in unit
mega	M	1,000,000 (one million)
kilo	k	1,000 (one thousand)
hecto	h	100 (one hundred)
deka	da	10 (ten)
deci	d	0.1 (one-tenth)
centi	c	0.01 (one-hundredth)
milli	m	0.001 (one-thousandth)
micro	μ	0.000001 (one-millionth)

When the prefix *centi* is added to *meter*, the result is *centimeter*. The symbol for centimeter is cm. A centimeter is *one-hundredth* of a meter.

$$1 \text{ cm} = 0.01 \text{ m} \qquad 1 \text{ m} = 100 \text{ cm}$$
$$25 \text{ cm} = 0.25 \text{ m} \qquad 3.5 \text{ m} = 350 \text{ cm}$$

m is the symbol for meter.

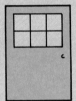

A door is about 1 m wide.

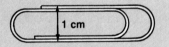

A paper clip is about 1 cm wide.

Exercises

1. Name 3 things that are best measured in meters.
2. Name 3 things that are best measured in centimeters.

Complete. *km stands for kilometer and mm stands for millimeter.*

3. 35 cm = ____ m
4. 57 cm = ____ m
5. 136 cm = ____ m
6. 395 cm = ____ m
7. 3 m = ____ cm
8. 4.7 m = ____ cm
9. 1 km = ____ m
10. 4 km = ____ m
11. 5000 m = ____ km
12. 1 cm = ____ mm
13. 14 cm = ____ mm
14. 55 mm = ____ cm

1-5 The Distributive Property

Angie and Maria are clerks in a local department store. Each one earns $4.65 per hour. Angie works 24 hours per week while Maria works 32 hours per week. What are their total earnings?

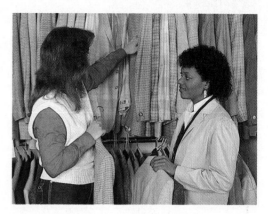

This problem can be solved in two ways. You could find Angie's earnings and Maria's earnings, then add to find the total earnings. Or, you could find the total number of hours worked, then multiply by the hourly wage.

Angie's Earnings	+	Maria's Earnings	=	Total Earnings
($4.65)(24)	+	($4.65)(32)	=	($4.65)(24 + 32)
$111.60	+	$148.80	=	($4.65)(56)
		$260.40	=	$260.40

The total earnings of $260.40 are distributed between Angie and Maria, each being paid $4.65 per hour for each hour worked. This is an example of the **distributive property**.

> For any numbers a, b, and c
> 1. $a(b + c) = ab + ac$ and $(b + c)a = ba + ca$.
> 2. $a(b - c) = ab - ac$ and $(b - c)a = ba - ca$.

Distributive Properties

Example

1 Use two ways to evaluate $8(5 + 4)$.

$$8(5 + 4) = 8(9)$$
$$= 72$$

$$8(5 + 4) = 8(5) + 8(4)$$
$$= 40 + 32$$
$$= 72$$

The distributive property is needed to simplify algebraic expressions containing **like terms**. A **term** of an expression is a number, a variable, or a product or quotient of numbers and variables. Some examples of terms are $5x^2$, $\frac{ab}{4}$, $\frac{x}{y}$, and $7k$. Some pairs of like terms are $5x$ and $3x$, $2xy$ and $7xy$, and $7ax^2$ and $11ax^2$.

> **Like terms are terms that contain the same variables, with corresponding variables raised to the same power.**

Definition of Like Terms

An expression in **simplest form** has no like terms and no parentheses.

Examples

2 **Simplify: $5a + 7a$**

$5a + 7a = (5 + 7)a$ *Use the Distributive Property: $ba + ca = (b + c)a$.*

$ = 12a$ *Substitution Property*

3 **Simplify: $6x^2y - 2x^2y$**

$6x^2y - 2x^2y = (6 - 2)x^2y$ *Distributive Property*

$ = 4x^2y$ *Substitution Property*

Like terms may also be defined as terms which are the same, or which differ only in their coefficients. The **coefficient**, or **numerical coefficient**, is the numerical part of a term. For example, the coefficient of $6ab$ is 6. *The coefficient of rs is 1 since by the multiplicative identity property $1 \cdot rs = rs$.*

Examples

4 **Name the coefficient of each term.**

    a. $19g^2h$ The coefficient is 19.

    b. xy^2z^2   The coefficient is 1 since $1xy^2z^2 = xy^2z^2$.

    c. $\dfrac{mn}{2}$ The coefficient is $\frac{1}{2}$ since $\frac{mn}{2}$ can be written as $\frac{1}{2}(mn)$.

    d. $\dfrac{2x^3}{5}$ The coefficient is $\frac{2}{5}$ since $\frac{2x^3}{5}$ can be written as $\frac{2}{5}(x^3)$.

5 **Simplify: $8n^2 + n^2 + 7n + 3n$**

$8n^2 + n^2 + 7n + 3n = 8n^2 + 1n^2 + 7n + 3n$ *Multiplicative Identity Property*

$ = (8 + 1)n^2 + (7 + 3)n$ *Distributive Property*

$ = 9n^2 + 10n$

6 **Simplify: $\dfrac{b}{2} + b$**

$\dfrac{b}{2} + b = \dfrac{1}{2}b + 1b$ *Multiplicative Identity Property*

$\phantom{\dfrac{b}{2} + b} = \left(\dfrac{1}{2} + 1\right)b$ *Distributive Property*

$\phantom{\dfrac{b}{2} + b} = \left(\dfrac{1}{2} + \dfrac{2}{2}\right)b$ *Substitution Property*

$\phantom{\dfrac{b}{2} + b} = \dfrac{3}{2}b$ *Substitution Property*

Simplify: $8a^2 + (8a + a^2) + 7a$

a. $8a^2 + (8a + a^2) + 7a = 8a^2 + (a^2 + 8a) + 7a$

b. $\qquad = (8a^2 + a^2) + (8a + 7a)$

c. $\qquad = (8a^2 + 1a^2) + (8a + 7a)$

d. $\qquad = (8 + 1)a^2 + (8 + 7)a$

e. $\qquad = 9a^2 + 15a$

Written Exercises

State the property shown in each of the following.

1. $5a + 2b = 2b + 5a$

2. $1 \cdot a^2 = a^2$

3. $(a + 3b) + 2c = a + (3b + 2c)$

4. $x^2 + (y + z) = x^2 + (z + y)$

5. $ax + 2b = xa + 2b$

6. $(3 \cdot x) \cdot y = 3 \cdot (x \cdot y)$

7. $29 + 0 = 29$

8. $5(a + 3b) = 5a + 15b$

9. $5a + 3b = 3b + 5a$

10. $5a + \left(\frac{1}{2}b + c\right) = \left(5a + \frac{1}{2}b\right) + c$

11. $(m + n)a = ma + na$

12. $0 + 7 = 7$

13. $1(a + b) = a + b$

14. $3m + nq = 3m + qn$

Simplify.

15. $5a + 6b + 7a$

16. $8x + 2y + x$

17. $3x + 2y + 2x + 8y$

18. $x^2 + 3x + 2x + 5x^2$

19. $\frac{2}{3}x^2 + 5x + x^2$

20. $\frac{3}{4}a^2 + 5ab + \frac{1}{2}a^2$

21. $3a + 5b + 2c + 8b$

22. $2x^2 + 3y + z^2 + 8x^2$

23. $5 + 7(ac + 2b) + 2ac$

24. $3(4x + y) + 2x$

25. $3(x + 2y) + 4(3x + y)$

26. $6(2x + y) + 2(x + 4y)$

27. $\frac{3}{4} + \frac{2}{3}(x + 2y) + x$

28. $\frac{3}{5}\left(\frac{1}{2}x + 2y\right) + 2x$

29. $0.2(3x + 0.2) + 0.5(5x + 3)$

30. $0.3(0.2 + 3y) + 0.21y$

31. $3[4 + 5(2x + 3y)]$

32. $4[1 + 4(5x + 2y)]$

Excursions in Algebra _____ History

The use of the term *associative* is due to Sir William Rowan Hamilton (1805-1865). Hamilton was a mathematician who studied and taught at Trinity College in Dublin, Ireland. He worked in astronomy and physics as well as higher forms of algebra. Some of his algebraic work is used in exactly the same form today. At the age of 30 Hamilton was knighted. He holds the honor of being the first foreign associate named to the United States Academy of Sciences.

Exploratory Exercises

State the coefficient in each term.

1. $5m$

2. $3am$

3. $0.2mp$

4. a^2q

5. $\frac{1}{5}mn^2$

6. $\frac{am}{3}$

7. $0.5abm$

8. $\frac{4am^2}{5}$

Name the like terms in each list of terms.

9. $6b, 6bc, bc$

10. $7a, 7a^2, 29a, 7a^3$

11. $4xy, 5xy, 6xy^2, 6x^2y$

12. $2rs^2, r^2s, rs^2$

13. $\frac{m^2n}{2}, 3mn, 5m^2n, \frac{mn^2}{4}$

14. $a^3, b^3, 3a^2, 4b^3$

15. $v^3, 3v^4, v^2, 4v^3$

16. $\frac{3d^2}{4}, \frac{d^2}{2}, d^3, \frac{3}{4}d$

17. $2cd^2, 3d^2c, 5c^2d$

Use the distributive property to write each expression in a different form.

18. $6(a + b)$

19. $3(a + c)$

20. $8(3x - 7)$

21. $4(7 - 2a)$

22. $ax + ay$

23. $cx + dx$

24. $4m - 4n$

25. $3r - kr$

Written Exercises

Simplify.

1. $3a + 7a$

2. $9c + 7c$

3. $13a + 5a$

4. $21x - 10x$

5. $5am - 4am$

6. $4np + 10np$

7. $18mn + 20mn$

8. $6xy + 28xy$

9. $15x^2 + 7x^2$

10. $23y^2 + 32y^2$

11. $10a + 30a + a$

12. $16b + 17b - 1b$

13. $9y^2 + 13y^2 + 3$

14. $11a^2 - 11a^2 + 12a^2$

15. $16a + 17b + 6$

16. $14a^2 + 13b^2 + 27$

17. $5a + 7a + 10b - 5b$

18. $16a + 21a + 30b - 7b$

19. $2(a + b) + b$

20. $3(x + 2y) - 2y$

21. $5x + 3(x - y)$

22. $9a + 14(a + 3)$

23. $6(5a + 3b - 2b)$

24. $2(3a + 2a + b)$

25. $5ab^2 + 2a^2b + ab^2$

26. $3xy^3 - 2y^3 + 5xy^3$

27. $4(3x + 2) + 2(x + 3)$

28. $\frac{3}{4}y + \frac{x}{4} + 3x$

29. $x^2 + \frac{7}{8}x - \frac{x}{8}$

30. $1.4a^2 + 3.8a + 5a$

31. $0.38k^2 + 0.6k^2 + 8.5k$

32. $m + 3(0.2m + 2.8m^3)$

33. $\frac{n}{2} + 3\left(\frac{n}{4} + n^2\right)$

Using Calculators _____ Simplifying Expressions

Use a calculator to do the arithmetic when simplifying expressions.

Example: Simplify $374n + 582n + 52.3y + 36y$.

$374n + 582n + 52.3y + 36y$

$= (374 + 582)n + (52.3 + 36)y$ *Distributive Property*

$= 956n + 88.3y$

Exercises Simplify.

1. $1436x^2 - 789x^2 + 5689x^2$

2. $8946y^3 + 9744y - 438y$

3. $485m^2n + 203m^2n + 168m^2 - 87m^2$

4. $5.86rs^3 - 4.06rs^3 + 0.92r^3s + 8.69r^3s$

1-6 Commutative and Associative Properties

The order in which two numbers are added or multiplied does *not* change their sum or product.

$$6 + 5 = 5 + 6 \qquad 12 + 9 = 9 + 12 \qquad 37 + 82 = 82 + 37$$
$$4 \cdot 5 = 5 \cdot 4 \qquad 7 \cdot 2 = 2 \cdot 7 \qquad 83 \cdot 37 = 37 \cdot 83$$

For any numbers a and b, $a + b = b + a$ and $a \cdot b = b \cdot a$.	Commutative Properties

How do you evaluate $5 + 7 + 4$? You could add the 5 and 7 and then add the 4 to the sum, or you could add the 7 and 4 and then add the 5.

$$5 + 7 + 4 = (5 + 7) + 4 \qquad\qquad 5 + 7 + 4 = 5 + (7 + 4)$$
$$= 12 + 4 \qquad\qquad\qquad = 5 + 11$$
$$= 16 \qquad\qquad\qquad\qquad = 16$$

The sum is 16 in each case.

How do you evaluate $3 \cdot 8 \cdot 7$?

$$3 \cdot 8 \cdot 7 = (3 \cdot 8) \cdot 7 \qquad\qquad 3 \cdot 8 \cdot 7 = 3 \cdot (8 \cdot 7)$$
$$= 24 \cdot 7 \qquad\qquad\qquad = 3 \cdot 56$$
$$= 168 \qquad\qquad\qquad\qquad = 168$$

Notice that the product is 168 in each case.

Thus, the way you group, or associate, three numbers does not change the sum or product.

For any numbers a, b, and c, $(a + b) + c = a + (b + c)$ and $(ab)c = a(bc)$.	Associative Properties

The commutative, associative, and distributive properties are used when simplifying expressions.

Example

1 **Simplify $3x + (5 + 6x)$ indicating all properties used.**

$3x + (5 + 6x) = 3x + (6x + 5)$	*Commutative Property for Addition*
$= (3x + 6x) + 5$	*Associative Property for Addition*
$= (3 + 6)x + 5$	*Distributive Property*
$= 9x + 5$	*Substitution Property*

Notice that in Example 1 the commutative and associative properties were used to group like terms.

Example

2 **Simplify $5n + 2(n^2 + 4n) + n^2$ indicating all properties used.**

$5n + 2(n^2 + 4n) + n^2 = 5n + (2n^2 + 8n) + n^2$	*Distributive Property*
$= 5n + (8n + 2n^2) + n^2$	*Commutative Property*
$= (5n + 8n) + (2n^2 + n^2)$	*Associative Property for*
$= (5n + 8n) + (2n^2 + 1n^2)$	*Multiplicative Identity*
$= (5 + 8)n + (2 + 1)n^2$	*Distributive Property*
$= 13n + 3n^2$	*Substitution Property*

The chart below summarizes the properties that are used when simplifying expressions.

The following properties are true for any numbers a, b, and c.		
	Addition	**Multiplication**
Commutative:	$a + b = b + a$	$ab = ba$
Associative:	$(a + b) + c = a + (b + c)$	$(ab)c = a(bc)$
Identity:	0 is the identity. $a + 0 = 0 + a = a$	1 is the identity. $a \cdot 1 = 1 \cdot a = a$
Zero:		$a \cdot 0 = 0 \cdot a = 0$
Distributive:	$a(b + c) = ab + ac$ and $(b + c)a = ba + ca$ $a(b - c) = ab - ac$ and $(b - c)a = ba - ca$	
Substitution:	If $a = b$, then a may be substituted for b.	

Exploratory Exercises

State the property shown in each of the following.

1. $(8 + 4) + 2 = 8 + (4 + 2)$
2. $5 + 3 = 3 + 5$
3. $8(a + b) = 8a + 8b$
4. $(3 + 8) + x = 11 + x$
5. $3x = x \cdot 3$
6. $(a + b) + 3 = a + (b + 3)$
7. $5(ab) = (5a)b$
8. $cb + ab = (c + a)b$
9. $10(x + y) = 10(y + x)$
10. $3(a + 2b) = (a + 2b) \cdot 3$
11. Is $12 - 8 = 8 - 12$? Is $27 - 10 = 10 - 27$? Is subtraction a commutative operation?
12. Is $24 \div 6 = 6 \div 24$? Is $36 \div 9 = 9 \div 36$? Is division a commutative operation?

State the property that justifies each step.

13. Simplify: $6a + (8b + 2a)$
    a. $6a + (8b + 2a) = 6a + (2a + 8b)$
    b. $\qquad\qquad = (6a + 2a) + 8b$
    c. $\qquad\qquad = (6 + 2)a + 8b$
    d. $\qquad\qquad = 8a + 8b$

Suppose you are to write each of the following in symbols.

Words	**Symbols**
Three times x plus y	$3x + y$
Three times the sum of x and y	$3(x + y)$

In the second expression, parentheses are used to show that the *sum*, x plus y, is multiplied by three. In algebraic expressions, terms enclosed by parentheses are treated as one quantity. The expression $3(x + y)$ can be read *three times the quantity x plus y*. Suppose you are to read each expression below.

Symbols	**Words**
$a + 5^2$	a plus five squared
$(a + 5)^2$	the quantity a plus 5 squared

The phrase *the quantity* tells you that the sum, $a + 5$, is squared. To avoid confusion, read $(a - b)^2$ as *a minus b the quantity squared*. Read $a - b^2$ as *a minus b squared*.

Try an experiment. Have a classmate close his or her book. Read the following expressions to your classmate. Then have him or her write the symbols for each expression.

   a. Seven times the quantity b minus 4
   b. The quantity 6 plus x cubed
   c. Two times the quantity a plus 3 times the quantity b minus 9

The correct answers are $7(b - 4)$, $(6 + x)^3$, and $2(a + 3)(b - 9)$, respectively. Compare your classmate's answers with the correct answers. How do they compare?

In verbal problems, look for key words that indicate that parentheses are to be used. Sometimes the words *sum, difference, quantity,* and *total* signal the use of parentheses. Study the following examples.

Words	**Symbols**
Four divided by the difference of a number and 6	$4 \div (n - 6)$
The quantity a plus b divided by x	$(a + b) \div x$

Exercises

Write each expression in symbols.

1. Eight times four plus x squared

2. Eight times the quantity four plus x squared

3. Add n to your age and double it.

Write each algebraic expression in words.

4. $3a + 2$

5. $3(a + 2)$

6. $\frac{5}{9}(F - 32)$

7. $(r + s) - (r - s)$

8. $8 \div (4 - c)^2$

9. $8 \div 4 - c^2$

1-7 Using Formulas

Marie wants to find the area of the picture shown at the right. The length is 51 cm and the width is 41 cm. She knows that the area of a rectangle is equal to the product of the length and width. She uses the formula $A = lw$ to express this relationship. The variables A, l, and w represent the measures of the area, length, and width.

$$A = lw$$
$$= 51 \cdot 41$$
$$= 2091$$

Marie finds that the area is 2091 square centimeters (cm^2).

A **formula** is an equation that states a rule for the relationship between certain quantities.

Examples

1 **Find the area of a rectangle of length 17 cm and width 13 cm.**

$$A = lw$$
$$A = 17 \cdot 13$$
$$= 221$$

The area is 221 cm^2.

2 **The formula for the area of a triangle is $A = \frac{1}{2}bh$. Find the area of a triangle with a base (b) of 6 units and a height (h) of 9 units.**

$$A = \frac{1}{2}bh$$
$$A = \frac{1}{2}(6)(9)$$
$$= 3 \cdot 9$$
$$= 27$$

The area of the triangle is 27 square units.

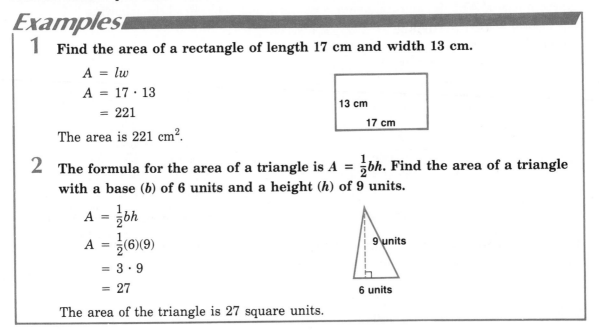

Many sentences can be written as equations or formulas. Use variables to represent the unspecified numbers or measures referred to in the sentence. Then write the verbal expressions as algebraic expressions. Some verbal expressions that suggest the equals sign are listed below.

is	is equal to	is as much as
equals	is the same as	is identical to

Example

3 Translate each sentence into an equation or formula.

a. The number z equals twice the sum of x and y.
The equation is $z = 2(x + y)$.

b. The area of a circle is equal to the product of π and the square of the radius (r).
The formula is $A = \pi r^2$.

Exploratory Exercises

Write a formula for each of the following. Use the variables indicated.

1. The area (A) of a square is the square of the length of one of its sides (s).

2. The perimeter (P) of a parallelogram is twice the sum of the lengths of two adjacent sides $(a$ and $b)$.

3. The perimeter (P) of a square is the product of 4 and the length of a side (s).

4. The circumference (C) of a circle is the product of 2, π, and the radius (r).

Written Exercises

The formula for the surface area (S) of a rectangular solid as shown at the right is $S = 2(lh + wh + lw)$. Copy and complete the charts.

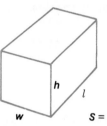

$S = 2(lh + wh + lw)$

	l	w	h	S
1.	5	8	6	
2.	18	10	4	
3.	$20\frac{1}{2}$	3	8	
4.	$5\frac{1}{2}$	12	$3\frac{1}{2}$	

	l	w	h	S
5.	12.9	11	4.6	
6.	21.8	6.5	9.7	

The formula for the area (A) of a trapezoid as shown at the right is $A = \frac{1}{2}h(a + b)$. Copy and complete the charts.

$A = \frac{1}{2}h(a + b)$

	h	a	b	A
7.	6	24	19	
8.	11	37	23	
9.	12	24	40	
10.	10	19	54	
11.	$\frac{5}{8}$	$\frac{3}{4}$	$\frac{1}{2}$	

	h	a	b	A
12.	$3\frac{1}{3}$	12	$8\frac{1}{4}$	
13.	4	18.9	12.7	
14.	2.4	8.25	3.15	

The formula for the area (A) of the shaded region of the figure below is $A = \frac{1}{2}\pi a^2 - a^2$. Find the area of the region for the following values of a. Use 3.14 for π. Round each answer to the nearest whole number.

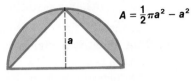

$A = \frac{1}{2}\pi a^2 - a^2$

15. 6   **16.** 4   **17.** 81   **18.** 64

19. 3.8   **20.** 5.6   **21.** 18.3   **22.** 27.4

Translate each sentence into an equation.

23. Twice x increased by the square of y is equal to z.

24. The square of a decreased by the cube of b is equal to c.

25. The sum of x and the square of a is equal to n.

26. The square of the sum of x and a is equal to m.

27. The number r equals the cube of the difference of a and b.

28. The number b equals x decreased by the cube of m.

29. The square of the product of a, b, and c is equal to k.

30. The product of a, b, and the square of c is f.

31. Y is the sum of twice m and the square of n.

32. A is equal to the sum of m and the square of n.

33. Z is equal to 29 decreased by the product of x and y.

34. R is the product of a and m decreased by z.

The distance (d) traveled is equal to the rate (r) times the time (t). The formula for this is $d = rt$. Use this formula to solve each problem.

35. Find the distance from Danville to the beach if it takes 3 hours to drive there at an average rate of 50 miles per hour.

36. George runs for 30 minutes every day. Find the distance he runs if he averages 660 feet per minute.

37. The speed of sound through air is about 330 meters per second. Find the distance between Carl and an explosion if it takes 10 seconds for the sound to reach him.

38. The speed of light is about 300,000 kilometers per second. Find the distance between Karen and a flash of light if it takes 6 seconds for Karen to see the light.

Challenge _____

Write a formula for the area of each figure.

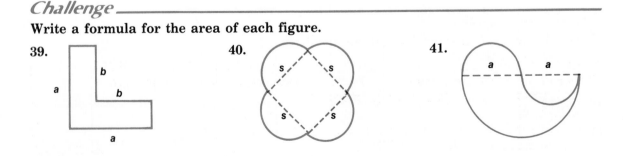

39.

40.

41.

1-8 Exploring Verbal Problems

Many problems in algebra are solved by translating the verbal problem into symbols. To do this accurately, you must explore the problem until you completely understand the relationships among the given information. You can explore a problem situation by asking and answering questions. Study the following examples.

Examples

1 **Peggy Richards has \$3.25 in nickels and dimes. She has 7 more dimes than nickels.**

Questions	Answers
a. Does she have more nickels or dimes?	**a.** more dimes
b. How much money does she have in all?	**b.** \$3.25
c. Do you know how many nickels and dimes she has?	**c.** no
d. If she has n nickels, how many dimes does she have?	**d.** $7 + n$ or $n + 7$
e. If she has x dimes, how much money does she have in dimes?	**e.** $10x$ cents

2 **One day John and Inger picked peaches for 4 hours. In all they picked 30 baskets of peaches. Inger picked 6 baskets less than John.**

Questions	Answers
a. How many baskets were picked in all?	**a.** 30
b. How long did John and Inger work?	**b.** 4 hours
c. Who worked longer?	**c.** They worked the same.
d. Who picked more?	**d.** John
e. If Inger picked n baskets, how many did John pick?	**e.** $n + 6$
f. If John picked r baskets, how many did Inger pick?	**f.** $r - 6$

Written Exercises

For each problem, answer the related questions.

1. Mr. Limotta checked his cash register at the end of the day. He found that he had 7 fewer \$5 bills than \$1 bills. He had eleven \$10 bills and no larger bills. In all he had \$267.
   a. Did he have more \$5 bills or \$1 bills?
   b. How many more?
   c. How much money did he have in all?
   d. How many \$20 bills did he have?

e. How much money did he have in $1 and $5 bills together?

f. When did he check his cash register?

g. If he had *n* $5 bills, how much money did he have in $5 bills?

2. Michelle has 20 books on crafts and cooking. She also has 21 novels. She has 6 more cookbooks than craft books.
   a. Does she have more cookbooks or craft books?
   b. How many more?
   c. Does she have more novels than craft books?
   d. How many books does she have in all?
   e. If she has *n* cookbooks, how many craft books has she?
   f. Of what kind of book does she have the least?

3. Two breakfast cereals, Kornies and Krispies, together cost $3.59. One of them costs 7¢ more than the other.
   a. Which one costs more?
   b. What is the difference in their prices?
   c. How much would two boxes of each cost?
   d. Would two boxes of the more expensive cereal cost more or less than $3.59?
   e. If the more expensive cereal costs *n* cents, what is the cost of the other cereal?

4. Marvin is 6 inches taller than Ira and Ira is 4 inches shorter than Bruce.
   a. Who is the tallest?
   b. Who is the shortest?
   c. Is Marvin taller or shorter than Bruce?
   d. How much taller than Ira is Marvin?
   e. How much taller than Bruce is Marvin?

5. Brenda Summer has 3 more nickels than dimes and 5 fewer pennies than nickels. She has 70 coins in all.
   a. Of which coin does she have the most?
   b. Of which coin does she have the fewest?
   c. How many fewer dimes than nickels does she have?
   d. How many fewer pennies than dimes does she have?
   e. How much money does she have in all?
   f. Does she have more money in nickels or dimes?

6. The Vegetable Mart offers corn at 18¢ per ear, cucumbers at 12¢ each, and tomatoes at 59¢ per basket. Norma has only $3 to spend and wants one basket of tomatoes and 5 fewer ears of corn than cucumbers.
   a. How many baskets of tomatoes does she want?
   b. How much more is a basket of tomatoes than an ear of corn?
   c. After buying the tomatoes, how much money does she have remaining?
   d. Will she buy more cucumbers or ears of corn?
   e. If she buys *n* cucumbers, how many ears of corn will she buy?

7. Chris can mow the lawn in 4 hours and Mark can do it in 3 hours.

    a. Alone, how much of the lawn will Chris mow in 3 hours?

    b. Alone, how much of the lawn will Mark mow in an hour?

    c. In n hours, how much of the lawn will Chris mow?

    d. If they both start mowing at the same time, using two mowers, can they finish the lawn in 2 hours?

8. Phoebe goes to Pluto's Platters to buy her stereo records. She bought 3 more rock records than classical and 2 less western records than rock. Including 5 jazz records, she bought 18.

    a. Did she buy more classical than rock?

    b. Did she buy more rock than western?

    c. Which did she buy the most of?

    d. How many rock, classical, and western records did she buy?

    e. If she bought n classical records, how many rock records did she buy?

9. Ninety-six students signed up for football at East High School. Eight are not eligible because of grades. There are eight fewer sophomores than juniors. There are 26 seniors and no freshmen.

    a. Are there more sophomores than juniors?

    b. If there are x juniors, how many sophomores are there?

    c. Are there more juniors or seniors?

    d. Which class has the most players?

10. Craig said, "I am 24 years younger than my mom and the sum of our ages is 68 years."

    a. How old was Craig's mother when Craig was born?

    b. How much older than Craig is his mother now?

    c. What will be the sum of their ages in 5 years?

    d. How old was Craig's mother when Craig was 10 years old?

    e. In ten years, how much younger than his mother will Craig be?

11. Doug was working some math problems. He thought that he could finish 3 pages of 24 problems per page in 2 hours. After $1\frac{1}{2}$ hours, he had finished 2 pages.

    a. How many problems had Doug completed in $1\frac{1}{2}$ hours?

    b. How many problems are there in all?

    c. At the rate he is working, will he finish the three pages in 2 hours?

12. Darryl is 7 years younger than Ernie. In 5 years the sum of their ages will be 75 years.

    a. Who is older?

    b. In 5 years, who will be younger?

    c. If Darryl is n years old now, how old will he be in 5 years?

    d. Ernie is x years old now. How old is Darryl?

    e. Who was younger seven years ago?

    f. What is the sum of their ages now?

Laura Sheppard is a computer programmer for a large bank. She uses data from the computer to find any errors in her programs. The data is in the hexadecimal numeration system.

The hexadecimal numeration system is a base 16 system. It uses the sixteen symbols 0, 1, 2, 3, 4, 5, 6, 7, 8, 9, A, B, C, D, E, and F. Notice that $B_{sixteen} = 11_{ten}$.

The position of each symbol gives its place value as a power of sixteen. Study how the hexadecimal numeral 9F3 is changed to a decimal numeral.

$$9F3_{sixteen} = 9 \cdot 16^2 + F \cdot 16^1 + 3$$
$$= 9 \cdot 256 + 15 \cdot 16 + 3$$
$$= 2304 + 240 + 3$$
$$= 2547_{ten}$$

The hexadecimal numeration system provides a shorter way of representing numbers than the binary system. Suppose you want to change a binary numeral to a hexadecimal. Separate the numeral into groups of 4 digits starting at the right. Each group can be changed to one hexadecimal digit.

$$11010011010010 = \underbrace{11}_{3} \quad \underbrace{0100}_{4} \quad \underbrace{1101}_{D} \quad \underbrace{0010}_{2}$$

$$1101_{two} = 13_{ten} = D_{sixteen}$$

Exercises
Change each hexadecimal numeral to a decimal numeral.

1. $53_{sixteen}$

2. $C6_{sixteen}$

3. $2E5_{sixteen}$

4. $10A3_{sixteen}$

Change each binary numeral to a hexadecimal numeral.

5. 1001_{two}

6. 10101100_{two}

7. 100101010_{two}

8. 10111010111_{two}

Challenge
9. Subtract the hexadecimals: 6E7 − 542

1-9 Problem Solving: Writing Equations

Four steps that can be used to solve verbal problems are listed below.

> 1. **Explore the problem.**
> 2. **Plan the solution.**
> 3. **Solve the problem.**
> 4. **Examine the solution.**

Problem-Solving Plan

 To solve a verbal problem, first read the problem carefully and *explore* what the problem is about.

- Identify what information is given.
- Identify what you are asked to find.
- Choose a variable to represent one of the unspecified numbers in the problem. This is called defining the variable.
- Use the variable in writing expressions for other unspecified numbers in the problem.

 Next, *plan* how to solve the problem. One way to solve a problem is to use an equation.

- Read the problem again. Decide how the unspecified numbers relate to other given information.
- Write an equation to represent the relationship.

Example

1 **Write an equation for the following problem.**

One number is 12 greater than a second number. The sum of the two numbers is 86. Find the numbers.

 Read the problem carefully.

Let n = the lesser number.

Then $n + 12$ = the greater number.

 The problem states the sum of the two numbers is 86.

So, the equation is $n + (n + 12) = 86$.

2 Write an equation for the following problem.

Jennifer Winter is in the ninth grade. Six years ago, twice her age was 16 years. How old is she now?

Explore   Let j = Jennifer's age now.

Then $j - 6$ = Jennifer's age 6 years ago.

Plan   The problem states that twice her age six years ago was 16 years. So, the equation is $2(j - 6) = 16$.

Verbal problems can be developed from equations. First, you must know what the variable in the equation represents. Then you can use the equation to establish the conditions of the problem. Study the following examples.

Examples

3 Write a problem based on the given information.

Let x = Mary's age now.

$x - 5 = 17$

Since Mary's age is represented by x, then $x - 5$ must be her age 5 years ago, which was 17.

Thus, the following problem can be written.

If Mary's age 5 years ago was 17, how old is she now?

4 Write a problem based on the given information.

Let w = Steve's weight in kilograms.

$w - 12$ = *Perry's weight in kilograms.*

$w + (w - 12) = 118$

The following problem can be written.

Perry weighs 12 kg less than Steve. The sum of their weights is 118 kg. How much does Steve weigh? How much does Perry weigh?

Exploratory Exercises

Write an expression for each of the following.

1. Mr. Jackson is now 49 years old. How old was he n years ago?
2. The sum of two numbers is 18. The lesser number is t. What is the greater number?
3. The length of a rectangle is 4 more than the width. The width is w. Find the length.
4. Sheldon is 8 years older than Jane. If Sheldon is n years old, how old is Jane?
5. Harold has 8 more than twice as many red marbles as blue marbles. He has t blue marbles. How many red marbles does he have?

6. This year's senior class has 117 fewer students than last year's class. This year's class has 947 students. How many were in last year's class?

7. The cost of gasoline has tripled in the past 8 years. Gasoline now costs $1.59 per gallon. What was the cost 8 years ago?

8. Tess types 42 words per minute. How many minutes would it take for her to type a 3000-word paper?

9. Anthony is paid $5.65 per hour. How much is he paid for working n hours?

10. Buzz graduated from high school y years ago at the age of 17. How old is he now?

Written Exercises

Define the variable, then write an equation for each problem.

1. A number increased by 24 is 89. Find the number. $X+24=89$

2. Twice a number decreased by 84 is 40. Find the number.

3. A number decreased by 19 is 83. Find the number.

4. 67 decreased by twice a number is 39. Find the number.

5. How old is Tyrone if twice his age increased by 17 is 53? X $2X+17=53$

6. Twenty-seven years ago Clarice was 21. How old is she now?

7. Peggy is 3 years older than Melissa. The sum of their ages in 4 years will be 59 years. How old is Peggy now?

8. Three times Cecile's age 4 years ago is 42. How old is Cecile now?

9. Bill is 5 inches taller than Bob and the sum of their heights is 137 inches. How tall is Bob?

10. Twice Mary Lou's height increased by 17 inches is 141 inches. How tall is Mary Lou?

11. Bob's dad is 27 years older than Bob. The sum of their ages 5 years ago was 45 years. How old is Bob now?

12. The sum of Mrs. Black's age and her daughter's age is 56 years. In 8 years, Mrs. Black will be twice as old as her daughter. How old is her daughter now?

13. In a football game, Michael gained 134 yards running. This was 17 yards more than the previous game. How many yards did he gain in both games?

14. Ponderosa pines grow about $1\frac{1}{2}$ feet each year. If a pine is now 17 feet tall, about how long will it take the tree to become $33\frac{1}{2}$ feet tall?

15. For 6 consecutive weeks, Connie lost the same amount of weight. Six weeks ago she weighed 145 pounds. She now weighs 125 pounds. How many pounds did Connie lose each week?

16. Each week for 7 weeks Sav-A-Buk stores reduced the price of a sofa by $18.25. The final reduced price was $252.50. What was the original price?

Write a problem based on the given information.

17. Let x = Olivia's age now.
$x + 7 = 29$

18. Let a = Quincy's age now.
$2(a - 7) = 58$

19. Let x = greater of two numbers.
$x - 7$ = lesser of two numbers.
$x + (x - 7) = 33$

20. Let x = lesser of two numbers.
$x + 29$ = greater of two numbers.
$x + (x + 29) = 135$

Write a problem based on the given information.

21. Let n = Anne's age now.
$n + 26$ = Anne's mother's age now.
$n + (n + 26) = 58$

22. Let w = Willie's age now.
$w + 4$ = Ellen's age now.
$(w + 10) + (w + 4 + 10) = 54$

23. Let x = weight of Seth's car in pounds.
$x + 250$ = weight of Terry's car in pounds.
$x + (x + 250) = 7140$

24. Let h = Roxanne's height in inches.
$h + 7$ = Sven's height in inches.
$2h + (h + 7) = 193$

25. Let x = the number of students present in Mr. Wyatt's class.
$x + 5 = 33$

26. Let n = the number of students in Alan's class.
$n - 7$ = the number of students in Jim's class.
$n + (n - 7) = 189$

27. Let m = Elroy's height in centimeters.
$m - 31$ = Reggie's height in centimeters.
$m + 2(m - 31) = 502$

28. Let n = number of nickels that Yvette has.
$n - 17$ = number of pennies that Yvette has.
$n + (n - 17) = 64$

29. Let x = distance that Cheryl drove east.
$x + 80$ = distance that Bonnie drove west.
$x + (x + 80) = 520$

30. Let p = number of pages in Ira's book.
$p - 27$ = number of pages in Danny's book.
$p + (p - 27) = 873$

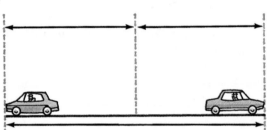

31. Let n = number of games that Greg won.
$n - 12$ = number of games that Alex won.
$n = 2(n - 12)$

32. Let x = Carol's height in inches 5 years ago.
$x + 7$ = Carol's height in inches now.
$x + 3$ = Martha's height in inches now.
$(x + 7) + (x + 3) = 124$

33. Let n = number of $5 bills that Lloyd has.
$n - 7$ = number of $10 bills that Lloyd has.
$n + 3$ = number of $1 bills that Lloyd has.
$n + (n + 3) + (n - 7) = 29$

34. Let d = number of dimes that Teresa has.
$d + 4$ = number of nickels that Teresa has.
$d - 9$ = number of quarters that Teresa has.
$d + (d + 4) + (d - 9) = 37$

35. Let x = number of albums that Anna has.
$x - 3$ = number of albums that Barbara has.
$x + 4$ = number of albums that Chris has.
$x + (x - 3) + (x + 4) = 43$

mini-review

Write *true* or *false*.

1. $5^2 = 5 + 5$

2. $7(0) = 7$

3. $1(4.2) = 4.2$

4. $3(4 \times 1) = 3(4) + 3(1)$

5. $7.2 + (3 + 2.8) =$
$(7.2 + 2.8) + 3$

Formulas

The formula for the area of a rectangle is $A = \ell w$. To find the area of a rectangle with length 51 cm and width 34 cm, you assign the variable ℓ the value 51 and the variable w the value 34. The area of the rectangle is (51)(34) or 1734 cm².

In the BASIC computer language, READ-DATA statements are used to assign values to variables. Consider the following program.

```
10  READ L,W          The computer locates the data and reads
20  DATA 51,34        them in the order in which they are listed.
30  LET A = L * W      In line 30 the variable A is assigned the
40  PRINT A            value of (51)(34).
```

When this program is executed, the value of A, 1734, is printed.

READ-DATA statements are very useful when working with many calculations. For example, the following program can be used to help complete the chart for exercises 1-6 on page 23.

```
 10  PRINT "L","W","H","S"
 20  PRINT
 30  READ L,W,H
 40  IF L = 0 THEN 110       When the value of L is zero,
 50  DATA 5,8,6,18,10,4,20.5,3,8      the program will end.
 60  DATA 5.5,12,3.5,12.9,11,4.6     Notice that more than one set of data
 70  DATA 21.8,6.5,9.7,0,0,0         can be included in each DATA statement.
 80  LET S = 2 * (L * H + W * H + L * W)   A LET statement is used in line 80
 90  PRINT L,W,H,S                    to write the formula as a BASIC
100  GOTO 30                          statement.
110  END
```

Enter and run this program on your computer. Compare the output with the chart that you have already completed.

Exercises

Write each formula as a BASIC statement.

1. $A = s^2$

2. $P = 2(\ell + w)$

3. $I = P \cdot r \cdot t$

4. $A = \frac{1}{2}bh$

5. $D = rt$

6. $A = \frac{1}{2}h(a + b)$

7. Write a program similar to the one above to print a chart for exercises 7-14 on page 23. Enter and run the program.

8. Write a program to find the area for each of the figures described in exercises 15-22 on page 24. Enter and run the program.

9. Write a program to find the distance in problems 35-38 on page 24. Enter and run the program.

Vocabulary

variable (3)
expression (3)
factor (3)
product (3)
dividend (3)
divisor (3)
quotient (3)
base (4)
exponent (4)
open sentence (9)
solution (9)
equals sign (9)
equation (9)
additive identity (12)
multiplicative identity (12)
multiplicative property of
  zero (12)
distributive property (15)

properties of equality:
  reflexive (12)
  symmetric (12)
  transitive (12)
  substitution (13)
term (15)
like terms (15)
simplest form (16)
coefficient (16)
commutative property for
  addition (18)
commutative property for
  multiplication (18)
associative property for
  addition (18)
associative property for
  multiplication (18)
formula (22)

Chapter Summary

1. Variables are symbols that are used to represent unspecified numbers. (3)

2. An algebraic expression consists of one or more numbers and variables with the operations of addition, subtraction, multiplication, and/or division. (3)

3. In a multiplication expression, the quantities being multiplied are called factors and the result is called the product. In a division expression, the dividend is divided by the divisor. The result is called the quotient. (3)

4. Parentheses or a dot can be used instead of × to indicate multiplication. When variables are used to represent factors, the multiplication sign is usually omitted. (3)

5. An exponent indicates the number of times the base is used as a factor. (4)

6. Order of Operations:
    1. Evaluate all powers.
    2. Do all multiplications and divisions from left to right.
    3. Do all additions and subtractions from left to right. (6)

7. Grouping symbols, such as parentheses and brackets, are used to clarify or change the order of operations. Evaluate expressions within grouping symbols first. (7)

8. In an open sentence, the variable must be replaced in order to determine if the sentence is true or false. (9)

9. Finding the replacements for the variable that make a sentence true is called solving the open sentence. Each replacement is called a solution of the open sentence. (9)

10. A mathematical sentence that contains an equals sign, $=$, is called an equation. (9)

11. The following properties of equality are true for any numbers a, b, and c.
    Reflexive: $a = a$ (12)
    Symmetric: If $a = b$, then $b = a$. (12)
    Transitive: If $a = b$ and $b = c$, then $a = c$. (12)
    Substitution: If $a = b$, then a may be replaced by b. (13)

12. Like terms are terms that contain the same variables, with corresponding variables raised to the same power. (15)

13. The coefficient, or numerical coefficient, is the numerical part of a term. (16)

14. The following properties are true for any numbers a, b, and c. (19)

	Addition	Multiplication
Commutative:	$a + b = b + a$	$ab = ba$
Associative:	$(a + b) + c = a + (b + c)$	$(ab)c = a(bc)$
Identity:	0 is the identity. $a + 0 = 0 + a = a$	1 is the identity. $a \cdot 1 = 1 \cdot a = a$
Zero:		$a \cdot 0 = 0 \cdot a = 0$
Distributive:	$a(b + c) = ab + ac$ and $(b + c)a = ba + ca$ $a(b - c) = ab - ac$ and $(b - c)a = ba - ca$	

15. A formula is an equation that states a rule for the relationship between certain quantities. (22)

16. To understand a verbal problem, you should explore the problem situation by asking and answering questions. (25)

17. A four-step problem-solving plan is given below. (29)
    1. Explore the problem.
    2. Plan the solution.
    3. Solve the problem.
    4. Examine the solution.

Chapter Review

1-1 **Write each of the following as an expression using exponents.**

1. $a \cdot a \cdot a \cdot a$ a^4

2. $15 \cdot x \cdot x \cdot x \cdot y \cdot y$

Write an algebraic expression for each verbal expression. Use x as the variable.

3. twice a number decreased by 17

4. a number increased by 14

5. the product of 8 and a number

6. twice the cube of a number

1-2 **Evaluate if $a = 5$, $b = 8$, $c = \frac{2}{3}$, $d = \frac{1}{2}$, and $e = 0.3$.**

7. ab^2

8. $3ac - bd$

9. $(2a - b)^2$

10. bcd

11. $5e^2$

12. $b + c + 2d$

1-3 **Solve each equation.**

13. $a = 29 - 5^2$

14. $5(6) - 3(5) = y$

15. $8 - 2 \cdot 3 = b$

16. $r = (29 - 5)^2$

17. $w = (0.2)(8 + 3)$

18. $m = \frac{2}{3}\left(3 - \frac{1}{2}\right)$

1-4 **State the property shown in each of the following.**

19. $7 + 0 = 7$

20. $2(1) = 2$

21. $11 \cdot 0 = 0$

22. If $a + b = 5$ then $5 = a + b$.

23. $r = r$

24. If $a = 7$ and $7 = 9 - 2$, then $a = 9 - 2$.

1-5 **Simplify.**

25. $10x + x$

26. $9a - 7a$

27. $5b + 3(b + 2)$

28. $9(r + s) - 2s$

1-6 **State the property shown in each of the following.**

29. $5(a + c) = 5(c + a)$

30. $10(ab) = (10a)b$

31. $4 + (x + y) = (4 + x) + y$

32. $a(b + c) = (b + c)a$

Simplify.

33. $6a + 7b + 8a + 2b$

34. $\frac{3}{4}a^2 + \frac{2}{3}ab + ab$

1-7 **Write each sentence as an equation.**

35. Eighteen decreased by the square of d is equal to f.

36. The number c equals the cube of the product of 2 and x.

1-8 **Two cans of vegetables together cost \$1.08. One of them costs 10¢ more than the other.**

37. Would 2 cans of the less expensive vegetable cost more or less than \$1.08?

38. How much would 3 cans of each cost?

1-9 **Define the variable, then write an equation for each problem.**

39. Carol weighs 8 pounds less than Claudia. Together they weigh 182 pounds. How much does Carol weigh?

40. Three times a number decreased by 21 is 57. Find the number.

Chapter Test

Write an algebraic expression for each verbal expression. Use x as the variable.

1. a number increased by 17
2. twice the square of a number
3. the sum of a number and its cube
4. twice Nica's age decreased by 23 years

Evaluate.

5. $(12 - 10)^4$
6. $(17 - 4)^2$
7. $0.7(1.4 + 0.6)$
8. $\frac{3}{4}(8 + 28)$
9. $23 - 12(1.5)$
10. $6 + 3(3.4)$

Evaluate if $m = 8$, $n = 3$, $p = \frac{3}{4}$, $q = \frac{2}{3}$, and $r = 0.5$.

11. $(mn)^2$
12. pq^2
13. $n + r^2$

Solve each equation.

14. $v = \frac{6^2 - 2^3}{7}$
15. $8(0.03) - 0.05 = y$
16. $\frac{3}{4} - \left(\frac{1}{2}\right)^2 = k$

State the property shown in each of the following.

17. $7a = 7a$
18. $7(m + 2n) = 7(2n + m)$
19. $34 \cdot 1 = 34$
20. $3(2a + b) = 6a + 3b$
21. If $m = a + b$ then $a + b = m$.
22. $3(2) = 2(3)$
23. $a + (2b + 5c) = (a + 2b) + 5c$
24. If $6 = 2 \cdot 3$ and $2 \cdot 3 = 8 - 2$, then $6 = 8 - 2$.

Simplify.

25. $n + 5n$
26. $2.5x - x + y + 3.5y$
27. $5a^2 + 7a + 3a + 11a^2$
28. $4an + \frac{2}{3}am + 8an + \frac{1}{3}am$

Write each sentence as an equation.

29. The product of π and the square of r is A.
30. The sum of a, b, and c is equal to P.

Define the variable, then write an equation for each problem.

31. Peggy is two years younger than Seymour. The sum of their ages is 68. How old is Peggy?
32. 79 decreased by 5 times a number is 49. Find the number.

CHAPTER 2

Adding and Subtracting Rational Numbers

Fresh water freezes at 0° Celsius. However, ocean water freezes at two degrees *less than zero*, or −2°C. The symbol "−" is used in expressing numbers less than 0. In this chapter you will learn more about such numbers.

2-1 Integers on the Number Line

Consider these subtraction sentences.

$$6 - 2 = 4 \qquad 5 - 1 = 4$$
$$6 - 4 = 2 \qquad 5 - 3 = 2$$
$$6 - 6 = 0 \qquad 5 - 5 = 0$$
$$6 - 8 = \underline{\ ?\ } \qquad 5 - 7 = \underline{\ ?\ }$$

There are no answers to $6 - 8$ and $5 - 7$ among the set of whole numbers. Thus, the whole numbers lack *closure* for subtraction. That is, the answer to a subtraction problem involving whole numbers is not always a whole number.

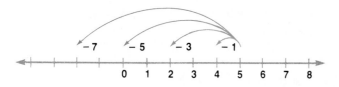

The number line shows that the answer for $5 - 7$ should be *two less than* zero. "Less than" is like taking away, or subtraction. You can write the number *two less than zero* as -2. This is an example of a **negative** number.

You can make a number line which includes negative numbers. Draw a line. Choose a starting point on the line and mark it 0. Then mark off equal distances from this point. To avoid confusion, name points to the right of 0 using the *positive sign* $(+)$ and to the left of zero using the *negative sign* $(-)$, as shown below.

0 is neither positive nor negative.

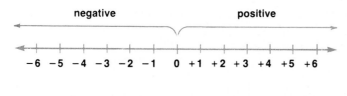

-3 is read *negative* 3 $\qquad$ $+4$ is read *positive* 4

Usually $+4$ is written as 4, without the positive sign.

The set of numbers used to name the points marked on the number line above is called the set of **integers**. This set can be written $\{\ldots, -5, -4, -3, -2, -1, 0, 1, 2, 3, 4, 5, \ldots\}$ where . . . means continued indefinitely.

To graph a set of numbers means to locate the points named by those numbers on the number line. The number that corresponds to a point on the number line is called the **coordinate** of the point.

Examples

1 **Name the coordinate of point _E_.**

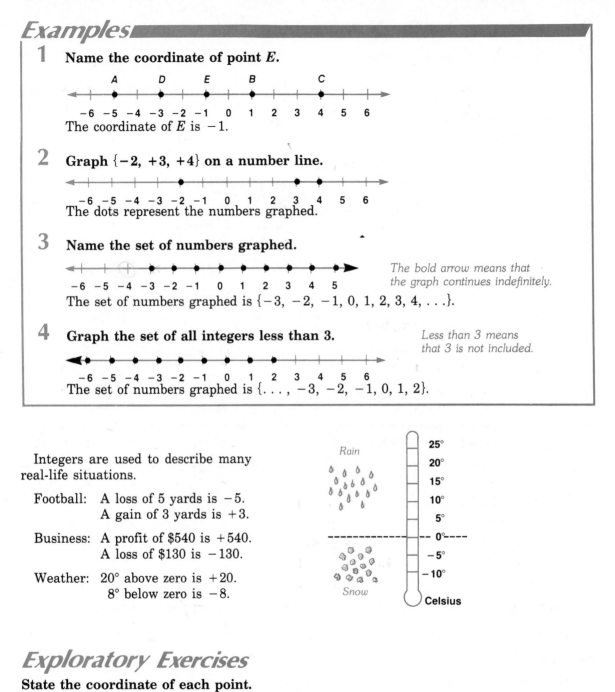

The coordinate of _E_ is −1.

2 **Graph {−2, +3, +4} on a number line.**

The dots represent the numbers graphed.

3 **Name the set of numbers graphed.**

The bold arrow means that the graph continues indefinitely.

The set of numbers graphed is {−3, −2, −1, 0, 1, 2, 3, 4, . . .}.

4 **Graph the set of all integers less than 3.**

Less than 3 means that 3 is not included.

The set of numbers graphed is {. . . , −3, −2, −1, 0, 1, 2}.

Integers are used to describe many real-life situations.

Football: A loss of 5 yards is −5.
A gain of 3 yards is +3.

Business: A profit of $540 is +540.
A loss of $130 is −130.

Weather: 20° above zero is +20.
8° below zero is −8.

Rain

25°
20°
15°
10°
5°
0°
−5°
−10°

Snow

Celsius

Exploratory Exercises

State the coordinate of each point.

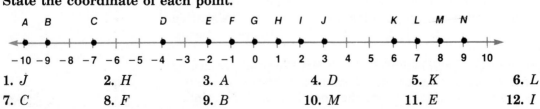

| 1. _J_ | 2. _H_ | 3. _A_ | 4. _D_ | 5. _K_ | 6. _L_ |
| 7. _C_ | 8. _F_ | 9. _B_ | 10. _M_ | 11. _E_ | 12. _I_ |

Name the set of numbers graphed.

13.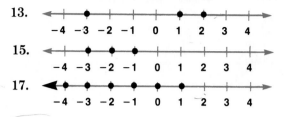

14.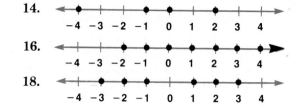

15.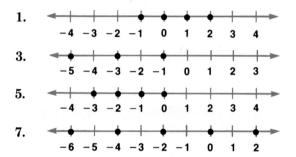

16.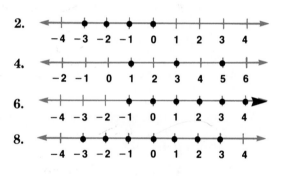

17.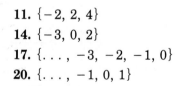

18.

Name an integer to describe each situation.

19. 3 yard loss

20. 12 yard gain

21. 650 meters above sea level

22. 189 meters below sea level

23. up 12 floors

24. down 3 floors

25. $450 loss

26. $325 profit

27. 37° above zero

28. 25° below zero

Written Exercises

Name the set of numbers graphed.

1.

2.

3.

4.

5.

6.

7.

8.

Graph each set of numbers on a number line.

9. $\{-1, 1, 3, 5\}$

10. $\{0, 2, 6\}$

11. $\{-2, 2, 4\}$

12. $\{-2, -4, -6\}$

13. $\{-2, 1, 4\}$

14. $\{-3, 0, 2\}$

15. $\{-4, -3, -2, 1\}$

16. $\{-3, -2, 2, 3\}$

17. $\{\ldots, -3, -2, -1, 0\}$

18. $\{-3, -2, -1, \ldots\}$

19. $\{4, 5, 6 \ldots\}$

20. $\{\ldots, -1, 0, 1\}$

21. {all integers less than -2}

22. {all integers greater than 3}

Find the next three numbers in each pattern.

23. 33, 25, 17, ___, ___, ___.

24. $-6, -3, 0,$ ___, ___, ___.

25. 19, 11, 3, ___, ___, ___.

26. 37, 26, 15, ___, ___, ___.

27. 22, 14, 6, ___, ___, ___.

28. 12, 3, -6, ___, ___, ___.

Challenge

Find the next three numbers in each pattern.

29. 1, 3, 9, 27, ___, ___, ___.

30. $1, \frac{1}{2}, \frac{1}{4},$ ___, ___, ___.

31. 0, 1, -2, 3, -4, 5, ___, ___, ___.

32. 1, 1, 2, 3, 5, 8, ___, ___, ___.

2-2 Addition on the Number Line

In Saturday's football game the Brookfield Warriors lost 3 yards on one play. On the next play they gained 7 yards. The diagram at the right shows that the net gain was 4 yards.

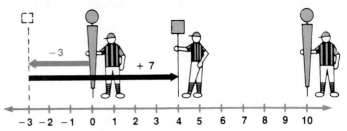

A number line is often used to show addition of integers. For example, to find the sum of 4 and −6, follow these steps.

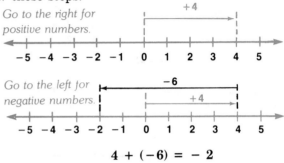

Step 1 Draw an arrow, starting at 0 and going to 4.

Go to the right for positive numbers.

Step 2 Starting at 4, draw an arrow 6 units to the left.

Go to the left for negative numbers.

Step 3 The sum is shown at the head of the second arrow.

$$4 + (-6) = -2$$

Note that parentheses are used in the expression $4 + (-6)$ so that the sign of the number is not confused with the operation symbol.

Examples

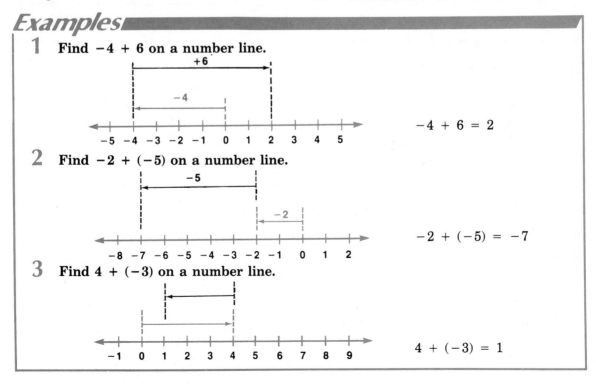

1 Find $-4 + 6$ on a number line.

$$-4 + 6 = 2$$

2 Find $-2 + (-5)$ on a number line.

$$-2 + (-5) = -7$$

3 Find $4 + (-3)$ on a number line.

$$4 + (-3) = 1$$

Exploratory Exercises

State the corresponding addition sentence for each diagram.

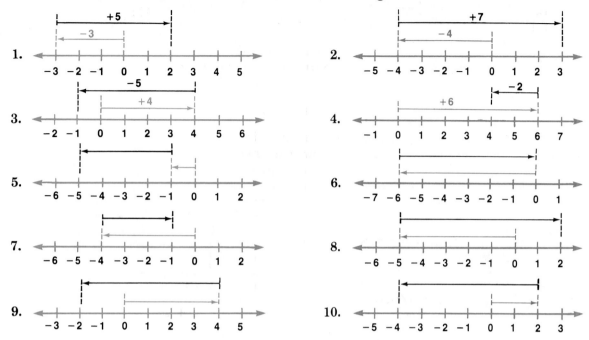

11. How is the meaning of the parentheses in $4 + (-6)$ different from those used in $4 + (5 - 3)$?

Written Exercises

Find each sum. If necessary, use a number line.

1. $7 + 6$	**2.** $9 + 7$	**3.** $-9 + (-7)$	**4.** $-8 + (-11)$
5. $-5 + 0$	**6.** $0 + (-9)$	**7.** $-9 + 4$	**8.** $6 + (-11)$
9. $4 + (-4)$	**10.** $-11 + 11$	**11.** $9 + (-5)$	**12.** $-3 + 9$
13. $2 + (-7)$	**14.** $-11 + 10$	**15.** $9 + (-4)$	**16.** $-14 + 6$
17. $-3 + 12$	**18.** $8 + 3$	**19.** $4 + (-7)$	**20.** $-11 + 5$
21. $7 + (-7)$	**22.** $-491 + 491$	**23.** $0 + 12$	**24.** $-13 + 0$
25. $-6 + (-11)$	**26.** $-13 + (-9)$	**27.** $-15 + (-11)$	**28.** $-18 + (-24)$

For each problem, state an addition sentence. Then solve the problem.

29. One night in Burlington, Vermont, the temperature was $-24°C$. During the day the temperature rose $12°C$. What was the temperature then?

30. A traffic helicopter ascended to a height of 400 meters to monitor traffic. Then it descended 300 meters. How high was it then?

31. An elevator went up to the 36th floor. Then it came down 11 floors. At what floor was it then?

32. A scuba diver was exploring at a depth of 75 meters. She then went up 30 meters. At what depth was she then?

2-3 Adding Integers

It would be difficult to use a number line to add -713 and 425. You need a mathematical concept called absolute value to make the job easier.

Looking at -4 and 4 on the number line, you can see that they are different numbers. However, they are the same number of units from 0. The numbers -4 and 4 have the same **absolute value**.

The absolute value of a number is the number of units it is from 0 on the number line.

Definition of Absolute Value

$\left| -4 \right|$ represents the absolute value of -4.

$\left| 4 \right|$ represents the absolute value of 4.

$$\left| -4 \right| = 4 \qquad\qquad \left| 4 \right| = 4 \qquad\qquad \left| 0 \right| = 0$$

Absolute value can be used to find the sum of integers. Consider the following facts learned from the number line.

$$+6 + (+7) = +13 \qquad\qquad -6 + (-7) = -13$$

Notice that the sign of each addend is positive. The sum is positive.

Notice that the sign of each addend is negative. The sum is negative.

These and other similar examples suggest the following rule.

To add integers with the same sign, add their absolute values. Give the sum the same sign as the addends.

Adding Integers with the Same Sign

Example

1 **Add:** $-5 + (-7)$

$$\begin{aligned} -5 + (-7) &= -(\left| -5 \right| + \left| -7 \right|) && \textit{Both numbers are negative.} \\ &= -(5 + 7) && \textit{Add absolute values.} \\ &= -12 && \textit{The sum is negative.} \end{aligned}$$

Study these facts learned from the number line.

$$4 + (-9) = -5 \qquad\qquad -5 + 8 = 3$$

$|4| = 4$ and $|-9| = 9.$ $\qquad\qquad$ $|-5| = 5$ and $|8| = 8.$

Notice that $9 - 4$ is 5. Which integer, 4 or -9, has the greater absolute value? The sum has the same sign as this addend.

Notice that $8 - 5$ is 3. Which integer, -5 or 8 has the greater absolute value? The sum has the same sign as this addend.

These and other similar examples suggest the following rule.

To add integers with different signs, subtract the lesser from the greater absolute value. Give the result the same sign as the addend with the greater absolute value.	*Adding Integers with Different Signs*

Examples

2 **Add: $3 + (-7)$**

$$\begin{aligned} 3 + (-7) &= -(|-7| - |3|) \\ &= -(7 - 3) \\ &= -4 \end{aligned}$$

-7 has the greater absolute value. The sum is negative.
Subtract absolute values.

3 **Add: $9 + (-2)$**

$$\begin{aligned} 9 + (-2) &= +(|9| - |-2|) \\ &= +(9 - 2) \\ &= +7 \end{aligned}$$

$+9$ has the greater absolute value. The sum is positive.
Subtract absolute values.

Exploratory Exercises

State the absolute value of each integer.

1. $+8$ 2. $+14$ 3. -6 4. -24 5. 17
6. 321   7. -21 8. -271 9. 0   10. 59

State the sign of each sum.

11. $-6 + (-11)$ 12. $-14 + (-15)$ 13. $+8 + (+9)$ 14. $13 + 21$
15. $-8 + (+16)$ 16. $-11 + (+7)$ 17. $+8 + (-35)$ 18. $+7 + (-27)$
19. $18 + (-3)$ 20. $17 + (-38)$ 21. $-27 + 31$ 22. $-17 + 12$

Complete each statement.

23. If $n > 0$, then $|n| = \underline{\ ?\ }$.   24. If $n < 0$, then $|n| = \underline{\ ?\ }$.
25. If $n > 0$, then $|-n| = \underline{\ ?\ }$.   26. If $n < 0$, then $|-n| = \underline{\ ?\ }$.

Written Exercises

Find each sum.

1. $+7 + (+9)$
2. $18 + 22$
3. $-6 + (-13)$
4. $-13 + (-8)$
5. $-3 + (+16)$
6. $14 + (-9)$
7. $-5 + 31$
8. $-10 + 4$
9. $24 + (-3)$
10. $-15 + 12$
11. $13 + (-21)$
12. $-8 + 11$
13. $-18 + (-11)$
14. $-23 + (-47)$
15. $82 + (-78)$
16. $43 + (-67)$
17. $38 + (-47)$
18. $-25 + 47$
19. $63 + (-47)$
20. $-21 + 52$
21. $102 + (-12)$
22. $-104 + 16$
23. $-93 + 39$
24. $97 + (-79)$

Evaluate each expression if $a = -5$, $k = 3$, and $m = -6$.

25. $a + 13$
26. $-5 + k$
27. $15 + m$
28. $8 + a$
29. $k + (-18)$
30. $m + (-31)$
31. $-17 + a$
32. $-21 + k$
33. $m + 6$
34. $k + (-7)$
35. $a + (-13)$
36. $m + 17$
37. $|m|$
38. $|a|$
39. $|m + 4|$
40. $|7 + a|$
41. $|-8 + k|$
42. $|a + k|$
43. $|k + m|$
44. $|k| + |m|$
45. $-|3 + a|$
46. $-|k + 8|$
47. $-|-24 + m|$
48. $-|a + (-11)|$

Find each sum.

49. $+374 + 239$
50. $521 + 124$
51. $-374 + (-165)$
52. $-179 + (-826)$
53. $-582 + 379$
54. $573 + (-336)$
55. $1982 + (-1482)$
56. $-1492 + 876$
57. $294 + |-49|$
58. $|-931| + (-643)$
59. $|871 + (-284)|$
60. $|-285 + (-641)|$
61. $|-857 + 931|$
62. $-|-423 + (-148)|$
63. $|-429| + 243$
64. $-197 + |-483|$
65. $-||-843| + |-231||$

Using Calculators _____ Change-Sign Key

Most calculators have a **change-sign key**, labeled $\boxed{+/-}$. When this key is pressed, the calculator changes the sign of the number in the display.

You can use the change-sign key to enter negative numbers. For example, you can enter -7 by pressing 7 and then pressing the change-sign key.

Example: Use the calculator to add -9 and 5.

Press the following sequence of keys.

9 $\boxed{+/-}$ $\boxed{+}$ 5 $\boxed{=}$

The sum is -4.

Exercises

Use a calculator to find each sum.

1. $-25 + (-18)$
2. $173 + (-200)$
3. $-618 + 52$

2-4 Adding Rational Numbers

Some points on a number line cannot be named by integers. For example, the number line below is separated into fourths to show a sample of numbers that appear in the form of common fractions and decimals. The numbers shown on this number line are all **rational numbers**.

$$-\frac{6}{4} \quad -\frac{5}{4} \quad -1 \quad -\frac{3}{4} \quad -\frac{2}{4} \quad -\frac{1}{4} \quad 0 \quad \frac{1}{4} \quad \frac{2}{4} \quad \frac{3}{4} \quad 1 \quad \frac{5}{4} \quad \frac{6}{4}$$

$$-1.5 \quad -1.25 \quad -1 \quad -0.75 \quad -0.5 \quad -0.25 \quad 0 \quad 0.25 \quad 0.5 \quad 0.75 \quad 1 \quad 1.25 \quad 1.5$$

> **A rational number is a number that can be expressed in the form $\frac{a}{b}$, where a and b are integers and b is not equal to 0.**

Definition of Rational Numbers

Examples of rational numbers expressed in the form $\frac{a}{b}$ are shown in this chart.

Rational Number	Fraction
3	$\frac{3}{1}$
$-2\frac{3}{4}$	$-\frac{11}{4}$
0.125	$\frac{1}{8}$
0	$\frac{0}{1}$
0.333 . . .	$\frac{1}{3}$

Terminating decimals and repeating decimals can be expressed as fractions.

Addition of rational numbers can be represented on a number line by following the same steps as addition of integers.

Consider the addition $\frac{1}{4} + \left(-\frac{3}{8}\right)$. First replace $\frac{1}{4}$ with $\frac{2}{8}$. Then add $\frac{2}{8}$ and $-\frac{3}{8}$.

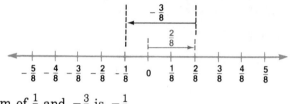

The sum of $\frac{1}{4}$ and $-\frac{3}{8}$ is $-\frac{1}{8}$.

Using the number line to add rational numbers is difficult. However, the rules used to add integers and to add positive rational numbers can be used to add all rational numbers.

Examples

1 Add: $-\frac{3}{8} + \left(-\frac{5}{16}\right)$

$$-\frac{3}{8} + \left(-\frac{5}{16}\right) = -\frac{6}{16} + \left(-\frac{5}{16}\right) \qquad \textit{Replace } -\frac{3}{8} \textit{ with } -\frac{6}{16}.$$

$$= -\left(\left|-\frac{6}{16}\right| + \left|-\frac{5}{16}\right|\right) \qquad \textit{Since the numbers have the same sign, add their absolute values.}$$

$$= -\left(\frac{6}{16} + \frac{5}{16}\right)$$

$$= -\frac{11}{16} \qquad \textit{The sum is negative.}$$

2 Add: $1.354 + (-0.765)$

$$1.354 + (-0.765) = +(|1.354| - |-0.765|) \qquad \textit{1.354 has the greater absolute value.}$$

$$= +(1.354 - 0.765) \qquad \textit{Since the addends have different signs, find the difference of their absolute values.}$$

$$= 0.589 \qquad \textit{The sum is positive.}$$

3 Add: $-1\frac{2}{3} + 4\frac{3}{4}$

$$-1\frac{2}{3} + 4\frac{3}{4} = -1\frac{8}{12} + 4\frac{9}{12} \qquad \textit{Replace } -1\frac{2}{3} \textit{ with } -1\frac{8}{12} \textit{ and } 4\frac{3}{4} \textit{ with } 4\frac{9}{12}.$$

$$= +\left(\left|4\frac{9}{12}\right| - \left|-1\frac{8}{12}\right|\right) \qquad \textit{4}\frac{9}{12} \textit{ has the greater absolute value.}$$

$$= +\left(4\frac{9}{12} - 1\frac{8}{12}\right) \qquad \textit{Since the addends have different signs, find the difference of their absolute values.}$$

$$= +3\frac{1}{12} \textit{ or } 3\frac{1}{12} \qquad \textit{The sum is positive.}$$

---

1. **If the numbers have the same sign, add their absolute values. Give the sum the same sign as the numbers.**

2. **If the numbers have different signs, subtract the lesser from the greater absolute value. Give the result the same sign as the number with the greater absolute value.**

Summary of Rules for Addition of Rational Numbers

Exploratory Exercises

State the absolute value of each number.

1. $+\frac{3}{4}$ 　　　　2. $+\frac{9}{8}$ 　　　　3. -1.76 　　　　4. -2.53 　　　　5. $-\frac{3}{11}$

6. -16.7 　　　　7. 1.82 　　　　8. $-\frac{7}{16}$ 　　　　9. $+\frac{3}{82}$ 　　　　10. 1.48

State the sign of each sum.

11. $-\frac{3}{4} + \frac{7}{8}$

12. $\frac{15}{16} + \left(-\frac{13}{16}\right)$

13. $-1.354 + 1.265$

14. $37.42 + (-45.36)$

15. $-\frac{12}{31} + \frac{13}{62}$

16. $-\frac{9}{13} + \left(-\frac{3}{13}\right)$

17. $-394.1 + 427.6$

18. $-85.32 + 76.3$

19. $-\frac{5}{12} + \left(-\frac{5}{24}\right)$

20. $\frac{2}{5} + \left(-\frac{2}{7}\right)$

21. $-0.0034 + 0.034$

22. $-0.0759 + 0.4$

Written Exercises

Find each sum.

1. $-\frac{11}{9} + \left(-\frac{7}{9}\right)$

2. $\frac{17}{21} + \left(-\frac{13}{21}\right)$

3. $\frac{5}{11} + \left(-\frac{6}{11}\right)$

4. $-\frac{8}{13} + \left(-\frac{11}{13}\right)$

5. $-\frac{7}{12} + \frac{5}{12}$

6. $-\frac{9}{28} + \frac{13}{28}$

7. $4.57 + (-3.69)$

8. $-4.8 + 3.2$

9. $-1.7 + (-3.9)$

10. $-2.31 + 7.62$

11. $-38.9 + 24.2$

12. $-0.007 + 0.06$

13. $\frac{3}{4} + \left(-\frac{7}{12}\right)$

14. $-\frac{2}{7} + \frac{3}{14}$

15. $-\frac{3}{8} + \frac{5}{24}$

16. $-\frac{5}{6} + \left(-\frac{7}{12}\right)$

17. $-\frac{1}{8} + \left(-\frac{5}{2}\right)$

18. $\frac{2}{3} + \left(-\frac{2}{9}\right)$

19. $-1.543 + 2.165$

20. $-3.948 + 4.826$

21. $-0.376 + (-0.289)$

22. $-0.006 + 0.0052$

23. $-0.0005 + (-0.3)$

24. $0.0007 + (-0.001)$

25. $-\frac{3}{5} + \frac{5}{6}$

26. $\frac{3}{8} + \left(-\frac{7}{12}\right)$

27. $-\frac{4}{15} + \frac{3}{4}$

28. $-\frac{9}{4} + \left(-\frac{4}{3}\right)$

29. $\frac{17}{5} + \left(-\frac{13}{4}\right)$

30. $-\frac{7}{15} + \left(-\frac{5}{12}\right)$

Challenge

Find each sum. Express each result in decimal form.

31. $-\frac{4}{5} + (-3.8)$

32. $-0.37 + \left(-\frac{21}{8}\right)$

33. $-5\frac{3}{4} + 6.25$

34. $-8.66 + 6\frac{7}{8}$

35. $7.43 + \left(-\frac{9}{4}\right)$

36. $4\frac{7}{8} + -3.754$

37. $-11\frac{7}{16} + 7.225$

38. $-3.276 + \left(-\frac{15}{8}\right)$

mini-review

Simplify.

1. $7(x + y) + 2y$

2. $7a^2 + 3(a^2 + b) + 6a$

Evaluate.

3. $2^4 - 2^2 \div 2^2$

Write an equation for each sentence.

4. The square of the difference of a and b is equal to twice c.

5. The circumference (C) of a circle is equal to the product of π and the diameter (d).

Problem Solving

Many different strategies can be used to solve problems. One strategy is to write an equation. Another important strategy is called *guess and check*. To use this strategy, guess the answer to the problem, then check whether the guess is correct. If the first guess is incorrect, guess again until you find the right answer. Often, the results of one guess can help you make a better guess. Always keep a record of your guesses so you do not make the same guess twice.

Sometimes there will not be one right answer. You may have to find the best answer.

Example: **Insert parentheses so that a true equation results.**

$$10 - 4 \cdot 2 - 1 = 3$$

Copy the expression to the left of the equals sign.
Then insert parentheses and evaluate the expression.

$10 - 4 \cdot (2 - 1) = 6$ *Try again since the value does not equal 3.*
$(10 - 4) \cdot 2 - 1 = 11$ *Try again.*
$10 - (4 \cdot 2 - 1) = 3$ *Correct!*

Exercises

Use the guess-and-check strategy to solve each problem.

1. When a certain number is multiplied by itself the product is 2916. Find the number.

2. Find an odd number between 10 and 25 which is divisible by 3, but is not divisible by 5.

3. Using each of the digits 1, 2, . . ., 6 only once, write two whole numbers whose product is as large as possible.

4. If it costs a nickel each time you cut and weld a link, what is the minimum cost to make a chain out of 5 links?

5. Paper plates can be purchased in packages of 15 or 25. Joe bought 7 packages and got 125 plates. How many packages of 25 did he buy?

6. The cube of a certain whole number is close to 4000. Find the number.

7. Copy the figure at the right. Then fill in the digits 1, 2, . . ., 8 in such a way that no two consecutive numbers are in boxes which touch at a point or side.

8. Gina and Jim raise cats and birds. They counted all the heads and got 10. They counted all the feet and got 34. How many birds and cats do they have?

For each of the following, insert parentheses so that a true equation results.

9. $4 \cdot 5 - 2 + 7 = 19$

10. $25 - 4 \cdot 2 + 3 = 5$

11. $3 + 5 \cdot 8 - 2 = 48$

12. $3 + 6 \cdot 4 \cdot 2 = 54$

2-5 More About Addition

Previously you have added pairs of numbers. To add three or more rational numbers, first group the numbers in pairs. Use the commutative and associative properties to rearrange the addends if necessary.

Examples

1 Add: $(-4) + 5 + (-6)$

$$-4 + 5 + (-6) = (-4 + 5) + (-6) \quad \text{Group two of the addends.}$$
$$= 1 + (-6)$$
$$= -5 \quad \text{Do you get the same result if you find the sum } -4 + [5 + (-6)]?$$

2 Add: $-\frac{4}{3} + \frac{5}{8} + \left(-\frac{7}{3}\right)$

$$-\frac{4}{3} + \frac{5}{8} + \left(-\frac{7}{3}\right) = \left[-\frac{4}{3} + \left(-\frac{7}{3}\right)\right] + \frac{5}{8} \quad \text{Commutative and Associative Properties.}$$
$$= -\frac{11}{3} + \frac{5}{8}$$
$$= -\frac{88}{24} + \frac{15}{24}$$
$$= -\frac{73}{24}$$
$$= -3\frac{1}{24}$$

3 Add: $28.32 + (-56.17) + 32.41 + (-75.13)$

Group the positive numbers and group the negative numbers.

$$28.32 + (-56.17) + 32.41 + (-75.13) = 28.32 + 32.41 + (-56.17) + (-75.13)$$
$$= (28.32 + 32.41) + [(-56.17) + (-75.13)]$$
$$= 60.73 + (-131.30)$$
$$= -70.57$$

You can use the distributive property and what you know about rational numbers to simplify expressions that have like terms.

Example

4 Simplify: $-5x + a + 7x + (-4a)$

$$-5x + a + 7x + (-4a) = (-5x + 7x) + [1a + (-4a)] \quad \text{Group the like terms.}$$
$$= (-5 + 7)x + [1 + (-4)]a \quad \text{Use the distributive property.}$$
$$= 2x + (-3a)$$

Exploratory Exercises

Find each sum.

1. $2 + (-6) + 4$
2. $5 + 2 + (-5)$
3. $0.6 + (-0.3) + (-0.4)$
4. $-0.2 + 0.4 + (-0.7)$
5. $\frac{1}{2} + \left(-\frac{1}{4}\right) + \frac{3}{4}$
6. $-\frac{1}{5} + \frac{3}{5} + \left(-\frac{4}{5}\right)$
7. $-4m + 8m$
8. $-8x + (-10x)$
9. $r + (-2r) + 5r$
10. $-k + 6k + (-3k)$
11. $-b + y + 4b + (-5y)$
12. $s + (-5t) + 9t + 8s$

Written Exercises

Find each sum.

1. $4 + (-12) + (-18)$
2. $7 + (-11) + 32$
3. $8 + (-15) + 13$
4. $-41 + (-78) + 51$
5. $83 + (-19) + 16$
6. $16 + (-9) + (-94)$
7. $-3a + 12a + (-14a)$
8. $5y + (-12y) + (-21y)$
9. $14b + (-21b) + 37b$
10. $5x + (-21x) + 29x$
11. $-3z + (-17z) + (-18z)$
12. $9m + 43m + (-16m)$
13. $-\frac{3}{4} + \frac{5}{12} + \left(-\frac{5}{4}\right)$
14. $\frac{7}{3} + \left(-\frac{5}{6}\right) + \left(-\frac{2}{3}\right)$
15. $-\frac{2}{7} + \frac{3}{14} + \frac{3}{7}$
16. $-\frac{3}{5} + \frac{6}{7} + \left(-\frac{2}{35}\right)$
17. $\frac{5}{8} + \left(-\frac{3}{16}\right) + \left(-\frac{7}{24}\right)$
18. $\frac{3}{4} + \left(-\frac{5}{8}\right) + \frac{3}{32}$
19. $12 + (-17) + 36 + (-45)$
20. $81 + (-31) + (-9) + 62$
21. $-75 + 47 + 32 + (-16)$
22. $28 + (-56) + 32 + (-75)$
23. $6.7 + (-8.1) + (-7.3)$
24. $-7.6 + 1.8 + (-3.5)$
25. $-37.12 + 42.18 + (-12.6)$
26. $-4.13 + (-5.18) + 9.63$
27. $-7.9 + (-5.3) + (-4.2)$
28. $-9.7 + 5.3 + 4.2$
29. $-14a + 36k + 12k + (-83a)$
30. $16b + (-22xy) + 31b + (-36xy)$
31. $13mp + (-3ps) + 76mp + (-21ps)$
32. $-17px + 22bg + 35px + (-37bg)$

33.
$$\begin{array}{r} 12a \\ +(-9a) \\ \hline \end{array}$$

34.
$$\begin{array}{r} -15m \\ +\quad 6m \\ \hline \end{array}$$

35.
$$\begin{array}{r} -23w \\ +\quad 47w \\ \hline \end{array}$$

36.
$$\begin{array}{r} -13c \\ +(-28c) \\ \hline \end{array}$$

37.
$$\begin{array}{r} 5.8k \\ +(-3.6k) \\ \hline \end{array}$$

38.
$$\begin{array}{r} -7.9s \\ +(-3.8s) \\ \hline \end{array}$$

39.
$$\begin{array}{r} -0.23x \\ +(-0.5\ x) \\ \hline \end{array}$$

40.
$$\begin{array}{r} 0.81h \\ +(-0.93h) \\ \hline \end{array}$$

Solve each problem.

41. Julie Thomas shot rounds in a recent golf tournament in which her scores relative to par were -3, $+2$, -4, and -1. What was her score for the tournament relative to par?

42. Last week, the following day-to-day changes in the noon temperatures were recorded: Sun., $+3$; Mon., -7; Tues., -5; Wed., $+4$; Thurs., $+6$; Fri., -3; Sat., -8. What was the net change for the week?

43. On Tuesday, Johnny Lomax wrote checks for $35.76 and $41.32. On Wednesday, he deposited $135.59. Friday he wrote a check for $63.17. What was the net increase or decrease in his account for the week?

44. Last week, the following day-to-day changes for the Dow-Jones stock averages were recorded: Mon., $+5\frac{3}{8}$; Tues., $-6\frac{1}{4}$; Wed., $+11\frac{1}{8}$; Thurs., $+3\frac{5}{8}$; Fri., $-7\frac{1}{2}$. What was the net change for the week?

2-6 Subtraction

There are many patterns in nature. On an oak leaf, points match each other *opposite* a center line. Similar patterns are helpful in understanding subtraction.

Notice that -3 and 3 are the same distance but in *opposite* directions from 0 on the number line.

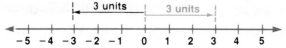

What is the result when you add two numbers such as 3 and -3?

$$3 + (-3) = 0 \qquad -7 + 7 = 0 \qquad -\tfrac{4}{7} + \tfrac{4}{7} = 0 \qquad 19.3 + (-19.3) = 0$$

If the sum of two numbers is 0, the numbers are called **additive inverses** or **opposites**.

> -3 is the additive inverse, or opposite, of 3.
>
> 7 is the additive inverse, or opposite, of -7.
>
> $\tfrac{4}{7}$ is the additive inverse, or opposite, of $-\tfrac{4}{7}$.
>
> -19.3 is the additive inverse, or opposite, of 19.3

Is 3 the additive inverse of -3?

Zero is its own opposite.

These and many other similar examples suggest the following property.

> **For every number *a*,   *a* + (−*a*) = 0**

Additive Inverse Property

If a is negative, then (−a) is positive.

Additive inverses are used in the subtraction of rational numbers. Observe the following patterns.

| *Subtraction* | *Addition* | *Subtraction* | *Addition* |

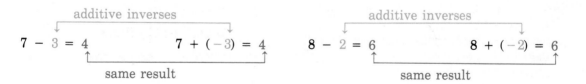

It appears that subtracting a number is equivalent to adding its additive inverse. These and other similar examples suggest the rule for subtracting rational numbers.

> **To subtract a rational number, add its additive inverse. For rational numbers a and b, $a - b = a + (-b)$.**   *Subtraction Rule*

Examples

1 **Subtract: $5 - (-8)$**

$$5 - (-8) = 5 + (+8) \qquad \textit{To subtract } -8, \textit{ add } +8.$$
$$= 13$$

2 **Subtract: $6 - 11$**

$$6 - 11 = 6 + (-11) \qquad \textit{To subtract } 11, \textit{ add } -11.$$
$$= -5$$

3 **Subtract: $-4 - (-7)$**

$$-4 - (-7) = -4 + (+7) \qquad \textit{To subtract } -7, \textit{ add } +7.$$
$$= 3$$

4 **Subtract: $7.32 - (-6.85)$**

$$7.32 - (-6.85) = 7.32 + (+6.85) \qquad \textit{To subtract } -6.85, \textit{ add } +6.85.$$
$$= 14.17$$

5 **Subtract: $-\frac{7}{8} - \left(-\frac{3}{16}\right)$**

$$-\frac{7}{8} - \left(-\frac{3}{16}\right) = -\frac{7}{8} + \frac{3}{16} \qquad \textit{To subtract } -\frac{3}{16} \textit{ add } +\frac{3}{16}.$$
$$= -\frac{14}{16} + \frac{3}{16}$$
$$= -\frac{11}{16}$$

The distributive property is used to simplify expressions that contain like terms as shown in the next example.

Example

6 Simplify: $7x - 12x$

$$7x - 12x = 7x + (-12x) \quad \text{To subtract } 12x, \text{ add } -12x.$$
$$= [7 + (-12)]x \quad \text{Distributive Property}$$
$$= -5x$$

Exploratory Exercises

State the additive inverse of each of the following.

1. $+6$ **2.** -6 **3.** 5 **4.** -14 **5.** -13

6. a **7.** $-a$ **8.** $-2y$ **9.** 0 **10.** $4x$

11. 3.7 **12.** -7.4 **13.** $\frac{3}{7}$ **14.** $-\frac{4}{9}$ **15.** $-\frac{8}{17}$

State the number named.

16. $-(-5)$ **17.** $-(+7)$ **18.** $-(4)$ **19.** $-(-13)$ **20.** $-(-36)$

21. $-(-7)$ **22.** $-(18)$ **23.** $-(-16)$ **24.** $-(-43)$ **25.** $-(+56)$

26. $-(-1.8)$ **27.** $-(+7.1)$ **28.** $-\left(\frac{8}{11}\right)$ **29.** $-\left(-\frac{3}{4}\right)$ **30.** $-(6.5)$

State an addition expression for each of the following.

31. $8 - 13$ **32.** $-18 - 7$ **33.** $-17 - 8$ **34.** $11 - (-2)$

35. $-1.7 - (-1.5)$ **36.** $\frac{3}{8} - \left(-\frac{2}{3}\right)$ **37.** $9y - 3y$ **38.** $-8a - (-7a)$

Written Exercises

Find each difference.

1. $27 - 19$ **2.** $47 - 32$ **3.** $52 - 37$ **4.** $8 - 13$

5. $13 - 31$ **6.** $27 - 43$ **7.** $17 - (-23)$ **8.** $29 - (-25)$

9. $18 - (-34)$ **10.** $-21 - (-14)$ **11.** $-23 - (-12)$ **12.** $-47 - 35$

13. $\frac{3}{5} - \left(-\frac{1}{5}\right)$ **14.** $\frac{1}{6} - \frac{2}{3}$ **15.** $-\frac{1}{2} - \left(-\frac{3}{4}\right)$ **16.** $-5\frac{7}{8} - 2\frac{3}{4}$

17. $0 - 21$ **18.** $69 - (-95)$ **19.** $7.3 - (-4.2)$ **20.** $-4.5 - 8.6$

21. $-67.1 - (-38.2)$ **22.** $89.3 - (-14.2)$ **23.** $-72.5 - 81.3$ **24.** $3.81 - (-4.65)$

25. $\quad 19$
$\underline{\quad -36}$

26. $\quad 61$
$\underline{-(-43)}$

27. $\quad -5.2$
$\underline{-(-3.8)}$

28. $\quad -1.7$
$\underline{-(+3.9)}$

29. $19m - 12m$ **30.** $8h - 23h$ **31.** $-18p - 4p$ **32.** $-21a - 3a$

33. $24b - (-9b)$ **34.** $-31x - (-33x)$ **35.** $-52z - (-17z)$ **36.** $41y - (-41y)$

Evaluate each of the following.

37. $m - 7$, if $m = 5$

38. $a - 12$, if $a = -8$

39. $p - 14$, if $p = 72$

40. $y - 0.5$, if $y = -0.8$

41. $a - (-7)$, if $a = 1.9$

42. $b - (-0.5)$, if $b = -13$

43. $h - (-1.3)$, if $h = -18$

44. $k - (-12)$, if $k = 2.7$

45. $w - 3.7$, if $w = -1.8$

46. $\frac{3}{5} - n$, if $n = -\frac{7}{5}$

47. $\frac{11}{2} - m$, if $m = -\frac{5}{2}$

48. $\frac{8}{13} - a$, if $a = -\frac{9}{13}$

49. $\frac{11}{4} - x$, if $x = \frac{27}{8}$

50. $-\frac{8}{5} - y$, if $y = \frac{12}{5}$

51. $-\frac{12}{7} - z$, if $z = \frac{16}{21}$

52. $-\frac{13}{6} - k$, if $k = -\frac{11}{12}$

53. $-\frac{18}{17} - q$, if $q = \frac{31}{34}$

54. $-\frac{33}{38} - r$, if $r = -\frac{16}{19}$

mini-review

Find each sum.

1. $-83 + 24$

2. $-0.25 + (-1.873)$

3. $-3x + 5x + (-9x)$

State the property that is shown.

4. $6(x + 3y) = 6(3y + x)$

Define a variable, then write an equation for the following.

5. 55 decreased by three times a number is 31. Find the number.

Excursions in Algebra ──────────── Magic Squares

Magic squares are square arrays of numbers. The sum of the numbers in each row, column, and diagonal is the same.

1	2	−3
−4	0	4
3	−2	−1

The sum of the numbers in each row, column, and diagonal of this magic square is 0.

New magic squares can be formed by adding the same number to each entry in the magic square above. In the squares below, how was each entry obtained? Find each new magic square.

3	4	−1

−2		
	−3	
		−4

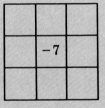

56 *Adding and Subtracting Rational Numbers*

2-7 Solving Equations Involving Addition

A scale, as shown below on the left is in balance when both sides hold equal weights. If you add weight to only one side, as shown on the right, then the scale is no longer in balance.

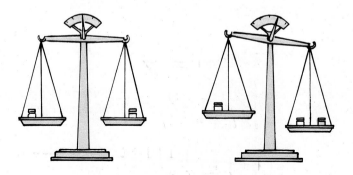

However, if you add the same weight to both sides, the scale will balance.

Think of an equation as a scale in balance. If the same number is added to both sides of the equation, then the result is an equivalent equation. **Equivalent equations** are equations that have the same solution.

$$11 = x + 3 \qquad \textit{The solution to this equation is 8.}$$
$$11 + 5 = (x + 3) + 5 \quad \textit{Add 5 to both sides.}$$
$$16 = x + 8 \qquad \textit{The solution to this equation is also 8.}$$

The property that is used to add the same number to both sides of an equation is called the **addition property of equality**.

For any numbers a, b, and c, if $a = b$, then $a + c = b + c$.	*Addition Property of Equality*

Also, if the same number is *subtracted* from both sides of an equation, the result is an equivalent equation.

$$11 = x + 3$$
$$11 - 3 = (x + 3) - 3 \qquad \textit{Subtract 3 from both sides.}$$
$$8 = x \qquad \qquad \textit{Why is this equation equivalent to } 11 = x + 3?$$

The property that is used to subtract the same number from both sides of an equation is called the **subtraction property of equality**.

For any numbers a, b, and c,
if $a = b$, then $a - c = b - c$.

Subtraction Property of Equality

Both the addition and subtraction properties of equality can be used to solve equations involving addition.

Examples

1 **Solve: $k + 15 = -6$**

$$k + 15 = -6 \qquad \textit{Use the subtraction property of equality.}$$
$$k + 15 - 15 = -6 - 15 \quad \textit{Subtract 15 from both sides.}$$
$$k + 0 = -21$$
$$k = -21$$

To check that -21 is the solution, substitute -21 for k in $k + 15 = -6$.

Check: $k + 15 = -6$
$$-21 + 15 \overset{?}{=} -6$$
$$-6 = -6 \quad \textit{The check verifies that the solution to the equation is } -21.$$

2 **Solve: $r + 16 = -7$**

$$r + 16 = -7 \qquad \qquad \textit{Use the addition property of equality and the additive inverse.}$$
$$r + 16 + (-16) = -7 + (-16) \quad \textit{Add } -16 \textit{ to both sides.}$$
$$r + 0 = -23 \qquad \qquad \textit{The sum of 16 and } -16 \textit{ is 0.}$$
$$r = -23$$

Check: $r + 16 = -7$
$$-23 + 16 \overset{?}{=} -7$$
$$-7 = -7 \quad \textit{The check verifies that the solution to the equation is } -23.$$

Example

3 Solve: $m + \left(-\frac{3}{4}\right) = -\frac{1}{2}$ **Check:** $m + \left(-\frac{3}{4}\right) = -\frac{1}{2}$

$$m + \left(-\frac{3}{4}\right) + \frac{3}{4} = -\frac{1}{2} + \frac{3}{4}$$

$$\frac{1}{4} + \left(-\frac{3}{4}\right) \stackrel{?}{=} -\frac{1}{2}$$

$$m + 0 = -\frac{2}{4} + \frac{3}{4}$$

$$-\frac{1}{2} = -\frac{1}{2}$$

$$m = \frac{1}{4} \quad \text{The solution is } \frac{1}{4}.$$

Exploratory Exercises

State the number you add to both sides of each equation to solve it.

1. $y + 21 = -7$

2. $13 + x = -16$

3. $y + (-5) = 11$

4. $z + (-9) = 34$

5. $-10 + k = 34$

6. $y + 13 = 45$

State the number you subtract from both sides of each equation to solve it.

7. $m + 16 = 14$

8. $k + 9 = -16$

9. $t + 5 = 8$

10. $y + 9 = -53$

11. $z + (-3) = -8$

12. $x + (-4) = -37$

Written Exercises

Solve each equation.

1. $m + 10 = 7$

2. $y + 16 = 7$

3. $5 + a = -14$

4. $9 = x + 13$

5. $k + 11 = -21$

6. $b + 15 = -32$

7. $-11 = a + 8$

8. $18 + m = -57$

9. $14 + c = -5$

10. $y + 3 = -15$

11. $p + 12 = -4$

12. $w + 42 = -51$

13. $r + (-8) = 7$

14. $z + (-17) = 0$

15. $z + (-18) = 34$

16. $-12 + b = 12$

17. $-15 + d = 13$

18. $x + (-7) = 36$

19. $r + (-11) = -21$

20. $y + (-13) = -27$

21. $h + (-13) = -5$

22. $d + (-6) = -9$

23. $-11 = k + (-5)$

24. $-23 = -19 + n$

25. $-4.1 = m + (-0.5)$

26. $0 = t + (-1.4)$

27. $y + 2.3 = 1.5$

28. $x + 4.2 = 1.5$

29. $2.4 = m + 3.7$

30. $4.4 = b + 6.3$

31. $y + \frac{7}{16} = -\frac{5}{8}$

32. $x + \frac{4}{9} = -\frac{2}{27}$

33. $-\frac{7}{6} + k = \frac{5}{6}$

34. $-\frac{5}{7} + w = \frac{5}{7}$

35. $m + \frac{5}{9} = -\frac{3}{5}$

36. $m + \left(-\frac{7}{8}\right) = \frac{5}{12}$

Using Calculators _____ Checking Solutions

A calculator can help you check the solution to an equation. For example, enter the following sequence to check if -2.4 is the solution to $x + (-7.3) = -9.7$.

ENTER: 2.4 $\boxed{+/-}$ $\boxed{+}$ 7.3 $\boxed{+/-}$ $\boxed{=}$

Because -9.7 shows in the display screen, -2.4 is the solution.

Exercises   Use a calculator to check the solutions for Written Exercises 19-30.

2-8 Solving Equations Involving Subtraction

Many equations involving subtraction may be solved by using the addition property of equality.

Example

1 Solve: $m - 9 = -13$.

$$m - 9 = -13$$
$$m - 9 + 9 = -13 + 9 \quad \text{Add 9 to both sides.}$$
$$m = -4$$

Check: $m - 9 = -13$
$$-4 - 9 \overset{?}{=} -13$$
$$-13 = -13 \quad \text{The solution is } -4.$$

Sometimes an equation can be solved more easily if it is first rewritten in a different form. Recall that subtracting a number is the same as adding its inverse. For example, the equation $b - (-8) = 23$ may be rewritten as $b + 8 = 23$. Also, $y + (-7.5) = -12.2$ may be rewritten as $y - 7.5 = -12.2$.

Examples

2 Solve: $b - (-8) = 23$

This equation is equivalent to $b + 8 = 23$.

$$b + 8 = 23$$
$$b + 8 - 8 = 23 - 8 \quad \text{Subtract 8 from both sides.}$$
$$b = 15$$

Check: $b - (-8) = 23$
$$15 - (-8) \overset{?}{=} 23$$
$$23 = 23 \quad \text{The solution is 15.}$$

3 Solve: $y + (-7.5) = -12.2$

This equation is equivalent to $y - 7.5 = -12.2$

$$y - 7.5 = -12.2$$
$$y - 7.5 + 7.5 = -12.2 + 7.5 \quad \text{Add 7.5 to both sides.}$$
$$y = -4.7 \quad \text{Check this result.}$$

The solution is -4.7.

Solving some equations requires two steps. Study the following example.

Example

4 **Solve:** $-8 - k = 13$

$$-8 - k = 13$$
$$-8 - k + k = 13 + k \qquad \text{Add } k \text{ to both sides.}$$
$$-8 = 13 + k$$
$$-13 + (-8) = -13 + 13 + k \qquad \text{Add } -13 \text{ to both sides (or subtract 13).}$$
$$-21 = k$$

Check:
$$-8 - k = 13$$
$$-8 - (-21) \overset{?}{=} 13$$
$$13 = 13 \qquad \text{The solution is } -21.$$

Exploratory Exercises

Rename the following expressions by using their inverse operations.

1. $m + (-8)$ **2.** $r + (-12)$ **3.** $y - (-11)$ **4.** $k - (-12)$

5. $b + (-17)$ **6.** $a - (-21)$ **7.** $n - (-23)$ **8.** $x + (-36)$

9. $z + (-31)$ **10.** $s - (-18)$ **11.** $p - (-47)$ **12.** $q + (-62)$

Written Exercises

Solve each equation.

1. $a - 15 = -32$ **2.** $h - 26 = -29$ **3.** $y - 7 = -32$

4. $r - 21 = -37$ **5.** $y + (-7) = -19$ **6.** $x + (-8) = -31$

7. $b + (-14) = 6$ **8.** $k + (-13) = 21$ **9.** $d - (-27) = 13$

10. $m - (-13) = 37$ **11.** $r - (-31) = 16$ **12.** $t - (-16) = 9$

13. $-8 + m = -11$ **14.** $-7 + y = -12$ **15.** $g + 27 = 8$

16. $j + 13 = -27$ **17.** $k - 12 = -14$ **18.** $n + (-5) = 27$

19. $m - (-21) = 9$ **20.** $-9 + s = 17$ **21.** $p + (-23) = -14$

22. $x - (-33) = 14$ **23.** $-12 + z = -36$ **24.** $x - 13 = 45$

25. $d - 27 = -63$ **26.** $y + (-18) = 7$ **27.** $w - (-37) = 28$

28. $13 - m = 41$ **29.** $16 - y = 37$ **30.** $65 = 12 - x$

31. $41 = 32 - r$ **32.** $-7 = -16 - k$ **33.** $-27 = -6 - p$

34. $-14 - a = -21$ **35.** $-27 - b = -7$ **36.** $-19 - s = 41$

37. $r - 6.5 = -9.3$ **38.** $y - 7.3 = 5.1$ **39.** $p - (-1.3) = -7.1$

40. $s - (-7.1) = 2.4$ **41.** $-1.43 + w = 0.89$ **42.** $-0.0056 + z = 0.065$

43. $m - \frac{6}{7} = \frac{3}{14}$ **44.** $a - \frac{2}{3} = -\frac{4}{9}$ **45.** $b + \left(-\frac{3}{4}\right) = \frac{4}{5}$

46. $j + \left(-\frac{3}{5}\right) = \frac{5}{3}$ **47.** $x - \left(-\frac{5}{6}\right) = \frac{2}{7}$ **48.** $h - \left(-\frac{7}{8}\right) = \frac{5}{9}$

Applications in Meteorology

Anna Lopez is a meteorologist. When forecasting the weather, Anna predicts the high and low temperatures for each day. In addition, she predicts the equivalent temperatures due to the wind-chill factor, which depends on the actual temperature and the speed of the wind. Anna uses a chart similar to this to predict the wind-chill factor.

Wind Chill Chart

Wind speed in mph	Actual temperature (°Fahrenheit)								
	50	40	30	20	10	0	−10	−20	−30
	Equivalent temperature (°Fahrenheit)								
0	50	40	30	20	10	0	−10	−20	−30
5	48	37	27	16	6	−5	−15	−26	−36
10	40	28	16	4	−9	−21	−33	−46	−58
15	36	22	9	−5	−18	−36	−45	−58	−72
20	32	18	4	−10	−25	−39	−53	−67	−82
25	30	16	0	−15	−29	−44	−59	−74	−88
30	28	13	−2	−18	−33	−48	−63	−79	−94

In Chicago on January 11, the low temperature was −10°F. If the wind speed was 15 mph, the wind-chill factor made the temperature equivalent to −45°F.

Exercises

Use the wind chill chart to find each equivalent temperature.

1. 30°F, 10 mph
2. 20°F, 20 mph
3. −10°F, 15 mph
4. −20°F, 5 mph
5. 0°F, 15 mph
6. 40°F, 30 mph

7. Find the difference between the equivalent temperatures in problems 1 and 2.

8. Find the difference between the equivalent temperatures in problems 3 and 4.

9. Find the difference between the equivalent temperatures in problems 5 and 6.

10. Find the difference between the equivalent temperatures in problems 2 and 6.

2-9 Problem Solving: **Rational Numbers**

Before you solve a problem, you must study the problem carefully. Consider the following problem and its solution.

Death Valley is about 86 meters below sea level. The top of Mt. McKinley is 6194 meters above sea level. What is the difference in these elevations?

 Read the problem to find out what is asked. Identify important facts from the problem.

The problem asks for the difference in elevations.

Death Valley	86 m below sea level
Mt. McKinley	6194 m above sea level

Then think about how the facts are related. Sometimes it is helpful to draw a chart or diagram.

Elevation above sea level can be represented with a positive number. Elevation below sea level can be represented with a negative number.

Mt. McKinley	6194 m
Sea Level	0 m
Death Valley	−86 m

 Decide how to solve the problem.

To solve the problem, find the difference between 6194 and −86. Recall that difference is the result of subtraction. Find $6194 - (-86)$.

 Do the computation and answer the problem.

$6194 - (-86) = 6280$
The difference in elevations is 6280 m.

 See if the solution makes sense for the given problem. If not, try another way to solve the problem.

Since Mt. McKinley is about 6200 m above sea level and Death Valley is about 90 m below sea level, the distance between elevations should be approximately 6290 m. The solution 6280 makes sense.

Sometimes a problem can be solved by translating it into a mathematical equation. Study this example.

Example

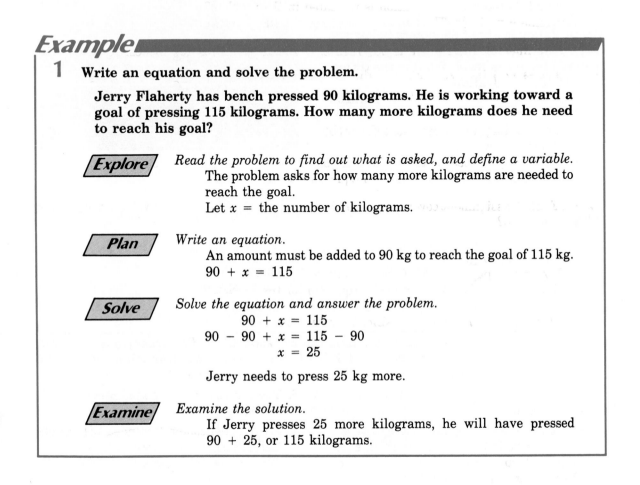

1 **Write an equation and solve the problem.**

Jerry Flaherty has bench pressed 90 kilograms. He is working toward a goal of pressing 115 kilograms. How many more kilograms does he need to reach his goal?

Explore Read the problem to find out what is asked, and define a variable.
The problem asks for how many more kilograms are needed to reach the goal.
Let x = the number of kilograms.

Plan Write an equation.
An amount must be added to 90 kg to reach the goal of 115 kg.
$90 + x = 115$

Solve Solve the equation and answer the problem.
$$90 + x = 115$$
$$90 - 90 + x = 115 - 90$$
$$x = 25$$

Jerry needs to press 25 kg more.

Examine Examine the solution.
If Jerry presses 25 more kilograms, he will have pressed $90 + 25$, or 115 kilograms.

Exploratory Exercises

State the answer to each question.

1. Frieda traveled 110 kilometers by boat up the Rhine River last summer. She then traveled 320 kilometers down along the river by train. How far downstream was she from her starting point?

   a. What is asked?
   b. How far up the river did Frieda travel?
   c. How far down the river did she travel?
   d. How can these distances be represented using positive and negative numbers?
   e. Define a variable. Then state an equation for the problem.

2. The sum of two integers is -23. One of the integers is $+9$. What is the other integer?

   a. What is asked?
   b. What is one of the integers?
   c. What is the sum of the integers?
   d. What mathematical operation is indicated in the problem?
   e. Define a variable. Then state an equation for the problem.

3. The perimeter of a triangle is $35\frac{3}{8}$ inches. One side measures $10\frac{1}{8}$ inches. A second side measures $12\frac{3}{16}$ inches. What does the third side measure?

   a. What is the perimeter of the triangle?
   b. What are the measures of the known sides?
   c. Draw a diagram to represent the problem.
   d. What is unknown?
   e. What do you need to know about the perimeter to solve this problem?
   f. Define a variable. Then state an equation for the problem.

4. An English assignment covers 182 pages. Kristina has 79 pages yet to read. How many pages has she read?

   a. What is asked?
   b. How many pages does the assignment cover?
   c. How many pages has Kristina yet to read?
   d. Define a variable. Then state an equation for the problem.

For each problem, define a variable. Then state an equation.

5. An elevator started at the first floor and went up 14 floors. Then it went down 9 floors. At what floor was it then located?

6. Fairmeadow High School has 1283 students. On Friday 1116 were present. How many were absent?

7. Thirteen subtracted from a number is -5. Find the number.

8. The sum of a number and 12 is equal to 47. Find the number.

9. In a mid-season slump the Yankees scored only 17 runs in 9 games. Their opponents scored 41 runs. By how many runs did their opponents outscore them?

10. A traffic helicopter descended 160 meters to observe road conditions. It leveled off at 225 meters. What was its original altitude?

Written Exercises

1-10. Solve the problems in Exploratory Exercises 1-10.

Read and explore each problem. Make a diagram if necessary. Then define a variable, write an equation, and solve the problem.

11. Jeff Simons sold 27 cars last month. This amount is 36 less than the same time period one year ago. What were his sales one year ago?

12. A rancher lost 47 cattle because of the summer heat. His herd now numbers 396. How large was the herd before the summer heat?

13. The temperature at mid-afternoon was 12°C. By early evening the temperature was −7°C. What was the temperature change?

14. On February 2 the highest temperature in the United States was 87°F in Miami, Florida. The lowest temperature was −19°F in Rice Lake, Wisconsin. What was the difference between the high and low temperatures?

15. Gary Carson skied down the slalom run in 131.3 seconds. This was 21.7 seconds faster than his sister. What was her time?

16. Lisa Thorson skied down the slalom run in 139.8 seconds. This was 13.7 seconds slower than her best time. What is her best time?

17. Agnes Graham bought a jacket on sale and saved $27.35. The regular price was $81.79. What was the sale price?

18. The total of Barbara Orfanello's gas bill and electric bill for January was $210.87. Her electric bill was $95.25. How much was her gas bill?

19. Thirteen less than some number is 64. What is the number?

20. Some number subtracted from 161 yields 87. What is the number?

21. The sum of two integers is −32. One of the integers is +6. What is the other integer?

22. The difference of two integers is 26. The lesser integer is −11. What is the greater integer?

23. A scuba diver swam to a depth of 53 meters below sea level. Then he saw a shark 10 meters above him. At what depth was the shark?

24. The entrance to a South Dakota gold mine is 3273 feet above sea level. The mine is 4386 feet deep, measured from the entrance. What is the elevation of the bottom of the mine?

25. Eagle's Bluff is about 143 meters above sea level. From the peak of the bluff to the floor of Sulphur Springs Canyon is 217 meters. How far below sea level is Sulphur Springs Canyon?

26. A 4-sided city lot has a perimeter of 340.8 feet. Two sides have lengths of 60.23 feet. A third side has a length of 109.13 feet. What is the length of the fourth side?

27. Four cave explorers descended to a depth of 112 meters below the cave entrance. They discovered a large cavern whose ceiling was 27 meters above them. At what depth below the cave entrance was the cavern ceiling?

28. The area of a triangular courtyard is 1520.2 square feet. The area occupied by a circular fountain in the middle is 132.7 square feet. A walkway covers 253.6 square feet. If the remaining area is used for gardens, how much area is set aside for gardens?

29. Shares of stock in Olympia Motors were listed at $37\frac{3}{4}$ per share. The shares then dropped $2\frac{1}{8}$ points. What was the new listing?

30. A triangle has sides of $16\frac{3}{8}$, $14\frac{1}{16}$, and $17\frac{3}{4}$ inches. What is its perimeter?

Temperature

Temperature is commonly measured in Celsius degrees or Fahrenheit degrees. Celsius and Fahrenheit thermometers are shown at the right.

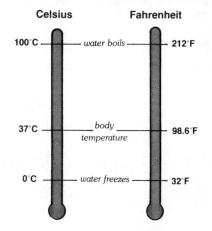

The following program converts a Fahrenheit reading to the equivalent Celsius reading.

```
10  INPUT F
20  LET C = 5/9*(F-32)
30  PRINT "F = ";F,"C = ";C
40  END
```

Note how the formula $C = \dfrac{5}{9}(F - 32)$ is written in line 20.

When you input the Fahrenheit degrees shown on the thermometer, the corresponding Celsius degrees will be printed.

There is one temperature at which the value of F is the same as C. The program can be modified so that the computer will evaluate all integer values of F from −50 to 50 and print only the value of F that is the same as C.

```
10  FOR F = -50 TO 50
20  LET C = 5/9*(F-32)
25  IF C< >F THEN 35
30  PRINT "F = ";F,"C = ";C
35  NEXT F
40  END
```

In line 25, the symbol < > represents not equal.

Exercises

1. At what temperature is the value of F the same as C?
2. If line 25 was removed from the program, how would the output change?
3. Change lines 10 and 25 of the program to determine if there is a Fahrenheit temperature that is 100 more than the corresponding Celsius temperature.
4. Modify the program to determine if there is a Fahrenheit temperature that is 50 more than the corresponding Celsius temperature.

Vocabulary

negative (39)

integers (39)

coordinate (39)

absolute value (44)

rational number (47)

additive inverse (53)

opposite (53)

equivalent equations (57)

Chapter Summary

1. On a number line, points to the right of zero are named with a positive sign $(+)$ and points to the left of zero are named with a negative sign $(-)$. (39)

2. The set of integers can be written $\{\ldots, -5, -4, -3, -2, -1, 0, 1, 2, 3, 4, 5, \ldots\}$ where ... means continued indefinitely. (39)

3. To graph a set of numbers means to locate the points named by those numbers on the number line. (39)

4. A number line can be used to add integers. Move to the right for positive integers and to the left for negative integers. (42)

5. Definition of Absolute Value: The absolute value of a number is the number of units it is from 0 on the number line. (44)

6. Adding Integers with the Same Sign: To add integers with the same sign, add their absolute values. Give the sum the same sign as the addends. (44)

7. Adding Integers with Different Signs: To add integers with different signs, subtract the lesser from the greater absolute values. Give the result the same sign as the addend with the greater absolute value. (45)

8. A rational number is a number that can be expressed in the form $\frac{a}{b}$, where a and b are integers and b is not equal to zero. (47)

9. The rules used to add integers can also be used to add rational numbers. (47)

10. If the sum of two numbers is 0, the numbers are called additive inverses or opposites. (53)

11. Additive Inverse Property: For every number a, $a + (-a) = 0$. (53)

12. To subtract a rational number, add its additive inverse. For rational numbers a and b, $a - b = a + (-b)$. (54)

13. Addition Property of Equality: For any numbers a, b, and c, if $a = b$ then $a + c = b + c$. (57)

14. Subtraction Property of Equality: For any numbers a, b, and c, if $a = b$ then $a - c = b - c$. (58)

15. Equations involving addition may be solved by using the subtraction property of equality or by using the additive inverse. (58)

16. Equations involving subtraction may be solved by using the addition property of equality. Sometimes it is easier to write and solve an equivalent equation involving addition. (60)

17. Before you solve a problem, you must explore the problem and plan carefully. It is often helpful to draw a chart or diagram. Sometimes a problem can be solved by translating it into a mathematical equation. (64)

Chapter Review

2-1 **Name the set of numbers graphed.**

1.

2.

3.

4.

Graph each set of numbers on a number line.

5. $\{-2, 1, 4\}$

6. $\{5, 3, -1, -3\}$

7. $\{-3, -2, -1, 0, \ldots\}$

8. $\{\ldots, 3, 4, 5\}$

2-2 **Use a number line to find each sum.**

9. $4 + (-5)$

10. $-3 + 6$

11. $-2 + (-4)$

12. $-4 + 1$

2-3 **Find each sum.**

13. $17 + (-9)$

14. $-9 + (-12)$

15. $-12 + 8$

16. $13 + (-51)$

17. $-74 + 21$

18. $-17 + (-31)$

2-4 **Find each sum.**

19. $\frac{6}{7} + \left(-\frac{13}{7}\right)$

20. $-\frac{5}{8} + \frac{3}{16}$

21. $-7.5 + 10.2$

22. $-0.37 + (-0.812)$

23. $3.707 + (-0.058)$

24. $-4.375 + 5.432$

2-5   **Find each sum.**

25. $84 + (-31) + 13$

26. $65 + (-13 + 28)$

27. $-4b + 17b + (-36b)$

28. $a + 9a + (-12a)$

29. $\frac{7}{3} + \frac{5}{12} + \left(-\frac{5}{6}\right)$

30. $-\frac{4}{3} + \frac{5}{6} + \left(-\frac{7}{3}\right)$

31. $-6.7 + 8.1 + (-5.3)$

32. $-5 + (-3.7) + 9.4$

33. $-13pq + 41k + 12k + (-38pq)$

34. $61mb + (-51pg) + (-48mb) + 13pg$

2-6   **Find each difference.**

35. $14 - 36$

36. $8 - (-5)$

37. $-7 - (-11)$

38. $-13 - 16$

39. $3.72 - (-8.65)$

40. $0.702 - 0.98$

41. $-13x - (-7x)$

42. $-4.5y - 8.1y$

43. $\begin{array}{r} 36 \\ -19 \\ \hline \end{array}$

44. $\begin{array}{r} -61 \\ -(-43) \\ \hline \end{array}$

45. $\begin{array}{r} -2.8 \\ -(+3.9) \\ \hline \end{array}$

46. $\frac{4}{5} - \left(-\frac{9}{5}\right)$

47. $-\frac{4}{7} - \frac{3}{14}$

48. $-\frac{3}{2} - \frac{5}{4}$

2-7   **Solve each equation.**

49. $k + 13 = 5$

50. $19 = y + 7$

51. $z + 15 = -9$

52. $m + (-5) = -17$

53. $p + (-7) = 31$

54. $19 = -8 + d$

2-8   **Solve each equation.**

55. $x - 16 = 37$

56. $15 - y = 9$

57. $r - (-5) = -8$

58. $m - (-4) = 21$

59. $-13 = 6 - k$

60. $y + (-9) = -35$

2-9   **For each problem, define a variable. Then use an equation to solve the problem.**

61. Some number added to -16 is equal to 39. What is the number?

62. When 9 is subtracted from another integer, the difference is -13. What is the other integer?

63. The temperature at sunrise was $-2°$ F. At noon the temperature was $15°$F. What was the temperature change?

64. Darlene's score at the end of the first half of a game was -7.8. At the end of the game her score was 19.2. How many points did she score during the second half of the game?

Chapter Test

Graph each set on a number line.

1. $\{1, 2, -5\}$

2. $\{\ldots, -2, -1, 0, 1\}$

Find each sum.

3. $-11 + (-13)$

4. $-15 + 23$

5. $36 + (-42)$

6. $1.654 + (-2.367)$

7. $\frac{3}{7} + \left(-\frac{9}{7}\right)$

8. $-\frac{1}{8} + \frac{3}{4}$

9. $12x + (-21x)$

10. $-7 + (-6) + 37$

11. $[4 + (-13)] + (-12)$

12. $\frac{5}{8} + \left(-\frac{3}{16}\right) + \left(-\frac{3}{4}\right)$

13. $-7.9 + 3.5 + 2.4$

14. $18b + 13xy + (-46b)$

Find each difference.

15. $12 - 19$

16. $-14 - 3$

17. $21 - (-7)$

18. $-41 - (-52)$

19. $-\frac{7}{16} - \frac{3}{8}$

20. $6.32 - (-7.41)$

Solve each equation.

21. $m + 13 = -9$

22. $k + 16 = -4$

23. $y + (-3) = 14$

24. $x + (-6) = 13$

25. $k - (-3) = 28$

26. $-5 - k = 14$

27. $r - (-1.2) = -7.3$

28. $b - \frac{2}{3} = -\frac{5}{6}$

Solve each problem.

29. The sum of two integers is -11. One integer is 8. Find the other integer.

30. Joe's golf score was 68. This was 4 less than Marie's golf score. What was Marie's score?

1. Write a mathematical expression for twice a number decreased by 17.

2. Write the expression $3 \cdot 3 \cdot 3 \cdot a \cdot a \cdot b \cdot b \cdot b$ using exponents.

Evaluate.

3. $3 + 2(4) - 10 \div 2$

4. $[(4 + 8)^2 \div 4 \times 2] + 3 \times 2$

5. $4(5b - 3a)^2$ if $a = 6$ and $b = 4$

6. $3ab - 4c$ if $a = 2$, $b = 3$, and $c = \frac{1}{2}$

7. Solve: $x = \frac{3 + 7}{10}$

8. What number is called the additive identity?

State the property shown.

9. $(3 + 8)4 = (11)4$

10. $(7 \cdot x) \cdot a = (x \cdot 7) \cdot a$

11. $y + 8 = y + 8$

12. $6(7a + 3) = 42a + 18$

Simplify.

13. $4mn + 12mn$

14. $16x^2 + 12xy - 13x^2$

15. $3(a + 0.2b) - 0.4b$

16. $4(x + 3y) + 2(2x + y)$

Write each sentence as an equation.

17. The sum of y and the cube of n equals x.

18. The square of a side (s) is equal to the area (A).

19. Name the set of numbers graphed.

Graph each set of numbers on a number line.

20. $\{-3, -1, 2, 5\}$

21. $\{\ldots, -6, -5, -4\}$

22. Find $4 + (-6)$ on a number line.

Find each sum or difference.

23. $36 + (-73)$

24. $-8 + (-21)$

25. $-9.3 + 4.7$

26. $-\frac{1}{2} + \left(-\frac{1}{6}\right) + \left(-\frac{2}{3}\right)$

27. $-21 - (-28)$

28. $3.6 - 7.9$

29. $-3a + 5m + 16m + (-25a)$

30. $-7t - 16t$

Solve.

31. $r + 17 = 23$

32. $-13 + a = 14$

33. $y - 8 = -12$

34. $-20 = m - (-14)$

35. $7 - x = -10$

36. $m - \frac{1}{2} = \frac{2}{5}$

Problem Solving

For the following problem, answer the related question.

37. Heather is 4 years older than Brian. How old was Brian when Heather was 11 years old?

Define the variable, then write an equation for the following problem.

38. A number decreased by 11 is 40. Find the number.

Read and explore the following problems. Then define a variable, write an equation, and solve.

39. Ryan scored 32 points in a basketball game. This was 8 points more than the last game. How many points did he score in the last game?

40. The sum of two integers is -38. One of the integers is -56. What is the other integer?

The test questions on this page deal with number concepts and basic operations. The information at the right may help you with some of the questions.

Directions: Choose the best answer. Write A, B, C, or D.

1. Which of the following numbers is *not* a prime number?

   (A) 17 **(B)** 23 **(C)** 37 **(D)** 87

2. How many integers between 325 and 400, inclusive, are divisible by 4?

   (A) 18 **(B)** 19 **(C)** 20 **(D)** 24

3. How many integers between 99 and 201 are divisible by 2 or 5?

   (A) 60 **(B)** 61 **(C)** 70 **(D)** 71

4. How many integers are between, but not including, 5 and 1995?

   (A) 1988   **(B)** 1989
   (C) 1990   **(D)** 2000

5. A person is standing in line, thirteenth from the front and eleventh from the back. How many people are in the line?

   (A) 22 **(B)** 23 **(C)** 24 **(D)** 25

6. What number is missing from the sequence 2, 5, 15, 18, 54, 171, 174, 522?

   (A) 36 **(B)** 56 **(C)** 57 **(D)** 398

7. What digit is represented by △ in this subtraction problem?

$$\begin{array}{r} 80\square \\ -602 \\ \hline \triangle 98 \end{array}$$

   (A) 1 **(B)** 2 **(C)** 3 **(D)** 4

8. How many fourths of a mile will a car travel on a 400-mile trip.

   (A) 100 **(B)** 400 **(C)** 1000 **(D)** 1600

---

1. A number is *divisible* by another number if it can be divided exactly with no remainder. A number is divisible by each of its factors.

2. A number is *prime* if it has no factors except itself and 1.

   7 is a prime number.
   8 is not *prime* since it has factors other than itself and 1.
   2 and 4 are factors of 8.

---

9. $8(916) + 916 =$

   (A) $4(916) + 3(916)$
   (B) $5(916) + 4(916)$
   (C) $6(916) + 4(916)$
   (D) $3(916) + 4(916)$

10. Nancy has 9 more marbles than James. If she gives him 13 of her marbles, how many more will he have than she?

    (A) 4 **(B)** 11 **(C)** 17 **(D)** 21

11. A person has 100 green, 100 orange, and 100 yellow jelly beans. How many jars can be filled if each jar must contain 8 green, 5 orange, and 6 yellow jelly beans?

    (A) 12 **(B)** 15 **(C)** 16 **(D)** 25

12. A hospital patient must be given medication every 5 hours, starting at 10 A.M. Thursday. On what day will the patient first receive medication at noon?

    (A) Thursday   **(B)** Friday
    (C) Saturday   **(D)** Sunday

13. Which of the following is the difference of two consecutive prime numbers less than 30?

    (A) 5 **(B)** 6 **(C)** 7 **(D)** 8

14. The sum of five consecutive integers is always divisible by

    (A) 2 **(B)** 4 **(C)** 5 **(D)** 10

CHAPTER 3

Multiplying and Dividing Rational Numbers

Steve Bernard earns 3% commission on sales of all new cars. To earn $850.00 per week in commission, what must his weekly sales be? In this chapter, you will learn to use equations to solve problems such as this.

3-1 Multiplying Rational Numbers

How can you multiply positive and negative numbers? One way is to consider multiplication as repeated addition. For example, $4(-2)$ may be expressed as $(-2) + (-2) + (-2) + (-2)$.

$$(-2) + (-2) + (-2) + (-2) = -8$$
$$4(-2) = -8$$

The product of *positive* 4 and *negative* 2 is *negative* 8.

Another way to find the product of a positive number and a negative number is to consider the following example.

$0 = 7(0)$	*Multiplication Property of Zero*
$0 = 7[5 + (-5)]$	*Substitution and Additive Inverse Property*
$0 = 7(5) + 7(-5)$	*Distributive Property*
$0 = 35 + 7(-5)$	*Substitution*

Using the additive inverse property, 0 is equal to $35 + (-35)$. Therefore $7(-5)$ must equal -35. Using the commutative property, $(-5)(7)$ must also equal -35. These and many other similar examples suggest the following rule.

The product of two numbers that have different signs is negative.	*Multiplying Two Numbers with Different Signs*

Examples

1 **Simplify:** $9(-4)$

$9(-4) = -36$

2 **Simplify:** $(-3a)(4b)$

$(-3a)(4b) = (-3)(4)ab$ *Commutative and Associative Properties*
$\qquad\qquad = -12ab$

3 **Simplify:** $(0.5)(-6)$

$(0.5)(-6) = -3$

You know that the product of two positive numbers is positive. What is the sign of the product of two negative numbers?

$0 = -6(0)$	*Multiplicative Property of Zero*
$0 = -6[8 + (-8)]$	*Substitution*
$0 = -6(8) + (-6)(-8)$	*Distributive Property*
$0 = -48 + (-6)(-8)$	*Substitution*

The additive inverse of -48 is 48. Thus, $(-6)(-8)$ must equal 48. The product of *negative* 6 and *negative* 8 is *positive* 48.

These and many other similar examples lead to the following rule.

The product of two numbers that have the same sign is positive.	*Multiplying Two Numbers with the Same Sign*

Examples

4 **Multiply:** $(-4)(-13)$

$(-4)(-13) = 52$ *Both factors are negative, so the product is positive.*

5 **Multiply:** $\left(-\frac{2}{3}\right)\left(-\frac{1}{5}\right)$

$\left(-\frac{2}{3}\right)\left(-\frac{1}{5}\right) = \frac{2}{15}$ *Why is the product positive?*

6 **Simplify:** $6x(-7y) + (-3x)(-5y)$

$$6x(-7y) + (-3x)(-5y) = -42xy + 15xy$$
$$= (-42 + 15)xy \quad \textit{Distributive Property}$$
$$= -27xy$$

What is the result if a number is multiplied by -1?

$$-1(3) = -3 \qquad \frac{4}{5}(-1) = -\frac{4}{5} \qquad -1(-4) = 4 \qquad (-0.3)(-1) = 0.3$$

These examples are summarized in the multiplicative property of -1.

The product of any number and -1 is its additive inverse. $-1(a) = -a$ **and** $a(-1) = -a$	*Multiplicative Property of -1*

To find the product of 3 or more numbers, first group the numbers in pairs.

Example

7 **Simplify:** $(-2)(-3)(-1)(4)$

$$(-2)(-3)(-1)(4) = 6(-1)(4) \qquad \textit{First multiply } -2 \textit{ by } -3.$$
$$= -6(4) \qquad\qquad \textit{Then multiply 6 by } -1.$$
$$= -24$$

Recall that the product of *two* negative factors is positive. Why are the following statements true?

The product of an *even* number of negative factors is positive.
The product of an *odd* number of negative factors is negative.

Exploratory Exercises

Determine if each product is positive or negative.

1. $3(-2)$
2. $(-2)(-8)$
3. $7(8)$
4. $3(-5)$
5. $(-6)(-5)$
6. $(-9)(7)$
7. $(-11)(10)$
8. $(-9)(-8)$
9. $\left(\frac{2}{3}\right)\left(-\frac{1}{4}\right)$
10. $\left(\frac{7}{3}\right)\left(\frac{7}{3}\right)$
11. $\left(-\frac{7}{9}\right)\left(\frac{9}{14}\right)$
12. $\left(-\frac{3}{4}\right)\left(\frac{4}{3}\right)$
13. $(-3)(4)(-2)$
14. $(-6)(4)(-3)$
15. $\left(\frac{3}{5}\right)\left(\frac{2}{3}\right)(-3)$
16. $\left(-\frac{4}{5}\right)\left(-\frac{1}{5}\right)(-5)$

17. Under what conditions is ab positive?
18. Under what conditions is ab negative?
19. If a^2 is positive, what can you conclude about a?
20. If a^3 is positive, what can you conclude about a?
21. If ab is negative, what is the sign of the inverse of ab?
22. Under what conditions is ab equal to zero?

Written Exercises

1-16. Find each product for Exploratory Exercises 1-16.

Find each product.

17. $5(12)$
18. $(-6)(11)$
19. $\left(\frac{3}{5}\right)\left(-\frac{4}{7}\right)$
20. $\left(-\frac{7}{8}\right)\left(-\frac{1}{3}\right)$
21. $4\left(-\frac{7}{8}\right)$
22. $(-5)\left(-\frac{2}{5}\right)$
23. $\frac{3}{5}(5)(-2)\left(-\frac{1}{2}\right)$
24. $\frac{2}{11}(-11)(-4)\left(-\frac{3}{4}\right)$
25. $\left(-\frac{1}{3}\right)\left(-\frac{3}{4}\right)\left(-\frac{4}{5}\right)$
26. $\left(-\frac{7}{12}\right)\left(\frac{6}{7}\right)\left(-\frac{3}{4}\right)$
27. $(-4)(0)(-2)(-3)$
28. $(4)(-2)(-1)(-3)$

Simplify each expression.

29. $3(-4) + 2(-7)$
30. $-3(2) + (-2)(-3)$
31. $-4(4) + (-2)(-3)$
32. $(-7)(8) + 8(-7)$
33. $5(-2) - 3(-8)$
34. $4(-1) - 2(-6)$
35. $4(7) - 3(11)$
36. $8(9) - 6(3)$
37. $\frac{2}{3}\left(\frac{1}{2}\right) - \left(-\frac{3}{2}\right)\left(\frac{2}{3}\right)$
38. $\left(-\frac{1}{2}\right)\left(-\frac{1}{2}\right) - \frac{2}{3}\left(\frac{3}{2}\right)$
39. $\left(\frac{5}{8}\right)\left(-\frac{1}{2}\right) - \left(\frac{5}{8}\right)\left(\frac{1}{2}\right)$
40. $\frac{5}{6}\left(\frac{6}{7}\right) - \left(\frac{5}{6}\right)\left(-\frac{6}{7}\right)$
41. $5(3t - 2t) + 2(4t - 3t)$
42. $3(5x + 3x) - 4(2x + 6x)$
43. $4[3x + (-2x)] - 5(3x + 2x)$
44. $6(3x + 7x) + 7[8x + (-4x)]$
45. $\frac{1}{2}(6x + 8x) - \frac{1}{3}(6x + 9x)$
46. $-\frac{2}{7}(21x + 35a) + \frac{4}{7}(35x - 21a)$
47. $\frac{3}{4}(4a - 12b) + \frac{1}{8}(16a + 48b)$
48. $\frac{5}{6}(-24a + 36b) + \left(-\frac{1}{3}\right)(60a - 42b)$
49. $\frac{1}{2}\left(-\frac{1}{3}a + \frac{2}{3}b\right) + \frac{2}{3}\left(\frac{1}{2}a - \frac{3}{4}b\right)$
50. $\frac{1}{2}(-3a - 4b) + \left(-\frac{2}{9}\right)(-4a - 7b)$

mini-review

Add or subtract.

1. $-3 - (-4)$
2. $51 + (-93)$
3. $-0.187 + (-8.15)$
4. $-3.2x - 8.4x$
5. $-5 + (-4.8) + 10.4$

3-2 Dividing Rational Numbers

Study the following examples.

$$\frac{60}{6} \cdot 6 = 10 \cdot 6$$ *Multiplying by 6* $$\frac{38 \cdot 2}{2} = \frac{76}{2}$$ *Dividing by 2 undoes*
$$= 60$$ *undoes dividing by 6.* $$= 38$$ *multiplying by 2.*

These and other examples show that multiplication and division are inverse operations. You can use this fact to derive rules for dividing positive and negative numbers.

$$3 \cdot 4 = 12 \quad \text{so} \quad 12 \div 4 = 3$$

same   positive
signs   quotient

$$5 \cdot (-6) = -30 \quad \text{so} \quad -30 \div (-6) = 5$$

The quotient of two numbers with the same sign is *positive*.

What happens if the numbers have different signs?

$$-7 \cdot 9 = -63 \quad \text{so} \quad -63 \div 9 = -7$$

different   negative
signs   quotient

$$-8 \cdot (-6) = 48 \quad \text{so} \quad 48 \div (-6) = -8$$

The quotient of two numbers with different signs is *negative*.

> **The quotient of two numbers is positive if the numbers have the same sign. The quotient of two numbers is negative if the numbers have different signs.**

Division of Rational Numbers

Notice that the rule for finding the sign of the quotient of two numbers is the same as the rule for finding the sign of their product.

Examples

1 Simplify: $-36 \div 3$

Since the numbers have different signs, the quotient is negative.
$$-36 \div 3 = -12$$

2 Simplify: $\frac{-45}{-9}$

$$\frac{-45}{-9} = 5$$ *The fraction bar indicates division.*
The quotient is positive.

Two numbers whose product is 1 are **multiplicative inverses** or **reciprocals**.

The reciprocal of $\frac{4}{9}$ is $\frac{9}{4}$ because $\frac{4}{9} \cdot \frac{9}{4} = 1$.

The reciprocal of -5 is $-\frac{1}{5}$ because $-5\left(-\frac{1}{5}\right) = 1$

The reciprocal of 1 is 1 because $1 \cdot 1 = 1$

Zero has no reciprocal because the product of zero and any rational number is zero, not 1.

These examples can be summarized in the multiplicative inverse property.

> **For every nonzero number a, there is exactly one number $\frac{1}{a}$, such that $a\left(\frac{1}{a}\right) = \frac{1}{a}(a) = 1$.**

Multiplicative Inverse Property

Recall that it is possible to subtract a number by adding its opposite. In a similar manner, it is possible to divide a number by multiplying by its reciprocal.

Consider this example.

$$\frac{2}{3} \div \frac{3}{4} = \frac{2}{3} \cdot \frac{4}{3} \qquad \frac{3}{4} \text{ and } \frac{4}{3} \text{ are reciprocals.}$$
$$= \frac{8}{9}$$

In general, *any* division expression can be changed to an equivalent multiplication expression.

> **For all numbers a and b, with $b \neq 0$,**
> $$a \div b = \frac{a}{b} = a\left(\frac{1}{b}\right) = \frac{1}{b}(a).$$

Division Rule

Examples

3 Divide: $-\frac{3}{4} \div 8$

$-\frac{3}{4} \div 8 = -\frac{3}{4} \cdot \frac{1}{8}$ *Multiply by the reciprocal of 8.*

$= -\frac{3}{32}$

4 Simplify: $\frac{4a + 32}{4}$

$\frac{4a + 32}{4} = (4a + 32) \div 4$

$= (4a + 32)\left(\frac{1}{4}\right)$

$= 4a\left(\frac{1}{4}\right) + 32\left(\frac{1}{4}\right)$

$= a + 8$

Exploratory Exercises

State the reciprocal of each number.

1. 3
2. -5
3. 0
4. -1
5. -14
6. 7

7. $\frac{2}{3}$
8. $\frac{1}{15}$
9. $-\frac{3}{11}$
10. $-\frac{1}{11}$
11. $\frac{10}{7}$
12. $\frac{21}{5}$

13. $-\frac{3}{5}$
14. $-\frac{8}{15}$
15. $3\frac{1}{4}$
16. $2\frac{1}{8}$
17. $-2\frac{3}{7}$
18. $-6\frac{5}{11}$

Written Exercises

Simplify.

1. $\frac{-30}{-5}$
2. $\frac{-48}{8}$
3. $\frac{30}{-6}$
4. $\frac{-55}{11}$
5. $\frac{70}{5}$
6. $\frac{80}{20}$

7. $\frac{-40}{8}$
8. $\frac{-48}{6}$
9. $\frac{-96}{-16}$
10. $\frac{-84}{-7}$
11. $\frac{-36}{-9}$
12. $\frac{42}{-6}$

13. $\frac{-38}{2}$
14. $\frac{54}{-9}$
15. $\frac{-200}{50}$
16. $\frac{-450}{10}$
17. $\frac{-36a}{-6}$
18. $\frac{45b}{9}$

19. $\frac{63a}{-9}$
20. $\frac{77b}{-11}$
21. $49 \div 7$
22. $-16 \div 8$
23. $65 \div (-13)$
24. $75 \div (-15)$

25. $\frac{-\frac{5}{6}}{8}$
26. $\frac{-\frac{3}{4}}{9}$
27. $\frac{\frac{7}{8}}{-10}$
28. $\frac{\frac{3}{11}}{-6}$
29. $\frac{\frac{1}{3}}{4}$
30. $\frac{\frac{3}{8}}{6}$

31. $\frac{7}{-\frac{2}{5}}$
32. $\frac{11}{-\frac{5}{6}}$
33. $\frac{-6}{-\frac{4}{7}}$
34. $\frac{-5}{\frac{2}{7}}$
35. $\frac{-6}{-\frac{4}{9}}$
36. $\frac{-9}{-\frac{10}{17}}$

37. $\frac{3a + 9}{3}$
38. $\frac{6a + 24}{6}$
39. $\frac{7a + 35}{-7}$
40. $\frac{14a + 56}{-7}$

41. $\frac{20a + 30b}{-2}$
42. $\frac{-5x + (-10y)}{-5}$
43. $\frac{60a - 30b}{-6}$
44. $\frac{70x - 30y}{-5}$

Using Calculators_____The Reciprocal Key

The key labeled $\frac{1}{x}$ on your calculator is the reciprocal key. When this key is pressed, the calculator replaces the number in the display with its reciprocal.

Exercises

Use a calculator to evaluate each expression. Round each result to the nearest thousandth.

1. $\frac{1}{2.5}$
2. $\frac{1}{7}$
3. $\frac{1}{3(5)}$
4. $\frac{1}{3} \cdot \frac{1}{5}$
5. $\frac{1}{0.618}$
6. $\frac{1}{5 - 2(0.8)}$

7. Enter a number. Then press the reciprocal key twice. What happens? Predict what will happen if you press the key n times.

8. Enter 0 and then press the reciprocal key. What happens? Why?

3-3 Solving Equations Using Multiplication and Division

A certain basket holds $\frac{1}{4}$ case of apples. There are 30 apples in the basket. About how many apples would a case hold?

An equation can be used to solve this problem. If x is the number of apples in a case, then the equation is $\frac{1}{4}x = 30$. To solve this equation, you would use the **multiplication property of equality**. It states that if both sides of an equation are multiplied by the same nonzero number, the result is an equivalent equation.

Recall that equivalent equations have the same solution.

For any numbers a, b, and c,	
if $a = b$, then $ac = bc$.	*Multiplication Property of Equality*

Example

1 **Solve:** $\frac{1}{4}x = 30$

$\frac{1}{4}x = 30$ *The coefficient of x is $\frac{1}{4}$.*

$4\left(\frac{1}{4}x\right) = 4(30)$ *Multiply both sides by 4, the reciprocal of $\frac{1}{4}$.*

$1x = 120$

$x = 120$

Check: $\frac{1}{4}x = 30$

$\frac{1}{4}(120) \stackrel{?}{=} 30$ *Replace x with 120.*

$30 = 30$

The solution is 120.

In the equation $\frac{1}{4}x = 30$, the variable x represented the number of apples in a case. Thus, there are about 120 apples in a case.

2 **Solve:** $\frac{k}{7} = -45$

$$\frac{k}{7} = -45$$

$$\frac{1}{7}k = -45 \qquad \text{Substitute } \frac{1}{7}k \text{ for } \frac{k}{7}.$$

$$7 \cdot \frac{1}{7}k = 7(-45) \qquad \text{Multiply both sides by 7.}$$

$$k = -315 \qquad \text{Check this result.}$$

The solution is -315.

3 **Solve:** $\left(2\frac{1}{3}\right)m = 3\frac{1}{9}$

$$\left(2\frac{1}{3}\right)m = 3\frac{1}{9}$$

$$\frac{7}{3}m = \frac{28}{9} \qquad \text{Rewrite the mixed numbers as improper fractions.}$$

$$\frac{3}{7}\left(\frac{7}{3}m\right) = \frac{3}{7}\left(\frac{28}{9}\right) \qquad \text{Multiply both sides by } \frac{3}{7}.$$

$$m = \frac{4}{3} \qquad \text{Check this result.}$$

The solution is $\frac{4}{3}$ or $1\frac{1}{3}$.

4 **Solve:** $24 = -2a$

$$24 = -2a$$

$$-\frac{1}{2}(24) = -\frac{1}{2}(-2a) \qquad \text{Multiply both sides by } -\frac{1}{2}.$$

$$-12 = a \qquad \text{Check this result.}$$

The solution is -12.

The equation $24 = -2a$ was solved by multiplying both sides by $-\frac{1}{2}$. The same result could have been obtained by dividing both sides by -2. In general, dividing both sides of an equation by the same nonzero number results in an equivalent equation. This is called the **division property of equality**.

The division property of equality is a special case of the multiplication property of equality.

> **For any numbers a, b, and c, with $c \neq 0$,**
> **if $a = b$, then $\frac{a}{c} = \frac{b}{c}$.**

Division Property of Equality

Example

5 Solve: $-6x = 11$

$$-6x = 11$$

$$\frac{-6x}{-6} = \frac{11}{-6} \qquad \text{Divide both sides by } -6.$$

$$x = -\frac{11}{6} \qquad \text{Check this result.}$$

The solution is $-\frac{11}{6}$.

Exploratory Exercises

State the number that you would multiply both sides of each equation by to solve it.

1. $\frac{b}{3} = -6$ 　 2. $\frac{b}{5} = 10$ 　 3. $\frac{3}{4}n = 30$ 　 4. $\frac{5}{7}t = -10$ 　 5. $\frac{4}{9}n = -24$

6. $-\frac{5}{9}x = 15$ 　 7. $-8n = 24$ 　 8. $3n = -18$ 　 9. $1 = \frac{k}{9}$ 　 10. $-14 = \frac{k}{2}$

State the number that you would divide both sides of each equation by to solve it.

11. $4x = 24$ 　 12. $28 = 7x$ 　 13. $35 = 4y$ 　 14. $-36 = 4z$ 　 15. $-7x = 21$

16. $-5x = 14$ 　 17. $-8x = -9$ 　 18. $-14x = -30$ 　 19. $-6x = -36$ 　 20. $-10x = 40$

Written Exercises

Solve each equation.

1. $-4r = -28$ 　 2. $-7w = -49$ 　 3. $-8t = 56$ 　 4. $5t = -45$ 　 5. $6x = -42$

6. $11y = -77$ 　 7. $-5s = -85$ 　 8. $-7h = -91$ 　 9. $9x = 40$ 　 10. $-3y = 52$

11. $3w = -11$ 　 12. $5c = 8$ 　 13. $6x = 28$ 　 14. $4x = 62$ 　 15. $-11q = -81$

16. $-13s = -64$ 　 17. $434 = -31y$ 　 18. $17b = -391$ 　 19. $\frac{k}{8} = 6$ 　 20. $11 = \frac{k}{5}$

21. $-10 = \frac{b}{-7}$ 　 22. $-13 = \frac{b}{-8}$ 　 23. $\frac{h}{11} = -25$ 　 24. $\frac{h}{12} = -24$ 　 25. $\frac{d}{3} = -30$

26. $\frac{d}{4} = -5$ 　 27. $-65 = \frac{f}{29}$ 　 28. $-70 = \frac{f}{25}$ 　 29. $\frac{2}{3}x = -6$ 　 30. $\frac{3}{5}x = 9$

31. $\frac{2}{5}t = -10$ 　 32. $\frac{4}{9}t = 72$

33. $\frac{4}{7}r = 20$ 　 34. $\frac{3}{4}x = -12$

35. $\frac{4}{9}x = -9$ 　 36. $\frac{9}{11}y = 20$

37. $-\frac{3}{5}y = -50$ 　 38. $-\frac{2}{3}x = -41$

39. $-\frac{11}{8}x = 42$ 　 40. $-\frac{13}{5}y = -22$

41. $3x = 4\frac{2}{3}$ 　 42. $\frac{5}{2}x = -25$

43. $\left(5\frac{1}{2}\right)x = 33$ 　 44. $-5x = -3\frac{2}{3}$

45. $\left(-4\frac{1}{2}\right)x = 36$ 　 46. $\left(3\frac{1}{2}\right)x = -1\frac{1}{6}$

mini-review

Solve each equation.

1. $y + 14 = -3$

2. $m - (-43) = 17$

Simplify.

3. $\frac{4}{5}\left(-\frac{5}{9}\right)$ 　 4. $\frac{8a + 32}{-4}$

5. $14a + (-18b) + 6a^2 + 10b$

3-4 Solving Equations Using More than One Operation

Each of these equations can be solved by performing the inverse of the operation indicated in the equation.

$$x + 2 = 5 \qquad 3x = 4.8 \qquad \frac{x}{2} = -11$$

But each of the following equations contains more than one operation.

$$\frac{x}{4} + 7 = 10 \qquad \frac{a + 10}{3} = 6 \qquad -5x - 7 = 28$$

These equations can be solved using the same methods that were used to solve the first set of equations. However, more than one step is involved.

Recall the order of operations for evaluating an expression. To solve an equation with more than one operation, undo the operations in reverse order.

Examples

1 **Solve: $3x + 7 = 13$**

$3x + 7 = 13$	*Addition of 7 is indicated.*
$3x + 7 - 7 = 13 - 7$	*Therefore, subtract 7 from both sides.*
$3x = 6$	*Multiplication by 3 is also indicated.*
$\dfrac{3x}{3} = \dfrac{6}{3}$	*Therefore, divide both sides by 3.*
$x = 2$	

Check:
$$\begin{aligned}
3x + 7 &\overset{?}{=} 13 \\
3(2) + 7 &\overset{?}{=} 13 \\
6 + 7 &\overset{?}{=} 13 \\
13 &= 13
\end{aligned}$$

The solution is 2.

2 **Solve: $\frac{x}{4} + 9 = 6$**

$\dfrac{x}{4} + 9 = 6$	
$\dfrac{x}{4} + 9 - 9 = 6 - 9$	*First subtract 9 from both sides. Why?*
$\dfrac{x}{4} = -3$	
$4\left(\dfrac{x}{4}\right) = 4(-3)$	*Then multiply both sides by 4. Why?*
$x = -12$	*Check this result.*

The solution is -12.

Examples

3 Solve: $7 = 14 - 3x$

$$7 = 14 - 3x$$
$$7 - 14 = 14 - 3x - 14$$
$$7 - 14 = 14 - 14 - 3x$$
$$-7 = -3x$$
$$\frac{-7}{-3} = \frac{-3x}{-3}$$
$$\frac{7}{3} = x \qquad \textit{Check this result.}$$

The solution is $\frac{7}{3}$ or $2\frac{1}{3}$.

4 Solve: $\frac{d-4}{3} = 5$

$$\frac{d-4}{3} = 5$$
$$3\left(\frac{d-4}{3}\right) = 3(5)$$
$$d - 4 = 15$$
$$d - 4 + 4 = 15 + 4$$
$$d = 19 \qquad \textit{Check this result.}$$

The solution is 19.

Exploratory Exercises

State the steps that you would use to solve each equation.

1. $3x - 7 = 2$
2. $5n - 4 = -7$
3. $2x + 5 = 13$
4. $8 + 3x = 5$
5. $\frac{a+2}{5} = 10$
6. $\frac{a-7}{15} = -30$
7. $\frac{3}{11}x + 2 = 5$
8. $-\frac{4}{13}y - 7 = 6$

Written Exercises

Solve and check each equation.

1. $4t - 7 = 5$
2. $6 = 4n + 2$
3. $4 + 7x = 39$
4. $7n - 4 = 17$
5. $5n + 3 = 9$
6. $34 = 8 - 2t$
7. $5 - 3x = 32$
8. $2 - 7s = -19$
9. $-3x - 7 = 18$
10. $-4y + 2 = 29$
11. $\frac{x}{2} + 5 = 7$
12. $\frac{m}{3} - 6 = 14$
13. $\frac{y}{3} + 6 = -45$
14. $\frac{a}{6} - 7 = 13$
15. $\frac{b}{3} + 2 = -21$
16. $\frac{c}{-4} - 8 = -42$
17. $\frac{c}{-3} - 1 = 26$
18. $\frac{c}{-9} + 18 = 40$
19. $\frac{d+5}{3} = -9$
20. $\frac{3+n}{7} = -5$
21. $\frac{m-5}{4} = 5$
22. $\frac{t-6}{7} = 8$
23. $\frac{s-8}{-7} = 16$
24. $7 = \frac{r-8}{6}$
25. $\frac{4d+5}{7} = 7$
26. $\frac{4r+8}{16} = 7$
27. $\frac{7n+(-1)}{8} = 8$
28. $\frac{-3n-(-4)}{-6} = -9$
29. $0.2n + 3 = 8.6$
30. $0.5x + 1.5 = 12$
31. $8 - 1.2s = -1.6$
32. $4 + 2.3y = -5.2$
33. $8 = 4.1n - 24.8$
34. $-7 = 2.6t + 8.6$
35. $\frac{3}{4}n - 3 = 9$
36. $\frac{1}{3}x + 4 = 6$
37. $3 - \frac{n}{3} = 7$
38. $5 + \frac{t}{4} = 8$
39. $5 - \frac{2}{3}n = 7$
40. $8 + \frac{3}{4}n = 26$

Challenge

41. $2[x + 3(x - 1)] = 18$
42. $4(2x - 7) + 3(x - 1) = 46$
43. $\frac{1}{4}\left[\frac{3}{2}(x - 2) + 2x\right] = -6$
44. $-\frac{1}{2}\left[4 - 3\left(x + \frac{1}{5}\right)\right] = -\frac{4}{5}$

Applications in Physics

Suppose an automobile is moving at a speed of 50 mph. Wishing to pass another car, the driver increases the speed to 55 mph in 10 seconds. The driver has accelerated the car.

Acceleration is the rate at which speed is changing with respect to time. To compute acceleration (a) you divide the change in speed by the time (t) needed to make the change. The change in speed is the difference between the final speed (f) and the starting speed (s). This can be summarized in the following formula.

$$a = \frac{f - s}{t}$$

Example: A race car goes from 44 m/s to 77 m/s in 11 seconds. Find the change in speed per second.

$$a = \frac{f - s}{t}$$

$$a = \frac{77 - 44}{11} \text{ or } 3 \qquad \textit{Substitute 77 for f, 44 for s, and 11 for t.}$$

The car accelerates 3 meters per second each second or 3 m/s^2.

Consider what happens when the racing car slows down from 77 m/s to 44 m/s during the 11 seconds. The same equation can be used. Subtracting the starting speed from the final speed gives a negative value. This means that the acceleration is negative. *Negative acceleration is* <u>deceleration</u> .

$$a = \frac{44 - 77}{11} = -3$$

The acceleration is -3 m/s^2.

Exercises

For each problem, find the acceleration.

1. A motorcycle goes from 2 m/s to 14 m/s in 6 seconds.

2. A skateboard goes from 5 m/s to 0 m/s in 1 second.

3. A train is traveling for 1 hour at a constant speed of 50 mph.

4. A car starts from a standstill. It accelerates to 40 mph in 10 seconds.

5. A jet plane decreases its speed from 500 km/h to 350 km/h in 30 seconds.

6. A car traveling at 35 mph is stopped in 5 seconds.

3-5 More Equations

Many equations contain variables on both sides. To solve such equations, first use the addition or subtraction property of equality to write an equivalent equation that has all the variables on one side. Then finish solving the equation by using the methods shown earlier in this chapter.

Examples

1 Solve: $5n - 7 = 3n + 2$

$$5n - 7 = 3n + 2$$

$$5n - 3n - 7 = 3n - 3n + 2 \qquad \text{\textit{Subtract 3n from both sides}}$$

$$2n - 7 = 2$$

$$2n - 7 + 7 = 2 + 7 \qquad \text{\textit{Add 7 to both sides.}}$$

$$2n = 9$$

$$\frac{2n}{2} = \frac{9}{2} \qquad \text{\textit{Divide both sides by 2.}}$$

$$n = \frac{9}{2} \text{ or } 4\frac{1}{2}$$

Check: $5n - 7 = 3n + 2$

$$5\left(\frac{9}{2}\right) - 7 \stackrel{?}{=} 3\left(\frac{9}{2}\right) + 2$$

$$\frac{45}{2} - \frac{14}{2} \stackrel{?}{=} \frac{27}{2} + \frac{4}{2}$$

$$\frac{31}{2} = \frac{31}{2}$$

The solution is $\frac{9}{2}$ or $4\frac{1}{2}$.

2 Solve: $\frac{2}{5}x + 3 = \frac{1}{5}x - 7$

$$\frac{2}{5}x + 3 = \frac{1}{5}x - 7$$

$$\frac{2}{5}x - \frac{1}{5}x + 3 = \frac{1}{5}x - \frac{1}{5}x - 7 \qquad \text{\textit{Subtract $\frac{1}{5}$x from both sides.}}$$

$$\frac{1}{5}x + 3 = -7$$

$$\frac{1}{5}x + 3 - 3 = -7 - 3 \qquad \text{\textit{Subtract 3 from both sides.}}$$

$$\frac{1}{5}x = -10$$

$$5\left(\frac{1}{5}x\right) = 5(-10) \qquad \text{\textit{Multiply both sides by 5.}}$$

$$x = -50 \qquad \text{\textit{Check this result.}}$$

The solution is -50.

Many equations also contain grouping symbols. When solving
equations of this type, first use the distributive property to remove
the grouping symbols.

Example

3   **Solve: $2(2r + 5) + 1 = 5 - 2(3 - r)$**

$$2(2r + 5) + 1 = 5 - 2(3 - r)$$
$$4r + 10 + 1 = 5 - 6 + 2r \qquad \textit{Use the distributive property.}$$
$$4r + 11 = -1 + 2r \qquad \textit{Simplify.}$$
$$4r - 2r + 11 = -1 + 2r - 2r$$
$$2r + 11 = -1$$
$$2r + 11 - 11 = -1 - 11$$
$$2r = -12$$
$$\frac{2r}{2} = \frac{-12}{2}$$
$$r = -6 \qquad \textit{Check this result.}$$

The solution is -6.

Some equations may have *no* solutions. Other equations may have
all numbers in their solution sets. An equation that is true for every
value of the variable is called an **identity**.

Examples

4   **Solve: $2x + 5 = 2x - 3$**

$$2x + 5 = 2x - 3$$
$$2x + 5 - 5 = 2x - 3 - 5$$
$$2x = 2x - 8$$
$$2x - 2x = 2x - 8 - 2x$$
$$0 = -8 \quad \textit{This is a false statement.}$$

This equation has no solutions.

5   **Solve: $3(x + 1) - 5 = 3x - 2$**

$$3(x + 1) - 5 = 3x - 2$$
$$3x + 3 - 5 = 3x - 2$$
$$3x - 2 = 3x - 2$$
$$3x - 2 + 2 = 3x - 2 + 2 \quad \textit{Add 2 to both sides.}$$
$$3x = 3x$$
$$3x - 3x = 3x - 3x \qquad \textit{Subtract 3x from both sides.}$$
$$0 = 0 \quad \textit{This statement is true for all values of x.}$$

This equation is an identity.

Exploratory Exercises

State the steps that you would use to solve each equation.

1. $3x + 2 = 4x - 1$ 2. $6x - 8 = 9 + 2x$ 3. $4y - 3 = -5y + 7$ 4. $2y + 7 = -3y - 7$

5. $3(x + 1) = 7$ 6. $4(x - 1) = 5$ 7. $6(2x - 3) = -9$ 8. $-7(x - 3) = -4$

Written Exercises

Solve and check each equation.

(handwritten: $6x + 18 = 4x - 4$; $2x = 14$)

1. $6x + 7 = 8x - 13$
2. $3x - 5 = 7x + 7$
3. $3 - 4x = 10x + 10$
4. $13 - 8x = 5x + 2$
5. $17 + 2x = 21 + 2x$
6. $-5x - 1 = -5x - 1$
7. $6x + 3 = 6x + 3$
8. $18 - 4x = 42 - 4x$
9. $3(x + 2) = 12$
10. $3(x - 5) = -6$
11. $7(x - 3) - 2 = 5$
12. $3x - 2(x + 3) = x$
13. $7 + 2(x + 1) = 2x + 9$
14. $6(x + 2) - 4 = -10$
15. $6 = 3 + 5(x - 2)$
16. $-2(2x - 3) = 6 - 4x$
17. $4(x - 2) = 4x$
18. $-5 = 4 - 2(x - 5)$
19. $6(x + 3) = 4(x - 1)$
20. $8(x - 9) = -8(x + 5)$
21. $-3(x + 5) = 3(x - 1)$
22. $5x - 7 = 5(x - 2) + 3$
23. $7 - 3x = x - 4(2 + x)$
24. $4(2x - 1) = -10(x - 5)$
25. $2(x - 3) + 5 = 3(x - 1)$
26. $5x + 4 = 7(x + 1) - 2x$
27. $2x - 4(x - 5) = 2(10 - x)$
28. $6(x - 2) = 5(x - 11) - 21$
29. $\frac{1}{3}(x + 6) = 7$
30. $5 - \frac{1}{2}(x - 6) = 4$
31. $3(x - 5) = \frac{1}{5}(10x - 25)$
32. $4(2x - 8) = \frac{1}{7}(49x + 70)$
33. $\frac{2}{3}n + 8 = \frac{1}{3}n - 2$
34. $\frac{3}{4}n + 16 = 2 - \frac{1}{8}n$
35. $3 + \frac{2}{5}x = 11 - \frac{2}{5}x$
36. $\frac{1}{2}t + 6 = \frac{1}{3}t$
37. $2.1k - 50 = 7.3k - 3.2$
38. $18 - 3.8x = 7.36 - 1.9x$
39. $8n - 11.35 = 1.2n + 17.21$
40. $3.1x - 2.78 = 7.22 - 1.9x$
41. $3(4x - 8) = -7(2x - 3)$
42. $16(2x - 5) = -2(5x - 18)$
43. $3(5 - t) = 14$
44. $10\left(t - \frac{3}{5}\right) = 8$
45. $8 + 10x = 5x + 11$
46. $5\left(2w - \frac{3}{5}\right) = w - 3$
47. $3(2x + 1) = 6(x - 1)$
48. $12(4 - y) = 57$
49. $9(2 + w) = 33$
50. $2(3v - 1) = 6v - 2$

mini-review

Write an equation.

1. The product of π and the square of r is A.

State the property.

2. $a + 0 = a$ 3. $x(yz) = (yz)x$

Simplify.

4. $4.75 - (-7.63)$ 5. $a + (-12a)$

3-6 Still More Equations

You can solve equations containing fractions and decimals by first using the multiplication property of equality to eliminate the fractions and decimals.

Examples

1 Solve: $\frac{2x}{5} + \frac{x}{4} = \frac{26}{5}$

$$\frac{2x}{5} + \frac{x}{4} = \frac{26}{5}$$ *The least common denominator is 20.*

$$20\left(\frac{2x}{5} + \frac{x}{4}\right) = \left(\frac{26}{5}\right)20$$ *Multiply both sides of the equations by 20.*

$$20\left(\frac{2x}{5}\right) + 20\left(\frac{x}{4}\right) = \left(\frac{26}{5}\right)20$$ *Use the distributive property.*

$$8x + 5x = 104$$ *The fractions are eliminated.*

$$13x = 104$$

$$x = 8$$

Check: $\frac{2x}{5} + \frac{x}{4} = \frac{26}{5}$

$$\frac{2(8)}{5} + \frac{8}{4} = \frac{26}{5}$$

$$\frac{16}{5} + \frac{8}{4} \stackrel{?}{=} \frac{26}{5}$$

$$\frac{64}{20} + \frac{40}{20} \stackrel{?}{=} \frac{104}{20}$$

$$\frac{104}{20} = \frac{104}{20}$$

The solution is 8.

2 Solve: $2.1x + 45.2 = -7.3 - 8.4x$

$$2.1x + 45.2 = -7.3 - 8.4x$$

$$10(2.1x + 45.2) = 10(-7.3 - 8.4x)$$ *Multiply both sides of the equation by 10.*

$$10(2.1x) + 10(45.2) = 10(-7.3) - 10(8.4x)$$

$$21x + 452 = -73 - 84x$$ *The decimals are eliminated.*

$$21x + 84x + 452 = -73 - 84x + 84x$$

$$105x + 452 - 452 = -73 - 452$$

$$105x = -525$$

$$x = -5$$ *Check this result.*

The solution is −5.

Some equations contain more than one variable. It is often necessary to solve such equations for a specific variable.

Example

3 Solve for x: $ax + b = dx + c$

$$ax + b = dx + c$$
$$ax + b - b = dx + c - b$$
$$ax = dx + c - b$$
$$ax - dx = dx + c - b - dx$$
$$(a - d)x = c - b$$
$$\frac{(a - d)x}{a - d} = \frac{c - b}{a - d} \qquad \text{\textit{Division by zero is undefined.}}$$
$$\qquad\qquad\qquad\quad \text{\textit{Therefore } a - d \neq 0.}$$
$$x = \frac{c - b}{a - d}$$

Exploratory Exercises

State the number that each side of the equation must be multiplied by to remove the fractions or decimals. Then rewrite the equation.

1. $\frac{3}{4}x - 7 = 8 + \frac{2}{3}x$

2. $\frac{2}{5}x = 7 - \frac{3}{4}x$

3. $4t - 7 = \frac{5t}{2} - 3$

4. $1.2s + 8.1 = 3.5 - 2s$

5. $5.2z = 3 + 1.7z$

6. $8.17y = 4.2 - 3.7y$

Written Exercises

Solve and check each equation.

1. $\frac{y + 5}{-3} = 7$ $\quad Y + 5 = 21$
$\quad -5 \quad +26$

2. $\frac{x - 7}{5} = 12$

3. $\frac{3n - 2}{5} = \frac{7}{10}$

4. $0.2x + 1.7 = 3.9$

5. $5.3 - 0.3x = -9.4$

6. $1.9s + 6 = 3.1 - s$

7. $\frac{3}{4}x - 4 = 7 + \frac{1}{2}x$

8. $\frac{3}{8} - \frac{1}{4}x = \frac{1}{2}x - \frac{3}{4}$

9. $\frac{5}{8}x + \frac{3}{5} = x$

10. $3y - \frac{4}{5} = \frac{1}{3}y$

11. $\frac{1}{3}y + 3 = \frac{1}{2}y$

12. $\frac{2}{5}x - 1 = \frac{1}{4}x$

13. $\frac{4y + 3}{7} = \frac{9}{14}$

14. $\frac{4 - x}{5} = \frac{1}{5}x$

15. $\frac{7 + 3t}{4} = -\frac{1}{8}t$

16. $1.3x - 4 = 2.1x + 8$

17. $0.8 - 0.2z = 0.3z - 4$

18. $2.1y + 7 = 1.2y - 2$

19. $\frac{2}{3}x + \frac{1}{2} = \frac{1}{3}x + 4$

20. $\frac{3y}{2} - y = 4 + \frac{1}{2}y$

21. $\frac{x}{2} - \frac{1}{3} = \frac{x}{3} - \frac{1}{2}$

Solve for x.

22. $5x = y$

23. $x + r = 2d$

24. $\frac{x + a}{3} = c$

25. $\frac{d + x}{e} = f$

26. $ax + b = c$

27. $ex - 2y = 3z$

Solve for y.

28. $ay - b = c$

29. $c - 2y = d$

30. $ay + z = am - n$

31. $a(y + 1) = b$

32. $\frac{x}{y} = 4$

33. $\frac{3}{5}y + a = b$

3-7 Problem Solving: Using Equations

In cross-country, a team's score is found by adding the place numbers of the first five finishers. For example, five runners for a team finished 2nd, 6th, 8th, 9th, and 13th. Their team's score is found as follows.

$$2 + 6 + 8 + 9 + 13 = 38$$

Rick and Tad ran in an invitational meet. Rick finished 3 places ahead of Tad. Their combined score was 27. In what place did each runner finish?

Use the problem solving plan to find the solution.

Explore

Define a variable.
Let x = Rick's place number.
$x + 3$ = Tad's place number.

Plan

Write an equation.
The combined score was 27.

$$\underbrace{x + (x + 3)}\ \ \underbrace{=}\ \ \underbrace{27}$$

Solve

Solve the equation and answer the problem.
$$x + (x + 3) = 27$$
$$2x + 3 = 27$$
$$2x + 3 - 3 = 27 - 3$$
$$2x = 24$$
$$\frac{2x}{2} = \frac{24}{2}$$
$$x = 12$$

Since x represents Rick's place number, Rick finished in 12th place. Since $x + 3$ represents Tad's place number, Tad finished in 15th place.

Examine

Check whether the answer makes sense.

Read the problem again and compare your answer to the statements given in the problem. For the problem above you could ask the following questions.

    1. If Rick finished 12th and Tad finished 15th, did Rick finish 3 places ahead of Tad?

    2. Was their combined score 27?

Example 1

Use an equation to solve the problem. Then examine the solution.

Rylynn wants to buy a 10-speed bicycle which costs $117. This is $12 more than three times the amount that she saved last month. How much did she save last month?

Explore   Let x = amount of money saved last month.

Plan   Cost is $12 more than 3 times amount saved last month.

$$117 = 12 \quad + \quad 3x$$

Solve

$$117 = 12 + 3x$$
$$117 - 12 = 12 + 3x - 12$$
$$105 = 3x$$
$$\frac{105}{3} = \frac{3x}{3}$$
$$35 = x$$

Rylynn saved $35 last month.

Examine   Is $117 equal to $12 more than three times $35?

$$117 \stackrel{?}{=} 3(35) + 12$$
$$117 \stackrel{?}{=} 105 + 12$$
$$117 = 117$$

Since this is a true statement, $35 is the correct answer.

Consecutive numbers are numbers in counting order such as 3, 4, 5. Beginning with an even integer and counting by two gives **consecutive even integers**. For example, $-6, -4, -2, 0, 2, 4$ are consecutive even integers. Beginning with an odd integer and counting by two gives **consecutive odd integers**. For example, $-3, -1, 1, 3, 5$ are consecutive odd integers.

Example 2

Find three consecutive even integers whose sum is -12.

Let x = the least even integer.
$x + 2$ = the next greater even integer.
$x + 4$ = the greatest of the three even integers.

$$x + (x + 2) + (x + 4) = -12 \qquad \textit{The sum of the integers is } -12.$$
$$3x + 6 = -12$$
$$3x = -18$$
$$x = -6$$

Therefore, $x + 2 = -4$ and $x + 4 = -2$. The integers are $-6, -4,$ and -2.

Exploratory Exercises

Solve each problem.

1. State three consecutive integers if the greatest one is 4.

2. State three consecutive integers if the least one is −2.

3. State three consecutive even integers if the least one is −4.

4. State three consecutive even integers if the greatest one is 10.

5. State four consecutive odd integers if the least one is 13.

6. State four consecutive odd integers if the least one is −7.

For each sentence, define a variable. Then state an equation.

7. The sum of two consecutive integers is 17.

8. The sum of three consecutive even integers is 48.

9. The sum of two consecutive odd integers is −36.

10. The sum of four consecutive integers is −46.

11. Three times a number increased by 4 is −11.

12. Seventeen decreased by twice a number is 5.

Written Exercises

For each problem, define a variable. Then use an equation to solve the problem. Some problems have no solutions.

1. Find three consecutive integers whose sum is 87.

2. Find three consecutive integers whose sum is 114.

3. Find four consecutive integers whose sum is 130.

4. Find four consecutive integers whose sum is 278.

5. Find two consecutive even integers whose sum is 115.

6. Find two consecutive even integers whose sum is 138.

7. Find two consecutive odd integers whose sum is 64.

8. Find two consecutive odd integers whose sum is 35.

9. Find three consecutive odd integers whose sum is 99.

10. Find three consecutive even integers whose sum is 72.

11. Twice a number increased by 20 is 62. Find the number.

12. Three times a number decreased by 11 is 58. Find the number.

13. Karen has 6 more than twice as many newspaper customers as when she started. She now has 98 customers. How many did she have when she started?

14. Bonnie sold some stock for $42 a share. This was $10 a share more than twice what she paid for it. At what price did she buy the stock?

15. Last year Marc Ames sold 7 sedans more than twice the number of vans Lola Kaplan sold. Marc sold 83 sedans. How many vans did Lola sell?

16. One season Reggie Walker scored 9 more runs than twice the number of runs he batted in. He scored 117 runs that season. How many runs did he bat in?

17. A rectangular playground is 60 meters longer than it is wide. It can be enclosed by 920 meters of fencing. Find its length.

18. A soccer field is 75 yards shorter than 3 times its width. Its perimeter is 370 yards. Find its dimensions.

19. The captain of the cross-country team placed second in a meet. The other four members placed in consecutive order, but farther behind. The team score was 40. In what places did the other members finish?

20. One member of the cross-country team placed fourth in a meet. The other four members placed in consecutive order, but farther behind. The team score was 70. In what places did the other members finish?

21. Brad bought a used bike for $8 more than half its original price. Brad paid $40 for the bike. What was the original price?

22. The lengths of the sides of a triangle are consecutive odd integers. The perimeter is 27. What are the lengths of the sides?

23. Twice a number increased by 4 times the number is 96. Find the number.

24. Twice a number increased by 12 is 31 less than three times the number. Find the number.

25. A number increased by 5 less than twice itself is 415. Find the number.

26. Five times a number decreased by 4 more than twice the number is 119. Find the number.

27. Find four consecutive even integers such that twice the least increased by the greatest is 96.

28. Find 4 consecutive odd integers such that the sum of the first and twice the second is 175.

29. Twice the greater of two consecutive odd integers is 13 less than three times the lesser. Find the integers.

30. Three times the greatest of 3 consecutive even integers exceeds twice the least by 38. Find the integers.

31. Find two consecutive integers such that 3 times the first integer plus 2 times the second integer is equal to 107.

32. Find two consecutive integers such that 2 times the first integer plus 4 times the second integer is equal to 256.

Challenge

33. The length of a rectangle is 40 m less than 2 times its width. Its perimeter is 220 m. Find its dimensions.

34. The length of a rectangle is 35 m more than 3 times its width. Its perimeter is 390 m. Find its dimensions.

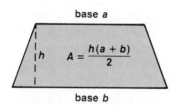

base a

$$A = \frac{h(a + b)}{2}$$

base b

35. A trapezoid has an area of 96 m^2 and a height of 12 m. One base is 2 m longer than the other base. How long is each base?

36. A trapezoid has an area of 117 sq ft and a height of 9 ft. One base is 4 ft shorter than the other base. How long is each base?

mini-review

Solve.

1. $x - (-7.4) = 5.92$

2. $\frac{7}{8} + y = \frac{11}{20}$

3. $4x = 62$

4. $0.5x + 1.5 = 12$

5. $6(x + 3) = 4(x - 1)$

Problem Solving

Many problems can be solved more easily if you draw a picture or diagram to represent the situation. Sometimes a picture will help you decide how to work a problem. Other times the picture will show the answer to the problem.

The length of a rectangle is twice its width. The perimeter is 39 m. Find the length and width.

Draw one side and mark it x.

Then draw an adjacent side twice as long as the first side.

Finish drawing the rectangle.

Label all four sides.

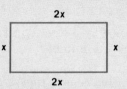

You can use the diagram to write an equation for the problem.

$$x + 2x + x + 2x = 39$$
$$6x = 39$$
$$x = 6.5$$

The width is 6.5 m and the length is twice the width, or 13 m.

Solve each problem. Use pictures and diagrams.

1. Two sides of a triangle have the same length. The third side is 2 m longer. If the perimeter of the triangle is 20 m, find the lengths of the sides.

2. You can cut a pizza into 7 pieces with only 3 straight cuts. What is the greatest number of pieces you can make with 5 straight cuts?

3. A row of 20 seats has some red seats and some blue seats. The first two are red, the next two are blue, the next two are red, and so on. What color is the 14th seat?

4. Three spiders are on a 9-ft wall. Susie spider is 4 feet from the top. Sam spider is 7 feet from the bottom. Shirley spider is 3 feet below Sam spider. Which spider is nearest the top of the wall?

5. A row of coins is arranged in the following pattern: 1 dime, followed by 3 nickels, then 5 dimes, 7 nickels, and so on. What is the 40th coin in the row?

6. An ant is climbing a 30-ft flagpole. Each day he climbs up 7 feet. Each night he slips back 4 feet. How many days will it take to reach the top of the flagpole?

7. A staircase with 3 steps was built with 6 blocks. Can a staircase be built with 28 blocks? How many steps would it have?

8. There were 9 people at a party. Everyone shook hands with everyone else exactly once. How many handshakes occurred?

3-8   Ratio and Proportion

As gear A revolves 4 times, it will cause gear B to revolve 3 times. Hence, we say that the gear ratio is 4 to 3.

In mathematics, a **ratio** is a comparison of two numbers by division. The gear ratio above can be expressed in the following ways.

$$4 \text{ to } 3 \qquad 4 : 3 \qquad \frac{4}{3}$$

A ratio is most commonly expressed as a fraction in simplest form.

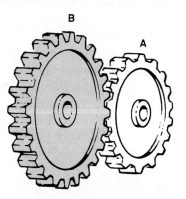

Examples

1 **What is the ratio of 10 m to 6 m?** $\frac{10}{6} = \frac{5}{3}$

The ratio is $\frac{10}{6}$ or $\frac{5}{3}$.

2 **What is the ratio of 20 inches to 4 feet?**

The units should be the same.
    4 feet = 48 inches

The ratio is $\frac{20}{48}$ or $\frac{5}{12}$.

An equation of the form $\frac{a}{b} = \frac{c}{d}$ which states that two ratios are equal is called a proportion.

Definition of Proportion

Every proportion consists of four terms.

$$\overset{\textit{first}}{\underset{\textit{second}}{\frac{a}{b}}} = \overset{\textit{third}}{\underset{\textit{fourth}}{\frac{c}{d}}}$$

The first and fourth terms are called the **extremes**.

The second and third terms are called the **means**.

In a proportion, the product of the extremes is equal to the product of the means.

$$\text{If } \frac{a}{b} = \frac{c}{d}, \text{ then } ad = bc.$$

Means-Extremes Property of Proportions

You can use this property to solve some equations. The equation must be in the form of a proportion.

3 **Solve:** $\frac{21}{27} = \frac{x}{18}$

$$\frac{21}{27} = \frac{x}{18}$$

$21(18) = 27x$ *Means-Extremes Property*

$378 = 27x$

$14 = x$ *Check this result.*

The solution is 14.

4 **Solve:** $\frac{x}{5} = \frac{x + 3}{10}$

$$\frac{x}{5} = \frac{x + 3}{10}$$

$10x = 5(x + 3)$ *Means-Extremes Property*

$10x = 5x + 15$ *Distributive Property*

$5x = 15$

$x = 3$ *Check this result.*

The solution is 3.

Proportions are often used to solve problems.

Example

5 **A trip of 96 miles required 6 gallons of gasoline. At that rate, how many gallons would be required for a 152-mile trip?**

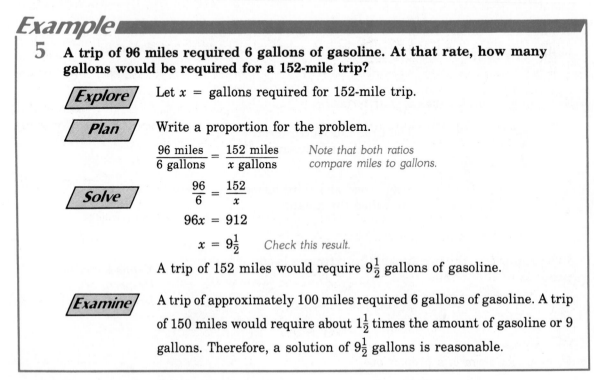

Explore Let x = gallons required for 152-mile trip.

Plan Write a proportion for the problem.

$$\frac{96 \text{ miles}}{6 \text{ gallons}} = \frac{152 \text{ miles}}{x \text{ gallons}} \quad \begin{array}{l} \textit{Note that both ratios} \\ \textit{compare miles to gallons.} \end{array}$$

Solve $$\frac{96}{6} = \frac{152}{x}$$

$96x = 912$

$x = 9\frac{1}{2}$ *Check this result.*

A trip of 152 miles would require $9\frac{1}{2}$ gallons of gasoline.

Examine A trip of approximately 100 miles required 6 gallons of gasoline. A trip of 150 miles would require about $1\frac{1}{2}$ times the amount of gasoline or 9 gallons. Therefore, a solution of $9\frac{1}{2}$ gallons is reasonable.

Exploratory Exercises

Write each ratio as a fraction in simplest form.

1. 3 grams to 11 grams
2. 7 feet to 3 feet
3. 21 meters to 16 meters
4. 16 cm to 5 cm
5. 12 ounces to 6 ounces
6. 15 km to 5 km
7. 8 feet to 28 inches
8. 4 pounds to 100 ounces
9. 16 cm to 40 mm
10. 72 mm to 90 cm

Written Exercises

Solve each proportion.

1. $\frac{3}{4} = \frac{x}{8}$

2. $\frac{3}{15} = \frac{b}{45}$

3. $\frac{2}{10} = \frac{1}{y}$

4. $\frac{10}{a} = \frac{20}{28}$

5. $\frac{6}{8} = \frac{7}{x}$

6. $\frac{x}{9} = \frac{7}{16}$

7. $\frac{9}{m} = \frac{15}{10}$

8. $\frac{6}{5} = \frac{18}{t}$

9. $\frac{x + 2}{5} = \frac{7}{5}$

10. $\frac{6}{14} = \frac{7}{x - 3}$

11. $\frac{3}{5} = \frac{x + 2}{6}$

12. $\frac{14}{10} = \frac{5 + x}{x - 3}$

Use a proportion to solve each problem.

13. Stewart earns $97 in 4 days. At that rate, how many days will it take him to earn $485?

14. Peggy saves $18 in 4 weeks. How long will it take her to save $81 at the same rate?

15. Shan Wong used 25 gallons of gasoline in traveling 350 miles. How much gasoline will he use in traveling 462 miles?

16. Andrea Jones drove 244 kilometers in 4 hours. At that rate, how long will it take her to drive 366 kilometers?

17. The scale on a map is 1 centimeter to 57 kilometers. Fargo and Bismarck are 4.7 centimeters apart on the map. What is the actual distance between these cities?

18. The scale on a map is 2 centimeters to 5 kilometers. Dove Creek and Kent are 15.75 kilometers apart. How far apart are they on the map?

19. One gear has 36 teeth. The ratio of this gear to a second gear is 4 to 3. How many teeth does the second gear have?

20. One gear has 45 teeth. The ratio of this gear to a second gear is 3 to 2. How many teeth does the second gear have?

Using Calculators _____ Solving Proportions

It is sometimes helpful to use a calculator when solving a proportion. Follow these steps to solve the proportion $\frac{6}{2.56} = \frac{9}{m}$.

ENTER: 9 ☒ 2.56 ☐ 6 ☐   *Multiply the values shown diagonally. Then divide by the third value.*

The solution is 3.84.

Exercises Solve each proportion by using a calculator.

1. $\frac{x}{4.8} = \frac{5}{16}$

2. $\frac{2.4}{3.6} = \frac{q}{1.8}$

3. $\frac{s}{9.6} = \frac{7}{16}$

4. $\frac{19.2}{a} = \frac{7}{29.4}$

The basic unit of length in the metric system is the meter. A unit of capacity, the **liter**, is defined in terms of the meter.

The large cube shown on this page is 10 centimeters along each edge. A cube this size has a volume of 1000 cubic centimeters and a capacity of one **liter** (L). The usual metric prefixes are used with liter.

1 cm³

A **milliliter** is $\frac{1}{1000}$ of a liter. One milliliter of water will fill a cube that is 1 cm along each edge. A thimble holds about 1 milliliter (1 mL).

There is also a relationship between capacity and mass in the metric system. A milliliter of water has a mass of one gram. A liter of water has a mass of one kilogram.

Exercises

Would you use milliliter or liter to measure each of the following?

1. gasoline for a car
2. eye drops
3. a large bottle of soda pop
4. vanilla for a cake
5. liquid detergent for laundry
6. water for the garden

Complete each of the following.

7. 3000 mL = ___ L
8. 2 L = ___ mL
9. 4.6 L = ___ mL
10. 2100 mL = ___ L
11. 4200 mL = ___ L
12. 5.06 L = ___ mL
13. 0.54 L = ___ mL
14. 236 mL = ___ L
15. 20 mL = ___ L
16. 3 mL = ___ L
17. 3.05 L = ___ mL
18. 17.98 L = ___ mL

Challenge

19. How many liters of water will fill a cube that has a volume of 1 cubic meter?

3-9 Percent

Les is the quarterback for the JFK High School football team. In last week's game he completed 17 out of 25 passes. What is his rate per 100?

You can solve this problem by using ratios. Write a ratio which is equivalent to $\frac{17}{25}$ and has a denominator of 100.

$$\frac{17}{25} = \frac{17 \cdot 4}{25 \cdot 4} = \frac{68}{100}$$

Les completed passes at a rate of 68 per 100 or 68 percent. The word **percent** means per hundred, or hundredths. The symbol for percent is %.

$$68\% = \frac{68}{100} = 0.68$$

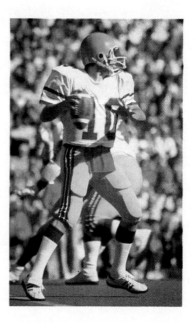

You can use a proportion to change a fraction to a percent, as shown in the following examples.

Examples

1 **Change $\frac{3}{5}$ to a percent.**

$$\frac{3}{5} = \frac{n}{100}$$

$$5n = 300 \qquad \text{\textit{Means-Extremes}}$$
$$\text{\textit{Property}}$$
$$n = 60$$

Thus, $\frac{3}{5}$ is equal to $\frac{60}{100}$ or 60%.

2 **Change $\frac{7}{8}$ to a percent.**

$$\frac{7}{8} = \frac{n}{100}$$

$$8n = 700 \qquad \text{\textit{Means-Extremes}}$$
$$\text{\textit{Property}}$$
$$n = 87\frac{1}{2}$$

Thus, $\frac{7}{8}$ is equal to $87\frac{1}{2}\%$.

Proportions can also be used to solve percent problems. One of the ratios in such proportions is always a comparison of two numbers called the **percentage** and the **base**. If the number 17 is being compared to the number 25, then 17 is the percentage and 25 is the base. The other ratio is formed by expressing the percent as a fraction, called the **rate**.

$$\frac{\text{Percentage}}{\text{Base}} = \text{Rate} \quad \text{or} \quad \frac{\text{Percentage}}{\text{Base}} = \frac{r}{100}$$

Percent Proportion

In the percent proportion, the rate is $\frac{r}{100}$.

Example

3 **50 is what percent of 60?**

$$\frac{\text{Percentage}}{\text{Base}} = \frac{r}{100}$$

$$\frac{50}{60} = \frac{r}{100} \qquad \text{The number 50 is being compared to 60.}$$

$$5000 = 60r$$

$$83\tfrac{1}{3} = r$$

Thus, 50 is $83\tfrac{1}{3}\%$ of 60.

Sometimes it is easier to solve a percent problem by translating the problem into a mathematical equation. Recall that the word "of" suggests multiplication, and the word "is" suggests equality. The problem in Example 3 can be translated into an equation as follows. The percent is represented by $\frac{x}{100}$.

50 is what percent of 60?

$$50 = \qquad \frac{x}{100} \qquad \cdot 60 \qquad \text{Compare this equation to the one in Example 3.}$$

Examples

4 **What number is 36% of 150?**

$$x \qquad = \frac{36}{100} \cdot 150$$

$$x = 54$$

Thus, 54 is 36% of 150.

5 **40% of what number is 30?**

$$\frac{40}{100} \cdot \qquad x \qquad = 30$$

$$40x = 3000$$

$$x = 75$$

Thus, 40% of 75 is 30.

There are many applications of percent, such as sales tax, discounts, and commission. Example 6 involves commission.

Example

6 Jim Byars earns 3% commission on sales of all new cars. If he earned $861 in commission last week, what was the dollar amount of his total sales?

Explore | Let x = total sales in dollars.

Plan | 3% of total sales equals $861

$$\frac{3}{100} \cdot x = 861$$

Solve |
$$\frac{3}{100}x = 861$$
$$3x = 86,100$$
$$x = 28,700 \quad \textit{Check this result.}$$

The total sales amount was $28,700.

Examine | 3% of $28,700 is $861.

Exploratory Exercises

Change each ratio or fraction to a percent.

1. $\frac{31}{100}$ 2. $\frac{9}{100}$ 3. $\frac{3}{10}$ 4. $\frac{1}{25}$ 5. $\frac{4}{5}$

6. $\frac{7}{20}$ 7. $\frac{3}{8}$ 8. $\frac{1}{3}$ 9. $\frac{7}{4}$ 10. $\frac{9}{5}$

Use a proportion to solve each problem.

11. 6 is what percent of 15?
12. 18 is what percent of 60?
13. What percent of 50 is 35?
14. What percent of 17 is 34?
15. 5 is what percent of 40?
16. What percent of 60 is 20?
17. What percent of 75 is 225?
18. 10 is what percent of 50?

Use an equation to solve each problem.

19. What number is 40% of 80?
20. 35 is 50% of what number?
21. 17 is 25% of what number?
22. What number is 0.3% of 6270?
23. 14 is what percent of 56?
24. What percent of 72 is 12?

Written Exercises

Solve each problem.

1. What is 40% of 60?
2. Seventy-five is what percent of 250?
3. Twenty-one is 35% of what number?
4. Find 37.5% of 80.
5. Fifty-two is what percent of 80?
6. Thirty-six is 45% of what number?
7. Find 7.5% of 405.
8. Find 81% of 32.
9. Twenty-eight is 20% of what number?
10. Sixteen is 40% of what number?
11. 19 is what percent of 76?
12. 37 is what percent of 296?
13. Find 4% of $6070.
14. Find 6% of $9.40.
15. 55 is what percent of 88?
16. 88 is what percent of 55?

17. $7030.50 is 107.5% of how many dollars?

18. $54,000 is 108% of how many dollars?

19. Find 112% of $500.

20. Find 113.4% of $1000.

21. 96 is what percent of 60?

22. 84 is what percent of 96?

23. 8 is 20% of what number?

24. 90 is 60% of what number?

25. Find 0.1% of $5000.

26. What is 98% of $140?

27. A theater was filled to 75% of capacity. How many of the 720 seats were filled?

28. The sales tax on a $20 purchase was $0.90. What was the rate of sales tax?

29. Janice scored 85% on the last test. She answered 34 questions correctly. How many questions were on the test?

30. In a 180-kilogram sample of ore, there was 3.2% metal. How many kilograms of metal were in the sample?

31. Suppose 6% of 8000 people polled regarding an election expressed no opinion. How many people expressed no opinion?

32. Bob Stapleton earns 2% of sales on all truck bodies he sells. Last week he earned $974. What were his sales?

33. Henri Rici paid $5000 for a car. After one year, its value had decreased by $1500. By what percent had the car depreciated in value?

34. June Carlos earns $125 per week in salary and 8% commission on all sales. How much must she sell in order to earn $200 per week?

35. A store advertised tires at 20% off. What was the original price of a tire that was marked $13 off?

36. The price of a coat was marked down $6. The original price was $60. What was the rate of discount?

Challenge

37. Jim Hunts works as a salesman in a men's clothing store. One day, he began with $75 in the cash register. At the end of the day he had $1422.79. If he charged 6% sales tax on all items sold, what were his total sales for the day?

▱▱▱▱▱▱▱ Using Computers ▱▱▱▱▱▱▱

Successive Discounts

A store may give a second discount on an item that is already being sold at a discount. Perhaps the item is out of style or slightly damaged. Consider this example.

Example The regular price of a sofa is $825. What is the final sale price if an additional 20% discount is given on this sofa which is already selling at a discount of 10%?

Regular price	$ 825		$742.50	*A 20% discount is the same as*
A 10% discount	× 0.90		× 0.80	*80% of $742.50.*
is the same as	$742.50		$594.00	**Sale price**
90% of the				
regular price.				

The two successive discounts can be summarized as follows.

($825 × 0.90) × 0.80 = $594

The following program will help you determine whether two successive discounts or one combined discount will give a lower sale price.

```
10   PRINT "ENTER ORIGINAL PRICE AND TWO DISCOUNTS
         AS DECIMALS"
20   INPUT P,X1,X2
30   LET S1 = P * (1 - X1) * (1 - X2)      Computes sale price with successive discounts
40   LET S2 = P * (1 - (X1 + X2))          Computes sale price with one combined discount
50   PRINT "TWO SUCCESSIVE DISCOUNTS", "$";S1
60   PRINT "COMBINED DISCOUNT", "$";S2
70   IF S2 < S1 THEN PRINT "ONE COMBINED DISCOUNT HAS A LOWER
         SALE PRICE."
80   IF S1 < S2 THEN PRINT "SUCCESSIVE DISCOUNTS HAVE A LOWER
         SALE PRICE"
90   IF S1 = S2 THEN PRINT "THERE IS NO DIFFERENCE"
100  END
```

Exercises

Find the sale price of each item using successive discounts and one combined discount.

1. Price, $49.00; Discounts, 20% and 15%
2. Price, $185; Discounts, 25% and 10%
3. Price, $12.50; Discounts, 30% and $12\frac{1}{2}$%
4. Price, $156.95; Discounts, $33\frac{1}{3}$% and 10%
5. What is the relationship between the sale price using successive discounts and one combined discount?
6. Modify the program to determine whether the order in which the discounts are applied affects the sale price.

Vocabulary

multiplicative inverse (79)	ratio (97)	percent (101)
reciprocal (79)	proportion (97)	percentage (101)
identity (88)	extremes (97)	base (101)
consecutive numbers (93)	means (97)	rate (101)

Chapter Summary

1. The product of two numbers that have different signs is negative. (75)
2. The product of two numbers that have the same sign is positive. (76)
3. The product of any number and -1 is its additive inverse.
$$-1(a) = -a \text{ and } a(-1) = -a \quad (76)$$
4. The quotient of two numbers is positive if the numbers have the same sign, negative if the numbers have different signs. (78)
5. Multiplicative Inverse Property: For every nonzero number a, there is exactly one number $\frac{1}{a}$, such that $\frac{1}{a}(a) = a\left(\frac{1}{a}\right) = 1$. (79)
6. Division Rule: For all numbers a and b, with $b \neq 0$, $a \div b = \frac{a}{b} = a\left(\frac{1}{b}\right) = \frac{1}{b}(a)$. (79)

7. Multiplication Property of Equality: For any numbers a, b, and c, if $a = b$ then $ac = bc$. (81)

8. Division Property of Equality: For any numbers a, b, and c, with $c \neq 0$, if $a = b$ then $\frac{a}{c} = \frac{b}{c}$. (82)

9. An equation that is true for every value of the variable is called an identity. (88)

10. An equation of the form $\frac{a}{b} = \frac{c}{d}$ is called a proportion. (97)

11. In a proportion, the product of the extremes is equal to the product of the means. If $\frac{a}{b} = \frac{c}{d}$, then $ad = bc$. (97)

12. Proportions can be used to solve percent problems. (101)

13. Percent Proportion: $\dfrac{\text{Percentage}}{\text{Base}} = \dfrac{r}{100}$ (102)

Chapter Review

3-1   **Find each product.**

1. $(-11)(9)$ 2. $(-8)(-12)$ 3. $\frac{3}{5}\left(-\frac{5}{7}\right)$

Simplify each expression.

4. $-3(7) + (-8)(-9)$ 5. $\frac{1}{2}(6a + 8b) - \frac{2}{3}(12a + 24b)$

3-2   **Simplify.**

6. $\dfrac{-54}{6}$ 7. $\dfrac{63b}{-7}$ 8. $\dfrac{\frac{4}{5}}{-7}$ 9. $\dfrac{-12}{-\frac{2}{3}}$ 10. $\dfrac{33a + 66}{-11}$

3-3   **Solve each equation.**

11. $-7r = -56$ 12. $23y = 1035$ 13. $\frac{3}{4}x = -12$ 14. $\frac{x}{5} = 7$

3-4   15. $3x - 8 = 22$ 16. $-4y + 2 = 32$ 17. $0.5n + 3 = -6$

18. $-6 = 3.1t + 6.4$ 19. $\frac{x}{-3} + 2 = -21$ 20. $\frac{r - 8}{-6} = 7$

3-5   21. $5a - 5 = 7a - 19$ 22. $-3(x + 2) = -18$

23. $4(2y - 1) = -10(y - 5)$ 24. $11.2n + 6 = 5.2n$

3-6   25. $\frac{2}{3}x + 5 = \frac{1}{2}x + 4$ 26. $2.9m + 1.7 = 3.5 + 2.3m$ 27. $\frac{3t + 1}{4} = \frac{3}{4}t - 5$

Solve for x.

28. $x + r = q$ 29. $\frac{x + y}{c} = d$

Solve for y.

30. $5(2a + y) = 3b - y$ 31. $\frac{2y - a}{3} = \frac{y + 3b}{4}$

3-7   **32.** Find two consecutive even integers whose sum is 94.

33. Find three consecutive odd integers whose sum is 81.

34. Find four consecutive integers such that the sum of the second and twice the third is 68.

35. Four times a number decreased by twice the number is 100. What is the number?

3-8   **Solve each proportion.**

36. $\frac{6}{15} = \frac{n}{45}$

37. $\frac{4}{8} = \frac{11}{t}$

38. $\frac{5}{6} = \frac{n-2}{4}$

3-9   **Change each fraction to a percent.**

39. $\frac{6}{10}$

40. $\frac{7}{8}$

41. $\frac{17}{100}$

Solve each problem.

42. 9 is what percent of 15?

43. What number is 60% of 80?

44. Twenty-one is 35% of what number?

45. 84 is what percent of 96?

Chapter Test

Simplify each expression.

1. $\frac{8(-3)}{2}$

2. $(-5)(-2)(-2) - (-6)(-3)$

3. $\frac{2}{3}\left(\frac{1}{2}\right) - \left(-\frac{3}{2}\right)\left(-\frac{2}{3}\right)$

4. $\frac{3}{4}(8x + 12y) - \frac{5}{7}(21x - 35y)$

5. $\frac{70a - 42b}{-14}$

6. $\frac{\frac{11}{5}}{-6}$

Solve each equation.

7. $-3y = 63$

8. $\frac{3}{4}y = -27$

9. $3x + 1 = 16$

10. $5n + 7 = 28 + 2n$

11. $5(8 - 2n) = 4n - 2$

12. $3(n + 5) - 6 = n + 5$

13. $7x + 9 = 3(x + 3)$

14. $-2(3n - 5) + 3n = 2 - n$

15. $\frac{3}{4}n - \frac{2}{3}n = 5$

16. $\frac{t - 7}{4} = 11$

17. $\frac{2r - 3}{-7} = 5$

18. $8r - \frac{r}{3} = 46$

Solve for x.

19. $\frac{x + y}{b} = c$

20. $yx + a = c$

Solve each proportion.

21. $\frac{7}{8} = \frac{5}{t}$

22. $\frac{9}{11} = \frac{x - 3}{x + 5}$

23. $\frac{y + 2}{8} = \frac{7}{5}$

24. $\frac{2}{5} = \frac{x - 3}{-2}$

Solve each problem.

25. Find 6.5% of 80.

26. 42 is what percent of 126?

27. 84 is 60% of what number?

28. Find three consecutive odd integers whose sum is 93.

29. Twice a number increased by 12 is 31 less than three times the number. Find the number.

30. Find two consecutive integers such that twice the lesser integer, increased by the greater integer, is 50.

When a fair coin is tossed, only 2 **outcomes** are possible. The coin will land either heads or tails. Each outcome is *equally likely* to happen.

The probability that a tossed coin will land heads is $\frac{1}{2}$. This means that there is one way for a successful outcome (a head) to occur out of two possible outcomes (a head or a tail). The results of similar experiments lead to the following definition.

> If all of the outcomes of an event are equally likely, the probability of that event occurring is
>
> $$P(\text{event}) = \frac{\text{number of favorable outcomes}}{\text{total number of possible outcomes}}.$$

Probability of a Successful Event

When one die is rolled, there are 6 possible outcomes. Thus, the probability of rolling a 3 is $\frac{1}{6}$. The probability of rolling a number between 1 and 6, inclusive, is $\frac{6}{6}$ or 1. The probability of rolling a 7 is $\frac{0}{6}$ or 0.

> The probability of an impossible event is 0.
> The probability of an event that is certain to occur is 1.

Probabilities of 1 and 0

Example 1:   A five-person committee is comprised of 3 women and 2 men: Annette, Barbara, Claudia, David, and Eddie. A chairperson is selected at random.   *Selected at random means that it is equally likely for each person to be selected.*

a. What is the probability that the chairperson is Annette?

$$P(\text{Annette}) = \frac{1}{5} \qquad \frac{1 \text{ favorable outcome}}{5 \text{ possible outcomes}}$$

The probability that the chairperson is Annette is $\frac{1}{5}$.

b. What is the probability that the chairperson is a man?

$$P(\text{man}) = \frac{2}{5} \qquad \frac{2 \text{ men}}{5 \text{ possible outcomes}}$$

The probability that the chairperson is a man is $\frac{2}{5}$.

Example 2: **A card is chosen at random from a standard deck of 52 playing cards. What is the probability of choosing a king or queen?**

There are 4 kings and 4 queens in a standard deck of 52 cards.

$$P(\text{king or queen}) = \frac{8}{52} = \frac{2}{13}$$

The probability that the card is a king or queen is $\frac{2}{13}$.

Exercises

The spinner shown at the right is equally likely to stop at any of the six numbers. It is spun once. Find the probability for each of the following.

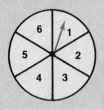

1. 1
2. 3
3. an even number
4. an odd number
5. a number less than 5
6. a number greater than 5
7. 3 or 4
8. 1, 2, or 3

The spinner shown at the right is divided into four sectors. It is spun once. Find the probability for each of the following.

9. $P(A)$
10. $P(B)$
11. $P(C)$
12. $P(D)$
13. $P(A \text{ or } B)$
14. $P(\text{not } C)$

A card is chosen at random from a standard deck of 52 playing cards. Find the probability of choosing each of the following.

15. the king of hearts
16. a red ace
17. a queen
18. the jack of spades
19. a club
20. not a 7

21. Copy the chart at the right. Flip a coin 50 times, recording your results in groups of 10 as indicated in the chart. Find the ratio of heads to the number of flips for each group of 10 and record this ratio. After 50 flips, find the total number of heads and tails. Determine the ratio of heads to flips for the total and record the ratio. Compare your results to your classmates' results. What ratio of heads to flips is expected?

Number of Flips	Heads	Tails	Heads Flips
1-10			
11-20			
21-30			
31-40			
41-50			
Totals			

CHAPTER 4

Inequalities

Tim has scores of 9.7, 9.9, 9.4, and 9.2 in the Olympic tryouts. He has one more trial. The leading opponent has completed the competition with an average score of 9.52. What must Tim score on his final trial if he is to win the competition? In this chapter, you will learn how to solve problems such as this using inequalities.

4-1 Inequalities and their Graphs

You know that 3 is less than 8. This can be shown in two ways.

$3 < 8$ means 3 *is less than* 8.

$8 > 3$ means 8 *is greater than* 3.

Note that the $<$ and $>$ point to the numeral for the lesser number.

Any mathematical sentence containing $<$ or $>$ is called an **inequality**.

Think about $3 < 8$. This sentence is true. Is $3 > 8$ true? Is $3 = 8$ true? Note that only one of the three sentences is true. This can be summarized by the following property.

For any two numbers a and b, exactly one of the following sentences is true.

$$a < b \qquad a = b \qquad a > b$$

Comparison Property

Examples

1 **Is $4 < 5\frac{1}{2}$ true or false?**

$4 < 5\frac{1}{2}$ means 4 *is less than* $5\frac{1}{2}$. This sentence is true.

The inequalities $4 < 5\frac{1}{2}$ and $5\frac{1}{2} > 4$ have the same meaning.

2 **Is $9 > 4 + 3 + 2 + 1$ true or false?**

$9 \overset{?}{>} 4 + 3 + 2 + 1$ *Is 9 greater than the sum of 4, 3, 2, and 1?*

$9 \overset{?}{>} 10$ *Simplify the right side of the inequality.*

Since 9 is not greater than 10, the sentence is false.

Recall that there are three properties of equality. Equality is reflexive, symmetric, and transitive. Do inequalities have these same properties?

Decide whether the sentences below are true or false.

Reflexive:	$6 > 6$	*False*
Symmetric:	If $4 > 3$, then $3 > 4$.	*False*
Transitive:	If $6 > 2$ and $2 > 1$, then $6 > 1$.	*True*

Check whether the transitive property is true for other examples.

The relation $>$ is not reflexive or symmetric. However, it is transitive. Explore some similar examples to verify that $<$ is transitive.

For all numbers a, b, and c,
1. If $a < b$ and $b < c$, then $a < c$.
2. If $a > b$ and $b > c$, then $a > c$.

Transitive Property of Order

Example

3 State whether the following sentence is true or false.

If $-3 < 1$ and $1 < 4$, then $-3 < 4$.

The sentence is true by the transitive property of order.

The symbols $\neq$, $\leq$, and $\geq$ can also be used when comparing numbers. The following chart shows several inequality symbols and their meanings.

Symbol	Meaning
$<$	is less than
$>$	is greater than
$\neq$	is not equal to
$\leq$	is less than or equal to
$\geq$	is greater than or equal to

Example

4 Is $5.1 \leq 7 + 0.9$ true or false?

$5.1 \overset{?}{\leq} 7 + 0.9$ *Is 5.1 less than or equal to 7 + 0.9?*

$5.1 \leq 7.9$

Since 5.1 is less than 7.9, the sentence is true.

Consider the graphs of -3, -1, $2\frac{1}{2}$, and 4.5, shown on the number line below.

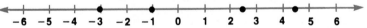

The following statements can be made about the numbers and their graphs.

The graph of -3 is to the left of the graph of -1. $-3 < -1$

The graph of -1 is to the left of the graph of $2\frac{1}{2}$. $-1 < 2\frac{1}{2}$

The graph of $2\frac{1}{2}$ is to the right of the graph of -3. $2\frac{1}{2} > -3$

The graph of 4.5 is to the right of the graph of $2\frac{1}{2}$. $4.5 > 2\frac{1}{2}$

If a and b represent any numbers and the graph of a is to the left of the graph of b, then $a < b$. If the graph of a is to the right of the graph of b, then $a > b$.

Comparing Numbers on the Number Line

Recall that an equation such as $x + 6 = 7$ is an open sentence. An inequality can also be an open sentence. The set of all replacements for the variable which make the inequality true is called the **solution set** of the inequality.

What replacements for x make $x < 5$ true? All numbers less than 5 make the inequality true. This can be shown by the solution set {all numbers less than 5}, read *the set of all numbers less than 5*. Study the graph of this solution set in Example 5 below.

Examples

5   **Graph the solution set of $x < 5$.**

The graph extends indefinitely in the negative direction.

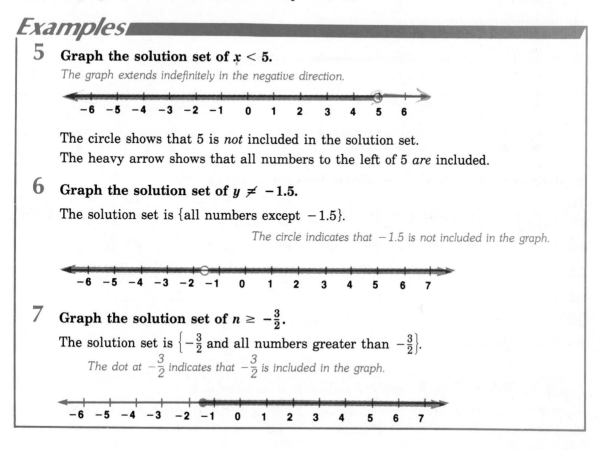

The circle shows that 5 is *not* included in the solution set.
The heavy arrow shows that all numbers to the left of 5 *are* included.

6   **Graph the solution set of $y \neq -1.5$.**

The solution set is {all numbers except -1.5}.

The circle indicates that -1.5 is not included in the graph.

7   **Graph the solution set of $n \geq -\frac{3}{2}$.**

The solution set is $\left\{-\frac{3}{2} \text{ and all numbers greater than } -\frac{3}{2}\right\}$.

The dot at $-\frac{3}{2}$ indicates that $-\frac{3}{2}$ is included in the graph.

Exploratory Exercises

State whether each sentence is true or false.

1. $7 < 4$ 　　　　　　　　**2.** $-3 < 3$ 　　　　　　　**3.** $2 > 0$ 　　　　　　　**4.** $-9 > -4$

5. $4\frac{1}{2} \neq 6\frac{1}{2}$ 　　　　　　**6.** $-\frac{8}{3} \leq \frac{8}{3}$ 　　　　　**7.** $\frac{1}{2} \geq \frac{1}{2}$ 　　　　　　**8.** $-5\frac{2}{3} \neq -6\frac{2}{3}$

9. $-4 < 2 - 8$ 　　　　**10.** $-8 + 4 < -5$ 　　　**11.** $-0.5 - 3 \geq -4$ 　　**12.** $-0.6 \leq -1 + 0.4$

13. If $4 > 3$ and $3 < 5$, then $4 > 5$. 　　　　　**14.** If $1 < 3$, then $1 > 3$.

State the solution set of each inequality.

15. $n > 3$ 　　　　**16.** $y < -5$ 　　　**17.** $z < 6$ 　　　　**18.** $y > -1$ 　　　**19.** $y \geq -4$ 　　　**20.** $m \neq 0$

State whether each number is included on the graph below.

21. -1 　　　　　**22.** 4 　　　　　**23.** 3.9 　　　　　**24.** -4.5 　　　　**25.** $-1\frac{1}{2}$ 　　　　**26.** $2\frac{1}{2}$

Written Exercises

State an inequality for each graph.

1. 　　　　**2.**

3. 　　　　**4.**

5. 　　　　**6.**

7. 　　　　**8.**

9. 　　　**10.**

Replace each ? with $<$, $>$, or $=$ to make each sentence true.

11. $-5 \underline{\ ?\ } 7$ 　　　　　**12.** $-2 \underline{\ ?\ } -3$ 　　　　**13.** $6 \underline{\ ?\ } 4 + 2$ 　　　　**14.** $-7 - 2 \underline{\ ?\ } -9$

15. $-5 \underline{\ ?\ } 0 - 3$ 　　**16.** $3 \underline{\ ?\ } \frac{15}{3}$ 　　　　**17.** $10 \underline{\ ?\ } \frac{27}{3}$ 　　　**18.** $12 \underline{\ ?\ } -15 - (-27)$

19. $8 \underline{\ ?\ } 4.1 + 3.9$ 　**20.** $5 \underline{\ ?\ } 8.4 - 1.5$ 　**21.** $-7 \underline{\ ?\ } -\frac{3.6}{0.6}$ 　　**22.** $\frac{5.4}{18} \underline{\ ?\ } -4 + 1$

23. $(-7.5)(0.4) \underline{\ ?\ } 3.1$ 　　　　**24.** $(6.3)(-0.4) \underline{\ ?\ } 25.2$ 　　　**25.** $\frac{4}{3}(6) \underline{\ ?\ } 4\left(\frac{3}{2}\right)$

26. $8\left(\frac{3}{4}\right) \underline{\ ?\ } 6\left(\frac{2}{3}\right)$ 　　　　　　**27.** $3 + 1.7 \underline{\ ?\ } \frac{9.6}{2}$ 　　　　**28.** $\frac{2.7}{3} \underline{\ ?\ } 2(4.5)$

29. If $-6 < -2$ and $-2 < 5$, then $-6 \underline{\ ?\ } 5$. 　　**30.** If $-6 < -2$ and $-2 < 5$, then $5 \underline{\ ?\ } -6$.

31. If $2\frac{2}{3} > -1\frac{1}{2}$ and $-1\frac{1}{2} > -3$, then 　　　**32.** If $4.5 > 2.1$ and $2.1 > -3.6$, then

　　$-3 \underline{\ ?\ } 2\frac{2}{3}$. 　　　　　　　　　　　　　　　$4.5 \underline{\ ?\ } -3.6$.

Graph the solution set of each inequality on a number line.

33. $n > 5$ 　　　**34.** $x > -3$ 　　　**35.** $m < 1$ 　　　**36.** $y < -2$ 　　　**37.** $x \neq -1$ 　　　**38.** $y \neq 3$

39. $y \leq 6$ 　　　**40.** $n \leq -2$ 　　**41.** $a \geq -3$ 　　　**42.** $x \geq -2$ 　　**43.** $x < -10$ 　　**44.** $m < 3$

In algebra a compound statement consists of two simple statements that are connected by the words *and* or *or*. You must read compound statements very carefully. Understanding the meaning of the words *and* and *or* will help you decide if a compound statement is true or false. Study the statements below.

The star is red *and* the square is blue.

For this compound statement to be true, both parts must be true. Since the star is red, the first part is true. However, the square is not blue, so the second part is false. Therefore, the compound statement is false.

The star is red *or* the square is blue.

For this compound statement to be true, at least one part needs to be true. You know that the star is red, so the compound statement is true.

The compound statements described above can be defined as follows.

A compound statement formed by joining two statements with the word *and* is called a conjunction. For a conjunction to be true, both statements must be true.	*Conjunction*

A compound statement formed by joining two statements with the word *or* is called a disjunction. For a disjunction to be true, at least one statement must be true.	*Disjunction*

Exercises

Decide whether each statement is a disjunction or a conjunction. Write true or false.

1. The circle is blue and the triangle is yellow.

2. The triangle is yellow or the circle is blue.

3. The square is red and the triangle is blue.

4. The circle is orange and the star is not red.

5. The star is blue or the triangle is red.

6. The triangle is blue or the circle is blue.

7. $3 < 4$ or $7 < 6$

8. $-4 > 0$ and $2 < 5$

9. $6 > 0$ and $-6 < 0$

10. $2 = 0$ or $-2 > -3$

11. $7 \neq 7$ and $6 > 4$

12. $0 > -4$ or $2 < -2$

Kristina had $267.23 in her savings account and Mike had $134.53 in his account. They each received $10 from their grandmother and deposited it in their accounts. Whose account has more money?

	Kristina	**Mike**
	$267.23 >	$134.53
$267.23 + $10.00		$134.53 + $10.00
	$277.23 >	$144.53

Kristina had more money at the beginning and at the end. Notice that adding the same number to both sides of the inequality did not change the truth of the inequality.

Suppose Kristina and Mike each withdrew, or subtracted, $25 from their accounts. Kristina would still have more money than Mike.

You know that the sentence $-1 < 3$ is true. Is $-1 + 1 < 3 + 1$ a true sentence? Is $-1 - 2 < 3 - 2$ a true sentence? These examples suggest the following rules that may be used in solving inequalities.

For all numbers a, b, and c,	*Addition and Subtraction*
1. If $a > b$, then $a + c > b + c$ and $a - c > b - c$.	*Properties for*
2. If $a < b$, then $a + c < b + c$ and $a - c < b - c$.	*Inequalities*

Examples

1 **Solve:** $m + 7 > 12$

$$m + 7 > 12$$
$$m + 7 - 7 > 12 - 7 \quad \text{Subtract 7 from both sides.}$$
$$m > 5$$

The solution set is {all numbers greater than 5}.

Check: First check whether 5 is the correct *boundary*. Is 5 the value of m in $m + 7 = 12$?

$$m + 7 \stackrel{?}{=} 12$$
$$5 + 7 \stackrel{?}{=} 12$$
$$12 = 12$$

Next substitute one or two numbers greater than 5, such as 6 and 10, into the inequality. For numbers greater than 5, the inequality should be true.

$$m + 7 > 12 \qquad\qquad m + 7 > 12$$
$$6 + 7 \stackrel{?}{>} 12 \quad \text{Try 6} \qquad 10 + 7 \stackrel{?}{>} 12 \quad \text{Try 10}$$
$$13 > 12 \quad \checkmark \qquad\qquad 17 > 12 \quad \checkmark$$

2 **Solve:** $9y - 14 < 8y + 3$

$$9y - 14 < 8y + 3$$
$$9y - 8y - 14 < 8y - 8y + 3 \quad \text{Subtract 8y from both sides.}$$
$$y - 14 < 3$$
$$y - 14 + 14 < 3 + 14 \quad \text{Add 14 to both sides.}$$
$$y < 17$$

The solution set is {all numbers less than 17}. *Try checking 10 and 16.*

Exploratory Exercises

State the number you would add to both sides to solve each inequality.

1. $r + 7 < 21$
2. $y + 2 < -16$
3. $m - 13 \geq 41$
4. $y - 18 \geq -3$
5. $4y < 3y + 12$
6. $7x < 6x - 12$
7. $6z > 5z - 21$
8. $7n > 6n - 4$
9. $12 > m - (-3)$
10. $16 \leq k - (-9)$
11. $14 < b - 7$
12. $9 > p - 21$

Written Exercises

Solve each inequality.

1. $a + 2 < 10$
2. $x + 3 < -17$
3. $r - 9 \geq 23$
4. $y - 15 \geq -2$
5. $5b < 4b + 8$
6. $6y < 5y - 11$
7. $3m > 2m - 19$
8. $9z > 8z - 8$
9. $y + 2 \leq -6$
10. $x + 7 \leq 10$
11. $n - 3 > 8$
12. $x - 5 > 3$
13. $6 + n > 40$
14. $3 + y \geq -4$
15. $-7 + n \leq -16$
16. $-8 + y < 10$
17. $n - (-5) < -6$
18. $y - (-4) > -7$
19. $-12 < s - (-3)$
20. $-21 > r - (-8)$

Solve each inequality.

21. $t + 13.1 \le 47.7$ **22.** $y + 18.7 < 81.6$ **23.** $m - 1.73 > 4.65$ **24.** $p - 7.35 \ge 6.81$

25. $\frac{3}{4} + r > \frac{7}{4}$ **26.** $r + \frac{5}{3} \le \frac{2}{3}$ **27.** $x - \frac{1}{3} < \frac{1}{2}$ **28.** $x + \left(-\frac{1}{4}\right) \ge -\frac{7}{4}$

29. $9f - 6 > 10f$

30. $8x - 31 > 7x$

31. $6n > 5n + 6$

32. $3m < 2m - 7$

33. $14 + 7x > 8x$

34. $-3 + 14z < 15z$

35. $6a + 4 \ge 5a$

36. $9y - 6 > 10y$

37. $2r - 2.1 < -8.7 + r$

38. $5s - 6.5 < -13.4 + 4s$

39. $12.37 + 4z > 181.3 + 3z$

40. $16.83 + p < 14.65 + 2p$

41. $y + \frac{3}{8} \le \frac{7}{24} + 2y$

42. $7x + \frac{3}{16} < -\frac{11}{16} + 6x$

43. $2r - \frac{3}{4} < r + \frac{5}{3}$

44. $y + \frac{16}{9} > 2y + \frac{5}{6}$

mini-review

Use the formula $d = rt$ to solve the following problem.

1. Kim can drive from her home to Denver in $6\frac{1}{2}$ hours. If her average speed is 52 miles per hour, how far does she live from Denver?

Solve.

2. In Anchorage, Alaska, the average high temperature in January is $-7°C$. The average high temperature in July is $18°C$. Find the difference between the two temperatures.

3. Find four consecutive integers whose sum is 110.

4. 36 is 150% of what number?

Solve for x.

5. $ax + m = c - 2m$

Excursions in Algebra _____ Set-Builder Notation

You have written the solutions of an inequality as a set. For example, the solution set of $16 + x > 19$ is {all numbers greater than 3}. Another way of writing such a solution set is called **set-builder notation**.

Example: **Solve $x + 4 < 16$. Write the solution set in set-builder notation.**

$$x + 4 < 16$$
$$x + 4 - 4 < 16 - 4 \quad \textit{Subtract 4 from both sides.}$$
$$x < 12$$

The solution set in set-builder notation is $\{x \mid x < 12\}$, read *the set of all numbers x such that x is less than 12.*

Exercises

Solve each inequality. Write the solution set in set-builder notation.

1. $x + 5 < 7$ **2.** $6 + n \ge 9$ **3.** $4x \le 5x - 4$

4. $-2 + m > 2m + 5$ **5.** $9x + 4 \le 13x - 7$ **6.** $5(y - 3) \ge 15$

4-3 Solving Inequalities Using Multiplication and Division

You know that the sentence $-4 < 6$ is true. Suppose both sides of the inequality are multiplied by the same positive number. Study the following examples. Are the resulting sentences true?

$$-4 < 6$$
$$-4(3) \overset{?}{<} 6(3)$$
$$-12 \overset{?}{<} 18 \quad \textit{True}$$

$$-4 < 6$$
$$-4\left(\tfrac{1}{2}\right) \overset{?}{<} 6\left(\tfrac{1}{2}\right)$$
$$-2 \overset{?}{<} 3 \quad \textit{True}$$

Notice that dividing both sides by 2 would have given the same result as multiplying by $\frac{1}{2}$.

The inequalities $-12 < 18$ and $-2 < 3$ are true. Thus, if both sides of a true inequality are multiplied by the same positive number, the result is also true.

What happens if both sides of an inequality are multiplied by the same negative number?

$$-4 < 6$$
$$-4(-3) \overset{?}{<} 6(-3)$$
$$12 \overset{?}{<} -18 \quad \textit{False}$$

$$-4 < 6$$
$$-4\left(-\tfrac{1}{2}\right) \overset{?}{<} 6\left(-\tfrac{1}{2}\right)$$
$$2 \overset{?}{<} -3 \quad \textit{False}$$

The inequality $12 < -18$ is false, but $12 > -18$ is true. Also, $2 < -3$ is false, but $2 > -3$ is true. Thus, when both sides of an inequality are multiplied by the same negative number, the direction of the inequality must be reversed.

> **For all numbers a, b, and c,**
> 1. **If c is positive and $a < b$, then $ac < bc$.**
>   **If c is positive and $a > b$, then $ac > bc$.**
> 2. **If c is negative and $a < b$, then $ac > bc$.**
>   **If c is negative and $a > b$, then $ac < bc$.**

Multiplication Property for Inequalities

You can use this property to solve inequalities.

Example

1 **Solve:** $\dfrac{k}{4} > 13$

$$\frac{k}{4} > 13$$
$$4\left(\frac{k}{4}\right) > 4(13) \qquad \textit{Multiply both sides by 4.}$$
$$k > 52$$

The solution set is {all numbers greater than 52}.

2 **Solve:** $\frac{a}{-7} > -2$ *Another way to write $\frac{a}{-7}$ is $-\frac{a}{7}$.*

$$\frac{a}{-7} > -2$$

$$-7\left(\frac{a}{-7}\right) < -7(-2)$$ *Multiply both sides by -7 and reverse the direction of the inequality.*

$$a < 14$$

The solution set is {all numbers less than 14}.

3 **Solve:** $\frac{4}{3}x \leq -12$ *Another way to write $\frac{4}{3}x$ is $\frac{4x}{3}$.*

$$\frac{4}{3}x \leq -12$$

$$\frac{3}{4}\left(\frac{4}{3}x\right) \leq \frac{3}{4}(-12)$$ *The reciprocal of $\frac{4}{3}$ is $\frac{3}{4}$. Multiply both sides by $\frac{3}{4}$.*

$$x \leq -9$$

The solution set is {all numbers less than or equal to -9}.

Recall that $\frac{a}{b}$ (or $a \div b$) is equivalent to $a\left(\frac{1}{b}\right)$ for all numbers when b is *not* zero. Thus, the multiplication property for inequalities can also apply to division. When solving inequalities, you can multiply (or divide) both sides by the same positive number. You can also multiply (or divide) both sides by the same negative number if you reverse the direction of the inequality.

> **For all numbers a, b, and c,**
> 1. If c is positive and $a < b$, then $\frac{a}{c} < \frac{b}{c}$.
>   If c is positive and $a > b$, then $\frac{a}{c} > \frac{b}{c}$.
> 2. If c is negative and $a < b$, then $\frac{a}{c} > \frac{b}{c}$.
>   If c is negative and $a > b$, then $\frac{a}{c} < \frac{b}{c}$.

Division Property for Inequalities

The following example shows two methods to solve the inequality $-6m \geq -72$.

Choose the method which is easiest for you.

4 **Solve:** $-6m \geq -72$

a. $-6m \geq -72$ *Multiply both sides by $-\frac{1}{6}$. Change $\geq$ to $\leq$.*

$$\left(-\frac{1}{6}\right)(-6m) \leq \left(-\frac{1}{6}\right)(-72)$$

$$m \leq 12$$

b. $-6m \geq -72$ *Divide both sides by -6. Change $\geq$ to $\leq$.*

$$\frac{-6m}{-6} \leq \frac{-72}{-6}$$

$$m \leq 12$$

The solution set is {all numbers less than or equal to 12}.

Example

5 **Solve:** $(-0.4)x < 0.6$

$(-0.4)x < 0.6$

$\dfrac{(-0.4)x}{-0.4} > \dfrac{0.6}{-0.4}$ *Divide both sides by -0.4 and reverse the direction of the inequality.*

$x > -1.5$

The solution set is {all numbers greater than -1.5}.

Exploratory Exercises

State the number by which you would multiply both sides of each inequality to solve it. Then state if the direction of the inequality reverses.

1. $\dfrac{r}{3} > -4$ 2. $\dfrac{s}{-6} < -11$ 3. $\dfrac{d}{-8} < -9$ 4. $\dfrac{d}{-11} > 3$

5. $3y < 21$ 6. $-6z < 18$ 7. $-4x > 8$ 8. $5a < -20$

9. $\dfrac{1}{6}j \geq -9$ 10. $-\dfrac{1}{8}h \leq 10$ 11. $-\dfrac{s}{11} < 2$ 12. $-\dfrac{t}{12} < -4$

13. $\dfrac{4}{3}k > 16$ 14. $\dfrac{2}{7}m < 12$ 15. $-\dfrac{5n}{3} \leq -10$ 16. $-\dfrac{3r}{8} \geq 9$

Written Exercises

Solve each inequality.

1. $14p < 84$ 2. $-16q > -128$ 3. $-17s > 119$ 4. $4z < -6$

5. $-2r \geq 35$ 6. $23b > 276$ 7. $-8s < -34$ 8. $5m \leq -17$

9. $\dfrac{h}{-18} > -25$ 10. $\dfrac{k}{-32} \leq 50$ 11. $\dfrac{b}{8} \leq -16$ 12. $\dfrac{a}{-7} < -35$

13. $7r < -4.9$ 14. $-\dfrac{1}{4}m \geq 19$ 15. $-\dfrac{1}{5}y < -\dfrac{2}{3}$ 16. $-3n \leq -6.6$

17. $-\dfrac{5s}{8} \geq \dfrac{15}{4}$ 18. $\dfrac{2}{5}z < \dfrac{4}{3}$ 19. $-\dfrac{3}{4}k > \dfrac{6}{7}$ 20. $\dfrac{4z}{7} > -\dfrac{2}{5}$

21. $-5.1m < -3.57$ 22. $6.1g < 3.66$ 23. $0.7t \leq -0.98$ 24. $-1.2x \leq 4.08$

25. $-13z > -1.04$ 26. $\dfrac{3b}{4} < \dfrac{2}{5}$ 27. $-\dfrac{5x}{6} < \dfrac{2}{3}$ 28. $1.8z > -54$

29. $\dfrac{13}{18} \leq \dfrac{2}{3}w$ 30. $-2.58 > 4.3n$ 31. $51.3 < -5.7a$ 32. $-\dfrac{3}{14} \geq -\dfrac{5m}{7}$

Challenge

Solve each inequality. Round solutions to the nearest hundredth.

33. $8.7x < 40$ 34. $0.07x \geq 0.93$ 35. $-0.41y \leq 2.5$ 36. $-3.1y > -4.2$

37. $843a \geq 25$ 38. $-207a < 30.2$ 39. $-5.04 \leq -15b$ 40. $3x < 5x$

State the conditions under which each sentence is true.

41. If $x > y$, then $x^2 > y^2$.

42. If $x < y$, then $x^2 < y^2$.

4-4   Inequalities with More Than One Operation

You can solve inequalities containing more than one operation by applying the methods you have already used.

Examples

1   **Solve: $16 - 5b > 29$**

$$16 - 5b > 29$$
$$16 - 16 - 5b > 29 - 16 \qquad \textit{Subtract 16 from both sides.}$$
$$-5b > 13$$
$$\frac{-5b}{-5} < \frac{13}{-5} \qquad \textit{Divide both sides by } -5 \left(\textit{or multiply by } -\tfrac{1}{5} \right).$$
$$\textit{Change} > \textit{to} <.$$
$$b < -\frac{13}{5}$$

The solution set is $\left\{ \text{all numbers less than } -\frac{13}{5} \right\}$.

2   **Solve: $9x + 4 < 13x - 7$**

$$9x + 4 < 13x - 7$$
$$9x - 13x + 4 < 13x - 13x - 7 \qquad \textit{Subtract 13x from both sides.}$$
$$-4x + 4 < -7$$
$$-4x + 4 - 4 < -7 - 4 \qquad \textit{Subtract 4 from both sides.}$$
$$-4x < -11$$
$$\frac{-4x}{-4} > \frac{-11}{-4} \qquad \textit{Divide both sides by } -4 \left(\textit{or multiply by } -\tfrac{1}{4} \right)$$
$$\textit{Change} < \textit{to} >.$$
$$x > \frac{11}{4}$$

The solution set is $\left\{ \text{all numbers greater than } \frac{11}{4} \right\}$.

Use the distributive property to eliminate grouping symbols.

Example

3   **Solve: $(0.7)(m + 3) \le (0.4)(m + 5)$**

$$(0.7)(m + 3) \le (0.4)(m + 5)$$
$$0.7m + 2.1 \le 0.4m + 2.0 \qquad \textit{Use the distributive property.}$$
$$0.7m + 2.1 - 2.1 \le 0.4m + 2.0 - 2.1 \qquad \textit{Subtract 2.1 from both sides.}$$
$$0.7m \le 0.4m - 0.1$$
$$0.7m - 0.4m \le 0.4m - 0.4m - 0.1 \qquad \textit{Subtract 0.4m from both sides.}$$
$$0.3m \le -0.1$$
$$\frac{0.3m}{0.3} \le \frac{-0.1}{0.3} \qquad \textit{Divide both sides by 0.3.}$$
$$m \le -\frac{1}{3}$$

The solution set is $\left\{ \text{all numbers less than or equal to } -\frac{1}{3} \right\}$.

Example

4 **Solve:** $-3(2x - 7) \geq 4x - (x - 3)$

$$-3(2x - 7) \geq 4x - (x - 3)$$
$$-3(2x - 7) \geq 4x + (-1)(x - 3) \qquad \text{To subtract, add the inverse.}$$
$$-3(2x) + (-3)(-7) \geq 4x + (-1)x + (-1)(-3) \qquad \text{Use the distributive property.}$$
$$-6x + 21 \geq 4x + (-x) + 3 \qquad \text{Simplify.}$$
$$-6x + 21 \geq 3x + 3 \qquad \text{Combine 4x and } -x.$$
$$-3x + (-6x) + 21 \geq (-3x) + 3x + 3 \qquad \text{Add } -3x \text{ to both sides.}$$
$$-9x + 21 \geq 3$$
$$-9x + 21 + (-21) \geq 3 + (-21) \qquad \text{Add } -21 \text{ to both sides.}$$
$$-9x \geq -18$$
$$x \leq 2 \qquad \text{Divide both sides by } -9.$$
$$\qquad \text{Change } \geq \text{ to } \leq.$$

The solution set is {all numbers less than or equal to 2}.

Exploratory Exercises

State the steps you would use to solve each inequality.

1. $3x - 1 > 14$

2. $9x + 2 > 20$

3. $4y - 7 > 21$

4. $-7y + 6 < 48$

5. $32 + 14t < 4$

6. $5 + 9a > -67$

7. $-12 + 11y \leq 54$

8. $-9 + 6r \leq -33$

9. $\frac{z}{4} + 7 \geq -5$

10. $\frac{b}{-3} + 5 \leq -13$

11. $\frac{d}{-4} - 5 < 23$

12. $\frac{m}{3} - 7 > 11$

13. $13 - 2a \leq 15$

14. $5 - 6g > -19$

15. $2k + 7 > k - 10$

16. $5y + 4 > y + 13$

Written Exercises

Solve each inequality.

1. $13r - 11 > 7r + 37$

2. $6a + 9 < -4a + 29$

3. $10p - 14 < 8p - 17$

4. $9q + 2 \leq 7q - 25$

5. $3y + 7 \leq 4y + 8$

6. $5 + 10b > 12b + 10$

7. $0.1x < 0.2x - 8$

8. $0.3x + 6.8 \geq 2.0x$

9. $7(x + 8) < 3(x + 12)$

10. $-5(y + 5) \geq 5(y - 1)$

11. $3n - 8n + 21 > 0$

12. $9d - 5 + d < -8$

13. $0.6(y + 7) \geq 0.7(2y + 6)$

14. $0.3(m + 4) \leq 0.4(2m + 3)$

15. $8c - (c - 5) < c + 17$

16. $10x - 2(x - 4) \leq 0$

17. $1.3x - 12 < 0.9x + 4$

18. $4x - 13 > 2.7x + 13$

19. $-3(2x - 8) < 2(x + 14)$

20. $5x \leq 10 + 3(2x + 4)$

21. $-4(2x - 3) + 5(2x + 10) \geq 0$

22. $y - 3(y + 1) \leq 5y - 10$

23. $6 - (3y + 5) > 4 - (2y + 7)$

24. $3y - 2(8y - 11) > 5 - (2y + 6)$

Challenge

25. $\frac{3x + 8}{12} < \frac{5}{12}$

26. $\frac{5y - 4}{3} > \frac{y + 5}{3}$

27. $\frac{2n + 1}{7} \geq \frac{n + 4}{5}$

28. $\frac{c + 8}{4} \leq \frac{-c + 5}{9}$

4-5 Comparing Rational Numbers

You know that $\frac{6}{9}$ is less than $\frac{7}{9}$ because the denominators are the same and 6 is less than 7. How can you compare $\frac{3}{8}$ and $\frac{4}{11}$? If you change both fractions so that they have a common denominator of 88, you can see that $\frac{33}{88}$ is greater than $\frac{32}{88}$. Thus, $\frac{3}{8} > \frac{4}{11}$.

A shortcut for comparing two rational numbers is to use cross products. Study the property stated below.

> **For any rational numbers $\frac{a}{b}$ and $\frac{c}{d}$, with $b > 0$, $d > 0$,**
>
> **1. If $\frac{a}{b} < \frac{c}{d}$, then $ad < bc$.**
>
> **2. If $ad < bc$, then $\frac{a}{b} < \frac{c}{d}$.**

Comparison Property for Rational Numbers

This property also holds if $<$ is replaced by $>$, $\leq$, $\geq$, or $=$.

The following example shows how this property is used to compare $\frac{3}{8}$ and $\frac{4}{11}$.

You can use the multiplication property for inequalities to prove the comparison property.

Find the product of the extremes. 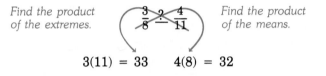 *Find the product of the means.*

$$3(11) = 33 \qquad 4(8) = 32$$

Since $33 > 32$, you can conclude that $\frac{3}{8} > \frac{4}{11}$.

Examples

1 **Replace the ? with $<$, $>$, or $=$ to make a true sentence.** $\frac{6}{11}\ \underline{?}\ \frac{7}{12}$

Find the cross products.

$$\frac{6}{11}\ \underline{?}\ \frac{7}{12}$$

$$72 < 77$$

The true sentence is $\frac{6}{11} < \frac{7}{12}$.

2 **Replace the ? with $<$, $>$, or $=$ to make a true sentence.** $-\frac{1}{4}\ \underline{?}\ -\frac{1}{5}$

Rewrite $-\frac{1}{4}$ as $\frac{-1}{4}$ and $-\frac{1}{5}$ as $\frac{-1}{5}$. Then find the cross products.

$$\frac{-1}{4}\ \underline{?}\ \frac{-1}{5}$$

$$-5 < -4$$

The true sentence is $-\frac{1}{4} < -\frac{1}{5}$.

The comparison property can help you decide which of two items is the better buy. Study the following example.

Example

3 **Super Saver Mart advertised a 9.4-ounce tube of toothpaste for $1.61. Is this a better buy than another brand of 6 ounces for 95 cents?**

Compare the unit costs. If the quality of the two items is the same, the item with the smaller unit cost is the better buy. Make sure to express costs using the same unit.

$$\text{unit cost} = \frac{\text{total cost}}{\text{number of units}} \text{ or } \frac{\text{total cents}}{\text{number of ounces}}$$

$$\text{unit cost of first brand} = \frac{161}{9.4}$$

$$\text{unit cost of second brand} = \frac{95}{6}$$

In each case the unit cost is expressed as cents per ounce.

Compare $\frac{161}{9.4}$ and $\frac{95}{6}$ by finding the cross products.

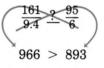

$$966 > 893$$

Thus, $\frac{161}{9.4} > \frac{95}{6}$.

The lesser number is $\frac{95}{6}$, so 6 ounces for 95¢ is the better buy.

Exploratory Exercises

State which ratio in each pair is greater.

1. $\frac{3}{4}, \frac{4}{5}$

2. $\frac{11}{12}, \frac{7}{8}$

3. $\frac{9}{10}, \frac{10}{11}$

4. $\frac{7}{8}, \frac{8}{9}$

5. $\frac{6}{5}, \frac{7}{6}$

6. $\frac{11}{9}, \frac{12}{10}$

7. $-\frac{1}{3}, -\frac{1}{4}$

8. $-\frac{1}{7}, -\frac{1}{6}$

9. $-\frac{9}{7}, -\frac{7}{5}$

10. $-\frac{3}{4}, -\frac{2}{3}$

11. $-\frac{13}{11}, -\frac{15}{13}$

12. $-\frac{6}{5}, -\frac{7}{6}$

13. $\frac{0.3}{4}, \frac{0.2}{2}$

14. $\frac{3}{0.4}, \frac{5}{0.6}$

15. $\frac{0.8}{3}, \frac{0.2}{4}$

16. $\frac{0.06}{0.4}, \frac{0.9}{5}$

Write a ratio for the unit cost of each of the following.

17. 10 ounces of coffee for $4.59

18. $3.79 for 8 ounces of coffee

Written Exercises

Replace each ? with <, >, or = to make each sentence true.

1. $\frac{6}{7}$? $\frac{7}{8}$

2. $\frac{8}{7}$? $\frac{9}{8}$

3. $\frac{7}{19}$? $\frac{6}{17}$

4. $\frac{8}{15}$? $\frac{9}{16}$

5. $-\frac{5}{16}$? $-\frac{3}{10}$

6. $-\frac{4}{11}$? $-\frac{1}{3}$

7. $-\frac{11}{15}$? $-\frac{9}{11}$

8. $-\frac{6}{11}$? $-\frac{4}{7}$

9. $-\frac{2}{3}$? $-\frac{3}{5}$

10. $-\frac{1}{3}$? $-\frac{2}{7}$

11. $-\frac{7}{6}$? $-\frac{21}{18}$

12. $\frac{5}{14}$? $\frac{25}{70}$

13. $\frac{0.4}{3}$? $\frac{1.2}{2}$

14. $\frac{1.1}{4}$? $\frac{2.2}{5}$

15. $-\frac{3.2}{1.06}$? $-\frac{2.8}{2.13}$

16. $-\frac{5.35}{2.4}$? $-\frac{6.9}{4.01}$

Write a ratio for the unit cost of each item. Then compare the ratios to determine which of the two items is the better buy.

17. a 21-ounce can of baked beans for 79¢ or a 28-ounce can for 97¢

18. a 10-ounce jar of coffee for $4.27 or an 8-ounce jar for $3.64

19. a 184-gram can of peanuts for 91¢ or a 340-gram can for $1.89

20. a half-pound bag of cashews for $2.93 or a $\frac{3}{4}$-pound bag for $4.19

21. a six-pack of cola containing 2.1 liters for $1.79, or a six-pack containing 1.9 liters for $1.69

22. three liters of soda for $2.25 or two liters for $1.69

23. a 27-ounce loaf of bread for 93¢ or a 20-ounce loaf for 79¢

24. a dozen extra-large eggs weighing 27 ounces for $1.09, or a dozen large eggs weighing 24 ounces for 99¢

25. a 100-count package of paper plates for $1.49, or a 75-count package for 98¢

26. a 25-pound bag of dog food for $9.85 or a 20-pound bag for $6.50

Solve each problem.

27. At Whittaker's Market a head of lettuce is 79¢. A head of lettuce weighs approximately $\frac{3}{4}$-pound. Dudley's Market sells lettuce at 44¢ for $\frac{1}{2}$-pound. Which store has the better price on lettuce?

28. Melody Morrison wanted to buy soda for a party. Eight 1-liter bottles of Brand X cost $3.92. Six 1-liter bottles of Brand Y cost $3.08. A 2-liter bottle of Brand Z costs $1.09. Which soda is least expensive per liter?

29. Mrs. Fischer saw 3 packaged pumpkin pies on sale. The first was 99¢ for a 26-ounce pie, the second was $1.19 for a 28-ounce pie, and the third was $1.25 for a 30-ounce pie. Which pie was least expensive per ounce?

mini-review

Define the variable, then write an equation for the following problem. Do not solve.

1. Half of a number increased by 14 is 25. Find the number.

Solve.

2. $5t = -3 + 4t$

3. $r - 23 = -10$

4. $-8k = 102$

Use a proportion to solve the following problem.

5. In 3 minutes, a printing press printed 1700 pages. How many pages could be printed in an hour?

30. The following is a proof of the first part of the comparison property for rational numbers. State the property that justifies each step of the proof.

Given: $\frac{a}{b} < \frac{c}{d}$, $b > 0$, $d > 0$

Prove: $ad < bc$

Proof: $b\left(\frac{a}{b}\right) < b\left(\frac{c}{d}\right)$

$a < \frac{bc}{d}$

$a \cdot d < \left(\frac{bc}{d}\right)d$

$ad < bc$

Write a proof similar to the one from Challenge Exercise 30 for each of the following.

31. If $\frac{a}{b} > \frac{c}{d}$ with $b > 0$ and $d > 0$, then $ad > bc$.

32. If $ad < bc$ with $b > 0$ and $d > 0$, then $\frac{a}{b} < \frac{c}{d}$.

Using Calculators _____ Comparing Numbers

You can use a calculator to compare rational numbers. First change each fraction to a decimal by dividing the numerator by the denominator. Then compare the decimals.

Example: Change the fractions $\frac{6}{17}$, $\frac{17}{49}$, and $\frac{35}{99}$ to decimals. Then write the fractions in order from least to greatest.

$\frac{6}{17} = 0.3529412$

$\frac{17}{49} = 0.3469388$

$\frac{35}{99} = 0.3535354$

It is not always necessary to copy all the decimal places shown in the calculator display. Usually, you can round results to the nearest hundredth or to the nearest thousandth.

Therefore $\frac{17}{49} < \frac{6}{17} < \frac{35}{99}$.

Exercises

Write the fractions in order from least to greatest.

1. $\frac{17}{21}$, $\frac{20}{27}$, $\frac{19}{24}$

2. $\frac{5}{13}$, $\frac{8}{23}$, $\frac{7}{18}$

3. $\frac{11}{15}$, $\frac{5}{7}$, $\frac{9}{13}$

4. $\frac{8}{19}$, $\frac{10}{23}$, $\frac{11}{27}$

5. $\frac{17}{19}$, $\frac{32}{35}$, $\frac{45}{49}$

6. $\frac{3}{14}$, $\frac{5}{23}$, $\frac{9}{43}$

Use a calculator to determine which of the two items is the better buy.

7. a dozen oranges for $1.59 or half a dozen for 85¢

8. five pounds of green beans for $3.50 or 2 pounds for $1.38

9. a 48-ounce bottle of dish soap for $2.39 or a 22-ounce bottle for $1.09

10. a 1-pound package of lunch meat for $1.98 or a 12-ounce package for $1.80

4-6 Compound Sentences

Megan Peroni works part-time. Last year she paid $280 in federal income tax. The tax table that she used is shown at the right. According to the table, her taxable income must have been at least $4650 but less than $4700.

Let I represent her income. Then the two inequalities below describe the amount of her income.

$$I \geq 4650 \quad \text{and} \quad I < 4700$$

When considered together, these inequalities form a **compound sentence**. A compound sentence containing *and* is true only if both inequalities are true.

If line 37 (taxable income) is—		And you are—			
At least	But less than	Single	Married filing jointly *	Married filing separately *	Head of a household
			Your tax is—		
4,000	4,050	196	69	273	190
4,050	4,100	202	74	280	195
4,100	4,150	208	80	287	201
4,150	4,200	214	85	294	206
4,200	4,250	220	91	301	212
4,250	4,300	226	96	308	217
4,300	4,350	232	102	315	223
4,350	4,400	238	107	322	228
4,400	4,450	245	113	329	234
4,450	4,500	252	118	336	240
4,500	4,550	259	124	343	246
4,550	4,600	266	129	350	252
4,600	4,650	273	135	357	258
4,650	4,700	280	140	364	264
4,700	4,750	287	146	371	270
4,750	4,800	294	151	378	276
4,800	4,850	301	157	385	282
4,850	4,900	308	162	392	288
4,900	4,950	315	168	399	294
4,950	5,000	322	173	406	300

Another way of writing $I \geq 4650$ and $I < 4700$ without *and* is shown below.

$$4650 \leq I < 4700$$

This sentence is read, *I is greater than or equal to 4650 and less than 4700.*

Examples

1 Write the compound sentence $x > -5$ and $x < 1$ without *and.*

$x > -5$ and $x < 1$ can be written $-5 < x < 1$ or $1 > x > -5$.

2 Write the compound sentence $y \geq 0$ and $y \leq 5$ without *and.*

$y \geq 0$ and $y \leq 5$ can be written $0 \leq y \leq 5$ or $5 \geq y \geq 0$.

The graph of a compound sentence containing *and* is the *intersection* of the graphs of the two inequalities.

3   **Graph the solution set of $x > -5$ and $x < 1$.**

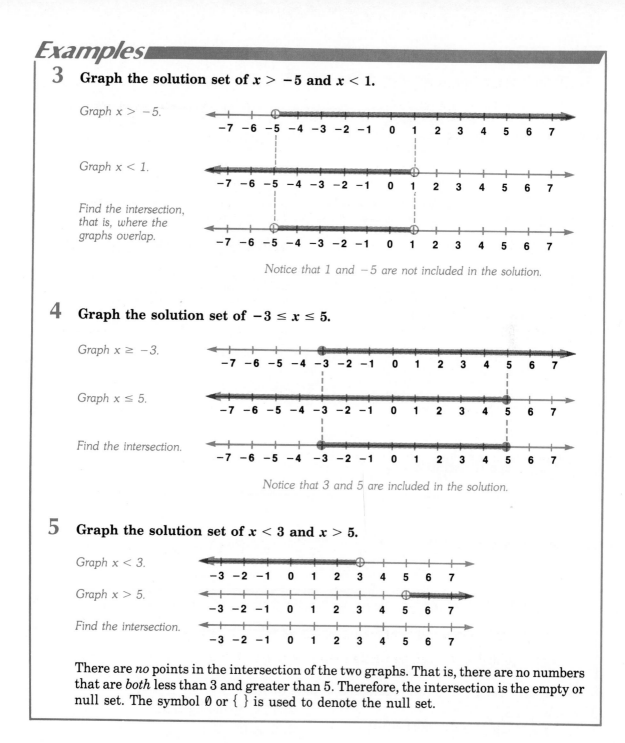

Graph $x > -5$.

Graph $x < 1$.

Find the intersection, that is, where the graphs overlap.

Notice that 1 and -5 are not included in the solution.

4   **Graph the solution set of $-3 \leq x \leq 5$.**

Graph $x \geq -3$.

Graph $x \leq 5$.

Find the intersection.

Notice that 3 and 5 are included in the solution.

5   **Graph the solution set of $x < 3$ and $x > 5$.**

Graph $x < 3$.

Graph $x > 5$.

Find the intersection.

There are *no* points in the intersection of the two graphs. That is, there are no numbers that are *both* less than 3 and greater than 5. Therefore, the intersection is the empty or null set. The symbol $\emptyset$ or $\{\ \}$ is used to denote the null set.

A compound sentence may contain *or* instead of *and*. Only one inequality in such a sentence needs to be true for the sentence to be true. The solution of an *or* sentence is the *union* of the solution sets of each inequality.

Examples

6 **Graph the solution set of $x \geq 3$ or $x < -2$.**

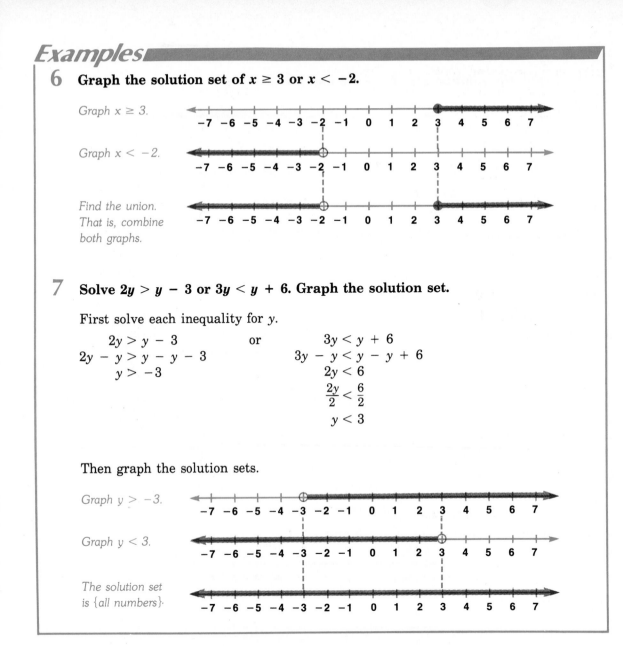

Graph $x \geq 3$.

Graph $x < -2$.

Find the union. That is, combine both graphs.

7 **Solve $2y > y - 3$ or $3y < y + 6$. Graph the solution set.**

First solve each inequality for y.

$$2y > y - 3 \qquad \text{or} \qquad 3y < y + 6$$
$$2y - y > y - y - 3 \qquad \qquad 3y - y < y - y + 6$$
$$y > -3 \qquad \qquad \qquad 2y < 6$$
$$\qquad \qquad \qquad \qquad \frac{2y}{2} < \frac{6}{2}$$
$$\qquad \qquad \qquad \qquad y < 3$$

Then graph the solution sets.

Graph $y > -3$.

Graph $y < 3$.

The solution set is {all numbers}.

Exploratory Exercises

State whether each compound sentence is true or false.

1. $8 < 3$ and $8 > 3$
2. $13 > 9$ and $13 > 12$
3. $5 < 7$ and $-8 < -6$
4. $9 \neq 0$ and $12 < 17$
5. $5 \geq -4$ and $11 \leq 7$
6. $5 > -3$ and $-5 > -1$
7. $7 > 4$ or $5 < 6$
8. $13 > 6$ or $0 < -2$
9. $-11 < -19$ or $3 > 0$
10. $8 \leq 8$ or $7 > 15$
11. $8 \neq 9$ or $16 < -7$
12. $-21 > -19$ or $-7 > 0$

Written Exercises

Write each compound sentence without *and*.

1. $0 \le m$ and $m < 9$

2. $0 < y$ and $y \le 12$

3. $p > \frac{3}{4}$ and $p \le \frac{11}{9}$

4. $r > -\frac{1}{2}$ and $r < \frac{8}{3}$

5. $z > -\frac{4}{5}$ and $z < \frac{2}{3}$

6. $y \le \frac{4}{9}$ and $y \ge -\frac{4}{3}$

7. $m < -\frac{6}{5}$ and $m > -\frac{13}{7}$

8. $r > -\frac{3}{4}$ and $r \le -\frac{1}{10}$

9. $a \le -2.4$ and $a \ge -4.9$

10. $m \ge 0.35$ and $m \le 0.99$

Graph the solution set of each compound sentence.

11. $m < -7$ or $m \ge 0$

12. $x \ge -2$ and $x \le 5$

13. $n \le -5$ and $n \ge -1$

14. $r > 2$ or $r \le -2$

15. $b > 5$ or $b \le 0$

16. $p < -3$ and $p > 3$

17. $x > -5$ and $x < 0$

18. $d \ge -6$ and $d \le -3$

19. $q \ge -5$ and $q \le 1$

20. $w > -3$ or $w < 1$

21. $d > 0$ or $d < 4$

22. $s \le 8$ or $s \ge 3$

23. $a > 8$ or $a < 5$

24. $r > -4$ or $r \le 0$

25. $p \le 6$ and $p \ge -1$

Solve each inequality and graph the solution set.

26. $3 + x < -4$ or $3 + x > 4$

27. $-1 + b > -4$ or $-1 + b < 3$

28. $2 > 3t + 2$ and $3t + 2 > 14$

29. $9 - 2m > 11$ and $5m < 2m + 9$

30. $2x + 4 \le 6$ or $x \ge 2x - 4$

31. $7 + 3q < 1$ or $-12 < 11q - 1$

32. $x \ne 6$ and $3x + 1 > 10$

33. $-2 \le x + 3$ and $x + 3 < 4$

34. $-5 < 4 - 3x < 13$

35. $-3 - x < 2x < 3 + x$

36. $2x - 1 < 2x + 8 < 2x + 4$

37. $x - 1 < 2x + 3 < x + 4$

38. $5(x - 3) + 2 < 7$ and $5x > 4(2x - 3)$

39. $2 - 5(2x - 3) > 2$ or $3x < 2(x - 8)$

Write the compound sentence whose solution set is graphed.

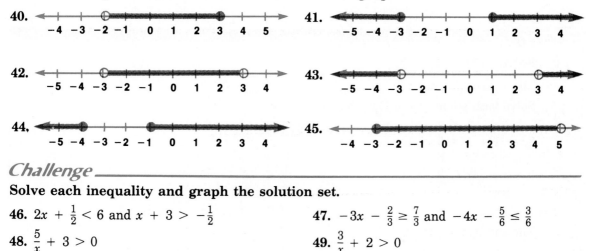

40.

41.

42.

43.

44.

45.

Challenge

Solve each inequality and graph the solution set.

46. $2x + \frac{1}{2} < 6$ and $x + 3 > -\frac{1}{2}$

47. $-3x - \frac{2}{3} \ge \frac{7}{3}$ and $-4x - \frac{5}{6} \le \frac{3}{6}$

48. $\frac{5}{x} + 3 > 0$

49. $\frac{3}{x} + 2 > 0$

4-7 Open Sentences Containing Absolute Value

The **absolute value** of a number is the number of units it is from 0 on the number line. An open sentence that contains absolute value must be interpreted carefully. Study the graph and interpretation of each open sentence given below.

$|x| = 2$

The distance from 0 to x is 2 units.
Therefore, $x = -2$ or $x = 2$.

2 units   2 units

$|x| < 2$

The distance from 0 to x is less than 2 units.
Therefore, $x > -2$ and $x < 2$.
This can also be written as $-2 < x < 2$.

2 units   2 units

$|x| > 2$

The distance from 0 to x is greater than 2 units.
Therefore, $x < -2$ or $x > 2$.

2 units   2 units

Notice that an open sentence containing absolute value should be interpreted as a compound sentence.

Example

1 **Solve: $|3x - 1| = 5$**

$|3x - 1| = 5$ means $3x - 1 = 5$ or $3x - 1 = -5$.
Solve both equations to find the solution set.

$$3x - 1 = 5 \qquad \text{or} \qquad 3x - 1 = -5$$
$$3x - 1 + 1 = 5 + 1 \qquad 3x - 1 + 1 = -5 + 1$$
$$3x = 6 \qquad\qquad 3x = -4$$
$$\frac{3x}{3} = \frac{6}{3} \qquad\qquad \frac{3x}{3} = \frac{-4}{3}$$
$$x = 2 \qquad \text{or} \qquad x = -\frac{4}{3}$$

The solution set is $\left\{2, -\frac{4}{3}\right\}$.

Examples

2 **Solve $|2x + 1| < 8$ and graph the solution set.**

$|2x + 1| < 8$ means $2x + 1 > -8$ *and* $2x + 1 < 8$.

$$2x + 1 > -8 \qquad \text{and} \qquad x + 1 < 8$$
$$2x + 1 + (-1) > -8 + (-1) \qquad\qquad 2x + 1 + (-1) < 8 + (-1)$$
$$2x > -9 \qquad\qquad\qquad\qquad 2x < 7$$
$$\frac{2x}{2} > \frac{-9}{2} \qquad\qquad\qquad\qquad \frac{2x}{2} < \frac{7}{2}$$
$$x > -\frac{9}{2} \qquad \text{and} \qquad x < \frac{7}{2}$$

The solution set is $\left\{$all numbers greater than $-\frac{9}{2}$ and less than $\frac{7}{2}\right\}$.

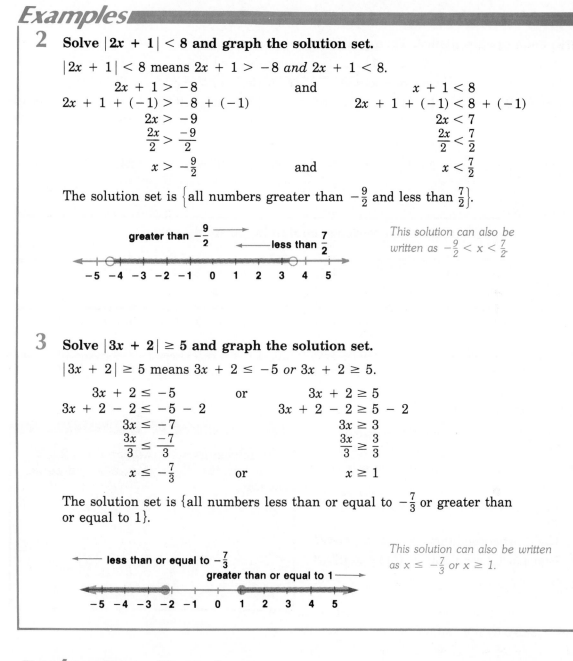

This solution can also be written as $-\frac{9}{2} < x < \frac{7}{2}$.

3 **Solve $|3x + 2| \geq 5$ and graph the solution set.**

$|3x + 2| \geq 5$ means $3x + 2 \leq -5$ *or* $3x + 2 \geq 5$.

$$3x + 2 \leq -5 \qquad \text{or} \qquad 3x + 2 \geq 5$$
$$3x + 2 - 2 \leq -5 - 2 \qquad\qquad 3x + 2 - 2 \geq 5 - 2$$
$$3x \leq -7 \qquad\qquad\qquad\qquad 3x \geq 3$$
$$\frac{3x}{3} \leq \frac{-7}{3} \qquad\qquad\qquad\qquad \frac{3x}{3} \geq \frac{3}{3}$$
$$x \leq -\frac{7}{3} \qquad \text{or} \qquad x \geq 1$$

The solution set is {all numbers less than or equal to $-\frac{7}{3}$ or greater than or equal to 1}.

This solution can also be written as $x \leq -\frac{7}{3}$ or $x \geq 1$.

Exploratory Exercises

State each open sentence as a compound sentence.

1. $|x| = 4$
2. $|y| = 7$
3. $|y| > 3$
4. $|x| > 5$
5. $|y| < \frac{5}{2}$
6. $|x| < \frac{7}{2}$
7. $|x + 2| > 3$
8. $|y + 1| > 0$
9. $|x + 2| < 3$
10. $|y + 1| < 4$
11. $|2x - 5| \geq 3$
12. $|2x + 3| \geq 5$
13. $|7 - x| = 4$
14. $|7 + x| = 2$
15. $|3x + 1| > 6$
16. $|3x - 1| < 6$

Written Exercises

Solve each open sentence. Then graph its solution set.

1. $|y + 1| > 4$ **2.** $|x + 1| > -2$ **3.** $|y - 1| < 4$ **4.** $|x - 7| < 2$

5. $|2 - y| \le 1$ **6.** $|6 - x| \le 2$ **7.** $|9 - y| \ge -3$ **8.** $|7 - x| \ge 4$

9. $|2y - 10| \ge 6$ **10.** $|12 - 3x| \ge 12$ **11.** $|3 - 3x| = 0$ **12.** $|14 - 2y| = 16$

13. $|4x + 4| \le 14$ **14.** $|6x + 6| \le 28$ **15.** $|10x + 10| \ge 90$ **16.** $|9x + 9| \ge -72$

17. $|2y - 5| \ge 4$ **18.** $|2y - 7| \ge -6$ **19.** $|4 - 3x| = 0$ **20.** $|13 - 2y| = 8$

21. $\left|3t - \frac{1}{2}\right| < \frac{7}{2}$ **22.** $\left|\frac{1}{2} - 3t\right| \ge \frac{11}{2}$ **23.** $|y| + 6 = 8$ **24.** $|y| - 7 = 4$

Challenge

For each graph write an open sentence containing absolute value.

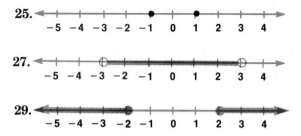

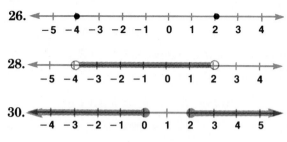

Solve each problem.

31. State all integer solutions of $|x| \le 2$.

32. State all integer solutions of $|x| \le 4$.

33. If $|x| \le a$, how many integer solutions exist?

34. If $|x| < a$, how many integer solutions exist?

35. Under what conditions is $-|a|$ negative?

36. Under what conditions is $-|a|$ positive?

37. Suppose $x < 0$, $y > 0$, and $x + y = 0$. Is $|x| > |y|$?

mini-review

Match each expression on the left with one on the right that has the same value.

1. $-6 + (-2)$ **a.** $-6 \div 2$

2. $-6\left(\frac{1}{2}\right)$ **b.** 3

3. $(-6)(-2)$ **c.** $-(6 + 2)$

4. $-6 \div (-2)$ **d.** $6 - (-2)$

5. $6 + 2$ **e.** $6(2)$

Using Calculators _____ Inequalities

Use a calculator to help you solve each open sentence. If necessary, round answers to the nearest hundredth.

1. $|8.36 - r| < 29.4$ **2.** $|13.04 - a| \ge 2.34$

3. $|4.96x + 8.9| \le 10.8$ **4.** $|194t + 2.36| \le 14.8$

5. $|263 + 94.8y| \ge 13.9$ **6.** $|88.6 - 433m| < 849$

Applications in Industry

Parts used in automobiles must have very precise measurements. Otherwise, they will not work properly. However, it is impossible to produce parts with exact dimensions. Thus, the dimensions of the parts must be between specified limits.

For example, a certain ball bearing that is 1 centimeter in diameter will only work if it is slightly larger or slightly smaller. The diameter may not differ from 1 centimeter by more than 0.001 centimeter. The 0.001 centimeter is called the **tolerance** of the ball bearing. The diameter of the ball bearing must be 1 ± 0.001 centimeter. That is, the diameter can vary between $1 + 0.001$ centimeter and $1 - 0.001$ centimeter. The acceptable diameter can be represented by the following inequality.

$$1 - 0.001 \le x \le 1 + 0.001$$
$$0.999 \le x \le 1.001$$

The tolerance interval is 0.999 cm to 1.001 cm.

That is, the least possible diameter is 0.999 cm, and the greatest possible diameter is 1.001 cm.

Exercises

Write each expression as an inequality.

1. $x = 3 \pm 0.01$
2. $x = 5 \pm 0.003$
3. $x = 7 \pm 0.0002$
4. $y = 6 \pm 0.0015$
5. $y = 1 \pm 0.15$
6. $y = 2 \pm 0.003$
7. $r = 0.5 \pm 0.0001$
8. $r = 1.5 \pm 0.001$
9. $d = \frac{1}{2} \pm 0.0035$

Solve each problem.

10. A chemical supply company guarantees the precision weighing of its products. They advertise that a certain product weighs 8 oz $\pm$ 0.03 oz. What is the tolerance interval?

11. A pane of glass should be 26 inches wide by 32 inches long. The tolerance is $\frac{3}{16}$ inch. Find the tolerance interval for each dimension.

4-8   Problem Solving: Inequalities

Problems containing the phrases *greater than* or *less than* can often be solved using inequalities. Other phrases that suggest inequalities are *at least*, *at most*, and *between*. Study the inequalities that correspond to each statement below.

The number x is *at least* 8. $x \geq 8$ *At least 8 means 8 or greater.*

The number y is *at most* 4. $y \leq 4$ *At most 4 means 4 or less.*

The number z is *between* 7 and 10. $7 < z < 10$ *Between 7 and 10 means greater than 7 and less than 10.*

The number w is *between* 7 and 10, $7 \leq w \leq 10$ *Between 7 and 10, inclusive, means greater than or equal to 7 and less than or equal to 10.*
inclusive.

Examples

1 **Jerry wishes to spend at most $12.50 on new equipment for his model railroad. He has chosen a new railroad car that costs $7.98. How much can he spend on other equipment?**

 Explore   At most $12.50 means $12.50 or less.

Let x = the amount that Jerry can spend for other equipment.

 Plan   Total spent ≤ 12.50
$7.98 + x \leq 12.50$

Solve $7.98 - 7.98 + x \leq 12.50 - 7.98$
$x \leq 4.52$

Jerry can spend $4.52 or less for other equipment.

Examine   Jerry can spend at most $4.52 since $7.98 + $4.52 = $12.50. The answer given above is correct.

2 **Roberto has scores of 9.3, 9.2, 9.7, and 8.9 in a figure skating competition. He has one more trial. Roberto will win the competition if his total score is greater than 46.3. What must Roberto's fifth score be?**

Explore   You must find Roberto's fifth score so that his total score will be greater than 46.3.

Let x = Roberto's fifth score.

Plan   Roberto's total score $>$ Opponent's total score
$9.3 + 9.2 + 9.7 + 8.9 + x >$ 46.3

Solve $37.1 + x > 46.3$
$37.1 - 37.1 + x > 46.3 - 37.1$
$x > 9.2$

Roberto's final score must be greater than 9.2.   *Examine this solution.*

Written Exercises

Use an inequality to solve each problem.

1. Five times a number increased by 12 is at least 37. What is the number?

2. Seven times a number decreased by 4 times the number is less than 30. What is the number?

3. The sum of two consecutive positive odd integers is at most 18. What are the integers?

4. The sum of two consecutive positive even integers is at most 22. What are the integers?

5. The Two Rivers Tribune pays 5¢ per paper to the carrier. How many papers must the carrier deliver to earn at least $3.50 per day?

6. A bookstore makes a profit of $4.30 on each two-volume set of books sold. How many sets must the store sell to make a profit of at least $175.00?

7. A stove and a freezer weigh at least 260 kg. The stove weighs 115 kg. What is the weight of the freezer?

8. Bill and his father spent at least $110.00 while shopping. Bill spent $47.32. How much did his father spend?

9. Duane earns $12,000 per year in salary and 6% commission on his sales. How much were his sales if his annual income was between $21,000 and $27,000?

10. Sheila bought between 10 and 18 gallons of paint for her house. The paint cost $9.75 per gallon. What was the total cost of the paint?

11. George plans to spend at most $40 for shirts and ties. He bought 2 shirts for $13.95 each. How much can he spend for ties?

12. Jerry plans to spend at most $10.00 on model airplanes and supplies. If he buys two models for $3.49 each, how much will he have left for supplies?

13. If 4 times an integer is increased by 3, the result is between 13 and 25. What is the integer?

14. If 9 less than 6 times a number lies between 31 and 37, what is the number?

15. Glenda has scores of 8.7, 9.3, 8.8, and 9.4 in a figure skating competition. She has one more trial. The leading opponent has a total score of 45.9. What must Glenda's fifth score be if she is to at least tie for first place?

16. Jenny has a total score of 45.9 in five trials of a skating competition. The leading opponent has scores of 9.1, 8.7, 9.5, and 9.3, and has one more trial. What can Jenny's opponent score to assure Jenny of first place?

17. Keith has scores of 9.1, 9.3, 9.6, and 8.7 in a pommel horse competition. He has one more trial. The leading opponent has completed all five trials and has an average score of 9.22. What must Keith score on his final trial if he is to win the competition?

18. Nancy has scores of 9.9, 9.5, 8.9, and 8.7 on the uneven parallel bars. She has one more trial. The leading opponent has completed the competition with an average score of 9.12. What must Nancy score on her final trial if she is to win the competition?

19. The sum of two consecutive even integers is greater than 75. Find the pair with the least sum.

20. Find all sets of three consecutive positive even integers whose sum is less than 30.

Comparisons

In the BASIC language conditional program branches are like railroad branches that are controlled by switches. Whether a train takes a branch, or does not, depends on whether the switch is open or closed. Whether or not a computer takes a conditional branch depends on whether a statement (the condition) is true or false.

A conditional branch uses an IF-THEN statement. In the following program, IF-THEN statements are used to compare two rational numbers.

```
10   INPUT "ENTER THE FIRST NUMERATOR AND DENOMINATOR ";A,B
20   INPUT "ENTER THE SECOND NUMERATOR AND DENOMINATOR ";C,D
30   IF A/B > C/D THEN 60
40   IF A/B < C/D THEN 70
50   PRINT A;"/";B;"=";C;"/";D:GOTO 80        A colon is used to connect
60   PRINT A;"/";B;">";C;"/";D:GOTO 80        two statements.
70   PRINT A;"/";B;"<";C;"/";D:GOTO 80
80   END
```

Notice how the comparison property is used in the program. By this property, you know that either $\frac{A}{B} > \frac{C}{D}$, $\frac{A}{B} < \frac{C}{D}$, or $\frac{A}{B} = \frac{C}{D}$. Line 30 checks the first possibility. If the condition is true, the computer branches to line 60. If not, the second possibility is checked in line 40. The branching continues until the appropriate PRINT statement is executed and the program ends.

Exercises

Compare each of the following pairs of rational numbers. If the rational number is negative, enter the negative sign with the numerator.

1. $\frac{9}{11}, \frac{15}{19}$ **2.** $\frac{7}{8}, \frac{13}{15}$ **3.** $-\frac{7}{8}, -\frac{13}{15}$ **4.** $\frac{16}{17}, \frac{17}{18}$

5. $-\frac{7}{6}, -\frac{21}{18}$ **6.** $\frac{-6}{-5}, \frac{5}{6}$ **7.** $\frac{-6}{5}, \frac{5}{6}$ **8.** $-\frac{15}{33}, -\frac{22}{45}$

9. Determine which of the following two items is a better buy: a 16-ounce box of crackers for $1.69 or a 9-ounce box for $1.09.

10. Determine which of the following two items is a better buy: $1\frac{1}{4}$ pounds of cheese for $3.90 or $1\frac{3}{4}$ pounds for $4.25.

Vocabulary

inequality (111)
comparison property (111)
transitive property of
  order (112)
solution set (113)
absolute value (132)

properties for inequalities:
  addition (116)
  subtraction (116)
  multiplication (119)
  division (120)
compound sentence (128)

Chapter Summary

1. A mathematical sentence containing $<$ or $>$ is called an inequality. (111)

2. Comparison Property:
   For any two numbers a and b, exactly one of the following sentences is true.
   $$a < b \qquad a = b \qquad a > b \qquad (111)$$

3. Transitive Property of Order:
   For all numbers a, b, and c,
   1. If $a < b$ and $b < c$, then $a < c$.
   2. If $a > b$ and $b > c$, then $a > c$. (112)

4. The symbols $\neq$, $\leq$, and $\geq$ can also be used when comparing numbers. The symbol $\neq$ means *is not equal to*, $\leq$ means *is less than or equal to*, and $\geq$ means *is greater than or equal to*. (112)

5. If a and b represent any numbers and the graph of a is to the left of the graph of b, then $a < b$. If the graph of a is to the right of the graph of b, then $a > b$. (113)

6. Addition and Subtraction Properties for Inequalities:
   For all numbers a, b, and c,
   1. If $a > b$, then $a + c > b + c$ and $a - c > b - c$.
   2. If $a < b$, then $a + c < b + c$ and $a - c < b - c$. (116)

7. Multiplication and Division Properties for Inequalities:
   For all numbers a, b, and c,
   1. If c is positive and $a < b$, then $ac < bc$ and $\dfrac{a}{c} < \dfrac{b}{c}$.

      If c is positive and $a > b$, then $ac > bc$ and $\dfrac{a}{c} > \dfrac{b}{c}$.
   2. If c is negative and $a < b$, then $ac > bc$ and $\dfrac{a}{c} > \dfrac{b}{c}$.

      If c is negative and $a > b$, then $ac < bc$ and $\dfrac{a}{c} < \dfrac{b}{c}$.
      (119-120)

8. Comparison Property for Rational Numbers:
   For any rational numbers $\dfrac{a}{b}$ and $\dfrac{c}{d}$ with $b > 0$, $d > 0$,
   1. If $\dfrac{a}{b} < \dfrac{c}{d}$, then $ad < bc$.
   2. If $ad < bc$, then $\dfrac{a}{b} < \dfrac{c}{d}$.

   This property also holds if you replace $<$ by $>$, $\leq$, $\geq$, or $=$. (124)

9. A compound sentence containing *and* is true only if both inequalities are true. (128)

10. A compound sentence containing *or* is true if at least one of the inequalities is true. (129)

11. An open sentence containing absolute value should be interpreted as a compound sentence. (132)

Chapter Review

4-1 State whether each sentence is true or false.

1. $4 < -5$
2. $13 > 4$
3. $7 - 8 \leq 0$
4. $\frac{6}{2} - 3 \geq 0$

Replace each __?__ with $<$, $>$, or $=$ to make each sentence true.

5. -9 __?__ -11
6. 5 __?__ $\frac{13}{3}$
7. $(4.1)(0.2)$ __?__ 8.2

Graph the solution set of each inequality on a number line.

8. $y \geq -4$
9. $x \leq 5$
10. $n < 4$
11. $r \neq -2$

4-2 Solve each inequality.

12. $m - 4 < 9$
13. $5y - 6 \geq 4y$
14. $r - 2.3 \geq -7.8$
15. $n + 8 < -3$
16. $2x + 7 < 3x$
17. $y + \frac{5}{8} < \frac{11}{24}$

4-3 Solve each inequality.

18. $4p > -52$
19. $\frac{h}{-8} \leq 13$
20. $\frac{b}{-7} < -12$
21. $6a \leq -24$

22. $\frac{4}{3}k > 16$
23. $-\frac{3}{8}r > 9$
24. $-7c \leq 91$
25. $0.7t < -0.98$

26. $-5m > 17$
27. $\frac{2}{3}k > \frac{2}{15}$
28. $-0.3x < 4.5$
29. $\frac{4}{7}z > -\frac{2}{5}$

4-4 Solve each inequality.

30. $7m - 12 < 30$
31. $2r - 0.5 > 3.1$
32. $14a - 11 > 6a + 37$
33. $7y + 8 \leq 4y - 11$
34. $4(m - 1) < 7m + 8$
35. $4z - 11 > 7.3z + 22$

4-5 Replace each __?__ with $<$, $>$, or $=$ to make each sentence true.

36. $\frac{3}{8}$ __?__ $\frac{4}{11}$
37. $\frac{10}{11}$ __?__ $\frac{11}{12}$
38. $-\frac{3}{4}$ __?__ $-\frac{7}{9}$

39. Which is a better buy: 0.75 liter of soda for 89¢ or 1.25 liter of soda for $1.31?

4-6 Write each compound sentence without *and*.

40. $-4 < y$ and $y \leq 7$
41. $-3 \leq x$ and $x \leq 17$

Graph the solution set of each compound sentence.

42. $y > -1$ and $y \leq 3$
43. $x \leq -3$ or $x > 0$
44. $2m + 5 \leq 7$ or $2m \geq m - 3$
45. $4r \geq 3r + 7$ and $3r < 33$

4-7 Solve each inequality. Then graph its solution set.

46. $|y| > 2$
47. $|m - 1| \leq 5$
48. $\left| 2t - \frac{1}{2} \right| > \frac{9}{2}$

4-8 Use an inequality to solve each problem.

49. If 8 times a number is decreased by 2, the result is between 5 and 15. What is the number?

50. Linda plans to spend at most $85 for jeans and shirts. She bought 2 shirts for $15.30 each. How much can she spend on jeans?

Chapter Test

State whether each sentence is true or false.

1. $4 > -8$

2. $-2 > 0$

3. $0.3 < -0.6$

Replace each ? with >, <, or = to make each sentence true.

4. $2 \; \underline{?} \; -7$

5. $-4 \; \underline{?} \; -3$

6. $\frac{7}{6} \; \underline{?} \; \frac{13}{12}$

State an inequality for each graph.

7.

8.

Graph the solution set of each inequality on a number line.

9. $y \leq 2$

10. $-3 \leq x < 4$

11. $y \neq 4$

Solve each inequality.

12. $y - 2 > 11$

13. $7y > 6y - 11$

14. $\frac{r}{5} > -4$

15. $\frac{a}{-3} > -8$

16. $3z \leq 4.2$

17. $5p \geq -19$

18. $\frac{3}{4}r + 7 \leq -8$

19. $\frac{2}{3}r > -\frac{7}{12}$

20. $8x + 3 < 13x - 7$

21. $0.3(m + 4) \leq 0.5(m - 4)$

Graph the solution set of each compound sentence.

22. $x > -3$ and $x < 2$

23. $x \geq 7$ or $x \leq -1$

Solve each inequality. Then graph its solution set.

24. $|n| < 5$

25. $|n| > 3$

26. $|2x - 1| < 5$

27. $|3x - 5| \geq 1$

Use an inequality to solve each problem.

28. Jim plans to spend at most $35 for record albums and tapes. He bought 2 albums for $7.95 each. How much can he spend on tapes?

29. Seven less than twice a number is less than 83. What is the number?

30. The average of four consecutive positive odd integers is less than 20. What are the greatest integers that will satisfy this condition?

1. Write a mathematical expression for the square of a number increased by twice the number.

2. Evaluate $\dfrac{c^2 - a^2}{(c - a)^2}$ if $a = 5$ and $c = 7$.

3. Solve: $x = \dfrac{2}{3} \cdot \dfrac{3}{4} \div \dfrac{3}{5}$.

4. State the property shown by $0 + 96 = 96$.

Simplify.

5. $13a + 21a + 14b - 11b$

6. $5x^2 + 2 + 3x - 4x^2$

Write each sentence as an equation.

7. Twice x decreased by y is z.

8. The product of a, b, and the square of c is f.

9. Graph $\{-1, 0, 1, \ldots\}$ on a number line.

Find each sum or difference.

10. $12 + (-6)$

11. $-11 + (-5)$

12. $-38.6 + 42.73$

13. $11a + (-3a)$

14. $13 - (-18)$

Solve.

15. $y + (-9) = 19$

16. $p - 13 = 27$

17. $-18.3 = x - 11.6$

Simplify.

18. $(-9)(7)(2)$

19. $\dfrac{3}{4}(12a - 72b) + \dfrac{2}{5}(10a + 15b)$

20. $\dfrac{-36}{-12}$

21. $\dfrac{20x + 30y}{-10}$

Solve.

22. $\dfrac{a}{-3} = 42$

23. $4x + 2 = -10$

24. $3(7m - 2) = 4(-7m + 2)$

25. $\dfrac{y - 3}{6} = \dfrac{2}{3}$

26. $\dfrac{4}{9} = \dfrac{8}{r}$

27. What is 35% of 70?

28. State an inequality for the graph.

Solve each inequality.

29. $y - 9 > 4$ 30. $-\dfrac{3}{8}x \geq 6$

31. $7 + 3t \leq 14$

32. $4(a + 6) > 7a - 8$

33. Replace $\underline{\ ?\ }$ with $<$, $>$, or $=$ to make the sentence $-\dfrac{7}{8}$ $\underline{\ ?\ }$ $-\dfrac{28}{32}$ true.

Solve each inequality and graph the solution set.

34. $x - 4 < 0$ and $2x + 5 > 1$

35. $|7 - x| \geq 2$

Problem Solving

Solve each problem.

36. The difference of two integers is -117. One of the integers is -68. What is the other integer?

37. Two meters of copper wire weigh 0.4 kg. How much will 50 meters of wire weigh?

38. The sales tax on a $44 purchase is $2.31. What is the rate of sales tax?

39. Connie earns $17,000 per year in salary and a 7% commission on her sales. How much must her sales be for her income to be at least $25,000?

The test questions on this page deal with fraction concepts. The information at the right may help you with some of the questions. Study the examples.

Directions: Choose the best answer. Write A, B, C, or D.

1. In a class of 27 students, six are honor students. What part of the class are *not* honor students?

    (A) $\frac{7}{11}$ (B) $\frac{7}{9}$ (C) $\frac{2}{7}$ (D) $\frac{2}{9}$

2. Which of the following fractions is less than $\frac{1}{5}$?

    (A) $\frac{3}{14}$ (B) $\frac{21}{100}$ (C) $\frac{2}{11}$ (D) $\frac{101}{501}$

3. Which fraction is greater than $\frac{1}{4}$ but less than $\frac{1}{3}$?

    (A) $\frac{5}{12}$ (B) $\frac{1}{5}$ (C) $\frac{4}{13}$ (D) $\frac{3}{4}$

4. Which of the following is the least?

    (A) 0.77   (B) $\frac{7}{9}$ (C) $\frac{8}{11}$ (D) $\frac{3}{4}$

5. Which of the following is the greatest?

    (A) $\frac{1}{2}$ (B) $\frac{7}{13}$ (C) $\frac{4}{9}$ (D) $\frac{8}{15}$

6. The months from April through December, inclusive, are what fractional part of a year?

    (A) $\frac{7}{12}$ (B) $\frac{3}{4}$ (C) $\frac{5}{12}$ (D) $\frac{2}{3}$

7. What fractional part of a week is one-sixth of a day?

    (A) $\frac{1}{42}$ (B) $\frac{1}{30}$ (C) $\frac{4}{7}$ (D) $\frac{7}{168}$

8. The difference between $42\frac{3}{8}$ minutes and $41\frac{2}{3}$ minutes is approximately how many seconds?

    (A) 18   (B) 63   (C) $22\frac{1}{2}$ (D) 43

---

1. The fraction $\frac{a}{b}$ means $a \div b$. The *numerator* is a and the *denominator* is b.

2. As the numerator of a positive fraction increases, the value of the fraction increases.

    Example: $\frac{1}{5} < \frac{2}{5} < \frac{3}{5} < \frac{10}{5} < \frac{13}{5}$

3. As the denominator of a positive fraction increases, the value of the fraction decreases.

    Example: $\frac{3}{2} > \frac{3}{3} > \frac{3}{4} > \frac{3}{8} > \frac{3}{11}$

4. A fraction may be used to indicate part of a group.

    $$\frac{\text{part}}{\text{whole}} = \text{fractional part}$$

    Example: If there are 4 boys in a class of 9 students, then boys represent $\frac{4}{9}$ of the class.

---

9. Which group of numbers is arranged in descending order?

    (A) $\frac{5}{7}, \frac{7}{12}, \frac{6}{11}, \frac{3}{13}$ (B) $\frac{7}{12}, \frac{5}{7}, \frac{6}{11}, \frac{3}{13}$

    (C) $\frac{5}{7}, \frac{6}{11}, \frac{7}{12}, \frac{3}{13}$ (D) $\frac{3}{13}, \frac{7}{12}, \frac{6}{11}, \frac{5}{7}$

10. Which group of numbers is arranged from greatest to least?

    (A) $3, \frac{1}{4}, -1, -0.5$ (B) $-1, -0.5, \frac{1}{4}, 3$

    (C) $3, \frac{1}{4}, -0.5, -1$ (D) $-0.5, \frac{1}{4}, -1, 3$

11. A car was driven twice as many miles in July as in each of the other 11 months of the year. What fraction of the total mileage for the year occurred in July?

    (A) $\frac{2}{11}$ (B) $\frac{2}{13}$ (C) $\frac{1}{6}$ (D) $\frac{1}{7}$

CHAPTER 5

Powers

We live in the Milky Way galaxy. The galaxy closest to us is the Large Magellanic Cloud. It is about 160,000 light years or 1,500,000,000,000,000,000 kilometers from Earth. The number 1,500,000,000,000,000,000 can be expressed more concisely by using powers of ten. You will learn more about powers in this chapter.

5-1 Multiplying Monomials

A **monomial** is a number, a variable, or a product of numbers and variables. Some examples of monomials are $-9, y, 7a, 3y^3$, and $\frac{1}{2}abc^5$. Monomials such as -9 and $\frac{5}{3}$, which do not contain variables, are called **constant monomials**, or **constants**.

The following expressions are *not* monomials.

$$m + n \qquad \frac{x}{y} \qquad 3a - 4ab \qquad \frac{1}{x^2}$$

Why is each expression not a monomial?

Consider each of the following products.

$$4 \cdot 16 = 64 \qquad 8 \cdot 16 = 128 \qquad 8 \cdot 32 = 256$$

Replace each factor by a power of 2.

$$2^2 \cdot 2^4 = 2^6 \qquad 2^3 \cdot 2^4 = 2^7 \qquad 2^3 \cdot 2^5 = 2^8$$

Recall that an expression of the form x^n is a power. The base is x and the exponent is n.

Consider the exponents only. How do you obtain the exponent 6 from the exponents 2 and 4? How do you obtain 7 from 3 and 4? How do you obtain 8 from 3 and 5?

Think about $a^2 \cdot a^3$.

a^2 **means** $a^1 \cdot a^1$ and a^3 **means** $a^1 \cdot a^1 \cdot a^1$.

$a^2 \cdot a^3$ **means** $(a^1 \cdot a^1) \cdot (a^1 \cdot a^1 \cdot a^1)$.

$$\underbrace{a^1 \cdot a^1}_{2} \cdot \underbrace{a^1 \cdot a^1 \cdot a^1}_{3} = a^5$$
$$2 + 3 = 5$$
$$a^2 \cdot a^3 = a^{2+3} = a^5$$

These and many similar examples suggest that you can multiply powers that have the same base by adding exponents.

For any number a and positive integers m and n,
$$a^m \cdot a^n = a^{m+n}.$$

Product of Powers

Examples

1 **Simplify:** $x^3 \cdot x^4$

$x^3 \cdot x^4 = x^{3+4}$ *To multiply powers that have*

      $= x^7$ *the same base, add the exponents.*

2 **Simplify:** $(3a^2)(4a)$

$(3a^2)(4a) = 3(4)(a^2)(a)$ *Use the commutative and associative properties.*

      $= 12a^{2+1}$ *Recall $a = a^1$.*

      $= 12a^3$

3 **Simplify:** $(a^3b^2)(a^2b^4)$

$$(a^3b^2)(a^2b^4) = (a^3 \cdot a^2)(b^2 \cdot b^4)$$
$$= a^{3+2}b^{2+4}$$
$$= a^5b^6$$

4 **Simplify:** $(-5x^2)(3x^3y^2)(\frac{2}{5}xy^4)$

$$(-5x^2)(3x^3y^2)(\tfrac{2}{5}xy^4)$$
$$= (-5 \cdot 3 \cdot \tfrac{2}{5})(x^2 \cdot x^3 \cdot x)(y^2 \cdot y^4)$$
$$= -6x^6y^6$$

The variables in a monomial are usually arranged in alphabetical order.

Exploratory Exercises

Verify each product by multiplication.

1. $3^1 \cdot 3^2 = 3^3$
2. $2^3 \cdot 2^2 = 2^5$
3. $4^2 \cdot 4^2 = 4^4$
4. $2^5 \cdot 2^2 = 2^7$
5. $5^2 \cdot 5 = 5^3$
6. $3^2 \cdot 3^4 = 3^6$

Simplify.

7. $x^3 \cdot x^5$
8. $y^7 \cdot y^7$
9. $a^4 \cdot a^4$
10. $b^5 \cdot b^2$
11. $m \cdot m^3$
12. $d \cdot d^6$
13. $(3a^2)(4a^3)$
14. $(-5x^3)(4x^4)$
15. $(-10x^3y)(2x^2)$
16. $(3y^3z)(7y^4)$
17. $(y^3z^4)(y^2)$
18. $m^4(m^3b^2)$

Written Exercises

Simplify.

1. $a^2(a^5)$
2. $b^4 \cdot b^2$
3. $m^5 \cdot m$
4. $m^2(m^2)$
5. $t^2(t^2)(t^2)$
6. $r^2(r^3)(r^3)$
7. $a^5(a)(a^7)$
8. $(b^4)(b^4)(b)$
9. $(a^2b)(ab^4)$
10. $(x^3y)(xy^3)$
11. $(m^3n)(mn^2)$
12. $(r^3t^4)(r^4t^4)$
13. $(3a^2b)(2ab^5)$
14. $(4x^2y^3)(2xy^6)$
15. $(3x^4)(-2x^4y^3)$
16. $(-8x^3y)(2x^4)$
17. $(3x^4y)(4x^2y^2)$
18. $(-2x^2y)(-6x^4y^7)$
19. $(-3x^5y)(2x^4)$
20. $(-2n^4y^3)(3ny^4)$
21. $(3x^2y^2z)(2x^2y^2z^3)$
22. $(r^2xy)(-2r^3x)$
23. $(5a^2b^2c)(-7a^3)$
24. $(2am^3n)(-3am^4)$
25. $(2am)(3a^2m^2n)$
26. $(4r^2st)(-6s^2t^2)$
27. $(ab)(ac)(bc)$
28. $(m^2n)(am)(an^2)$
29. $\frac{3}{4}a(12b^2)$
30. $-\frac{5}{6}c(12a^3)$
31. $(\frac{1}{2}a^2)(6ab^2)$
32. $(-27ay^3)(-\frac{1}{3}ay^3)$
33. $ab(\frac{1}{2}a)(\frac{1}{2}b)(\frac{1}{2}c)$
34. $(bc)(\frac{2}{3}b)(\frac{2}{3}a)$
35. $(-\frac{1}{8}a)(-\frac{1}{6})(b)(48c)$
36. $(-\frac{1}{3}c^2b^3a)(18a^2b^2c^3)$

Challenge

Simplify. Consider all exponents to be positive integers.

37. $y^2 \cdot y^b$
38. $3^x \cdot 3^2$
39. $a^{x-2} \cdot a^5$
40. $2^{4a} \cdot 2^{5a}$
41. $x^{2a} \cdot x^{4a}$
42. $(2^{7x+6})(2^{3x-4})$
43. $(y^{3a+1})(y^{a-6})$
44. $(x+3)^a \cdot (x+3)^6$
45. $(x+3)^{2a} \cdot (x+3)^{b-a}$

Problem Solving

Another problem-solving strategy is to look for a pattern. When using this strategy, it is important to organize information about the problem. Study the following example.

Example: **How many diagonals can be drawn for a polygon with n sides, where n is less than or equal to 12?**

Try several cases. That is, draw several polygons and see how many diagonals you can draw for each polygon. Use a table to record the number of sides and the number of diagonals for each polygon. Then study the pattern formed by the numbers in the table.

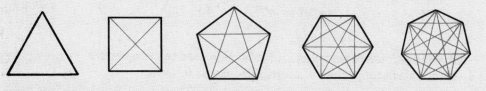

Number of Sides	3	4	5	6	7	8	9	10	11	12
Number of Diagonals	0	2	5	9	14					

+2 +3 +4 +5

Continue the pattern to find the number of diagonals for a polygon with 8, 9, 10, 11, or 12 sides. Thus, the rest of the numbers that belong in the table above are 20, 27, 35, 44, and 54. Do you see why?

Exercises

Solve each problem.

1. There were 10 people at a party. Each person shook hands with each of the other people exactly once. How many handshakes occurred?

2. How many squares are shown at the right? (Hint: There are more than 16.)

3. How many rectangles are shown below?

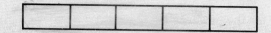

4. How many triangles are shown at the right?

5. Imagine 25 lockers, all closed, and 25 people. Suppose the first person opens every locker. Then the second person closes every second locker. Next the third person changes the state of every third locker. (If it's open, she closes it. If it's closed, she opens it.) Suppose this procedure is continued until the 25th person changes the state of the 25th locker. Which lockers will be open at the end of the procedure?

5-2 Powers of Monomials

Mary wanted to rewrite the expressions $(5^2)^4$ and $(x^6)^2$ using only a single exponent. She wrote the expressions correctly as follows.

$$(5^2)^4 = (5^2)(5^2)(5^2)(5^2) \qquad (x^6)^2 = (x^6)(x^6)$$
$$= 5^{2+2+2+2} \qquad\qquad\qquad = x^{6+6}$$
$$= 5^8 \qquad\qquad\qquad\qquad = x^{12}$$

How can you obtain the exponent 8 from the exponents 2 and 4? How can you obtain 12 from 6 and 2? These and many similar examples suggest the following rule.

> **For any number a and any integers m and n,**
> $$(a^m)^n = a^{mn}.$$

Power of a Power

Next Mary wanted to find $(xy)^3$ and $(ab)^4$. She used the associative and commutative properties of multiplication as follows.

$$(xy)^3 = (xy)(xy)(xy) \qquad (ab)^4 = (ab)(ab)(ab)(ab)$$
$$= (x \cdot x \cdot x)(y \cdot y \cdot y) \qquad = (a \cdot a \cdot a \cdot a)(b \cdot b \cdot b \cdot b)$$
$$= x^3 y^3 \qquad\qquad\qquad = a^4 b^4$$

These examples suggest that the power of a product is the product of the powers.

> **For all numbers a and b and any integer m,**
> $$(ab)^m = a^m b^m.$$

Power of a Product

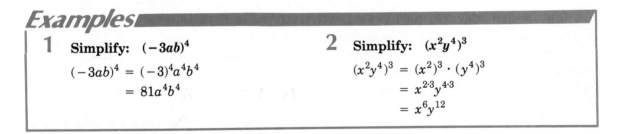

Examples

1 Simplify: $(-3ab)^4$

$$(-3ab)^4 = (-3)^4 a^4 b^4$$
$$= 81a^4 b^4$$

2 Simplify: $(x^2 y^4)^3$

$$(x^2 y^4)^3 = (x^2)^3 \cdot (y^4)^3$$
$$= x^{2\cdot3} y^{4\cdot3}$$
$$= x^6 y^{12}$$

Example 2 shows the combined use of the rules for the power of a power and the power of a product. This can be stated as follows.

> **For all numbers a and b and any integers m, n, and p,**
> $$(a^m b^n)^p = a^{mp} b^{np}.$$

Power of a Monomial

3 Simplify: $\left(-\frac{2}{3}a^2x^3\right)^3$

$\left(-\frac{2}{3}a^2x^3\right)^3 = \left(-\frac{2}{3}\right)^3(a^2)^3(x^3)^3$

$= -\frac{8}{27}a^6x^9$

4 Simplify: $(9b^4y)^2[(-b)^2]^3$

$(9b^4y)^2[(-b)^2]^3 = 9^2(b^4)^2y^2(b^2)^3$

$= 81b^8y^2b^6$

$= 81b^{14}y^2$

Exploratory Exercises

Simplify.

1. $(m^2)^4$ **2.** $(n^4)^3$ **3.** $(3y)^2$ **4.** $(4x)^3$ **5.** $[(-x)y]^4$ **6.** $[(-p)q]^2$

7. $[(-a)b^2]^3$ **8.** $[(-x)y^2]^5$ **9.** $(x^2y^5)^2$ **10.** $(n^3r^2)^4$ **11.** $\left(\frac{2}{3}a^2\right)^3$ **12.** $\left(-\frac{1}{2}a^4\right)^3$

Written Exercises

Simplify.

1. $(5^3)^3$ **2.** $(10^2)^2$ **3.** $[(-5)^2]^3$ **4.** $[(-4)^2]^2$

5. $(x^4)^3$ **6.** $(m^2)^5$ **7.** $[(-y)^3]^6$ **8.** $[(-m)^5]^2$

9. $(5c)^3$ **10.** $(10y)^2$ **11.** $(-7z)^3$ **12.** $(-3n)^4$

13. $\left(\frac{1}{2}c\right)^2$ **14.** $\left(\frac{2}{5}d\right)^2$ **15.** $(0.4d)^2$ **16.** $(0.6d)^3$

17. $(ab^2)^3$ **18.** $(a^3x^2)^4$ **19.** $(2a^2b)^2$ **20.** $(3x^2y^3)^3$

21. $4(a^2b^3)^3$ **22.** $-3(ax^3y)^2$ **23.** $(-5x^3y)^3$ **24.** $(-3a^2b^5)^2$

25. $\left(\frac{1}{2}xy^2\right)^3$ **26.** $\left(\frac{3}{4}x^2y^5\right)^2$ **27.** $(0.2a^2)^3$ **28.** $(0.3x^3y^2)^2$

29. $(-0.1x^2)^2$ **30.** $(-0.2x^3y)^3$ **31.** $10^2 \cdot 10^3$ **32.** $4^2 \cdot 4^3 \cdot 4^4$

33. $(4xy)^2(-3x)$ **34.** $(2a)^2(3y)$ **35.** $(2a)^3(-3b)$ **36.** $(-3ab)^3(2b^2)$

37. $(4x^2y^3)^3$ **38.** $(3ab^4)^3$ **39.** $(-2a^2b^3)^4$ **40.** $(-6a^3x^5)^2$

41. $(2x^2)^2\left(\frac{1}{2}y^2\right)^2$ **42.** $\left(\frac{3}{10}y^2\right)^2(10y^2)^3$ **43.** $(4ab)^2(a^3b)^4$ **44.** $(-3x^2y)^2(2x)^3$

45. $(3a^2)^3 + (5a^2)^3$ **46.** $(5y)^2 + (3y)(7y)$ **47.** $(-3x^2y)^3(x^3) - 3(x^2y)^2(x^5y)$

48. $(3ab)^2(2a^2b) + 5a^3(ab^3)$ **49.** $(a^2)^3 + (10a^3)^2 + (5ab)^6$ **50.** $(-3a^2b)^3 + (5a^6b^3)^2 + 10a^6b^3$

Challenge

Evaluate if $x = 2$, $y = 3$, and $z = 4$.

51. x^x **52.** y^x **53.** z^y **54.** $(2x)^2(3)^y$ **55.** $(4x)^y(2x)^y$ **56.** $(y + x)^z$

Using Calculators   Powers of Numbers

Some calculators have a power key, labeled y^x. The following example shows how you can use this key to find 7^8.

ENTER: 7 $\boxed{y^x}$ 8 $\boxed{=}$ The display shows 5764801. So, $7^8 = 5,764,801$.

Exercises   Use a calculator to simplify each expression.

1. $(40.8)^3$ **2.** $(0.018)^4$ **3.** $(4^2)^2$ **4.** $(9^2)^3$ **5.** $[(2^3)^2]^4$ **6.** $[(3^2)^4]^2$

5-3   Dividing Monomials

Consider quotients **a**, **b**, and **c** shown below.

a. $\dfrac{81}{27} = 3$ **b.** $\dfrac{27}{3} = 9$ **c.** $\dfrac{243}{9} = 27$

A power of 3 can be substituted for each number.

a. $\dfrac{3^4}{3^3} = 3^1$ **b.** $\dfrac{3^3}{3^1} = 3^2$ **c.** $\dfrac{3^5}{3^2} = 3^3$

Consider the exponents only. In example **a**, how do you obtain the exponent 1 from the exponents 4 and 3? Look at examples **b** and **c**. How do you obtain 2 from 3 and 1? How do you obtain 3 from 5 and 2?

You can use your knowledge of exponents to simplify $\dfrac{b^5}{b^2}$, $b \neq 0$.

$$\frac{b^5}{b^2} = \frac{\not{b} \cdot \not{b} \cdot b \cdot b \cdot b}{\not{b} \cdot \not{b}}$$ *Notice that $\frac{b \cdot b}{b \cdot b}$ is equal to 1.*

$$= b \cdot b \cdot b$$ *The quotient has $(5 - 2)$ or 3 factors.*

$$= b^3$$

Notice that you can divide powers that have the same base by subtracting exponents.

> **For all integers *m* and *n*, and any nonzero number *a*,**
> $$\frac{a^m}{a^n} = a^{m-n}.$$

Dividing Powers

Why is 0 not an acceptable replacement for a?

Examples

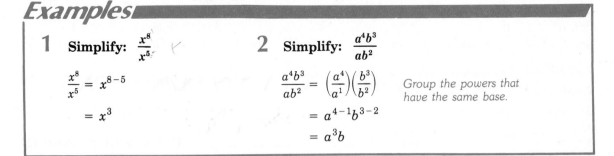

1 **Simplify:** $\dfrac{x^8}{x^5}$

$$\frac{x^8}{x^5} = x^{8-5}$$

$$= x^3$$

2 **Simplify:** $\dfrac{a^4 b^3}{ab^2}$

$$\frac{a^4 b^3}{ab^2} = \left(\frac{a^4}{a^1}\right)\left(\frac{b^3}{b^2}\right)$$ *Group the powers that have the same base.*

$$= a^{4-1} b^{3-2}$$

$$= a^3 b$$

Study the two ways to simplify $\dfrac{a^3}{a^3}$, $a \neq 0$, shown below.

$$\frac{a^3}{a^3} = \frac{a \cdot a \cdot a}{a \cdot a \cdot a}$$ $$\frac{a^3}{a^3} = a^{3-3}$$ *Use the rule for dividing powers.*

$$= 1$$ $$= a^0$$

Since $\dfrac{a^3}{a^3}$ cannot have two different values, you can conclude that a^0 is equal to 1. In general, *any* nonzero number raised to the zero power is equal to 1.

0^0 is not defined.

> **For any nonzero number a, $a^0 = 1$.**

Zero Exponent

Study the two ways to simplify $\dfrac{k^2}{k^7}$, $k \neq 0$, shown below.

$$\dfrac{k^2}{k^7} = \dfrac{\cancel{k} \cdot \cancel{k}}{\cancel{k} \cdot \cancel{k} \cdot k \cdot k \cdot k \cdot k \cdot k} \qquad \dfrac{k^2}{k^7} = k^{2-7}$$

$$= \dfrac{1}{k \cdot k \cdot k \cdot k \cdot k} \qquad\qquad = k^{-5} \quad \text{Use the rule for dividing powers.}$$

$$= \dfrac{1}{k^5}$$

Since $\dfrac{k^2}{k^7}$ cannot have two different values, you can conclude that k^{-5} is equal to $\dfrac{1}{k^5}$. This example suggests the following rule.

> **For any nonzero number a and any integer n, $a^{-n} = \dfrac{1}{a^n}$.**

Negative Exponents

To simplify a quotient of monomials, write an equivalent expression that has positive exponents and no powers of powers. Also, each base should appear only once and all fractions should be in simplest form.

Examples

3 Simplify: $\dfrac{-2r^3s^5}{6r^7s^5}$

$$\dfrac{-2r^3s^5}{6r^7s^5} = \left(-\dfrac{2}{6}\right)\left(\dfrac{r^3}{r^7}\right)\left(\dfrac{s^5}{s^5}\right)$$

$$= -\dfrac{1}{3}r^{-4}s^0$$

$$= \left(-\dfrac{1}{3}\right)\left(\dfrac{1}{r^4}\right)(1)$$

$$= -\dfrac{1}{3r^4}$$

4 Simplify: $\dfrac{20b^2c^{-4}}{15a^{-2}b^7c^{-3}}$

$$\dfrac{20b^2c^{-4}}{15a^{-2}b^7c^{-3}} = \left(\dfrac{20}{15}\right)\left(\dfrac{1}{a^{-2}}\right)\left(\dfrac{b^2}{b^7}\right)\left(\dfrac{c^{-4}}{c^{-3}}\right)$$

$$= \left(\dfrac{4}{3}\right)(a^2b^{-5}c^{-1}) \quad \text{Note: } \dfrac{1}{a^{-2}} = \dfrac{1}{\frac{1}{a^2}} = 1 \cdot a^2 = a^2$$

$$= \dfrac{4a^2}{3b^5c}$$

Exploratory Exercises

Simplify. Remember to express the results with positive exponents. Assume no denominator is equal to zero.

1. k^0

2. b^0

3. y^{-3}

4. m^{-8}

5. $r^0 s^4$

6. $m^{-5} n^0$

7. $a^0 c^{-7}$

8. $f^6 g^0$

9. $\frac{1}{2} x^3 y^{-6}$

10. $\frac{2}{3} a^{-7} b^{-4}$

11. $c^0 d^{-2} e^{-1}$

12. $x^5 y^0 z^{-5}$

13. $\frac{k^9}{k^4}$

14. $\frac{r^5}{r^2}$

15. $\frac{x^2}{x^3}$

16. $\frac{c^4}{5c^5}$

17. $\frac{5n^5}{n^8}$

18. $\frac{w^2}{w^9}$

19. $\frac{a^2 b^7}{a^4}$

20. $\frac{b^9}{b^4 c^3}$

21. $\frac{1}{x^{-1}}$

22. $\frac{1}{r^{-4}}$

23. $\frac{a^{-4}}{b^{-3}}$

24. $\frac{r^{-5}}{k^{-1}}$

Written Exercises

Simplify. Assume no denominator is equal to zero.

1. $\frac{n^8}{n^5}$

2. $\frac{w^9}{w^2}$

3. $\frac{x^2}{x^3}$

4. $\frac{b^6}{b^7}$

5. $\frac{a^0}{a^{-2}}$

6. $\frac{1}{r^{-3}}$

7. $\frac{k^{-2}}{k^4}$

8. $\frac{m^2}{m^{-4}}$

9. $\frac{an^6}{n^5}$

10. $\frac{xy^7}{y^4}$

11. $\frac{an^3}{n^5}$

12. $\frac{kn^2}{n^4}$

13. $\frac{b^6 c^5}{b^3 c^2}$

14. $\frac{(-a)^4 b^8}{a^4 b^7}$

15. $\frac{(-x)^3 y^3}{x^3 y^6}$

16. $\frac{a^2 b^2}{a^4 b^5}$

17. $\frac{12b^5}{4b^4}$

18. $\frac{48a^8}{12a}$

19. $\frac{12b^4}{60b}$

20. $\frac{10m^4}{30m}$

21. $\frac{x^3 y^6}{x^3 y^3}$

22. $\frac{a^6 b^3}{a^2 b^9}$

23. $\frac{a^3 b^4}{a^2 b^2}$

24. $\frac{b^6 c^5}{b^{14} c^2}$

25. $\frac{w^5 t^7}{w^3 t^{12}}$

26. $\frac{(-r)^5 s^8}{r^5 s^2}$

27. $\frac{30x^4 y^7}{-6x^{13} y^2}$

28. $\frac{24a^3 b^6}{-2a^2 b^2}$

29. $\frac{16b^4 c}{-4bc^3}$

30. $\frac{-8a^3 b^7}{a^2 b^6}$

31. $\frac{22a^2 b^5 c^7}{-11abc^2}$

32. $\frac{24x^2 y^7 z^3}{-6x^2 y^3 z^1}$

33. $\frac{9xyz^5}{x^4}$

34. $\frac{ab^5 c}{ac}$

35. $\frac{7x^3 z^5}{4z^{15}}$

36. $\frac{27a^4 b^6 c^9}{15a^3 c^{15}}$

37. $\frac{a^7 b^2}{a^{-2} b}$

38. $\frac{r^{-5} s^{-2}}{r^2 s^5}$

39. $\frac{5r^{-1} s}{s^2}$

40. $\frac{r^{-4} k^2}{5k^2}$

41. $\frac{3m^2 n^2}{6m^{-1} k}$

42. $\frac{-b^{-1} c}{4a^{-1} c^2}$

43. $\frac{2xy^{-2} z^4}{3xyz^{-1}}$

44. $\frac{7m^{-1} n^3}{n^2 r^{-2}}$

Challenge

Simplify.

45. $\frac{x^{y+2}}{x^{y-3}}$

46. $\frac{y^{x-3}}{y^{x+4}}$

47. $\frac{(a^{x+2})^2}{(a^{x-3})^2}$

48. $\frac{a^b}{a^{a-b}}$

Solve each of the following for k.

49. $x^{k-12} = (x^2)^{-k-3}$

50. $m^k \cdot m^{-15} = (m^3)^{k+2}$

51. $x^{2k} \cdot x^{3k} = x^{15}$

52. $x^{2k+1} = (x^5)^{k-4}$

53. $a^k \cdot a^3 = \frac{1}{a^{2k}}$

54. $4^k \cdot (4^2)^k = 4^6$

5-4 Scientific Notation

Astronomers use large numbers when measuring the distance from a star to earth. Sometimes it is not desirable to record these numbers in decimal notation.

For example, the earth is about 93,000,000 miles away from the sun.

$93,000,000 = 9.3 \times 10,000,000$ *The decimal point was moved 7 places to the left, and placed after the first nonzero digit.*

$ = 9.3 \times 10^7$ $10,000,000 = 10^7.$

This form of writing numbers is called **scientific notation**. To write a number in scientific notation, express it as the product of a number between 1 and 10 and a power of 10.

A number is expressed in scientific notation when it is in the form $$a \times 10^n$$ **where $1 \leq a < 10$ and n is an integer.**

Definition of Scientific Notation

Examples

1   **Express 38,245 in scientific notation.**

38,245   *The decimal point must be moved 4 places to the left.*

$38,245 = 3.8245 \times 10^4$

2   **Express 5,093.4 in scientific notation.**

5,093.4   *The decimal point must be moved 3 places to the left.*

$5,093.4 = 5.0934 \times 10^3$

3   **Express 2.6×10^5 in decimal notation.**

$2.6 \times 10^5 = 2.6 \times 100,000$

$ = 260,000$ *Notice that the decimal point was moved 5 places to the right. Why?*

Scientific notation is also used to express very small numbers.

$$0.000034 = 3.4 \times 0.00001 \quad \textit{The decimal point was moved 5 places to the right.}$$
$$= 3.4 \times \frac{1}{100,000}$$
$$= 3.4 \times \frac{1}{10^5}$$
$$= 3.4 \times 10^{-5} \quad \textit{The exponent of 10 is } -5.$$

When numbers between zero and one are written in scientific notation, the exponent of 10 is negative.

Examples

4 **Express 0.00319 in scientific notation.**

0.00319   *The number is less than 1. The decimal point must be moved 3 places to the right.*

$$0.00319 = 3.19 \times 10^{-3}$$

5 **Express 3.2×10^{-7} in decimal notation.**

$$3.2 \times 10^{-7} \doteq 3.2 \times 0.0000001$$
$$= 0.00000032 \quad \textit{Notice that the decimal point was moved 7 places to the left.}$$

You can find products or quotients of numbers that are expressed in scientific notation.

Examples

6 **Evaluate $\dfrac{5.6 \times 10^{-8}}{8.0 \times 10^{-3}}$. Express the result in scientific notation and decimal notation.**

$$\frac{5.6 \times 10^{-8}}{8.0 \times 10^{-3}} = \frac{5.6}{8.0} \times \frac{10^{-8}}{10^{-3}} \quad \textit{Note } -8-(-3) = -8 + 3 = -5$$
$$= 0.7 \times 10^{-5} \quad \textit{Change } 0.7 \times 10^{-5} \textit{ to scientific notation.}$$
$$= 7 \times 10^{-6} \text{ or } \quad 0.000007$$

7 **Use scientific notation to find the product of 0.000008 and 3,500,000,000. Express the result in scientific notation and decimal notation.**

$$(0.000008)(3,500,000,000) = (8 \times 10^{-6})(3.5 \times 10^9)$$
$$= (8)(3.5)(10^{-6})(10^9) \quad \textit{Use the commutative and associative}$$
$$= 28(10^3) \quad \textit{properties.}$$
$$= 2.8 \times 10^4 \text{ or } 28,000$$

Exploratory Exercises

Express each number in the second column in decimal notation. Express each number in the third column in scientific notation.

	Planet	Diameter (km)	From sun (km)
1.	Mercury	5.0×10^3	57,900,000
2.	Venus	1.218×10^4	108,230,000
3.	Earth	1.276×10^4	149,590,000
4.	Mars	6.76×10^3	227,720,000
5.	Jupiter	1.427×10^5	778,120,000
6.	Saturn	1.21×10^5	1,428,300,000

Written Exercises

Express each number in scientific notation.

1. 4293   **2.** 5280   **3.** 240,000   **4.** 389,500

5. 0.000319   **6.** 0.004296   **7.** 0.000000092   **8.** 0.00000000317

9. 32×10^5 **10.** 284×10^3 **11.** 0.76×10^7 **12.** 0.0031×10^3

Evaluate. Express each result in scientific notation and decimal notation.

13. $\dfrac{4.8 \times 10^3}{1.6 \times 10^1}$ **14.** $\dfrac{5.2 \times 10^5}{1.3 \times 10^2}$ **15.** $\dfrac{7.8 \times 10^{-5}}{1.3 \times 10^{-7}}$

16. $\dfrac{8.1 \times 10^2}{2.7 \times 10^{-3}}$ **17.** $\dfrac{1.32 \times 10^{-6}}{2.4 \times 10^2}$ **18.** $\dfrac{2.31 \times 10^{-2}}{3.3 \times 10^{-9}}$

19. $(2 \times 10^5)(3 \times 10^{-8})$ **20.** $(4 \times 10^2)(1.5 \times 10^6)$ **21.** $(3.1 \times 10^{-2})(2.1 \times 10^5)$

22. $(3.1 \times 10^4)(4.2 \times 10^{-3})$ **23.** $(78 \times 10^6)(0.01 \times 10^3)$ **24.** $(0.2 \times 10^5)(31 \times 10^{-6})$

25. $(0.000003)(70,000)$ **26.** $(86,000,000)(0.005)$

27. $24,000 \div 0.00006$ **28.** $0.0000039 \div 650,000$

Using Calculators _____ Scientific Notation

Scientific notation can be used to enter very large or very small numbers into many calculators. These numbers are entered using the key labeled ⃞EE or ⃞Exp. Use the following steps to enter 230×10^{15}.

ENTER: 230   ⃞EE↓   15   ⃞=

DISPLAY: 230   230.00   230.15   2.3   17

Notice that the numeral on the far right is the exponent of 10. That is, 2.3   17 means 2.3×10^{17}. The calculator has expressed 230×10^{15} in scientific notation as 2.3×10^{17}.

Exercises   Express each of the following numbers in scientific notation.

1. 234.6×10^9 **2.** 723.4×10^{13} **3.** 8061×10^{15} **4.** 9382×10^{10}

5. 0.0083×10^{21} **6.** 0.0642×10^{11} **7.** 0.03×10^{19} **8.** 0.458×10^{25}

5-5   Problem Solving: Age Problems

To solve verbal problems you must analyze each sentence carefully. Decide what is asked and explore how the given facts are related. Many problems contain extra information. Other problems do not contain enough information. Study the following problems.

Examples

1 **Maria is 8 years older than Jose. Carla is 2 years younger than Maria. The sum of Maria's age and Jose's age is 38. How old is Jose?**

Explore   This problem asks for Jose's age. What facts are given?

Maria is 8 years older than Jose.
The sum of Maria's age and Jose's age is 38.

You do not need the information about Carla's age to solve this problem.

Define variables, then use an equation to solve the problem.

Let a = Jose's age now.
$a + 8$ = Maria's age now.

Plan $\underbrace{\text{Jose's age}}_{a} + \underbrace{\text{Maria's age}}_{(a + 8)} = \underbrace{38}_{38}$

Solve
$$a + (a + 8) = 38$$
$$2a + 8 = 38$$
$$2a + 8 - 8 = 38 - 8$$
$$2a = 30$$
$$a = 15$$

Examine   If Jose is 15 years old, then Maria must be 23 years old. Since the sum of their ages is 38, the solution is correct.

2 **Luanne is 7 years younger than Jolene. Jolene is 2 years older than Beth. How old is Beth?**

Explore   Let b = Beth's age now.
$b + 2$ = Jolene's age now.
$(b + 2) - 7$ = Luanne's age now.

Plan   There is no other information given about how the ages are related. You cannot write an equation.

This problem does not contain enough information.

Example

3 Six years ago, Mr. Winters was five times as old as his son Mark. How old is Mark now if his age is one-third of his father's present age?

Explore
Let a = Mark's age now.
$3a$ = Mr. Winters' age now.   *Why?*
$a - 6$ = Mark's age 6 years ago.
$3a - 6$ = Mr. Winters' age 6 years ago.

Plan
$$\underbrace{\text{Mr. Winters' age}}_{3a - 6} = \underbrace{5 \text{ times}}_{5 \times} \underbrace{\text{Mark's age.}}_{(a - 6)}$$

Solve
$$3a - 6 = 5(a - 6)$$
$$3a - 6 = 5a - 30$$
$$-2a = -24$$
$$a = 12$$

Mark is now 12 years old.   *Examine this solution.*

Exploratory Exercises

State an expression for each of the following.

1. Marilyn is now n years old. Represent her age:
   a. 5 years ago.
   b. in 11 years.
   c. x years ago.

2. Don is now x years old. Represent his age:
   a. 7 years ago.
   b. in 12 years.
   c. in d years.

3. Paul is now $(n + 7)$ years old. Represent his age:
   a. in 7 years.
   b. 4 years ago.
   c. n years ago.
   d. in $(n + 2)$ years.
   e. $(n - 4)$ years ago.
   f. in $5n$ years.

4. Helene is now $(2n + 8)$ years old. Represent her age:
   a. 5 years ago.
   b. in 6 years.
   c. n years ago.
   d. in $(n - 3)$ years.
   e. $(n + 1)$ years ago.
   f. in $3n$ years.

5. Mary is m years old. Represent John's age if he is:
   a. twice as old as Mary.
   b. one-third as old as Mary.
   c. 5 years younger than Mary.
   d. 8 years older than Mary.

Written Exercises

Use an equation to solve each problem. If there is not enough information given, write *not enough information*.

1. Abe is 3 years older than Mindy. The sum of their ages is 39. What are their ages now?

2. Charlie is 14 years younger than Jack. The sum of their ages is 74. What are their ages now?

3. Nica is five times as old as his sister. The sum of their ages is 12. How old is Nica's sister?

4. Joshua is 7 years younger than his brother, and 30 years younger than his father. How old is Joshua?

5. Erin is 25 years younger than her father. The sum of their ages is 75. How old is Erin?

6. Matt is 5 years older than his sister, and 23 years younger than his mother. If the sum of Matt's age and his mother's age is 35, how old is Matt?

7. Lisa is 6 years older than her brother Tom. Their father's age is twice the sum of their ages. How old is Lisa if her father is 32?

8. Todd is 12 years older than Delores. In 2 years, Todd will be twice as old as Delores. How old is Todd now?

9. Twelve years ago, Thea was 7 years old. In 8 years, Thea will be three times as old as Nancy. Nancy is two years younger than Cindy. How old is Nancy now?

10. The sum of David's age and Ben's age is 40. Ann is 3 years older than David. David is 4 years older than Ben. How old is David?

11. Barney is 54 years old and Hugh is 38. How many years ago was Barney three times as old as Hugh?

12. Hector is now 28 years old and Henry is 8 years old. In how many years will Hector be twice as old as Henry?

13. Ramona is 5 years older than Alex. Six years ago, Alex was twice as old as Maria. How old is Alex now?

14. Felicia is 23 years younger than her mother and 25 years younger than her father. How old is Felicia?

15. Eight years ago, the sum of Pete's age and Matt's age was 26. Matt is 4 years older than Pete. How old is Pete now?

16. Dana is 3 years younger than Natalie. In 7 years, the sum of their ages will be 63. What are their ages now?

Challenge

Use an equation to solve each problem.

17. Shannon is 8 years younger than Susie and in 6 years will be four-fifths as old as Susie. What are their ages now?

18. Mr. Dunn is 7 times as old as his son, Jeff. In 5 years, he will be four times as old as Jeff. What are their ages now?

19. Erica is $\frac{2}{3}$ as old as Gerda. In 6 years, she will be $\frac{3}{4}$ as old as Gerda. What are their ages now?

20. Violet is $\frac{5}{6}$ as old as Lynne. In 20 years, Violet will be $\frac{10}{11}$ as old as Lynne. What are their ages now?

21. Harvey is now one-half as old as his mother. Harvey is 12 years older than his brother Henry. Henry is one-fourth as old as his mother. How old is Harvey?

22. The sum of Arlie's age and Bert's age is 39. In 7 years, Arlie will be 3 years older than Bert was 5 years ago. How old is Arlie?

mini-review

Graph the set of numbers on a number line.

1. $\{\ldots -3, -2, -1, 0, 1, 2\}$

Solve.

2. $r - (-3) = -15$

3. $\frac{s + 5}{s + 1} = \frac{7}{6}$

4. $6t - 14 < 10$

5. $-0.7m > 4.2$

5-6 Problem Solving: Percents

A jacket that cost $50 last year is now priced at $60. The price increased by $10 since last year. You can write a ratio that compares the amount of increase to the price last year. The ratio can be changed to a percent.

$$\frac{amount\ of\ increase}{price\ last\ year} \qquad \frac{10}{50} = \frac{20}{100} \quad or \quad 20\% \qquad \textit{A percent is a ratio of a number to 100.}$$

The amount of increase is 20% of the price last year. Therefore, you could say that the price of the jacket *increased by 20%* since last year. The **percent of increase** was 20%.

The **percent of decrease** can be found in a similar manner, as shown in the following example.

Example

1 **A sweater that originally cost $35 is now on sale for $28. Find the percent of decrease.**

Explore The price decreased from $35 to $28. The amount of decrease was $7.

Plan You need to write a ratio that compares the amount of decrease with the original price. Then, express the ratio as a percent.

$$\frac{amount\ of\ decrease}{original\ price} \qquad \frac{7}{35} = \frac{x}{100} \qquad \textit{To express } \frac{7}{35} \textit{ as a percent,}$$
$$\textit{change it to the ratio of}$$
$$\textit{some number to 100.}$$

Solve
$$\frac{7}{35} = \frac{x}{100}$$
$$700 = 35x$$
$$\frac{700}{35} = x$$
$$20 = x \qquad \textit{The percent of decrease was 20\%.}$$

Examine Check the solution with the words of the problem. The original price of the sweater was $35. Find 20% of $35 and subtract the result from $35.

$$20\%\ of\ 35 = \frac{20}{100}(35)$$
$$= \frac{1}{5}(35)$$
$$= 7 \qquad \text{The amount of decrease was \$7.}$$

Since $35 − $7 = $28, the solution is correct.

Sometimes an increase or decrease is given as a percent, and you must find the amount. The following problem involves a discount. A discount of 35% means that the price is *decreased* by 35%.

In advertisements, discounts are often stated as %-off.

Example

2 Amy bought a television set that had an original price of $495.50. She received a 35% discount. What was the discount price?

Explore The original price was $495.50, and the discount was 35%.

Plan You need to find the amount of discount, then subtract that amount from $495.50. The result is the discount price.

Solve 35% of 495.50 = 0.35(495.50)   *Note 35% = $\frac{35}{100}$ or 0.35.*

$\quad\quad\quad\quad\quad\quad\quad$ = 173.425   *Round 173.425 to 173.43.*

The amount of discount is $173.43. Subtract this amount from the original price.

$\quad\quad$ 495.50 − 173.43 = 322.07

The discount price was $322.07.

Examine Here is another way to solve the problem. The discount was 35%, so the discount price was 65% of the original price. Find 65% of $495.50.

$\quad\quad$ 0.65 (495.50) = 322.075

This method produces the same discount price, $322.07.

The sales tax on a purchase is a *percent* of the purchase price. To find the total price, you must calculate the *amount* of sales tax and add it to the purchase price.

Example

3 Frank Orfanello purchased a new tennis racket for $31.78. He also had to pay a sales tax of 5%. Find the amount of tax and the total price.

Explore The price is $31.78 and the tax rate is 5%.

Plan First find 5% of $31.78. Then add the result to $31.78.

Solve 5% of 31.78 = 0.05(31.78)   *Note 5% = 0.05.*

$\quad\quad\quad\quad\quad\quad\quad$ = 1.589   *Round 1.589 to 1.59.*

The amount of tax is $1.59. Now find the total price.

$\quad\quad$ $\underbrace{\text{purchase price}}$ + $\underbrace{\text{amount of tax}}$ = $\underbrace{\text{total price}}$

$\quad\quad\quad\quad$ 31.78 $\quad\quad$ + $\quad\quad$ 1.59 $\quad\quad$ = 33.37

The total price is $33.37.

Examine Since 100 + 5 = 105, the total price is 105% of the purchase price. Find 105% of $31.78 and compare the result to $33.37.

$\quad\quad$ 1.05(31.78) = 33.369   The total price of $33.37 is correct.

Sometimes it is helpful to use equations to solve percent problems.

Example

4 **Jane Shriver works as a sales person in a department store. One of her benefits is a 20% discount on all items she buys for herself. She paid $54 for a new dress. What was the price before the discount?**

 Let x = price of dress before discount.
Then $0.20x$ = amount of discount.   *Note 20% = 0.20.*

 price − discount = discount price
        x − $0.20x$ =   54

Solve $x - 0.20x = 54$
        $(1 - 0.20)x = 54$ *Distributive Property*
        $0.80x = 54$
        $x = 67.5$

The price before the discount was $67.50.

Examine If the price before the discount was $67.50 and Jane paid $54 for the dress, the amount of discount was $13.50. Since $13.50 is 20% of $67.50, the solution is correct.

Exploratory Exercises

Solve each problem.

1. What is 50% of 20?
2. What is 50% of 350?
3. What is 25% of 32?
4. What is 25% of 60?
5. What is 75% of 60?
6. What is 75% of 120?
7. 18 is 50% of what number?
8. 92 is 50% of what number?
9. 10 is 25% of what number?
10. 30 is 75% of what number?

Written Exercises

Solve each problem.

1. A number x increased by 40% is equal to 14.
2. A number x decreased by 20% is equal to 16.
3. 14 is 50% less than n.
4. 55 is 10% more than n.
5. The price in dollars (p) plus 5% tax is equal to $3.15.
6. The price in dollars (p) minus a 15% discount is $3.40.

Copy and complete the following chart. The first line is given as a sample.

	Earlier Amount	Later Amount	Did the amount increase (I) or decrease (D)?	Amount of Increase or Decrease	Percent of Increase or Decrease
	$50	$70	I	$20	40%
7.	$100	$94	a.	b.	c.
8.	$100	$108	a.	b.	c.
9.	$200	b.	D	a.	14%
10.	$300	b.	I	a.	32%
11.	a.	$60	I	$12	b.
12.	a.	$36	D	$36	b.

Notice that 20 is 40% of 50.

Solve each problem.

13. What is 30% more than 30?

14. What is 75% less than 80?

15. What percent of 11 is 6?

16. What percent of 80 is 60?

17. A price decreased from $50 to $40. Find the percent of decrease.

18. A price increased from $40 to $50. Find the percent of increase.

19. An item priced $36 has a 25% discount. Find the discount price.

20. Sales tax of 6% is added to a purchase of $11. Find the total price.

Find the customer price for each of the following. When there is a discount and sales tax, compute the discount price first.

21. Stereo Set: $345.00
    Discount: 12%

22. Ten-speed Bike: $148.00
    Discount: 18%

23. Clothing: $74.00
    Sales Tax: 6.5%

24. Books: $38.50
    Sales Tax: 6%

25. Shoes: $44.00
    Discount: 10%
    Sales Tax: 4%

26. Auto Tires: $154.00
    Discount: 20%
    Sales Tax: 5%

Solve each problem.

27. Wilma paid $92.04 for new school clothes. This included 4% sales tax. What was the cost of the clothes before taxes?

28. Millie paid $45.10, including $7\frac{1}{2}$% tax, for a pair of jeans. What was the cost of the jeans before taxes?

29. Jason paid $13.96 for a new shirt, after receiving a 20% discount. What was the price before the discount?

30. Ben received a discount of $4.35 on a new radio. The discount price was $24.65. What was the percent of discount?

31. A group of 25 people share equally in the profit from a bake sale. What percent does each person receive?

32. The original selling price of a stove was $550. This price was increased by 20%. The increased price was then discounted by 10%. What was the new selling price?

33. Forty percent of the students who auditioned for the school play were cut in the first week. Twenty percent of the remaining students were chosen for the play. If 12 students were chosen, how many students were in the original audition?

34. If a is 180% of b, then b is what percent of a?

Challenge

Solve each problem.

35. Which is better, a discount of 30%, or successive discounts of 15% and 15%?

36. Which is better, successive discounts of 10%, 5%, and 5%, or successive discounts of 5%, 5%, and 10%?

37. A coat that sells for $80 is discounted 20%. The sales tax is 6%. Is it better for the buyer to have the discount applied before the sales tax is added or after the sales tax is added?

Using Calculators_____The Percent Key

Most calculators have a key labeled $\boxed{\%}$. This key can be used to find percents of numbers. The way this key is used varies for different types of calculators. Two possible key sequences are shown in the following example.

Example: Find 18% of 46.

ENTER: 46 $\boxed{\times}$ 18 $\boxed{\%}$
DISPLAY: 46   18 8.28

or

ENTER: 46 $\boxed{\times}$ 18 $\boxed{\%}$ $\boxed{=}$
DISPLAY: 46   18 0.18 8.28

The correct answer is 8.28.

Try to obtain the same result using the percent key on your calculator. Refer to the instruction manual if necessary.

Exercises
Use a calculator to find the value of each of the following.

1. 20% of 96

2. 38% of 600

3. 32.7% of 91

4. 123% of 60

5. 0.7% of 90

6. 88% of 93

7. 3.75% of 509

8. 0.92% of 92

9. 0.002% of 80

Applications in Business

The Consumer Price Index is used to keep track of the change in the prices of goods and services bought by most people in the United States. Current prices are compared to average prices during 1967. For example, an index of 310 points means that goods and services that cost $100 in 1967 would now cost $310. Monthly changes in the CPI are often expressed as percents.

Example: **The CPI was 308.8 in April, 1984 and 309.7 in May, 1984. Find the monthly percent increase.**

$309.7 - 308.8 = 0.9$ *Subtract the earlier value from the later value.*

$\dfrac{0.9}{308.8} = \dfrac{x}{100}$ *Express the difference as a percent of the earlier value.*

$90 = 308.8x$

$\dfrac{90}{308.8} = x$

$0.29 = x$ *Round to the nearest tenth.*

The monthly percent increase was 0.3%

Exercises
Compute the monthly percent increase in the CPI to the nearest tenth.

1. March 245.1
   April 247.8

2. Jan. 179.3
   Feb. 180.7

3. June 234.8
   July 236.4

4. August 294.3
   Sept. 295.4

5. Oct. 301.4
   Nov. 306.1

6. April 280.6
   May 281.8

Compute the yearly percent increase in the CPI to the nearest tenth. The CPI for two successive years is given.

7. Jan. 195.3
   Jan. 209.4

8. July 223.7
   July 251.4

9. Dec. 245.1
   Dec. 283.8

10. Aug. 291.4
    Aug. 310.8

11. May 263.1
    May 295.6

12. Nov. 236.4
    Nov. 275.2

5-7   Problem Solving: Mixtures

Sue Murphy sold tickets for the basketball game. Each adult ticket costs $2.50 and each student ticket costs $1.10. The total number of tickets sold was 105 and the total income was $202.30. How many of each kind of ticket were sold?

Equations can be used to solve problems such as this. It is often helpful to use a chart to organize the information.

Example

1   **Use an equation to solve the problem above.**

Explore   Let a = the number of adult tickets sold.
$105 - a$ = the number of student tickets sold.

Plan

	Number of Tickets	Price per Ticket	Total Price
Adult	a	2.50	$2.50a$
Student	$105 - a$	1.10	$1.10(105 - a)$

$$\underbrace{\text{Income from}}_{\substack{\text{Adult Tickets} \\ 2.50a}} + \underbrace{\text{Income from}}_{\substack{\text{Student Tickets} \\ 1.10(105 - a)}} = \underbrace{\text{Total}}_{\substack{\text{Income} \\ 202.30}}$$

Solve
$$2.50a + 1.10(105 - a) = 202.30$$
$$2.50a + 115.50 - 1.10a = 202.30$$
$$2.50a - 1.10a = 202.30 - 115.50$$
$$1.40a = 86.80$$
$$a = 62$$

There were 62 adult tickets sold. There were $105 - 62$, or 43 student tickets sold.

Examine   If 62 adult tickets were sold, the total income from adult tickets was $155. If 43 student tickets were sold, the total income from student tickets was $47.30.
Since $155 + 47.30 = \$202.30$, the solution is correct.

Some problems involve mixtures of solutions. When solving such problems, compare the amounts of the substances in the solutions. Sometimes these amounts are given as percents.

Example

2

Hal is doing a chemistry experiment that calls for a 30% solution of copper sulfate. Hal has 40 mL of 25% solution. How many milliliters of a 60% solution should Hal add to obtain the required 30% solution?

Explore   Let x = amount of 60% solution to be added.

Plan

	Amount of Solution (mL)	Amount of Copper Sulfate
25% solution	40	0.25(40)
60% solution	x	0.60x
30% solution (mixture)	40 + x	0.30(40 + x)

$$\underbrace{\text{Amount of Copper Sulfate in 25\% Solution}}_{0.25(40)} + \underbrace{\text{Amount of Copper Sulfate in 60\% Solution}}_{0.60x} = \underbrace{\text{Amount of Copper Sulfate in Mixture}}_{0.30(40 + x)}$$

Solve

$$0.25(40) + 0.60x = 0.30(40 + x)$$
$$10 \quad + \quad 0.6x = 12 + 0.3x$$
$$0.3x = 2$$
$$x = 6.7 \quad \text{\textit{Round to the nearest tenth.}}$$

Hal should add 6.7 mL of the 60% solution to the 40 mL of 25% solution. *Examine this solution.*

Exploratory Exercises

Copy and complete the chart for each problem. Then state an equation.

1. Bonnie bought 16 paperback books for $10.95. Some costs 60¢ each and the rest cost 75¢ each. How many of each did she buy?

	Number	Total Price
60¢ books	x	
75¢ books		

2. Ralph has $2.55 in dimes and quarters. He has eight more dimes than quarters. How many quarters does he have?

	Number	Total Value
Quarters	x	
Dimes		

3. Peanuts sell for $3.00 a pound. Cashews sell for $6.00 a pound. How many pounds of cashews should be mixed with 12 pounds of peanuts to obtain a mixture selling for $4.20 a pound?

	Pounds	Total Price
$3.00 peanuts	12	
$6.00 cashews		
$4.20 mixture		

4. How much whipping cream (9% butterfat) should be added to 1 gallon of milk (4% butterfat) to obtain a 6% butterfat mixture?

	Gallons	Amount of Butterfat
9% butterfat	x	
4% butterfat		
6% butterfat		

Written Exercises

Solve each problem.

1. A chemist has 2.5 liters of a solution which is 70% acid. How much water should be added to obtain a 50% acid solution?

2. How much pure copper must be added to 50 kg of an alloy containing 12% copper to raise the copper content to 21%?

3. Matt has 500 mL of a 60% solution of silver nitrate. How many milliliters of a 30% silver nitrate solution should be added to obtain a 50% solution?

4. A liter of cream has 9.2% butterfat. How much skim milk containing 2% butterfat should be added to the cream to obtain a mixture with 6.4% butterfat?

5. Adrienne has 5 more dimes than nickels. In all, she has $2.30. How many nickels does she have?

6. Lois has 27 coins in nickels and dimes. In all she has $1.90. How many of each does she have?

7. How much coffee costing $3 a pound should be mixed with 5 pounds of coffee costing $3.50 a pound to obtain a mixture costing $3.25 a pound?

8. Theatre tickets cost $2.50 for children and $3.50 for adults. The price for 8 tickets was $23.00. How many adult tickets were purchased?

9. On the first day of school, 264 notebooks were sold. Some sold for 95¢ each and the rest sold for $1.25 each. How many of each were sold if the total sales were $297.00?

10. Ground chuck sells for $1.75 a pound. How many pounds of ground round selling for $2.45 a pound should be mixed with 20 pounds of ground chuck to obtain a mixture that sells for $2.05 a pound?

11. Drew has twice as many quarters as nickels and three more dimes than nickels. He has $4.20 in all. How many of each does he have?

12. Norbert has 42 coins in nickels, dimes, and quarters. If he has 8 more nickels than dimes and has $7.15 in all, how many of each does he have?

Challenge

13. A 60 mL mixture of alcohol and iodine is 2% iodine. How much alcohol must be evaporated away to leave a mixture that is 8% iodine?

14. Don has twice as much money in nickels as in dimes. He has 30 coins in all. How many of each coin does he have?

15. Jackie's car radiator has a 9-liter capacity. The radiator contains a solution that is 20% antifreeze. To be safe, she would like the solution to contain 25% antifreeze. How much of the solution should she drain and replace with 100% antifreeze?

16. A storage battery contains 1000 mL of a solution of 18% acid. The battery should contain a 21% solution for best efficiency. How much of the 18% solution should be drained and replaced with 100% acid?

mini-review

Find each sum.

1. $-84 + 17$ 2. $-\frac{7}{8} + \frac{3}{5}$

3. $41ab + (-13cd) + (-12ab) + 56cd$

Graph the solution set.

4. $5r \geq 4r + 6$ and $3r < 30$

5. $|m - 3| \leq 5$

Powers and E Notation

In the BASIC language, powers are written using the symbols ↑ or ∧. For example, $(2ab^2)^3$ can be written (2*A*B ↑ 2) ↑ 3. The following program evaluates this expression if $a = 9$ and $b = 10$.

```
10   READ A,B          Lines 10 and 20 assign the variables
20   DATA 9,10         A the value 9 and B the value 10.
30   PRINT (2 * A * B↑2)↑3
40   END

RUN
5.832E + 09
```

Notice that the output for this program is in E notation. This is the computer equivalent of scientific notation. Thus, 5.832E + 09 means 5.832×10^9. The computer used E notation because there were more than six significant digits in the output. (Some computers allow nine significant digits.)

Expressions such as $\dfrac{3.8 \times 10^{-9}}{1.3 \times 10^{-4}}$ can be evaluated using E notation.

This can be done by entering the following command into a computer.

```
PRINT (3.8E-09)/(1.3E-04)
```

The answer will be printed.

```
2.92307692 E-05
```

Exercises

Write a program that will evaluate each of the following expressions if $a = 4, b = 6$, and $c = 8$.

1. $a^2b^3c^4$ **2.** $(-2a)^2(4b)^3$ **3.** $(4a^2b^4)^3$ **4.** $(-6ab^3c^2)^4$

5. $\left(\frac{1}{2}ab\right)^2(2c)^2$ **6.** $(-5a^2c^3)^2(2b^2)^2$ **7.** $(ac)^3 + (3b)^2$ **8.** $(2a^3)^2 + (ab^2)^2$

Write PRINT commands that will evaluate each of the following expressions.

9. $\dfrac{4.2 \times 10^8}{2.3 \times 10^{15}}$ **10.** $\dfrac{3.4 \times 10^{-10}}{1.2 \times 10^{10}}$ **11.** $\dfrac{4.24 \times 10^{-12}}{3.1 \times 10^{-9}}$

12. $(5 \times 10^{19})(6 \times 10^{-8})$ **13.** $(2 \times 10^{12})(1.3 \times 10^7)$ **14.** $(1.4 \times 10^{-10})(2.7 \times 10^{-8})$

Chapter Summary

1. A monomial is a number, a variable, or a product of numbers and variables. (145)

2. Monomials that do not contain variables are called constants. (145)

3. Product of Powers Rule: For any number a and positive integers m and n,

$$a^m \cdot a^n = a^{m+n}. \quad (145)$$

4. Power of a Power Rule: For any number a and any integers m and n,

$$(a^m)^n = a^{mn}. \quad (148)$$

5. Power of a Product Rule: For all numbers a and b and any integer m,

$$(ab)^m = a^m b^m. \quad (148)$$

6. Power of a Monomial Rule: For all numbers a and b and any integers m, n, and p,

$$(a^m b^n)^p = a^{mp} b^{np}. \quad (148)$$

7. Dividing Powers: For all integers m and n and any nonzero number a,

$$\frac{a^m}{a^n} = a^{m-n}. \quad (150)$$

8. Zero Exponent: For any nonzero number a, $a^0 = 1$. (151)

9. Negative Exponents: For any nonzero number a and any integer n,

$$a^{-n} = \frac{1}{a^n}. \quad (151)$$

10. Scientific Notation: A number is expressed in scientific notation when it is in the form $a \times 10^n$ where $1 \le a < 10$ and n is an integer. (153)

Chapter Review

5-1 **Simplify.**

1. $b^2 \cdot b^7$
2. $y^3 \cdot y^3 \cdot y^l$
3. $(a^2b)(a^2b^2)$

4. $(a^2)(a^2b)$
5. $(3ab)(-4a^2b^3)$
6. $(-4a^2x)(-5a^3x^4)$

5-2 **Simplify.**

7. $(7a)^2$
8. $(4a^2b)^3$
9. $\left(\frac{1}{3}b^2\right)^2$

10. $(-0.5)^3a^4$
11. $(-3xy)^2(4x)^3$
12. $(5a^2)^3 + 7(a^6)$

5-3 **Simplify. Assume no denominator is equal to zero.**

13. $\dfrac{y^{10}}{y^6}$
14. $\dfrac{(3y)^0}{6a}$
15. $\dfrac{42b^7}{14b^4}$

16. $\dfrac{27b^{-2}}{14b^{-3}}$
17. $\dfrac{3a^3bc^2}{18a^2b^3c^4}$
18. $\dfrac{-16a^3b^2c^4d}{-48a^4bcd^3}$

5-4 **Express each number in scientific notation.**

19. 240,000
20. 0.000314

Evaluate. Express each result in scientific notation.

21. $(2 \times 10^5)(3 \times 10^6)$
22. $(3 \times 10^3)(1.5 \times 10^6)$

23. $\dfrac{5.4 \times 10^{-3}}{0.9 \times 10^4}$
24. $\dfrac{8.4 \times 10^{-6}}{1.4 \times 10^{-9}}$

5-5 **Use an equation to solve each problem.**

25. Joe is 10 years older than Jim. The sum of their ages is 64. What are their ages?

26. Mary is 20 years old. Her sister, Sara, is 5 years old. In how many years will Mary be twice as old as Sara?

5-6 **Solve each problem.**

27. What is 80% less than 90?

28. Gasoline prices increased from $1.10 to $1.20 per gallon. Find the percent of increase.

29. Find the total price if $5\frac{1}{4}\%$ sales tax is added to a purchase of $21.00.

30. Lee received a discount of $2.40 on an item marked $48.00. What was the percent of discount?

5-7 **Solve each problem.**

31. Joe has 32 coins in nickels and dimes. He has 10 more nickels than dimes and has $2.15 in all. How many of each kind of coin does he have?

32. How many pounds of nuts costing $2.00 per pound should be mixed with 10 pounds of nuts costing $3.00 per pound to obtain a mixture costing $2.25 per pound?

Chapter Test

Simplify. Assume no denominator is equal to zero.

1. $y^2 \cdot y^{13}$

2. $a^2 \cdot a^3 \cdot b^4 \cdot b^5$

3. $(a^2 b)(a^3 b^2)$

4. $(-12abc)(4a^2 b^3)$

5. $(9a)^2$

6. $(-3a)^4 (a^5 b)$

7. $\left(\frac{1}{5} r^2\right)^2$

8. $(-0.3a)^3$

9. $(-5a^2)(-6b)^2$

10. $(5a)^2 b + 7a^2 b$

11. $\dfrac{y^{11}}{y^6}$

12. $\dfrac{y^3 x}{yx}$

13. $\dfrac{63a^2 bc}{9abc}$

14. $\dfrac{49a^2 bc}{21ab^3 c^2}$

15. $\dfrac{14ab^{-3}}{21a^2 b^{-5}}$

16. $\dfrac{10a^2 bc}{20a^{-1} b^{-1} c}$

Express in scientific notation.

17. 5280

18. 0.00378

Evaluate. Express each result in scientific notation.

19. $(3 \times 10^3)(2 \times 10^4)$

20. $(4 \times 10^{-3})(2 \times 10^{16})$

21. $\dfrac{25 \times 10^3}{5 \times 10^{-3}}$

22. $\dfrac{91 \times 10^{18}}{13 \times 10^{14}}$

Solve each problem.

23. Jim is 5 years older than Les. The sum of their ages is 105. What are their ages?

24. What is 0.5% of 234?

25. What percent of 200 is 86?

26. 42 is 20% of what number?

27. A tire listed for $63.00 is sold for $49.00. What is the percent of discount?

28. Don has 42 coins in dimes, nickels, and quarters. He has twice as many dimes as quarters and two more nickels than quarters. In all he has $5.10. How many of each kind of coin does Don have?

Kyong Song wishes to travel from Chatsworth to Northridge to Granada Hills. She can travel from Chatsworth to Northridge on Lassen Street, Devonshire Street, or Plummer Street. She can travel from Northridge to Granada Hills on Henderson Street or Rinaldi Street. Her possible routes can be shown on a **tree diagram** as follows.

Lassen Street —— Henderson Street / Rinaldi Street

Devonshire Street —— Henderson Street / Rinaldi Street

Plummer Street —— Henderson Street / Rinaldi Street

A set of all of the possible outcomes, called a **sample space**, is { Lassen-Henderson, Lassen-Rinaldi, Devonshire-Henderson, Devonshire-Rinaldi, Plummer-Henderson, Plummer-Rinaldi }. Notice that there are six possible routes and that six is the product of the number of routes from Chatsworth to Northridge (3), and from Northridge to Granada Hills (2). Assuming that each route is equally likely, you can use the tree diagram or the sample space to find the following probabilities.

$$P(\text{Devonshire as the first street}) = \frac{1}{3}.$$

$$P(\text{Rinaldi as the second street}) = \frac{3}{6} = \frac{1}{2}.$$

$$P(\text{Devonshire, Rinaldi}) = \frac{1}{6}.$$

$$P(\text{Devonshire, Rinaldi}) = P(\text{Devonshire as first Street}) \cdot P(\text{Rinaldi as second street})$$

$$= \frac{1}{3} \cdot \frac{1}{2}$$

$$= \frac{1}{6}$$

In this example, Kyong's choice of the second street is not affected by her choice of the first street. When the outcome of the second event is not affected by the outcome of the first, the events are **independent**.

> **The probability of two independent events, A and B, occurring is the product of their individual probabilities.**
>
> $$P(A \text{ and } B) = P(A) \cdot P(B)$$

Probability of Two Independent Events

Example 1: A bag contains 4 red marbles and 3 white marbles. One marble is selected, returned to the bag, and then a second marble is selected. Find the probability of each of the following.

a. *P*(both red)

$$P(\text{both red}) = P(\text{red}) \cdot P(\text{red})$$

$$= \frac{4}{7} \cdot \frac{4}{7} = \frac{16}{49}$$

b. *P*(red and white)   *Select red followed by white.*

$$P(\text{red and white}) = P(\text{red}) \cdot P(\text{white})$$

$$= \frac{4}{7} \cdot \frac{3}{7} = \frac{12}{49}$$

Exercises

State whether the following events are independent.

1. flip a coin then flip it again

2. toss a die and flip a coin

3. draw a marble from a bag and then draw a second without replacement

4. draw a card from a deck, replace it and draw again

A nickel is flipped and then a dime is flipped. Find the probability of each of the following outcomes in the indicated order.

5. *P*(head and tail)

6. *P*(both tails)

7. *P*(both heads)

8. *P*(tail and head)

A bag contains 5 red, 3 blue, and 7 white marbles. A marble is selected, returned to the bag, and a second marble is selected. Find the probability of each of the following outcomes in the indicated order.

9. *P*(both red)

10. *P*(white and red)

11. *P*(both blue)

12. *P*(red and blue)

13. *P*(blue and red)

14. *P*(both white)

Suppose three marbles are selected and returned to the bag of marbles in Exercises 9-14. Find the probability of each of the following outcomes in the indicated order.

15. *P*(all three red)

16. *P*(red, white, blue)

17. *P*(all three blue)

18. *P*(white, blue, blue)

19. *P*(red, blue, red)

20. *P*(all three white)

Theo and Luke Mallinson play on the Cherry Creek High School basketball team. Theo can make 3 out of 5 free throws and Luke can make 4 out of 7 free throws. What is the probability of each of the following?

21. Luke will make his next two free throws.

22. Theo will make his next two free throws.

23. Luke and Theo (in that order) will both make their next free throws.

24. Theo will miss his next three free throws.

CHAPTER 6

Polynomials

Poly-, a prefix meaning many or several, is used in some mathematical words. There are many *poly*gons, plane figures with many angles, in the photograph above. In algebra, expressions consisting of one or more monomials are called *poly*nomials. In this chapter you will learn to add, subtract, and multiply polynomials.

6-1 Polynomials

A **polynomial** is a monomial or a sum of monomials. Recall that a monomial is a number, a variable, or a product of numbers and variables. A **binomial** is a polynomial with two terms, and a **trinomial** is a polynomial with three terms.

A monomial has one term.

Examples of each of these types of polynomials are given in the following chart.

monomial	binomial	trinomial
$5x^2$	$3x + 2$	$5x^2 - 2x + 7$
$4abc$	$4x + 5y$	$a^2 + 2ab + b^2$
-7	$3x^2 - 8xy$	$4a + 2b^2 - 3c$

The expression $x + \dfrac{3}{b}$ is not a polynomial because $\dfrac{3}{b}$ is not a monomial.

Example

1 State whether each expression is a polynomial. If the expression is a polynomial, identify it as either a monomial, binomial, or trinomial.

a. $8x^2 - 3xy$

The expression $8x^2 - 3xy$ can be written as $8x^2 + (-3xy)$. Therefore, $8x^2 - 3xy$ is a polynomial because it can be written as the sum of two monomials, $8x^2$ and $-3xy$. Since it has two terms, $8x^2 - 3xy$ is a binomial.

b. $\dfrac{5}{2y^2} + 7y + 6$

The expression $\dfrac{5}{2y^2} + 7y + 6$ is not a polynomial because $\dfrac{5}{2y^2}$ is not a monomial.

c. $3x^2 + 2x + 4$

The expression $3x^2 + 2x + 4$ is a polynomial because it is the sum of three monomials, $3x^2$, $2x$, and 4. Since it has three terms, $3x^2 + 2x + 4$ is a trinomial.

The **degree** of a monomial is the sum of the exponents of its variables.

monomial	degree
$5x^2$	2
$4ab^3c^4$	$1 + 3 + 4 = 8$
-9	0

What is the degree of $-\frac{1}{2}x$?

To find the degree of a polynomial, first find the degree of each of its terms. The degree of the polynomial is the greatest of the degrees of its terms.

Example

2 State the degree of each polynomial.

a. $8x^3 - 2x^2 + 7$

The polynomial $8x^3 - 2x^2 + 7$ has three terms, $8x^3$, $-2x^2$, and 7. Their degrees are 3, 2, and 0. Therefore, the degree of $8x^3 - 2x^2 + 7$ is 3.

b. $6x^2y + 5x^3y^2z - x + x^2y^2$

The polynomial $6x^2y + 5x^3y^2z - x + x^2y^2$ has four terms, $6x^2y$, $5x^3y^2z$, $-x$, and x^2y^2. Their degrees are 3, 6, 1, and 4. Therefore, the degree of $6x^2y + 5x^3y^2z - x + x^2y^2$ is 6.

The terms of a polynomial are usually arranged so that the powers of one variable are in either ascending or descending order.

Ascending Order	Descending Order
$3 + 5a - 8a^2 + a^3$	$a^3 - 8a^2 + 5a + 3$
(in x) $5xy + x^3y^2 - x^4 + x^5y^2$	(in x) $x^5y^2 - x^4 + x^3y^2 + 5xy$
(in y) $x^3 - 3x^2y + 4x^2y^2 - y^3$	(in y) $-y^3 + 4x^2y^2 - 3x^2y + x^3$

Exploratory Exercises

State whether each expression is a polynomial. If the expression is a polynomial, identify it as either a monomial, binomial, or trinomial.

1. $5x^2y + 3xy + 7$

2. $\frac{5}{k} - k^2y$

3. 17

4. $4t^2 + 3t$

5. $\frac{3}{a^3}$

6. $5a^2b^3$

7. $k^3 - \frac{2}{k}$

8. $\frac{a^3}{3}$

9. $3a^2x - 5a$

10. $4x^2 + 3y^2z$

11. $4b^2c - 8abc + b^3$

12. -12

13. 0

14. $x^2 - \frac{x}{2} + \frac{1}{3}$

15. $5a^2b - \frac{1}{2}ab^2 + \frac{1}{b^3}$

State the degree of each monomial.

16. $100x$

17. -18

18. $29xyz$

19. $8x^2$

20. $17x^2y$

21. $-14x^3z$

22. 0

23. $51x^5yz$

24. $28xst^3$

25. $14m^2n^3$

26. $4x$

27. $-36xw^4$

State the degree of each polynomial.

28. $12s + 21t$

29. 19

30. $14x + 3y$

31. $22x + 5y^4$

32. $-5m^2 + 9m^5$

33. $7x^3 + 4xy + 3xz^3$

34. $17r^2t + 3r + t^2$

35. $29x + x^{29}$

36. $17x^3y^4 - 11xy^5$

37. $22m^4n^2 - 14mn^6$

38. $-2a^2b^{10} + 3a^9b$

39. $13s^2t^2 + 4st^2 - 5s^5t$

Written Exercises

Find the degree of each polynomial.

1. $11x^2$

2. $5r - 3s + 7t$

3. $x + 2y^2 + 3z^3$

4. $n - 2p^2$

5. $27x^4 - 3x^3yz$

6. $12x^4y^5 + xy^6$

7. $29n^2 + 17n^2t^2$

8. $32xyz + 11x^2y + 17xz^2$

9. $4xy + 9xz^2 + 17rs^3$

10. $11wxyz - 9w^4$

11. $2xy^2z + 5xyz^5 + x^4$

12. $5x^2 - 2x^5$

13. $n^2 + r^3 + s^{14} + z^2$

14. $-4yzw^4 + 10x^4z^2w - 2z^2w^3$

15. $6mn^4t - 3m^4nt^2 + mn^6$

16. $2x^3yz - 5xy^3z + 11z^5$

17. 2^2r^2

18. $3^3xy + 5x$

Arrange the terms of each polynomial so that the powers of x are in ascending order.

19. $3 + x^4 + 2x^2$

20. $1 + x^3 + x^5 + x^2$

21. $2x^2 + 5ax + a^3$

22. $-2x^2y + 3xy^3 + x^3$

23. $17bx^2 + 11b^2x - x^3$

24. $21p^2x + 3px^3 + p^4$

Arrange the terms of each polynomial so that the powers of x are in descending order.

25. $-7 + x^2 + 4x$

26. $-6x + x^5 + 4x^3 - 20$

27. $5x^2 - 3x^3 + 2x + 7$

28. $a^2x + x^3 - 3$

29. $5b + \frac{2}{3}bx + b^3x^2$

30. $\frac{3}{4}x^3y - x^2 + 4 + \frac{2}{3}x$

31. $a + x$

32. $11x^2 + 7ax^3 - 3x + 2a$

33. $4x^3y + 3xy^4 - x^2y^3 + y^4$

34. $7a^3x - 8a^3x^3 + \frac{1}{5}x^5 + \frac{2}{3}x^2$

35. $\frac{1}{3}s^2x^3 + 4x^4 - \frac{2}{5}s^4x^2 + \frac{1}{4}x$

36. $0.2mx^4 - 1.3x^5 + 0.4m^2 + 2.6x^3$

37. $1.7t^3x + 2.4tx^5 - 0.3tx^2 + 5.1x^3$

mini-review

Simplify.

1. $x^2 + y^2 + 3xy + 2x^2 - y^2$

2. $\dfrac{-18}{-\frac{2}{3}}$

3. $y^4 \cdot y^3 \cdot y$

4. $(2ab^2c^3)^4$

5. $\dfrac{5x^4yz^2}{20x^2y^3z^2}$

6-2 Adding and Subtracting Polynomials

You have used properties to simplify expressions.

$$4a + 3a - 2 = (4 + 3)a - 2 \qquad \textit{Distributive Property}$$
$$= 7a - 2 \qquad \textit{Substitution Property of Equality}$$

$$5x^2 + 3y + 2x^2 - y = 5x^2 + 2x^2 + 3y - y \qquad \textit{Commutative Property for Addition}$$
$$= (5 + 2)x^2 + (3 - 1)y \qquad \textit{Distributive Property}$$
$$= 7x^2 + 2y \qquad \textit{Substitution Property of Equality}$$

Suppose you want to add the polynomials $(3x + 2y)$ and $(8x + 3y)$.
You can use the same properties to find such sums.

Examples

1   **Add:** $(3x + 2y) + (8x + 3y)$

To add polynomials, add their like terms.

$$(3x + 2y) + (8x + 3y) = (3x + 8x) + (2y + 3y) \qquad \textit{Associative and Commutative Properties for Addition}$$
$$= (3 + 8)x + (2 + 3)y \qquad \textit{Distributive Property}$$
$$= 11x + 5y \qquad \textit{Substitution Property of Equality}$$

2   **Add:** $(-3x^2 + 2x + 7) + (6x^2 - 5x - 3)$

$$(-3x^2 + 2x + 7) + (6x^2 - 5x - 3) = (-3x^2 + 6x^2) + [2x + (-5x)] + [7 + (-3)]$$
$$= (-3 + 6)x^2 + [2 + (-5)]x + [7 + (-3)]$$
$$= 3x^2 + (-3x) + 4$$
$$= 3x^2 - 3x + 4$$

Sometimes it is convenient to find the sum by writing the polynomials in column form.

Examples

3   **Add in column form:** $(5x^2 - 3xy + 7y^2) + (4x^2 + xy - 3y^2)$

$$\begin{array}{l} 5x^2 - 3xy + 7y^2 \\ \underline{4x^2 + xy - 3y^2} \\ 9x^2 - 2xy + 4y^2 \end{array}$$

4   **Add in column form:** $(3y^2 + 5y - 6) + (7y^2 - 9)$

$$\begin{array}{l} 3y^2 + 5y - 6 \\ \underline{7y^2 - 9} \qquad \textit{Notice that like terms are aligned.} \\ 10y^2 + 5y - 15 \end{array}$$

Recall that you can subtract a rational number by adding its additive inverse or opposite.

$a - b = a + (-b)$

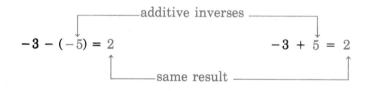

$$-3 - (-5) = 2 \qquad\qquad -3 + 5 = 2$$

Similarly, you can subtract a polynomial by adding its additive inverse. To find the additive inverse of a polynomial, replace each term by its additive inverse.

Another way to find the additive inverse is to multiply each term by -1.

Polynomial	Additive Inverse
$x + 2y$	$-x - 2y$
$2x^2 - 3x + 5$	$-2x^2 + 3x - 5$
$-8x + 5y - 7z$	$8x - 5y + 7z$
$3x^3 - 2x^2 - 5x$	$-3x^3 + 2x^2 + 5x$

Examples

5 **Subtract:** $(5x^2 - 2x + 7) - (2x^2 + 4x - 3)$

Add the additive inverse of $(2x^2 + 4x - 3)$.

$$
\begin{aligned}
(5x^2 - 2x + 7) - (2x^2 + 4x - 3) &= (5x^2 - 2x + 7) + [-(2x^2 + 4x - 3)] \\
&= (5x^2 - 2x + 7) + (-2x^2 - 4x + 3) \\
&= 5x^2 - 2x + 7 - 2x^2 - 4x + 3 \\
&= (5x^2 - 2x^2) + (-2x - 4x) + (7 + 3) \\
&= 3x^2 - 6x + 10
\end{aligned}
$$

6 **Subtract:** $(2x^2 - 3xy + 5y^2) - (x^2 - 3xy - 2y^2)$

$$
\begin{aligned}
(2x^2 - 3xy + 5y^2) - (x^2 - 3xy - 2y^2) &= (2x^2 - 3xy + 5y^2) + [-(x^2 - 3xy - 2y^2)] \\
&= (2x^2 - 3xy + 5y^2) + (-x^2 + 3xy + 2y^2) \\
&= (2x^2 - x^2) + (-3xy + 3xy) + (5y^2 + 2y^2) \\
&= x^2 + 7y^2
\end{aligned}
$$

7 **Subtract in column form:** $(4x^2 + 5xy - 3y^2) - (6x^2 + 8xy + 3y^2)$

$$
\begin{array}{r}
4x^2 + 5xy - 3y^2 \\
(-)\ \underline{6x^2 + 8xy + 3y^2}
\end{array}
\qquad
\begin{array}{c}
-(6x^2 + 8xy + 3y^2) \\
\text{\textit{additive inverse}}
\end{array}
\qquad
\begin{array}{r}
4x^2 + 5xy - 3y^2 \\
(+)\ \underline{-6x^2 - 8xy - 3y^2} \\
-2x^2 - 3xy - 6y^2
\end{array}
$$

Example

8 Subtract and check by addition: $(5a^3 + 2a^2 - 7) - (3a^3 + 8a^2 - 2a + 4)$

$$5a^3 + 2a^2 \qquad - 7$$
$$(-)3a^3 + 8a^2 - 2a + 4 \qquad -(3a^3 + 8a^2 - 2a + 4)$$
$$\text{additive inverse}$$

$$5a^3 + 2a^2 \qquad - 7$$
$$(+)\underline{-3a^3 - 8a^2 + 2a - 4}$$
$$2a^3 - 6a^2 + 2a - 11$$

Check:
$$2a^3 - 6a^2 + 2a - 11 \qquad \textit{difference}$$
$$(+) \underline{\ 3a^3 + 8a^2 - 2a + \ 4} \qquad \textit{second polynomial}$$
$$5a^3 + 2a^2 \qquad - \ 7 \qquad \textit{first polynomial}$$

Exploratory Exercises

State the additive inverse of each polynomial.

1. 29
2. $-15x^2y$
3. $3x + 2y$
4. $5a + 9b$
5. $7a - 6b$
6. $4x^2 - 5$
7. $-8m + 7n$
8. $-11x + 13y$
9. $x^2 + 3x + 7$
10. $x^2 + 7xy + y^2$
11. $2y^2 - 7y + 12$
12. $6a^2 - 3ab + b^2$
13. $-10r^2 + 4rs - 6s$
14. $-6a + 5b - c$
15. $-x^3 - x - 1$
16. $-4h^2 - 5hk - k^2$
17. $-3ab^2 + 5a^2b - b^3$
18. $x^3 + 5x^2 - 3x - 11$

Add or subtract.

19. $(2n + 7p) + (8n + 2p)$
20. $(3r - 9s) + (4r + 8s)$
21. $(2a + 3b) + (5a - 2b)$
22. $(7m + 3n) - (3m + 5n)$
23. $(5x + 8y) - (-3x + 5y)$
24. $[-5a + (-8b)] + (4a + 8b)$
25. $(5n + r) + (7n - 3r)$
26. $(-5r + 2s) - (-3r - 2s)$
27. $(5r - 3s) - (5r + 3s)$
28. $(7m + 2n) - (-6m + 7n)$

Written Exercises

Add or subtract.

1. $(5x + 6y) + (2x + 8y)$
2. $(4a + 6b) + (2a + 3b)$
3. $(7n + 11m) - (4m + 2n)$
4. $(7y + 9x) - (6x + 5y)$
5. $(3x - 7y) + (3y + 4x)$
6. $(3x - 2y) + (5x + 8y)$
7. $(5a - 6m) - (2a + 5m)$
8. $(3s - 5t) - (8t + 2s)$
9. $(5m + 3n) + 8m$
10. $(12x + 7y) + 8y$
11. $(13x + 9y) - 11y$
12. $(9x + 3y) - 9y$
13. $(n^2 + 5n + 3) + (2n^2 + 8n + 8)$
14. $(5a^2 + 7a + 5) + (a^2 + 6a + 3)$
15. $(3 + 2a + a^2) - (5 + 8a + a^2)$
16. $(3x^2 - 7x + 4) - (2x^2 + 8x - 6)$
17. $\left(\frac{1}{2}x^2 + \frac{5}{3}x - \frac{1}{4}\right) + \left(\frac{1}{2}x^2 - \frac{1}{3}x + \frac{1}{2}\right)$
18. $\left(\frac{3}{4}x^2 + \frac{2}{3}x - 7\right) + \left(\frac{5}{4}x^2 - 6x + 4\right)$
19. $(5ax^2 + 3a^2x - 5x) + (2ax^2 - 5ax + 7x)$
20. $\left(\frac{5}{7}a^2 - \frac{3}{4}a + \frac{1}{2}\right) - \left(\frac{3}{7}a^2 + \frac{1}{2}a - \frac{1}{2}\right)$
21. $(2xy + 6xy^2 + y^2) - (3x^2y + 2xy + 3y^2)$
22. $\left(\frac{3}{8}m^2 - 4m + \frac{2}{3}\right) + \left(\frac{5}{8}m^2 - 2m + \frac{1}{3}\right)$

23. $(3mn^2 + 3mn - n^3) - (5mn^2 + n + 2n^3)$

24. $(x^3 - 3x^2y + 4xy^2 + y^3) - (7x^3 + x^2y - 9xy^2 + y^3)$

Add.

25. $\begin{array}{l} 4a + 5b - 6c + d \\ 3a - 7b + 2c + 8d \\ 2a - b + 7d \end{array}$

26. $\begin{array}{l} 2x^2 - 5x + 7 \\ 5x^2 + 7x - 3 \\ x^2 - x + 11 \end{array}$

27. $\begin{array}{l} 5ax^2 + 3a^2x - 7a^3 \\ 2ax^2 - 8a^2x + 4 \end{array}$

28. $\begin{array}{l} a^3 - b^3 \\ 3a^3 + 2a^2b - b^2 + 2b^3 \end{array}$

Subtract.

29. $\begin{array}{l} 6x^2y^2 - 3xy - 7 \\ 5x^2y^2 + 2xy + 3 \end{array}$

30. $\begin{array}{l} 5x^2 - 4 \\ 3x^2 + 8x + 4 \end{array}$

31. $\begin{array}{l} 11m^2n^2 + 2mn - 11 \\ 5m^2n^2 - 6mn + 17 \end{array}$

32. $\begin{array}{l} 2a - 7 \\ 5a^2 + 8a - 11 \end{array}$

Subtract and check by addition.

33. $\begin{array}{l} 11m^2n^2 + 4mn - 6 \\ 5m^2n^2 - 6mn + 17 \end{array}$

34. $\begin{array}{l} 7z^2 + 4 \\ 3z^2 + 2z - 6 \end{array}$

35. $\begin{array}{l} 4y - 11 \\ 3y^2 + 4y - 11 \end{array}$

Find the measure of the third side of each triangle. P is the measure of the perimeter.

36. $P = 3x + 3y$

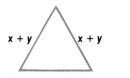

$x + y$ $\quad$ $x + y$

37. $P = 7x + 2y$

$2x + y$ $\quad$ $3x - 5y$

38. $P = 11x^2 - 29x + 10$

$5x^2 - 13x + 24$

$x^2 + 7x + 9$

Challenge _____

Two angles are **complementary** if the sum of their degree measures is 90. Find the complement of each angle below.

39. 85 $\qquad$ **40.** $3x$ $\qquad$ **41.** $x - 2$ $+y=90$ $\qquad$ **42.** $2x + 40$

Two angles are **supplementary** if the sum of their degree measures is 180. Find the supplement of each angle below.

43. 45 $\qquad$ **44.** $2x$ $\qquad$ **45.** $8x - 10$ $\qquad$ **46.** $5x + 130$

The sum of the degree measures of the three angles of a triangle is 180. Find the degree measure of the third angle of each triangle given the degree measures of the other two angles.

47. 80; 70 $\qquad$ **48.** $3x$; $x + 2$ $\qquad$ **49.** $x - 1$; $x + 5$ $\qquad$ **50.** $2x - 3$; $3x - 8$

51. $5 - 2x$; $7 + 8x$ $\qquad$ **52.** $x^2 - 8x + 2$; $x^2 - 3x - 1$

53. $3x^2 - 5$; $4x^2 + 2x + 1$ $\qquad$ **54.** $4 - 2x$; $x^2 - 1$

Powers containing the exponent 2 or 3 can be read in two ways.

x^2 is read "x squared" or "x to the second power."
x^3 is read "x cubed" or "x to the third power."

Powers containing numerical exponents other than 2 or 3 are usually read as follows.

x^0 is read "x to the zero power."
x^6 is read "x to the sixth power."
x^n is read "x to the nth power."

Recall that an exponent indicates the number of times that the base is used as a factor. Suppose you are to write each of the following in symbols.

Words	Symbols
3 times x squared	$3x^2$
3 times x the quantity squared	$(3x)^2$

In the second expression, parentheses are used to show that the expression $3x$ is used as a factor twice.

$$(3x)^2 = (3x)(3x)$$

The phrase *the quantity* is used to indicate parentheses when reading expressions.

Exercises
State how you would read each of the following expressions.

1. 4^2
2. 3^3
3. a^5
4. m^9
5. $5b^2$
6. $(12r)^5$
7. $9x^3y$
8. $(x + 2y)^2$
9. $4m^2n^4$
10. $(6a^2b)^4$
11. $a - b^3$
12. $(2a + b)^4$

Decide if the expressions are equivalent. Write *yes* or *no*.

13. $12 \cdot x^3$ and $12 \cdot x \cdot x \cdot x$
14. $3xy^5$ and $3(xy)^5$
15. $(2a)^3$ and $8a^3$
16. $(ab)^2$ and $a^2 \cdot b^2$
17. xy^3 and x^3y^3
18. $4(x^3)^2$ and $4x^6$

6-3   Multiplying a Polynomial by a Monomial

You can use the distributive property to multiply a polynomial by a monomial.

Examples

1   **Multiply:** $5a(3a^2 + 4)$

$5a(3a^2 + 4) = 5a(3a^2) + 5a(4)$ *Use the distributive property.*

$\qquad\qquad\quad = 15a^3 + 20a$

2   **Multiply:** $2m^2(5m^2 - 7m + 8)$

$2m^2(5m^2 - 7m + 8) = 2m^2(5m^2) + 2m^2(-7m) + 2m^2(8)$ *Use the product*

$\qquad\qquad\qquad\qquad = 10m^4 - 14m^3 + 16m^2$ *of powers rule.*

3   **Multiply:** $-3xy(2x^2y + 3xy^2 - 7y^3)$

$-3xy(2x^2y + 3xy^2 - 7y^3) = -3xy(2x^2y) + (-3xy)(3xy^2) + (-3xy)(-7y^3)$

$\qquad\qquad\qquad\qquad\quad = -6x^3y^2 - 9x^2y^3 + 21xy^4$

4   **Simplify:** $2a(5a^2 + 3a - 2) + 8(3a^2 - 7a + 1)$

$2a(5a^2 + 3a - 2) + 8(3a^2 - 7a + 1)$

$\quad = 2a(5a^2) + 2a(3a) + 2a(-2) + 8(3a^2) + 8(-7a) + 8(1)$

$\quad = 10a^3 + 6a^2 - 4a + 24a^2 - 56a + 8$

$\quad = 10a^3 + 30a^2 - 60a + 8$ *Combine like terms.*

Exploratory Exercises

Multiply.

1. $-5a(12a^2)$
2. $4x^2(7x^3)$
3. $2(5x - 3)$
4. $8(3a + 5)$
5. $7a(5a + 8)$
6. $3m(8m + 7)$
7. $3ab(5a - 3)$
8. $2mn(m - 7)$
9. $-8a^2(3a^2 + 7a)$
10. $-4m^3(5m^2 + 2m)$
11. $3xy(3xy + 2x)$
12. $7ab(5ab^2 + b^2)$

$9x^2y^2 + 6x^2y$

Written Exercises

Multiply.

1. $5(3a + 7)$
2. $8(7m + 2)$
3. $-3(8x + 5)$
4. $-7(5x + 8)$
5. $\frac{1}{2}x(8x + 6)$
6. $\frac{2}{3}a(6a + 15)$
7. $3b(5b + 8)$
8. $7a(8a + 11)$
9. $-2x(5x + 11)$
10. $-5y(7y + 12)$
11. $1.1a(2a + 7)$
12. $2.6b(5b - 1)$
13. $7a(3a^2 - 2a)$
14. $5b(8b^2 - 7b)$
15. $3st(5s^2 + 2st)$
16. $5mn(5m^2 + 3mn)$
17. $7xy(5x^2 - y^2)$
18. $4ab(3a^2 - 7b^2)$

19. $2a(5a^3 - 7a^2 + 2)$

20. $5a(a^2 + 9a - 3)$

21. $7x^2y(5x^2 - 3xy + y)$

22. $8cd^2(7c^2d - cd + d^2)$

23. $5y(8y^3 + 7y^2 - 3y)$

24. $8v(7v^3 + v^2 - 7v)$

25. $-4x(7x^2 - 4x + 3)$

26. $-8a(5a^2 + 8a - 3)$

27. $5x^2y(3x^2 - 7xy + y^2)$

28. $7a^2b^2(a^4 - 5a^2b + 6b^2)$

29. $4m^2(9m^2n + mn - 5n^2)$

30. $2x^2(9x^2y - 7xy + y^2)$

31. $-8xy(4xy + 7x - 14y^2)$

32. $-7ab(ab + 11a^2b - 11b^2)$

33. $-\frac{1}{3}x(9x^2 + x - 5)$

34. $\frac{2}{5}a(10a^2 - 15a + 8)$

35. $-2mn(8m^2 - 3mn + n^2)$

36. $-7am(2a^2m^2 - 7am + 11)$

37. $-\frac{3}{4}ab^2\left(\frac{1}{3}b^2 - \frac{4}{9}b + 1\right)$

38. $-\frac{1}{3}xy\left(12x^2 + 8xy - \frac{2}{3}y^2\right)$

Simplify.

39. $2a(a^3 - 2a^2 + 7) + 5(a^4 + 5a^3 - 3a + 5)$

40. $6m(m^2 - 11m + 4) - 7(m^3 + 8m - 11)$

41. $5m^2(m + 7) - 2m(5m^2 - 3m + 7) + 2(m^3 - 8)$

42. $6a^2(3a - 4) + 5a(7a^2 - 6a + 5) - 3(a^2 + 6a)$

43. $3a^2(a - 4) + 6a(3a^2 + a - 7) - 4(a - 7)$

44. $8r^2(r + 8) - 3r(5r^2 - 11) - 9(3r^2 - 8r + 1)$

45. $2.5t(8t - 12) + 5.1(6t^2 + 10t - 20)$

46. $3.2a(5a + 1.1) + 9.3(6a^2 - 1.1a + 3.5)$

47. $\frac{3}{4}m(8m^2 + 12m - 4) + \frac{3}{2}(8m^2 - 9m)$

48. $\frac{1}{2}a(a^2 + 7a - 8) + \frac{1}{4}(5a^3 + 8a^2 - 3a)$

Challenge

49. $\frac{3}{4}a(a^2 + 0.79a + 0.345) - \frac{4}{5}a\left(\frac{1}{4}a^2 + 0.295a + \frac{1}{2}\right)$

50. $\frac{2}{5}x^2(x^3 + 0.86x^2 - 0.49) - 0.67x\left(0.34x^4 - \frac{2}{5}x^3 - 0.631\right)$

Excursions in Algebra _____ History

Amalie Emmy Noether (1882–1935) was a German mathematician who worked with the structure of algebra. She studied non-commutative algebras. In the period 1930–1933 she was the center of mathematical activity at the University of Göttingen with her research program and her influence on many students.

Noether's strength as a mathematician lay in her ability to operate abstractly with concepts. In her hands the axiomatic method (using axioms or properties) became a powerful tool of mathematical research. Albert Einstein paid her a great tribute in 1935: "In the realm of algebra . . . , she discovered methods which have proved of enormous importance in the development of the present day younger generation of mathematicians."

6-4 Multiplying Polynomials

The distributive property can be used to multiply polynomials as well as to multiply a monomial by a polynomial. To find the product of two binomials, use the distributive property twice.

Example

1   **Multiply:** $(2x + 3)(5x + 8)$

$$
\begin{aligned}
(2x + 3)(5x + 8) &= 2x(5x + 8) + 3(5x + 8) && \text{Use the distributive property.}\\
&= 2x(5x) + 2x(8) + 3(5x) + 3(8) && \text{Use the distributive property again.}\\
&= 10x^2 + 16x + 15x + 24 && \text{Simplify each term.}\\
&= 10x^2 + 31x + 24 && \text{Combine like terms.}
\end{aligned}
$$

Although two binomials can always be multiplied as shown above, the following shortcut called the **FOIL method** is used frequently.

	$2x \cdot 5x$	
Multiply the **F**irst terms.	$(2x + 3)\,(5x + 8)$	$10x^2$
	$2x \cdot 8$	$+$
Multiply the **O**uter terms.	$(2x + 3)\,(5x + 8)$	$16x$
	$3 \cdot 5x$	$+$
Multiply the **I**nner terms.	$(2x + 3)\,(5x + 8)$	$15x$
	$3 \cdot 8$	$+$
Multiply the **L**ast terms.	$(2x + 3)\,(5x + 8)$	24

$$
\begin{aligned}
(2x + 3)(5x + 8) &= 10x^2 + 16x + 15x + 24\\
&= 10x^2 + 31x + 24 && \text{Combine the like terms}\\
& && 16x \text{ and } 15x.
\end{aligned}
$$

To multiply two binomials, find the sum of the products of	
F the first terms,	*FOIL Method*
O the outer terms,	*for Multiplying Two*
I the inner terms, and	*Binomials*
L the last terms.	

Examples

2 **Multiply:** $(x + 5)(x + 7)$

$$(x + 5)(x + 7) = \overbrace{x \cdot x}^{F} + \overbrace{x \cdot 7}^{O} + \overbrace{5 \cdot x}^{I} + \overbrace{5 \cdot 7}^{L}$$

$$= x^2 + 7x + 5x + 35$$

$$= x^2 + 12x + 35$$

3 **Multiply:** $(3x - 5)(5x + 2)$

$$\begin{array}{cccc} \text{F} & \text{O} & \text{I} & \text{L} \end{array}$$

$$(3x - 5)(5x + 2) = 3x(5x) + 3x(2) + (-5)(5x) + (-5)(2)$$

$$= 15x^2 + 6x - 25x - 10$$

$$= 15x^2 - 19x - 10$$

4 **Multiply:** $\left(\frac{1}{3}a - \frac{2}{3}\right)\left(\frac{1}{2}a + \frac{1}{3}\right)$

$$\left(\frac{1}{3}a - \frac{2}{3}\right)\left(\frac{1}{2}a + \frac{1}{3}\right) = \left(\frac{1}{3}a\right)\left(\frac{1}{2}a\right) + \left(\frac{1}{3}a\right)\left(\frac{1}{3}\right) + \left(-\frac{2}{3}\right)\left(\frac{1}{2}a\right) + \left(-\frac{2}{3}\right)\left(\frac{1}{3}\right)$$

$$= \frac{1}{6}a^2 + \frac{1}{9}a - \frac{1}{3}a - \frac{2}{9}$$

$$= \frac{1}{6}a^2 + \frac{1}{9}a - \frac{3}{9}a - \frac{2}{9}$$

$$= \frac{1}{6}a^2 - \frac{2}{9}a - \frac{2}{9}$$

The distributive property can be used to multiply any two polynomials.

Examples

5 **Multiply:** $(2x + 5)(3x^2 - 5x + 4)$

$$(2x + 5)(3x^2 - 5x + 4) = (2x + 5)(3x^2) + (2x + 5)(-5x) + (2x + 5)(4)$$

$$= 6x^3 + 15x^2 - 10x^2 - 25x + 8x + 20$$

$$= 6x^3 + 5x^2 - 17x + 20$$

6 **Multiply:** $(x^2 - 5x + 4)(2x^2 + x - 7)$

$$(x^2 - 5x + 4)(2x^2 + x - 7)$$

$$= (x^2 - 5x + 4)(2x^2) + (x^2 - 5x + 4)(x) + (x^2 - 5x + 4)(-7)$$

$$= 2x^4 - 10x^3 + 8x^2 + x^3 - 5x^2 + 4x - 7x^2 + 35x - 28$$

$$= 2x^4 - 10x^3 + x^3 + 8x^2 - 5x^2 - 7x^2 + 4x + 35x - 28$$

$$= 2x^4 - 9x^3 - 4x^2 + 39x - 28$$

Polynomials can also be multiplied in column form.

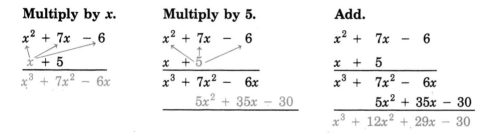

Multiply by x.

$$x^2 + 7x - 6$$
$$x + 5$$
$$\overline{}$$
$$x^3 + 7x^2 - 6x$$

Multiply by 5.

$$x^2 + 7x - 6$$
$$x + 5$$
$$\overline{}$$
$$x^3 + 7x^2 - 6x$$
$$5x^2 + 35x - 30$$

Add.

$$x^2 + 7x - 6$$
$$x + 5$$
$$\overline{}$$
$$x^3 + 7x^2 - 6x$$
$$5x^2 + 35x - 30$$
$$\overline{x^3 + 12x^2 + 29x - 30}$$

In the partial products, notice that like terms are aligned.

Examples

7 **Multiply in column form:** $(4x + 7)(5x^2 - 3x + 7)$

$$5x^2 - 3x + 7$$
$$4x + 7$$
$$\overline{}$$
$$20x^3 - 12x^2 + 28x \longleftarrow \text{This is the product of } 4x \text{ and } 5x^2 - 3x + 7.$$
$$35x^2 - 21x + 49 \longleftarrow \text{This is the product of } 7 \text{ and } 5x^2 - 3x + 7.$$
$$\overline{20x^3 + 23x^2 + 7x + 49}$$

8 **Multiply in column form:** $(x^3 + 5x - 6)(2x - 9)$

Since there is no x^2 in $x^3 + 5x - 6$, $0x^2$ is used as a placeholder.

$$x^3 + 0x^2 + 5x - 6$$
$$2x - 9$$
$$\overline{}$$
$$2x^4 + 0x^3 + 10x^2 - 12x \qquad \text{This is the product of } 2x \text{ and } x^3 + 5x - 6.$$
$$- 9x^3 + 0x^2 - 45x + 54 \qquad \text{This is the product of } -9 \text{ and } x^3 + 5x - 6.$$
$$\overline{2x^4 - 9x^3 + 10x^2 - 57x + 54}$$

Exploratory Exercises

State the sum of the product of the inner terms and the product of the outer terms.

1. $(x + 5)(x + 3)$
2. $(r - 3)(r + 7)$
3. $(2a + 1)(a + 5)$
4. $(3y + 2)(y - 3)$
5. $(x + 5)(5x - 3)$
6. $(x + 2)(4x - 7)$
7. $(3x + 2)(2x + 3)$
8. $(3a - 4)(4a + 1)$
9. $(5b - 3)(2b + 1)$
10. $(3z + 5)(5z - 3)$
11. $(2m + 4)(m + 5)$
12. $(3x + 7)(5x - 1)$

Written Exercises

$2m^2 + 10m + 4m + 20$

Multiply.

1. $(a + 3)(a + 7)$
2. $(c + 2)(c + 8)$
3. $(m - 5)(m - 11)$
4. $(x - 4)(x - 8)$
5. $(x + 11)(x - 4)$
6. $(y + 3)(y - 7)$
7. $(2x + 1)(x + 8)$
8. $(5y - 3)(y + 2)$
9. $(4a + 3)(2a - 1)$

10. $(5a + 3)(3a + 1)$

11. $(8a + 3)(5a + 4)$

12. $(2x + 3y)(5x + 2y)$

13. $(2a + 3b)(5a - 2b)$

14. $(2b + 5d)(4b + 8d)$

15. $(7y - 1)(2y - 3)$

16. $(5q + 2r)(8q - 3r)$

17. $(5r - 7s)(4r + 3s)$

18. $\left(2x - \frac{1}{2}\right)\left(5x + \frac{1}{2}\right)$

19. $\left(4x - \frac{2}{3}\right)\left(5x + \frac{1}{3}\right)$

20. $\left(3x + \frac{1}{4}\right)\left(6x - \frac{1}{2}\right)$

21. $\left(4x - \frac{1}{2}\right)\left(3x + \frac{3}{4}\right)$

22. $\left(\frac{1}{3}x + \frac{1}{2}\right)\left(\frac{2}{3}x - \frac{1}{2}\right)$

23. $\left(\frac{1}{4}y + \frac{1}{3}x\right)\left(\frac{3}{4}y - \frac{2}{3}x\right)$

24. $(2r + 0.1)(5r - 0.3)$

25. $(2a + 0.7)(3a + 0.8)$

26. $(0.2x + 0.5y)(0.2x - 0.5y)$

27. $(0.7x + 2y)(0.9x + 3y)$

28. $(0.5x + 0.3)(0.8x - 0.6)$

29. $(0.3a - 1.2)(0.8a + 1.1)$

30. $(a + 2)(a^2 - 5a + 9)$

31. $(m + 7)(m^2 + 7m - 2)$

32. $(2x + 1)(x^2 + 7x - 9)$

33. $(5a + 2)(a^2 - 3a + 11)$

34. $(3x + 5)(2x^2 - 5x + 11)$

35. $(4s + 5)(3s^2 + 8s - 9)$

36. $(4x - 3y)(3x^2 + 5xy + y^2)$

37. $(5x - 2y)(6x^2 - 5xy + 9y^2)$

38. $(0.3m + 2)(0.2m^2 - 1.1m + 0.7)$

39. $(0.3n + 8)(0.5n^2 - 3.1n + 1.5)$

40. $(0.6a + 0.5)(0.7a^2 - 0.2a - 1.1)$

41. $(0.9t + 0.2)(0.7t^2 - 0.6t + 1.7)$

42. $\left(\frac{1}{2}a + \frac{2}{3}\right)\left(a^2 + \frac{2}{3}a + \frac{1}{6}\right)$

43. $\left(\frac{2}{3}x - \frac{1}{2}y\right)\left(\frac{2}{3}x^2 - \frac{3}{4}xy + \frac{1}{4}y^2\right)$

44. $\left(\frac{1}{4}m + \frac{3}{4}\right)\left(\frac{1}{2}m^2 - 6\right)$

45. $\left(\frac{1}{3}a + \frac{2}{3}\right)\left(\frac{1}{4}a^2 + \frac{3}{4}a - \frac{5}{4}\right)$

46. $(x^2 - 7x + 4)(2x^2 - 3x - 6)$

47. $(a^2 + 2a + 5)(a^2 - 3a - 7)$

48. $(6a^2 + 5ab + 4b^2)(5a^2 - 3ab - 2b^2)$

Multiply in column form.

49. $(5x^2 - 6x + 9)(4x^2 + 3x + 11)$

50. $(-2x^2 + 3x - 8)(3x^2 + 7x - 5)$

51. $(3a + 5)(2a - 8a^2 + 3)$

52. $(5x - 2)(7 - 5x^2 + 2x)$

53. $(5x^4 - 2x^2 + 1)(x^2 - 5x + 3)$

54. $(-7b^3 + 2b - 3)(5b^2 - 2b + 4)$

55. $\left(\frac{1}{2}a^3 - 3a + 2\right)\left(\frac{1}{2}a^3 + 3a + 2\right)$

56. $\left(\frac{2}{3}x^3 - \frac{1}{3}x^2 + x\right)(-5x^2 + x - 1)$

57. $(0.2x^2 + 3x - 2)(3x^3 - 0.3x - 3)$

58. $(0.5a^2 - ab + b^2)(a^2 - 2ab + 7b^2)$

Challenge _____

Multiply.

59. $(3x^a + y)(5x^a + 2y)$

60. $(8x^n + x^{2n})(4x^n - x^{2n})$

61. $(2a^n + b^m)(3a^n + 5b^m)$

62. $(2y^a - 5y^{2b})(3y^{3a} - 4y^b)$

63. $(4x^{2y} + 6x^{3y})(2x^y - 5x^{4y})$

64. $(9z^r - 8z^{5r})(2z^{2r} + 4z^{4r})$

65. $(6m^{2x} - 10m^{2x})(2m^{5x} + 6m^{3x})$

66. $(7r^{4a} + 2r^{4a})(11r^{6a} - 3r^{4a})$

6-5 Some Special Products

Study the following diagram. There are two ways to find the area of the large square.

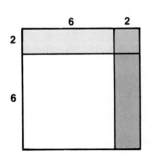

Method 1. The length of each side is $6 + 2$ units. Find the square of $(6 + 2)$.

$$(6 + 2)^2 = 8^2$$
$$= 64$$

Method 2. The area of the large square is the sum of the areas of the smaller parts.

$$6^2 + 6 \cdot 2 + 6 \cdot 2 + 2^2$$
$$= 36 + 12 + 12 + 4$$
$$= 64$$

Notice that $(6 + 2)^2 = 6^2 + 6 \cdot 2 + 6 \cdot 2 + 2^2$

Using a similar procedure, the general form $(a + b)^2$ can be simplified as follows.

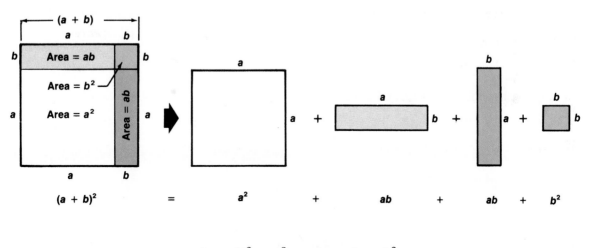

$$(a + b)^2 = a^2 + ab + ab + b^2$$
$$= a^2 + 2ab + b^2$$

Check this result using the FOIL method.

$$(a + b)^2 = a^2 + 2ab + b^2$$

Square of a Sum

Examples

1 **Multiply:** $(x + 3)^2$

Use the square of a sum, $(a + b)^2 = a^2 + 2ab + b^2$.

$$(x + 3)^2 = x^2 + 2(x)(3) + (3)^2 \quad \text{\textit{Replace a with x and b with 3.}}$$
$$= x^2 + 6x + 9$$

2 **Multiply:** $(5m + 3n)^2$

Use $(a + b)^2 = a^2 + 2ab + b^2$.

$$(5m + 3n)^2 = (5m)^2 + 2(5m)(3n) + (3n)^2$$
$$= 25m^2 + 30mn + 9n^2$$

To find $(a - b)^2$, express $(a - b)$ as $[a + (-b)]$ and square it as a sum.

$$(a - b)^2 = [a + (-b)]^2$$
$$= a^2 + 2(a)(-b) + (-b)^2$$
$$= a^2 - 2ab + b^2$$

$$(a - b)^2 = a^2 - 2ab + b^2$$

*Square of
a Difference*

Compare the square of a sum and the square of a difference. How do they differ?

Examples

3 **Multiply:** $(c - 2)^2$

Use the square of a difference, $(a - b)^2 = a^2 - 2ab + b^2$.

$$(c - 2)^2 = c^2 - 2(c)(2) + (2)^2 \quad \text{\textit{Replace a with c and b with 2.}}$$
$$= c^2 - 4c + 4$$

4 **Multiply:** $(3x - 2y)^2$

Use $(a - b)^2 = a^2 - 2ab + b^2$.

$$(3x - 2y)^2 = (3x)^2 - 2(3x)(2y) + (2y)^2$$
$$= 9x^2 - 12xy + 4y^2 \quad \text{\textit{You can use the distributive property to check this.}}$$

You can use the FOIL method to find the product of a sum and a difference of the same two numbers. For example find $(a + b)(a - b)$.

$$(a + b)(a - b) = a(a) + a(-b) + b(a) + b(-b)$$
$$= a^2 - ab + ba - b^2$$
$$= a^2 - b^2$$

This product is called the **difference of squares**.

$$(a + b)(a - b) = a^2 - b^2$$

Product of a Sum and a Difference

Examples

5 Multiply: $(x + 5)(x - 5)$

$(a + b)(a - b) = a^2 - b^2$

$(x + 5)(x - 5) = x^2 - 5^2$ *Replace a with x and b with 5.*
$= x^2 - 25$

6 Multiply: $(5a + 6b)(5a - 6b)$

$(a + b)(a - b) = a^2 - b^2$

$(5a + 6b)(5a - 6b) = (5a)^2 - (6b)^2$
$= 25a^2 - 36b^2$

Exploratory Exercises

Multiply.

1. $(a + 2b)^2$
2. $(a - 3b)^2$
3. $(2x + y)^2$
4. $(3x - 2y)^2$
5. $(3m^2 + 2n)^2$
6. $(3m - 4x)^2$
7. $(a^2 + b)^2$
8. $(2a + 3)(2a - 3)$
9. $(3a - 8b)^2$
10. $(4x - 3)(4x + 3)$
11. $(5a - 3b)(5a - 3b)$
12. $(4x^2 + y)^2$
13. $(3x - y)^2$
14. $(5m^2 + 7n)^2$
15. $(2x^2 - 3y^3)^2$

Written Exercises

Multiply.

1. $(4x + y)^2$
2. $(5x + y)^2$
3. $(2a - b)^2$
4. $(5a - b)^2$
5. $(6m + 2n)^2$
6. $(7x + 3y)^2$
7. $(4x - 9y)^2$
8. $(5r - 7s)^2$
9. $(5a - 12b)^2$
10. $(6a - 5b)^2$
11. $(5x + 6y)^2$
12. $(11m + 7n)^2$
13. $\left(\frac{1}{2}a + b\right)^2$
14. $\left(\frac{1}{3}x + y\right)^2$
15. $\left(\frac{4}{3}x - 2y\right)^2$
16. $\left(\frac{3}{4}a - 2b\right)^2$
17. $(0.7x - 1.1)^2$
18. $(0.3a - 2.5)^2$
19. $(1.1x + y)^2$
20. $(3.1 + 2y)^2$
21. $(a^2 - 3b^3)^2$
22. $(x^3 - 5y^2)^2$
23. $(3x + 5)(3x - 5)$
24. $(8a + 2b)(8a - 2b)$

25. $(3.2x^2 - 1.4y)^2$

26. $(1.8a^2 - 2.3y^2)^2$

27. $\left(\frac{1}{3}a + \frac{3}{2}b\right)\left(\frac{1}{3}a - \frac{3}{2}b\right)$

28. $\left(\frac{4}{3}x^2 - y\right)\left(\frac{4}{3}x^2 + y\right)$

29. $(7a^2 - b)^2$

30. $(8x^2 - 3y)^2$

31. $(3a^2 + b)^2$

32. $(4x^3 - 3y^2)^2$

33. $(6a^3 - a^2)^2$

34. $\left(\frac{3}{5}x^2 - \frac{2}{5}y\right)^2$

35. $\left(\frac{1}{4}a^2 - \frac{1}{3}b^3\right)^2$

36. $(0.2a^3 + 0.1b^2)^2$

37. $(1.3x^2 + 2.1y^3)^2$

38. $(x^{2a} + y^{2a})^2$

39. $(x^{3n} - y^{2n})^2$

40. $(a^{2n} - b^{5n})(a^{2n} - b^{5n})$

41. $(x^{2n} + y^n)(x^{2n} - y^n)$

42. $(a^{3n} - b^{5n})(a^{3n} + b^{5n})$

43. $(x^{3n} + y^{5n})(x^{3n} + y^{5n})$

Challenge

Multiply.

44. $(a + b)^4$

45. $(2x - y)^4$

46. $(3m + 2n)^4$

47. $(a + b)^5$

48. $(a - b)^5$

49. $(x - 2y)^3$

50. $(2x - 3y)^4$

51. $\left(\frac{1}{2}x + y\right)^3$

52. $(0.3m - n)^4$

Using Calculators _____ The Store and Recall Keys

Many calculators have keys labeled STO and RCL. The key labeled STO is the store key. When you enter a number and then press this key, the number is *stored* in the memory of the calculator.

The key labeled RCL is the recall key. When you press this key, the calculator retrieves a stored number from the memory and displays it.

The store and recall keys are helpful when evaluating expressions.

Example: Evaluate $5 - 4x^2$ when x is 7.29.

First, store 7.29.

Some calculators have different labels for store. and recall keys.

ENTER: 7.29 $\boxed{\text{STO}}$

DISPLAY: 7.29

Then evaluate the expression.

ENTER: 5 $\boxed{-}$ 4 $\boxed{\times}$ $\boxed{\text{RCL}}$ $\boxed{x^2}$ $\boxed{=}$

DISPLAY: 5   4   7.29 53.1441 −207.5764

When x is 7.29, the value of $5 - 4x^2$ is -207.5764.

Exercises

Evaluate each expression for the given value.

1. $2 - 3x^2$, when $x = 1.03$

2. $-6 - 7a$, when $a = 0.358$

3. $2a^2 + 5a - 7$, when $a = 3.81$

4. $4c^2 + c - 9$, when $c = -0.006$

5. $(7 - x)^2$, when $x = -0.007$

6. $7 - x^2$, when $x = -0.007$

6-6 Solving Equations

Many equations contain polynomials that must be added, subtracted, or multiplied before the equation can be solved.

Examples

1 **Solve:** $-8 - (9 - 4m) = 15$

$$-8 - (9 - 4m) = 15$$
$$-8 - 9 + 4m = 15 \qquad \text{\textit{Replace each term in the parentheses}}$$
$$-17 + 4m = 15 \qquad \text{\textit{with its additive inverse.}}$$
$$-17 + 17 + 4m = 15 + 17$$
$$4m = 32$$
$$\frac{4m}{4} = \frac{32}{4}$$
$$m = 8$$

The solution is 8.   *Check this result.*

2 **Solve:** $5(x - 3) + 3x = 8(9 - x) + 21$

$$5(x - 3) + 3x = 8(9 - x) + 21$$
$$5x - 15 + 3x = 72 - 8x + 21$$
$$8x - 15 = 93 - 8x$$
$$8x + 8x - 15 + 15 = 93 + 15 - 8x + 8x$$
$$16x = 108$$
$$\frac{16x}{16} = \frac{108}{16}$$
$$x = 6.75$$

The solution is 6.75.   *Check this result.*

3 **Solve:** $x(x - 3) + 4x - 3 = 8x + 4 + x(3 + x)$

$$x(x - 3) + 4x - 3 = 8x + 4 + x(3 + x)$$
$$x^2 - 3x + 4x - 3 = 8x + 4 + 3x + x^2$$
$$x^2 + x - 3 = x^2 + 11x + 4$$
$$x - 3 = 11x + 4 \qquad \text{\textit{Subtract } } x^2 \text{ \textit{from both}}$$
$$x - 11x - 3 + 3 = 11x - 11x + 4 + 3 \qquad \text{\textit{sides of the equation.}}$$
$$-10x = 7$$
$$\frac{-10x}{-10} = \frac{7}{-10}$$
$$x = -\frac{7}{10} \text{ or } -0.7$$

The solution is -0.7.   *Check this result.*

Exploratory Exercises

Simplify.

1. $3x + 4x - 5 - 6$
2. $12 - 3y + 12y - 23$
3. $3y + 5y - 8 - 34$
4. $17 - (3a + 4) - 6a$
5. $6y - 8y + 34 - 34y$
6. $8r + 34 + 39r - 8r$
7. $12(q + 4) - 2q$
8. $5(x - 3) + 22 - 8x$
9. $-3(x - 12) + 5(x - 23)$
10. $-9(9 - y) - 8(12 - y) + 23$

Written Exercises

Solve each equation.

1. $3x + 8x - 7 = 21x - 5$
2. $9x - 8 + 4x = 7x + 16$
3. $4y + 8y - 7 = 30y + 19$
4. $8y + 16 + 8y = 21 - 9y$
5. $-8 + 12a = 14a - 23 + 5a$
6. $7a + 23 - 12a = 34 + 23a$
7. $-9a + 34 - 2a = 28 - 5a + 27$
8. $9a - 11 = 23 + 24a - 27a$
9. $11(a - 3) + 5 = 2a + 44$
10. $-3(2a - 12) + 48 = 3a - 3$
11. $26 + 4(3a - 5) = 14a - 15$
12. $-13 + 3(3a + 11) = -33 - 3a$
13. $57 + 2a = 3a - 5(a - 9)$
14. $29 - 3a = 2(3a - 4) + 3$
15. $3a - 35 = 4(a + 12)$
16. $13 - 3a = 23(2a - 3)$
17. $2(5w - 12) = 6(-2w + 3) + 2$
18. $-11(3a - 4) = -3(-4a - 14)$
19. $-6(12 - 2w) = 7(-2 - 3w)$
20. $15(3a - 4) = -4(3a - 3)$
21. $-5(2x - 13) + 12 = 3(2x - 5)$
22. $7(x - 12) = 13 + 5(3x - 4)$
23. $\frac{1}{2}(2x - 34) = \frac{2}{3}(6x - 27)$
24. $\frac{3}{4}(8z - 12) = \frac{5}{6}(12z - 18)$
25. $19 - (2y + 3) = 2(y + 3) + y$
26. $2(a + 2) + 3a = 13 - (2a + 2)$
27. $x(x + 2) + 3x = x(x - 3)$
28. $w(w + 12) = w(w + 14) + 12$
29. $a(a - 6) + 2a = 3 + a(a - 2)$
30. $q(2q + 3) + 20 = 2q(q - 3)$
31. $x(x + 8) - x(x + 3) - 23 = 3x + 11$
32. $y(y - 12) + y(y + 2) + 25 = 2y(y + 5) - 15$

Challenge

Solve each equation for x or y.

33. $2x = 5a$
34. $4aby = 8a^2bc$
35. $30b^2c^2d = 10bc^2y$
36. $y - 2a = 0$
37. $4n + 3y = 2m$
38. $ax + 3 = b$
39. $2x - 7 = 8 + a$
40. $2y + b = 3 - 5y$
41. $7ax - 2d = 3ax + 6d$
42. $4x + 5mn = 7mn + 2x$
43. $by - c = a - d$
44. $3(y - 2a) = 24a$
45. $a(x + b) = 3ab + 5$
46. $2(3a - 2x) = 5a + x$
47. $4(y + 3a) = 4a - y$

6-7   Problem Solving: Perimeter and Area

Recall that a **polygon** is a closed plane figure formed by line segments. The **perimeter** of a polygon is the sum of the lengths of its sides. Some common units of length are inches (in.), feet (ft), yards (yd), centimeters (cm), and meters (m).

Example

1   **In a certain isosceles triangle the third side is 3 inches shorter than either of the congruent sides. If the perimeter is 69 inches, find the lengths of the sides.**

An isosceles triangle has at least two congruent sides.

Explore   Let the following expressions represent the lengths of the sides.

s *length of each congruent side*

$(s - 3)$ *length of third side*

Plan   Recall that the perimeter of a triangle is the sum of the lengths of its sides. To find these lengths, solve the following equation.

$$\underset{\text{Side}}{\text{First}} + \underset{\text{Side}}{\text{Second}} + \underset{\text{Side}}{\text{Third}} = \underset{\text{the Triangle}}{\text{Perimeter of}}$$

Solve

$$s + s + (s - 3) = 69$$
$$3s - 3 = 69$$
$$3s = 72$$
$$s = 24$$

Therefore, the length of each congruent side is 24 inches. The length of the third side is 24 − 3 or 21 inches.

Examine   The sum of the lengths of the three sides is 24 + 24 + 21 or 69 inches.

The **area** of a polygon is the measurement of the region bounded by the polygon. Area is measured in square units. Some common units of area are square inches, square feet, square yards, square centimeters, and square meters.

Example

2 Maria Coulson has a rectangular garden that is 10 feet longer than it is wide. A sidewalk that is 3 feet in width surrounds the garden. The total area of the sidewalk is 396 square feet. What are the dimensions of the garden?

Explore

Let x = width of garden.
$(x + 10)$ = length of garden.

$(x + 6)$ = width of garden and sidewalk.
$(x + 16)$ = length of garden and sidewalk.

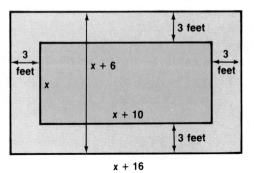

Since the area of a rectangle is the product of its length and width, the following expressions represent area.

$$x(x + 10) \quad \textit{area of garden}$$
$$(x + 6)(x + 16) \quad \textit{area of garden and sidewalk}$$

Plan

To find the dimensions of the garden, solve the following equation.

$$\begin{array}{c} \textit{area of garden} \\ \textit{and sidewalk} \end{array} - \begin{array}{c} \textit{area of} \\ \textit{garden} \end{array} = \begin{array}{c} \textit{area of} \\ \textit{sidewalk} \end{array}$$

Solve

$$(x + 6)(x + 16) - x(x + 10) = 396$$
$$x^2 + 22x + 96 - x^2 - 10x = 396$$
$$12x + 96 = 396$$
$$12x = 300$$
$$x = 25$$

Therefore, the width is 25 feet. The length is $(x + 10)$ or 35 feet.

Examine

To examine the solution, compute the total area of the garden and sidewalk in two ways and compare the results.

$$\textit{area of garden} + \textit{area of sidewalk}$$
$$25 \times 35 \quad + \quad 396 \quad = 1271$$

$$\textit{total length} \times \textit{total width}$$
$$(35 + 6) \quad \times \quad (25 + 6)$$
$$41 \quad \times \quad 31 \quad = 1271$$

Exploratory Exercises

Write an expression that represents each of the following.

1. The length of a rectangle is 5 units more than the width. Find the length if the measure of the width is: **a.** n **b.** $2t$
   c. $2n + 3$ **d.** $t - 1$

2. The length of a rectangle is 2 units less than twice the width. Find the length if the measure of the width is: **a.** t **b.** $2x$
   c. $3a + 2$ **d.** $2t + 1$

Written Exercises

Use an equation to solve each problem.

1. The length of a rectangle is 4 feet more than twice the width. The perimeter is 116 feet. Find the dimensions of the rectangle.

2. A certain triangle has two congruent sides. The third side is 17 cm shorter than either of the equal sides. If the perimeter is 91 cm, what is the length of the third side?

3. To get a square photograph to fit into a square frame, Linda LaGuardia had to trim a 1-inch strip from each side of the photo as shown below. In all, she trimmed off 40 square inches. What were the original dimensions of the photograph?

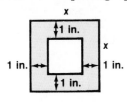

4. A rectangular garden is 5 feet longer than twice its width. It has a sidewalk 3 feet wide on two of its sides, as shown below. The area of the sidewalk is 213 square feet. Find the dimensions of the garden.

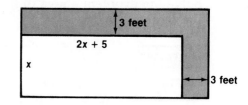

5. The second side of a triangle is twice the length of the first. The third side is 3 cm less than the second side. What are the lengths of the sides if the perimeter is 37 cm?

6. The three sides of a triangle have measures that are consecutive odd numbers. What are the lengths of the sides if the perimeter is 87 m?

7. The length of a rectangle is 20 yards greater than the width. If the length was decreased by 5 yards, and the width increased by 4 yards, the area would remain unchanged. Find the original dimensions of the rectangle.

8. The length of a rectangle is 7 cm less than twice its width. If the length was increased by 11 cm and the width decreased by 6 cm, the area would be decreased by 40 square centimeters. Find the original dimensions of the rectangle.

mini-review

Simplify.

1. $\dfrac{mn^3}{n^6}$ 2. $\left(\frac{1}{4}x^3\right)^2$

Solve.

3. What number is 70% less than 80?

4. Find three consecutive odd integers whose sum is 261.

5. The sum of two consecutive positive even integers is at most 10. What are the integers?

Challenge

9. Mr. Herrera had a concrete sidewalk built on three sides of his yard as shown at the right. The yard measures 24 by 42 feet. The longer walk is 3 feet wide. The price of the concrete was $22 per square yard, and the total bill was $902. What is the width of the walk on the remaining two sides?

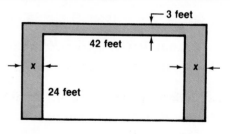

6-8 Problem Solving: Simple Interest

Anita Seltzer deposited an amount of money in the bank at 7% annual interest. After 6 months, she received $52.50 interest. How much money had Anita deposited in the bank?

The formula $I = Prt$ is used to solve **simple interest** problems such as the one above. In the formula, I represents interest, P represents the amount of money invested or principal, r represents the annual interest rate, and t represents time in years.

Examples

1 Solve the problem above to find out how much money Anita had deposited in the bank.

 Let P = amount of money Anita deposited.

 $I = Prt$
$52.50 = P(0.07)\left(\frac{1}{2}\right)$ *Change 7% to 0.07. Change 6 months to $\frac{1}{2}$ year.*

Solve $52.50 = 0.035\,P$
$1500 = P$

Anita had deposited $1500 in the bank.

Examine   When P is 1500, I is $(1500)(0.07)\left(\frac{1}{2}\right)$ or $52.50.

2 Marilyn Mallinson invested $15,000, part at 12% annual interest and the balance at 15% annual interest. Last year she earned $1995 in interest. How much money did she invest at each rate?

Let n = amount of principal invested at 12%.
$(15,000 - n)$ = amount of principal invested at 15%.

Since $I = Prt$, the following expressions represent the interest earned on each portion of the investment.

Interest on 12% investment   Interest on 15% investment
$I = n \cdot 0.12 \cdot 1$ $I = (15,000 - n) \cdot 0.15 \cdot 1$
$\quad = 0.12n$ $\quad = 2250 - 0.15n$

Use the following equation to find the amount of money invested at each rate.

Interest at 12% + Interest at 15% = Total Interest

$$0.12n + 2250 - 0.15n = 1995$$
$$-0.03n = -255$$
$$n = 8500$$

Therefore, Marilyn invested $8500 at 12% and $(15,000 - n)$ or $6500 at 15%.

Exploratory Exercises

Use $I = Prt$ to find the missing quantity.

1. Find I, if $P = \$8,000$, $r = 6\%$, and $t = 1$ year.

2. Find I, if $P = \$5,000$, $r = 12\frac{1}{2}\%$, and $t = 5$ years.

3. Find t, if $I = \$1890$, $P = \$6000$, and $r = 9\%$.

4. Find t, if $I = \$2160$, $P = \$6,000$, and $r = 8\%$.

5. Find r, if $I = \$2430$, $P = \$9,000$, and $t = 2$ years, 3 months.

6. Find r, if $I = \$780$, $P = \$6500$, and $t = 1$ year.

7. Find P, if $I = \$756$, $r = 9\%$, and $t = 3\frac{1}{2}$ years.

8. Find P, if $I = \$196$, $r = 10\%$ and $t = 7$ years.

9. Find r, if $I = \$3,487.50$, $P = \$6,000$, and $t = 3$ years, 9 months.

10. Find t, if $I = \$3528$, $P = \$8,400$, and $r = 10\frac{1}{2}\%$.

Written Exercises

Solve each problem.

1. Michele Limotta invested $10,000 for one year, part at 8% annual interest and the balance at 12% annual interest. Her total interest for the year was $944. How much money did she invest at each rate?

2. Steve Devine invested $7,200 for one year, part at 10% annual interest and the balance at 14% annual interest. His total interest for the year was $960. How much money did he invest at each rate?

3. Fred Ferguson invested $5,000 for one year, part at 9% annual interest and the balance at 12% annual interest. The interest from the investment at 9% was $198 more than the interest from the investment at 12%. How much money did he invest at 9%?

4. Angela Raimondi wants to invest $8500, part at 14% annual interest and part at 12% annual interest. If she wants to earn the same amount of interest from each investment, how much should she invest at 14%? (Answer to the nearest cent.)

5. In one year, Charlotte earned the same interest from an investment at 8% annual interest as an investment at 12% annual interest. She had invested $1500 more in the 8% account. How much money did she have invested at 12%?

6. John and Inger Johnson have $8000 to invest. They want to earn $1050 interest for the year. Money can be invested at annual interest rates of either 12% or 15%. What is the minimum amount at 15%, with the balance at 12%, that will give $1050 in interest?

7. Charlie and Bonnie Hall have invested $2500 at 10% annual interest. They have $6000 more to invest. At what rate must they invest the $6000 to have a total annual interest of $1120?

8. Ken Bauman invested $7525, part at 16% annual interest and the balance at 11% annual interest. He earned twice as much interest from the 11% investment as from the 16% investment. How much money did he have invested at 11%?

Del Vargas has a checking account. He records his checks and deposits in the check register below. To find his balance, Del adds any deposits to his previous balance and subtracts the checks he has written.

CHECK NO.	DATE	CHECK ISSUED TO	AMOUNT OF DEPOSIT	AMOUNT OF CHECK	BALANCE	
					35.72	← to previous balance
—	11/10	Deposit	115.00		150.72	← add deposits
428	11/12	S.E. Electric		25.50	125.22	← subtract checks
429	11/12	Star Oil Co.		21.35		
430	11/19	Kelly's Casuals		42.14		
431	11/23	Photo Journal Inc		6.50		
432	11/25	Palmer's Market		29.83		
—	11/25	Deposit	119.75			
433	11/28	Central Loan		90.00		

Each month Del receives a bank statement along with his canceled checks and deposit slips. The statement shows which checks and deposits the bank has processed. Unprocessed checks and deposits are said to be outstanding. Parts of the statement are shown below.

ENDING BALANCE
$31.90

CHECK NO.	AMOUNT
CHECKS	
428	25.50
429	21.35
430	42.14
432	29.83
DEPOSITS	
	115.00

Del must bring his statement and register ending balances into agreement. To the bank's ending balance, he adds any outstanding deposits. Then he subtracts any outstanding checks or service charges. This number should equal the ending balance in Del's check register.

Exercises

1-6. In Del's check register, find the balance after each check or deposit is made.

7. What checks and deposits are outstanding?

8. Bring the ending balance (from Exercise 6) into agreement with the bank balance.

6-9 Problem Solving: Uniform Motion

When an object moves at a constant speed, or rate, it is said to be in **uniform motion**. The formula $d = rt$ is used to solve uniform motion problems. In the formula, d represents distance, r represents rate, and t represents time. When solving uniform motion problems, it is often helpful to draw a diagram and to organize relevant information in a chart.

In the formula, r can represent an <u>average</u> rate instead of a constant rate.

Examples

1 **Manuel Fernandez rides his bicycle at a speed of 8 mph (miles per hour). How long will it take him to ride 28 miles?**

 Explore Let t = the time it takes Manuel to ride 28 miles

Plan
$$d = rt$$
$$28 = 8t$$

Solve
$$3\tfrac{1}{2} = t$$

Manuel will take $3\tfrac{1}{2}$ hours to ride 28 miles.

Examine When t is $3\tfrac{1}{2}$, d is $8 \cdot 3\tfrac{1}{2}$ or 28 miles.

2 **Dan and Donna Wyatt leave their home in Chatsworth at the same time. They travel in opposite directions. Dan travels at 80 km/h (kilometers per hour) and Donna travels at 72 km/h. In how many hours will they be 760 km apart?**

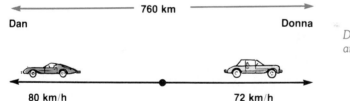

Draw a diagram to help analyze the problem.

Let t represent the number of hours.

Organize the information in a chart.

	r	$\cdot\ t$	$=\ d$
Dan	80	t	$80t$
Donna	72	t	$72t$

Dan travels $80t$ km.
Donna travels $72t$ km.

They travel a total of 760 km.

Dan's distance + Donna's distance = Total distance
$$80t \quad + \quad 72t \quad = 760$$
$$152t = 760$$
$$t = 5$$

In 5 hours, Dan and Donna will be 760 km apart. *Examine this solution.*

Example

3 **At 8:00 A.M. Peggy leaves home driving at 35 mph. A half hour later, Doug discovers that she left her briefcase, so he drives 50 mph to catch up with her. If Doug is delayed 15 minutes with a flat tire, at what time will he catch up to Peggy?**

Let x = the time Peggy travels until Doug arrives

	r ·	t =	d
Peggy	35	x	$35x$
Doug	50	$\left(x - \frac{3}{4}\right)$	$50\left(x - \frac{3}{4}\right)$

Peggy travels x hours.

Doug starts $\frac{1}{2}$ hour later and is delayed for $\frac{1}{4}$ hour. Doug travels $\left(x - \frac{3}{4}\right)$ hours.

Peggy and Doug travel the same distance.

$$35x = 50\left(x - \frac{3}{4}\right)$$
$$35x = 50x - \frac{75}{2}$$
$$-15x = -\frac{75}{2}$$
$$x = 2\frac{1}{2}$$

Peggy has been traveling for $2\frac{1}{2}$ hours when Doug catches up to her.

Doug catches up to Peggy at 8 A.M. + $2\frac{1}{2}$ hours or 10:30 A.M.

Exploratory Exercises

Use $d = rt$ to answer each question.

1. Pat is driving 80 km/h. How far will she travel: **a.** in 2 hours? **b.** in 6 hours? **c.** in h hours?

2. Bob is driving 40 mph. How far will he travel: **a.** in 3 hours? **b.** in $4\frac{1}{2}$ hours? **c.** in 15 minutes? **d.** in k minutes?

3. Marilyn traveled 240 miles. What was her rate if she made the trip: **a.** in 6 hours? **b.** in t hours?

4. Juan traveled 270 miles. What was his rate if he made the trip: **a.** in 5 hours? **b.** in x hours?

5. Rudy rode his bicycle 72 km. How long did it take him if his rate was: **a.** 9 km/h? **b.** 18 km/h?

6. Patsy traveled 360 miles. How long did it take her if her rate was: **a.** 40 mph? **b.** 30 mph? **c.** x mph?

Written Exercises

Solve each problem. Use charts and diagrams if necessary.

1. Two trains leave Bridgeport at the same time, one traveling north, the other south. The first train travels at 40 mph and the second at 30 mph. In how many hours will the trains be 245 miles apart?

2. Ike and Mike leave home traveling on their bicycles in opposite directions. Mike travels 10 km/h and Ike travels 12 km/h. In how many hours will they be 110 kilometers apart?

3. Rosita drives from Boston to Cleveland, a distance of 616 miles. Her rest, gasoline, and food stops amount to 2 hours. What was her rate if the trip took 16 hours?

4. At the same time Kris leaves Washington, D.C. for Detroit, Amy leaves Detroit for Washington, D.C. The distance between the cities is 510 miles. Amy drives 5 mph faster than Kris. How fast is Kris driving if they pass each other in 6 hours?

5. Two cyclists are traveling in the same direction on the same course. One travels 20 mph and the other 14 mph. After how many hours will they be 15 miles apart?

6. Art leaves at 10:00 A.M., traveling at 50 mph. At 11:30 A.M., Jennifer starts in the same direction at 45 mph. When will they be 100 miles apart?

7. Boat A leaves the pier at 9:00 A.M., at 8 knots (nautical miles per hour). A half hour later, Boat B leaves the same pier in the same direction traveling at 10 knots. At what time will Boat B overtake Boat A?

8. Bob is driving 40 mph. After Bob has driven 30 miles, Jack starts driving in the same direction. At what rate must Jack drive to catch up to Bob in 5 hours?

9. An express train travels 80 km/h from Wheaton to Whitfield. A passenger train, traveling 48 km/h, takes 2 hours longer for the same trip. How far apart are Wheaton and Whitfield?

10. Farmer Brown drives to town at 36 mph and returns at 48 mph. If his total driving time is $3\frac{1}{2}$ hours, how far is his home from town?

11. Two airplanes leave Dallas at the same time and fly in opposite directions. One plane travels 80 mph faster than the other. After three hours, they are 2940 miles apart. What is the rate of each plane?

12. Jackson runs a 440 yard run in 55 seconds and Owen runs it in 88 seconds. To have Jackson and Owen finish at the same time, how many yards headstart should Owen be given?

13. At 1:30 P.M., a plane leaves Tucson for Baltimore, a distance of 2240 miles. The plane flies 280 mph. A second plane leaves Tucson at 2:15 P.M., and is scheduled to land in Baltimore 15 minutes before the first plane. At what rate must the second plane travel to arrive on schedule?

14. Sherry leaves Columbus, Ohio, on a train traveling 70 mph to Dallas. Twelve hours later, Don leaves Columbus by plane traveling 500 mph to Dallas. If Columbus and Dallas are 1050 miles apart, will Don arrive before or after Sherry?

Challenge

15. Two trains are 240 miles apart traveling toward each other on parallel tracks. One travels 35 mph and the other travels 45 mph. At the front of the faster train is a bee that can fly 75 mph. Assume that the bee can change direction instantaneously. It flies from one train to the other until the trains pass each other. When the trains pass, what distance has the bee flown?

Compound Interest

Suppose you have deposited $1000 in a savings account that pays 7.5% interest compounded annually. If you do not withdraw or deposit any additional money to the account, in how many years will your money double?

The formula $I = Prt$ is used to solve this problem:
$$I = Prt$$
$$I = 1000 \cdot 0.075 \cdot 1$$
$$I = 75$$

The interest earned after 1 year is $75. The new principal is $1075. This procedure is now repeated using $1075 as the principal and continues until the principal is greater than $2000.

Certainly you could solve the problem with a calculator, but a computer has the advantage of performing the operations very quickly. Use this BASIC program to determine in how many years your money will double.

```
10   PRINT "ENTER THE PRINCIPAL, THE RATE AS A DECIMAL,
     AND THE TIME IN YEARS"
20   INPUT P,R,T        When interest is compounded annually, T = 1.
30   LET DEP = P        DEP is the amount deposited.
40   LET Y = 0
50   PRINT "YEAR", "PRINCIPAL"
60   LET I = P * R * T      Line 60 calculates the interest.
70   LET P = P + I          Line 70 adds interest to the principal.
80   LET Y = Y + T          Line 80 keeps a count of the years.
90   PRINT Y, "$";P
100  IF P > 2 * DEP THEN 120
110  GOTO 60
120  PRINT "IT TOOK ";Y;" YEARS TO DOUBLE YOUR MONEY"
130  END
```

Exercises

1. If $P = \$1000$, $r = 7.5\%$, and $t = 1$, in how many years will your money double?

2. If $P = \$1000$, $r = 10\%$, and $t = 1$, in how many years will your money double?

3. Run the program several times using $P = \$1000$ and $t = 1$, but vary the rate of interest. What is the relationship between the interest rate and the number of years it takes to double the principal?

4. If interest is compounded semiannually, $t = 0.5$. In how many years would your money double if $P = 1000$, $r = 10\%$ and $t = 0.5$?

5. Run the program several times using $P = \$1000$ and $r = 10\%$, but vary the time, t. What is the relationship between t and the number of years it takes to double the principal?

Vocabulary

polynomial (175)
binomial (175)
trinomial (175)
degree (175)
ascending order (176)
descending order (176)
FOIL method (185)

square of a sum (190)
square of a difference (190)
difference of squares (191)
perimeter (195)
area (195)
simple interest (198)
uniform motion (201)

Chapter Summary

1. The degree of a monomial is the sum of the exponents of its variables. The degree of a nonzero constant is 0. (175)

2. Expressions like $8x + y$, $3x^2 + 2x + 4$, and $5 - 3y + 5xy^2$ are called polynomials. (175)

3. A polynomial is an expression that can be written as a sum of monomials. A polynomial with two terms is called a binomial. A polynomial with three terms is called a trinomial. (175)

4. The degree of a polynomial is the greatest of the degrees of its terms. (176)

5. The terms of a polynomial are usually arranged so that the powers of one variable are in ascending or descending order (176)

6. The same properties used to simplify expressions can be used to add polynomials. (178)

7. To subtract a polynomial from a polynomial, add the additive inverse. (179)

8. To multiply two binomials, find the sum of the products of the **F**irst terms, the **O**uter terms, the **I**nner terms, and the **L**ast terms. This method is called FOIL. (185)

9. Square of a Sum:
   $(a + b)^2 = (a + b)(a + b) = a^2 + 2ab + b^2$. (190)

10. Square of a Difference:
    $(a - b)^2 = (a - b)(a - b) = a^2 - 2ab + b^2$. (190)

11. Product of a Sum and a Difference:
    $(a + b)(a - b) = a^2 - b^2$. (191)

12. The formula $I = Prt$ is used to solve simple interest problems. (198)

13. The formula $d = rt$ is used to solve uniform motion problems. (201)

Chapter Review

6-1 Arrange the terms of each polynomial so that the powers of x are in descending order.

1. $3x^4 - x + x^2 - 5$

2. $ax^2 - 5x^3 + a^2x - a^3$

6-2 Add or subtract.

3. $(2x^2 - 5x + 7) - (3x^3 + x^2 + 2)$

4. $(x^2 - 6xy + 7y^2) + (3x^2 + xy - y^2)$

5. $(x^2 - 5x + 3) - (3x - 4)$

6. $\left(-\frac{1}{2}x^2 - \frac{1}{3}x + 2\right) + \left(\frac{3}{2}x^2 + \frac{1}{3}x - 4\right)$

6-3 Multiply. Simplify when possible.

7. $7xy(x^2 + 4xy - 8y^2)$

8. $x(3x - 5) + 7(x^2 - 2x + 9)$

9. $4x^2(x + 8) - 3x(2x^2 - 8x + 3) + 3(x^3 - 7x + 1)$

6-4 Multiply.

10. $(x + 5)(3x - 2)$

11. $(4x - 3)(x + 4)$

12. $(x - 4)(x^2 + 5x - 7)$

13. $\left(\frac{1}{2}a + 1\right)\left(\frac{3}{4}a^2 - 2a + 4\right)$

6-5 Multiply.

14. $(x - 6)(x + 6)$

15. $(5x - 3y)(5x + 3y)$

16. $(4x + 7)^2$

17. $(8x - 5)^2$

6-6 Solve each equation.

18. $4a + 9a - 7 = 14a + 6$

19. $4 + 6x = 2(4x - 2)$

Solve each problem.

6-7 20. Bill McClure is making a picture frame whose length will be 4 in. greater than its width. The frame will have a uniform width of 2 in. If the area of the frame will be 192 square inches, what will the inside dimensions of the picture frame be?

21. The sum of two congruent sides of a certain triangle is 22 in. greater than the base. If the perimeter is 50 inches, what is the length of each congruent side?

6-8 22. Brenda Smith invested $8000 for one year, part at 8% and the remainder at 12%. Her total interest for the year was $744. How much money did she invest at each rate?

23. Francie earned $786 interest on a one year investment earning 15% annual interest. How much money did Francie invest?

6-9 24. At 8:00 A.M., Alan drove west at 35 mph. At 9:00 A.M., Winnie drove east from the same point at 42 mph. When will they be 266 miles apart?

25. Karen leaves home driving 32 mph. A half hour later, her sister Gail drives 40 mph to catch up to her. When will Gail catch up to Karen?

Arrange the terms of each polynomial so that the powers of x are in descending order.

1. $5x^2 - 3 + x^3 + 5x$

2. $5 - xy^3 + x^3y^2 - x^2$

Simplify each of the following.

3. $(a + 5)(a - 5)$

4. $(2x - 5)(7x + 3)$

5. $(3a^2 + 3)[2a - (-6)]$

6. $3x^2y^3(2x - xy^2)$

7. $-4xy(5x^2 - 6xy^3 + 2y^2)$

8. $(4x^2 - y^2)(4x^2 + y^2)$

9. $\left(\frac{1}{2}x + 4\right)\left(\frac{1}{2}x + 3\right)$

10. $(0.2a - 0.4)^2$

11. $0.3b(0.4b^2 - 0.7b + 4)$

12. $(2a^2b + b^2)^2$

13. $x^2(x - 8) - 3x(x^2 - 7x + 3) + 5(x^3 - 6x^2)$

14. $a^2(a + 5) + 7a(a^2 + 8) - 7(a^3 - a + 2)$

Solve each equation.

15. $5y - 8 - 13y = 12y + 6$

16. $3(4m + 5) = 6m - 9$

Solve each problem.

17. The length of a rectangle is 3 inches less than twice the width. The perimeter is 84 inches. Find the dimensions of the rectangle.

18. The length of a rectangle is eight times its width. If the length was decreased by 10 meters and the width was decreased by 2 meters, the area would be decreased by 162 square meters. Find the original dimensions.

19. Peggy invested $5,000 for one year. Maureen also invested $5,000 for one year. Maureen's account earned interest at a rate of 10% per year. At the end of the year, Maureen's account earned $125 more than Peggy's account. What was the rate of interest on Peggy's account?

20. The second side of a triangle is twice the length of the first side. The length of the third side is 12 inches more than the length of the first side. If the perimeter is 304 inches, what is the length of each side?

21. Two cyclists start toward each other from two towns that are 96 miles apart. One cyclist rides at 18 mph and the other rides at 14 mph. In how many hours will they meet?

22. Joe invested $5000 for one year at 9% interest. Harry invested some money at the same time at 8% interest. At the end of the year, Joe and Harry together had earned $810 in interest. How much money did Harry invest?

Cumulative Review

1. Evaluate $3b^3y$ if $b = -4$ and $y = -\frac{4}{3}$.

State the property shown.

2. If $a = 6 + 1$ and $6 + 1 = b$ then $a = b$.

3. $12x^2 + 4xy = 4x(3x + y)$

4. $(4 + x) + 6 = 4 + (x + 6)$

Simplify.

5. $4a + 3(a + 4)$

Find each sum or difference.

6. $-21 + 13$

7. $\frac{3}{5} + \left(-\frac{3}{10}\right)$

8. $-21 + (-5) + (-18)$

9. $-13.4 - 14.3$

Solve.

10. $5 + a = 17$

11. $-13 = -42 - p$

Simplify.

12. $-3(-6) - 6(-5)$

13. $\dfrac{-\frac{3}{5}}{9}$

Solve.

14. $\frac{3}{5}x = -8$

15. $7a - 5 = 30$

16. $7 = 3 + 4(m - 1)$

17. 48 is what percent of 144?

18. Graph the solution set of the inequality $x \geq -3$ on a number line.

Solve each inequality.

19. $2a < a + 3$

20. $-16r \geq -48$

21. $10y - 3(y + 4) \leq 0$

22. Which is a better buy, a gallon of milk for $1.67 or a half-gallon of milk for $0.96?

23. Write the following compound sentence without *and*: $x > 4$ and $x \leq 7$.

24. Solve: $|x + 4| \leq 1$

Simplify.

25. $(2r^2s)(8rs^3)$

26. $(4a^2b^3)^3$

27. y^{-4}

28. $\dfrac{52m^8}{14m^5}$

29. Express 983,000,000 in scientific notation.

30. Find the degree of $27x^2 + 4xy - 13y^3$.

Simplify.

31. $(4x^2 - 7xy + 8y^2) - (3x^2 - 2xy - 5y^2)$

32. $\frac{1}{2}y\left(2y + \frac{1}{y}\right)$

33. $(2x + 5)(3x - 8)$

34. $(3m + 4)^2$

Solve.

35. $4z - 2 + 3z = 2(8 - z)$

Problem Solving

Solve each problem.

36. Find three consecutive integers whose sum is 117.

37. Six times an integer decreased by 5 is greater than 67. What is the least integer that will satisfy this condition?

38. Maggie is 3 years older than Agnes. The sum of their ages is 35. What are their ages now?

39. Mike has 400 mL of 75% solution of silver nitrate. How many milliliters of a 30% solution should be added to obtain a 50% solution?

40. Use $I = Prt$ to find t, if $I = \$1192.50$, $P = \$4500$, and $r = 13\frac{1}{4}\%$.

The test questions on this page deal with ratios, proportions, and percents. The information at the right may help you with some of the questions.

Directions: Choose the best answer. Write A, B, C, or D.

1. 0.7% is the ratio of 7 to

   (A) 100 (B) $\frac{1}{10}$

   (C) $\frac{1}{1000}$ (D) 1000

2. 37.5% of a pound is equivalent to what fractional part of a pound?

   (A) $\frac{37}{100}$ (B) $\frac{3}{8}$ (C) $\frac{37}{99}$ (D) $37\frac{1}{2}$

3. Five-sixths is how many sevenths?

   (A) $5\frac{5}{7}$ (B) $8\frac{2}{5}$ (C) $5\frac{5}{6}$ (D) $4\frac{2}{7}$

4. How many elevenths is 75%?

   (A) $8\frac{1}{4}$ (B) $\frac{3}{4}$ (C) $6\frac{9}{11}$ (D) $\frac{12}{11}$

5. 90% of 270 is 2.7% of

   (A) 729 (B) 900

   (C) 2000 (D) 9000

6. A box contains 60 red, blue, and green pens. If 35% are red and 9 are blue, what percent are green?

   (A) 40 (B) 50 (C) 60 (D) 65

7. Thirty-six of 90 students in a high school graduating class are boys. Nine boys and 18 girls plan to attend college. What percent of the class are girls who plan to attend college?

   (A) 20 (B) 40 (C) 60 (D) $66\frac{2}{3}$

8. 150% of $5c$ is b. What percent of $2b$ is c?

   (A) $5\frac{1}{2}$ (B) $6\frac{2}{3}$ (C) 15 (D) 75

9. Two-fifths times five-sevenths is equal to what number times six-elevenths?

   (A) $\frac{11}{21}$ (B) $\frac{55}{63}$ (C) $\frac{20}{77}$ (D) $\frac{22}{43}$

1. A ratio is an expression that compares two quantities.

   Example: If a container holds 4 pens and 7 pencils, the ratio of pencils to pens is 7:4 or $\frac{7}{4}$.

2. Two equivalent ratios form a proportion. The cross products of a proportion are equal. That is, if $\frac{a}{b} = \frac{c}{d}$, then $ad = bc$.

3. *Percent* means *hundredths*.

   7% means $\frac{7}{100}$ or 7 out of 100.

10. A woman owns $\frac{3}{4}$ of a business. She sells half of her share for $30,000. What is the total value of the business?

    (A) $45,000 (B) $75,000
    (C) $80,000 (D) $112,000

11. On a map, a line segment 1.75 inches long represents 21 miles. What distance in miles is represented by a segment 0.6 inches long?

    (A) 6 (B) 7.2 (C) 12.6 (D) 24.15

12. A cake recipe that serves 6 people calls for 2 cups of flour. How many cups of flour would be needed to bake a smaller cake that serves 4 people?

    (A) $\frac{3}{4}$ (B) 1 (C) $1\frac{1}{4}$ (D) $1\frac{1}{3}$

13. The price of an item was reduced by 10%, then later reduced by 20%. The two reductions were equivalent to a single reduction of

    (A) 15% (B) 28% (C) 30% (D) 70%

14. The discount price for a $50 item is $40. What is the discount price for a $160 item if the rate of discount is $1\frac{1}{2}$ times the rate of discount for the $50 item?

    (A) 20 (B) 48 (C) 96 (D) 112

Factoring

The measure of the area of a certain square garden can be represented by the polynomial $y^2 - 16y + 64$. What is the measure of one side of the garden? To answer questions such as this one, you can use *factoring*. In this chapter, you will learn to factor certain types of polynomials.

7-1   Factors, Greatest Common Factors

If two or more numbers are multiplied, each number is a **factor** of the product. For example, you can express 18 as the product of different pairs of positive integers.

$$18 = 1 \cdot 18 \qquad 18 = 2 \cdot 9 \qquad 18 = 3 \cdot 6$$

The integers 1, 18, 2, 9, 3, and 6 are factors of 18.

Some integers have only two whole-number factors, the integer itself and 1. These integers are called **prime numbers**.

> **A prime number is an integer, greater than 1, whose only whole number factors are 1 and itself.**

Definition of Prime Number

The prime numbers less than 50 are 2, 3, 5, 7, 11, 13, 17, 19, 23, 29, 31, 37, 41, 43, and 47.

> **A composite number is any positive integer, except 1, that is not prime.**

Definition of Composite Number

The first few composite numbers are 4, 6, 8, 9, 10, and 12.

The number 9 is a factor of 18, but 9 is not a *prime* factor because it is not a prime number. When a composite number is expressed as a product of factors that are all prime, the expression is called the **prime factorization** of the number. The prime factorization of 18 is $2 \cdot 3 \cdot 3$ or $2 \cdot 3^2$.

The number 1 is neither prime nor composite.

Example

1   **Express the composite number 84 as a product of prime factors.**

Begin by dividing 84 by the least prime number that is a factor. Then use each prime in order as many times as it is a factor.

$$84 = 2 \cdot 42$$
$$2 \cdot 2 \cdot 21$$
$$2 \cdot 2 \cdot 3 \cdot 7$$

The least prime number that is a factor of 84 is 2.

When all factors are prime the process stops.

The expression $2 \cdot 2 \cdot 3 \cdot 7$ or $2^2 \cdot 3 \cdot 7$ is the prime factorization of 84.

A negative integer may be expressed as a product of a positive integer and -1. For example, to find the factors of -525, first write it as the product of -1 and 525. Then find the prime factors of 525.

$$-525 = -1 \cdot 525$$
$$= -1 \cdot 3 \cdot 5^2 \cdot 7$$

$525 = 3 \cdot 5^2 \cdot 7$

A monomial such as $20a^2b$ may be expressed in factored form as a product of prime numbers and variables with no exponent greater than 1.

$$20a^2b = 2 \cdot 10 \cdot a \cdot a \cdot b$$
$$= 2 \cdot 2 \cdot 5 \cdot a \cdot a \cdot b$$

Two or more integers may have some common factors. Consider the prime factorizations of 90 and 105.

$$90 = 2 \cdot 3 \cdot 3 \cdot 5 \qquad 105 = 3 \cdot 5 \cdot 7$$

The integers 90 and 105 have the common factors 3, 5, and $3 \cdot 5$ or 15. The greatest of these, 15, is called the **greatest common factor** (**GCF**) of 90 and 105.

The number 1 is also a common factor.

> **The greatest common factor of two or more integers is the greatest of the factors common to each integer.**

Definition of Greatest Common Factor.

The GCF of two or more monomials is the product of their common factors, when each monomial is in factored form.

Examples

2 **Find the GCF of 54, 63, and 180.**

$54 = 2 \cdot \textcircled{3} \cdot \textcircled{3} \cdot 3$ *Find the common factors.*

$63 = \textcircled{3} \cdot \textcircled{3} \cdot 7$

$180 = 2 \cdot 2 \cdot \textcircled{3} \cdot \textcircled{3} \cdot 5$

The GCF of 54, 63, and 180 is $3 \cdot 3$, or 9.

3 **Find the GCF of $8a^2b$ and $18a^2b^2c$.**

$8a^2b = \textcircled{2} \cdot 2 \cdot 2 \cdot \textcircled{a} \cdot \textcircled{a} \cdot \textcircled{b}$

$18a^2b^2c = \textcircled{2} \cdot 3 \cdot 3 \cdot \textcircled{a} \cdot \textcircled{a} \cdot \textcircled{b} \cdot b \cdot c$

The GCF of $8a^2b$ and $18a^2b^2c$ is $2a^2b$.

Exploratory Exercises

State whether the second integer is a factor of the first.

1. 16; 8   **2.** 15; 3   **3.** 41; 6   **4.** 55; 11   **5.** 72; 36

State whether each number is prime or composite. If the number is composite, find its prime factorization.

6. 89   **7.** 39   **8.** 24   **9.** 91   **10.** 53

Find the GCF of each pair of numbers.

11. 4, 12	**12.** 10, 15	**13.** 9, 36	**14.** 15, 5	**15.** 11, 22
16. 15, 45	**17.** 20, 30	**18.** 18, 35	**19.** 36, 72	**20.** 16, 18

Written Exercises

Find the prime factorization of each number.

1. 21	**2.** 28	**3.** 60	**4.** 51	**5.** 39
6. 63	**7.** 34	**8.** 72	**9.** 112	**10.** 150
11. 304	**12.** 216	**13.** 300	**14.** 1000	**15.** 1540

Factor each expression. Do not use exponents.

16. -64	**17.** -26	**18.** -240	**19.** -500	**20.** -231
21. $98a^2b$	**22.** $44ab^2c^3$	**23.** $196b^2$	**24.** $756(ab)^3$	**25.** $-102x^3y$

Find the GCF for each of the following.

26. 16, 60	**27.** 15, 50	**28.** -80, 45
29. 29, -58	**30.** 305, 55	**31.** 252, 126
32. 128, 245	**33.** 95, 304	**34.** $7y^2$, $14y^3$
35. $17a$, $34a^2$	**36.** $-12ab$, $4a^2b^2$	**37.** $4xy$, $-6x$
38. 6, 8, 4	**39.** 5, 10, 15	**40.** 16, 24, 30
41. 18, 30, 54	**42.** 24, 84, 168	**43.** 16, 22, 30
44. $50n^4$, $40n^2p^2$	**45.** $20a^2$, $24ab^5$	**46.** $60x^2y^2$, $35xz^3$
47. $12an^2$, $40a^4$	**48.** $56x^3y$, $49ax^2$	**49.** $12mn$, $10mn$, $15mn$
50. $6a^2$, $18b^2$, $9b^3$	**51.** $8b^4$, $5c$, $3a^2b$	**52.** $15abc$, $35a^2c$, $105a$
53. $14a^2b^2$, $18ab$, $2a^3b^3$	**54.** $18a^2b^2$, $6b$, $42a^2b^3$	**55.** $24a^2b$, $28axy$, $36ay$

Excursions in Algebra _____ Sieve of Eratosthenes

Eratosthenes was an early Greek (c. 200 B.C.) who was one of the first to calculate the circumference of the earth. He is also remembered in mathematics for the "sieve of Eratosthenes," a method for finding prime numbers.

To use his method, list the positive integers beginning with 2. Each multiple of a prime is to be crossed out. For example, cross out every second number after 2, every third number after 3, every fifth number after 5, and so on. When the process is finished, the numbers not crossed out are prime. *Begin by crossing out every second number after two.*

2 3 4̸ 5 6̸ 7 8̸ 9 1̸0̸ 11 1̸2̸ 13 1̸4̸ 15 1̸6̸ 17
1̸8̸ 19 2̸0̸ 21 2̸2̸ 23 2̸4̸ 25 2̸6̸ 27 2̸8̸ 29 3̸0̸

Exercises

1. Copy and complete the sieve of Eratosthenes above for integers to 30.
2. List the positive integers from 2 to 100. Use the sieve of Eratosthenes to find the prime numbers between 2 and 100.

7-2 Factoring Using the Distributive Property

The distributive property has been used to multiply a polynomial by a monomial. It can also be used to write a polynomial in factored form.

Multiplying	Factoring
$3(a + b) = 3a + 3b$	$3a + 3b = 3(a + b)$
$x(y - z) = xy - xz$	$xy - xz = x(y - z)$
$3y(4x + 2) = 3y(4x) + 3y(2)$	$12xy + 6y = 3y(4x) + 3y(2)$
$\quad\quad\quad\quad = 12xy + 6y$	$\quad\quad\quad\quad = 3y(4x + 2)$

Examples

1 **Use the distributive property to write $10y^2 + 15y$ in factored form.**

First, find the greatest common factor of $10y^2$ and $15y$.

$10y^2 = 2 \cdot \boxed{5} \cdot \boxed{y} \cdot y$
$\;15y = 3 \cdot \boxed{5} \cdot \boxed{y}$ *The GCF is 5y.*

Then, express each term as a product of the GCF and its remaining factors.

$10y^2 + 15y = 5y(2y) + 5y(3)$
$\quad\quad\quad\quad = 5y(2y + 3)$ *Use the distributive property.*

2 **Factor: $21ab^2 - 33a^2bc$**

$21ab^2 = \boxed{3} \cdot 7 \cdot \boxed{a} \cdot \boxed{b} \cdot b$
$33a^2bc = \boxed{3} \cdot 11 \cdot \boxed{a} \cdot a \cdot \boxed{b} \cdot c$ *The GCF is 3ab.*

Express the terms as products.

$21ab^2 - 33a^2bc = 3ab(7b) - 3ab(11ac)$
$\quad\quad\quad\quad\quad\quad = 3ab(7b - 11ac)$ *Use the distributive property.*

3 **Factor: $12a^5b + 8a^3 - 24a^3c$**

$12a^5b = 2 \cdot 2 \cdot 3 \cdot a \cdot a \cdot a \cdot a \cdot a \cdot b$
$\;\;8a^3 = 2 \cdot 2 \cdot 2 \cdot a \cdot a \cdot a$
$24a^3c = 2 \cdot 2 \cdot 2 \cdot 3 \cdot a \cdot a \cdot a \cdot c$ *The GCF is $4a^3$.*

$12a^5b + 8a^3 - 24a^3c = 4a^3(3a^2b) + 4a^3(2) - 4a^3(6c)$
$\quad\quad\quad\quad\quad\quad\quad\quad = 4a^3(3a^2b + 2 - 6c)$

4 **Factor: $6x^3y^2 + 14x^2y + 2x^2$**

$6x^3y^2 = 2 \cdot 3 \cdot x \cdot x \cdot x \cdot y \cdot y$
$14x^2y = 2 \cdot 7 \cdot x \cdot x \cdot y$
$\;\;2x^2 = 2 \cdot x \cdot x$ *The GCF is $2x^2$.*

$6x^3y^2 + 14x^2y + 2x^2 = 2x^2(3xy^2 + 7y + 1)$

Exploratory Exercises

Find the GCF of the terms in each expression.

1. $3y^2 + 12$
2. $4a + 2b$
3. $5y - 9y^2$
4. $6a + 3b$
5. $9b + 5c$
6. $3a + 6a$
7. $9y^2 + 3y$
8. $11a + 10q$
9. $8x^2 - 4x$
10. $12a^2b + 6a$
11. $7ac - 21a^2$
12. $16c - 21b$
13. $21xyz - xy$
14. $14b^2 - 42c$
15. $42a - 13r$

Written Exercises

Factor each expression.

1. $16x + 4y$
2. $24x^2 + 12y^2$
3. $12xy + 12x^2$
4. $5a^2b + 10ab$
5. $11x + 44x^2y$
6. $16x^2 + 8x$
7. $25a^2b^2 + 30ab^3$
8. $18xy^2 - 24x^2y$
9. $14xy - 18xy^2$
10. $27a^2b + 9b^3$
11. $36a^2b^2 - 12ab$
12. $3a^2b - 6a^2b^2$
13. $14xy^2 + 2xy$
14. $15xy^3 + y^4$
15. $x^5y - x$
16. $29xy - 3x$
17. $17a - 41a^3b$
18. $a + a^4b^3$
19. $3x^2y + 9y^2 + 6$
20. $5a^2 + 10ab - 15b^2$
21. $2a^3b^2 - 16a^2b^3 + 8ab$
22. $3x^3y + 9xy^2 + 36xy$
23. $24x^2y^2 + 12xy + x$
24. $28a^2b^2c^2 + 21a^2bc^2 - 14abc$
25. $12ax + 20bx + 32cx$
26. $a + a^2b + a^3b^3$
27. $ax^3 + 5bx^3 + 9cx^3$
28. $14a^3x + 19a^3y + 11a^3z$
29. $6x^2 - 9xy + 24x^2y^2$
30. $42abc - 12a^2b^2 + 3a^2c^2$
31. $24abx + 12ax^2 + 6x^3$
32. $x^5 + 5x^4 + 3x^2 + 2x$
33. $\frac{1}{2}x^2 - \frac{1}{4}ax$
34. $\frac{2}{3}x + \frac{1}{3}y$
35. $\frac{4}{5}x^2y + \frac{3}{5}y^2$
36. $\frac{2}{5}a - \frac{2}{5}b + \frac{4}{5}c$

Excursions in Algebra _____ Divisibility Rules

Some simple rules can help you determine if a number is divisible by 2, 3, 5, or 10.

If the ones digit is 0, 2, 4, 6, or 8, the number is divisible by 2.
If the ones digit is 0 or 5, the number is divisible by 5.
If the ones digit is 0, the number is divisible by 10.
If the *sum* of the digits is divisible by 3, the number is divisible by 3.

For example, the sum of the digits of 741 is $7 + 4 + 1$ or 12.
741 is divisible by 3 because 12 is divisible by 3.

Exercises

Determine whether each number is divisible by 2, 3, 5, or 10.

1. 44
2. 75
3. 110
4. 123
5. 405
6. 570

You can simplify equations involving area by using the distributive property and factoring. Consider this example.

A deck 3 meters wide is to be built around a swimming pool that is shown in the diagram at the right. In order to determine the amount of material that is needed to build the deck, it is necessary to calculate the area of the deck.

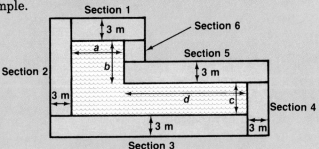

To find the area of the deck, find the sum of the areas of the rectangular regions.

$$\underbrace{3(a + 3)}_{Section\ 1} + \underbrace{3(b + c + 3)}_{Section\ 2} + \underbrace{3(a + d + 3)}_{Section\ 3} + \underbrace{3(c + 3)}_{Section\ 4} + \underbrace{3(d + 3)}_{Section\ 5} + \underbrace{3(b - 3)}_{Section\ 6}$$

Area =

Use the distributive property.
$A = 3a + 9 + 3b + 3c + 9 + 3a + 3d + 9 + 3c + 9 + 3d + 9 + 3b - 9$
Combine like terms.
$A = 6a + 6b + 6c + 6d + 36$
Factor the polynomial.
$A = 6(a + b + c + d + 6)$
The area of the deck can be represented by $A = 6(a + b + c + d + 6)$.

Exercises

For each diagram, write an equation that represents the area of the shaded region.

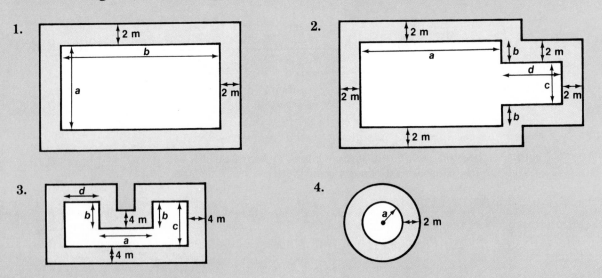

7-3   Factoring Differences of Squares

Consider the two squares that are shown. The area of the larger square is a^2, and the area of the smaller square is b^2.

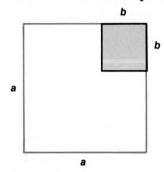

The area $a^2 - b^2$ can be found by subtracting the area of the smaller square from the area of the larger square.

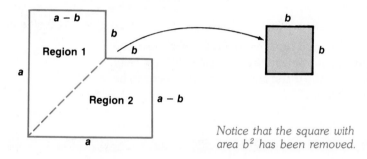

Notice that the square with area b^2 has been removed.

Rearranging these regions as shown below, you can see that $a^2 - b^2$ is equal to the product of $(a - b)$ and $(a + b)$.

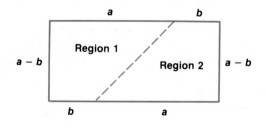

The area of the rectangle is $(a - b)(a + b)$. This is the same as $a^2 - b^2$.

$$a^2 - b^2 = (a - b)(a + b) = (a + b)(a - b)$$

Difference of Squares

You can use the difference of squares to factor binomials of the form $a^2 - b^2$.

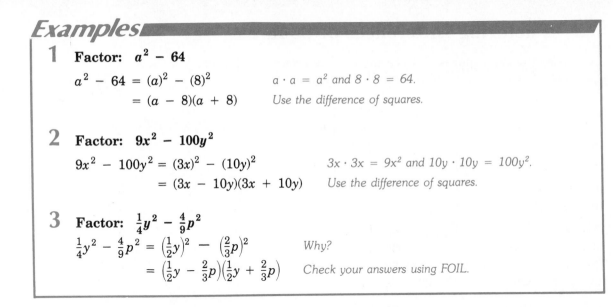

Examples

1 **Factor:** $a^2 - 64$

$$a^2 - 64 = (a)^2 - (8)^2 \qquad a \cdot a = a^2 \text{ and } 8 \cdot 8 = 64.$$
$$= (a - 8)(a + 8) \qquad \textit{Use the difference of squares.}$$

2 **Factor:** $9x^2 - 100y^2$

$$9x^2 - 100y^2 = (3x)^2 - (10y)^2 \qquad 3x \cdot 3x = 9x^2 \text{ and } 10y \cdot 10y = 100y^2.$$
$$= (3x - 10y)(3x + 10y) \qquad \textit{Use the difference of squares.}$$

3 **Factor:** $\frac{1}{4}y^2 - \frac{4}{9}p^2$

$$\frac{1}{4}y^2 - \frac{4}{9}p^2 = \left(\frac{1}{2}y\right)^2 - \left(\frac{2}{3}p\right)^2 \qquad \textit{Why?}$$
$$= \left(\frac{1}{2}y - \frac{2}{3}p\right)\left(\frac{1}{2}y + \frac{2}{3}p\right) \qquad \textit{Check your answers using FOIL.}$$

Sometimes the terms of a binomial have common factors. If so, the GCF should always be factored out before factoring the difference of squares. Occasionally, factoring the difference of squares needs to be used more than once in a problem.

Examples

4 **Factor:** $16x^2 - 36y^2$

$$16x^2 - 36y^2 = 4(4x^2 - 9y^2) \qquad 4 \text{ is the GCF of } 16x^2 \text{ and } 36y^2.$$
$$= 4(2x - 3y)(2x + 3y) \qquad 2x \cdot 2x = 4x^2 \text{ and } 3y \cdot 3y = 9y^2.$$

5 **Factor:** $162a^4 - 32y^8$

$$162a^4 - 32y^8 = 2(81a^4 - 16y^8) \qquad \textit{Why?}$$
$$= 2(9a^2 - 4y^4)(9a^2 + 4y^4) \qquad 9a^2 + 4y^4 \text{ cannot be factored.}$$
$$= 2(3a - 2y^2)(3a + 2y^2)(9a^2 + 4y^4)$$

Exploratory Exercises

State whether each binomial can be factored as the difference of squares.

1. $x^2 - y^2$

2. $a^2 + b^2$

3. $b^2 - 25$

4. $a^2 - 4b^4$

5. $9y^2 + a^2$

6. $25a^2 - 16$

7. $9x^2 - 5$

8. $a - 9$

9. $8c^2 - 7$

10. $36a^2 - 49$

11. $\frac{4}{9}a^2 - \frac{1}{4}$

12. $\frac{16}{25}a^2 + 1$

Written Exercises

Factor each polynomial completely.

1. $a^2 - 9$
2. $x^2 - 49$
3. $4x^2 - 9y^2$
4. $x^2 - 36y^2$
5. $a^2 - 4b^2$
6. $1 - 9y^2$
7. $16a^2 - 9b^2$
8. $3m^2 - 6n^2$
9. $16a^2 - 25$
10. $2a^2 + 18a$
11. $6x^2 + 12$
12. $8x^2 - 12y^2$
13. $2z^2 - 98$
14. $12a^2 - 48$
15. $8x^2 - 18$
16. $45x^2 - 20z^2$
17. $25y^2 - 49z^4$
18. $9x^4 - 25y^4$
19. $17 - 68a^2$
20. $144x^2 - 9y^2$
21. $25a^2x^2 - 1$
22. $4x^2 - 64y^2$
23. $12a^2 - 12$
24. $9x^4 - 16y^2$
25. $36x^2 - 81y^4$
26. $28x^2 - 7$
27. $81 - 9x^2$
28. $-16 + 9x^2$
29. $-9 + 4y^2$
30. $15x^2 - 60y^2$
31. $x^4 - y^4$
32. $a^4 - b^2$
33. $x^4 - 1$
34. $\frac{1}{4}x^2 - 16$
35. $\frac{9}{2}x^2 - \frac{49}{2}y^2$
36. $\frac{2}{3}x^2 - \frac{8}{3}$
37. $x^8 - 1$
38. $(a + b)^2 - m^2$
39. $(x - y)^2 - y^2$
40. $p^2 - (m + n)^2$
41. $a^2 - (b - c)^2$
42. $y^4 - 81$
43. $x^4 - 16$
44. $162a^5 - 32ab^4$
45. $98x^6 - 128y^8$

Challenge

46. Find positive integers m and n such that $m^2 - n^2 = 11$.
47. Find positive integers x and y such that $x^2 - y^2 = 15$.

Using Calculators _____ Solving Equations

You can use your calculator to solve and check equations such as $0.35x + 6.789x = 15$. First, find the sum of 0.35 and 6.789 and store it.

ENTER: .35 $+$ 6.789 $=$ STO   *When you enter .35,*
DISPLAY: 0.35   6.789 7.139   7.139   *the display shows 0.35.*

Then, divide 15 by 7.139. *You are dividing both sides of the equation by 7.139*

ENTER: 15 $\div$ RCL $=$
DISPLAY: 15   7.139   2.1011346

The solution is about 2.101 *Use your calculator to check this solution.*

Exercises

Solve and check each equation.

1. $0.02y + 3.87y = 45$
2. $6.09x + 0.089x = 9$
3. $2.5x + 7.3x - 5.06x = -1$
4. $7.8y + 9.2y - 0.06y = -20$
5. $35 = 56.7a - 60.02a$
6. $75 = 0.008c - 4.2c + 9.01c$

In the metric system, a unit of mass is the gram (g). One gram is defined as the mass of one cubic centimeter of water at its maximum density.

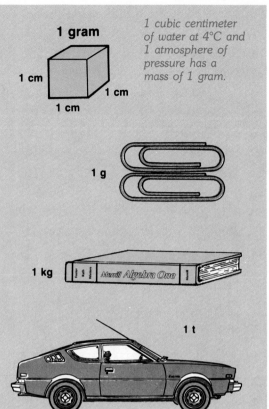

1 gram

1 cm
1 cm
1 cm

1 cubic centimeter of water at 4°C and 1 atmosphere of pressure has a mass of 1 gram.

You can think of a gram as about the mass of two paper clips.

1 g

A gram is too small to use conveniently. Therefore, the kilogram (kg) is used as the basic unit for mass. There are 1000 grams in a kilogram. The mass of this textbook is about one kilogram.

1 kg   Merrill Algebra One

A metric ton (t) equals 1000 kilograms. Shippers measure grain in metric tons. A metric ton is about the mass of a small automobile.

1 t

The milligram (mg) is used to measure very small quantities. One gram equals 1000 milligrams.

Exercises

Would you use gram or kilogram to measure the mass of each object?

1. bag of groceries
2. pencil
3. mouse
4. wrestler
5. suitcase
6. pepper

Complete the following.

7. 3 kg = ___ g
8. 8.5 kg = ___ g
9. 5000 g = ___ kg
10. 6700 g = ___ kg
11. 8 g = ___ mg
12. 6.5 g = ___ mg
13. 3000 mg = ___ g
14. 3900 mg = ___ g
15. 9.52 kg = ___ g
16. 3852 g = ___ kg
17. 3598 mg = ___ g
18. 6.257 g = ___ mg
19. 38.575 kg = ___ g
20. 875 g = ___ kg
21. 575 mg = ___ g
22. 5 t = ___ kg
23. 5300 kg = ___ t
24. 88,000 kg = ___ t
25. 40 mg = ___ kg
26. 260 mg = ___ kg
27. 2 kg = ___ mg
28. 1.93 kg = ___ mg
29. 10 mg = ___ t
30. 10 t = ___ mg

7-4 Perfect Squares and Factoring

Recall $1^2 = 1, 2^2 = 4, 3^2 = 9, 4^2 = 16$, and so on. Numbers such as 1, 4, 9, and 16 are called **perfect squares**. Products of the form $(a + b)^2$ and $(a - b)^2$ are also called perfect squares and these expansions are called **perfect square trinomials**.

You should learn to recognize these patterns.

$$(a + b)^2 = a^2 + 2ab + b^2$$
$$(a - b)^2 = a^2 - 2ab + b^2$$

Perfect Square Trinomials

These patterns can help you factor trinomials such as
$$y^2 + 16y + 64 \text{ and } 4x^2 - 20xy + 25y^2.$$

Finding a Product

$$\begin{aligned}(y + 8)^2 &= y^2 + 2(8)y + (8)^2 \\ &= y^2 + 16y + 64\end{aligned}$$

$$\begin{aligned}(2x &- 5y)^2 \\ &= (2x)^2 - 2(2x)(5y) + (5y)^2 \\ &= 4x^2 - 20xy + 25y^2\end{aligned}$$

Factoring

$$\begin{aligned}y^2 + 16y + 64 &= (y)^2 + 2(8y) + (8)^2 \\ &= (y + 8)^2\end{aligned}$$

$$\begin{aligned}4x^2 &- 20xy + 25y^2 \\ &= (2x)^2 - 2(2x)(5y) + (5y)^2 \\ &= (2x - 5y)^2\end{aligned}$$

To determine if a trinomial can be factored in this way, first decide if it is a perfect square. In other words, decide if it can be written in either the form $a^2 + 2ab + b^2$ or $a^2 - 2ab + b^2$. Study the following examples.

Example

1 **Determine if $x^2 + 22x + 121$ is a perfect square. If it is, factor it.**

To decide if $x^2 + 22x + 121$ is a perfect square, answer each question below.

a. Is x^2 a perfect square? $x^2 = (x)^2$ *Yes*
b. Is 121 a perfect square? $121 = (11)^2$ *Yes*
c. Is the middle term twice
   the product of x and 11? $22x = 2(x)(11)$ *Yes*

Since all three answers are "yes," the trinomial $x^2 + 22x + 121$ is a perfect square. It can be factored as follows.

$$\begin{aligned}x^2 + 22x + 121 &= (x)^2 + 2(x)(11) + (11)^2 \\ &= (x + 11)^2\end{aligned}$$

Examples

2 **Determine if $16a^2 + 72a + 81$ is a perfect square. If it is, factor it.**

    a. Is the first term a square? $16a^2 = (4a)^2$ *Yes*
    b. Is the last term a square? $81 = (9)^2$ *Yes*
    c. Is the middle term twice the
        product of $4a$ and 9? $72a = 2(4a)(9)$ *Yes*

    $16a^2 + 72a + 81$ is a perfect square.

$$16a^2 + 72a + 81 = (4a)^2 + 2(4a)(9) + (9)^2$$
$$= (4a + 9)^2$$

3 **Determine if $4a^2 - 20a + 15$ is a perfect square. If it is, factor it.**

    a. Is the first term a square? $4a^2 = (2a)^2$ *Yes*
    b. Is the last term a square? $15 = (?)^2$ *No*

    $4a^2 - 20a + 15$ is not a perfect square.

4 **Determine if $16x^2 - 26x + 49$ is a perfect square. If it is, factor it.**

    a. Is the first term a square? $16x^2 = (4x)^2$ *Yes*
    b. Is the last term a square? $49 = (7)^2$ *Yes*
    c. Is the middle term 2 times
        the product of $4x$ and 7? $26x \neq 2(4x)(7)$ *No*

    $16x^2 - 26x + 49$ is *not* a perfect square.

5 **Factor $9x^2 - 12xy + 4y^2$.**

    $9x^2 - 12xy + 4y^2$ is a perfect square.   *Why?*
$$9x^2 - 12xy + 4y^2 = (3x)^2 - 2(3x)(2y) + (2y)^2$$
$$= (3x - 2y)^2$$

Exploratory Exercises

Determine whether each trinomial is a perfect square trinomial. If it is, state its factors.

1. $a^2 + 4a + 4$ 2. $b^2 + 14b + 49$ 3. $x^2 - 10x - 100$
4. $y^2 + 10y - 100$ 5. $n^2 - 13n + 36$ 6. $p^2 + 12p + 36$
7. $y^2 - 8y + 10$ 8. $x^2 + 17x + 21$ 9. $4x^2 - 4x + 1$
10. $9y^2 - 10y + 4$ 11. $9b^2 - 6b + 1$ 12. $4a^2 - 20a + 25$

Written Exercises

Factor, if possible.

1. $a^2 + 12a + 36$
2. $b^2 + 10b + 25$
3. $x^2 + 16x + 64$
4. $y^2 + 14y + 49$
5. $4a^2 + 4a + 1$
6. $64b^2 + 16b + 1$
7. $1 - 10a + 25a^2$
8. $1 - 12y + 36y^2$
9. $9a^2 + 6a + 2$
10. $16c^2 - 8c + 49$
11. $25x^2 + 20x + 4$
12. $9a^2 - 24a + 16$
13. $121y^2 + 22y + 1$
14. $81n^2 + 36n + 4$
15. $25b^2 - 30b + 9$
16. $25x^2 - 120x + 144$
17. $64b^2 - 72b + 81$
18. $49m^2 - 126m + 81$
19. $m^2 + 16mn + 64n^2$
20. $25a^2 + 40a + 9$
21. $9x^2 + 24xy + 16y^2$
22. $16p^2 - 40pq + 25q^2$
23. $144p^2 + 72p + 9$
24. $144n^2 + 168n + 49$
25. $64x^2 - 80x + 25$
26. $2x^2 - 20x + 50$
27. $3x^2 + 36x + 108$
28. $3x^2 + 18x + 48$
29. $6x^2 + 18x + 24$
30. $3b^2 - 18bc + 27c^2$
31. $4x^2 + 4xz^2 + z^4$
32. $4x^2 - 28xy^2 + 49y^4$
33. $\frac{1}{4}a^2 + 3a + 9$
34. $\frac{4}{9}b^2 - \frac{16}{3}b + 16$
35. $m^4 + 12m^2n^2 + 36n^4$
36. $16x^2y^2 - 72xy + 81$
37. $9a^2 + \frac{24}{5}a + \frac{16}{25}$
38. $a^2 - \frac{4}{3}a + \frac{16}{36}$

Find the replacement for c that would make a perfect square.

39. $9x^2 + cxy + 49y^2$
40. $16m^2 + cmp + 25p^2$
41. $cx^2 + 28x + 49$
42. $cy^2 + 50y + 25$
43. $4x^2 + 4xy + c$
44. $9a^2 + 24ab + c$
45. $9x^2 - 12xy + c$
46. $64x^2 - 16xy + c$

Challenge

47. What is the length of a side of a square whose area is represented by the expression $x^2 - 20x + 100$?

48. The area of a square is represented by $y^2 + 40y + 400$. What is its perimeter?

mini-review

1. Express 0.00000253 in scientific notation.

Solve.

2. Les is 6 years younger than twice Jim's age. The sum of their ages is 30. What are their ages?

Simplify.

3. $x(2x + 5) - 7(x^2 + 3x - 2)$
4. $(2y^2 + 5y - 3) + (7y^2 - 8y + 9)$
5. $(2y + 5)(3y - 7)$

7-5 Factoring $x^2 + bx + c$

Recall that if two numbers are multiplied, each number is a *factor* of the product. Similarly, if two binomials are multiplied, each binomial is a *factor* of the product.

Use the FOIL method to find the product $(x + 3)(x + 7)$.

$$\begin{array}{ccccc} \text{F} & \text{O} & \text{I} & \text{L} \end{array}$$
$$\begin{aligned} (x + 3)(x + 7) &= x \cdot x + x \cdot 7 + 3 \cdot x + 3 \cdot 7 \\ &= x^2 + 7x + 3x + 3 \cdot 7 \\ &= x^2 + (7 + 3)x + 3 \cdot 7 \\ &= x^2 + 10x + 21 \qquad \text{\textit{21 is the product of 3 and 7.}} \\ &\qquad\qquad\qquad\qquad\quad \text{\textit{10 is the sum of 3 and 7.}} \end{aligned}$$

The binomials $(x + 3)$ and $(x + 7)$ are factors of $x^2 + 10x + 21$.

In general, the product of the binomials $(x + m)$ and $(x + n)$ can be found by using FOIL.

$$\begin{aligned} (x + m)(x + n) &= x^2 + nx + mx + mn \\ &= x^2 + (m + n)x + mn \end{aligned}$$

This pattern can be used to factor certain types of trinomials. For example, to factor $x^2 + 7x + 10$ into the form $(x + m)(x + n)$, find the factors of 10 whose sum is 7. Consider only positive factors of 10 since $(m + n)$ and mn are both positive.

mn = 10
m + n = 7

Factors of 10	Sum of Factors
1, 10	1 + 10 = 11
2, 5	2 + 5 = 7

Since the sum must be 7, the factors are 2 and 5.

$$x^2 + 7x + 10 = (x + 2)(x + 5) \qquad \text{\textit{Check by using FOIL.}}$$

Example

1 **Factor:** $y^2 + 8y + 12$

$y^2 + 8y + 12 = y^2 + (m + n)y + mn \qquad m + n = 8 \text{ and } mn = 12$
Find the factors of 12 whose sum is 8. Consider only positive integers.

Factors of 12	Sum of Factors
1, 12	1 + 12 = 13
2, 6	2 + 6 = 8
3, 4	3 + 4 = 7

The factors are 2 and 6. Therefore, $y^2 + 8y + 12 = (y + 2)(y + 6)$.
Check that $(y + 2)(y + 6) = y^2 + 8y + 12$ by using FOIL.

Example

2 **Factor:** $a^2 - 9a + 18$

$a^2 - 9a + 18 = a^2 + (m + n)a + mn \qquad m + n = (-9)$ and $mn = 18$
Since $(m + n)$ is negative and mn is positive, the factors of 18 must *both* be *negative*. Do you see why?

Factors of 18	Sum of Factors
$-1, -18$	$-1 + (-18) = -19$
$-2, -9$	$-2 + (-9) = -11$
$-3, -6$	$-3 + (-6) = -9$

Therefore, $a^2 - 9a + 18 = (a - 3)(a - 6)$.   *Check by using FOIL.*

Notice that in the trinomial $x^2 + 5x - 6$ the value of c is *negative*. Since $x^2 + 5x - 6$ can be expressed as $x^2 + 5x + (-6)$, the same pattern can be used to factor trinomials in which c is negative.

Examples

3 **Factor:** $x^2 + 5x - 6$

$x^2 + 5x - 6 = x^2 + (m + n)x + mn$ where $m + n = 5$ and $mn = -6$. Since $(m + n)$ is positive and mn is negative, exactly one factor of each pair of factors below must be negative. Do you see why?

Factors of -6	Sum of Factors
$1, -6$	$1 + (-6) = -5$
$-1, 6$	$-1 + 6 = 5$
$2, -3$	$2 + (-3) = -1$
$-2, 3$	$-2 + 3 = 1$

Select the factors -1 and 6. Therefore, $x^2 + 5x - 6 = (x - 1)(x + 6)$.
Check by using FOIL.

4 **Factor:** $a^2 - 3a - 10$

$a^2 - 3a - 10 = a^2 + (m + n)a + mn \qquad m + n = -3$ and $mn = -10$
$2 + (-5) = -3$ and $2(-5) = -10$.

Therefore, $a^2 - 3a - 10 = (a + 2)(a - 5)$.

When the value of c is negative, the factors of a trinomial are a *difference* and a *sum*. For $x^2 + 5x - 6$, the difference is $(x - 1)$ and the sum is $(x + 6)$. For $a^2 - 3a - 10$ the difference is $(a - 5)$ and the sum is $(a + 2)$.

Example

5 **Factor:** $14 + 13x + x^2$

The polynomial $14 + 13x + x^2$ can be written as $x^2 + 13x + 14$.
$x^2 + 13x + 14 = x^2 + (m + n)x + mn$ $m + n = 13$ and $mn = 14$

Factors of 14	Sum of Factors
1, 14	$1 + 14 = 15$
2, 7	$2 + 7 = 9$

Why should you test only positive factors?

There are no factors m and n such that $m + n = 13$ and $mn = 14$.
Therefore, $x^2 + 13x + 14$ cannot be factored using integers.

A polynomial that *cannot* be written as a product of two polynomials is called a **prime polynomial**. In Example 5 the trinomial $x^2 + 13x + 14$ is prime.

Example

6 **Find all values of k so that the trinomial $x^2 + kx + 8$ can be factored using integers.**

For $x^2 + kx + 8$, the value of k is the sum of the factors of 8.

Factors of 8	Sum of Factors
1, 8	$1 + 8 = 9$
2, 4	$2 + 4 = 6$
$-1, -8$	$-1 + (-8) = -9$
$-2, -4$	$-2 + (-4) = -6$

The values of k are 9, 6, -9, and -6.

Exploratory Exercises

For each polynomial, find integers m and n whose product is the last term and whose sum is the coefficient of the second term.

1. $x^2 + 15x + 14$ **2.** $y^2 + 9y + 14$ **3.** $b^2 - 8b + 12$
4. $x^2 - 19x + 34$ **5.** $p^2 + 5p - 36$ **6.** $r^2 - 10r - 24$
7. $y^2 - 7y - 30$ **8.** $g^2 + 5g - 24$ **9.** $x^2 + 18x + 45$
10. $t^2 - 19t + 48$ **11.** $c^2 - 17c - 60$ **12.** $a^2 + 13a - 48$

Complete the factoring.

13. $p^2 + 9p - 10 = (p + \blacksquare)(p - 1)$ **14.** $y^2 + 3y - 28 = (y + 7)(y \ \blacksquare \ 4)$
15. $x^2 - 2x - 35 = (x + 5)(x - \blacksquare)$ **16.** $a^2 - 4a - 21 = (a + \blacksquare)(a - 7)$
17. $h^2 + 6h - 16 = (h - 2)(h \ \blacksquare\blacksquare)$ **18.** $x^2 - 9x - 36 = (x - 12)(x \ \blacksquare\blacksquare)$
19. $a^2 + 4am - 21m^2 = (a - 3m)(a \ \blacksquare\blacksquare)$ **20.** $p^2 + 16rp + 63r^2 = (p \ \blacksquare\blacksquare)(p + 9r)$

Written Exercises

Factor each trinomial, if possible. At least two cannot be factored using integers. If the trinomial cannot be factored using integers, write *prime*.

1. $y^2 + 12y + 27$
2. $a^2 + 22a + 21$
3. $c^2 + 2c - 3$
4. $x^2 + 2x - 15$
5. $y^2 - 8y + 15$
6. $a^2 - 12a + 35$
7. $m^2 - m - 20$
8. $x^2 - 5x - 24$
9. $h^2 + 5h + 8$
10. $c^2 + 3c + 6$
11. $z^2 - 10z - 39$
12. $y^2 - 7y + 60$
13. $r^2 - 10r - 24$
14. $y^2 - 9y - 36$
15. $y^2 + 8y - 20$
16. $n^2 + 12n - 45$
17. $p^2 + 10p + 16$
18. $g^2 + 15g + 26$
19. $b^2 - 11b + 28$
20. $x^2 - 9x + 14$
21. $15 + 16m + m^2$
22. $36 + 15a + a^2$
23. $y^2 + 11y + 28$
24. $x^2 + 14x + 33$
25. $a^2 - 18a - 40$
26. $b^2 + 13b - 30$
27. $x^2 - 3x - 18$
28. $y^2 - 7y - 30$
29. $36 - 16m + m^2$
30. $36 - 13y + y^2$
31. $m^2 - 6m - 55$
32. $h^2 - 3h - 108$
33. $66 - 17j + j^2$
34. $90 - 19c + c^2$
35. $42 - 23a + a^2$
36. $50 - 27x + x^2$
37. $c^2 - 2cd - 8d^2$
38. $x^2 - 4xy - 5y^2$
39. $a^2 + 2ab - 3b^2$
40. $n^2 + 4an - 32a^2$
41. $(a + b)^2 - 5(a + b) - 6$
42. $(c + q)^2 - 8(c + q) - 9$

Find all values of k so that each trinomial can be factored using integers.

43. $x^2 + kx + 10$
44. $m^2 + km + 6$
45. $r^2 + kr - 13$
46. $y^2 + ky - 4$
47. $n^2 + kn + 7$
48. $p^2 + kp + 17$
49. $a^2 + ka - 5$
50. $b^2 + kb - 16$
51. $t^2 + kt + 21$
52. $c^2 + kc + 12$
53. $s^2 + ks - 14$
54. $y^2 + ky - 15$

Excursions in Algebra ———————————— Factoring Cubes

You know how to factor the difference of two squares. Can you factor the difference of two cubes? Consider $a^3 - b^3$.

$$a^3 - b^3 = a^3 - a^2b + a^2b - b^3 \qquad \text{Notice that } -a^2b + a^2b = 0.$$
$$= a^2(a - b) + b(a^2 - b^2)$$
$$= a^2(a - b) + b(a - b)(a + b)$$
$$= (a - b)[a^2 + b(a + b)]$$
$$= (a - b)(a^2 + ab + b^2)$$

Example: Factor $y^3 - 27$.

y^3 is the cube of y. 27 is the cube of 3. Now use the pattern above.
$$y^3 - 27 = (y - 3)(y^2 + 3y + 9)$$

Exercises

Factor using the pattern above.

1. $x^3 - 64$
2. $8x^3 - y^3$
3. $27a^3 - 64b^3$
4. Find a pattern for factoring $a^3 + b^3$ by using a method similar to the one above.

7-6 Factoring by Grouping

Some polynomials have four terms. It may be possible to factor these polynomials by first grouping the terms in pairs and factoring a monomial from each group. Then use the distributive property again to factor the common binomial.

Examples

1
Factor: $3xy - 21y + 5x - 35$

$$3xy - 21y + 5x - 35 = (3xy - 21y) + (5x - 35)$$

Group pairs of terms that have a common monomial factor.

$$= 3y(x - 7) + 5(x - 7)$$

Factor the GCF from each group.

$$= 3y(x - 7) + 5(x - 7)$$

Notice that $(x - 7)$ is a common factor.

$$= (3y + 5)(x - 7)$$

Use the distributive property.

Check by using FOIL.

$$\qquad\qquad \text{F} \qquad \text{O} \qquad \text{I} \qquad \text{L}$$
$$(3y + 5)(x - 7) = 3y(x) + 3y(-7) + 5(x) + 5(-7)$$
$$= 3xy - 21y + 5x - 35$$

2
Factor: $8x^2y - 5x - 24xy + 15$

$$8x^2y - 5x - 24xy + 15 = (8x^2y - 5x) + (-24xy + 15)$$

Why are the terms grouped this way?

$$= x(8xy - 5) + (-3)(8xy - 5)$$

What is the common factor?

$$= (x - 3)(8xy - 5)$$

Check: $(x - 3)(8xy - 5) = x(8xy) + x(-5) + (-3)(8xy) + (-3)(-5)$
$$= 8x^2y - 5x - 24xy + 15$$

Sometimes you can group the terms in more than one way. The following example shows another way to factor the polynomial in Example 2 above.

Example

3
Factor: $8x^2y - 5x - 24xy + 15$

$$8x^2y - 5x - 24xy + 15 = (8x^2y - 24xy) + (-5x + 15)$$

$$= 8xy(x - 3) + (-5)(x - 3)$$

$$= (8xy - 5)(x - 3)$$ *The result is the same as in Example 2.*

Recognizing binomials that are additive inverses is often helpful in factoring. For example, the binomials $(3 - a)$ and $(a - 3)$ are additive inverses since $(3 - a)$ and $-1(a - 3)$ are equivalent. What is the additive inverse of $(5 - y)$?

$-1(a-3) = (-1)(a) + (-1)(-3)$
$= -a + 3$
$= 3 - a$

Example

4 **Factor:** $15x - 3xy + 4y - 20$

$$15x - 3xy + 4y - 20 = (15x - 3xy) + (4y - 20)$$
$$= 3x(5 - y) + 4(y - 5)$$
$$= -3x(y - 5) + 4(y - 5)$$
$$= (-3x + 4)(y - 5)$$

The binomials $(5-y)$ and $(y-5)$ are additive inverses.

$(5 - y) = -1(y - 5).$

Check: $(-3x + 4)(y - 5) = (-3x)(y) + (-3x)(-5) + 4(y) + 4(-5)$
$$= -3xy + 15x + 4y - 20$$
$$= 15x - 3xy + 4y - 20$$

Exploratory Exercises

Express each polynomial in factored form.

1. $k(r + s) - m(r + s)$

2. $y(m + n) - 4(m + n)$

3. $4b(x - y) + y(x - y)$

4. $t(t - s) + s(t - s)$

5. $7rp\,(r - 3p) - 4q(r - 3p)$

6. $3ab(a - 4) - 8(a - 4)$

7. $8m(x + y) + (x + y)$

8. $p(p - 3r) - (p - 3r)$

9. $5mp(2m + 3p) - 3bc(2m + 3p)$

10. $5z(5x^2 - 3y^2) + m^2(5x^2 - 3y^2)$

11. $4m(y - 5) + 3p(5 - y)$

12. $5y(z - 6) - 3m(6 - z)$

13. $7x(a + b) + 3m(a + b) - 4p(b + a)$

14. $3a(x - y) - 4b(y - x) + 5c(x - y)$

15. $a(8r - 3y) + b(8r - 3y) + c(3y - 8r)$

16. $x(4a^2 + 3b^2) - 3y(4a^2 + 3b^2) + z(3b^2 + 4a^2)$

Written Exercises

Find the common factor for the grouped binomials.

> **Sample:** $(2a^2 + ab) + (4ac + 2bc)$
>
> $(2a^2 + ab) + (4ac + 2bc) = a(2a + b) + 2c(2a + b)$
>
> The common factor is $(2a + b)$.

1. $(bx + by) + (3ax + 3ay)$

2. $(3mx + 2my) + (3kx + 2ky)$

3. $(a^2 + 3ab) + (2ac + 6bc)$

4. $(rx + 2ry) + (kx + 2ky)$

5. $(a^2 - 4ac) + (ab - 4bc)$

6. $(10x^2 - 6xy) + (15x - 9y)$

7. $(4m^2 - 3mp) + (3p - 4m)$

8. $(16k^2 - 28kp) + (7p^2 - 4kp)$

9. $(6x^3 + 7x^2y) + (6x + 7y)$

10. $(5a + 2b) + (10a^2 + 4ab)$

11. $(3a^2b + 2ab^3) + (6ab + 4b^3)$

12. $(15a^2 - 21ab) + (20ab - 28b^2)$

Factor. Check by using FOIL.

13. $2ax + 6xc + ba + 3bc$

14. $6mx - 4m + 3rx - 2r$

15. $ay + 4p + 4a + yp$

16. $3my - ab + am - 3by$

17. $2my + 7x + 7m + 2xy$

18. $zr + 6q + rq + 6z$

19. $ay - ab + cb - cy$

20. $3ax - 6bx + 8b - 4a$

21. $a^2 - 2ab + a - 2b$

22. $2ab + 2am - b - m$

23. $4ax + 3ay + 4bx + 3by$

24. $x^2 + 5xy + ax + 5ay$

25. $3m^2 - 5m^2p + 3p^2 - 5p^3$

26. $10x^2 - 14xy + 5xy - 7y^2$

27. $5a^2 - 4ab + 12b^3 - 15ab^2$

28. $4ax - 14bx + 35by - 10ay$

29. $6a^2 - 6ab + 3cb - 3ca$

30. $5a^2 + 5ab + 5cd + 5c^2$

31. $ax + a^2x - a - 2a^2$

32. $5xy + 15x - 6y - 18$

33. $7mp^2 + 2np^2 - 7mq^2 - 2nq^2$

34. $5a^3 + 3a^2b - 5ab^2 - 3b^3$

35. $x^3 + 2x^2 - x - 2$

36. $y^3 + y^2 - y - 1$

37. $a^3 - a^2b + ab^2 - b^3$

38. $2a^3 - 5ab^2 - 2a^2b + 5b^3$

39. $7m(a^2 - b^2) + 5y(b^2 - a^2)$

40. $3x(k^2 - m^2) - 4a(m^2 - k^2)$

41. $a^2(m - 2) + 5a(m - 2) + 6(m - 2)$

42. $x^2(a + 1) - 2x(a + 1) - 15(a + 1)$

43. $2a^2x + 3a^2y - 14ax - 21ay + 24x + 36y$

44. $ax^2 - 3bx^2 - 7ax + 21bx - 18a + 54b$

Excursions in Algebra ———————— Grouping Three Terms

In the following example, the first three terms have been grouped to form a perfect square trinomial.

Factor: $a^2 + 4a + 4 - 9b^2$

$$a^2 + 4a + 4 - 9b^2 = (a^2 + 4a + 4) - 9b^2$$
$$= (a + 2)^2 - 9b^2$$
$$= [(a + 2) - 3b][(a + 2) + 3b]$$
$$= (a + 2 - 3b)(a + 2 + 3b)$$

The perfect square trinomial $a^2 + 4a + 4$ can be factored as $(a + 2)^2$.

Use the difference of squares.

Exercises
Factor each polynomial.

1. $x^2 + 4x + 4 - 25y^2$

2. $y^2 + 8y + 16 - 36z^2$

3. $x^2 + 2xy + y^2 - r^2$

4. $m^2 - k^2 + 6k - 9$

5. $9 - 9y^2 - x^2 + 6xy$

6. $c^2 - 10ab - a^2 - 25b^2$

7. $4a^2 + 12ab + 9b^2 - 16x^2$

8. $4a^2 + 4ax + x^2 - b^2$

When you read mathematics, do not expect to read rapidly. Mathematics is a concise language. Try reading aloud each of these statements.

Liquids have no definite shape.

$$x^2 + 5x + 4 = 0$$

The equation takes longer to read because the mathematical symbols are compact forms of words and concepts. In words, it would be read as *x squared plus five x plus four equals zero*. The following concepts are involved.

x is a variable.

The raised 2 in x^2 means x is used as a factor twice.

$5x$ means 5 multiplied by x.

You must also know the meaning of $+$, $=$, 5, 4, and 0.

For understanding, you need to translate the symbols into words and concepts.

Suppose you read a section in this book. First read it rapidly to get a general idea of the content. Then reread it slowly so that you understand all of the ideas in the section. Turn to page 236 and read section 7-8 rapidly to find the main ideas in that section.

The main ideas in the section are listed here.

The section gives a summary of the methods used to factor polynomials.

If there is a greatest common factor, factor it out first.

Continue factoring until each of the remaining factors is prime.

Now reread section 7-8 carefully to find out how to factor a polynomial completely.

Exercises

Write each expression in words.

1. $3x^2 + 14x + 15$

2. $(3x + 5)(x + 3)$

3. $3xy - 6x + 5y - 10$

4. $(3x + 5)(y - z)$

5. List the concepts contained in exercise 1.

6. List the concepts contained in exercise 2.

7. List the methods of factoring polynomials that are discussed in section 7-8.

7-7   Factoring $ax^2 + bx + c$

In the trinomial $x^2 - 3x - 18$, the coefficient of x^2 is 1. To factor this trinomial, you find the factors of -18 whose sum is -3.

Consider the trinomial $2y^2 + 7y + 6$. In this trinomial the coefficient of y^2 is not 1. To factor a trinomial such as this one, another method is needed.

What is the coefficient of y^2 in $2y^2 + 7y + 6$?

Study how FOIL is used to multiply $(3x + 4)$ by $(2x + 7)$.

$$
\begin{array}{cccc}
\text{F} & \text{O} & \text{I} & \text{L}
\end{array}
$$
$$(3x + 4)(2x + 7) = 6x^2 + 21x + 8x + 28$$

$$= 6x^2 + (21 + 8)x + 28$$

$$21 \cdot 8 = 168$$

$$6 \cdot 28 = 168$$

Notice that the *product* of 6 and 28 is the same as the *product* of 21 and 8. You can use this method to factor the trinomial $2y^2 + 7y + 6$.

$2y^2 + 7y + 6$

$2y^2 + (\blacksquare + \blacksquare)\,y + 6$

The product of 2 and 6 is 12. You need to find two integers whose *product is 12* and whose *sum is 7*.

Factors of 12	Sum of Factors
1, 12	$1 + 12 = 13$
2, 6	$2 + 6 = 8$
3, 4	$3 + 4 = 7$

$2y^2 + (3 + 4)y + 6$ Select the factors 3 and 4.

$2y^2 + 3y + 4y + 6$

$(2y^2 + 3y) + (4y + 6)$ Group pairs of terms that have a common monomial factor.

$y(2y + 3) + 2(2y + 3)$ Factor the GCF from each group.

$(y + 2)(2y + 3)$ Use the distributive property.

Therefore, $2y^2 + 7y + 6 = (y + 2)(2y + 3)$.   *Check by using FOIL.*

Example 1, which follows, illustrates that the order in which the factors are selected does not affect the result.

1 **Factor:** $3x^2 + 11x + 6$

$3x^2 + 11x + 6$ *The product of 3 and 6 is 18.*

Factors of 18	Sum of Factors
1, 18	$1 + 18 = 19$
2, 9	$2 + 9 = 11$
3, 6	$3 + 6 = 9$

$3x^2 + (\boxed{} + \boxed{})x + 6$ *Select the factors 2 and 9.*

$3x^2 + (2 + 9)x + 6$ or $3x^2 + (9 + 2)x + 6$

$3x^2 + 2x + 9x + 6$ $3x^2 + 9x + 2x + 6$

$(3x^2 + 2x) + (9x + 6)$ $(3x^2 + 9x) + (2x + 6)$

$x(3x + 2) + 3(3x + 2)$ $3x(x + 3) + 2(x + 3)$ *Factor the GCF from each group.*

$(x + 3)(3x + 2)$ $(3x + 2)(x + 3)$ *Use the distributive property.*

          Notice that $(x + 3)(3x + 2) = (3x + 2)(x + 3)$.

Therefore, $3x^2 + 11x + 6 = (x + 3)(3x + 2)$.   *Check by using FOIL.*

2 **Factor:** $5x^2 - 17x + 14$

$5x^2 - 17x + 14$ *The product of 5 and 14 is 70.*
Both factors of 70 must be negative. Why?

Factors of 70	Sum of Factors
$-1, -70$	$-1 + (-70) = -71$
$-2, -35$	$-2 + (-35) = -37$
$-5, -14$	$-5 + (-14) = -19$
$-7, -10$	$-7 + (-10) = -17$

$5x^2 + (\boxed{} + \boxed{})x + 14$

$5x^2 + [-10x + (-7)x] + 14$

$(5x^2 - 10x) + (-7x + 14)$

$5x(x - 2) + (-7)(x - 2)$ *What is the common factor?*

$(5x - 7)(x - 2)$

Therefore, $5x^2 - 17x + 14 = (5x - 7)(x - 2)$.   *Check by using FOIL.*

Example

3 **Factor:** $8y^2 - 6y - 9$

$$8y^2 - 6y - 9$$

The product of 8 and −9 is −72.
Exactly one factor of −72 in each pair must be negative.
Why? Since the sum is negative, the factor with the
greater absolute value is negative.

Factors of −72	Sum of Factors
1, −72	1 + (−72) = −71
2, −36	2 + (−36) = −34
3, −24	3 + (−24) = −21
4, −18	4 + (−18) = −14
6, −12	6 + (−12) = −6

$8y^2 + (\blacksquare + \blacksquare)y - 9$

$8y^2 + [6y + (-12)y] - 9$

$(8y^2 + 6y) + (-12y - 9)$ *You can stop listing factors when you find a pair that works.*

$2y(4y + 3) + (-3)(4y + 3)$

$(2y - 3)(4y + 3)$

Therefore, $8y^2 - 6y - 9 = (2y - 3)(4y + 3)$.   *Check by using FOIL.*

Exploratory Exercises

For each trinomial $ax^2 + bx + c$, supply the missing numbers so that the sum will equal b and the product will equal ac.

1. $3y^2 + 11y + 6 = 3y^2 + (\blacksquare + \blacksquare)y + 6$
2. $3c^2 + 14c + 8 = 3c^2 + (\blacksquare + \blacksquare)c + 8$
3. $4y^2 + 11y + 6 = 4y^2 + (\blacksquare + \blacksquare)y + 6$
4. $6b^2 + 31b + 5 = 6b^2 + (\blacksquare + \blacksquare)b + 5$
5. $4x^2 - 8x + 3 = 4x^2 + (\blacksquare + \blacksquare)x + 3$
6. $2y^2 - 11y + 15 = 2y^2 + (\blacksquare + \blacksquare)y + 15$
7. $2k^2 - 9k + 10 = 2k^2 + (\blacksquare + \blacksquare)k + 10$
8. $4a^2 - 25a + 6 = 4a^2 + (\blacksquare + \blacksquare)a + 6$
9. $5c^2 + 6c - 8 = 5c^2 + (\blacksquare + \blacksquare)c - 8$
10. $2x^2 + x - 21 = 2x^2 + (\blacksquare + \blacksquare)x - 21$
11. $5r^2 - 13r - 6 = 5r^2 + (\blacksquare + \blacksquare)r - 6$
12. $6a^2 + 7a - 3 = 6a^2 + (\blacksquare + \blacksquare)a - 3$
13. $3m^2 + 11m - 20 = 3m^2 + (\blacksquare + \blacksquare)m - 20$
14. $3d^2 - 5d - 28 = 3d^2 + (\blacksquare + \blacksquare)d - 28$

Written Exercises

Factor each trinomial, if possible. At least two of the trinomials cannot be factored using integers.

1. $3y^2 + 8y + 5$
2. $7a^2 + 22a + 3$
3. $3x^2 + 8x + 4$
4. $3a^2 + 14a + 15$
5. $8m^2 - 10m + 3$
6. $2y^2 - 7y + 3$
7. $2h^2 - h - 3$
8. $3y^2 + 5y - 2$
9. $3k^2 + 7k - 6$
10. $3m^2 - 7m - 6$
11. $6p^2 - p - 2$
12. $4b^2 + 5b - 6$
13. $2a^2 + 3a - 14$
14. $2x^2 + 5x - 12$
15. $6t^2 + 5t - 6$
16. $7n^2 - 22n + 3$
17. $2y^2 - 5y + 3$
18. $3x^2 + 4x - 15$

19. $2q^2 - 9q - 18$ **20.** $6y^2 - 11y + 4$ **21.** $6m^2 + 19m + 10$

22. $4y^2 - 17y - 15$ **23.** $6x^2 - 19x - 11$ **24.** $10n^2 - 19n + 7$

25. $12r^2 - 11r + 3$ **26.** $9k^2 - 12k + 4$ **27.** $8p^2 - 18p + 9$

28. $5b^2 - 13b - 10$ **29.** $15p^2 + 14p - 8$ **30.** $3t^2 - 32t + 20$

31. $6y^2 - 19y + 15$ **32.** $10k^2 - 11k - 6$ **33.** $6s^2 + 7s - 20$

34. $12b^2 + 17b + 6$ **35.** $18x^2 + 55x + 25$ **36.** $16m^2 + 14m - 15$

37. $18c^2 + 41c - 10$ **38.** $15y^2 + 17y - 18$ **39.** $18r^2 - 19r - 12$

40. $15x^2 - 13xy + 2y^2$ **41.** $8m^2 - 14mn + 3n^2$ **42.** $3s^2 - 10st - 8t^2$

43. $16x^2 - 16xy - 5y^2$ **44.** $16a^2 - 38ab - 5b^2$ **45.** $20p^2 + 11pq - 4q^2$

46. $25r^2 + 25rs + 6s^2$

47. $9k^2 + 30km + 25m^2$

48. $36a^2 + 9ab - 10b^2$

49. $20s^2 + 17st - 24t^2$

50. $3x^2 - 30xy + 56y^2$

51. $8x^2 - 42xq + 27q^2$

52. $12r^2 - 16rs - 11s^2$

53. $14c^2 + 41cd + 15d^2$

54. $21x^2 + 52xy + 32y^2$

mini-review

Find each product.

1. $\left(-\frac{7}{12}\right)\left(\frac{6}{7}\right)\left(-\frac{3}{4}\right)$

2. $(4x^2y)(-3x^3y^2)$

3. $8ay(-2ax + 4y^2)$

4. $(2x - 5)^2$

5. $(a + 2)(2a^3 + 7a - 3)$

Using Calculators _____ Checking Solutions

You can use your calculator to check whether $\frac{1}{18}$ is a solution of $243y^2 = \frac{3}{4}$.
First enter $\left(\frac{1}{18}\right)^2$ by using the reciprocal and square keys. Then store it.

ENTER: 18 $\boxed{1/x}$ $\boxed{x^2}$ $\boxed{STO}$

DISPLAY: 18   .05555556   .00308642   .00308642

Then, evaluate $243y^2$ for $y = \frac{1}{18}$ and compare it to the value of $\frac{3}{4}$.

ENTER: 243 $\boxed{\times}$ $\boxed{RCL}$ $\boxed{=}$

DISPLAY: 243   .00308642   0.75

ENTER: 3 $\boxed{\div}$ 4 $\boxed{=}$

DISPLAY: 3   4   0.75

Since $0.75 = 0.75$, the number $\frac{1}{18}$ is a solution of $243y^2 = \frac{3}{4}$.

Exercises

Use your calculator to check whether the given number is a solution of the equation.

1. $128x^2 = 2$; $\frac{1}{8}$ **2.** $108y^2 = 3$; $\frac{1}{5}$

3. $144a^2 - 16 = 0$; $-\frac{1}{3}$ **4.** $25x^2 - 30x = -9$; $\frac{3}{5}$

5. $49c^2 = -112c - 64$; $-\frac{8}{7}$ **6.** $4a^2 = -20a - 25$; $\frac{2}{5}$

7-8   Summary of Factoring

You have used many methods to factor polynomials. This table can help you decide which method to use.

Check for:	Two	Three	Four or More
		Number of Terms	
greatest common factor	✔	✔	✔
difference of squares	✔		
perfect square trinomial		✔	
trinomial that has two binomial factors		✔	
pairs of terms that have a common monomial factor			✔

If there is a GCF, factor it out first. Then, check the appropriate factoring methods in the order shown in the table. Using these methods, factor until each of the remaining factors is prime. When you follow this procedure, you are *factoring a polynomial completely*.

Examples

1   Factor: $3x^2 - 27$

Since $3x^2 - 27$ has two terms, first check for the GCF. Then check for the difference of squares.

$$3x^2 - 27 = 3(x^2 - 9)$$
$$= 3(x - 3)(x + 3)$$

3 is the GCF.
$x^2 - 9$ is the difference of squares.

Check: $3(x - 3)(x + 3) = 3(x^2 - 9)$
$$= 3x^2 - 27$$

The binomial $3x^2 - 27$ is completely factored as $3(x - 3)(x + 3)$.

2   Factor: $6y^2 - 20y - 16$

Since $6y^2 - 20y - 16$ has three terms, check for the GCF, a perfect square trinomial, and a trinomial that has two binomial factors.

$$6y^2 - 20y - 16 = 2(3y^2 - 10y - 8)$$ *2 is the GCF.*

The trinomial $3y^2 - 10y - 8$ is not a perfect square. Why? Try factoring $3y^2 - 10y - 8$ using two binomial factors.

$$6y^2 - 20y - 16 = 2(3y^2 - 10y - 8)$$
$$= 2(y - 4)(3y + 2)$$

The trinomial $6y^2 - 20y - 16$ is completely factored as $2(y - 4)(3y + 2)$.

Example

3 **Factor:** $2m^3 + 3m^2n - 8m - 12n$

Since $2m^3 + 3m^2n - 8m - 12n$ has four terms, first check for the GCF. Then, check for pairs of terms that have a common monomial factor.

$$2m^3 + 3m^2n - 8m - 12n = (2m^3 + 3m^2n) + (-8m - 12n)$$
$$= m^2(2m + 3n) + (-4)(2m + 3n)$$
$$= (m^2 - 4)(2m + 3n) \qquad m^2 - 4 \text{ is the}$$
$$\qquad\qquad\qquad\qquad\qquad\qquad \text{difference of squares.}$$
$$= (m - 2)(m + 2)(2m + 3n)$$

The polynomial $2m^3 + 3m^2n - 8m - 12n$ is completely factored as $(m - 2)(m + 2)(2m + 3n)$. *Check by multiplying the factors.*

Exploratory Exercises

Factor. Check by using FOIL or the distributive property.

1. $3x^2 + 15$
2. $4y^2 - 24$
3. $5ax + 6ay$
4. $8mn^2 - 13m^2n$
5. $12ax^2 + 18ay^2$
6. $4c^2d + 16bc^2$
7. $5x^2 - 10x^2y$
8. $4m^2 - 20m^2n$
9. $3a^2b + 6ab + 9ab^2$
10. $2x^2y + 8x^2y^2 + 10x^2y^3$
11. $a^2 - 9b^2$
12. $9x^2 - 16y^2$

Written Exercises

Factor completely. Check by using FOIL or the distributive property.

1. $2a^2 - 72$
2. $3y^2 - 147$
3. $m^3 + 6m^2 + 9m$
4. $18y + 12y^2 + 2y^3$
5. $4a^3 - 36a$
6. $3x^3 - 27x$
7. $m^4 - p^2$
8. $b^4 - 16$
9. $2k^2 + 3k + 1$
10. $6r^2 + 13r + 6$
11. $6y^2 - 24x^2$
12. $2m^2 - 32n^2$
13. $3y^2 + 21y - 24$
14. $6x^2 + 27x - 15$
15. $20y^2 + 34y + 6$
16. $5a^2 + 7a + 3$
17. $2b^2 + 6b + 2$
18. $3b^2 - 36$
19. $m^2 + 8mn + 16n^2$
20. $4a^2 + 12ab + 9b^2$
21. $6p^2 + 9p - 105$
22. $12c^2 + 10c - 42$
23. $3ax^2 + 16ax + 21a$
24. $4y^3 - 12y^2 + 8y$
25. $9a^3 + 66a^2 - 48a$
26. $2m^2 - mb - 10b^2$
27. $3x^2 - 9xy - 30y^2$
28. $a^2b^3 - 25b$
29. $m^3n^2 - 49m$
30. $2a^2 - 4ab - 70b^2$
31. $3x^2 + 24xy - 99y^2$
32. $3y^4 - 48$
33. $4x^4 - 324$
34. $m^2p + m^2 - 36p - 36$
35. $9y^4 + 8y^2 - 1$
36. $27k^2m + 27km^2 - 12m^3$
37. $60r^3 - 54r^2s + 12rs^2$
38. $8y^4 + 14y^2 - 4$
39. $x^2y^2 - z^2 - y^2 + x^2z^2$

Challenge

Factor completely by first factoring out a common decimal or fraction.

40. $0.3x^2 - 4.8$
41. $0.7y^2 - 6.3$
42. $\frac{1}{4}a^2 + a + 1$
43. $\frac{1}{3}b^2 + 2b + 3$
44. $y^2 + \frac{5}{12}y - \frac{1}{6}$
45. $\frac{1}{4}r^2 + \frac{3}{2}r + 2$
46. $0.4r^2 + 1.2r + 0.8$
47. $0.7y^2 + 3.5y + 4.2$
48. $m^2 - \frac{5}{12}m - \frac{1}{4}$

Bits and Bytes

The decimal numeration system is a base 10 system. The ten digits 0, 1, 2, 3, 4, 5, 6, 7, 8, and 9 are used to name numbers.

Powers of Two

$2^0 = 1$	$2^4 = 16$
$2^1 = 2$	$2^5 = 32$
$2^2 = 4$	$2^6 = 64$
$2^3 = 8$	$2^7 = 128$

Internally, a digital computer uses only two digits, 0 and 1. These two digits (bits) are used in a base two, or binary, numeration system.

In this system the position of each digit gives its place value as a power of 2. If 0 and 1 are used, then 11101 in base two means 1 sixteen, 1 eight, 1 four, 0 twos, and 1 one.

binary numeral $\rightarrow$ $11101 = 1 \cdot 2^4 + 1 \cdot 2^3 + 1 \cdot 2^2 + 0 \cdot 2^1 + 1$

$$= \ \ 16 \ + \ 8 \ + \ 4 \ + \ 0 \ + 1$$

$$= 29 \ \leftarrow \textit{decimal numeral}$$

To show which base is used, you can write $11101_{two} = 29_{ten}$.

The circuits of a computer store numbers in base 2. The diagram depicts how a computer would store 1010_{two}.

A color spot indicates a circuit that conducts electricity. It represents 1.

A grey spot indicates a circuit that does not conduct electricity. It represents 0.

Bits are the alphabet of machine language. The pattern formed by a group of bits stands for a number, and that number itself may stand for a character or even a whole word. Usually, eight bits make up one **byte**. Computer size is often stated in bytes of memory.

In mathematics and business 1K = 1000; in a computer, 1K = 1024. A small personal computer may have only 4K bytes of memory, but most have from 16K to 128K bytes. A time sharing computer may have 20 times as much.

Exercises

Change each binary numeral to a decimal numeral.

1. 1101_{two} **2.** 10110_{two} **3.** 11111_{two} **4.** 10101_{two}

Draw a diagram that depicts how a computer would store each of the following.

5. 1100_{two} **6.** 1001_{two} **7.** 19_{ten} **8.** 33_{ten}

factor (211)
prime number (211)
composite number (211)
prime factor (211)
prime factorization (211)

greatest common factor, GCF (212)
difference of squares (217)
perfect square trinomial (221)
prime polynomial (226)

Chapter Summary ▰▰▰▰▰▰▰▰▰▰▰▰▰

1. A prime number is an integer, greater than 1, whose only whole number factors are 1 and itself. (211)

2. A composite number is any positive integer, except 1, that is not prime. (211)

3. Expressing a composite number as a product of prime factors is called prime factorization. (211)

4. The greatest common factor (GCF) of two or more integers is the greatest of the factors common to each integer. (212)

5. The distributive property may be used to express a polynomial in factored form. (214)

6. Difference of Squares:
   $a^2 - b^2 = (a - b)(a + b) = (a + b)(a - b)$ (217)

7. The result of squaring an integer is called a perfect square. (221)

8. The square of a binomial is a perfect square trinomial. (221)

9. Factoring Perfect Square Trinomials:
   $a^2 + 2ab + b^2 = (a + b)^2$
   $a^2 - 2ab + b^2 = (a - b)^2$ (221)

10. The pattern $(x + m)(x + n) = x^2 + (m + n)x + mn$ can be used to factor trinomials of the form $x^2 + bx + c$. (224)

11. When the value of c is negative, the factors of $x^2 + bx + c$ are a difference and a sum. (225)

12. A polynomial that cannot be written as a product of two polynomials is called a prime polynomial. (226)

13. To factor a trinomial of the form $ax^2 + bx + c$, first find two factors whose product is $a \cdot c$ and whose sum is b. Then, rename b as the sum of these factors. Continue to factor by grouping the terms in pairs and factoring the GCF from each group. (232).

14. Summary of Factoring (236)

Check for:	Number of Terms		
	Two	Three	Four or More
greatest common factor	✔	✔	✔
difference of squares	✔		
perfect square trinomial		✔	
trinomial that has two binomial factors		✔	
pairs of terms that have a common monomial factor			✔

Chapter Review

7-1 **Find the prime factorization of each of the following.**

1. 42   **2.** 66   **3.** 80

4. $96y^3x^2$ **5.** $121(ab)^4$ **6.** $16a^3b$

Find the GCF of each of the following.

7. 35, 50   **8.** 12, 18, 40   **9.** $16abc, 30a^2b$

Factor each polynomial completely. If a polynomial cannot be factored using integers, write *prime*.

7-2 **10.** $13x + 26y$ **11.** $6x^2y + 12xy + 6$ **12.** $24a^2b^2 - 18ab$

13. $24ab + 18ac + 32a^2$ **14.** $\frac{3}{5}a - \frac{3}{5}b + \frac{6}{5}c$ **15.** $\frac{3}{4}x + \frac{1}{4}y$

7-3 **16.** $b^2 - 16$ **17.** $25 - 9y^2$ **18.** $16a^2 - 81b^4$

19. $2y^2 - 128$ **20.** $\frac{1}{4}y^2 - \frac{9}{16}z^2$ **21.** $x^4 - 1$

7-4 **22.** $a^2 + 18a + 81$ **23.** $16x^2 - 8x + 1$ **24.** $9x^2 - 12x + 4$

25. $32x^2 - 80x + 50$ **26.** $6a^2 - 24a + 6$ **27.** $y^2 - \frac{3}{2}y + \frac{9}{16}$

7-5 **28.** $y^2 + 7y + 12$ **29.** $b^2 - 8b + 15$ **30.** $y^2 - 9y - 36$

31. $b^2 + 5b - 6$ **32.** $r^2 + 23r + 132$ **33.** $a^2 - 3a - 28$

34. $x^2 - 13x + 30$ **35.** $s^2 + 10s - 39$ **36.** $x^2 + 11xy + 24y^2$

37. $m^2 - mn - 42n^2$ **38.** $a^2 - 10ab + 9b^2$ **39.** $r^2 - 8rs - 65s^2$

7-6 **40.** $a^2 - 4ac + ab - 4bc$ **41.** $4m^2 - 3mp + 3p - 4m$

42. $2rs + 6ps + rm + 3mp$ **43.** $bm + 7r + rm + 7b$

44. $10x^2 - 6xy + 15x - 9y$ **45.** $16k^2 - 4kp - 28kp + 7p^2$

7-7 **46.** $3y^2 + 14y + 8$ **47.** $4m^2 + 11m + 6$ **48.** $4y^2 - 7y + 3$

49. $2r^2 - 3r - 20$ **50.** $3a^2 - 13a + 14$ **51.** $4m^2 - 8m + 3$

52. $6b^2 + 7b + 3$ **53.** $3x^2 + 11x - 20$ **54.** $12x^2 + 31x + 20$

7-8 **55.** $3x^2 - 12$ **56.** $12mx + 3xb + 4my + by$ **57.** $12ay^2 + 31ay + 20a$

58. $2r^3 - 18r^2 + 28r$ **59.** $mx^2 + bx^2 - 49m - 49b$ **60.** $4y^2 + 2y - 6$

Chapter Test

Find the prime factorization of each of the following.

1. 95   **2.** 300   **3.** $18a^2b$

Find the GCF of each of the following.

4. 36, 20   **5.** $18a^2b$, $28a^3b^2$ **6.** $6x^2y^3$, $12x^2y^2z$, $15x^2y$

Factor, if possible.

7. $25y^2 - 49w^2$ **8.** $w^2 - 16w + 64$ **9.** $x^2 + 14x + 24$

10. $36a^2 - 48a + 16$ **11.** $y^2 - 8y + 7$ **12.** $a^2 - 11ab + 18b^2$

13. $28m^2 + 18m$ **14.** $m^2 + 7m + 10$ **15.** $5x^2 + 20y^2$

16. $h^2 - 3h - 10$ **17.** $8m^2 - 72n^2$ **18.** $r^2 + 3r - 18$

19. $x^2 + 18x + 81$ **20.** $a^2 - 12a - 13$ **21.** $r^2 - rs - 72s^2$

22. $36m^2 - 24mn + 4n^2$ **23.** $3x^2 + 19x + 28$ **24.** $5x^2 - 19x + 14$

25. $36m^2 + 60mn + 25n^2$ **26.** $192a^2 - 75b^2$ **27.** $6p^2 + 7p - 3$

28. $16a^2b^2 - c^2d^2$ **29.** $2m^2 + 11m + 12$ **30.** $36a^2b^3 - 45ab^4$

31. $4m^2 - 196$ **32.** $6x^3 + 15x^2 - 9x$

33. $3a^2b - 8a - 12ab - 32$ **34.** $4my - 20m + 15p - 3py$

35. $15a + 6b + 10a^2 + 4ab$ **36.** $y^2m + y^2n - 4m - 4n$

Applications in Probability

Cecile, Tom, Mike, Allison, Carl, and Eric would all like to help plan the senior prom. Two of them will be chosen to help. Mr. O'Donnell decides to choose the two students by writing their names on cards, putting the cards in a hat, and choosing two cards without replacing the first card. What is the probability that the cards he draws will contain the names Allison and Eric in that order?

Since there were six students originally, the probability of selecting Allison is $\frac{1}{6}$. After the first student is selected, only five remain. So, the probability of selecting Eric on the second draw is $\frac{1}{5}$. Thus, the probability of selecting Allison and then Eric is $\frac{1}{6} \cdot \frac{1}{5}$ or $\frac{1}{30}$.

Notice that selecting Eric on the second draw is more likely than selecting Allison on the first draw because the sample space was decreased from 6 to 5 elements. The outcome of the second event is affected by the outcome of the first event. Such events are called **dependent events**.

> The probability of two dependent events, *A* and *B*, occurring in that order is the product of the probability of *A* occurring and the probability of *B* occurring given that *A* has occurred.
>
> $$P(A \text{ and } B) = P(A) \cdot P(B \mid A)$$

Probability of Two Dependent Events

$P(B \mid A)$ is read "the probability of B given that A has occurred."

Example 1: A bag contains 5 blue marbles and 7 red marbles. Two marbles are to be selected, without replacing the first one. What is the probability of selecting a blue marble and then a red marble?

Since replacement does not occur, the probability of selecting the red marble is altered by selecting the blue marble. The event is dependent.

$$P(\text{blue and red}) = P(\text{blue}) \cdot P(\text{red} \mid \text{blue})$$

$$= \frac{5}{12} \cdot \frac{7}{11} \qquad P(A \text{ and } B) = P(A) \cdot P(B \mid A)$$

$$= \frac{35}{132}$$

Example 2: A bag contains 3 blue, 5 red, and 8 green marbles. If 3 marbles are selected in succession without replacement, what is the probability that they are all blue?

$$P(3 \text{ blue}) = P(\text{blue}) \cdot P(\text{blue} \,|\, \text{blue}) \cdot P(\text{blue} \,|\, \text{blue, blue})$$

$$= \frac{3}{16} \cdot \frac{2}{15} \cdot \frac{1}{14} \qquad \text{\textit{Each time there is one less blue marble.}}$$

$$= \frac{6}{3360} \quad \text{or} \quad \frac{1}{560}$$

Exercises

State whether the following events are dependent or independent.

1. choosing two names from a list of eight without replacement

2. tossing two 6's on a die on two consecutive rolls

3. drawing two kings from a deck of cards with replacement between draws

4. tossing a 5 then a 4 on a die

5. tossing a 1 on a die then drawing a queen from a deck of cards

6. drawing two hearts from a deck of cards without replacement between draws

A bag contains 5 red, 8 blue, and 3 green marbles. What is the probability of selecting each of the following in the indicated order?

7. two red with no replacement

8. two red with replacement

9. blue, then green, with replacement

10. blue, then green, with no replacement

11. red, then blue, then green, with no replacement

12. red, then blue, then green, with replacement

13. three green with replacement

14. three green with no replacement

15. four blue with replacement

16. four green with replacement

Cathy Bentz wishes to select two other students to help decorate for a party. There are 10 girls and 15 boys from which to choose. What is the probability that the following occurs?

17. Mary and Bill are selected in that order

18. a girl and a boy are selected in that order

19. two girls are selected

20. two boys are selected

CHAPTER 8

Applications of Factoring

A rocket travels at an average speed of 1920 feet per second. How many seconds after it is fired will it be 32,000 feet high? Problems such as this can be solved by using equations. In this chapter, you will learn how factoring can be used to solve some types of equations.

8-1 Solving Equations Already in Factored Form

Consider the following products.

$$3(0) = 0 \qquad -8(0) = 0 \qquad \left[\tfrac{1}{2} + \left(-\tfrac{1}{2}\right)\right](0) = 0 \qquad (x + 2)(0) = 0$$

The above products all equal zero. Notice that in each case *at least one* of the factors is zero.

For all numbers a and b, if $ab = 0$ then $a = 0$ or $b = 0$.	*Zero Product Property*

You can use this property to solve equations already written in factored form.

Examples

1 **Solve and check: $2x(x - 5) = 0$**

If $2x(x - 5) = 0$, then $2x = 0$ or $x - 5 = 0$ *Zero Product Property*
$2x = 0$ or $x - 5 = 0$ *Solve both equations.*
$x = 0$ or $x = 5$

Check: $2x(x - 5) = 0$
$\qquad\qquad 2(0)(0 - 5) \stackrel{?}{=} 0 \qquad$ or $\qquad 2(5)(5 - 5) \stackrel{?}{=} 0$
$\qquad\qquad\qquad\; 0(-5) \stackrel{?}{=} 0 \qquad\qquad\qquad\;\; 10(0) \stackrel{?}{=} 0$
$\qquad\qquad\qquad\qquad 0 = 0 \qquad\qquad\qquad\qquad\; 0 = 0$

The solutions of $2x(x - 5) = 0$ are 0 and 5. The solution set is $\{0, 5\}$.

2 **Solve and check: $(y + 2)(3y + 5) = 0$**

$(y + 2)(3y + 5) = 0$
$y + 2 = 0 \qquad$ or $\qquad 3y + 5 = 0 \qquad$ *Zero Product Property*
$\qquad y = -2 \qquad\qquad\qquad 3y = -5$
$\qquad\qquad\qquad\qquad\qquad\qquad\; y = -\dfrac{5}{3}$

Check: $(y + 2)(3y + 5) = 0$
$\qquad (-2 + 2)[3(-2) + 5] \stackrel{?}{=} 0 \qquad$ or $\qquad \left(-\dfrac{5}{3} + 2\right)\left[3\left(-\dfrac{5}{3}\right) + 5\right] \stackrel{?}{=} 0$
$\qquad\qquad\quad 0[3(-2) + 5] \stackrel{?}{=} 0 \qquad\qquad\qquad \left(-\dfrac{5}{3} + 2\right)(-5 + 5) \stackrel{?}{=} 0$
$\qquad\qquad\qquad\qquad\qquad 0 = 0 \qquad\qquad\qquad\qquad\qquad \left(-\dfrac{5}{3} + 2\right)(0) \stackrel{?}{=} 0$
$\qquad\qquad\qquad\qquad\qquad\qquad\qquad\qquad\qquad\qquad\qquad\qquad\qquad 0 = 0$

The solution set is $\left\{-2, -\dfrac{5}{3}\right\}$.

Example 3

Maria gave this puzzle to her friends. "The product of 4 times my age and 45 less than 3 times my age is 0. How old am I?" Find Maria's age now.

**Explore** | This problem, can be solved by using an equation.
Let y = Maria's age now.

Plan | $4y(3y - 45) = 0$

Solve | $4y = 0$ or $3y - 45 = 0$
$y = 0$ $3y = 45$
                       $y = 15$

Examine | Although 0 is a solution of the equation $4y(3y - 45) = 0$, Maria cannot be 0 years old. Therefore, disregard 0 as a solution. Maria is 15 years old.

Exploratory Exercises

State the conditions under which each equation will be true.
Sample: $x(x + 7) = 0$ will be true if $x = 0$ or $x + 7 = 0$.

1. $x(x + 3) = 0$
2. $y(y - 12) = 0$
3. $3r(r - 4) = 0$
4. $7a(a + 6) = 0$
5. $3t(4t - 32) = 0$
6. $2x(5x - 10) = 0$
7. $(x - 6)(x + 4) = 0$
8. $(b - 3)(b - 5) = 0$
9. $(a + 3)(3a - 12) = 0$
10. $(2y + 22)(y - 1) = 0$
11. $(2y + 8)(3y + 24) = 0$
12. $(4x + 4)(2x + 6) = 0$
13. $(x - 3)(x - 3) = 0$
14. $(3x - 9)(5x - 15) = 0$
15. $(3x + 2)(x - 7) = 0$
16. $(x - 8)(2x + 7) = 0$
17. $(4x - 7)(3x + 5) = 0$
18. $(3x - 5)(4x - 7) = 0$
19. $(2x + 3)(x + 7) = 0$
20. $\left(4x - \frac{1}{3}\right)\left(3x + \frac{1}{8}\right) = 0$

Written Exercises

1-20. Solve and check each equation in Exploratory Exercises 1-20.

Solve each problem. Disregard unreasonable solutions.

21. Sue told Jennifer, "The product of twice my age decreased by 32 and 5 times my age is zero. How old am I?" Find Sue's age.

22. The product of a certain positive number decreased by 5 and the same number increased by 7 is 0. What is the number?

23. The product of a certain negative number increased by 2 and the same number decreased by $\frac{3}{4}$ is 0. What is the number?

24. The result is 0 when 7 is multiplied by the sum of 6 and a certain number. What is the number?

Challenge

Write an equation in factored form that would have each given solution set.

25. $\{-3, 5\}$
26. $\{0, -6\}$
27. $\{-9, -11\}$
28. $\left\{2, -\frac{2}{3}\right\}$
29. $\left\{-\frac{3}{4}, -\frac{5}{6}\right\}$
30. $\left\{0, -7, -\frac{1}{3}\right\}$

Problem Solving

A useful problem-solving strategy is to organize relevant information by using a table. Study the following problem.

> **To mail a small package costs a certain amount for the first ounce and 17¢ for each additional ounce. A 5-ounce package costs 90¢ to mail. How much would a 10-ounce package cost?**

You know that a 5-ounce package costs 90¢ to mail. Write this specific case in your table. You also know that it costs 17¢ more for each additional ounce. Use this information to generate more cases.

Number of Ounces	1	2	3	4	5	6	7	8	9	10
Cost					0.90	1.07	1.24	1.41	1.58	1.75

Therefore, a 10-ounce package would cost $1.75 to mail.

Using the pattern in the table, you could find the cost of mailing a 1-ounce package.

A 4-ounce package costs 0.90 − 0.17 or 0.73 to mail.
↓

Number of Ounces	1	2	3	4	5	6	7	8	9	10
Cost	0.22	0.39	0.56	0.73	0.90	1.07	1.24	1.41	1.58	1.75

A 1-ounce package costs 22¢ to mail. The following expression represents the cost of mailing an n-ounce package.

cost of first ounce + (number of ounces − first ounce) 0.17
$$0.22 + (n - 1)\ 0.17$$

Exercises

Use a table to solve each problem.

1. Bob Hartschorn was charged $2.12 for a 20-minute call to Chicago. If Bob was charged $2.32 for a 22-minute call, how much should he be charged for an hour call?

2. Find the sum of the first three consecutive odd integers. What is the sum of the first five consecutive odd integers? What is the sum of the first fifty consecutive odd integers?

3. Find pairs of positive integers whose sum is 45 and whose difference is less than 9.

4. Find the positive integers less than 50 that have an odd number of factors.

5. To determine a grade point average, four points are given for an A, three for a B, two for a C, one for a D, and zero for an F. If a student has a total of 13 points for 5 classes, what combinations of grades could he have?

6. Joan tore a sheet of paper in half. Then she tore each of the resulting pieces in half. If she continued this process 15 more times, how many pieces of paper would she have at the end?

8-2 Factoring Review

Equations can be easily solved if the equation is factorable. You have used several methods to factor polynomials. A summary of these is given in the following chart.

Check for:	Number of Terms		
	Two	*Three*	*Four or More*
greatest common factor	✔	✔	✔
difference of squares	✔		
perfect square trinomial		✔	
trinomial that has two binomial factors		✔	
pairs of terms that have a common monomial factor			✔

Examples

1 **Factor: $2x^3 - 50x$**

$$2x^3 - 50x = 2x(x^2 - 25) \qquad \text{\textit{2x is the GCF.}}$$
$$= 2x(x - 5)(x + 5) \qquad \text{\textit{$x^2 - 25$ is the difference of two squares.}}$$

2 **Factor: $5a^2x^2 - 30ax^2 + 45x^2$**

$$5a^2x^2 - 30ax^2 + 45x^2 = 5x^2(a^2 - 6a + 9) \qquad \text{\textit{$5x^2$ is the GCF.}}$$
$$= 5x^2(a - 3)(a - 3) \qquad \text{\textit{$a^2 - 6a + 9$ is a perfect}}$$
$$= 5x^2(a - 3)^2 \qquad\qquad \text{\textit{square trinomial.}}$$

3 **Factor: $6m^3 - 11m^2n - 10mn^2$**

$$6m^3 - 11m^2n - 10mn^2 = m(6m^2 - 11mn - 10n^2) \qquad \text{\textit{m is the GCF.}}$$
$$= m(2m - 5n)(3m + 2n)$$

4 **Factor: $4ax^2 - 36ay^2 - 5bx^2 + 45by^2$**

$$4ax^2 - 36ay^2 - 5bx^2 + 45by^2 = (4ax^2 - 36ay^2) - (5bx^2 - 45by^2)$$
$$= 4a(x^2 - 9y^2) - 5b(x^2 - 9y^2)$$
$$= (x^2 - 9y^2)(4a - 5b)$$
$$= (x - 3y)(x + 3y)(4a - 5b)$$

Exploratory Exercises

Indicate which method of factoring you would apply first to each polynomial. Use the table from the previous page.

1. $x^3 - 5x^2$

2. $64c^2 - 25p^2$

3. $9x^2 - 12xy + 4y^2$

4. $16m^4 - 64n^2$

5. $35z^2 + 13z - 12$

6. $x^2 + y^2$

7. $8x^2 - 72x + 162$

8. $3x^2 - xy - 6x + 2y$

9. $1 - 49k^2$

10. $4x^4 - 3x^3y - 12x^2 + 9xy$

11. $x^2 - 5x + 6$

12. $x^2 - (y + z)^2$

Written Exercises

1-12. Factor each polynomial in Exploratory Exercises 1-12.

Factor each of the following polynomials.

13. $6x^2 + 10xy$

14. $35ab - 15b^3$

15. $4a^2 - 9b^2$

16. $25v^4 - 36w^4$

17. $x^2 + 12x + 36$

18. $a^2 - 8a + 16$

19. $12y^2 + 19y - 21$

20. $20m^2 + 17mn - 24n^2$

21. $x^3 + 5x^2 - 9x - 45$

22. $4x^3 + 12x^2 - x - 3$

23. $m^4 - m^2n^2$

24. $x^6 - x^4y^4$

25. $20a^2c^2 + 60a^2c + 45a^2$

26. $48a^2m^2 - 24a^2m + 3a^2$

27. $15x^3y - 6x^2y^3 + 3x^2yz$

28. $5ab^2c + 5ab^4 - 15a^3b^2$

29. $8x^3 - 32xy^4$

30. $48a^5y - 147ay^7$

31. $x^3 + 2x^2 + 8x + 16$

32. $4a^3 + 3a^2 + 8a + 6$

33. $12x^2 - 12xy - 72y^2$

34. $10ab^2 + 20abc - 80ac^2$

35. $(x + y)^2 - (a - b)^2$

36. $(3a + 2b)^2 - 9(x + 3y)^2$

37. $6x^2 + 2xy - 4y^2$

38. $10x^2 + 29xy + 10y^2$

39. $\dfrac{m^2}{4} - \dfrac{9}{25}$

40. $\dfrac{x^4}{9} - 49y^2$

41. $6ax - 21ay + 10bx - 35by$

42. $20ax - 4ay - 15bx + 3by$

43. $2x^2 - 7x - 8$

44. $2x^2 - 7x - 4$

45. $x^2 + 6x + 9 - y^2$

46. $a^4 - b^4 - 2b^2c^2 - c^4$

Challenge

47. $0.01x^2 - 0.06xy + 0.09y^2$

48. $0.15x^4 - 0.019x^2y + 0.0006y^2$

49. $0.12m^3n^2 - 0.001m^2n$

50. $\dfrac{3}{5}a^2b - \dfrac{4}{5}a^3b^2$

51. $\dfrac{1}{4}x^2 - \dfrac{3}{5}xy + \dfrac{9}{25}y^2$

52. $\dfrac{m^2}{3} + \dfrac{2}{3}m - \dfrac{35}{3}$

53. $x^4 - 2x^2y + 3x^3 - 6xy$

54. $4p^2m - 5p^2n - 8pm + 10pn$

mini-review

Solve.

1. $4x + 9 < 6x$

2. $-\dfrac{1}{6}x \le \dfrac{5}{3}$

3. $2r + 3.5 > 7.1$

4. $|m - 1| \le 3$

Graph the solution set.

5. $x \ge -3$ and $x < 4$

Applications in Banking   Factoring and Compound Interest

Many formulas are used daily in business and science. One such formula is used in finding **compound interest**. Compound interest is interest that is added to an original investment at specified time intervals. Thus, the interest becomes part of a new principal.

Suppose you deposited $500 in a savings account for 3 years at a rate of 6% annual interest.

	amount deposited +	interest	= new principal
End of first year	$500 +	$500(0.06)	= $530
End of second year	$530 +	$530(0.06)	= $561.80
End of third year	$561.80 +	$561.80(0.06)	= $595.51 *This result is approximate.*

To write a general formula, let P represent the amount deposited or principal and let r represent the annual interest rate. Then, $P \cdot r$ represents the amount of interest earned.

End of first year
$$P + P \cdot r = P(1 + r)^1$$ *Factor out P.*

End of second year
$$P(1 + r) + P(1 + r) \cdot r = P(1 + r)(1 + r)$$ *Factor out P(1 + r).*
$$= P(1 + r)^2$$

End of third year
$$P(1 + r)^2 + P(1 + r)^2 \cdot r = P(1 + r)^2(1 + r)$$ *Factor out P(1 + r)².*
$$= P(1 + r)^3$$
$$\vdots$$

End of t years
$$P(1 + r)^t$$

Therefore, at the end of t years the total amount of savings including interest could be represented by $P(1 + r)^t$.

Suppose that interest is compounded biannually for 1 year at an annual interest rate of 6%. The interest would be computed twice per year at 3% each time. Thus the total amount in savings could be represented by:

$$P\left(1 + \frac{0.06}{2}\right)^{2 \cdot 1} \leftarrow \textit{interest computed twice per year for 1 year}$$

$$\underset{\textit{interest computed each time at } \frac{0.06}{2} \textit{ or } 0.03}{\uparrow}$$

Exercises   Use a calculator to solve each problem.

1. Gloria invested $750 for 1 year at 8% annual interest. If interest is compounded biannually, how much will Gloria have at the end of the year?

2. Ann invested $600 in a savings account for 2 years. If the annual interest rate is 12% compounded biannually, what is the total amount Ann will have at the end of 2 years?

3. For interest compounded quarterly for 2 years at 12% annual interest the expression is $P\left(1 + \frac{0.12}{4}\right)^{4 \cdot 2}$. If Jim invested $600 in such an account, how much will he have at the end of 2 years?

4. In Exercises 2 and 3, Ann's money was compounded biannually and Jim's was compounded quarterly. Who had more money at the end of 2 years? How much more?

8-3   Solving Some Equations by Factoring

If a polynomial equation can be written in the form $ab = 0$, then the zero product property can be applied to solve the equation.

Examples

1 **Solve and check:** $x^2 - 9 = 0$

$$x^2 - 9 = 0 \qquad \textit{x}^2 - 9 \textit{ is the difference of two squares.}$$
$$(x - 3)(x + 3) = 0$$
$$x - 3 = 0 \quad \text{or} \quad x + 3 = 0 \qquad \textit{Use the zero product property.}$$
$$x = 3 \qquad\qquad\quad x = -3$$

Check: $x^2 - 9 = 0$
$$(3)^2 - 9 \overset{?}{=} 0 \qquad \text{or} \qquad (-3)^2 - 9 \overset{?}{=} 0$$
$$9 - 9 \overset{?}{=} 0 \qquad\qquad\qquad 9 - 9 \overset{?}{=} 0$$
$$0 = 0 \qquad\qquad\qquad\qquad 0 = 0$$

The solution set is $\{3, -3\}$.

2 **Solve and check:** $y^2 = -7y$

To use the zero product property, one side of the equation must be zero.

$$y^2 = -7y$$
$$y^2 + 7y = 0$$
$$y(y + 7) = 0 \qquad \textit{Use the distributive property.}$$
$$y = 0 \quad \text{or} \quad y + 7 = 0$$
$$y = -7$$

Check: $y^2 \overset{?}{=} -7y$
$$(0)^2 \overset{?}{=} -7(0) \qquad \text{or} \qquad (-7)^2 \overset{?}{=} -7(-7)$$
$$0 = 0 \qquad\qquad\qquad 49 = 49$$

The solution set is $\{0, -7\}$.

3 **Solve:** $\frac{2}{3}x^2 - 3x = 0$

$$\frac{2}{3}x^2 - 3x = 0$$
$$x\left(\frac{2}{3}x - 3\right) = 0$$
$$x = 0 \quad \text{or} \quad \frac{2}{3}x - 3 = 0$$
$$\frac{2}{3}x = 3$$
$$x = \frac{9}{2} \qquad \textit{Check the result.}$$

The solution set is $\left\{0, \frac{9}{2}\right\}$.

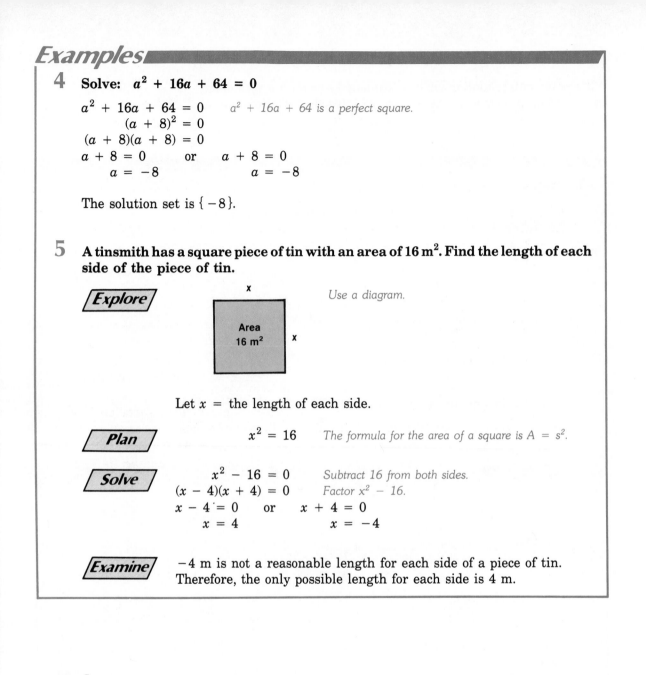

4 Solve: $a^2 + 16a + 64 = 0$

$a^2 + 16a + 64 = 0$ *$a^2 + 16a + 64$ is a perfect square.*
$(a + 8)^2 = 0$
$(a + 8)(a + 8) = 0$
$a + 8 = 0$ or $a + 8 = 0$
$a = -8$ $a = -8$

The solution set is $\{-8\}$.

5 A tinsmith has a square piece of tin with an area of $16\ m^2$. Find the length of each side of the piece of tin.

Explore   *Use a diagram.*

x

Area
16 m²

x

Let x = the length of each side.

Plan $x^2 = 16$ *The formula for the area of a square is $A = s^2$.*

Solve $x^2 - 16 = 0$ *Subtract 16 from both sides.*
$(x - 4)(x + 4) = 0$ *Factor $x^2 - 16$.*
$x - 4 = 0$ or $x + 4 = 0$
$x = 4$ $x = -4$

Examine -4 m is not a reasonable length for each side of a piece of tin. Therefore, the only possible length for each side is 4 m.

Exploratory Exercises

Express each equation in factored form so that the zero product property can be applied.

1. $n^2 - 3n = 0$
2. $y^2 - 6y = 0$
3. $8c^2 + 32c = 0$
4. $9d^2 + 36d = 0$
5. $3x^2 - \frac{3}{4}x = 0$
6. $x^2 + \frac{5}{3}x = 0$
7. $7y^2 = 14y$
8. $8y^2 = -4y$
9. $-13y = -26y^2$
10. $x^2 = 9$
11. $y^2 - 16 = 0$
12. $x^2 + 4x + 4 = 0$
13. $y^2 - 16y + 64 = 0$
14. $x^2 - 8x = -16$
15. $y^2 = 10y - 25$

Written Exercises

Solve and check.

1. $x^2 - 6x = 0$
2. $m^2 + 36m = 0$
3. $2x^2 + 4x = 0$
4. $4x^2 - 9 = 0$
5. $a^2 - 81 = 0$
6. $16x^2 = 64$
7. $4s^2 = -36s$
8. $y^2 = 7y$
9. $x^2 = -8x$
10. $6y = -3y^2$
11. $x^2 = 36$
12. $y^2 = 64$
13. $y^2 = -5y$
14. $\frac{1}{2}y^2 - \frac{1}{4}y = 0$
15. $3y^2 - \frac{4}{3} = 0$
16. $\frac{2}{3}y = \frac{1}{3}y^2$
17. $5x^2 = 45$
18. $2y^2 - 98 = 0$
19. $4y^2 - 16 = 0$
20. $m^2 - 24m + 144 = 0$
21. $y^2 + 10y = -25$
22. $25x^2 + 20x = -4$
23. $81n^2 + 36n = -4$
24. $9y^2 = -42y - 49$
25. $y^2 - \frac{16}{81} = 0$
26. $\frac{5}{6}x^2 = \frac{2}{3}x$
27. $\frac{3}{4}x^2 - \frac{1}{8}x = 0$

Use an equation to solve each problem. Disregard any unreasonable solutions.

28. The square of a number decreased by 144 is zero. Find the number.

29. The area of a square tabletop is $4\,\text{m}^2$. Find the length of one side of the tabletop.

30. The square of a number added to 6 times the number is zero. Find the number.

31. The square of a number is equal to 10 times the number decreased by 25. Find the number.

32. Jake is as many years less than 30 as Jackie is more than 30. The product of their ages is 884. How old is each?

33. A certain number decreased by 7 is multiplied by the same number increased by 7. The product is 51. Find the number.

34. The square of a number increased by 1070 is 1359. Find the number.

35. If the square of a number is subtracted from 900, the result is 275. Find the number.

Challenge

36. The height h in meters of a rocket with initial velocity v, t seconds after blast-off, is given by the formula $h = vt - 5t^2$. A toy rocket is launched with an initial velocity of 80 meters/second. How many seconds after blast-off will it hit the ground?

37. A tinsmith has a rectangular piece of tin with a 3-inch square cut from each corner.

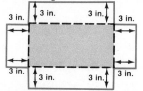

After folding up the sides to form a box, she notices the box is twice as long as it is wide and has a volume of 1350 in³. Find the length and width of the box.

8-4 Solving More Equations by Factoring

Some equations of second degree or higher can be written as a product of factors equal to zero. The zero product property can be applied to solve these equations.

Example

1 **Solve and check:** $2x^2 = 11x - 12$

$$2x^2 = 11x - 12$$

$2x^2 - 11x + 12 = 0$ *Rewrite the equation.*

$(2x - 3)(x - 4) = 0$ *Factor $2x^2 - 11x + 12$.*

$2x - 3 = 0$ or $x - 4 = 0$ *Use the zero-product property.*

$x = \dfrac{3}{2}$ or $x = 4$

Check: $2x^2 = 11x - 12$

$2\left(\dfrac{3}{2}\right)^2 \overset{?}{=} 11\left(\dfrac{3}{2}\right) - 12$ $2(4)^2 \overset{?}{=} 11(4) - 12$

$2\left(\dfrac{9}{4}\right) \overset{?}{=} \dfrac{33}{2} - \dfrac{24}{2}$ $2(16) \overset{?}{=} 44 - 12$

$\dfrac{9}{2} = \dfrac{9}{2}$ $32 = 32$

The solution set of $2x^2 = 11x - 12$ is $\left\{\dfrac{3}{2}, 4\right\}$.

You may have to use more than one method of factoring to solve an equation.

Example

2 **Solve and check:** $x^3 - 24x = 5x^2$

$$x^3 - 24x = 5x^2$$

$x^3 - 5x^2 - 24x = 0$ *Arrange terms in descending order.*

$x(x^2 - 5x - 24) = 0$ *Factor out the GCF, x.*

$x(x - 8)(x + 3) = 0$ *Factor $x^2 - 5x - 24$.*

$x = 0$ or $x - 8 = 0$ or $x + 3 = 0$

$x = 0$ or $x = 8$ or $x = -3$

Check: $x^3 - 24x = 5x^2$

$0^3 - 24(0) \overset{?}{=} 5(0)^2$ $8^3 - 24(8) \overset{?}{=} 5(8)^2$ $(-3)^3 - 24(-3) \overset{?}{=} 5(-3)^2$

$0 - 0 \overset{?}{=} 0$ $512 - 192 \overset{?}{=} 5(64)$ $-27 + 72 \overset{?}{=} 5(9)$

$0 = 0$ $320 = 320$ $45 = 45$

The solution set of $x^3 - 24x = 5x^2$ is $\{0, 8, -3\}$.

In Example 2, if you divide both sides of $x(x^2 - 5x - 24) = 0$ by x the result would not be an equivalent equation. This follows since 0 is a solution of the first equation. But 0 is *not* a solution of $x^2 - 5x - 24 = 0$. For this reason, when solving equations do not divide by expressions containing a variable.

Exploratory Exercises

Solve each equation.

1. $(a + 7)(a - 3) = 0$
2. $(x - 6)(x + 5) = 0$
3. $(r - 8)(r - 2) = 0$
4. $(b + 12)(b - 3) = 0$
5. $(2y + 3)(y + 1) = 0$
6. $(3z - 1)(z + 2) = 0$
7. $(3x - 4)(2x - 1) = 0$
8. $(2m - 1)(5m + 3) = 0$
9. $7(k - 5)(k + 3) = 0$
10. $4(s + 7)(s - 6) = 0$
11. $x(2x + 7)(3x + 4) = 0$
12. $z(5z + 4)(3z - 11) = 0$

Written Exercises

Solve and check each equation.

1. $x^2 + 13x + 36 = 0$
2. $y^2 + 19y + 34 = 0$
3. $a^2 + 4a - 21 = 0$
4. $b^2 - 8b - 33 = 0$
5. $s^2 + 2s - 63 = 0$
6. $c^2 + 17c + 72 = 0$
7. $r^2 - 49 = 0$
8. $y^2 - 64 = 0$
9. $x^2 - 12x = 0$
10. $k^2 - 13k = 0$
11. $p^2 = 5p + 24$
12. $r^2 = 18 + 7r$
13. $2t^2 + 7t = 15$
14. $3y^2 - 7y = 20$
15. $6z^2 + 5 = -17z$
16. $12m^2 + 3 = -20m$
17. $2x^2 + 13x = 24$
18. $3y^2 + 16y = 35$
19. $m^3 - 81m = 0$
20. $4b^3 - 36b = 0$
21. $r^3 - 6r^2 + 8r = 0$
22. $s^3 + 2s^2 - 35s = 0$
23. $5b^3 + 34b^2 = 7b$
24. $2k^3 + 5k^2 = 42k$
25. $2y^3 - 15y = y^2$
26. $6x^3 - 7x = 11x^2$
27. $\frac{x^2}{12} - \frac{2}{3}x - 4 = 0$
28. $x^2 - \frac{1}{6}x - \frac{35}{6} = 0$
29. $0.03x^2 - x + 3 = 0$
30. $0.3x^2 - 1.06x + 0.2 = 0$
31. $(x + 8)(x + 1) = -12$
32. $(r - 1)(r - 1) = 36$
33. $(3y + 2)(y + 3) = y + 14$
34. $(y + 4)(3y - 2) = -y - 14$
35. $h^3 + h^2 - 4h - 4 = 0$
36. $y^3 - y^2 - y + 1 = 0$
37. $9a^3 - 18a^2 - a + 2 = 0$
38. $2m^3 + 5m^2 - 18m - 45 = 0$
39. $y^4 - 8y^2 + 16 = 0$
40. $m^4 - 2m^2 + 1 = 0$
41. $xy + 4x - 3y - 12 = 0$
42. $2my + 5m + 8y + 20 = 0$
43. $3rs - 4r + 6s - 8 = 0$
44. $4pz - z + 12p - 3 = 0$

Challenge

Write an equation with integral coefficients in the form $ax^2 + bx + c = 0$ that would have the given solutions.

45. $\{2, 3\}$
46. $\{-3, 5\}$
47. $\left\{\frac{2}{3}, -1\right\}$
48. $\left\{-3, \frac{3}{4}\right\}$

8-5 Problem Solving: Integer Problems

Some types of integer problems can be solved by using factoring.

Examples

1 **Find two consecutive integers whose product is 72.**

Explore This problem can be solved by using an equation.
Let x = one integer.
Then $x + 1$ = the next greater integer.

Plan $x(x + 1) = 72$

Solve
$$x(x + 1) = 72$$
$$x^2 + x = 72$$
$$x^2 + x - 72 = 0$$
$$(x + 9)(x - 8) = 0$$
$$x + 9 = 0 \quad \text{or} \quad x - 8 = 0$$
$$x = -9 \quad \text{or} \quad x = 8$$

If $x = -9$, then $x + 1 = -8$.
If $x = 8$, then $x + 1 = 9$.

Examine Since $-9(-8) = 72$ and $8 \cdot 9 = 72$, the consecutive integers are -9 and -8 or 8 and 9.

2 **Find two integers whose sum is 15 and whose product is 54.**

Explore Let n = one integer.
Then $15 - n$ = the other integer.

Plan $n(15 - n) = 54$

Solve
$$n(15 - n) = 54$$
$$15n - n^2 = 54$$
$$-n^2 + 15n - 54 = 0$$
$$n^2 - 15n + 54 = 0 \qquad \textit{Multiply both sides by } -1.$$
$$(n - 9)(n - 6) = 0$$
$$n - 9 = 0 \quad \text{or} \quad n - 6 = 0$$
$$n = 9 \quad \text{or} \quad n = 6$$

If $n = 9$, then $15 - n = 6$.
If $n = 6$, then $15 - n = 9$.

Examine Since $6 + 9 = 15$ and $6 \cdot 9 = 54$, the two integers are 6 and 9.

Example

3

The sum of the squares of two consecutive odd integers is 130. Find the integers.

Explore

Let x = one odd integer.
Then $x + 2$ = the next greater odd integer.

Plan

$$x^2 + (x + 2)^2 = 130$$

Solve

$$x^2 + (x + 2)^2 = 130$$
$$x^2 + x^2 + 4x + 4 = 130$$
$$2x^2 + 4x - 126 = 0$$
$$2(x^2 + 2x - 63) = 0 \qquad \textit{Factor out the GCF, 2.}$$
$$x^2 + 2x - 63 = 0 \qquad \textit{Divide both sides by 2.}$$
$$(x + 9)(x - 7) = 0$$
$$x + 9 = 0 \quad \text{or} \quad x - 7 = 0$$
$$x = -9 \quad \text{or} \quad x = 7$$

If $x = -9$, then $x + 2 = -7$.
If $x = 7$, then $x + 2 = 9$.

Examine

Since $(-9)^2 + (-7)^2 = 130$ and $(7)^2 + (9)^2 = 130$,
the consecutive odd integers are -9 and -7 or 7 and 9.

Exploratory Exercises

Define a variable and state an equation for each sentence.

1. The product of two consecutive integers is 110.

2. The product of two consecutive integers is 156.

3. The product of two consecutive even integers is 168.

4. The product of two consecutive odd integers is 143.

5. The sum of two integers is 15 and their product is 44.

6. The sum of two integers is 22 and their product is 117.

7. The sum of the squares of two consecutive integers is 181.

8. The sum of the squares of two consecutive even integers is 100.

9. The difference of the squares of two consecutive integers is 17.

10. The difference of the squares of two consecutive even integers is 52.

Written Exercises

1-10. Solve each problem in Exploratory Exercises 1-10.

For each problem below, define a variable. Then use an equation to solve the problem.

11. Find two consecutive even integers whose product is 120.

12. Find two consecutive even integers whose product is 360.

13. Find two consecutive positive odd integers whose product is 195.

14. Find two consecutive odd integers whose product is 399.

15. Find two consecutive positive integers whose product is 182.

16. Find two consecutive positive integers whose product is 272.

17. Find two integers whose sum is 11 and whose product is 24.

18. Find two integers whose sum is 19 and whose product is 60.

19. Find two integers whose difference is 3 and whose product is 88.

20. Find two integers whose difference is 23 and whose product is -120.

21. The sum of the squares of two consecutive positive odd integers is 202. Find the integers.

22. The sum of the squares of two consecutive positive integers is 113. Find the integers.

23. The sum of two integers is 13. The sum of their squares is 97. Find the integers.

24. The sum of two integers is 3. The sum of their squares is 185. Find the integers.

25. When one integer is added to the square of the next consecutive integer, the sum is 41. Find the integers.

26. When one integer is added to the square of the next consecutive integer, the sum is 55. Find the integers.

27. When the square of the second of two consecutive even integers is added to twice the first integer, the sum is 76. Find the integers.

28. When the square of the second of two consecutive even integers is added to twice the first integer, the sum is 116. Find the integers.

29. Find 3 consecutive odd integers if the difference of the squares of the least and greatest is 120.

30. Lyle and Connie Fisher's ages are consecutive odd integers. The product of their ages is 399. If Lyle is older, find their ages.

31. Jim is a year older than Colleen and the difference of the squares of their ages is 97. How old is each?

32. Jennifer said to Peggy, "I am thinking of 2 consecutive even integers. The difference of their squares is 92." What are the numbers?

Using Calculators ——————————— Special Products

You know that $(x - y)(x + y) = x^2 - y^2$. This fact can be used to multiply numbers mentally. Suppose you want to find $36 \cdot 44$. Notice that $36 = 40 - 4$ and $44 = 40 + 4$.

$$
\begin{aligned}
36 \cdot 44 &= (40 - 4)(40 + 4) \\
&= 40^2 - 4^2 \\
&= 1600 - 16 \\
&= 1584
\end{aligned}
$$

Let $x = 40$ and $y = 4$ in $(x - y)(x + y) = x^2 - y^2$.

Exercises

Calculate each product mentally and check by using a calculator.

1. $27 \cdot 33$
2. $19 \cdot 21$
3. $53 \cdot 67$
4. $95 \cdot 105$

When you solve a polynomial equation by factoring, the zero product property is used.

$$\text{If } ab = 0, \text{ then } a = 0 \text{ or } b = 0.$$

Now consider the inequality $ab > 0$. For what values of a and b will this inequality be true? It will be true only when a and b are either both positive or both negative.

$$\text{If } ab > 0, \text{ then either } a > 0 \text{ and } b > 0, \text{ or } a < 0 \text{ and } b < 0.$$

Example: Solve $(x + 6)(x - 2) > 0$ and graph the solution.

$$x + 6 > 0 \text{ and } x - 2 > 0 \quad \text{or} \quad x + 6 < 0 \text{ and } x - 2 < 0$$
$$x > -6 \text{ and } x > 2 \quad\quad \text{or} \quad\quad x < -6 \text{ and } x < 2$$
$$x > 2 \quad\quad\quad \text{or} \quad\quad\quad x < -6 \quad\quad \text{\textit{Why?}}$$

Consider the inequality $ab < 0$. Either a must be positive and b negative or b must be positive and a negative.

$$\text{If } ab < 0, \text{ then either } a > 0 \text{ and } b < 0 \text{ or } a < 0 \text{ and } b > 0.$$

Example: Solve $(x + 7)(x - 8) < 0$ and graph the solution.

$$x + 7 > 0 \text{ and } x - 8 < 0 \quad \text{or} \quad x + 7 < 0 \text{ and } x - 8 > 0$$
$$x > -7 \text{ and } x < 8 \quad\quad \text{or} \quad\quad x < -7 \text{ and } x > 8$$

This can never be true.

The compound sentence $x > -7$ and $x < 8$ can be written $-7 < x < 8$.

Exercises

Solve each inequality and graph the solution.

1. $x(x + 4) > 0$
2. $x(x - 3) > 0$
3. $(x + 2)(x - 3) \geq 0$
4. $x(x - 5) < 0$
5. $(x + 6)(x - 3) \leq 0$
6. $x^2 + 5x + 6 > 0$
7. $x^2 - 2x - 15 \geq 0$
8. $x^2 + 6x + 5 < 0$
9. $y^2 < 9$
10. $y^2 + 2y > 35$
11. $x^2 > 36$
12. $x^2 - 3x \leq -2$

8-6 Problem Solving: Velocity and Area

If an object is launched into the air its height above the ground after t seconds is given by the formula $h = vt - 16t^2$. In this formula, h represents the height of the object in feet, and v represents the initial velocity in feet per second. Thus, the height of an object with an initial velocity of 144 feet per second is represented by $h = 144t - 16t^2$.

Example

1 **A flare is launched from a life raft with an initial velocity of 144 feet per second. How many seconds will it take for the flare to return to the sea?**

| Explore | Use the formula $h = vt - 16t^2$. |

The variable h represents the height of the flare in feet when it returns to the sea. Thus, $h = 0$.

The variable v represents the initial velocity of the flare, in feet per second.
Thus, $v = 144$.

Plan Substitute the appropriate values into the formula.

$$0 = 144t - 16t^2 \qquad \text{t is the time in seconds.}$$

Solve
$$0 = 16t(9 - t)$$
$$16t = 0 \quad \text{or} \quad 9 - t = 0$$
$$t = 0 \quad \text{or} \qquad 9 = t$$

Examine The flare returns to the sea in 9 seconds. The answer 0 is not reasonable since it represents the time when the flare is launched.

You can use factoring to solve some area problems. Recall that the area of a rectangle is equal to the product of the length and the width.

Example

2 Pat Bing has a photograph that is 8 cm long and 6 cm wide. Pat wants to reduce the length and width of the photo by the same amount. She also wants the reduced photo to have half the area of the original photo. By what amount should she reduce the length and width?

Let x = the amount the length and width should be reduced.

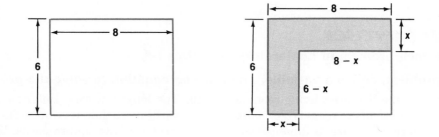

The dimensions of the reduced photo will be $(8 - x)$ and $(6 - x)$.

The area of the photo is $8 \cdot 6$, or 48 cm^2.

The area of the reduced photo will be $\frac{48}{2}$, or 24 cm^2.

$$\text{length} \cdot \text{width} = \text{area}$$

$(8 - x)(6 - x) = 24$	*Substitute the appropriate values into the formula.*
$48 - 8x - 6x + x^2 = 24$	*Solve the equation.*
$x^2 - 14x + 48 = 24$	
$x^2 - 14x + 24 = 0$	
$(x - 12)(x - 2) = 0$	
$x - 12 = 0 \quad \text{or} \quad x - 2 = 0$	
$x = 12 \quad \text{or} \quad x = 2$	*Why is 12 cm not a reasonable answer?*

Pat should reduce the length and width by 2 cm each.

The dimensions of the reduced photo will be $8 - 2$, or 6 cm and $6 - 2$, or 4 cm.

Exploratory Exercises

Define a variable and state an equation for each problem.

1. The length of a rectangle is 3 feet greater than its width. The area of the rectangle is 108 ft^2. Find the length and width.

2. The length of a rectangle is 4 cm greater than its width. The area of the rectangle is 117 cm^2. Find the length and width.

3. The width of a rectangle is 9 feet less than its length. The area of the rectangle is 90 ft^2. Find the length and width.

4. The width of a rectangle is 7 cm less than its length. The area of the rectangle is 120 cm^2. Find the length and width.

5. The side of one square is 7 in. longer than the side of a second square. The difference of their areas is 231 in^2. Find the length of their sides.

6. One square has sides three times as long as the sides of a second square. The combined area of the squares is 640 ft^2. Find their dimensions.

7. If the sides of a square are doubled, its area is increased by 363 in^2. What is the original length of the side?

8. A rectangle is 24 m long and 16 m wide. By how much must each dimension be decreased in order to decrease the area by 279 m^2?

Written Exercises

1-8. Solve each problem in Exploratory Exercises 1-8.

For each problem, define a variable. Then use an equation to solve the problem.

9. The area of Jane Redfern's living room is 40 m^2. The length of the room is 3 m more than the width. What are its dimensions?

10. The length of Mrs. Boland's garden is 5 yards more than its width. The area of the garden is 234 square yards. What are its dimensions?

11. A rectangle is 4 in. wide and 7 in. long. When the length and width are increased by the same amount, the area is increased by 26 in^2. What are the dimensions of the new rectangle?

12. A photo is 8 cm wide and 12 cm long. The length and width are increased by an equal amount in order to double the area of the photo. What are the dimensions of the new photo?

13. Mr. Steinborn wants to double the area of his garden by adding a strip of uniform width along each of the four sides. The original garden is 10 ft by 15 ft. How wide a strip must be added?

14. A strip of uniform width is plowed along both sides and both ends of a garden 120 ft by 90 ft. How wide is the strip if the garden is half plowed?

Use $h = vt - 16t^2$ to find the missing quantity.

15. Find v, if $t = 5$ seconds and $h = 480$ feet.

16. Find h, if $t = 7$ seconds and $v = 1700$ feet per second.

17. Find h, if $t = 2$ seconds and $v = 110$ feet per second.

18. Find 2 values for t, if $v = 120$ feet per second and $h = 224$ feet.

Use the formula $h = vt - 16t^2$ to solve each of the following problems.

19. A flare is launched from a life raft with an initial velocity of 192 feet per second. How many seconds will it take for the flare to return to the sea?

20. A golf ball is hit into the air with an initial velocity of 64 feet per second. How many seconds will it take for the golf ball to hit the ground?

21. A missile is fired with an initial velocity of 2320 feet per second. When will it be 40,000 feet high?

22. A rocket is fired with an initial velocity of 1920 feet per second. When will it be 32,000 feet high?

23. A rocket is fired with an initial velocity of 1640 feet per second. When will it be 816 feet high?

24. A flare is launched with an initial velocity of 128 feet per second. How many seconds will it take for the flare to return to the sea?

8-7 Simplifying Rational Expressions

Factoring polynomials is also a useful tool for simplifying **algebraic fractions.**

Rational numbers and algebraic fractions are similar. Recall that any rational number can be expressed as the quotient of two integers.

Algebraic fractions contain variables. The expressions $\frac{36a^2bc}{24b^2}$, $\frac{2x}{x-5}$, and $\frac{p^2-25}{p^2+4p+1}$ are examples of algebraic fractions.

Assume that the denominator does not equal zero.

To simplify a rational number such as $\frac{6}{21}$, first factor the numerator and denominator. Then eliminate common factors.

$$\frac{6}{21} = \frac{2\cdot 3}{7\cdot 3}$$

Notice that $\frac{3}{3} = 1$.

$$= \frac{2\cdot \cancel{3}}{7\cdot \cancel{3}} \text{ or } \frac{2}{7}$$

Eliminate common factors.

The same procedure can be used to simplify algebraic fractions.

Examples

1 **Simplify:** $\frac{42y^2}{18xy}$

Assume the denominator does not equal zero.

$$\frac{42y^2}{18xy} = \frac{2\cdot 3\cdot 7\cdot y\cdot y}{2\cdot 3\cdot 3\cdot x\cdot y}$$

Factor the numerator and denominator.

$$= \frac{\overset{1}{\cancel{2}}\cdot \overset{1}{\cancel{3}}\cdot 7\cdot y\cdot \overset{1}{\cancel{y}}}{\underset{1}{\cancel{2}}\cdot \underset{1}{\cancel{3}}\cdot 3\cdot x\cdot \underset{1}{\cancel{y}}}$$

Eliminate common factors.

$$= \frac{7y}{3x}$$

2 **Simplify:** $\frac{y^2-9}{y^2-y-6}$

$$\frac{y^2-9}{y^2-y-6} = \frac{(y+3)(y-3)}{(y-3)(y+2)}$$

$$= \frac{(y+3)\overset{1}{\cancel{(y-3)}}}{\underset{1}{\cancel{(y-3)}}(y+2)}$$

$$= \frac{y+3}{y+2}$$

3 **Simplify:** $\frac{a+2}{a^2-4}$

$$\frac{a+2}{a^2-4} = \frac{(a+2)\cdot 1}{(a+2)(a-2)}$$

$$= \frac{\overset{1}{\cancel{(a+2)}}\cdot 1}{\underset{1}{\cancel{(a+2)}}(a-2)}$$

$$= \frac{1}{a-2}$$

Exploratory Exercises

For each expression, find the greatest common factor (GCF) of the numerator and denominator. Then simplify each expression. Assume that no denominator is equal to zero.

1. $\dfrac{24}{72}$

2. $\dfrac{99}{132}$

3. $\dfrac{42y}{18xy}$

4. $\dfrac{13x}{39x^2}$

5. $\dfrac{38a^2}{42ab}$

6. $\dfrac{79a^2b}{158a^3bc}$

7. $\dfrac{-3x^2y^5}{18x^5y^2}$

8. $\dfrac{14y^2z}{49yz^3}$

9. $\dfrac{x(y + 1)}{x(y - 2)}$

10. $\dfrac{4a}{a(a + 7)}$

11. $\dfrac{m + 5}{2(m + 5)}$

12. $\dfrac{(a + b)(a - b)}{(a - b)(a - b)}$

Written Exercises

Simplify each algebraic fraction. Assume that no denominator is equal to zero.

1. $\dfrac{y - 4}{y^2 - 16}$

2. $\dfrac{z + 3}{z^2 - 9}$

3. $\dfrac{a + b}{a^2 - b^2}$

4. $\dfrac{x + y}{x^2 - y^2}$

5. $\dfrac{c^2 - 4}{(c + 2)^2}$

6. $\dfrac{y^2 - 81}{(y - 9)^2}$

7. $\dfrac{a^2 - a}{a - 1}$

8. $\dfrac{m^2 - 2m}{m - 2}$

9. $\dfrac{x^2 + 4}{x^4 - 16}$

10. $\dfrac{y^2 + 6}{y^4 - 36}$

11. $\dfrac{2x^2 + 6}{2x + 6}$

12. $\dfrac{3n^2 - 9}{3n - 9}$

13. $\dfrac{-4y^2}{2y^2 - 4y^3}$

14. $\dfrac{3a^3}{3a^3 + 6a^2b}$

15. $\dfrac{-4a^2}{a^3 + 6a^2b + 9ab}$

16. $\dfrac{2a^3 - 8a}{am^3 + am^2 + am}$

17. $\dfrac{x + y}{x^2 + 2xy + y^2}$

18. $\dfrac{x + 6}{x^2 + 7x + 6}$

19. $\dfrac{x - 3}{x^2 + x - 12}$

20. $\dfrac{x + 5}{x^2 + 7x + 10}$

21. $\dfrac{m^2 - 16}{m^2 + 8m + 16}$

22. $\dfrac{n^2 - y^2}{n^2 - 2ny + y^2}$

23. $\dfrac{y^2 - 9}{y^2 + 6y + 9}$

24. $\dfrac{y^2 + 8y - 20}{y^2 - 4}$

25. $\dfrac{x^2 + 8x + 15}{x + 3}$

26. $\dfrac{2m^2 - 13m + 15}{2m - 3}$

27. $\dfrac{6x^2 + 24x}{x^2 + 8x + 16}$

28. $\dfrac{8m^2 - 16m}{m^2 - 4m + 4}$

29. $\dfrac{4k^2 - 25}{4k^2 - 20k + 25}$

30. $\dfrac{x^2 - x - 20}{x^2 + 7x + 12}$

31. $\dfrac{3 - x}{6 - 17x + 5x^2}$

32. $\dfrac{2x - 14}{x^2 - 4x - 21}$

33. $\dfrac{5x^2 + 10x + 5}{3x^2 + 6x + 3}$

34. $\dfrac{3x^2 + 3x + 18}{7x^2 + 7x + 42}$

35. $\dfrac{m^2 - 2m - 8}{m^2 - m - 6}$

36. $\dfrac{b^2 + b - 12}{b^2 + 2b - 15}$

37. $\dfrac{p^2 - 4p + 4}{p^2 + 4p - 12}$

38. $\dfrac{b^2 - 5b + 6}{b^4 - 13b^2 + 36}$

39. $\dfrac{2x^2 - 5x + 3}{3x^2 - 5x + 2}$

40. $\dfrac{3m^2 + 8m - 3}{6m^2 + 17m - 3}$

41. $\dfrac{2y^2 - 18}{2y - 6}$

42. $\dfrac{8x^2 - x^3}{16 - 2x}$

43. $\dfrac{2x^2 + 8x}{x^2 - 11x}$

44. $\dfrac{6y^3 - 9y^2}{2y^2 + 5y - 12}$

45. $\dfrac{x^2 - x^2y}{x^3 - x^3y}$

Sums of Integers

One advantage of using a computer in problem solving is that the computer can perform many operations very quickly. Consider this problem.

> The sum of the first 5 positive even integers is 30. Find the sum of the first 100 positive even integers.

The following BASIC program can be used to find the sum.

```
10  INPUT "HOW MANY EVEN INTEGERS? ";N
20  LET SUM = 0
30  FOR I = 2 TO 2 * N STEP 2
40  LET SUM = SUM + I          Line 40 calculates the sum.
50  NEXT I
60  PRINT "THE SUM OF THE FIRST ";N;" EVEN INTEGERS IS ";SUM
70  END

]RUN
HOW MANY EVEN INTEGERS? 100
THE SUM OF THE FIRST 100 EVEN INTEGERS IS 10100
```

Exercises

1. Run the program several times. Input 1, 2, 3,...10 for the value of N. Write the corresponding sum.

2. Modify lines 10, 30, and 60 to find the sum of the first N positive odd integers.

3. For N = 1, 2, 3, . . . 10, write the sum of the first N positive odd integers.

4. Modify the program to find the sum of the first N positive integers. Run the program for N = 1, 2, 3, . . . 10.

Vocabulary

Zero Product Property   (245)   algebraic fractions   (263)

Chapter Summary

1. The Zero Product Property:
   For all numbers a and b, if $ab = 0$, then $a = 0$ or $b = 0$.   (245)

2. If an equation of second degree or higher can be written as a product of factors equal to zero, the zero product property can be applied to solve the equation.   (254)

3. To simplify an algebraic fraction, first factor the numerator and denominator. Then eliminate common factors.   (263)

8-1 **Solve and check each equation.**

1. $y(y + 11) = 0$
2. $7a(a - 7) = 0$
3. $4t(2t - 10) = 0$
4. $(2y - 9)(2y + 9) = 0$
5. $(3y - 2)(4y + 7) = 0$
6. $(y - 2)(y + 7) = 0$
7. The product of a positive number decreased by 6 and the same number increased by 11 is zero. What is the number?

8-2 **Factor.**

8. $50x^2 - 98y^2$
9. $6m^3 + m^2 - 15m$
10. $56a^2 - 93a + 27$
11. $24am - 9an + 40bm - 15bn$
12. $81x^8 - 16c^4$
13. $49m^2 + 70mn + 25n^2$
14. $14x^2 + \frac{13}{2}x - 3$
15. $8a^2 + 32b^2$

Solve and check each equation.

8-3
16. $y^2 - 9y = 0$
17. $y^2 = -7y$
18. $2y^2 - 98 = 0$
19. $\frac{3}{4}y = \frac{1}{4}y^2$
20. $a^2 + 10a + 25 = 0$
21. $25y^2 + 20y = -4$
22. The square of a number added to seven times the number is zero. What is the number?

8-4
23. $y^2 + 40 = -13y$
24. $x^2 + 12x = -35$
25. $2m^2 + 13m = 24$
26. $(x + 6)(x - 1) = 78$
27. $6p^2 - 11p + 4 = 0$
28. $6x^3 + 29x^2 + 28x = 0$

For each problem, define a variable. Then use an equation to solve the problem.

8-5
29. The product of two consecutive odd integers is 143. Find the integers.
30. The sum of the squares of two consecutive odd integers is 202. Find the integers.

8-6
31. A rectangle is 11 inches wide and 13 inches long. When its length and width are decreased by the same amount, its area is decreased by 63 square inches. What are the dimensions of the new rectangle?
32. For this exercise, use the formula $h = vt - 16t^2$. A baseball travels upward with an initial velocity of 80 feet per second. How long does it take to return to the ground?

8-7 **Simplify each algebraic fraction.**

33. $\dfrac{3x^2y}{12xy^3z}$
34. $\dfrac{x + y}{x^2 + 3xy + 2y^2}$
35. $\dfrac{x^2 - 9}{x^2 - 6x + 9}$
36. $\dfrac{x^2 + 10x + 21}{x^3 + x^2 - 42x}$

Chapter Test

Factor.

1. $9x^2 - 36y^4$

2. $12x^2 + 23x - 24$

3. $25a^2 - 20a + 4$

4. $15ac - 21ad + 10bc - 14bd$

5. $3a^2b - 5ab + 11ab^2$

6. $50a^2 - 25b^2$

7. $25m^2n^2 + 90mnp + 81p^2$

8. $x^3 - 5x^2 - 9x + 45$

9. $x^8 - y^8$

10. $98a^2 - 140ab + 50b^2$

Simplify.

11. $\dfrac{21x^2y}{28ax}$

12. $\dfrac{x^2 + 7x - 18}{x^2 + 12x + 27}$

13. $\dfrac{7x^2 - 28}{5x^3 - 20x}$

Solve each equation.

14. $(3w - 21)(w + 8) = 0$

15. $18s^2 + 72s = 0$

16. $x^2 - 6x + 9 = 0$

17. $6w(4w - 28) = 0$

18. $t^2 - 121 = 0$

19. $4x^2 = 36$

20. $(3m + 5)(2m - 3) = 0$

21. $x^2 - \dfrac{4}{9} = 0$

22. $x^2 + 25 = 10x$

23. $a^2 - 9a - 52 = 0$

24. $3x^2 - 7x - 20 = 0$

25. $12x^2 - 6 = x$

26. $10m^2 + 7m = 3$

27. $x^3 - 5x^2 - 66x = 0$

28. $x^3 + 7x^2 - 25x - 175 = 0$

For each problem, define a variable. Then use an equation to solve the problem.

29. The product of 5 times Joe's salary and 61,000 less than 4 times Joe's salary is zero. What is Joe's salary?

30. The sum of two integers is 21 and their product is 104. Find the integers.

31. When one integer is added to the square of the next consecutive integer, the sum is 55. Find the integers.

32. A photograph is 8 cm wide and 12 cm long. The length and width are increased by an equal amount in order to double the area of the photograph. What are the dimensions of the new photograph?

For problems 33 and 34, use $h = vt - 16t^2$.

33. An arrow is shot directly up with an initial velocity of 144 ft/sec. How long does it take to return to the ground?

34. A rocket is fired directly up at an initial velocity of 2240 ft/sec. How high will the rocket be after 70 seconds?

1. Write a mathematical expression for 37 increased by twice a number.
2. Evaluate: $[4(15 - 3) \div 6 \times 2] + 4^2$
3. State the property shown by $7 \cdot 0 = 0$.
4. Simplify: $\frac{3}{4}(20 - 10x)$
5. Graph $\{-2, -3, -4\}$ on a number line.
6. Evaluate $b + (-16)$ if $b = 6$.

Find each sum or difference.

7. $\frac{3}{4} + \left(-\frac{5}{6}\right) + \frac{3}{2}$
8. $-14 - 21$

9. Solve: $-14 = 6 - z$
10. Simplify: $5(4a - 2a) + 6(7a - 4a)$

Solve.

11. $\frac{a + 2}{7} = -10$
12. $7.6x + 11.2 = -13.4x - 9.8$
13. Find 1.8% of 15.

Solve each inequality.

14. $16 \le y - 5$
15. $-7p < 84$
16. $\frac{1}{3}x - 1 \ge -4$
17. Solve the following inequality and graph the solution set:
$2x + 5 \le 9$ and $3x \ge 2x - 3$

Simplify.

18. $(4a^2b)(-3b^3)$
19. $-2(ax^3y)^3$
20. $\frac{-64a^3b^5c^4d}{-16a^2b^6c^3d}$
21. $7m^2p^3(m^4 - 3mp^5 + 2p^4)$
22. $(2a + 3)(a^2 + 3a + 4)$
23. $(2x + 3y)(2x - 3y)$

Solve.

24. $q(q - 1) + 3q = 1 + q(q + 3)$

Factor, if possible.

25. $25x^4 + 5y^2$
26. $a^2 - 16y^2$
27. $b^2 - b - 20$
28. $12x^2 + 26x + 12$
29. $2a^2 + 10ab + 3ab + 15b^2$

Solve.

30. $(3y + 2)(y - 5) = 0$
31. $5m^2 + 5m = 0$
32. $a^3 + 6a^2 + 9a = 0$
33. $n^2 + n = 2$

Problem Solving

Solve each problem.

34. Darlene earned $340 in 4 days. At that rate how long will it take her to earn $935?
35. Alan paid $96.70 for a special computer program. The price included $7\frac{1}{2}\%$ sales tax. What was the price without the tax?
36. The length of a rectangle is 12 meters greater than the width. If the length was decreased by 5 meters and the width increased by 2 meters, the area would be decreased by 55 square meters. Find the original dimensions of the rectangle.
37. Dylana drives from home to town at an average speed of 30 mph. She returns home at an average speed of 40 mph. If her total driving time is $3\frac{1}{2}$ hours, what is the distance between her home and town?
38. When one integer is added to the square of the next consecutive integer, the sum is 155. Find the integers.

The questions on this page involve comparing two quantities, one in Column A and one in Column B. In certain questions, information related to one or both quantities is centered above them. All variables used stand for real numbers.

Directions:

Write A if the quantity in Column A is greater.

Write B if the quantity in Column B is greater.

Write C if the quantities are equal.

Write D if there is not enough information to determine the relationship.

Column A	Column B
$x \geq 13$	
1. $\frac{37}{3}$	x
2. $\frac{0.4}{20}$	0.002
3. $5 + 2 \cdot 4 - 2$	$10 \div 5 + 4 - 3$
$b > c + 1$	
4. b	c
$b < c + 1$	
5. b	c
6. The number of which 6 is 20%	10% of 310
$a = b$	
7. $-5(a - b)$	$7(3b - 3a)$
8. $6\left(\frac{3}{4}\right)0$	$24\left(\frac{1}{6}\right)$
9. 25% of $\frac{4}{7}$	$\frac{4}{7}$ of $\frac{1}{4}$
10. $0.02 \div 0.2$	$0.2 \cdot 0.02$
11. The value of $2y + 7$ when $y = -2$.	The value of $2x - 8$ when $x = 6$.

Examples

Column A	Column B
1. $\frac{x}{y}$	$\frac{y}{x}$

The answer is D because it is not known whether x and y are positive or negative.

The values of $\frac{x}{y}$ and $\frac{y}{x}$ depend on the choices for x and y.

$a > 0$

Column A	Column B
2. $4a - 3a$	$4 \cdot 3a$

The answer is B because $12a$ is greater than a for all positive values of a.

Column A	Column B
12.	

The number indicated by arrow A on the number line above.	The number indicated by arrow B on the number line above.
13. The price of a stereo increased by 20%, and then decreased by 20%.	
The original price of the stereo.	The new price of the stereo.
$a:b = c:d$	
14. ad	bc
$3x - 3y = 24$	
15. x	y
$r < 0 < s$	
16. r^2	$\frac{s}{2}$

CHAPTER 9

Functions and Graphs

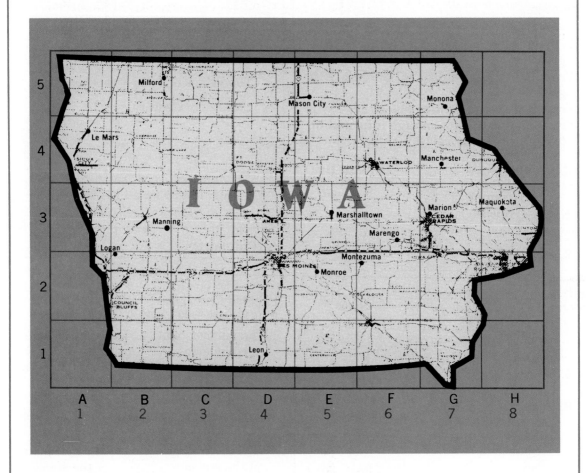

The letters and numbers shown beside the map above are used to identify regions on the map. For example, Manning is in region B–3. This region is above B and across from 3.

Suppose the letters were replaced by numbers as shown. Then the region containing Manning could be identified by 2–3, or by the **ordered pair** (2, 3). Would (3, 2) identify the same region? Why is the order of the numbers important?

In this chapter, you will learn to graph ordered pairs. You will also learn more about functions and their graphs.

9-1 Ordered Pairs

In mathematics, **ordered pairs** of numbers are used to locate points in the plane. The points are in reference to two perpendicular number lines, as shown at the right. Notice that the lines intersect at their zero points. The point of intersection is called the **origin**. The two number lines are often called the **x-axis** and **y-axis**. The first component of an ordered pair corresponds to a number on the horizontal, or x-axis. The second component of the ordered pair corresponds to a number on the vertical, or y-axis.

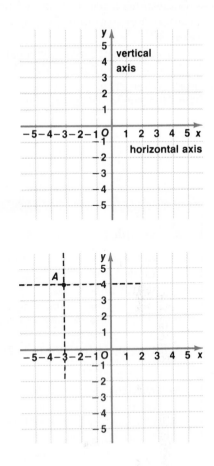

To find the ordered pair that locates point A, think of a horizontal line and vertical line through point A. Notice where these lines intersect the axes. The number on the x-axis that corresponds to A is -3. The number on the y-axis that corresponds to A is 4. Thus, the ordered pair for point A is $(-3, 4)$.

The first component, -3, is called the **x-coordinate** of point A. The second component, 4, is called the **y-coordinate** of point A. The plane is called the **coordinate plane**.

The first component is sometimes called the <u>abscissa</u>. The second component is sometimes called the <u>ordinate</u>.

Example

1 **Name the ordered pairs that locate points R, S, T, and U.**

The x-coordinate of point R is 4. The y-coordinate is -3. Thus, the ordered pair for R is $(4, -3)$.

The x-coordinate of point S is 1. The y-coordinate is 4. Thus, the ordered pair for S is $(1, 4)$.

The ordered pair for T is $(-3, -5)$ and the ordered pair for U is $(-5, 3)$. Do you see why?

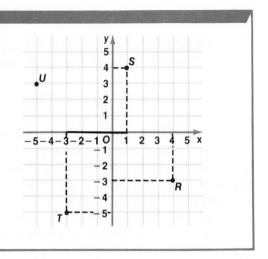

Sometimes a point is named not only by a letter but also by its location. For example, $R(4, 3)$ means that the location of point R is $(4, 3)$.

To **graph** an ordered pair means to place a dot at the point that is located by the ordered pair. This is sometimes called *plotting* the point. When graphing an ordered pair, you should start at the origin. The first component gives the number of units to move right or left. The second component gives the number of units to move up or down. Study these examples.

Examples

2 **Graph point $C(3, 1)$.**

Start at O. Move 3 units to the right. Then move 1 unit up and place a dot. Label the dot with the letter C.

> Check to make sure the dot corresponds to 3 on the x-axis and 1 on the y-axis.

3 **Graph point $D(-3, -2)$.**

Start at O. Move 3 units to the left. Do you see why the move was to the left? Then move 2 units down and place a dot. Do you see why the move was down? Label the dot with the letter D.

> Check to make sure the dot corresponds to -3 on the x-axis and -2 on the y-axis.

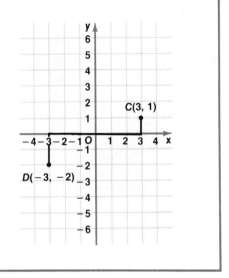

When plotting points, the following is true.

> 1. **Exactly one point in the plane is located by a given ordered pair of numbers.**
> 2. **Exactly one ordered pair of numbers locates a given point in the plane.**

Completeness Property for Points in the Plane

The x-axis and y-axis separate the plane into four regions, called **quadrants**. The quadrants are numbered as shown at the right. In which quadrant is the graph of $(5, -4)$? In which quadrant is the graph of $(-2, -7)$? In which quadrant is the graph of $(2, 0)$? The axes are not in any quadrant. Can you think of a reason why?

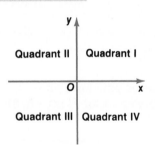

Quadrant II   Quadrant I

Quadrant III   Quadrant IV

Exploratory Exercises

State the ordered pair for each point.

1. A
2. B
3. C
4. D
5. E
6. F
7. G
8. H
9. I
10. J
11. K
12. L
13. M
14. N
15. P
16. Q
17. R
18. S
19. T
20. U

State the quadrant in which the point for each ordered pair is located.

21. $(5, 2)$
22. $(-3, -1)$
23. $(-2, 3)$
24. $(6, 0)$
25. $(0, -2)$
26. $(-6, -2)$
27. $(4, -3)$
28. $(5, 1)$
29. $(3, -2)$
30. $(3, 6)$
31. $(-4, 2)$
32. $(-3, 0)$
33. $(-3, 1)$
34. $(-4, 0)$
35. $(-1, -3)$
36. $(5, -1)$

State the quadrant for the graph of (x, y), given each condition.

37. $x > 0, y < 0$
38. $x < 0, y < 0$
39. $x = 0, y > 0$
40. $x < 0, y > 0$
41. $x > 0, y > 0$
42. $x > 0, y = 0$
43. $x = -1, y < 0$
44. $x < 0, y = 3$

Written Exercises

Graph each point.

1. $A(5, -2)$
2. $B(3, 5)$
3. $C(-6, 0)$
4. $D(-3, 4)$
5. $E(-3, -3)$
6. $F(-5, 1)$
7. $G(2, -1)$
8. $H(4, 0)$
9. $I(3, -4)$
10. $J(-3, 0)$
11. $K(-5, -2)$
12. $L(4, 2)$
13. $M(-5, -4)$
14. $N(1, 4)$
15. $P(2, -3)$
16. $Q(0, -2)$
17. $R(-2, 1)$
18. $S(-3, -1)$
19. $T(-3, 6)$
20. $U(6, 2)$

For each of the following, graph the points named. Then connect the points in alphabetical order and identify the figure.

21. $A(4, 6), B(3, 7), C(2, 6), D(1, 7), E(0, 6), F(1, 8), G(4, 9), H(7, 8), I(8, 6), J(7, 7), K(6, 6), L(5, 7), M(4, 6), N(4, 0), P(5, 0), Q(5, 1)$.

22. $A\left(-3, \frac{1}{2}\right), B(1, 0), C(4, 0), D(7, -4), E(8, -4), F(7, 0), G(10, 0), H(11, -2), I(12, -2), J\left(11\frac{1}{2}, 0\right),$
    $K\left(13, \frac{1}{2}\right), L\left(11\frac{1}{2}, 1\right), M(12, 3), N(11, 3), P(10, 1), Q(7, 1), R(8, 5), S(7, 5), T(4, 1), U(1, 1),$
    $V\left(-3, \frac{1}{2}\right)$.

9-2 Relations

Consider the ordered pairs (2, 2), (−2, 3), and (0, −1). In these examples, 2 is paired with 2, −2 is paired with 3, and 0 is paired with −1.

A relation is a set of ordered pairs.

Definition of Relation

A relation can be shown by a set of ordered pairs, a table, a mapping, or a graph.

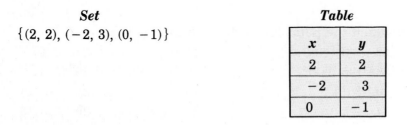

Set

{(2, 2), (−2, 3), (0, −1)}

Table

x	y
2	2
−2	3
0	−1

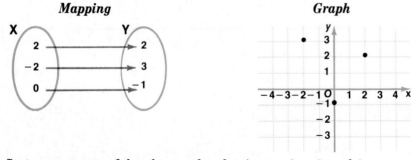

Mapping

Graph

The first components of the above ordered pairs are 2, −2, and 0. The **domain** of the relation is {2, −2, 0}.

The domain of a relation is the set of all *first* components from each ordered pair.

Definition of Domain

The second components are 2, 3, and −1. The **range** of the relation is {2, 3, −1}.

The range of a relation is the set of all *second* components from each ordered pair.

Definition of Range

Examples

1 State the set of ordered pairs shown by the table. Then state the domain and range of the relation.

x	y
0	5
2	3
1	−4
−3	3
−1	−2

The set of ordered pairs in the relation is
$\{(0, 5), (2, 3), (1, -4), (-3, 3), (-1, -2)\}$.

The domain is the set of first components
or $\{0, 2, 1, -3, -1\}$.

The range is the set of second components
or $\{5, 3, -4, -2\}$.

2 State the relation shown by the graph. Then state the domain and range.

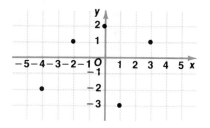

The relation is
$\{(3, 1), (0, 2), (-2, 1), (-4, -2), (1, -3)\}$.

The domain is $\{3, 0, -2, -4, 1\}$.

The range is $\{1, 2, -2, -3\}$.

3 State the relation for the mapping. Then state the domain and range.

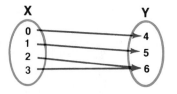

The relation is $\{(0, 4), (1, 5), (2, 6), (3, 6)\}$.

The domain is $\{0, 1, 2, 3\}$.

The range is $\{4, 5, 6\}$.

Exploratory Exercises

State the domain and range of each relation.

1. $\{(0, 2), (1, -2), (2, 4)\}$

2. $\{(-4, 2), (-2, 0), (0, 2), (2, 4)\}$

3. $\{(-3, 1), (-2, 0), (-1, 1), (0, 2)\}$

4. $\{(5, 2), (0, 0), (-9, -1)\}$

5. $\{(7, 5), (-2, -3), (4, 0), (5, -7), (-9, 2)\}$

6. $\{(1, 1), (2, 4), (-2, 4), (3, 9)\}$

7. $\{(-3, 0), (-2, -5), (-2, 6), (3, 7), (0, -17)\}$

8. $\{(-5, 2), (-4, 5), (-2, 1), (-4, 4)\}$

9. $\{(3.1, -1), (-4.7, 3.9), (2.4, -3.6), (-9, 12.12)\}$

10. $\{(4.7, -2.3), (5.1, 2.8), (-3.5, 1)\}$

11. $\left\{\left(\frac{1}{2}, \frac{1}{4}\right), \left(1\frac{1}{2}, -\frac{2}{3}\right), \left(-3, \frac{2}{5}\right), \left(-5\frac{1}{4}, -7\frac{2}{7}\right)\right\}$

12. $\left\{(0, 0), \left(\frac{1}{2}, \frac{1}{8}\right), \left(-\frac{1}{2}, -\frac{1}{8}\right)\right\}$

State each relation as a set of ordered pairs. Then state the domain and range of each.

13.

x	y
1	5
2	7
3	9
4	11

14.

x	y
1	3
2	2
4	9
6	5

15.

x	y
-4	1
-2	3
0	1
2	3
4	1

16.

x	y
1	-2
3	-4
5	-6
9	-4
11	-2

Written Exercises

Write the relation for each mapping as a set of ordered pairs.

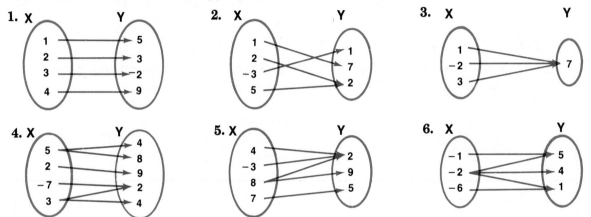

Draw a mapping for each relation. Then write the relation as a set of ordered pairs.

7.

x	y
1	3
2	4
3	5
4	6
5	7

8.

x	y
1	4
3	-2
4	4
6	-2

9.

x	y
8	1
7	3
6	5
2	-2

10.

x	y
4	2
1	3
3	3
6	4

11.

x	y
1	3
2	5
1	-7
2	9

12.

x	y
1	-2
$2\frac{1}{2}$	-3
3	8
4	-3

Write each relation as a set of ordered pairs. Then state the domain and range of each.

13.

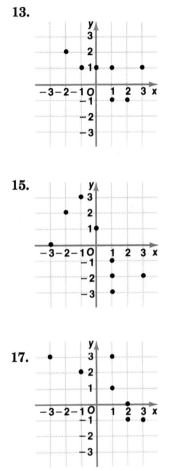

14.

15.

16.

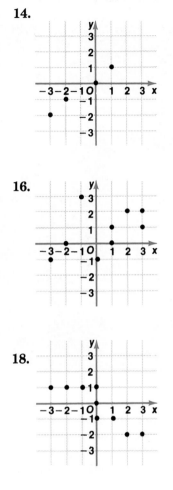

17.

18.

Draw a mapping for each relation.

19. $\{(1, 3), (2, 5), (8, 2), (5, -3)\}$

20. $\{(2, 3), (3, 2)\}$

21. $\{(8, 1), (4, 2), (6, -4), (5, -3), (6, 0)\}$

22. $\{(0, 1)\}$

23. $\{(2, 2), (3, 3), (4, 4)\}$

24. $\{(1, 3), (2, 7), (4, 1), (-3, 3), (3, 3)\}$

25. $\{(-6, 0), (-1, 2), (-3, 4)\}$

26. $\{(-3, 3), (-2, 2), (-1, 1), (0, 0), (1, -1)\}$

27. $\left\{\left(4\frac{1}{2}, \frac{1}{2}\right), \left(2\frac{1}{2}, 1\right), \left(-1\frac{1}{2}, 2\right)\right\}$

28. $\left\{\left(\frac{1}{3}, \frac{3}{4}\right), \left(\frac{2}{3}, -\frac{1}{2}\right), \left(-\frac{3}{4}, \frac{2}{3}\right), \left(\frac{2}{3}, \frac{3}{4}\right)\right\}$

mini-review

Arrange the terms of the polynomial so that the powers of x are in descending order.

1. $8 - xy^3 - 2x^3y^2 - 5x^2$

Factor.

2. $8m^2 - 72n^2$

3. $y^2 - \frac{3}{2}y + \frac{9}{16}$

Solve.

4. $(2m + 7)(5m - 3) = 0$

5. $a^2 + 2a = 63$

9-3 Equations as Relations

Anita works part-time in a bookstore. She earns $4 per hour. She made the following chart to show her earnings for different numbers of hours worked. She let x equal the number of hours she works per week, and y equal her total pay.

x (hours)	$4x$	y (pay)	(x, y)
1	4(1)	4	(1, 4)
5	4(5)	20	(5, 20)
8	4(8)	32	(8, 32)
10	4(10)	40	(10, 40)
12	4(12)	48	(12, 48)
15	4(15)	60	(15, 60)
20	4(20)	80	(20, 80)

The equation $y = 4x$ describes her pay (y) for any number of hours (x). Anita could have selected other values of x. Generally, however, these values are restricted. For example, Anita could not work less than 0 hours or more than 168 hours in a week. The ordered pairs in the chart above are *solutions* to the equation $y = 4x$.

Since the solutions to an equation in two variables are ordered pairs, such an equation describes a relation. The set of values of x is the domain of the relation. The set of corresponding values of y is the range.

Examples

1 Solve $y = 2x + 3$ if the domain is $\{-5, -3, -1, 0, 1, 3, 5, 7, 9\}$.

Make a table. The values of x come from the domain.

x	$2x + 3$	y	(x, y)
-5	$2(-5) + 3$	-7	$(-5, -7)$
-3	$2(-3) + 3$	-3	$(-3, -3)$
-1	$2(-1) + 3$	1	$(-1, 1)$
0	$2(0) + 3$	3	$(0, 3)$
1	$2(1) + 3$	5	$(1, 5)$
3	$2(3) + 3$	9	$(3, 9)$
5	$2(5) + 3$	13	$(5, 13)$
7	$2(7) + 3$	17	$(7, 17)$
9	$2(9) + 3$	21	$(9, 21)$

The solution set is
$\{(-5, -7), (-3, -3), (-1, 1), (0, 3), (1, 5), (3, 9), (5, 13), (7, 17), (9, 21)\}$.

2 Solve $2y + 4x = 8$ if the domain is $\{-4, -3, -2, 2, 3, 4\}$.

Values for y are usually easier to determine if the equation is first solved for y in terms of x.

$$2y + 4x = 8$$
$$2y = 8 - 4x$$
$$\frac{2y}{2} = \frac{8 - 4x}{2}$$
$$y = 4 - 2x$$

Now substitute the given values of x to determine the corresponding values of y.

x	$4 - 2x$	y	(x, y)
-4	$4 - 2(-4)$	12	$(-4, 12)$
-3	$4 - 2(-3)$	10	$(-3, 10)$
-2	$4 - 2(-2)$	8	$(-2, 8)$
2	$4 - 2(2)$	0	$(2, 0)$
3	$4 - 2(3)$	-2	$(3, -2)$
4	$4 - 2(4)$	-4	$(4, -4)$

The solution set is $\{(-4, 12), (-3, 10), (-2, 8), (2, 0), (3, -2), (4, -4)\}$.

When variables other than x and y are used, assume that the values of the letters that come first in the alphabet are from the domain.

Example

3 **Solve $3r + 2s = 11$ if the domain is $\{-3, 0, 1, 2, 5\}$.**

The values for r come from the domain. Therefore, first solve the equation so that s is expressed in terms of r.

$$3r + 2s = 11$$
$$2s = 11 - 3r$$
$$\frac{2s}{2} = \frac{11 - 3r}{2}$$
$$s = \frac{11 - 3r}{2}$$

Now substitute the given values of r to determine the corresponding values of s.

r	$\dfrac{11 - 3r}{2}$	s	(r, s)
-3	$\dfrac{11 - 3(-3)}{2}$	10	$(-3, 10)$
0	$\dfrac{11 - 3(0)}{2}$	$\dfrac{11}{2}$	$\left(0, \dfrac{11}{2}\right)$
1	$\dfrac{11 - 3(1)}{2}$	4	$(1, 4)$
2	$\dfrac{11 - 3(2)}{2}$	$\dfrac{5}{2}$	$\left(2, \dfrac{5}{2}\right)$
5	$\dfrac{11 - 3(5)}{2}$	-2	$(5, -2)$

The solution set is $\left\{(-3, 10), \left(0, \frac{11}{2}\right), (1, 4), \left(2, \frac{5}{2}\right), (5, -2)\right\}$.

Exploratory Exercises

Copy each table. Then find the solutions for each equation for the domain indicated.

1. $y = 3x$

x	y	(x, y)
-4		
-2		
0		
1		
2		
3		

2. $y = 4x - 3$

x	y	(x, y)
-3		
-2		
-1		
0		
2		
4		

3. $n = \dfrac{2m + 5}{3}$

m	n	(m, n)
-4		
-2		
0		
1		
3		

Written Exercises

Solve each equation for the variable indicated.

1. $x + y = 5$, for y

2. $3x + y = 7$, for y

3. $b - 5a = 3$, for b

4. $4m + n = 7$, for n

5. $8x + 2y = 6$, for y

6. $6x + 3y = 12$, for y

7. $4a + 3b = 7$, for b

8. $6r + 5s = 2$, for s

9. $6x = 3y + 2$, for y

10. $3a = 7b + 8$, for b

11. $4p = 7 - 2q$, for q

12. $7q = 4 + 5m$, for q

State which of the ordered pairs given are solutions of the equation.

13. $3x + y = 8$ **a.** $(2, 2)$ **b.** $(3, 1)$ **c.** $(4, -4)$ **d.** $(8, 0)$

14. $2x + 3y = 11$ **a.** $(3, 1)$ **b.** $(1, 3)$ **c.** $(-2, 5)$ **d.** $(4, -1)$

15. $2m - 5n = 1$ **a.** $(-2, -1)$ **b.** $(2, 1)$ **c.** $\left(-\frac{3}{2}, -\frac{1}{2}\right)$ **d.** $(-7, -3)$

16. $3r = 8s - 4$ **a.** $\left(\frac{2}{3}, \frac{3}{4}\right)$ **b.** $\left(0, \frac{1}{2}\right)$ **c.** $(4, 2)$ **d.** $(2, 4)$

17. $3y = x + 7$ **a.** $(-1, 2)$ **b.** $(2, -1)$ **c.** $(2, 3)$ **d.** $(2, 4)$

18. $4x = 8 - 2y$ **a.** $(2, 0)$ **b.** $(0, 2)$ **c.** $\left(\frac{1}{2}, -3\right)$ **d.** $(1, -2)$

Solve each equation if the domain is $\{-2, -1, 0, 2, 5\}$.

19. $y = 2x + 1$

20. $y = 5x - 3$

21. $x + y = 7$

22. $x - y = 4$

23. $2x + y = 7$

24. $5x + y = 4$

25. $2a + 3b = 13$

26. $4r + 3s = 16$

27. $3x = 5 + 2y$

28. $4y = 3 + 2x$

29. $5a = 8 - 4b$

30. $2t = 3 - 5s$

31. $a - 6b = -32$

32. $5x - y = -3$

33. $6x + 5y = 11$

34. $4m + 3n = 10$

35. $5y - 3x = 8$

36. $3z - 6w = 1$

Graphs are often used to help visualize the relationship between two variables. To fully understand the information presented in the graph, ask yourself the following three questions.

1. What does the title indicate will be represented in the graph?
2. What variable is represented along each axis?
3. What units are used along each axis?

Apply each of the three questions to the graph below. The bar graph shows information from a survey.

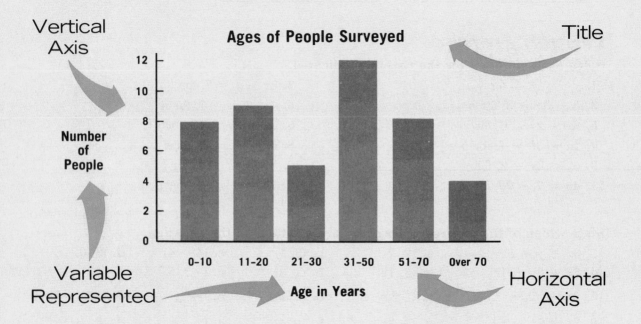

On the graph, the title indicates that the graph shows the number of people of each age who were surveyed. The vertical axis shows the number of people in each age group. The horizontal axis shows age groups in years. Each unit on the vertical axis represents two people. The horizontal axis is labeled to show what age groups were used. Notice that the units used for each axis do not have to be the same.

Exercises

Turn to page 293, *Misleading Graphs*. Answer the three questions at the top of this page about the graphs on page 293.

9-4 Graphing Relations

Some of the solutions of $y = 2x - 1$ are shown in the table. The solutions can also be shown by a graph.

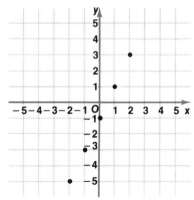

x	$2x - 1$	y	(x, y)
-2	$2(-2) - 1$	-5	$(-2, -5)$
-1	$2(-1) - 1$	-3	$(-1, -3)$
0	$2(0) - 1$	-1	$(0, -1)$
1	$2(1) - 1$	1	$(1, 1)$
2	$2(2) - 1$	3	$(2, 3)$

The domain of $y = 2x - 1$ is the set of all numbers. Therefore, an infinite number of ordered pairs are solutions to the equation.

Suppose you draw a line connecting the points in the graph above. All points for the solutions of $y = 2x - 1$ lie on this line. And the coordinates of every point on the line satisfy the equation. Hence, the line is called the graph of $y = 2x - 1$.

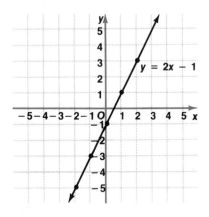

The equation $y = 2x - 1$ can be changed to equivalent forms such as $-y = 1 - 2x$ or $2x - y = 1$. All of these forms will have the same graph. An equation whose graph is a straight line is called a **linear equation**.

> A linear equation is an equation that can be written in the form $Ax + By = C$, where A, B, and C are any numbers, and A and B are not both 0.

Definition of Linear Equation

The equations $4x + 3y = 7$, $2x = 8 + y$, $5m - n = \frac{1}{2}$, $x = 3$, and $y = 7$ are linear equations. The equations $3x + y^2 = 7$ and $\frac{1}{x} + y = 4$ are *not* linear equations. Why?

Examples

1 **Draw the graph of $3x - y = 3$.**

Transform the equation to an equivalent one that expresses y in terms of x.

$$3x - y = 3$$
$$-y = 3 - 3x$$
$$y = 3x - 3$$

Now set up a table of values for x and y. Graph the ordered pairs and connect them with a line.

x	$3x - 3$	y	(x, y)
-2	$3(-2) - 3$	-9	$(-2, -9)$
-1	$3(-1) - 3$	-6	$(-1, -6)$
0	$3(0) - 3$	-3	$(0, -3)$
1	$3(1) - 3$	0	$(1, 0)$
2	$3(2) - 3$	3	$(2, 3)$

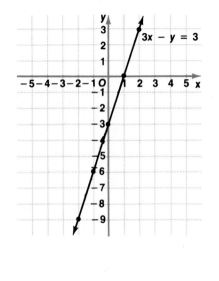

2 **Draw the graph of $3x + 2y = 4$.**

$$3x + 2y = 4$$
$$2y = 4 - 3x$$
$$y = \frac{4 - 3x}{2}$$

x	$\dfrac{4 - 3x}{2}$	y	(x, y)
-2	$\dfrac{4 - 3(-2)}{2}$	5	$(-2, 5)$
-1	$\dfrac{4 - 3(-1)}{2}$	$\dfrac{7}{2}$	$\left(-1, \dfrac{7}{2}\right)$
0	$\dfrac{4 - 3(0)}{2}$	2	$(0, 2)$
1	$\dfrac{4 - 3(1)}{2}$	$\dfrac{1}{2}$	$\left(1, \dfrac{1}{2}\right)$
2	$\dfrac{4 - 3(2)}{2}$	-1	$(2, -1)$

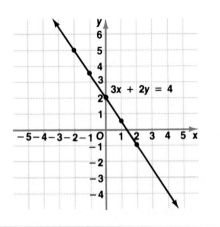

Exploratory Exercises

State whether each equation is a linear equation.

1. $5x + 2y = 7$

2. $3x^2 + 2y = 4$

3. $x + \dfrac{1}{y} = 7$

4. $\dfrac{1}{x} - \dfrac{1}{y} = \dfrac{1}{2}$

5. $\dfrac{3}{4}x + 2y = 3$

6. $\dfrac{3}{5}x - \dfrac{2}{3}y = 5$

7. $x = y^2$

8. $x = y$

9. $\dfrac{3}{5x} = y$

10. $\dfrac{3}{5}x = y$

11. $\dfrac{1}{3}x + \dfrac{1}{3y} = 4$

12. $5x - y = 4$

13. $xy^2 = y$

14. $xy = 4$

15. $\dfrac{y}{2} = 2$

16. $5m + 2n = 8$

17. $2w = 3z - 1$

18. $\dfrac{5}{3}x + \dfrac{2}{3}y = 7$

Written Exercises

State whether each equation is a linear equation.

1. $xy = 2$

2. $3x = 2y$

3. $x = y^2$

4. $y^2 = x^2$

5. $3m - 2n = 8$

6. $3mn^2 = 1$

7. $2x - 3 = y^2$

8. $5x - 7 = 3y$

9. $8a - 7b = 2a$

10. $3m - 2n = 0$

11. $4x^2 - 3x = y$

12. $2m + 5m = 7n$

Graph each equation.

13. $3m + n = 4$

14. $2x - y = 8$

15. $b = 5a - 7$

16. $y = 3x + 1$

17. $4x + 3y = 12$

18. $5x + 2y = 10$

19. $5x + 3y = 8$

20. $2x + 7y = 9$

21. $3x - 2y = 12$

22. $4x - 3y = 24$

23. $x = 4$

24. $y = -2$

25. $\dfrac{1}{2}x + y = 8$

26. $x + \dfrac{1}{3}y = 6$

27. $\dfrac{2}{3}x - \dfrac{1}{3}y = 2$

28. $\dfrac{3}{4}x + \dfrac{1}{2}y = 6$

29. $x = -\dfrac{5}{2}$

30. $y = \dfrac{4}{3}$

31. $\dfrac{2}{5}x - \dfrac{3}{5}y = 1$

32. $\dfrac{3}{4}x - \dfrac{2}{3}y = 7$

33. $\dfrac{3}{5}x = 6$

34. $\dfrac{3}{4}y = 6$

35. $\dfrac{5}{2}x + \dfrac{2}{3}y = 1$

36. $\dfrac{4}{3}x - \dfrac{3}{4}y = 1$

Challenge

37. $y = x^2$

38. $y = x^2 + 2$

39. $y = -(x^2) + 3$

40. $x = 2y^2$

41. $y = -(x^2) - 3$

42. $y - 2x^2 = 3$

43. $y = x^3$

44. $y = 2x^3 + 1$

45. $x = y^3 - 1$

mini-review

1. Find the prime factorization of 96.

2. Find the GCF of $6x^2y^3$, $12x^2y^2z$, and $15x^2y$.

Factor.

3. $m^2 + mn - 42n^2$

4. $y^2m + y^2n - 4m - 4n$

5. $\dfrac{2}{3}a - \dfrac{2}{3}b + \dfrac{4}{3}c$

9-5　Functions

The following graphs and accompanying tables describe two different relations.

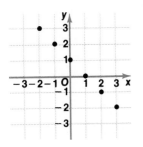

x	y
−2	3
−1	2
0	1
1	0
2	−1
3	−2

For each value of x, there is exactly one value of y.

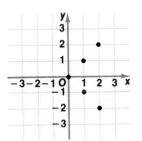

x	y
0	0
1	−1
1	1
2	−2
2	2

*For x = 1, there are two values of y, 1 and −1.
For x = 2, there are two values, 2 and −2.*

The first relation is an example of a special type of relation called a **function**.

A function is a relation in which each element of the domain is paired with exactly one element of the range.	***Definition of Function***

Examples

1　**Is {(5, −2), (3, 2), (4, −1), (−2, 2)} a function?**

Yes, because each element of the domain is paired with exactly one element of the range.

2　**Is {(−1, 3), (0, 5), (2, 3), (5, −2), (2, 4)} a function?**

No. The element 2 of the domain is paired with more than one element of the range, namely 3 and 4.

3   **Two relations are described by the following mappings. Which are functions?**

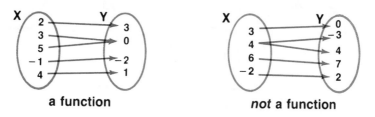

The relation at the left is a function. For each element in the domain of the relation, there is *only one* corresponding element in the range. Why is the relation at the right not a function?

4   **Is the relation described by $x + 2y = 8$ a function?**

Try substituting a value for x. For example, try 2. What is the corresponding value for y? Can there be more than one value for y when $x = 2$? No. If $x = 2$, the only value for y is 3. Can you find any values for x that will give more than one value for y? No. There are none. Therefore, $x + 2y = 8$ is a function. Specifically, we say that y is a function of x.

Suppose you graph the relation $x + 2y = 8$.

x	2	0	8
y	3	4	0

Now place your pencil at the left of the graph to represent a vertical line. Slowly move the pencil to the right across the graph.

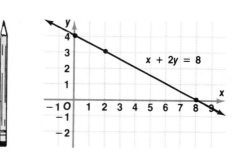

For each value of x, the vertical line passes through no more than one point of the graph. This is true for every function.

If any vertical line passes through no more than one point of the graph of a relation, then the relation is a function.

Vertical Line Test for a Function

5 Use the vertical line test to determine if the relation graphed is a function.

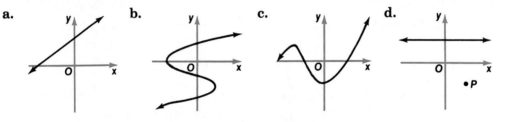

a.   **b.**   **c.**   **d.**

The relations in **a** and **c** are functions since any vertical line passes through no more than 1 point of the graph of the relation. The relation in **b** is *not* a function, since a vertical line near the *y*-axis passes through *three* points. The relation in **d** is *not* a function. A vertical line through point *P* also intersects the graph in another point.

Equations that describe functions are often written in a special way. The equation $y = 2x + 1$ can be written $f(x) = 2x + 1$. The symbol $f(x)$ is read "*f* of *x*" and represents the range of a function whose domain is represented by *x*. Specific values of the domain can then be substituted for *x* in the equation. For example, if $x = 3$, then $f(3) = 2(3) + 1$ or 7. Note $f(3)$ is a convenient way of referring to the value of *y* corresponding to $x = 3$. We say $f(3)$ is the **functional value** at $x = 3$.

Letters other than f are sometimes used for names of functions.

Examples

6 Find $f(2)$, $f(5)$, and $f(-3)$ if $f(x) = 2x - 7$.

$$f(x) = 2x - 7 \qquad f(x) = 2x - 7 \qquad f(x) = 2x - 7$$
$$f(2) = 2(2) - 7 \qquad f(5) = 2(5) - 7 \qquad f(-3) = 2(-3) - 7$$
$$= 4 - 7 \qquad\qquad = 10 - 7 \qquad\qquad = -6 - 7$$
$$= -3 \qquad\qquad\quad = 3 \qquad\qquad\qquad = -13$$

7 Find $g(2a)$ if $g(x) = x^2 - 2x + 1$.

$$g(x) = x^2 - 2x - 1$$
$$g(2a) = (2a)^2 - 2(2a) - 1 \qquad \text{Substitute 2a for x.}$$
$$= 4a^2 - 4a - 1$$

8 Find $4[f(3)]$ if $f(t) = 100t - 5t^2$.

$$f(t) = 100t - 5t^2$$
$$4[f(3)] = 4[100(3) - 5(3)^2]$$
$$= 4[300 - 45]$$
$$= 4 \cdot 255$$
$$= 1020$$

Exploratory Exercises

State whether each relation is a function.

1. $\{(3, 4), (5, 4), (-2, 3), (5, 3)\}$
2. $\{(8, 4), (5, -2), (6, 3), (2, 3)\}$
3. $\{(4, 1), (-2, 3), (0, 5), (5, 0), (3, 3)\}$
4. $\{(5, 1), (5, 2), (5, 3), (5, 4)\}$
5. $3x = 7y$
6. $2x - y^2 = 3$
7. $x^2 = y - 4$
8. $3m + 5n = 4$
9. $3s^2 + 2t^2 = 7$
10. $5a^2 - 7 = b$

Use the vertical line test to determine whether each graph represents a function.

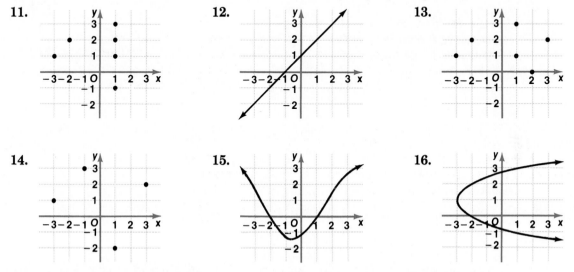

11.

12.

13.

14.

15.

16.

Given $g(x) = 2x - 1$, determine the value for each of the following.

17. $g(2)$
18. $g(-4)$
19. $g(-6)$
20. $g(0)$
21. $g\left(\frac{1}{2}\right)$
22. $g\left(\frac{5}{2}\right)$

Written Exercises

Determine whether each relation is a function.

1. $\{(3, 1), (5, 1), (7, 1)\}$
2. $\{(1, 3), (1, 5), (1, 7)\}$
3. $\{(-2, 4), (1, 3), (5, 2), (1, 4)\}$
4. $\{(-3, 3), (-2, 2), (-1, 1), (0, 0)\}$
5. $\{(6, -1), (1, 4), (2, 3), (6, 1)\}$
6. $\{(5, 4), (6, 1), (-2, 3), (0, 3)\}$
7. $\{(5, 4), (-6, 5), (4, 5), (0, 4)\}$
8. $\{(3, -2), (4, -1), (-2, 5), (4, 5)\}$
9. $3x + 5y = 7$
10. $y = 2$
11. $4x - 7y = 3$
12. $x^2 + y = 7$
13. $x + y^2 = 7$
14. $x = -3$
15. $\frac{1}{x} = y$
16. $3 = x - y$
17. $4x = 5y$
18. $x = -2$
19. $\frac{2}{3}x = \frac{3}{2}y + 1$
20. $x^2 - y^2 = 3$

Given $f(x) = 3x - 5$ and $g(x) = x^2 - x$, determine the value for each of the following.

21. $f(2)$
22. $f(-3)$
23. $g(-4)$
24. $g(3)$
25. $f\left(\frac{1}{2}\right)$
26. $f\left(\frac{2}{3}\right)$
27. $g\left(-\frac{1}{2}\right)$
28. $g\left(\frac{1}{3}\right)$
29. $f(2a)$
30. $g(2b)$
31. $3[f(5)]$
32. $2[g(-2)]$
33. $f(5.5)$
34. $1.5[f(-3)]$
35. $f(a + 3)$
36. $g(b - 3)$

Applications in Surveying

Many land regions have irregular shapes. Aerial surveyors often use coordinates when finding areas of such regions. The coordinate method described in the steps below can be used to find the area of *any* polygonal region. Study how this method is used to find the area of the region at the right.

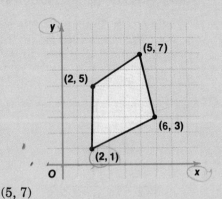

Step 1 List the ordered pairs for the vertices in counter-clockwise order, repeating the first ordered pair at the bottom of the list.

Step 2 Find D, the sum of the downward diagonal products (from left to right.)

$$D = (5 \cdot 5) + (2 \cdot 1) + (2 \cdot 3) + (6 \cdot 7)$$
$$= \quad 25 \quad + \quad 2 \quad + \quad 6 + 42 \text{ or } 75$$

Step 3 Find U, the sum of the upward diagonal products (from left to right.)

$$U = (2 \cdot 7) + (2 \cdot 5) + (6 \cdot 1) + (5 \cdot 3)$$
$$= 14 + 10 + 6 + 15 \text{ or } 45$$

(5, 7)

(2, 5)

(2, 1)

(6, 3)

(5, 7)

Step 4 Use the formula $A = \frac{1}{2}(D - U)$ to find the area.

$$A = \frac{1}{2}(D - U)$$
$$= \frac{1}{2}(75 - 45)$$
$$= \frac{1}{2}(30) \text{ or } 15$$

The area is 15 square units. Count the number of square units enclosed by the polygon. Does this result seem reasonable?

Exercises

Use the coordinate method to find the area of each region.

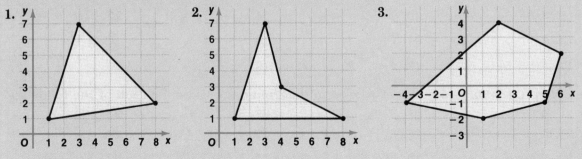

1.

2.

3.

9-6 Graphing Inequalities in Two Variables.

The graph of the equation $x = 3$ is a line
that separates the coordinate plane into two
regions. One region is shaded blue. The other
is shaded yellow. Each region is called a
half-plane. The line for $x = 3$ is called the
boundary for each half-plane.

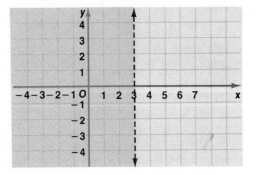

The inequality $x > 3$ describes the yellow region. The x-coordinate
of every point in that region is greater than 3. The inequality $x < 3$
describes the blue region. Points on the line for $x = 3$ are not part of
either region.

Consider the graphs of $y > x + 1$ and $y \le x + 1$. The boundary line
in both is the line for $y = x + 1$.

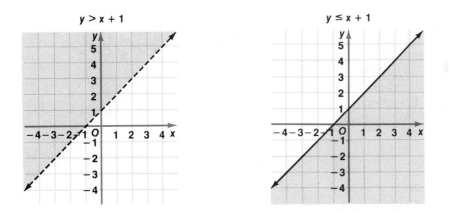

In the graph of $y > x + 1$, the boundary is *not* part of the graph.
Therefore the boundary is shown as a broken line. However, all
points above the broken line are part of the graph. The graph is called
an **open half-plane**.

The inequality $y \le x + 1$ means $y < x + 1$ or $y = x + 1$. In the graph
of $y \le x + 1$, the boundary *is* part of the graph and is shown as a solid
line. The graph also contains all points below the line. The graph is
called a **closed half-plane**.

Examples

1 Graph $y > -4x - 3$.

First graph $y = -4x - 3$. Draw it as a broken line since this boundary is *not* part of the graph. Test a point on either side of the boundary. This will tell you which half-plane is part of the graph. The origin is an easy point to check. The coordinates of the origin, $(0, 0)$, satisfy the inequality $y > -4x - 3$. So, the coordinates of all the points on that side of the boundary satisfy the inequality.

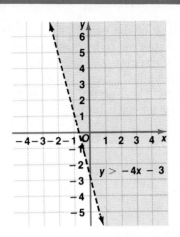

2 Graph $-2y + 3x \geq 8$.

First solve for y.

$$-2y + 3x \geq 8$$
$$-2y \geq -3x + 8$$
$$y \leq \frac{3}{2}x - 4$$

Then graph $y = \frac{3}{2}x - 4$. Draw it as a solid line since this boundary *is* part of the graph. Then test a point to determine which half-plane is part of the graph. The origin is not part of the graph. Therefore, the graph is the right half-plane including the boundary.

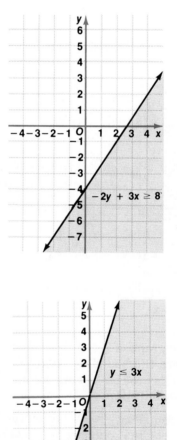

3 Graph $y \leq 3x$.

First graph $y = 3x$. Draw it as a solid line since this boundary *is* part of the graph. Then test a point to determine which half-plane is part of the graph. The origin is on the boundary, so you must test a point other than the origin. Try $(1, 1)$. Since $(1, 1)$ satisfies the inequality, the graph is the half-plane including $(1, 1)$.

Exploratory Exercises

State which of the ordered pairs given are solutions of the inequality.

1. $x + 2y \geq 3$ **a.** $(3, 1)$ **b.** $(4, -1)$ **c.** $(-2, 2)$
2. $2x - 3y \leq 1$ **a.** $(2, 1)$ **b.** $(5, -1)$ **c.** $(1, 1)$
3. $5x + 2 > 3y$ **a.** $(2, 3)$ **b.** $(4, 7)$ **c.** $(-2, -3)$
4. $4y - 8 \geq 0$ **a.** $(0, 2)$ **b.** $(2, 5)$ **c.** $(-2, 0)$
5. $3x - 2y \leq 6$ **a.** $(2, 0)$ **b.** $(4, -3)$ **c.** $(0, 3)$
6. $-2x < 8 - y$ **a.** $(5, 10)$ **b.** $(3, 6)$ **c.** $(-4, 0)$
7. $3x + 4y < 7$ **a.** $(1, 1)$ **b.** $(2, -1)$ **c.** $(-2, 4)$
8. $y > x - 1$ **a.** $(5, 8)$ **b.** $(3, 3)$ **c.** $(-2, -3)$

Written Exercises

Graph each inequality. Draw a separate set of axes for each.

1. $y > 3$
2. $y \leq -2$
3. $x \leq -1$
4. $x > 4$
5. $x + y > 1$
6. $x + y < 2$
7. $x + y < -2$
8. $x + y > 4$
9. $2x - y < 1$
10. $3x + y > 1$
11. $2x + 3y \geq -2$
12. $2x - 2y \leq 2$
13. $x - 2y < 4$
14. $4y + x < 16$
15. $2x > 3y$
16. $x < y$
17. $-x < -y$
18. $-y > x$
19. $y - x > 0$
20. $2x < -y$
21. $y > x - 1$
22. $y \leq x + 1$
23. $y \leq 3x - 1$
24. $y > 4x - 1$

Challenge

25. $y > |x|$
26. $|y| \geq 2$
27. $y > 2$ and $x < 3$
28. $y > 2$ or $y < 1$

Excursions in Algebra —————————————— Misleading Graphs

Greg Friedman had received scores of 72, 74, 75, 77, and 78 on his first five algebra exams. The two graphs below were made to show how his test scores increased. Do they show the same results?

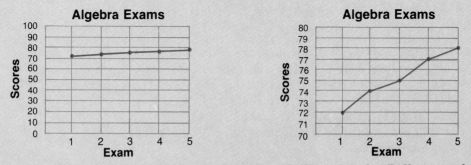

Both graphs use the same data but appear to show different results. Different scales change the appearance of the graphs. Sometimes different scales are used to make the graphs easier to read. Other times scales are chosen to make the data appear to support one point of view. Which graph do you think Greg showed his parents?

9-7 Finding Equations from Relations

Each package of chewing gum contains five sticks of gum. You can make a chart to show the relationship between the number of packages of gum and the number of sticks. Use x for the number of packages and y for the number of sticks.

x	1	2	3	4	5	6
y	5	10	15	20	25	30

This relation can also be shown as an equation. Since y is always five times x, the equation is $y = 5x$. Another way to discover this relationship is to study the differences between successive values of x and y.

	+1	+1	+1	+1	+1	
x	1	2	3	4	5	6
y	5	10	15	20	25	30
	+5	+5	+5	+5	+5	

Notice that the differences of the y-values are exactly five times the differences of the x-values. This suggests the relation $y = 5x$.

The following chart shows a different relationship.

	+1	+1	+1	+1	+1	
a	1	2	3	4	5	6
b	7	11	15	19	23	27
	+4	+4	+4	+4	+4	

Notice that the differences of the b-values are four times the differences of the a-values. This suggests the relation $b = 4a$. However, $b = 4a$ does *not* describe the relationship shown in the chart. If you substitute 1 for a in $b = 4a$, then $b = 4(1)$ or 4. According to the chart, the b-value should be 7, not 4. To make $b = 7$ when $a = 1$, you need to add 3. This suggests the relation $b = 4a + 3$. Check the relationship with other values.

If $a = 2$ and $b = 4a + 3$ If $a = 5$ and $b = 4a + 3$

  then $b = 4(2) + 3$ then $b = 4(5) + 3$

    $= 8 + 3$ $= 20 + 3$

    $= 11$ ✔ $= 23$ ✔

Examples

1 **Write an equation for the relation given in the chart.**

x	1	2	3	4	5	6
y	1	4	7	10	13	16

Find the differences.

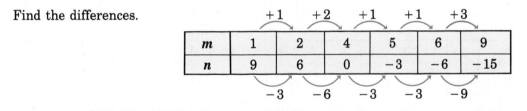

The differences suggest $y = 3x$, but this equation does *not* describe the relation. If $x = 1$ then $y = 3$ not 1. You need to subtract 2 from $3x$. Thus, $y = 3x - 2$ will describe the relation.

2 **Write an equation for the relation given in the chart.**

m	1	2	4	5	6	9
n	9	6	0	-3	-6	-15

Find the differences.

$$\overset{+1}{\quad} \overset{+2}{\quad} \overset{+1}{\quad} \overset{+1}{\quad} \overset{+3}{\quad}$$

m	1	2	4	5	6	9
n	9	6	0	-3	-6	-15

$$\underset{-3}{\quad} \underset{-6}{\quad} \underset{-3}{\quad} \underset{-3}{\quad} \underset{-9}{\quad}$$

Notice that the values for m are increasing, but the values for n are decreasing. The differences suggest $n = -3m$, but this equation does *not* describe the relation. If $m = 1$ then $n = -3$, not 9. For n to equal 9, you must add 12 to -3. Thus, the equation for the relation is $n = -3m + 12$, or $n = 12 - 3m$.

Exploratory Exercises

Find the missing terms in each sequence.

1. 1, 3, 5, 7, 9, ___, ___, ___

2. 4, 7, 10, 13, ___, ___, ___

3. 12, 9, 6, 3, ___, ___, ___

4. -11, -9, -7, -5, ___, ___, ___

5. 27, 34, 41, 48, ___, ___, ___

6. 31, 21, 11, ___, ___, ___

7. 4, 7, 12, 19, ___, ___, ___

8. 7, 19, 30, 40, 49, ___, ___, ___

9. 1, 4, 9, 16, ___, ___, ___

10. 4, 16, 36, 64, ___, ___, ___

11. 3, 5, 8, 13, 21, ___, ___, ___

12. -2, 4, -8, 16, ___, ___, ___

Written Exercises

Find the missing terms for each sequence.

1. 5, 7, 9, 11, ___, ___, ___
2. 12, 9, 6, 3, ___, ___, ___
3. −1, −4, −7, −10, ___, ___
4. 5, ___, ___, 20, 25, ___, ___
5. 6, 11, ___, ___, 26, ___
6. 1, 2, 4, 8, ___, ___, ___
7. 3, 1, $\frac{1}{3}$, ___, ___, ___
8. 4, −2, 1, −$\frac{1}{2}$, ___, ___, ___
9. 1, 0, 1, 0, ___, ___, ___
10. 1, 11, 21, 31, ___, ___, ___
11. 3, 1, −1, −3, ___, ___, ___
12. 17, 14, ___, ___, 5, ___

Write an equation for the relationship between the variables in each chart. Then copy and complete each chart.

13.

x	1	2	3	4	5	6
y	4	8	12	16		

14.

x	1	2	3	4	5	6
y	−3	−6	−9			−18

15.

m	−3	−2	−1	0	1	2	3
n	−5	−3	−1				

16.

a	−2	−1	0	1	2	3	4
b	−3	1	5				

17.

a	−4	−2	0	2	4	6	8
b	−13	−5	3	11			

18.

x	1	3	5	7	9	11	13
y	5	17	29	41			

19.

x	1	2	3	4	5	6	7
y	14	13	12		10		

20.

m	−2	−1	0	1	2	3	4
n	13	12	11	10			

21.

a	−5	−3	−1	1	2	4	7
b	28	18	8				

22.

x	−4	−2	0	2	4	6	8
y		22	18	14			

Challenge

Write an equation for each set of ordered pairs.

23. $\{(-2, 4), (-1, 1), (0, 0), (1, 1), (2, 4), (3, 9)\}$
24. $\{(1, 2), (2, 9), (3, 28), (4, 65), (5, 126)\}$
25. $\{(-2, 11), (-1, 14), (0, 15), (1, 14), (2, 11), (3, 6)\}$
26. $\{(1, 24), (2, 12), (3, 8), (4, 6), (6, 4)\}$

Using Calculators _____ Ordered Pairs

Write a linear equation for each set of ordered pairs.

1. $\{(-2, -5), (-1, -3.5), (-0.5, -2.75), (1, -0.5)\}$
2. $\{(5, -16.5), (-1.5, 3), (1.5, -6), (10, -31.5)\}$
3. $\{(2, -11), (4, -7), (8, 1), (16, 17), (32, 49)\}$
4. $\{(4, 69), (6, 91), (10, 135), (15, 190)\}$

FOR/NEXT Statements

An important step in graphing an equation is to select several values for x and then find the corresponding values for y. This means that the same expression is evaluated many times with different values for x. A computer can perform the operations easily using a loop.

FOR/NEXT statements provide the simplest means for establishing a loop.

This BASIC program uses a loop to generate several ordered pairs that could be used to graph the equation $y = 2x - 1$.

```
10  FOR X = -2 TO 2
20  LET Y = 2 * X - 1
30  PRINT "(";X;",";Y;")"
40  NEXT X
50  END
```

When the program is executed, five ordered pairs, $(-2, -5)$, $(-1, -3)$, $(0, -1)$, $(1, 1)$, and $(2, 3)$, are printed.

Exercises

1. Modify line 20 of the program to generate ordered pairs for $y = x + 2$, $y = 2x + 2$, $y = 3x + 2$, $y = 10x + 2$, and $y = 0.5x + 2$. Graph the five equations on the same axes. What effect does the coefficient of x have on the graph? At what point do the graphs intersect the y-axis?

2. Generate ordered pairs for $y = -x + 2$, $y = -2x + 2$, $y = -3x + 2$, $y = -10x + 2$, and $y = -0.5x + 2$. Graph the five equations on the same axes. If the coefficient of x is negative, describe the graphs. At what point do the graphs intersect the y-axis?

3. Generate ordered pairs for $y = 2x - 3$, $y = 2x$, and $y = 2x + 4$. Graph the three equations on the same axes. Describe the graphs. At what points do the graphs intersect the y-axis?

4. Generate ordered pairs for $y = -2x - 3$, $y = -2x$, and $y = -2x + 4$. Graph the three equations on the same axes. Describe the graphs. At what points do these graphs intersect the y-axis?

Vocabulary

Chapter Summary

1. Ordered pairs of numbers are used to locate points in the plane. The first component (x-coordinate) of an ordered pair corresponds to a number on the horizontal, or x-axis. The second component (y-coordinate) of the ordered pair corresponds to a number on the vertical, or y-axis.   (271)

2. Completeness Property for Points in the Plane: Exactly one point in the plane is located by a given ordered pair of numbers. Exactly one ordered pair of numbers locates a given point in the plane.   (272)

3. The x-axis and y-axis separate the plane into four regions, called quadrants.   (272)

4. Definition of Relation: A relation is a set of ordered pairs.   (274)

5. Definition of Domain: The domain of a relation is the set of all first components from each ordered pair.   (274)

6. Definition of Range: The range of a relation is the set of all second components from each ordered pair.   (274)

7. The solutions to equations in two variables are ordered pairs.   (279)

8. Definition of Linear Equation: A linear equation is an equation that can be written in the form $Ax + By = C$, where $A, B,$ and C are any numbers, and A and B are not both 0.   (283)

9. Definition of Function: A function is a relation in which each element of the domain is paired with exactly one element of the range.   (286)

10. Vertical Line Test for a Function: If any vertical line passes through no more than one point of the graph of a relation, then the relation is a function.   (287)

11. $f(x)$ is read "f of x" and represents the range of a function whose domain is represented by x.   (288)

12. When graphing inequalities, an open half-plane is used if the boundary is not part of the solution set. A closed half-plane is used if the boundary is part of the solution set.   (291)

Chapter Review

9-1 **State the quadrant in which the point for each ordered pair is located.**

   1. $(8, -2)$ **2.** $(-3, -3)$ **3.** $(5, 6)$ **4.** $(-2, 5)$

   Graph each point.

   5. $A(6, -5)$ **6.** $B(-4, 0)$ **7.** $C(-2, -3)$ **8.** $D(3, 5)$

9-2 **State the domain and range for each relation.**

   9. $\{(3, 5), (2, 6), (5, 7)\}$ **10.** $\{(4, 1), (4, -2), (4, 6), (4, -1)\}$

   11. $\{(-3, 5), (-3, 6), (4, 5), (4, 6)\}$ **12.** $\{(1, 3), (1, 5), (1, 7)\}$

State each relation as a set of ordered pairs. Then state the domain and range.

13.

x	y
-1	4
3	4
4	6
0	-4

14.

x	y
-1	1
-2	4
-3	9
-4	6

15.

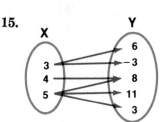

16.

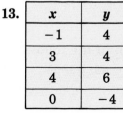

17.

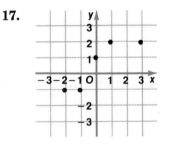

18.

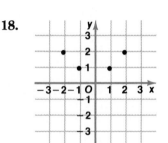

9-3 Solve each equation for y in terms of x.

19. $3x + y = 7$ **20.** $4x - 3y = 9$

State which of the ordered pairs are solutions of the given equation.

21. $2x - 3y = 8$ **a.** $(4, 4)$ **b.** $(6, 2)$ **c.** $(4, 0)$ **d.** $(2, 4)$

22. $y = 3x - 6$ **a.** $(0, 2)$ **b.** $(2, 0)$ **c.** $(6, 6)$ **d.** $(-6, 0)$

Solve each equation if the domain is $\{-4, -2, 0, 2, 4\}$.

23. $y = 4x + 5$ **24.** $x - y = 9$

25. $3x + 2y = 9$ **26.** $4x - 3y = 0$

9-4 State whether each equation is a linear equation.

27. $3x - y^2 = 6$ **28.** $xy = 8$

29. $y = 6$ **30.** $2x - 8y = 5$

Graph each equation.

31. $2x - 3y = 6$ **32.** $x + 5y = 4$

33. $y = 3x - 9$ **34.** $\frac{1}{2}x + \frac{1}{3}y = 3$

9-5 State whether each relation is a function.

35. $\{(3, 2), (5, 3), (4, 3), (5, 2)\}$ **36.** $\{(3, 8), (9, 3), (-3, 8), (5, 3)\}$

37. $3x - 4y = 7$ **38.** $x^2 - y = 4$

Given $g(x) = x^2 - x + 1$, determine the value for each of the following.

39. $g(2)$ **40.** $g(-2)$ **41.** $g(0)$ **42.** $g\left(\frac{1}{2}\right)$ **43.** $g(-1)$ **44.** $g(2a)$

9-6 Graph each inequality in the coordinate plane. Draw a separate set of axes for each.

45. $x + 2y > 5$ **46.** $4x - y \leq 8$

47. $3x - 2y < 6$ **48.** $\frac{1}{2}y \geq x + 4$

9-7 Write an equation for the relationship between the variables in each chart.

49.

x	0	1	2	3	4
y	5	8	11	14	17

50.

x	2	4	5	7	10
y	-2	0	1	3	6

Chapter Test

State the quadrant in which the point for each ordered pair is located.

1. $(-3, 5)$ **2.** $(-4, -1)$ **3.** $(5, -9)$

State each relation as a set of ordered pairs. Then state the domain and range.

4.

x	y
1	3
2	7
3	-3
5	-2

5.

6.

Solve each equation if the domain is $\{-2, -1, 0, 1, 3\}$.

7. $y = 3x + 10$ **8.** $2x - 5y = 4$ **9.** $2y - x = 8$

State whether each equation is a linear equation.

10. $5x = 17 - 4y$ **11.** $y = x^2 - y$ **12.** $y = \dfrac{1}{x}$

Graph each equation.

13. $x - 2y = 8$ **14.** $5x - 2y = 8$ **15.** $\frac{2}{3}x + \frac{3}{4}y = 1$

State whether each relation is a function.

16. $\{(2, 4), (4, 2), (5, 4), (4, 6)\}$ **17.** $\{(-6, 9), (4, 5), (8, -2), (0, 0)\}$

18. $8x - 3y = 7$ **19.** $2x = 9$

Given $f(x) = 2x - 3$, determine the value for each of the following.

20. $f(-3)$ **21.** $f(7)$ **22.** $f(0)$

Graph each of the following in the coordinate plane. Draw a separate set of axes for each.

23. $4x + 3y = 12$ **24.** $3x - 2y < 6$

25. $y \geq 5x + 1$ **26.** $4x + 2y = 9$

Write an equation for the relationship between the variables in the chart.

27.

x	1	2	3	4	7
y	3	8	13	18	33

Statistics provide techniques for collecting, organizing, analyzing, and interpreting numerical information called **data**. Organized data is easier to read and interpret. One way to organize data is by using frequency tables. Consider the following example.

Suppose a farmer recorded the number of eggs collected daily for 20 days. He recorded the following numbers:

8, 5, 6, 8, 7, 9, 8, 6, 4, 5, 8, 9, 11, 7, 6, 9, 4, 7, 8, 9

The table below was constructed to organize this data and to show the frequency distribution for the data.

Number of Eggs	Tally	Frequency
4	||	2
5	||	2
6	|||	3
7	|||	3
8	~~||||~~	5
9	||||	4
10		0
11	|	1
	Total	**20**

Note that the number in the frequency column corresponds to the number of tally marks.

This same data can be organized in intervals.

Number of Eggs	Frequency
4 – 5	4
6 – 7	6
8 – 9	9
10 – 11	1

Graphs are also used to present data and show relationships. There are several ways of presenting the data in the following table.

Students Enrolled in Graham College

Year	1960	1965	1970	1975	1980	1985
Enrollment	2870	3050	5000	7900	8550	10,400

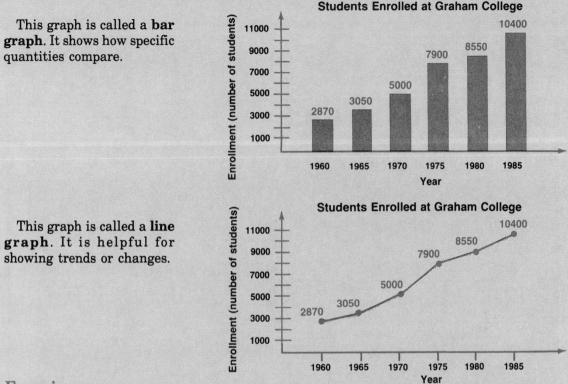

This graph is called a **bar graph**. It shows how specific quantities compare.

This graph is called a **line graph**. It is helpful for showing trends or changes.

Exercises

1. Make a frequency table from the following data. Organize the data using the following intervals: 60–65, 66–70, 71–75, 76–80, 81–85, 86–90, 91–95, and 96–100.

Test scores on a mathematics exam:

64	82	93	75	96	89	68	71	78	80
99	85	70	90	95	77	86	65	88	91
66	78	76	98	73	84	94	96	77	90

Draw a bar graph and a line graph for each of the following tables.

2. Number of Students at Broadview High School

Grade	9th	10th	11th	12th
Number of Students	250	400	325	230

3. Percent of 18 Year Olds with High School Diplomas

Year	1940	1950	1955	1960	1965	1970	1975	1980
Percent	49.3	60.0	62.5	70.0	73.9	75.6	74.8	74.5

4. Postal Rates for First Class Mail

Years	1966	1969	1972	1975	1978	1981	1985
Cost/ounce	5¢	6¢	8¢	13¢	15¢	20¢	22¢

CHAPTER 10

Lines and Slopes

The road sign shows the steepness or slope of the hill. This information aids drivers in gauging their speed. Slope is also used in mathematics to give information about the graphs of equations.

10-1 Slope

Jack Ferguson is a truck driver. When driving he
see many road signs similar to the one shown on the
preceding page. Suppose that the slope of a hill is 6%.
This means that for every 100 feet of *run* (horizontal
distance), there is a *rise* (vertical distance) of 6 feet.
The ratio of rise to run is called **slope**. The slope of a
line describes its steepness or rate of change.

On the graph below, the line passes through the origin, (0, 0), and
(4, 3). The rise (change in *y*-coordinates) is 3, while the run, (change
in the *x*-coordinates) is 4. Thus, the slope of this line is $\frac{3}{4}$.

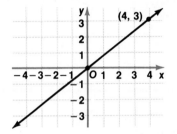

The slope of a line is the ratio of the change in *y* to the
corresponding change in *x*.

*Definition
of Slope*

$$\text{Slope} = \frac{\text{change in } y}{\text{change in } x}$$

Example

1 Determine the slope of each line.

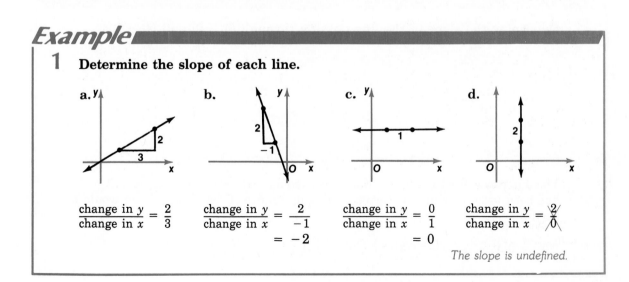

a. $\frac{\text{change in } y}{\text{change in } x} = \frac{2}{3}$

b. $\frac{\text{change in } y}{\text{change in } x} = \frac{2}{-1}$
$= -2$

c. $\frac{\text{change in } y}{\text{change in } x} = \frac{0}{1}$
$= 0$

d. $\frac{\text{change in } y}{\text{change in } x} = \frac{2}{0}$

The slope is undefined.

Notice that the line extending from lower left to upper right has a positive slope. The line extending from upper left to lower right has a negative slope. The slope of the horizontal line is 0.

For a vertical line the change in x would be zero. Since division by zero is not defined we say that *the slope of a vertical line is undefined.*

Example

2 **Determine the slope of the line containing the points listed.**

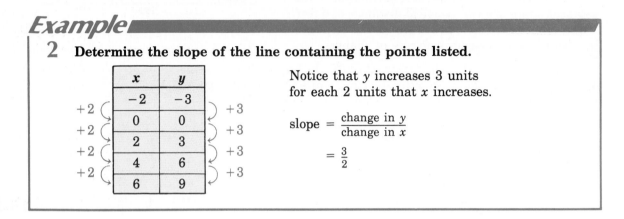

Notice that y increases 3 units for each 2 units that x increases.

$$\text{slope} = \frac{\text{change in } y}{\text{change in } x}$$

$$= \frac{3}{2}$$

From the above example and many other similar examples it is clear that the slope of a line can be determined from the coordinates of any two points on the line.

Given the coordinates of two points on a line, (x_1, y_1) and (x_2, y_2), the slope, m, can be found as follows.

$$m = \frac{y_2 - y_1}{x_2 - x_1} \text{ where } x_2 \neq x_1$$

Determining Slope Given Two Points

Example

3 **Determine the slope of the line passing through $(3, -9)$ and $(4, -12)$.**

$$m = \frac{y_2 - y_1}{x_2 - x_1} \qquad \text{y_2 is read "y sub 2." The 2 is a subscript.}$$

$$= \frac{-12 - (-9)}{4 - 3}$$

$$= \frac{-3}{1}$$

$$= -3$$

The difference of y-coordinates was expressed as $-12 - (-9)$. Suppose $-9 - (-12)$ had been used instead. The corresponding difference of the x-coordinates would have been $3 - 4$.

Notice that $\frac{-9 - (-12)}{3 - 4}$ is also equal to -3.

4 **Determine the value of *r* so the line through (*r*, 4) and (9, −2) has a slope of $-\frac{3}{2}$.**

$$m = \frac{y_2 - y_1}{x_2 - x_1}$$

$$-\frac{3}{2} = \frac{-2 - 4}{9 - r}$$

$$-\frac{3}{2} = \frac{-6}{9 - r}$$

$$-3(9 - r) = -6(2) \qquad \textit{Means-Extremes Property}$$

$$-27 + 3r = -12 \qquad \textit{Solve for r.}$$

$$3r = 15$$

$$r = 5$$

Exploratory Exercises

State the slope of each line.

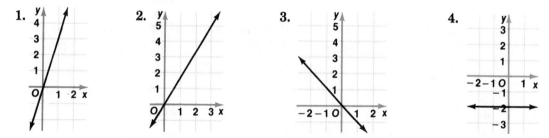

1.   2.   3.   4.

For each table, state the change in *y* and the change in *x*. Then determine the slope of the line passing through those points.

5.
x	y
0	0
1	2
2	4
3	6
4	8

6.
x	y
0	0
1	1
2	2
3	3
4	4

7.
x	y
−2	2
−1	1
0	0
1	−1
2	−2

8.
x	y
−2	−8
−1	−4
0	0
1	4
2	8

9.
x	y
−6	8
−3	4
0	0
3	−4
6	−8

Determine the slope of the line passing through each pair of points named below.

10. (3, 1), (5, 4)

11. (8, −1), (7, −2)

12. (6, 1), (6, 8)

13. (1, 4), (−2, −3)

14. (0, 0), (5, −2)

15. (6, 4), (−6, −4)

Written Exercises

Determine the slope of each line named below.

1. a
2. b
3. c
4. d
5. e
6. f
7. g
8. h

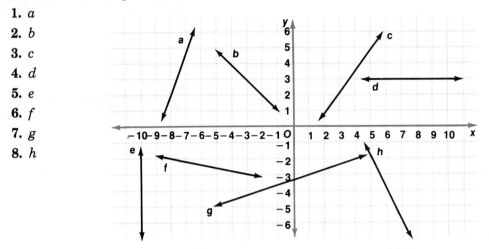

9. Look at lines a, c, and g above. These lines have positive slopes. What are the general directions of lines with positive slopes?

10. Look at lines b, f, and h above. These lines have negative slopes. What are the general directions of lines with negative slopes?

11. What is the slope of a horizontal line?

12. What is the slope of a vertical line?

Determine the slope of the line passing through each pair of points named below.

13. $(3, 4)$, $(4, 6)$
14. $(5, 2)$, $(7, 6)$
15. $(-3, 6)$, $(-5, 9)$
16. $(-2, 1)$, $(-6, 3)$
17. $(-3, 6)$, $(-8, 4)$
18. $(-1, 11)$, $(-5, 4)$
19. $(7, -4)$, $(9, -1)$
20. $(11, -1)$, $(14, -6)$
21. $(18, -4)$, $(6, -10)$
22. $(12, -3)$, $(14, -7)$
23. $(14, 3)$, $(-11, 3)$
24. $(-4, -6)$, $(-3, -8)$
25. $(0, 0)$, $\left(\frac{1}{3}, \frac{1}{6}\right)$
26. $\left(\frac{3}{4}, \frac{1}{2}\right)$, $\left(\frac{1}{2}, \frac{3}{4}\right)$
27. $\left(\frac{5}{8}, \frac{1}{3}\right)$, $\left(\frac{1}{8}, \frac{2}{3}\right)$
28. $\left(\frac{3}{4}, 1\right)$, $\left(\frac{3}{4}, -1\right)$
29. $\left(\frac{2}{3}, 5\right)$, $\left(\frac{1}{3}, 2\right)$
30. $\left(3\frac{1}{2}, 5\frac{1}{4}\right)$, $\left(2\frac{1}{2}, 6\right)$

Determine the value of r so that the line through each pair of points has the given slope.

31. $(9, r)$, $(6, 3)$, $m = -\frac{1}{3}$

32. $(r, 4)$, $(7, 3)$, $m = \frac{3}{4}$

33. $(4, -7)$, $(-2, r)$, $m = \frac{8}{3}$

34. $(6, -2)$, $(r, -6)$, $m = -4$

35. $(r, 7)$, $(11, r)$, $m = -\frac{1}{5}$

36. $(4, r)$, $(r, 2)$, $m = -\frac{5}{3}$

mini-review

Solve.

1. $\frac{3}{4}x = -36$

2. $\frac{r - 6}{-3} = 5$

3. $\frac{3}{4} = \frac{x + 5}{x + 7}$

4. $3y - 0.5 \geq 3.1$

5. The length of a rectangle is 5 feet more than 3 times the width. The perimeter is 250 feet. Find the dimensions of the rectangle.

10-2 Equations of Lines in Point-Slope and Standard Form

The graph at the right shows the nonvertical line, l, and point R having coordinates (x_1, y_1). The slope of line l is represented by m.

Let (x, y) represent any other point on line l. Since m is the slope of the line, all points (x, y) on the line satisfy the following equation.

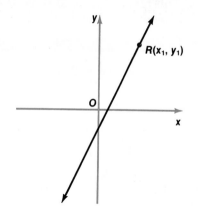

$$\frac{y - y_1}{x - x_1} = m \qquad \text{\textit{Assume } } x - x_1 \neq 0.$$

If both sides of the equation are multiplied by $(x - x_1)$ the result is the equation $y - y_1 = m(x - x_1)$. This form of an equation of a line is called the **point-slope form**.

> For a given point (x_1, y_1) on a nonvertical line, the point-slope form of a linear equation is
>
> $$y - y_1 = m(x - x_1).$$

Point-Slope Form

If you know the slope of a line and the coordinates of one point on the line, you can write the equation of the line.

Example

1 Write the equation of the line passing through $(2, -4)$ and having a slope of $\frac{2}{3}$.

Substitute in the point-slope form. Let $(x_1, y_1) = (2, -4)$ and $m = \frac{2}{3}$.

$$y - y_1 = m(x - x_1)$$
$$y - (-4) = \frac{2}{3}(x - 2)$$
$$y + 4 = \frac{2}{3}(x - 2)$$

The equation of the line is $y + 4 = \frac{2}{3}(x - 2)$.

Recall that any linear equation can be expressed in the form $Ax + By = C$. This is called the **standard form**. An equation that is written in point-slope form can be easily changed to standard form.

Example

2 Write $y + 4 = \frac{2}{3}(x - 2)$ in standard form.

$$y + 4 = \frac{2}{3}(x - 2)$$

$3(y + 4) = 2(x - 2)$ *Multiply both sides by 3.*

$3y + 12 = 2x - 4$

$-2x + 3y = -16$

$2x - 3y = 16$ *Multiply both sides by -1 to obtain a positive coefficient for x.*

$2x - 3y = 16$ is in standard form.

You can also find the equation of a line if you know the coordinates of two points on the line.

Example

3 Write the standard form of the equation for the line passing through $(5, -2)$ and $(-3, 8)$.

First determine the slope.

$$m = \frac{y_2 - y_1}{x_2 - x_1}$$

$$= \frac{8 - (-2)}{-3 - 5}$$ *Let $y_2 = 8$, $y_1 = -2$, $x_2 = -3$, and $x_1 = 5$.*

$$m = \frac{10}{-8} \text{ or } -\frac{5}{4}$$

Use the point-slope form. The slope is $-\frac{5}{4}$. The point (x_1, y_1) equals either $(5, -2)$ or $(-3, 8)$.

$y - y_1 = m(x - x_1)$ *Let $(x_1, y_1) = (5, -2)$*

$y - (-2) = -\frac{5}{4}(x - 5)$

$y + 2 = -\frac{5}{4}(x - 5)$ *This equation is in point-slope form.*

Now write the equation in standard form.

$$y + 2 = -\frac{5}{4}(x - 5)$$

$4(y + 2) = -5(x - 5)$

$4y + 8 = -5x + 25$

$5x + 4y = 17$ *This equation is in standard form.*

Check to see that you get the same result using the point $(-3, 8)$.

A horizontal line has a slope of zero. The point-slope form can be used to write the equation of horizontal lines. For example, the equation of a line through $(5, 2)$ and $(-9, 2)$ is $(y - 2) = 0(x - 5)$ or $y = 2$.

The slope of a vertical line is undefined. Therefore the point-slope form cannot be used for such lines. The equation of a line through $(3, 5)$ and $(3, -9)$ is $x = 3$ since the x-coordinate of every point on the line is equal to 3. Note that the equation $x = 3$ is in standard form.

Exploratory Exercises

State the slope and the point through which the line passes for each linear equation.

1. $y - 2 = 3(x - 5)$

2. $y - 3 = 4(x - 6)$

3. $y - (-5) = -2(x + 1)$

4. $y + 4 = -2[x - (-2)]$

5. $y + 6 = -\frac{3}{2}(x + 5)$

6. $y + 7 = -\frac{3}{4}(x + 4)$

7. $2(x - 3) = y + \frac{3}{2}$

8. $-\frac{2}{3}(x + 7) = y - \frac{3}{4}$

9. $-\frac{3}{5}(x + 6) = y + \frac{3}{8}$

10. $y = 3$

11. $y = -2$

12. $x = 1$

Express each equation in standard form.

13. $y - 3 = 2\left(x + \frac{3}{2}\right)$

14. $y + 5 = -3\left(x - \frac{1}{3}\right)$

15. $y + 1 = \frac{2}{3}(x + 2)$

16. $y + \frac{3}{2} = \frac{1}{2}(x + 4)$

17. $y - \frac{2}{3} = \frac{5}{3}(x + 7)$

18. $y - 1 = \frac{5}{6}\left(x + \frac{3}{5}\right)$

Written Exercises

Write the standard form of the equation for the line passing through the given point and having the given slope.

1. $(5, 4)$, $-\frac{2}{3}$

2. $(-6, -3)$, $-\frac{1}{2}$

3. $(9, 1)$, $\frac{2}{3}$

4. $(8, 2)$, $\frac{3}{4}$

5. $(4, -3)$, 2

6. $(-2, 4)$, -3

7. $(-6, 1)$, $\frac{3}{2}$

8. $(6, -2)$, $\frac{4}{3}$

9. $(5, 7)$, 0

10. $(-2, 6)$, 0

11. $(1, 3)$, undefined

12. $(-2, 1)$, undefined

Write the standard form of the equation for the line through each pair of points.

13. $(5, 4)$, $(6, 3)$

14. $(9, 1)$, $(8, 2)$

15. $(6, 1)$, $(7, -4)$

16. $(8, 3)$, $(5, -1)$

17. $(4, -2)$, $(8, -3)$

18. $(6, -1)$, $(4, -2)$

19. $(-6, 1)$, $(-8, 2)$

20. $(-5, 1)$, $(6, -2)$

21. $(-8, 2)$, $(-1, -2)$

22. $(4, -2)$, $(4, 8)$

23. $(5, -4)$, $(5, 5)$

24. $(5, 3)$, $(-6, 3)$

25. $\left(\frac{3}{4}, 1\right)$, $\left(2, \frac{1}{2}\right)$

26. $\left(\frac{1}{2}, \frac{3}{4}\right)$, $\left(\frac{2}{3}, \frac{4}{5}\right)$

27. $\left(2\frac{1}{2}, \frac{1}{3}\right)$, $\left(\frac{3}{4}, 1\frac{1}{2}\right)$

28. $(4, 2)$, $(-7, 2)$

29. $\left(-8, \frac{1}{2}\right)$, $\left(9, \frac{1}{2}\right)$

30. $(3, -2)$, $(3, 5)$

31. $(-2, 7)$, $\left(-2, \frac{16}{3}\right)$

32. $\left(-\frac{2}{9}, 3\right)$, $\left(\frac{8}{9}, 3\right)$

33. $\left(-2, \frac{2}{3}\right)$, $\left(-2, \frac{2}{7}\right)$

10-3   Slope-Intercept Form

The x-coordinate of the point where a line crosses the x-axis is called the **x-intercept** of the line. Line l crosses the x-axis at (4, 0). Therefore, the x-intercept is 4. Note that the corresponding y-coordinate is 0.

Similarly, the y-coordinate of the point where the line crosses the y-axis is called the **y-intercept** of the line. Line l crosses the y-axis at (0, 6). Therefore, the y-intercept is 6. Note that the corresponding x-coordinate is 0.

Consider the graph at the right. The line with slope m crosses the y-axis at $(0, b)$. You can write an equation for this line using the point-slope form. Let $(x_1, y_1) = (0, b)$.

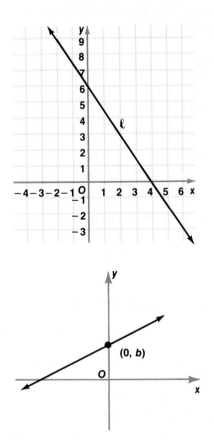

$y - y_1 = m(x - x_1)$ *Replace y_1 by b.*
$y - b = m(x - 0)$ *Replace x_1 by 0.*
$y = mx + b$
  ↑   ↑
slope   y-intercept

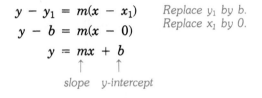

| An equation in the form $y = mx + b$ is said to be in slope-intercept form. | *Slope-Intercept Form* |

Example

1 **State the slope and y-intercept of the graph of $y = 5x - 3$.**

$y = mx + b$
$y = 5x + (-3)$

Since $m = 5$, the slope is 5.
Since $b = -3$, the y-intercept is -3.

Compare the slope-intercept form of a linear equation with the standard form, $Ax + By = C$.

Solve for y.

$$Ax + By = C$$
$$By = -Ax + C \qquad \textit{Assume } B \neq 0.$$
$$y = -\frac{A}{B}x + \frac{C}{B} \qquad \textit{This equation is in slope-intercept form.}$$
$$\underset{slope}{\uparrow} \qquad \underset{y\text{-}intercept}{\uparrow}$$

If the equation is given in standard form and B is *not* zero, the slope of the line can be determined by computing $-\frac{A}{B}$ and the y-intercept can be determined by computing $\frac{C}{B}$.

Example

2 **State the slope and y-intercept of the graph of $3x + 2y = 6$.**

In the equation $3x + 2y = 6$, $A = 3$, $B = 2$, and $C = 6$.

Slope: $-\frac{A}{B} = -\frac{3}{2}$ **y-intercept:** $\frac{C}{B} = \frac{6}{2}$ or 3

Check: Write the equation in slope-intercept form.

$$3x + 2y = 6$$
$$2y = -3x + 6$$
$$y = -\frac{3}{2}x + 3 \qquad \textit{The slope is } -\frac{3}{2} \textit{ and the } y\text{-intercept is 3.}$$

Recall that the x-coordinate of the y-intercept is 0 and the y-coordinate of the x-intercept is 0. You can use these facts to find the x- and y-intercepts of the graph of a linear equation.

Example

3 **Determine the x- and y-intercepts of the graph of $3x - 6y = 12$.**

To find the x-intercept, let $y = 0$.

$$3x - 6y = 12$$
$$3x - 6(0) = 12$$
$$3x = 12$$
$$x = 4$$

The x-intercept is 4.
The graph crosses the
x-axis at $(4, 0)$.

To find the y-intercept, let $x = 0$.

$$3x - 6y = 12$$
$$3(0) - 6y = 12$$
$$-6y = 12$$
$$y = -2$$

The y-intercept is -2.
The graph crosses the
y-axis at $(0, -2)$.

The y-intercept of an equation in the form $Ax + By = C$ is $\frac{C}{B}$. To find a formula for the x-intercept, let $y = 0$.

$$Ax + By = C$$
$$Ax + B(0) = C$$
$$Ax = C$$
$$x = \frac{C}{A}$$

The x-intercept is $\frac{C}{A}$, $A \neq 0$.

For the equation $2x - 3y = 8$, the x-intercept is $\frac{8}{2}$ or 4.

Exploratory Exercises

State the slope and y-intercept of the graph of each equation.

1. $y = 5x + 3$ **2.** $y = 2x + 1$ **3.** $y = 3x - 7$

4. $y = 6x - 8$ **5.** $y = \frac{1}{3}x$ **6.** $y = \frac{3}{4}x + 1$

7. $y = \frac{3}{5}x - \frac{1}{4}$ **8.** $y = \frac{2}{3}x$ **9.** $y = \frac{3}{5}x + \frac{1}{4}$

10. $2x + 3y = 5$ **11.** $-x + 4y = 3$ **12.** $2x - y = 1$
13. $y - 6x = 5$ **14.** $3y - 8x = 2$ **15.** $2y - 3x = 7$
16. $5y = -8x - 2$ **17.** $4y = 2x + 7$ **18.** $3y = -2x + 11$
19. State an equation for a line that has an undefined slope.
20. State an equation for a line that has no y-intercept.

Written Exercises

Write a linear equation in slope-intercept form for the line with the given slope and y-intercept.

1. $m = 3, b = 1$ **2.** $m = 2, b = 3$ **3.** $m = -3, b = 5$
4. $m = -4, b = 3$ **5.** $m = 4, b = -2$ **6.** $m = 2, b = -5$

7. $m = \frac{1}{2}, b = 5$ **8.** $m = \frac{2}{3}, b = 6$ **9.** $m = -\frac{5}{4}, b = 3$

Determine the x- and y-intercepts for the graph of each equation.

10. $3x + 2y = 6$ **11.** $5x + 3y = 15$ **12.** $5x + y = 10$
13. $2x + y = 6$ **14.** $3x + 4y = 24$ **15.** $2x - 7y = 28$
16. $3x - 2y = -5$ **17.** $2x + 5y = -11$ **18.** $8x + y = 4$
19. $6x + 2y = 3$ **20.** $3x - 7y = 9$ **21.** $-8x - 3y = 8$

Determine the slope and *y*-intercept for the graph of each equation. Then write each equation in slope-intercept form.

22. $2x + 5y = 10$

23. $3x + 4y = 12$

24. $5x - y = 15$

25. $3x - y = 9$

26. $2x + 5y = 8$

27. $7x + 4y = 8$

28. $5x - 4y = 11$

29. $7x - 3y = 10$

30. $2x + \frac{1}{3}y = 5$

31. $3x - \frac{1}{4}y = 6$

32. $\frac{1}{2}x + \frac{1}{4}y = 3$

33. $\frac{2}{3}x + \frac{1}{6}y = 2$

34. $3x = 2y - 7$

35. $5x = 8 - 2y$

36. $3y = 2x - 7$

37. $8y = 4x + 12$

38. $1.1x - 0.2y = 3.2$

39. $0.3x - 0.5y = 1.8$

Challenge

Solve each problem.

40. Find the coordinates of a point on the graph of $3x - 4y = -20$, if the *y*-coordinate is twice the *x*-coordinate.

41. Find the coordinates of a point on the graph of $4x - y = -2$, if the *y*-coordinate is three times the *x*-coordinate.

42. Find the coordinates of a point on the graph of $x + 2y = 11$, if the *y*-coordinate is 5 less than the *x*-coordinate.

43. Find the coordinates of a point on the graph of $7x + 3y = 2$, if the *y*-coordinate is 4 more than the *x*-coordinate.

Excursions in Algebra ———————————— **Rise Over Run**

Slope is sometimes defined as $\frac{\text{rise}}{\text{run}}$. In the coordinate plane, this is just another way of saying $\frac{\text{change in } y}{\text{change in } x}$.

When building a stairway, a carpenter considers the ratio of riser to tread. This ratio is equivalent to $\frac{\text{rise}}{\text{run}}$ and describes the steepness of the stairs.

$$\frac{\text{riser}}{\text{tread}} = \frac{\text{rise}}{\text{run}} = \frac{8}{12} = \frac{2}{3}$$

Exercises

Write the $\frac{\text{riser}}{\text{tread}}$ ratio for each of the following.

	Riser	Tread		Riser	Tread		Riser	Tread
1.	9″	12″	**2.**	6″	$7\frac{1}{2}″$	**3.**	7″	9″

4. For exercises 1-3, which stairs are the steepest?

10-4   Graphing Linear Equations

Previously you have graphed a linear equation by finding any two ordered pairs that satisfied the equation.

However, there are other methods that can be used. One such method is to use the x- and y-intercepts.

Example

1   **Graph $3x - 2y = 12$ by using the x- and y-intercepts.**

To find the x-intercept, let $y = 0$.

$$3x - 2y = 12$$
$$3x - 2(0) = 12$$
$$3x = 12$$
$$x = 4 \qquad \frac{C}{A} = 4$$

To find the y-intercept, let $x = 0$.

$$3x - 2y = 12$$
$$3(0) - 2y = 12$$
$$-2y = 12$$
$$y = -6 \qquad \frac{C}{B} = -6$$

Graph $(4, 0)$ and $(0, -6)$. Then draw the line that passes through these points.

To check, choose some other point on the line and see if it satisfies the equation. In this case, you could use $(2, -3)$.

$$3x - 2y = 12$$
$$3(2) - 2(-3) \stackrel{?}{=} 12$$
$$6 + 6 \stackrel{?}{=} 12$$
$$12 = 12 \quad \textit{It checks!}$$

If an equation is in standard form and A, B, or C is zero, the graph of the equation has only one intercept. In such cases, you must find some other ordered pairs that satisfy the equation.

When $A = 0$, the graph is horizontal. When $B = 0$, the graph is vertical. When $C = 0$, the graph passes through the origin.

If a linear equation is in slope-intercept form, then it is convenient to use the slope and *y*-intercept to draw the graph of the equation.

Example

2 Graph $y = 3x + 2$ by using the slope and *y*-intercept.

The *y*-intercept is 2 so the graph passes through $(0, 2)$. Since the slope is 3, we know

$$3 = \frac{3}{1} = \frac{\text{change in } y}{\text{change in } x} \quad .$$

Starting at $(0, 2)$ go up 3 units and to the right 1 unit to $(1, 5)$. Then draw the line through $(0, 2)$ and $(1, 5)$.

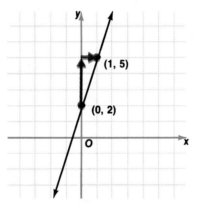

To check, you should find at least one other ordered pair whose graph should be on the line. Two such ordered pairs are $(2, 8)$ and $(-1, -1)$. Do you see how these ordered pairs can be obtained?

If the equation is in standard form, it is sometimes convenient to use the slope and *y*-intercept to draw the graph. Recall that for an equation in standard form, $-\frac{A}{B}$ is the slope of the line and $\frac{C}{B}$ is the *y*-intercept.

Consider the line $-4x + 3y = 12$. The slope, $-\frac{A}{B}$, is $\frac{4}{3}$. The *y*-intercept, $\frac{C}{B}$, is $\frac{12}{3}$ or 4. To draw the graph, use the slope and *y*-intercept, as in Example 2, and check the graph with at least one other ordered pair on the line.

Exploratory Exercises

State the x-intercept and y-intercept for each equation.

1. $4x + y = 8$ **2.** $6x + y = 6$ **3.** $3x + 4y = 6$

4. $5x + 2y = 20$ **5.** $2x - y = 8$ **6.** $3x - 2y = 6$

7. $7x + 2y = 10$ **8.** $5x + 6y = 8$ **9.** $5x - \frac{1}{2}y = 2$

10. $3x + \frac{1}{3}y = 2$ **11.** $y = 3x - 1$ **12.** $y = 4x + 3$

13. $2x = 5 - 3y$ **14.** $3x = 4y + 1$ **15.** $\frac{1}{2}x + \frac{1}{3}y = 0$

In each of the following the slope and a point on the line are given. Name two other points on each line.

16. $m = \frac{4}{3}, (0, 1)$ **17.** $m = 2, (0, 1)$ **18.** $m = \frac{5}{2}, (0, 3)$

19. $m = -7, (0, 4)$ **20.** $m = -\frac{1}{4}, (6, 1)$ **21.** $m = \frac{1}{2}, (5, 2)$

22. $m = -\frac{2}{3}, (-3, 2)$ **23.** $m = 8, (-3, 6)$ **24.** $m = 0, (3, 2)$

Written Exercises

Graph each equation using the x- and y-intercepts.

1. $6x - 3y = 6$ **2.** $4x + 5y = 20$ **3.** $5x - y = -10$

4. $2x + 10y = 5$ **5.** $2x + 5y = -10$ **6.** $7x - 2y = -7$

7. $y = 6x - 9$ **8.** $x + \frac{1}{2}y = 4$ **9.** $\frac{1}{2}x + \frac{2}{3}y = -3$

10. $x = 8y - 4$ **11.** $x = \frac{3}{4}y + 6$ **12.** $\frac{2}{3}y = \frac{1}{2}x + 6$

Graph each equation using the slope-intercept method.

13. $y = \frac{2}{3}x + 3$ **14.** $y = \frac{3}{4}x + 4$ **15.** $y = -\frac{3}{5}x - 1$

16. $y = -\frac{3}{4}x + 1$ **17.** $y = \frac{3}{2}x - 5$ **18.** $y = \frac{1}{2}x + 4$

19. $-4x + y = 6$

20. $-3x + 2y = 12$

21. $-2x + y = 3$

22. $3y - 7 = 2x$

23. $5x + 2 = 7y$

24. $\frac{3}{4}x + \frac{1}{2}y = 4$

mini-review

Simplify.

1. $(4xy^3)(-5x^3yz)$ **2.** $(-2a^2b^3)^4$

3. $\dfrac{5a^3b^2c^3}{-20a^4b^2}$ **4.** $\dfrac{x^2 - 5x - 24}{2x^2 - 4x - 30}$

5. $2x(x^3 - 3x^2 + 7) + 5(x^4 + 5x^3 - 3x + 5)$

Problem Solving

The freezing point of water on the Celsius and Fahrenheit scales can be represented by the ordered pair (0, 32), where 0 is the Celsius temperature and 32 is the Fahrenheit temperature. Similarly, the boiling point of water can be represented by (100, 212). With these two points you can draw the graph of the line showing the relationship between Celsius and Fahrenheit.

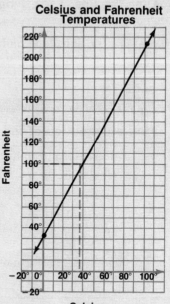

Celsius and Fahrenheit Temperatures

The graph above can be used to quickly estimate equivalent temperatures. For a Fahrenheit temperature of 100, for example, you can estimate the corresponding Celsius temperature by first locating 100 on the Fahrenheit scale. Follow the value horizontally until you reach the line, then drop vertically to the Celsius scale. The corresponding Celsius temperature is between 35° and 40°.

Many other relationships can be shown graphically. For example, the speed of sound through water is 1454 m/s, or about 1.5 km/s. The graph at the right shows the relationship between the time in seconds and the distance in kilometers. Note that the ordered pairs (4, 6) and (6, 9) were used to draw the graph.

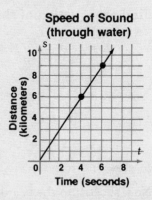

Speed of Sound (through water)

Exercises

Use the graph at the top of this page to estimate the Celsius or Fahrenheit equivalents.

1. 80°F   2. 65°F   3. 20°C   4. 50°C

Use the graph to solve each problem.

5. Using sonar, a ship finds that it takes sound waves 2.5 seconds to reach the ocean floor. Estimate the depth of the ocean at this point.

6. Estimate how many seconds it would take sound waves to reach a depth of 5 km.

10-5   Writing Slope-Intercept Equations of Lines

If you have enough information about a line, you can write an equation for the line. For example, you might know any of the following:

1. The slope and a point on the line.
2. Two points on the line.
3. The x- and y-intercepts.

Example

1   Find an equation of the line whose slope is 3 and that passes through $(4, -2)$.

$$y = mx + b \qquad \text{\textit{Use slope-intercept form.}}$$
$$y = 3x + b \qquad \text{\textit{The slope m is 3.}}$$
$$-2 = 3(4) + b \qquad \text{\textit{Substitute 4 for x and } -2 \text{ \textit{for y.}}}$$
$$-2 = 12 + b \qquad \text{\textit{Now solve for b.}}$$
$$-14 = b$$

The slope-intercept form of the equation for the line is $y = 3x + (-14)$. This can also be expressed as $y = 3x - 14$.   *In standard form the equation is $3x - y = 14$.*

The following procedure can be used to find an equation when two points on the line are known.

Example

2   Find an equation of the line that passes through $(5, 1)$ and $(8, -2)$.

$$m = \frac{y_2 - y_1}{x_2 - x_1} \qquad \text{\textit{First determine the slope.}}$$
$$= \frac{-2 - 1}{8 - 5}$$
$$= \frac{-3}{3}$$
$$= -1$$

In slope-intercept form $y = -1x + b$ or $y = -x + b$.

Now substitute the coordinates of either point into the equation and solve for b.

Using $(5, 1)$ **or**   Using $(8, -2)$

$$y = -x + b \qquad\qquad\qquad y = -x + b$$
$$1 = -(5) + b \qquad\qquad -2 = -(8) + b$$
$$6 = b \qquad\qquad\qquad\quad 6 = b$$

The slope-intercept form of the equation is $y = -x + 6$.   *The standard form is $x + y = 6$.*

You can also use the slope and y-intercept obtained from the graph to find the equation of a line.

Example

3 Find an equation for line PQ whose graph is shown below.

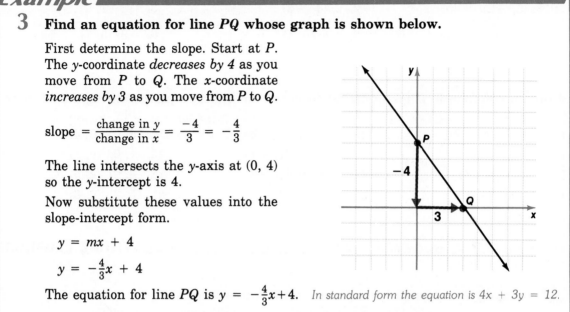

First determine the slope. Start at P. The y-coordinate *decreases by 4* as you move from P to Q. The x-coordinate *increases by 3* as you move from P to Q.

$$\text{slope} = \frac{\text{change in } y}{\text{change in } x} = \frac{-4}{3} = -\frac{4}{3}$$

The line intersects the y-axis at $(0, 4)$ so the y-intercept is 4.

Now substitute these values into the slope-intercept form.

$$y = mx + 4$$

$$y = -\frac{4}{3}x + 4$$

The equation for line PQ is $y = -\frac{4}{3}x + 4$.   *In standard form the equation is $4x + 3y = 12$.*

Exploratory Exercises

In each of the following a point on the line is given. Determine the y-intercept, b.

1. $(2, 1), y = 3x + b$ **2.** $(6, 2), y = -2x + b$ **3.** $(4, 5), y = -x + b$

4. $(2, 2), y = -\frac{3}{2}x + b$ **5.** $(8, 1), y = \frac{3}{4}x + b$ **6.** $(-6, 5), y = -\frac{2}{3}x + b$

7. $(1, -2), y = -\frac{5}{3}x + b$ **8.** $(3, -1), y = \frac{5}{6}x + b$ **9.** $(2, 3), y = \frac{4}{3}x + b$

State the slope and y-intercept for each line. Then express the equation of the line in slope-intercept form.

10. a
11. b
12. c
13. d
14. e
15. f

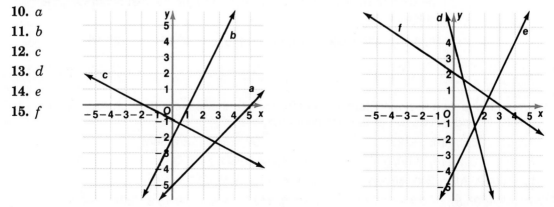

Written Exercises

Write an equation in slope-intercept form for the line having the given slope and passing through the indicated point.

1. 3; $(5, -2)$ **2.** 2; $(4, -2)$ **3.** $\frac{2}{3}$; $(-1, 0)$

4. $\frac{1}{2}$; $(5, 3)$ **5.** -5; $(5, 4)$ **6.** -3; $(3, 7)$

7. $\frac{3}{4}$; $(-2, -4)$ **8.** $-\frac{5}{3}$; $(-3, -5)$ **9.** $\frac{1}{4}$; $(0, 8)$

Write an equation in slope-intercept form for the line that passes through each pair of points.

10. $(-1, 7), (8, -2)$ **11.** $(5, 2), (-7, -4)$ **12.** $(6, 0), (0, 4)$

13. $(4, 1), (5, 2)$ **14.** $(8, -1), (7, -1)$ **15.** $(1, 0), (0, 1)$

16. $(6, 3), (-2, 4)$ **17.** $(-4, 3), (6, -5)$ **18.** $(8, 0), (2, 5)$

19. $(5, 7), (-1, 6)$ **20.** $(-6, 2), (3, -5)$ **21.** $(5, 7), (0, 6)$

Using Calculators _____ Writing Equations

Example: Determine slope-intercept form of the line passing through (7.6, 10.8) and (12.2, 93.7). Round values to the nearest hundredth.

First determine the slope, $m = \dfrac{y_2 - y_1}{x_2 - x_1}$

ENTER: $($ 93.7 $-$ 10.8 $)$ $\div$ $($ 12.2 $-$ 7.6 $)$ $=$

The display shows 18.021739. Rounded to the nearest hundredth, the slope is 18.02.

Recall that $y = mx + b$. To determine the y-intercept, solve for b. Thus, $b = -mx + y$. Let $(x, y) = (7.6, 10.8)$.

ENTER: 18.02 $+/-$ $\times$ 7.6 $+$ 10.8 $=$

The display shows -126.152. Rounded to the nearest hundredth, the y-intercept is -126.15.

Therefore, the slope intercept form is $y = 18.02x - 126.15$.

Exercises

Write an equation in slope-intercept form for the line that passes through each pair of points. Round values to the nearest hundredth.

1. $(5, -285), (10, -225)$ **2.** $(100, 293), (125, 368)$

3. $(5, -225), (16, -885)$ **4.** $(7, 12.7), (-1, 3.9)$

5. $(100, 257.5), (200, 507.5)$ **6.** $(1.3, 5.1), (2.7, 14.9)$

7. $(11.4, 25.8), (-2.4, -17.5)$ **8.** $(18.9, -3.4), (-15.3, 5.9)$

Applications in Aeronautics Airplane Flying Time

A light twin-engine aircraft has a useful carrying load of 2061 pounds. Of this a maximum of 1164 pounds of fuel can be carried. The remaining weight may be made up of people and cargo. If the plane is to carry more cargo or people, less fuel is carried and there is less flying time.

Shown below is a graph of the amount of fuel in pounds needed to fly a given number of hours.

Suppose a plane carries 519 pounds of cargo and 6 people weighing a total of 960 pounds. How many hours of flying time does the plane have?

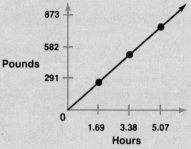

First, determine the amount of fuel the plane can carry. Then check the graph for the number of flying hours.

519	2061 *total pounds allowed*	582 pounds of fuel
+960	−1479	permit about 3.38
1479 *total pounds of cargo and people*	582 *pounds of fuel that can be carried*	hours of flying time.

Exercises

Solve.

1. How many hours of flying time does a plane have if it is carrying 1000 pounds of cargo and 4 people weighing a total of 770 pounds?

2. Approximately how many hours of flying time does a plane have if it is carrying 2 people weighing a total of 305 pounds and 906 pounds of cargo?

3. How many pounds of cargo can be carried if a plane must fly 3.38 hours to reach its destination? The pilot and copilot each weigh 145 pounds.

10-6   Parallel and Perpendicular Lines

The graphs below show parallel lines.

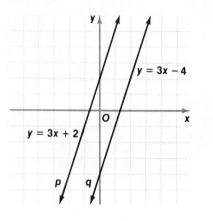

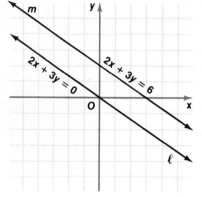

What is the slope of line p?
Line q?

What is the slope of line l?
Line m?

What is your guess about the relationship between the slopes of parallel lines?

| If two lines have the same slope, then they are parallel. All vertical lines are parallel. | *Definition of Parallel Lines* |

Example

1   **Find the equation of the line that is parallel to the graph of $5x - 2y = 6$ and that passes through $(4, -2)$. Use slope-intercept form.**

The slope of the graph of $5x - 2y = 6$ is $\frac{5}{2}$.

Therefore the slope-intercept form of an equation whose graph is parallel to the graph of $5x - 2y = 6$ is

$$y = \frac{5}{2}x + b.$$

Now substitute $(4, -2)$ into that equation and solve for b.

$$-2 = \frac{5}{2}(4) + b$$
$$-2 = 10 + b$$
$$-12 = b$$

The equation of the line is $y = \frac{5}{2}x - 12$.   *In standard form the equation is $5x - 2y = 24$.*

Line l is shown in the figure on the left below. Suppose the axes and the graph are rotated counterclockwise 90°. After the rotation, line l will coincide with line l' of the figure shown in color.

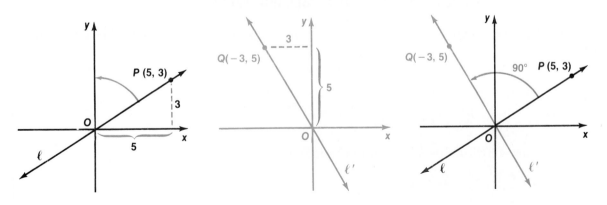

The figure at the right above shows lines l and l'. Note that line l' is perpendicular to line l. Study their slopes.

Compare the slopes. What is their product?

If the product of the slopes of two lines is -1, then the lines are perpendicular. In a plane, vertical lines are perpendicular to horizontal lines.	*Definition of Perpendicular Lines*

Example

2 **Show that the lines for $7x + 3y = 4$ and $3x - 7y = 1$ are perpendicular.**

The slope of the line for $7x + 3y = 4$ is $-\frac{7}{3}$.

The slope of the line for $3x - 7y = 1$ is $\frac{3}{7}$.

Since $-\frac{7}{3} \cdot \frac{3}{7} = -1$, the lines are perpendicular.

Example

3 Find an equation of the line that is perpendicular to the line for $2x - 5y = 3$ and that passes through $(-2, 7)$. Use slope-intercept form.

The slope of the line for $2x - 5y = 3$ is $\frac{2}{5}$. The slope of the line perpendicular to that line is $-\frac{5}{2}$. The equation in slope-intercept form for the line perpendicular to the line for $2x - 5y = 3$ is

$$y = -\frac{5}{2}x + b.$$

Now substitute $(-2, 7)$ into the equation.

$$7 = -\frac{5}{2}(-2) + b$$
$$7 = 5 + b$$
$$2 = b$$

The equation in slope-intercept form is $y = -\frac{5}{2}x + 2$.

In standard form the equation is $5x + 2y = 4$.

Exploratory Exercises

State the slopes of the lines parallel and perpendicular to the graphs of each equation.

1. $5x - y = 7$
2. $3x + 4y = 2$
3. $2x - y = 7$
4. $6x + 3y = 4$
5. $2x - 3y = 7$
6. $7x + y = 4$
7. $x = 7$
8. $2x + 7y = 8$
9. $5x - 3y = 4$
10. $y = -4$
11. $y = 4x + 2$
12. $y = 3x - 7$
13. $3y = 2x + 5$
14. $4x = 2y - 7$
15. $3x = 4 - 3y$

Written Exercises

Write an equation for the line that is parallel to the graph of each equation and that passes through the indicated point. Use slope-intercept form.

1. $y = -\frac{3}{5}x + 4$; $(0, -1)$
2. $6x + y = 4$; $(-2, 3)$
3. $y = \frac{3}{4}x - 1$; $(0, 0)$
4. $2x + 3y = 1$; $(4, 2)$
5. $5x - 2y = 7$; $(0, -4)$
6. $4x - 3y = 2$; $(4, 0)$
7. $y = \frac{3}{4}x - 1$; $(2, 2)$
8. $y = -\frac{1}{3}x + 7$; $(2, -5)$
9. $x = y$; $(7, -2)$

Write an equation for the line that is perpendicular to the graph of each equation and that passes through the indicated point. Use slope-intercept form.

10. $5x - 3y = 7$; $(8, -2)$
11. $3x + 8y = 4$; $(0, 4)$
12. $y = 3x - 2$; $(6, -1)$
13. $y = -3x + 7$; $(-3, 1)$
14. $y = 5x - 3$; $(0, -1)$
15. $y = \frac{2}{3}x + 1$; $(-3, 0)$
16. $3x + 7y = 4$; $(1, -3)$
17. $5x + 9y = 3$; $(0, 0)$
18. $y = 2x - 7$; $(4, -6)$

10-7 Midpoint of a Line Segment

The coordinate of the midpoint, P, of line segment AB
shown at the right can be found
as follows.

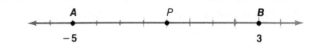

Find the distance from A to B on the number line. $\qquad |-5-3| = 8$

The distance from A to P on the number line is $\frac{1}{2}(8)$ or 4.

Add the distance, 4, to the coordinate of A, -5, to obtain the
coordinate of P. Thus, the coordinate of P is -1.

A simpler approach is to find the average of the coordinates.

$$P = \frac{x_1 + x_2}{2} = \frac{-5 + 3}{2} = \frac{-2}{2} = -1$$

The coordinate of the midpoint, P, of two points, x_1, and x_2,
on a number line is

$$P = \frac{x_1 + x_2}{2}.$$

*Midpoint on a
Number Line*

This method can be extended to find the coordinates of the
midpoint of a line segment in the coordinate plane.

The coordinates of the midpoint, (x, y), of a line segment
whose endpoints are (x_1, y_1) and (x_2, y_2) are

$$(x, y) = \left(\frac{x_1 + x_2}{2}, \frac{y_1 + y_2}{2} \right).$$

*Midpoint of a
Line Segment*

Example

1 Find the coordinates of the midpoint of the line segment from $(-2, 4)$ to $(8, 6)$.

$$(x, y) = \left(\frac{x_1 + x_2}{2}, \frac{y_1 + y_2}{2} \right)$$

$$= \left(\frac{-2 + 8}{2}, \frac{4 + 6}{2} \right)$$

$$= (3, 5)$$

Example

2 If one endpoint of a line segment is (2, 8) and the midpoint is (−1, 4), find the coordinates of the other endpoint.

$$(x, y) = \left(\frac{x_1 + x_2}{2}, \frac{y_1 + y_2}{2}\right)$$

$$(-1, 4) = \left(\frac{2 + x_2}{2}, \frac{8 + y_2}{2}\right) \qquad \text{Substitute } (-1, 4) \text{ for } (x, y).$$
$$\text{Substitute } (2, 8) \text{ for } (x_1, y_1).$$

Now separate this last expression into two equations.

$$-1 = \frac{2 + x_2}{2} \quad \text{Solve for } x_2. \qquad\qquad 4 = \frac{8 + y_2}{2} \quad \text{Solve for } y_2.$$

$$-2 = 2 + x_2 \qquad\qquad\qquad\qquad\qquad 8 = 8 + y_2$$

$$-4 = x_2 \qquad\qquad\qquad\qquad\qquad\qquad 0 = y_2$$

The coordinates of the endpoint are (−4, 0).

Exploratory Exercises

State the coordinate of the point midway between each pair of points on the number line.

1. 4 and 8   **2.** 3 and 1   **3.** 10 and 18

4. −2 and 6   **5.** −3 and 13   **6.** −4 and −10

7. −3 and 6   **8.** 5 and −6   **9.** −10 and 15

State the coordinates of the midpoint of the line segment whose endpoints are given.

10. (5, 1), (9, 3)   **11.** (2, 10), (8, −4)   **12.** (6, 5), (8, −3)

13. (15, −4), (3, −12)   **14.** (−11, 3), (3, −15)   **15.** (2, 0), (0, 12)

16. (9, −4), (1, 14)   **17.** (5, −6), (−7, 3)   **18.** (2, 5), (11, 2)

19. (5, −4), (6, −7)   **20.** (x, y), (a, b)   **21.** (2x, 3y), (6x, y)

Written Exercises

Write the coordinates of the midpoint of the line segment whose endpoints are given.

1. (8, 4), (12, 2)   **2.** (9, 5), (17, 3)   **3.** (11, 4), (9, 2)

4. (17, 9), (11, −3)   **5.** (14, 4), (2, 0)   **6.** (19, −3), (11, 5)

7. (4, 2), (8, −6)   **8.** (−6, 5), (8, −11)   **9.** (−6, 5), (8, −11)

10. (5, −2), (7, 3)   **11.** (8, 2), (12, −5)   **12.** (−11, 6), (13, 4)

13. (12, −3), (5, 8)   **14.** (4, 7), (8, 0)   **15.** (2, 5), (4, 1)

16. (9, 10), (−8, 4)   **17.** (−3, 6), (4, 5)   **18.** (−8, −5), (−2, 8)

19. $\left(\frac{1}{2}, 3\right)$, $(1, -2)$

20. $\left(\frac{5}{6}, \frac{1}{3}\right)$, $\left(\frac{1}{6}, \frac{1}{3}\right)$

21. $\left(3\frac{1}{2}, 2\frac{1}{4}\right)$, $\left(5\frac{1}{3}, 1\frac{1}{2}\right)$

22. $\left(2\frac{1}{5}, 3\frac{1}{3}\right)$, $\left(5\frac{3}{5}, 2\frac{1}{3}\right)$

If P is the midpoint of line segment AB, find the coordinates of the missing point A, B, or P.

23. $A(3, 5)$, $P(11, 7)$

24. $A(3, 5)$, $P(5, -7)$

25. $A(5, 9)$, $B(-7, 3)$

26. $B(11, -4)$, $P(3, 8)$

27. $B(5, 3)$, $P(9, 7)$

28. $A(11, -6)$, $B(5, -9)$

29. $P(5, -9)$, $A(4, -11)$

30. $P(3, 9)$, $B(-4, 1)$

31. $A(4, -7)$, $B(-8, 1)$

32. $A(7, 4)$, $P(9, -3)$

33. $P(3, -5)$, $A(-3, 8)$

34. $P(5, 6)$, $B(5, 7)$

35. The center of a circle is $(3, -2)$ and one endpoint of a diameter is $(8, 3)$. Find the other endpoint of the diameter.

36. The two endpoints of the diameter of a circle are $(8, -2)$ and $(4, -6)$. Find the coordinates of the center.

The coordinates on a map for certain cities are given below.

Los Angeles $(-6, -1)$ Dallas $(1, -3)$ Chicago $(3, 3)$

Atlanta $(5, -1)$ Miami $(6, -4)$ Boston $(7, 5)$

Find the coordinates of the point on the map midway between each pair of cities.

37. Los Angeles and Boston

38. Atlanta and Dallas

39. Chicago and Miami

40. Boston and Atlanta

41. Dallas and Boston

42. Miami and Dallas

43. Chicago and Los Angeles

44. Boston and Chicago

Challenge———

Find the coordinates of P on line segment AB if P is one-fourth of the distance from A to B.

45. $A(8, 4)$, $B(12, 12)$

46. $A(-3, 9)$, $B(5, 1)$

47. $A(-3, 2)$, $B(5, 4)$

48. $A(2, -6)$, $B(9, 5)$

For quadrilateral $ABCD$, determine whether the diagonals of $ABCD$ bisect each other.

49. $A(8, 6)$, $B(5, 5)$, $C(4, 2)$, $D(7, 3)$

50. $A(-2, 6)$, $B(2, 11)$, $C(3, 8)$, $D(-1, 3)$

51. $A(11, 6)$, $B(1, -2)$, $C(-2, 4)$, $D(3, 8)$

52. $A(8, -2)$, $B(3, -5)$, $C(-3, 5)$, $D(2, 8)$

Testing Points On A Line

Each of the two graphs has 3 points plotted. Are the points on the same line?

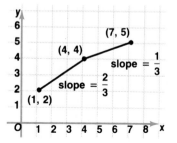

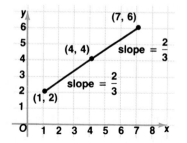

The points are not on the same line. The segments have different slopes.

The points are on the same line. The segments have the same slope and have a common point between.

You can write a computer program that tests if any 3 points are on the same line. Let the coordinates of the points to be tested be (A, B), (C, D), and (E, F).

```
10  REM THIS PROGRAM DETERMINES IF 3 POINTS
       LIE ON THE SAME LINE        REM statements often tell
20  INPUT A, B, C, D, E, F         how the program works.
30  IF (D-B)/(C-A)=(F-D)/(E-C) THEN 60
40  PRINT A;",";B,C;",";D,E;",";F,
    "POINTS ARE NOT ON SAME LINE"
50  GO TO 70
60  PRINT A;",";B,C;",";D,E;",";F,    Three points on the same
       "POINTS ARE ON THE SAME LINE"   line are called collinear.
70  END
```

When the ordered pairs (1, 2), (13, 23), and (5, 9) are used, the output is as follows.

```
1, 2     13, 23     5, 9
POINTS ARE ON THE SAME LINE
```

When the ordered pairs $(-5, 2)$, $(-5, 7)$, $(3, 8)$ are used, a division-by-zero error occurs in line 30. Add the following lines to the program to eliminate the error.

```
25  IF C - A=0 OR E - C=0 THEN PRINT "AT LEAST ONE LINE HAS AN
       UNDEFINED SLOPE": GOTO 70
```

Exercises　Use the computer program to determine if each set of points lie on one line.

1. (1, 5), (16, 14), $(-4, 2)$　　　　　　**2.** $(-2, -3)$, (2, 1), (5, 6)

3. $(-459, -80)$, (865, 163), (54, 1)　　**4.** (7, 14), $(-5, 10)$, $(-5, 8)$

5. Modify the program to print the slope for each segment.

slope (305)
point-slope form (309)
standard form (310)
x-intercept (312)
y-intercept (312)

slope-intercept form (312)
slopes of parallel lines (324)
slopes of perpendicular lines (325)
midpoint of a line segment (327)

Chapter Summary ▰▰▰▰▰

1. The slope of a line is the ratio of the change in y to the corresponding change in x. Slope $= \dfrac{\text{change in } y}{\text{change in } x}$. (305)

2. Given the coordinates of two points on a line, (x_1, y_1) and (x_2, y_2), the slope m can be found as follows.

$$m = \frac{y_2 - y_1}{x_2 - x_1} \quad (306)$$

3. For a given point (x_1, y_1) on a nonvertical line, the point-slope form of a linear equation is

$$y - y_1 = m(x - x_1). \quad (309)$$

4. The standard form of a linear equation is $Ax + By = C$ where $A, B,$ and C are integers and A and B are not both zero. (310)

5. The x-coordinate of the point where a line crosses the x-axis is called the x-intercept of the line. (312)

6. The y-coordinate of the point where a line crosses the y-axis is called the y-intercept of the line. (312)

7. An equation of the form $y = mx + b$ is said to be in slope-intercept form. (312)

8. If two lines have the same slope, then they are parallel. All vertical lines are parallel. (324)

9. If the product of the slopes of two lines is -1, then the lines are perpendicular. In a plane, vertical lines are perpendicular to horizontal lines. (325)

10. The coordinate of the midpoint, P, of two points, x_1 and x_2, on a number line is

$$P = \frac{x_1 + x_2}{2}. \quad (327)$$

11. The coordinates of the midpoint, (x, y), of a line segment whose endpoints are (x_1, y_1) and (x_2, y_2) are

$$(x, y) = \left(\frac{x_1 + x_2}{2}, \frac{y_1 + y_2}{2} \right). \quad (327)$$

Chapter Review

10-1   Determine the slope of the line passing through each pair of points named.

    1. $(-3, 5), (4, 5)$ **2.** $(8, 3), (2, 5)$

    3. $(-2, 5), (-2, 9)$ **4.** $(-3, -5), (9, -1)$

10-2   Write an equation in point-slope form and standard form for the line through each pair of points.

    5. $(8, 1), (-3, 5)$ **6.** $(-2, 5), (9, 5)$

    7. $(0, 5), (-2, 0)$ **8.** $(-3, 0), (0, -6)$

10-3   Determine the slope and y-intercept of the graph of each equation.

    9. $3x - 2y = 7$ **10.** $y = \frac{1}{4}x + 3$

    11. $8x + y = 4$ **12.** $x = 2y - 7$

    Determine the x- and y-intercepts for the graph of each equation.

    13. $2x + 5y = 10$ **14.** $3x + 4y = 15$

10-4   Graph each equation using the x- and y-intercepts.

    15. $3x - y = 9$ **16.** $5x + 2y = 12$

    Graph each equation using the slope-intercept method.

    17. $y = \frac{2}{3}x + 4$ **18.** $y = -\frac{3}{2}x - 6$

10-5   Write an equation for the line satisfying the given conditions. Use slope-intercept form.

    19. $m = 4$ and passes through $(6, -2)$

    20. Passes through $(9, 5)$ and $(-3, -4)$

    21. Passes through $(2, 2)$ and has y-intercept of 7

    22. Slope $= -\frac{3}{5}$ and y-intercept $= 3$

10-6   Write an equation for the line that is parallel to the graph of each equation and that passes through the indicated point. Use slope-intercept form.

    23. $4x - y = 7; (2, -1)$ **24.** $3x + 9y = 1; (3, 0)$

    Write an equation for the line that is perpendicular to the graph of each equation and that passes through the indicated point. Use slope-intercept form.

    25. $2x - 7y = 1; (-4, 0)$ **26.** $8x - 3y = 7; (4, 5)$

10-7   Find the coordinates of the midpoint of $\overline{AB}$.

    27. $A(3, 5), B(9, -3)$ **28.** $A(2, 7), B(8, 4)$

Chapter Test ▰▰▰▰▰▰▰

Determine the slope of the line passing through each pair of points.

1. $(9, 2), (3, -4)$　　　　　　　**2.** $(8, 3), (8, 1)$　　　　　　　**3.** $(4, -5), (-2, -5)$

Determine the slope and y-intercept for each equation.

4. $x - 8y = 3$　　　　　　　　　　　**5.** $3x - 2y = 9$

6. $\frac{1}{2}x + \frac{3}{4}y = 2$　　　　　　　　　　**7.** $y = 7$

Write an equation in standard form for the line satisfying the given conditions.

8. Passes through $(2, 5)$ and $(8, -3)$.

9. Passes through $(-2, -1)$ and $(6, -4)$.

10. Has slope of 2 and y-intercept $= 3$.

11. Has y-intercept -4 and passes through $(5, -3)$.

12. Slope $= \frac{3}{4}$ and passes through $(6, -2)$.

Write an equation in slope-intercept form for the line satisfying the given conditions.

13. Passes through $(4, -2)$ and the origin.

14. Passes through $(-2, -5)$ and $(8, -3)$.

15. Passes through $(6, 4)$ with y-intercept $= -2$.

16. Slope $= -\frac{2}{3}$ and y-intercept $= 5$.

17. Slope $= 6$ and passes through $(-3, -4)$.

Write the equation of the line satisfying the given conditions. Use slope-intercept form.

18. Parallel to $6x - y = 7$ and passes through $(-2, 8)$.

19. Parallel to $3x + 7y = 4$ and passes through $(5, -2)$.

20. Perpendicular to $5x - 3y = 9$ and passes through the origin.

21. Perpendicular to $x + 3y = 7$ and passes through $(5, 2)$.

Find the coordinates of the midpoint of the segment whose endpoints are named.

22. $(9, 3), (3, 6)$　　　　　　　　　　**23.** $(-2, -7), (6, -5)$

Graph each equation.

24. $4x - 3y = 24$　　　　　　　　　　**25.** $2x + 7y = 16$

1. Solve: $5\frac{2}{3} + 1\frac{1}{2} = x$

2. Simplify: $14a^2 + 13b^2 - 9a^2$

3. Find the sum: $-19.72 + (-13.81)$

4. Solve: $r + (-6) = -27$

5. Simplify: $\dfrac{-27}{-\frac{1}{3}}$

Solve.

6. $4y = -32$

7. $7 - \frac{1}{2}(x + 2) = 10$

8. State an inequality for the graph.

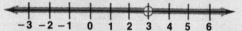

9. Replace $\underline{\ ?\ }$ with $<$, $>$, or $=$ to make the sentence $-\frac{3}{5} \ \underline{\ ?\ } \ -\frac{5}{7}$ true.

10. Solve $|2m - 1| \le 7$ and graph its solution set.

11. Simplify: $(-7z^2)^3$

12. Express the following product in scientific notation: $(0.00000004)(800)$

Simplify.

13. $(4m^2 + mp - 3p^2) - (-3m^2 + 4mp + 5p^2)$

14. $7y(9y^3 + 7y^2 - 3y + 4)$

15. $(3x + 4)^2$

16. Find the prime factorization of 230.

Factor, if possible.

17. $4a^2 - 8ab + 12ab^2$

18. $b^2 - 25$

19. $m^2 - 6m + 9$

20. $12a^2 + 29a + 15$

21. $8x^2y - 3x - 16xy + 6$

Solve.

22. $5x(2x - 3) = 0$

23. $3m^2 - 108 = 0$

24. Simplify: $\dfrac{p^2 + p - 2}{p^2 - p - 6}$

25. State the quadrant in which the point for the ordered pair $(-3, 5)$ is located.

26. Solve the equation $3x - y = 2$ if the domain is $\{-1, 0, 3, 5\}$.

27. Graph: $3x - 2y = 12$

28. Given $f(x) = 5x^2 - 3x + 2$, find $f(-3)$.

29. Write an equation for the relationship between the variables in the following chart.

x	0	2	4	6
y	-6	-9	-12	-15

30. Determine the slope of the line passing through $(4, -2)$ and $(8, 1)$.

31. Write an equation in slope-intercept form for the line with a slope of -4 and a y-intercept of 3.

32. Graph $2x + 3y = -6$ using the slope-intercept method.

33. Find the coordinates of the midpoint of the line segment whose endpoints are $(-6, 4)$ and $(2, 0)$.

Problem Solving

Solve each problem.

34. Five times a number decreased by 3 more than twice the number is 153. Find the number.

35. Find two integers whose sum is 12 and whose product is 32.

36. The area of a rectangle is 64 in². The length is 4 more than 3 times the width. Find the length and width.

37. A person invests $4000, part at 6% annual interest and the rest at 8% annual interest. If the investment earns $270 in interest at the end of one year, how much was invested at each rate?

The test questions on this page deal with expressions and equations. The information at the right may help you with some of the questions.

Directions: Choose the best answer. Write A, B, C, or D.

1. If $(-9)(-9)(-9) = (-9)(-9)(-9)n$, then $n =$

   (A) 1   (B) 0   (C) -9 (D) 9

2. If $(1 - 2 + 3 - 4 + 5 - 6) = -3$, then $2(-1 + 2 - 3 + 4 - 5 + 6) =$

   (A) -6 (B) 6   (C) 3   (D) -3

3. If $48k(5) = 20$, then $k =$

   (A) $\frac{5}{48}$ (B) $\frac{1}{12}$ (C) $\frac{1}{24}$ (D) $\frac{20}{48}$

4. If $23(66 + x) = 2300$, then $x =$

   (A) 1,185   (B) 782
   (C) 34   (D) 44

5. If $3y + 2$ is an odd integer, what is the next consecutive odd integer?

   (A) $3y + 4$ (B) $5y + 2$
   (C) $5y + 4$ (D) $y + 2$

6. $\dfrac{3(1.8 - 2.6) - (1.8 - 2.6)}{2} =$

   (A) 0.8   (B) -0.8
   (C) -1.5 (D) -3.4

7. $-3(a - b) =$

   (A) $3(b - a)$ (B) $3(a + b)$
   (C) $3(-b) + (-a)$ (D) $3ab$

8. If $3y = 7$, the value of $12y - 5$ is

   (A) 43   (B) 7 .   (C) 21   (D) 23

9. If $\frac{x}{8} + 3 = 1$, the value of $\frac{x}{2}$ is

   (A) -32 (B) -16 (C) -8 (D) 4

---

1. Many problems can be solved without much calculating if the basic mathematical concepts are understood. Always look carefully at what is asked, and think of possible shortcuts for solving the problem.

2. Check your solutions by substituting values for the variables.

---

10. If $x = 1$, $y = -2$, and $z = 2$, then

    $$\frac{x^2 y}{(x - z)^2} =$$

    (A) -2 (B) 2   (C) $-\frac{1}{3}$ (D) $\frac{1}{3}$

11. If $1 + \frac{c}{12} = 2\frac{3}{4}$, then $c =$

    (A) 33   (B) 32   (C) 21   (D) 12

12. A number added to one-third of itself results in a sum of 40. What is the number?

    (A) 32   (B) 30   (C) 10   (D) 27

13. How many dollars do you have if you have n nickels, d dimes, and k quarters?

    (A) $\dfrac{5n + 25k + 10d}{100}$

    (B) $\dfrac{25n + 10d + 4k}{100}$

    (C) $20n + 10d + 4k$

    (D) $\dfrac{20n + 10d + 4k}{100}$

14. Dave is twice as old as Bob, who is 3 years older than Steve. If Steve is 7 years old, how old is Dave?

    (A) 14   (B) 18   (C) 20   (D) 22

15. If $\frac{x}{5} = 2$, then $\frac{x}{2} =$

    (A) 10   (B) 5   (C) $\frac{1}{2}$ (D) $\frac{1}{5}$

16. If $20x$ cartons fill $\frac{x}{5}$ trucks, how many trucks are needed to hold 400 cartons?

    (A) 20   (B) 8,000 (C) 4   (D) 100

CHAPTER 11

Systems of Open Sentences

An airplane flies from New York to Los Angeles in 4 hours 20 minutes. The return trip from Los Angeles to New York takes 3 hours 50 minutes. The airplane can fly 600 mph in still air. What is the speed of the air current? In this chapter, you will learn how to solve problems such as this by using systems of equations.

11-1 Graphing Systems of Equations

The graphs of $y = 2x - 1$ and $3y + 2x = 13$ are shown at the right.
Notice that the graphs intersect at the point $(2, 3)$. Since this point
lies on the graph of each equation, it follows that the ordered pair
$(2, 3)$ satisfies both equations.

This can be checked by substituting $(2, 3)$ into each equation.

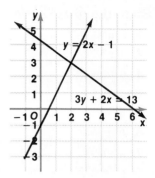

$$y \overset{?}{=} 2x - 1 \qquad\qquad 3y + 2x \overset{?}{=} 13$$
$$3 \overset{?}{=} 2(2) - 1 \qquad\qquad 3(3) + 2(2) \overset{?}{=} 13$$
$$3 = 3 \qquad\qquad\qquad 13 = 13$$

The equations $y = 2x - 1$ and $3y + 2x = 13$ together are called a
system of equations. The solution of this system of equations is
$(2, 3)$.

Examples

1   **Graph the equations $x + y = 6$ and $y = 2x$. Then find the solution of the system of equations.**

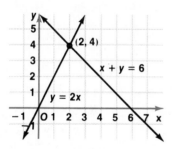

The graphs intersect at $(2, 4)$. Therefore,
$(2, 4)$ is the solution of the system of
equations $x + y = 6$ and $y = 2x$.

Check: $x + y = 6 \qquad y = 2x$
$$2 + 4 \overset{?}{=} 6 \qquad 4 \overset{?}{=} 2(2)$$
$$6 = 6 \qquad\quad 4 = 4$$

2   **Graph the equations $y = x - 4$ and $x + \frac{1}{2}y = \frac{5}{2}$. Then find the solution of the system of equations.**

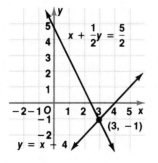

The graphs intersect at $(3, -1)$. Therefore,
$(3, -1)$ is the solution of the system of
equations $y = x - 4$ and $x + \frac{1}{2}y = \frac{5}{2}$.

Check: $y = x - 4 \qquad\qquad x + \frac{1}{2}y = \frac{5}{2}$
$$-1 \overset{?}{=} 3 - 4 \qquad 3 + \frac{1}{2}(-1) \overset{?}{=} \frac{5}{2}$$
$$-1 = -1 \qquad\qquad \frac{6}{2} - \frac{1}{2} \overset{?}{=} \frac{5}{2}$$
$$\frac{5}{2} = \frac{5}{2}$$

Exploratory Exercises

State the ordered pair for the intersection of each pair of lines.

1. a and b
2. a and c
3. a and d
4. a and e
5. b and c
6. b and d
7. b and e
8. c and d
9. c and e
10. d and e

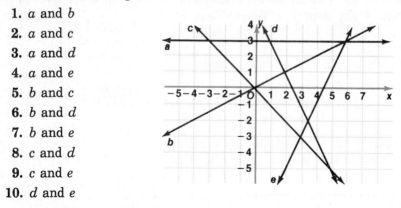

State which of the ordered pairs is a solution for the equation given.

11. $x + 2y = 7$ **a.** $(3, 2)$ **b.** $(6, 1)$ **c.** $(9, -1)$ **d.** $(-1, 4)$

12. $3x - 2y = 5$ **a.** $(1, 1)$ **b.** $(-1, 1)$ **c.** $(1, -1)$ **d.** $(5, 5)$

13. $1.5x + 0.3y = 3$ **a.** $(0, 10)$ **b.** $(2, 1)$ **c.** $(-3, 5)$ **d.** $(4, -10)$

14. $\frac{1}{2}x + \frac{2}{3}y = 3$ **a.** $(2, 3)$ **b.** $(2, 1)$ **c.** $(4, 5)$ **d.** $(3, 2)$

Written Exercises

Graph each pair of equations. Then state the solution of each system of equations.

1. $x - y = 2$
   $2x + 3y = 9$

2. $3x - 2y = 10$
   $x + y = 0$

3. $x + y = 8$
   $x - y = 2$

4. $5x - 3y = 12$
   $2x - 3y = 3$

5. $y = x$
   $x + y = 4$

6. $y = -3x$
   $4x + y = 2$

7. $x + y = 5$
   $x - 2y = -4$

8. $y = x - 1$
   $y + x = 11$

9. $y = -x$
   $y = 2x$

10. $x + y = 3$
    $y = x + 3$

11. $y = x + 3$
    $3y + x = 5$

12. $\frac{1}{2}x + y = -\frac{9}{2}$
    $x - y = 6$

13. $2x + 3y = -17$
    $y = x - 4$

14. $y = x - 3$
    $2x - y = 8$

15. $\frac{1}{3}x + 2y = 1$
    $\frac{3}{4}x + \frac{1}{4}y = -2$

16. $0.1x + 0.2y = 0.8$
    $0.5x - 0.5y = -0.5$

17. $0.4x + 0.3y = 2.4$
    $1.2x - 1.8y = -3.6$

18. $3x + y = -11$
    $\frac{1}{2}x + 2y = 0$

19. $\frac{1}{2}x + \frac{2}{3}y = -3$
    $4x - \frac{1}{3}y = -7$

20. $\frac{1}{3}x - \frac{1}{4}y = 2$
    $9x + \frac{3}{4}y = 24$

21. $0.2a = 0.3b$
    $0.4a - 0.2b = 0.2$

22. $3.4x + 6.3y = 4.4$
    $2.1x + 3.7y = 3.1$

23. $2x - 8y = 64$
    $\frac{1}{4}x + \frac{1}{7}y = 0$

24. $x + 2y = 0$
    $\frac{1}{3}x + \frac{1}{3}y = -1$

The Murphy Company, a leading gadget maker, wanted to know its break-even volume. This is the volume (number of gadgets) at which revenue (income) equals cost.

Jan Martinez, an accountant, made the following graph for the Murphy Company. Revenue is described by the equation $y = 5x$. Cost is described by the equation $y = 4x + 200$. Jan graphed these equations and found the point of intersection.

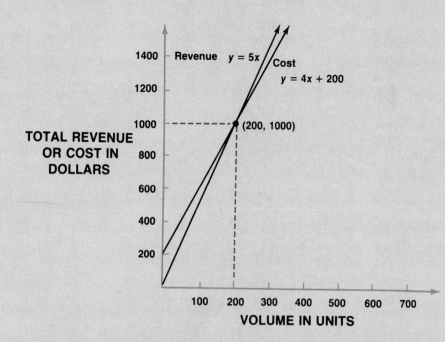

The graphs intersect at (200, 1000). This tells Jan that the Murphy Company must sell 200 gadgets to break even. At 200 units, the Murphy Company will incur $1000 of costs and receive $1000 in revenue. To make a profit, the Murphy Company must sell more than 200 gadgets.

Exercises

Make a break-even graph for each company. State the number of units necessary to break even and the revenue at that point.

1. Block Company   revenue: $y = 7x$
                        cost: $y = x + 300$

2. Zwik Company   revenue: $y = 4x$
                        cost: $y = 2x + 150$

3. Wu Company   revenue: $y = 11x$
                        cost: $y = 3x + 240$

4. Carilli Company   revenue: $y = 42x$
                        cost: $y = 3x + 780$

11-2   Systems of Equations

Not every system of equations has one ordered pair as its solution. Some systems have no solution. Others have infinitely many solutions.

A system of equations that has exactly one ordered pair as its solution is said to be consistent and independent.

Examples

1   **Graph the equations $x + y = 3$ and $x + y = 4$. Then state the number of solutions of the system of equations.**

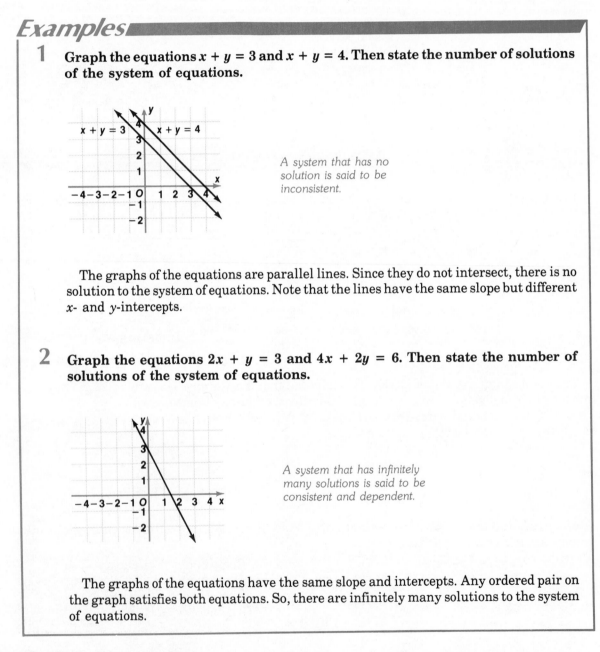

A system that has no solution is said to be inconsistent.

The graphs of the equations are parallel lines. Since they do not intersect, there is no solution to the system of equations. Note that the lines have the same slope but different x- and y-intercepts.

2   **Graph the equations $2x + y = 3$ and $4x + 2y = 6$. Then state the number of solutions of the system of equations.**

A system that has infinitely many solutions is said to be consistent and dependent.

The graphs of the equations have the same slope and intercepts. Any ordered pair on the graph satisfies both equations. So, there are infinitely many solutions to the system of equations.

Exploratory Exercises

State the slope and y-intercept for the graph of each equation. Then state whether the system of equations has one solution, no solution, or infinitely many solutions.

1. $x + y = 4$
   $2x + 3y = 9$

2. $x + y = 6$
   $x - y = 2$

3. $x + y = 6$
   $3x + 3y = 3$

4. $x + y = 1$
   $2x - 2y = 8$

5. $x + 2y = 5$
   $3x - 15 = -6y$

6. $2x + 4y = 8$
   $x + 2y = 4$

7. $y = -3x$
   $6y - x = -38$

8. $x + y = 1$
   $3x + 5y = 7$

9. $3x + 6 = 7y$
   $x + 2y = 11$

10. $x + 5y = 10$
    $x + 5y = 15$

11. $3x - 8y = 4$
    $6x - 42 = 16y$

12. $2x + 3y = 5$
    $-6x - 9y = -15$

Written Exercises

Graph each pair of equations. Then state whether the system has one solution, no solution, or infinitely many solutions. If the system has one solution, state it.

1. $3x + y = 6$
   $y + 2 = x$

2. $3x - y = 4$
   $6x + 2y = -8$

3. $x + 2y = 5$
   $2x + 4y = 1$

4. $2x - y = -4$
   $-3x + y = -9$

5. $2x + 5 = 3y$
   $x = 2$

6. $x + y = 4$
   $x + y = 9$

7. $y = 5$
   $y = 7$

8. $y = 6$
   $x = 9$

9. $2x + 3y = 4$
   $-4x - 6y = -8$

10. $9x - 2 = 4y$
    $x + y = 6$

11. $x + y = 4$
    $x - y = 10$

12. $x + 2y = 6$
    $x + 2y = 8$

13. $\frac{1}{2}x + y = 3$
    $\frac{1}{2}y + \frac{1}{4}x = 2$

14. $\frac{1}{2}x + \frac{1}{3}y = 6$
    $y = \frac{1}{2}x + 2$

15. $\frac{2}{3}x + \frac{1}{4}y = 4$
    $\frac{1}{3}x + \frac{1}{8}y = 2$

16. $\frac{1}{4}x - \frac{1}{3}y = -1$
    $\frac{1}{3}x - \frac{1}{2}y = -2$

17. $0.3y = 0.4x - 1.2$
    $1.2x + 0.9y = -3.6$

18. $0.2x + 0.1y = 1$
    $x = 1 - 0.5y$

11-3 Substitution

Most systems of equations are easier to solve by algebraic methods than by graphing. One such algebraic method is called **substitution**.

Consider the system of equations $y = 2x$ and $3x + 4y = 11$. In the first equation, y is equal to $2x$. Since y must have the same value in the second equation, you can substitute $2x$ for y in $3x + 4y = 11$.

$$3x + 4y = 11$$
$$3x + 4(2x) = 11 \quad \text{\textit{Substitute 2x for y. Now the equation has only one variable, x.}}$$
$$3x + 8x = 11 \quad \text{\textit{Solve to find the value of x.}}$$
$$11x = 11$$
$$x = 1$$

Now find the value of y by substituting 1 for x in $y = 2x$.

$$y = 2x \quad \text{\textit{Could you also substitute 1 for x in 3x + 4y = 11?}}$$
$$y = 2(1)$$
$$y = 2$$

$$
\begin{array}{lll}
\textit{Check:} & y = 2x & 3x + 4y = 11 \\
& 2 \overset{?}{=} 2(1) & 3(1) + 4(2) \overset{?}{=} 11 \\
& 2 = 2 & 3 + 8 \overset{?}{=} 11 \\
& & 11 = 11
\end{array}
$$

The solution of the system of equations is $(1, 2)$.

Example

1   **Use substitution to solve the system of equations $x + 6y = 1$ and $3x - 10y = 17$.**

Solve the first equation for x.

Then substitute $1 - 6y$ for x in the second equation and find the value of y.

$$x + 6y = 1$$
$$x = 1 - 6y$$

$$3x - 10y = 17$$
$$3(1 - 6y) - 10y = 17$$
$$3 - 18y - 10y = 17$$
$$-28y = 14$$
$$y = -\frac{1}{2}$$

Substitute $-\frac{1}{2}$ for y in one of the equations to find the value of x.

$$x + 6y = 1$$
$$x + 6\left(-\frac{1}{2}\right) = 1$$
$$x - 3 = 1$$
$$x = 4$$

The solution to this system is $\left(4, -\frac{1}{2}\right)$.   *Check this result.*

2 **Use substitution to solve the system of equations $\frac{3}{2}x + y = 3$ and $3x + 2y = 12$.**

Solve the first equation for y.

$\frac{3}{2}x + y = 3$

$y = 3 - \frac{3}{2}x$

Substitute $3 - \frac{3}{2}x$ for y in the second equation.

$3x + 2y = 12$

$3x + 2\left(3 - \frac{3}{2}x\right) = 12$

$3x + 6 - 3x = 12$

$6 = 12$

A false statement, $6 = 12$, occurs. When you graph the equations you will find that they have the same slope but different intercepts. The graphs are parallel lines. Therefore, no solution exists.

3 **Use substitution to solve the system of equations $\frac{1}{3}x + \frac{1}{2}y = 6$ and $\frac{2}{3}x + y = 12$.**

Solve the second equation for y.

$\frac{2}{3}x + y = 12$

$y = 12 - \frac{2}{3}x$

Substitute $12 - \frac{2}{3}x$ for y in the first equation.

$\frac{1}{3}x + \frac{1}{2}y = 6$

$\frac{1}{3}x + \frac{1}{2}\left(12 - \frac{2}{3}x\right) = 6$

$\frac{1}{3}x + 6 - \frac{1}{3}x = 6$

$6 = 6$

A true statement, $6 = 6$, occurs. When you graph the equations you will find they have the same slope and the same intercepts. The graphs coincide. Therefore, any solution to the first equation is also a solution to the second equation. The system has infinitely many solutions.

Exploratory Exercises

Solve each equation for x. Then, solve each equation for y.

1. $y + 1 = x$
2. $y + 2x = 3$
3. $2x + 3y = 6$
4. $y + 13 = \frac{1}{2}x$
5. $3y - \frac{1}{2}x = 7$
6. $x + y = 5$
7. $2x + 2y = -10$
8. $3x + 5y = 8$
9. $\frac{2}{3}x - \frac{1}{2}y = 10$
10. $1.6x + 2.3y = 3.2$
11. $0.75x + 6 = -0.8y$
12. $\frac{2}{3}x - \frac{4}{5}y = 3$

Written Exercises

Use substitution to solve each system of equations. State whether the system has no solution, one solution, or infinitely many solutions. If the system has one solution, state it.

1. $y = 2x$
$x + 2y = 8$

2. $y = 3x$
$x + 2y = -21$

3. $x = 2y$
$4x + 2y = 15$

4. $2x + 3y = 5$
$4x - 9y = 9$

5. $x = 3 - 2y$
$2x + 4y = 6$

6. $x - 3y = 3$
$2x + 9y = 11$

7. $3x + 2y = 14$
$x + \frac{2}{3}y = 4$

8. $3x + y = 2$
$2x - y = \frac{1}{2}$

9. $3x + 5y = 2x$
$x + 3y = y$

10. $x + \frac{1}{2}y = 4$
$y = -2x + 8$

11. $x - 2y = 5$
$3x - 5y = 8$

12. $2x - y = 7$
$\frac{3}{2}x = \frac{3}{4}y + 5$

13. $\frac{1}{4}x - 2y = -3$
$8x + 6y = 44$

14. $2x - y = 3x$
$2x + y = 3y$

15. $\frac{1}{2}x + \frac{1}{3}y = 3$
$-\frac{1}{4}x - \frac{2}{3}y = -3$

16. $-\frac{2}{5}x + \frac{2}{3}y = -8$
$\frac{1}{2}x + \frac{1}{2}y = 2$

17. $0.3x + 0.2y = 0.5$
$0.5x - 0.3y = 0.2$

18. $0.1x + 0.1y = 2$
$0.1x - 0.1y = 0$

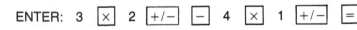

Using Calculators —————————— Checking Solutions

You can use a calculator to determine whether an ordered pair is a solution of a system of equations.

For example, follow the steps below to determine whether $(-2, -1)$ is the solution of the system $2x - 5y = 1$ and $3x - 4y = -2$.

ENTER: 2 $\boxed{\times}$ 2 $\boxed{+/-}$ $\boxed{-}$ 5 $\boxed{\times}$ 1 $\boxed{+/-}$ $\boxed{=}$

The display shows 1. Therefore $(-2, -1)$ is a solution of the first equation. Now check the second equation.

ENTER: 3 $\boxed{\times}$ 2 $\boxed{+/-}$ $\boxed{-}$ 4 $\boxed{\times}$ 1 $\boxed{+/-}$ $\boxed{=}$

The display shows -2. Therefore, $(-2, -1)$ is a solution of the system of equations.

Exercises

Use a calculator to determine whether the given ordered pair is a solution of each system of equations. If the ordered pair is not a solution, find the solution.

1. $5m + 2n = -8$ $\quad (-4, 6)$
$4m + 3n = 2$

2. $0.2a = 0.3b$ $\quad (0.75, 0.5)$
$0.4a - 0.2b = 0.2$

3. $x + y = 40$ $\quad (20, 20)$
$0.2x + 0.45y = 10.5$

4. $4x + 2y = 10.5$ $\quad (1.25, 2.75)$
$2x + 3y = 10.75$

5. $108x + 537y = -1395$ $\quad (2, 3)$
$-214x - 321y = 535$

6. $x + 5y = 20.25$ $\quad (2.25, 3.6)$
$x + 3y = 13.05$

11-4 Elimination Using Addition

In some systems of equations the coefficients of either the x or y terms are additive inverses of each other. The simplest way to solve these systems is to add the equations. Because one of the variables is eliminated, this method is called elimination.

Examples

1 **Use elimination to solve the system of equations $x - 2y = 5$ and $2x + 2y = 7$.**

Add the two equations.

$$
\begin{array}{ll}
x - 2y = 5 & \textit{The y-coefficients, 2 and } -2 \textit{, are additive inverses.} \\
\underline{2x + 2y = 7} & \textit{Add like terms.} \\
3x = 12 & \textit{Notice the variable y is eliminated.} \\
x = 4
\end{array}
$$

Substitute 4 for x in either equation and solve for y.

$$
\begin{aligned}
2x + 2y &= 7 \\
2(4) + 2y &= 7 \\
8 + 2y &= 7 \\
2y &= -1 \\
y &= -\tfrac{1}{2}
\end{aligned}
$$

The solution of the system is $\left(4, -\tfrac{1}{2}\right)$.   *Check this result.*

2 **The sum of two numbers is 42. Their difference is 6. Find the numbers.**

Explore   Let x = the greater number.
Let y = the lesser number.

Plan
$$
\begin{array}{ll}
x + y = 42 & \textit{sum} \\
x - y = 6 & \textit{difference}
\end{array}
$$

Solve
$$
\begin{array}{l}
x + y = 42 \\
\underline{x - y = 6} \\
2x = 48 \\
x = 24 \\
x + y = 42 \\
24 + y = 42 \\
y = 18
\end{array}
$$

The numbers are 18 and 24.   *Check the result.*

Exploratory Exercises

State whether addition can be used to solve each system.

1. $2x + y = 8$
$x - y = 3$

2. $m + 3n = 5$
$n = 3 - m$

3. $3a + b = 6$
$4a + b = 7$

4. $y + 3x = 12$
$3y - 3x = 6$

5. $y + 5x = 9$
$y = 7 + 5x$

6. $x = 5$
$x + y = 7$

7. $y = -3$
$2x + y = 6$

8. $\frac{1}{2}x - \frac{1}{5}y = 2$
$3x + \frac{1}{5}y = -6$

9. $\frac{1}{2}x + \frac{1}{2}y = 3$
$\frac{1}{4}x - \frac{1}{2}y = 3$

Written Exercises

Solve each system by elimination.

1. $x + y = 7$
$x - y = 9$

2. $r - s = -5$
$r + s = 25$

3. $-y + x = 6$
$x + y = 5$

4. $m - n = 3$
$n + m = 3$

5. $3x = 13 - y$
$2x - y = 2$

6. $x + y = 8$
$2x - y = 6$

7. $2x - 3y = -4$
$x = 7 - 3y$

8. $5s + 4t = 12$
$3s = 4 + 4t$

9. $0.6m - 0.2n = 0.9$
$0.3m = 0.9 - 0.2n$

10. $x + y = 0$
$\frac{1}{3}x = y$

11. $8x - 3y = 5$
$\frac{1}{3}x + 3y = 20$

12. $9x + 2y = 8$
$\frac{3}{2}x - 2y = 6$

13. $4x - \frac{1}{3}y = 8$
$5x + \frac{1}{3}y = 6$

14. $\frac{1}{2}x - \frac{1}{2}y = 10$
$\frac{3}{4}x + \frac{1}{2}y = 20$

15. $\frac{1}{3}x + \frac{1}{5}y = 5$
$\frac{1}{3}x - \frac{1}{5}y = -5$

Use a system of equations to solve each problem.

16. The sum of two numbers is 45. Their difference is 7. Find the numbers.

17. The sum of two numbers is 48. Their difference is 24. Find the numbers.

18. The sum of two numbers is 64. Their difference is 42. Find the numbers.

19. The sum of two numbers is 101. Their difference is 25. Find the numbers.

20. A room is 12 feet longer than it is wide. Half the perimeter of the rectangular floor is 72 feet. Find the length and width.

21. Half the perimeter of a rectangular garden is 100 m. The garden is 10 m longer than it is wide. Find its length and width.

22. The difference between twice one number and a lesser number is 21. The sum of the lesser number and twice the greater number is 27. Find the numbers.

23. The difference between twice one number and a lesser number is 32. The sum of the lesser number and twice the greater number is 60. Find the numbers.

24. Sara McMenemy's farm is 82 acres larger than Jim Underwood's farm. Together the farms contain 276 acres. How large is each farm?

25. At a meeting for mathematics editors, there were 7 more women than men. There were 43 editors present. How many men and how many women were there?

11-5 Elimination Using Multiplication

Some systems of equations cannot be solved directly by addition. Consider the following system.

$$6x + 12y = -5$$
$$6x + 9y = -3$$

Would a variable be eliminated by addition?

If either equation is multiplied by -1, the system can be solved by addition.

$$6x + 12y = -5$$ **Multiply by -1.** $$-6x - 12y = 5$$ *Then, add.*
$$6x + 9y = -3$$ $$\underline{6x + 9y = -3}$$
$$-3y = 2$$
$$y = -\frac{2}{3}$$

Substitute $-\frac{2}{3}$ for y in either of the original equations and solve for x.

$$6x + 12y = -5$$
$$6x + 12\left(-\frac{2}{3}\right) = -5$$
$$6x - 8 = -5$$
$$6x = 3$$
$$x = \frac{1}{2}$$

The solution of the system is $\left(\frac{1}{2}, -\frac{2}{3}\right)$. *Check this result.*

Example

1

Use elimination to solve the system of equations $\frac{1}{3}x + 2y = 6$ and $x + 3y = -6$.

Multiply the first equation by -3.

$$\frac{1}{3}x + 2y = 6$$ **Multiply by -3.** $$-x - 6y = -18$$ *Then, add.*
$$x + 3y = -6$$ $$\underline{x + 3y = -6}$$
$$-3y = -24$$
$$y = 8$$

Substitute 8 for y in either of the original equations and solve for x.

$$x + 3y = -6$$
$$x + 3(8) = -6$$
$$x + 24 = -6$$
$$x = -30$$

The solution to the system of equations is $(-30, 8)$. *Check this result.*

In some cases it is necessary to multiply *each* equation by some number in order to solve the system by addition. Consider the following example.

Example

2 **Use elimination to solve the system of equations $3a + 4b = -25$ and $2a - 3b = 6$.**

Multiply the first equation by 2 and the second equation by -3 to eliminate a.

$$3a + 4b = -25 \qquad \text{Multiply by 2.} \qquad 6a + 8b = -50$$

$$2a - 3b = 6 \qquad \text{Multiply by } -3. \qquad \underline{-6a + 9b = -18} \qquad \textit{Add.}$$

$$17b = -68$$

$$b = -4$$

Substitute -4 for b in either of the equations and solve for a.

$$3a + 4b = -25$$
$$3a + 4(-4) = -25$$
$$3a - 16 = -25$$
$$3a = -9$$
$$a = -3$$

The solution to the system of equations is $(-3, -4)$.

The above system of equations can also be solved by eliminating b. Multiply the first equation by 3 and the second equation by 4.

$$3a + 4b = -25 \qquad \text{Multiply by 3.} \qquad 9a + 12b = -75$$

$$2a - 3b = 6 \qquad \text{Multiply by 4.} \qquad \underline{8a - 12b = 24}$$

$$17a = -51$$

$$a = -3$$

Substitute -3 for a in either of the equations and solve for b.

$$2a - 3b = 6$$
$$2(-3) - 3b = 6$$
$$-6 - 3b = 6$$
$$-3b = 12$$
$$b = -4$$

The solution to the system of equations is $(-3, -4)$. Notice that the same result is obtained.

Exploratory Exercises

Explain how to eliminate the variable x in each system. Then, do the same for the variable y.

1. $x + 2y = 5$
   $3x + y = 7$

2. $4x + y = 8$
   $x - 7y = 2$

3. $x + 8y = 3$
   $4x - 2y = 7$

4. $y + x = 9$
   $2y - x = 1$

5. $4x - y = 4$
   $x + 2y = 3$

6. $y - 4x = 11$
   $2y + x = 6$

7. $3y - 8x = 9$
   $y - x = 2$

8. $0.6y + 0.9x = 1.1$
   $y + x = 2$

9. $\frac{3}{2}x + y = \frac{3}{2}$
   $\frac{3}{4}x + y = \frac{1}{4}$

10. $2x + y = 6$
    $3x - 7y = 9$

11. $1.2x + 1.4y = 3.6$
    $x - 2.8y = 7.3$

12. $3x + \frac{2}{3}y = 4$
    $4x + \frac{2}{3}y = 6$

Written Exercises

Use elimination to solve each system of equations.

1. $x - y = 6$
   $x + y = 5$

2. $x + y = 8$
   $2x - y = -6$

3. $y = 2x$
   $2x + y = 10$

4. $x + y = 1$
   $y = x$

5. $3x + 3y = 6$
   $2x - y = 1$

6. $3x + 4y = 7$
   $3x - 4y = 8$

7. $x + 2y = 8$
   $3x + 2y = 6$

8. $3x + 7y = -1$
   $6x + 7y = 0$

9. $3x + 0.2y = 7$
   $3x = 0.4y + 6$

10. $9x + 8y = 7$
    $18x - 14 = 16y$

11. $x - 5y = 0$
    $2x - 3y = 7$

12. $5x + 3y = 12$
    $4x - 3y = 15$

13. $12x - 9y = 114$
    $12x + 7y = 82$

14. $\frac{1}{4}x + y = \frac{7}{2}$
    $\frac{1}{2}x - \frac{1}{4}y = 1$

15. $\frac{1}{3}x - y = -1$
    $\frac{1}{5}x - \frac{2}{5}y = -1$

16. $\frac{2}{5}x - \frac{1}{2}y = 1$
    $\frac{1}{5}x + \frac{1}{2}y = -1$

17. $\frac{1}{8}(x + y) = 1$
    $x - y = 4$

18. $2x - y = 36$
    $3x - 0.5y = 26$

19. $3x + \frac{1}{3}y = 10$
    $2x - 5 = \frac{1}{3}y$

20. $\frac{1}{2}x - \frac{2}{3}y = 2\frac{1}{3}$
    $\frac{3}{2}x + 2y = -25$

21. $\frac{2x + y}{3} = 15$
    $\frac{3x - y}{5} = 1$

22. $x + y = 6000$
    $0.06x + 0.08y = 460$

23. $x + y = 20$
    $0.4x + 0.15y = 4$

24. $1.6x + 0.4y = 1$
    $0.4x - 0.1y = 1$

25. $3.2y + 7.3x = 0$
    $y = -3.5x$

26. $0.25(x + 4y) = 3.5$
    $0.5x - 0.25y = 1$

27. $0.4x - 0.5y = 1$
    $0.4x + y = -2$

For each problem, define two variables. Then, use a system of equations to solve the problem.

28. The sum of two numbers is 57 and their difference is 7. Find the two numbers.

29. The difference between two numbers is 20 and their sum is 48. Find the two numbers.

30. The sum of two numbers is 22. Five times one of the numbers equals six times the other number. Find the numbers.

31. The difference between two numbers is four. Twice the larger number equals three times the sum of the smaller number and 2. Find the numbers.

32. Mr. Abbott's farm is 32 acres smaller than Mr. Collins' farm. The two farms together contain 276 acres. How large is each farm?

33. A 140-meter rope is cut into two pieces. One piece is four times as long as the other. How long is each piece of rope?

34. The difference between the length and width of a rectangle is 7 cm. The perimeter of the rectangle is 50 cm. Find the length and width of the rectangle.

35. Layla is three times as old as Diana. In 10 years, Layla will be twice as old as Diana. Find their present ages.

36. A father is three times the age of his son. In six years, the father will be $2\frac{1}{2}$ times the age of the son. Find their present ages.

37. A rectangle has a perimeter of 40 cm. The length of the rectangle is 1 cm less than twice the width. Find the length and width of the rectangle.

38. The greater of two numbers is twice the lesser. If the greater is increased by 18, the result is 4 less than 4 times the lesser. Find the numbers.

39. The greater of two numbers is 1 less than 4 times the lesser. Three times the lesser number is 4 less than the greater. Find the numbers.

40. The perimeter of a rectangle is 86 cm. Twice the width exceeds the length by 2 cm. Find the dimensions of the rectangle.

41. The sum of Kari's age and her mother's age is 52. Kari's mother is 20 years older than Kari. How old is each?

Challenge

Use elimination to solve each of the following systems.

42. $\dfrac{1}{x} + \dfrac{1}{y} = 7$

$\dfrac{2}{x} + \dfrac{3}{y} = 16$

43. $\dfrac{1}{x + y} = 2$

$\dfrac{1}{x - y} = \dfrac{1}{y}$

44. Explain how the elimination method shows that a system is inconsistent.

45. Explain how the elimination method shows that a system is dependent.

mini-review

1. State whether $xy = 10$ is a linear equation.

Name the property shown by each of the following.

2. $5(a + b) = 5a + 5b$

3. If $a = 7$ and $7 = 9 - 2$, then $a = 9 - 2$.

4. $(3x)y = 3(xy)$

5. $a + (-a) = 0$

A system of three equations in three variables can be solved by elimination. Consider the following system of equations.

$$x + y + z = 6$$
$$x + 2y - z = 2$$
$$2x - 3y - z = -7$$

First, eliminate one of the variables. In this case, eliminate z by adding the first equation to each of the other equations.

$$\begin{array}{r} x + y + z = 6 \\ \underline{x + 2y - z = 2} \\ 2x + 3y \phantom{{}- z} = 8 \end{array} \qquad \begin{array}{r} x + y + z = 6 \\ \underline{2x - 3y - z = -7} \\ 3x - 2y \phantom{{}- z} = -1 \end{array}$$

In this way, a system of two equations in two variables is obtained. Then, solve the new system by elimination.

$$2x + 3y = 8 \quad \boxed{\text{Multiply by 2.}} \quad 4x + 6y = 16$$

$$3x - 2y = -1 \quad \boxed{\text{Multiply by 3.}} \quad \begin{array}{r} 9x - 6y = -3 \\ \hline 13x \phantom{{}- 6y} = 13 \\ x = 1 \end{array}$$

Substitute 1 for x in either of the two equations to solve for y.

$$2x + 3y = 8$$
$$2(1) + 3y = 8$$
$$3y = 6$$
$$y = 2$$

Finally, substitute 1 for x and 2 for y in any of the original equations to solve for z.

$$x + y + z = 6$$
$$1 + 2 + z = 6$$
$$z = 3$$

The solution of the system of equations is the ordered triple $(1, 2, 3)$. This can be checked by substituting these values into the original system of equations.

Exercises

Solve each system of equations.

1. $x - y + z = 5$
   $2x + y + z = 13$
   $4x + y - 2z = 12$

2. $-3x + y - z = 6$
   $3x - y + 2z = -7$
   $x + y + z = 0$

3. $x + 2y - z = 12$
   $x - 2y + z = -8$
   $2x - y + z = -3$

4. $2x - 2y - z = -1$
   $x + 2y + 2z = 9$
   $x + y - z = 8$

5. $x + y + z = 5$
   $2x + y - z = -1$
   $3x - y + z = 1$

6. $5x + 3y + z = -4$
   $3x + 2y - z = -4$
   $x - 3y + 5z = 4$

7. $a - 2b + c = -9$
   $2b + 3c = 16$
   $4b = 8$

8. $a + b + c = 0$
   $2a + b - c = 2$
   $2a + 2b + c = 5$

9. $m + n + p = 3$
   $m - p = 1$
   $n - p = -4$

11-6 Graphing Systems of Inequalities

Consider the following system of inequalities.

$$y \geq x + 2$$
$$y \leq -2x - 1$$

The solution of this system is the set of all ordered pairs that satisfy both inequalities. To find the solution of this system, graph each inequality. The intersection of the graphs represents the solution of the system.

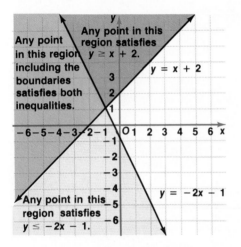

The graphs of $y = x + 2$ and $y = -2x - 1$ are the boundaries of the region. The solution of the system of inequalities is a region that contains an infinite number of ordered pairs.

Example

1 **Solve the system $y > x - 3$ and $y \leq -1$ by graphing.**

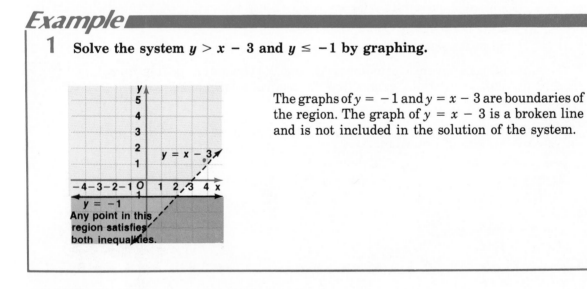

The graphs of $y = -1$ and $y = x - 3$ are boundaries of the region. The graph of $y = x - 3$ is a broken line and is not included in the solution of the system.

A system of inequalities may have no solution. This is illustrated by the next example.

Example

2 Solve the system $y > x + 2$ and $y < x - 3$ by graphing.

The graphs of the inequalities do not intersect. Thus, this system has no solutions.

An inequality containing an absolute value expression can be graphed by graphing the equivalent system of inequalities.

Example

3 Solve the inequality $|x| \le y$ by graphing.

The equivalent system of inequalities is $x \le y$ and $x \ge -y$.
The solution set is represented by the intersection of the shaded regions including the boundaries.

Exploratory Exercises

State whether each ordered pair is a solution of the system $x \le 3$ and $y > 6$.

1. $(3, 7)$ **2.** $(6, 2)$ **3.** $(0, 8)$ **4.** $(-3, -3)$

State which region on the graph is the solution of the system of inequalities.

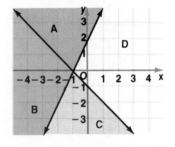

5. $y \ge 2x + 2$
$y \le -x - 1$

6. $y \ge 2x + 2$
$y \ge -x - 1$

7. $y \le 2x + 2$
$y \le -x - 1$

8. $y \le 2x + 2$
$y \ge -x - 1$

Written Exercises

Solve each system by graphing.

1. $x > 3$
   $y < 6$

2. $y < -2$
   $x < -3$

3. $y > 0$
   $x \le 0$

4. $x > y$
   $y < 4$

5. $y > 2$
   $y > -x + 2$

6. $y \ge 2x + 1$
   $y \le -x + 1$

7. $y < -2$
   $y - x > 1$

8. $x \le 2$
   $y - 3 \ge 5$

9. $y \le x + 3$
   $y \ge x + 2$

10. $x \ge 1$
   $y + x \le 3$

11. $y \ge 3x$
   $3y \le 5x$

12. $y \ge x - 3$
   $y \ge -x - 1$

13. $y > x + 1$
   $y < x + 3$

14. $y - x < 1$
   $y - x > 3$

15. $2y + x < 4$
   $3x - y > 6$

16. $y + 2 < x$
   $2y - 3 > 2x$

Solve each inequality by graphing.

17. $|y| < x$

18. $|x| \ge y$

19. $|y| + 1 < x$

20. $|x - 1| < y$

Write a system of inequalities for each graph.

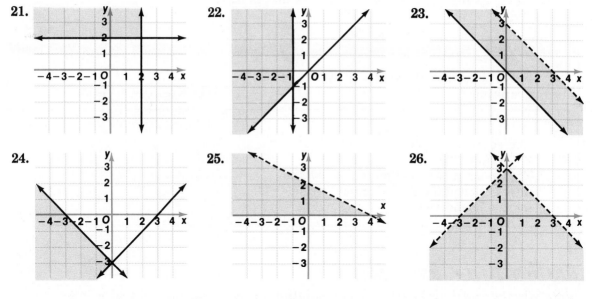

21.
22.
23.
24.
25.
26.

Challenge

Write a system of inequalities for each graph.

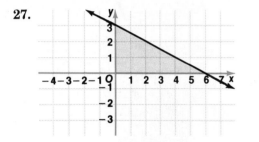

27.

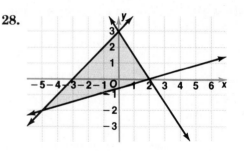

28.

Problem Solving

Organizing information into a chart can be a helpful tool in problem solving. Consider this problem.

> Mrs. Ruben, a grocer, mixes peanuts that sell for **$1.65 a pound and almonds that sell for $2.10 a pound. She wants to make 30 pounds of the mixture that sells for $1.83 a pound. How many pounds of each should Mrs. Ruben include in the mixture?**

Explore

First identify the variables.
Let x = the number of pounds of peanuts to use.
Let y = the number of pounds of almonds to use.

Plan

Organize the variables and the information from the problem into a chart.

	Number of Pounds	×	Cost per Pound	=	Total Cost
Peanuts	x		1.65		$1.65x$
Almonds	y		2.10		$2.10y$
Mixture	30		1.83		$1.83(30)$

Note that the quantities in red were obtained by multiplying the number of pounds by the cost per pound.

Using the first and last columns of the chart, write two equations.

$$x + y = 30$$
$$1.65x + 2.10y = 1.83(30)$$

The mixture weighs 30 pounds. The cost of the peanuts plus the cost of the almonds equals the cost of the mixture.

Solve the system of equations to find the answer.

Exercises

Complete each chart and write two equations for each problem.

1. Carla invested $7000, part at 6% and the rest at 10%. The total yearly interest was $580. How much did she invest at each rate?

	Principal	×	Rate	=	Interest
First part					
Second part					
Total			✕		

2. A barge travels 32 miles up a river in 4 hours. The return trip takes 2 hours. Find the rate of the barge in still water and the rate of the current.

	Rate	×	Time	=	Distance
Up River					
Down River					

11-7   Problem Solving: Digit Problems

Many problems relating to the digits of a number can be solved by
using systems of equations.

Consider the two-digit number 86.

$$86 = 10(8) + 6$$

Let t = the tens digit.
Let u = the units digit.

Then a two-digit number can be represented as
$$10(t) + u.$$

Examples

1   **The sum of the digits of a two-digit number is 9. The number is 6 times the units
digit. Find the number.**

Any two-digit number can be represented by $10t + u$.

 Let t = the tens digit.
Let u = the units digit.

 $t + u = 9$ *Write a system of equations.*
$10t + u = 6u$

 Solve $t + u = 9$ for u and use substitution.

$$\begin{aligned}
t + u &= 9 & 10t + u &= 6u \\
u &= 9 - t & 10t + (9 - t) &= 6(9 - t) \\
& & 10t + 9 - t &= 54 - 6t \\
& & 15t &= 45 \\
& & t &= 3
\end{aligned}$$

Solve for u.

$$\begin{aligned}
t + u &= 9 \\
3 + u &= 9 \\
u &= 6
\end{aligned}$$

The number is $10(3) + 6$, or 36.

Examine   Notice that the sum of the digits is 9 and that 36 is 6 times
the units digit, 6.

2   **The tens digit of a two-digit number is twice the units digit. If the digits are
reversed, the new number is 36 less than the original number. Find the original
number.**

Explore   Let t = the tens digit.
Let u = the units digit.
The original number can be represented by $10t + u$.
The new number can be represented by $10u + t$.

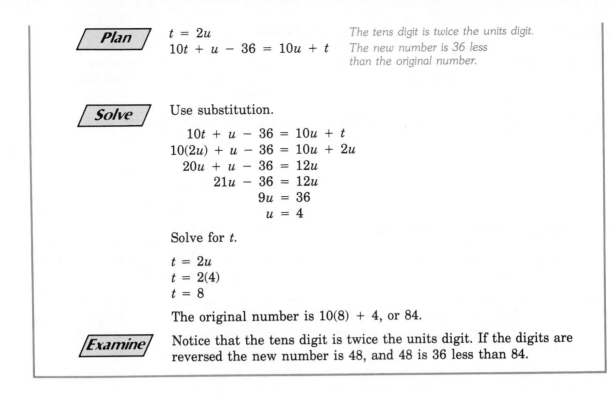

Plan

$t = 2u$ — *The tens digit is twice the units digit.*

$10t + u - 36 = 10u + t$ — *The new number is 36 less than the original number.*

Solve

Use substitution.

$$10t + u - 36 = 10u + t$$
$$10(2u) + u - 36 = 10u + 2u$$
$$20u + u - 36 = 12u$$
$$21u - 36 = 12u$$
$$9u = 36$$
$$u = 4$$

Solve for t.

$$t = 2u$$
$$t = 2(4)$$
$$t = 8$$

The original number is $10(8) + 4$, or 84.

Examine

Notice that the tens digit is twice the units digit. If the digits are reversed the new number is 48, and 48 is 36 less than 84.

Written Exercises

Use a system of equations to solve each problem.

1. A two-digit number is 6 times its units digit. The sum of the digits is 6. Find the number.

2. The sum of the digits of a two-digit number is 13. Twice the tens digit is two less than 5 times the units digit. Find the number.

3. The tens digit of a two-digit number is 6 more than the units digit. The number is 2 more than 8 times the sum of the digits. Find the number.

4. The sum of the digits of a two-digit number is 12. If the digits are reversed, the new number is 18 less than the original number. Find the original number.

5. The sum of the digits of a two-digit number is 7. If the digits are reversed, the new number is 3 less than 4 times the original number. Find the original number.

6. A bank teller reversed the digits in the amount of a check and overpaid a customer by $9. The sum of the digits in the two-digit amount was 9. Find the amount of the check.

7. The sum of the digits of a two-digit number is 12. The units digit is twice the tens digit. Find the number.

8. The units digit of a two-digit number exceeds twice the tens digit by one. The sum of the digits is 7. Find the number.

9. The sum of the digits of a two-digit number is 6. If the digits are reversed, the new number is three times the original tens digit. Find the original number.

10. The tens digit in a two-digit number exceeds twice its units digit by 1. If the digits are reversed, the number is 4 more than 3 times their sum. Find the original number.

11. A two-digit number is equal to 7 times the units digit. If 18 is added to the number, its digits are reversed. Find the number.

12. The tens digit of a two-digit number exceeds the units digit by 4. If the digits are reversed, the sum of the new number and the original number is 154. Find the original number.

13. The tens digit of a two-digit number exceeds twice the units digit by 1. If the digits are reversed, the sum of the new number and the original number is 143. Find the original number.

14. The ratio of the tens digit to the units digit of a two-digit number is 1 to 4. The number formed by reversing the digits is 2 less than 3 times the original number. Find the original number.

15. The sum of the digits of a two-digit number is 9. If 45 is subtracted from the number, the digits of the number are reversed. Find the number.

16. The sum of the digits of a three-digit number is 11. The tens digit is 3 times the hundreds digit and twice the units digit. Find the number.

17. The units digit of a three-digit number is 3. The sum of its digits is 9. If the units and hundreds digits are reversed, the sum of the new number and the original number is 909. Find the original number.

18. The units digit of a three-digit number is 5. The sum of its digits is 11. If the units and hundreds digits are reversed, the sum of the new number and the original number is 787. Find the original number.

19. The tens digit of a three-digit number is 7. The sum of its digits is 10. If the tens and hundreds digits are reversed, the sum of the new number and the original number is 1100. Find the original number.

20. The tens digit of a three-digit number is 3. The sum of its digits is 18. If the tens and hundreds digits are reversed, the sum of the new number and the original number is 1008. Find the original number.

21. The units digit of a two-digit number divided by the tens digit is 3. The sum of the digits is 12. Find the number.

22. The units digit of a two-digit number divides the tens digit twice with a remainder of 1. The sum of the digits is 10. Find the number.

23. Suppose that in a certain two-digit positive integer, the digits are reversed. The result is 36 less than the original integer. Find all integers for which this is true.

24. If the digits of a two-digit positive integer are reversed, the result is 6 less than twice the original. Find all integers for which this is true.

25. The numerator of a fraction is a positive two-digit integer. The denominator is found by reversing the digits of the numerator. If the value of the fraction is $\frac{7}{4}$, find all fractions that satisfy these conditions.

26. The sum of the digits of a three-digit number is 12. The tens digit is three less than the hundreds digit and the units digit is three times the hundreds digit. Find the number.

11-8 Problem Solving: Using Systems of Equations

Systems of equations can be used to solve many different problems.
Study these examples.

Example

1   **A barge travels 24 miles up a river in 3 hours. The return trip takes 2 hours. Find the rate of the barge in still water and the rate of the current.**

Explore   Let b = the rate of the barge in still water.
Let c = the rate of the current.

downstream   upstream ⟶

⟵ current

Because of the current, the barge travels slower upstream than downstream.

Use the formula distance = rate × time.

	$r \times t = d$		
Upstream	$b - c$	3	24
Downstream	$b + c$	2	24

Use a chart to organize the information.

Plan
$3(b - c) = 24 \;\rightarrow\; 3b - 3c = 24$
$2(b + c) = 24 \;\rightarrow\; 2b + 2c = 24$

Solve
$3b - 3c = 24$ Multiply by 2. $6b - 6c = 48$

$2b + 2c = 24$ Multiply by 3. $\underline{6b + 6c = 72}$ *Now add.*
$$12b \quad\quad = 120$$
$$b = 10$$

Solve for c.

$$3b - 3c = 24$$
$$3(10) - 3c = 24$$
$$30 - 3c = 24$$
$$-3c = -6$$
$$c = 2$$

Examine   The rate of the barge in still water is 10 mph.
The rate of the current is 2 mph.

Example

2 **A metal alloy is 25% copper. Another alloy is 50% copper. How much of each alloy should be used to make 1000 grams of an alloy that is 45% copper?**

 Let a = the number of grams of 25% copper alloy.
Let b = the number of grams of 50% copper alloy.

	25% Copper	50% Copper	45% Copper
Grams	a	b	1000
Percent	$0.25a$	$0.50b$	$0.45(1000)$

 $a + b = 1000$
$0.25a + 0.50b = 0.45(1000)$

Solve Use substitution.

$$a + b = 1000 \qquad\qquad 0.25a + 0.50b = 0.45(1000)$$
$$a = 1000 - b \qquad 0.25(1000 - b) + 0.50b = 450$$
$$250 - 0.25b + 0.50b = 450$$
$$0.25b = 200$$
$$b = 800$$

Find the value of a.

$$a + b = 1000$$
$$a + 800 = 1000$$
$$a = 200$$

200 grams of the 25% copper alloy and 800 grams of the 50% copper alloy should be used. *Check this result.*

Written Exercises

Use a system of equations to solve each problem.

1. A boat is rowed 10 miles downstream in two hours, then rowed the same distance upstream in $3\frac{1}{3}$ hours. Find the rate of the boat in still water and the rate of the current.

2. While traveling with the wind, a plane flies 300 miles between Chicago and Columbus in 40 minutes. It returns against the wind in 45 minutes. Find the air speed of the plane and the rate of the wind.

3. A box contains two different types of candy, weighs 10 pounds, and costs $14.55. One type of candy costs $1.50 a pound. The other type costs $1.35 a pound. How many pounds of each kind are there?

4. How many pounds of candy that sells for 80 cents a pound should be mixed with candy that sells for $1.50 a pound to make 20 pounds of a mixture to sell at $1.01 a pound?

5. Joe sold 30 peaches from his tree for a total of $7.50. He sold the small ones for 20 cents each and the large ones for 35 cents each. How many of each kind did he sell?

6. Louise walks from her home to the city in 4 hours. She can travel the same distance on her bicycle in one hour. If she rides 6 mph faster than she walks, what is her speed on the bicycle?

7. An airplane travels 1,800 miles in 3 hours flying with the wind. On the return trip, flying against the wind it takes 4 hours to travel 2,000 miles. Find the rate of the wind and the rate of the plane in still air.

8. A gas station attendant has some anti-freeze that is 40% alcohol and another type of antifreeze that is 60% alcohol. He wishes to make 1,000 gallons of antifreeze that is 48% alcohol. How much of each kind should he use?

9. A man invests $4000, part of it at 10% annual interest and the rest at 12% annual interest. If he receives $460 in interest at the end of one year, how much did he invest at each rate?

10. Jennifer broke open her "piggy bank" and found 83 coins in nickels and dimes. If she had $6.95 in all, how many coins of each has she?

11. While driving to Northridge, Mrs. Winters averages 40 mph. On the return trip she averages 56 mph and saves two hours of traveling time. How far from Northridge does she live?

12. Two boys are 15 miles apart. If they walk towards each other they meet in 3 hours. If they both walk in the same direction one boy overtakes the other in 8 hours. How fast does each boy walk?

13. Two trains start toward each other on parallel tracks at the same time from towns 450 miles apart. One train travels 6 mph faster than the other train. What is the rate of each train if they meet in 5 hours?

14. A car traveled due east from a certain point. One hour later another car started from the same point and traveled due west. Five hours after the first car started, they were 392 miles apart. The eastbound car traveled 10 mph faster than the westbound car. What is the speed of each car?

15. A riverboat travels 48 miles downstream in the same time that it takes to travel 32 miles upstream. The speed of the boat in still water is 16 miles per hour greater than the speed of the current. Find the speed of the current.

16. In still water, a motorboat can travel five times as fast as the current in the river. A trip upriver and back totaling 96 miles can be done in 5 hours. Find the rate of the current.

17. When George was 2 miles upstream from the starting point on a canoe trip, he passed a log floating downstream with the current. He paddled upstream for one more hour and returned to the starting point just as the log arrived. What was the rate of the current?

18. The Rent-A-Car company rents a compact car for a fixed amount each day plus a fixed amount for each mile driven. Joe spent $134 to rent a car for 5 days and drove it 450 miles. Patti spent $106 to rent the same kind of car for 4 days and drove 350 miles. Find the daily charge and the charge per mile for the compact car.

A square array of numbers, called a **determinant**, has a number associated with it. For a 2 × 2 array, the value is found by using the diagonals as shown.

$$\begin{vmatrix} 2 & 1 \\ 3 & 4 \end{vmatrix} = 2(4) - 3(1) \qquad \textit{The determinant is denoted by vertical bars.}$$

$$= 8 - 3$$

$$= 5$$

In general the determinant of a 2 × 2 array is found as follows.

$$\begin{vmatrix} a & b \\ c & d \end{vmatrix} = ad - bc \qquad \textit{\textbf{Value of a Determinant}}$$

Determinants can be used to solve a system of linear equations. Consider solving the following system of equations.

$$ax + by = c$$
$$dx + ey = f$$

To solve for the variable x in this system, the variable y is eliminated.

| $ax + by = c$ | Multiply by e. | $(ae)x + (be)y = ce$ | *Then, add.* |

| $dx + ey = f$ | Multiply by $-b$. | $-(bd)x - (be)y = -bf$ |

$$(ae - bd)x = ce - bf$$

$$x = \frac{ce - bf}{ae - bd}$$

To solve for y, eliminate the variable x.

| $ax + by = c$ | Multiply by d. | $(ad)x + (bd)y = cd$ | *Then, add.* |

| $dx + ey = f$ | Multiply by $-a$. | $-(ad)x - (ae)y = -af$ |

$$(bd - ae)y = cd - af$$

$$y = \frac{cd - af}{bd - ae}$$

$$= \frac{af - cd}{ae - bd}$$

The general solution to this system of equations is $\left(\dfrac{ce - bf}{ae - bd}, \dfrac{af - cd}{ae - bd} \right)$.

Notice that the denominator of each fraction is the same. It can be written as a determinant.

$$ae - bd = \begin{vmatrix} a & b \\ d & e \end{vmatrix}$$

Each numerator also may be written as a determinant.

$$ce - bf = \begin{vmatrix} c & b \\ f & e \end{vmatrix} \text{ and } af - cd = \begin{vmatrix} a & c \\ d & f \end{vmatrix}$$

Therefore, the solution to a system of equations in two variables can be found using determinants. This method is known as **Cramer's Rule**.

The solution to the system of equations $\begin{aligned} ax + by &= c \\ dx + ey &= f \end{aligned}$ **is** (x, y)

where $x = \dfrac{\begin{vmatrix} c & b \\ f & e \end{vmatrix}}{\begin{vmatrix} a & b \\ d & e \end{vmatrix}}$ and $y = \dfrac{\begin{vmatrix} a & c \\ d & f \end{vmatrix}}{\begin{vmatrix} a & b \\ d & e \end{vmatrix}}$ and $\begin{vmatrix} a & b \\ d & e \end{vmatrix} \neq 0.$

Cramer's Rule

Example:

Use Cramer's rule to solve the system $3x - 5y = -7$ and $x + 2y = 16$.

$$x = \frac{\begin{vmatrix} -7 & -5 \\ 16 & 2 \end{vmatrix}}{\begin{vmatrix} 3 & -5 \\ 1 & 2 \end{vmatrix}} \qquad\qquad y = \frac{\begin{vmatrix} 3 & -7 \\ 1 & 16 \end{vmatrix}}{\begin{vmatrix} 3 & -5 \\ 1 & 2 \end{vmatrix}}$$

$$= \frac{(-7)(2) - (16)(-5)}{(3)(2) - (1)(-5)} \qquad = \frac{(3)(16) - (1)(-7)}{(3)(2) - (1)(-5)}$$

$$= \frac{66}{11} \qquad\qquad\qquad\qquad = \frac{55}{11}$$

$$= 6 \qquad\qquad\qquad\qquad\quad = 5$$

The solution is $(6, 5)$.

Exercises

Solve each system by using Cramer's Rule.

1. $2x + 2y = 6$
   $3x - 4y = 2$

2. $x - y = -3$
   $4x + 3y = -5$

3. $3x + 2y = 10$
   $x + y = 6$

4. $x - y = 4$
   $x - 2y = 8$

5. $x = 3 - 2y$
   $y = 2x - 3$

6. $3x + 2y = 7$
   $4x - y = 2$

Solving Systems of Equations

Computers are often used as a tool for solving systems of equations. Consider the following system of equations.

$$ax + by = c$$
$$dx + ey = f$$

The general solution to the system of equations is $\dfrac{ce - bf}{ae - bd}$, $\dfrac{af - cd}{ae - bd}$.

This BASIC program will print the solution to a system of equations.

```
10   INPUT A,B,C,D,E,F                Line 20 checks whether the
20   IF A * E - B * D = 0 THEN 70     denominator is zero.
30   LET X = (C * E - B * F) / (A * E - B * D)
40   LET Y = (A * F - C * D) / (A * E - B * D)
50   PRINT "(";X;",";Y;") IS A SOLUTION"
60   GOTO 80
70   PRINT "NO UNIQUE SOLUTION"
80   END
```

Notice that line 70 makes no distinction between systems that have no solution and systems that have an infinite number of solutions. Study the following graphs.

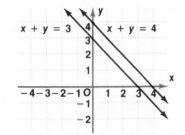

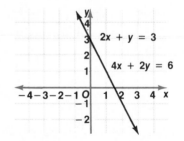

$x + y = 4$ $a = 1, b = 1, c = 4$
$x + y = 3$ $d = 1, e = 1, f = 3$

$ae - bd = 1 \cdot 1 - 1 \cdot 1 = 0$
$ce - bf = 4 \cdot 1 - 1 \cdot 3 = 1$
$af - cd = 1 \cdot 3 - 1 \cdot 4 = -1$

$2x + y = 3$ $a = 2, b = 1, c = 3$
$4x + 2y = 6$ $d = 4, e = 2, f = 6$

$ae - bd = 2 \cdot 2 - 4 \cdot 1 = 0$
$ce - bf = 3 \cdot 2 - 1 \cdot 6 = 0$
$af - cd = 2 \cdot 6 - 3 \cdot 4 = 0$

These and many other examples suggest that if only $ae - bd = 0$, the lines are parallel and the system has no solution. But if $ce - bf$ is also zero, the lines coincide and the system has an infinite number of solutions.

Exercises   Solve each system by using the computer program.

1. $5x + 5y = 16$
   $2x + 2y = 5$

2. $7x - 3y = 5$
   $14x - 6y = 10$

3. $x - 2y = 5$
   $3x - 5y = 8$

4. Modify the computer program so that it will check whether the system has no solution or an infinite number of solutions.

Vocabulary

Chapter Summary

1. A system of equations can be solved by graphing.   (337)
2. A system of equations may have either no solution, one solution, or infinitely many solutions.   (340)
3. Algebraic methods for solving systems of equations are as follows.
   substitution   (342)
   elimination   (345)
4. A system of inequalities can be solved by graphing.   (352)
5. Systems of equations can be used to solve digit problems   (356), uniform motion problems   (359), and mixture problems.   (360)

Chapter Review

11-1   **Solve each system of equations by graphing.**

1. $y = x$
   $y = 2 - x$

2. $x + y = 6$
   $x - y = 2$

3. $y = x - 1$
   $x + y = 11$

11-2   **Graph each pair of equations. Then state whether the system has one solution, no solution, or infinitely many solutions.**

4. $3x + y = -4$
   $6x + 2y = -8$

5. $y = 5$
   $y = 7$

6. $x - y = 10$
   $x + y = 11$

7. $9x + 2 = 4y$
   $x + y = 6$

11-3   **Solve each system of equations by substitution.**

8. $y = x - 1$
   $4x - y = 19$

9. $2m + n = 1$
   $m - n = 8$

10. $x = 2y$
    $x + y = 6$

11. $5x = -10y$
    $8x - 4y = 40$

12. $3m - 2n = -4$
    $3m + n = 2$

13. $3x - y = 1$
    $2x + 2y = 2$

11-4   Solve each system of equations by elimination using addition.

14. $x + y = 8$
    $x - y = 8$

15. $2m - n = 4$
    $m + n = 2$

16. $x + 2y = 6$
    $-x + 3y = 4$

17. $2m - n = 5$
    $2m + n = 3$

18. $3x - y = 11$
    $x + y = 5$

19. $6r + 2s = 32$
    $-6r + 9s = -21$

11-5   Solve each system of equations by elimination.

20. $3x + 3y = 6$
    $2x - y = 1$

21. $x - 2y = 5$
    $3x - 5y = 8$

22. $2x + 3y = 8$
    $x - y = 2$

23. $6x + 8y = 4$
    $2x - y = 5$

24. $2r + s = 9$
    $r + 11s = -6$

25. $5m + 2n = -8$
    $4m + 3n = 2$

11-6   Solve each system of inequalities by graphing.

26. $x \geq -3$
    $y \leq x + 2$

27. $y > -x - 1$
    $y \leq 2x + 1$

11-7   Use a system of equations to solve each problem.

28. The sum of two numbers is 42. Their difference is 18. What are the numbers?

29. The difference between the length and width of a rectangle is 7 cm. The perimeter is 50 cm. Find the length and width.

30. A two-digit number is 6 times its units digit. The sum of its digits is 3. Find the number.

31. A two-digit number is 7 times its units digit. If 18 is added to the number, its digits are reversed. Find the original number.

11-8   32. Bill mixes candy costing 45¢ per pound with candy costing 65¢ a pound. A 7-pound box of the mix costs $3.65. How much of each kind of candy should Bill use?

33. A speedboat travels 60 miles with the current in $1\frac{1}{2}$ hours. The return trip takes 2 hours. What is the rate of the current?

Chapter Test

Solve each system of equations by graphing.

1. $y = 3x$
$x + y = 4$

2. $y = x + 2$
$y = 2x + 7$

Graph each pair of equations. Then state whether the system has one solution, no solution, or infinitely many solutions.

3. $3x + y = 5$
$6x + 2y = 10$

4. $x + y = 11$
$x + y = 14$

5. $x + y = 5$
$x - y = 1$

6. $x = 2y$
$x + y = 3$

Solve each system of equations by substitution.

7. $y = 7 - x$
$y - x = 3$

8. $x + y = 8$
$x - y = 2$

9. $\frac{1}{8}(x + y) = 1$
$x - y = 4$

Solve each system of equations by elimination.

10. $-3x - y = -10$
$3x - 2y = 16$

11. $5x - 3y = 12$
$2x - 3y = 3$

12. $2x + 5y = 12$
$x - 6y = -11$

13. $x + y = 6$
$x - y = 4\frac{1}{2}$

14. $3x + \frac{1}{3}y = 10$
$2x + \frac{1}{3}y = 5$

15. $8x - 6y = 14$
$-6x + 9y = -15$

Use a system of equations to solve each problem.

16. The sum of the digits of a two-digit number is 10. If the digits are reversed, the new number is 18 less than the original number. Find the original number.

17. Mr. Salvatore mixes nuts costing $0.90 per pound and nuts costing $1.30 per pound. He wishes to make 50 pounds that cost $1.20 per pound. How many pounds of each should he use?

18. The units digit of a two-digit number exceeds twice the tens digit by 1. The sum of the digits is 10. Find the number.

19. Jodi rode her bicycle against the wind for a distance of 15 km in 1 hour. The return trip took 36 minutes. What was the rate of the wind?

20. Solve the system of inequalities $y > -x + 2$ and $y \le -3$ by graphing.

A measure of **central tendency** is a number that represents a set of data. Measures of central tendency may be used to *summarize* a set of data or to *compare* one set of data with another. Three measures of central tendency are the **median**, **mode**, and **mean**. They are defined as follows.

> The **mean** of a set of data is the sum of all the values divided by the number of values.
>
> The **median** of a set of data is the middle value. If there are two middle values, it is the value halfway between them.
>
> The **mode** of a set of data is the value that appears more frequently than any other. Some sets of data have multiple modes.

Definition of Mean, Median, and Mode

Example: Find the mean, median, and mode of the salaries of the 10 employees of the Rond Company. Three workers earn $15,500 each, two earn $13,200 each, and five earn $17,050 each.

To find the mean, add all 10 values. You can use multiplication to shorten the addition.

$$\text{mean} = \frac{5(17,050) + 3(15,500) + 2(13,200)}{10}$$

$$= \frac{85,250 + 46,500 + 26,400}{10}$$

$$= \frac{158,150}{10} \text{ or } 15,815 \qquad \text{The mean is \$15,815.}$$

To find the median, first arrange the salaries in descending order. The median is the middle value.

Notice that in this example there are two middle values, the 5th value, $17,050, and the 6th value, $15,500. The median is the mean of the two values. Therefore, the median is $\frac{17,050 + 15,500}{2}$ or $16,275.

17,050
17,050
17,050
17,050
17,050 ← median
15,500 ← median
15,500
15,500
15,500
13,200
13,200

More workers make $17,050 than any other salary. So it is the most frequently occurring value. Thus, the mode is $17,050.

The median is $16,275, the mode is $17,050, and the mean is $15,815.

The value of every item in a set of data affects the value of the mean. Thus, when extreme values are included, the mean may become less representative of the set. The values of the median and the mode are not affected by extreme values.

Example: **Find the mean of {1, 3, 6, 86} and {33, 34, 34, 35}.**

$$\{1, 3, 6, 86\}$$

$$\text{mean} = \frac{1 + 3 + 6 + 86}{4}$$

$$= \frac{96}{4} \text{ or } 24$$

$$\{33, 34, 34, 35\}$$

$$\text{mean} = \frac{33 + 34 + 34 + 35}{4}$$

$$= \frac{136}{4} \text{ or } 34$$

The mean is not close to any one of the four values in this set. In this case, it is not a particularly representative value.

There are no extreme values in this set. In this case, the mean is a representative value.

Exercises

Find the median, mode, and mean for each set of data.

1. {1, 2, 3, 4, 5}
2. {4, 6, 8, 10, 12}
3. {3, 3, 5, 6, 1}
4. {8, 8, 8, 8, 8, 8}
5. {7, 56, 8, 49, 3, 0, 10, 23}
6. {1, 6, 4, 2, 10, 12, 13, 12}
7. {2.4, 8.1, 2.4, 5.7, 6.5}
8. {3.3, 1.6, 8.2, 4.9, 6.7}

9. Two dice were tossed 25 times. Find the median, mode, and mean for the following results.

11	8	10	9	2
7	10	6	7	9
5	7	7	6	12
9	8	4	4	11
2	3	5	7	6

One of Isaac Newton's most famous quotes is, "If I have seen a little farther than others it is because I have stood on the shoulders of giants."

10. Make a frequency distribution chart for the number of letters in each word of the quote.

11. Find the median for the number of letters in each word.

12. Find the mode for the number of letters in each word.

13. Find the mean for the number of letters in each word.

CHAPTER 12

Radical Expressions

When a sky diver jumps from an airplane, the time it takes to reach the ground can be calculated by using the following equation.

$$t = \sqrt{\frac{2s_v}{g}}$$

In this equation s_v is the vertical distance the sky diver falls and g is the acceleration of gravity. Notice that it is necessary to find the square root of $\frac{2s_v}{g}$. In this chapter, you will learn how to find and use square roots.

12-1 Square Roots

Squaring a number means using that number as a factor two times.

$$8^2 = 8 \cdot 8 = 64 \qquad \text{\textit{8 is used as a factor two times.}}$$
$$(-8)^2 = (-8)(-8) = 64 \qquad \text{\textit{-8 is used as a factor two times.}}$$

The inverse of squaring is finding a **square root**. To find a square root of 64, you must find *two equal factors* whose product is 64.

$$x^2 = x \cdot x = 64$$

Since 8 times 8 is 64, one square root of 64 is 8. Since -8 times -8 is also 64, another square root of 64 is -8.

If $x^2 = y$, then x is a square root of y.	*Definition of Square Root*

An expression like $\sqrt{64}$ is called a **radical expression**. The symbol $\sqrt{}$ is a **radical sign**. It indicates the nonnegative or **principal square root** of the expression under the radical sign. This expression is called the **radicand**.

The square root of a negative number is not defined.

$$\text{radical sign} \longrightarrow \sqrt{64} \longleftarrow \text{radicand}$$

$\sqrt{64} = 8 \qquad \sqrt{64}$ indicates the *principal* square root of 64.

$-\sqrt{64} = -8 \qquad -\sqrt{64}$ indicates the *negative* square root of 64.

$\pm\sqrt{64} = \pm 8 \qquad \pm\sqrt{64}$ indicates *both* square roots of 64.

$\pm$ means positive or negative.

Examples

1 **Find $\sqrt{81}$.**

Since $9^2 = 81$, we know that $\sqrt{81} = 9$.

2 **Find $-\sqrt{36}$.**

Since $(6)^2 = 36$, we know that $-\sqrt{36} = -6$.

3 **Find $\pm\sqrt{0.09}$.**

Since $(0.3)^2 = 0.09$, we know that $\pm\sqrt{0.09} = \pm 0.3$.

To simplify a radical expression, find the square root of any factors of the radicand that are perfect squares. For example, to simplify $\sqrt{196}$, find any factors of 196 that are perfect squares. You can use the prime factorization of 196 as shown.

$$\begin{aligned}
\sqrt{196} &= \sqrt{2 \cdot 2 \cdot 7 \cdot 7} \\
&= \sqrt{2^2 \cdot 7^2} \\
&= \sqrt{2^2} \cdot \sqrt{7^2} \\
&= 2 \cdot 7 \\
&= 14 \quad \textbf{\textit{Check:}} \quad 14^2 = 196
\end{aligned}$$

The property used to simplify $\sqrt{196}$ is stated below.

For any numbers a and b, where $a \geq 0$ and $b \geq 0$, $$\sqrt{ab} = \sqrt{a} \cdot \sqrt{b}.$$	*Product Property of Square Roots*

Example

4 **Simplify:** $\sqrt{576}$

$$\begin{aligned}
\sqrt{576} &= \sqrt{2 \cdot 2 \cdot 2 \cdot 2 \cdot 2 \cdot 2 \cdot 3 \cdot 3} & \textit{Find the prime factorization of 576.} \\
&= \sqrt{2^6 \cdot 3^2} & \textit{Express the radicand using exponents.} \\
&= \sqrt{2^6} \cdot \sqrt{3^2} & \textit{Use the product property of square roots.} \\
&= 2^3 \cdot 3 & \textit{Simplify each radical.} \\
&= 24 & \textbf{\textit{Check:}} \quad 24^2 = 576
\end{aligned}$$

A similar property for quotients can also be used to simplify square roots.

For any numbers a and b, where $a \geq 0$ and $b > 0$, $$\sqrt{\frac{a}{b}} = \frac{\sqrt{a}}{\sqrt{b}}.$$	*Quotient Property of Square Roots*

Examples

5 **Simplify:** $\sqrt{\frac{9}{16}}$

$$\begin{aligned}
\sqrt{\frac{9}{16}} &= \frac{\sqrt{9}}{\sqrt{16}} \quad \textit{Use the quotient property of square roots.} \\
&= \frac{3}{4}
\end{aligned}$$

Check: $\left(\frac{3}{4}\right)^2 = \frac{9}{16}$

6 **Simplify:** $-\sqrt{\frac{81}{121}}$

$$\begin{aligned}
-\sqrt{\frac{81}{121}} &= -\frac{\sqrt{81}}{\sqrt{121}} \\
&= -\frac{9}{11}
\end{aligned}$$

Check: $\left(-\frac{9}{11}\right)^2 = \frac{81}{121}$

Exploratory Exercises

State the square of each number.

1. 10
2. 12
3. -7
4. -20
5. 0.3
6. 0.04
7. $\frac{1}{2}$
8. $\frac{4}{7}$
9. $-\frac{7}{8}$
10. $-\frac{11}{4}$

Simplify.

11. $\sqrt{121}$
12. $\pm\sqrt{36}$
13. $-\sqrt{81}$
14. $\sqrt{25}$
15. $\sqrt{\frac{4}{9}}$
16. $\sqrt{\frac{81}{64}}$
17. $\pm\sqrt{\frac{49}{121}}$
18. $-\sqrt{\frac{9}{100}}$
19. $\sqrt{0.0016}$
20. $\sqrt{0.09}$

Written Exercises

Find the principal square root of each number.

1. 49
2. 64
3. 16
4. 169
5. $\frac{25}{36}$
6. $\frac{81}{121}$
7. $\frac{36}{196}$
8. $\frac{25}{400}$
9. 0.0009
10. 0.0025
11. 0.0036
12. 0.16

Simplify.

13. $\sqrt{36}$
14. $\sqrt{9}$
15. $-\sqrt{100}$
16. $\pm\sqrt{144}$
17. $\pm\sqrt{25}$
18. $-\sqrt{169}$
19. $\sqrt{0.36}$
20. $\sqrt{0.0081}$
21. $\sqrt{529}$
22. $\sqrt{225}$
23. $\sqrt{676}$
24. $\sqrt{256}$
25. $-\sqrt{441}$
26. $-\sqrt{484}$
27. $\pm\sqrt{1024}$
28. $\pm\sqrt{289}$
29. $\sqrt{729}$
30. $\sqrt{961}$
31. $\sqrt{1764}$
32. $\sqrt{2025}$
33. $-\sqrt{\frac{289}{100}}$
34. $-\sqrt{\frac{169}{121}}$
35. $\sqrt{\frac{225}{25}}$
36. $\sqrt{\frac{144}{196}}$
37. $\sqrt{\frac{256}{361}}$
38. $\sqrt{\frac{196}{289}}$
39. $\pm\sqrt{\frac{961}{729}}$
40. $\pm\sqrt{\frac{484}{1024}}$
41. $\sqrt{\frac{576}{729}}$
42. $\sqrt{\frac{441}{529}}$
43. $\sqrt{\frac{0.09}{0.16}}$
44. $\sqrt{\frac{0.0025}{0.0036}}$

Excursions in Algebra _____Radical Sign

Ancient mathematicians commonly wrote the word for root to indicate square roots. Late medieval Latin writers commonly used ℞, a contraction of radix (root), to indicate a square root. The symbol $\sqrt{}$ first appeared in print in Rudolff's *Coss* (1525). It is uncertain whether Rudolff used the symbol because it resembled a small *r* for radix or whether he invented a new symbol.

12-2 Irrational Numbers and Real Numbers

You have encountered natural numbers, whole numbers, integers, and rational numbers. The capital letters **N**, **W**, **Z**, and **Q** are often used to denote these sets of numbers.

Counting or Natural Numbers, **N**　　{1, 2, 3, 4, . . . }

Whole Numbers, **W**　　{0, 1, 2, 3, 4, . . . }

Integers, **Z**　　{. . . , −3, −2, −1, 0, 1, 2, 3, . . . }

Rational Numbers, **Q**　　$\left\{ \begin{array}{l} \text{all numbers that can be expressed in the} \\ \text{form } \frac{a}{b}, \text{ where } a \text{ and } b \text{ are integers and } b \neq 0 \end{array} \right\}$

Recall that repeating or terminating decimals name rational numbers, since they can be represented as quotients of integers. The square roots of perfect squares also name rational numbers. For example, $\sqrt{0.16}$ is rational since it is equivalent to 0.4, a rational number. Consider the square roots of numbers that are *not* perfect squares.

$$\sqrt{2} = 1.414213 \ldots \qquad \sqrt{3} = 1.732050 \ldots \qquad \sqrt{7} = 2.645751 \ldots$$

Notice that none of these decimals terminate or repeat.

These numbers are *not* rational numbers. They are **irrational numbers**. The set of irrational numbers is often denoted by the capital letter **I**.

> **Irrational numbers are numbers that cannot be expressed in the form $\frac{a}{b}$, where a and b are integers and $b \neq 0$.**

Definition of Irrational Numbers

Example

1 **Name the set or sets of numbers to which each number belongs.**

a. −7

−7 is an integer. Since it can be expressed as $\frac{-7}{1}$, it is also a rational number.

b. 0.8888 . . .

This repeating decimal is equivalent to $\frac{8}{9}$. Thus, it names a rational number. This number can also be expressed as $0.\overline{8}$. The bar indicates repeating digits.

c. 0.101101110 . . .

This decimal does not terminate or repeat. Thus, it names an irrational number.

d. $\sqrt{9}$

Notice $\sqrt{9} = 3$. The number 3 is a natural number, a whole number, an integer, and a rational number.

Irrational numbers together with rational numbers form the set of **real numbers**, **R**. You have graphed some rational numbers on the number line. Yet, if you graphed *all* rational numbers, the number line still would not be complete. Irrational numbers complete the number line. Therefore, the graph of all real numbers is the entire number line.

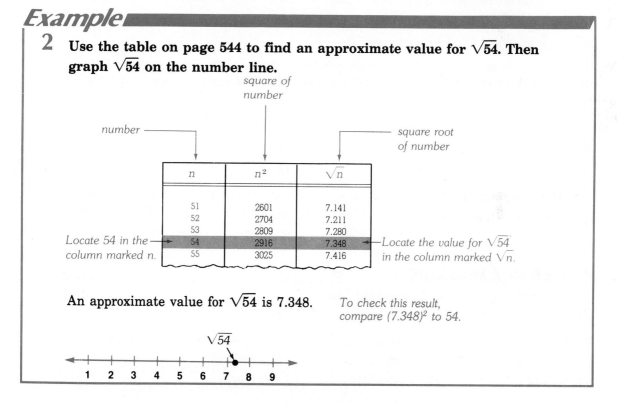

| **Each real number corresponds to exactly one point on the number line. Each point on the number line corresponds to exactly one real number.** | *Completeness Property for Points on the Number Line* |

You can approximate the graph of irrational numbers. The table of square roots on page 544 gives decimal approximations for square roots of integers from 1 to 100.

You can use a calculator or a table of square roots to approximate some irrational numbers.

Example

2   **Use the table on page 544 to find an approximate value for $\sqrt{54}$. Then graph $\sqrt{54}$ on the number line.**

square of number

number

square root of number

n	n^2	$\sqrt{n}$
51	2601	7.141
52	2704	7.211
53	2809	7.280
54	2916	7.348
55	3025	7.416

Locate 54 in the column marked n.

Locate the value for $\sqrt{54}$ in the column marked $\sqrt{n}$.

An approximate value for $\sqrt{54}$ is 7.348.   *To check this result, compare $(7.348)^2$ to 54.*

$\sqrt{54}$

Notice that the table on page 544 also has a column labeled n^2 that lists squares of integers from 1 to 100. You can use this column to determine if an integer between 1 and 10,000 is a perfect square. Any integer that is *not* listed in the n^2 column is *not* a perfect square and has an irrational square root. You can also use the table to find the integers whose values are nearest to the irrational square root.

Example

3 Use the table on page 544 to determine whether each square root is rational or irrational. Then state the two integers between which the value of the square root lies.

a. $\sqrt{9216}$

Look for 9216 in the column marked n^2. Since the number is listed, it is a perfect square. Thus, $\sqrt{9216}$ is a rational number. The corresponding value of n is 96. Thus, the value of $\sqrt{9216}$ is *exactly* 96.

n	n^2	$\sqrt{n}$
91	8281	9.539
92	8464	9.592
93	8649	9.644
94	8836	9.695
95	9025	9.747
96	9216	9.798

b. $\sqrt{8556}$

Notice that 8556 is *not* listed in the n^2 column. Thus, $\sqrt{8556}$ is irrational. Since 8556 is greater than 8464 and less than 8649, the value of $\sqrt{8556}$ is between 92 and 93.

Exploratory Exercises

Name the set or sets of numbers to which each number belongs. Use N for natural numbers, W for whole numbers, Z for integers, Q for rational numbers, and I for irrational numbers.

1. -5
2. $-\frac{1}{2}$
3. $\frac{6}{3}$
4. 16

5. $0.3333\ldots$
6. $\sqrt{11}$
7. $\sqrt{36}$
8. 0.125

9. $0.53694\ldots$
10. $0.\overline{35}$
11. 0.6125
12. $3.1416\ldots$

Use the table on page 544 to find an approximate value for each expression.

13. $\sqrt{2}$ **14.** $\sqrt{11}$ **15.** $\sqrt{20}$ **16.** $\sqrt{91}$ **17.** 16^2 **18.** 28^2

19. $\sqrt{31}$ **20.** $\sqrt{40}$ **21.** $\sqrt{89}$ **22.** $\sqrt{29}$ **23.** 66^2 **24.** $(-43)^2$

Written Exercises

Graph each number on the number line.

1. 3   **2.** -1.5 **3.** $1\frac{2}{3}$ **4.** $\sqrt{7}$ **5.** $-\sqrt{5}$ **6.** $\sqrt{20}$

State whether each decimal represents a rational number or an irrational number.

7. $0.10010001\ldots$ **8.** $1.23123412\ldots$ **9.** $0.\overline{571428}$ **10.** $0.3\overline{7}$

11. $0.4444\ldots$ **12.** $4.34334333\ldots$ **13.** $7.6567876\ldots$ **14.** $0.777\ldots$

Use the table on page 544 to determine if each number is rational or irrational. Then state the integers between which the value of the square root lies.

15. $\sqrt{6724}$ **16.** $\sqrt{350}$ **17.** $\sqrt{3800}$ **18.** $\sqrt{1156}$

19. $\sqrt{888}$ **20.** $\sqrt{289}$ **21.** $\sqrt{9025}$ **22.** $\sqrt{3640}$

23. $\sqrt{7166}$ **24.** $\sqrt{7511}$ **25.** $\sqrt{1444}$ **26.** $\sqrt{3249}$

12-3 Approximating Square Roots

One method for approximating square roots is called the **divide-and-average method**. This method is used below to approximate $\sqrt{88}$.

Step 1 Isolate 88 between two perfect squares. Choose 9 as an approximation for $\sqrt{88}$ because 88 is closer to 81 than 100.

$$81 < \ 88 \ < 100$$
$$9^2 < \ 88 \ < 10^2$$
$$9 < \sqrt{88} < 10$$

Step 2 Divide 88 by 9.
Carry the quotient to twice as many digits as in the divisor.

$$\begin{array}{r} 9.7 \quad \leftarrow \textit{two-digit quotient} \\ 9\overline{)88.0} \\ \uparrow \\ \textit{one digit divisor} \end{array}$$

Step 3 Average the quotient, 9.7, and the divisor, 9. Carry the average to the same number of digits as the quotient. Do not round.

$$\frac{9.7 + 9}{2} = \frac{18.7}{2}$$
$$\approx 9.3$$

The symbol $\approx$ means is approximately equal to.

Step 4 Use the average, 9.3, as the new divisor. Repeat steps 2 and 3.

Divide.
$$\begin{array}{r} 9.462 \\ 9.3_{\wedge}\overline{)88.0_{\wedge}000} \end{array}$$

Average.
$$\frac{9.3 + 9.462}{2} = \frac{18.762}{2}$$
$$\approx 9.381$$

An approximation for $\sqrt{88}$ is 9.381. More accurate approximations may be made by continuing the divide-and-average method.

Example

1 **Approximate $\sqrt{19.9}$. Use the divide-and-average method twice.**

$$16 < 19.9 < 25$$
$$4^2 < 19.9 < 5^2$$
$$4 < \sqrt{19.9} < 5$$

Choose 4 as the first approximation.

Divide.
$$\begin{array}{r} 4.9 \\ 4\overline{)19.9} \end{array}$$

Average.
$$\frac{4.9 + 4}{2} = \frac{8.9}{2}$$
$$\approx 4.4$$

Use 4.4 as the second approximation.

$$\begin{array}{r} 4.522 \\ 4.4_\wedge \overline{)19.9_\wedge 000} \end{array}$$

Divide.

Average. $\dfrac{4.522 + 4.4}{2} = \dfrac{8.922}{2}$ or 4.461

An approximation for $\sqrt{19.9}$ is 4.461. *To check this result, compare $(4.461)^2$ to 19.9.*

Exploratory Exercises

State the perfect square integer closest to each number.

1. 14	**2.** 3.2	**3.** 48	**4.** 79	**5.** 63	**6.** 41
7. 56	**8.** 27	**9.** 7.8	**10.** 29.3	**11.** 84	**12.** 69.7

State a first approximation for each of the following.

13. $\sqrt{13}$ **14.** $\sqrt{10}$ **15.** $\sqrt{31}$ **16.** $\sqrt{35}$ **17.** $\sqrt{27}$ **18.** $\sqrt{53}$

Written Exercises

State a first approximation for each of the following.

1. $\sqrt{68}$	**2.** $\sqrt{78}$	**3.** $\sqrt{42}$	**4.** $\sqrt{91}$	**5.** $\sqrt{95}$	**6.** $\sqrt{103}$
7. $\sqrt{150}$	**8.** $\sqrt{300}$	**9.** $\sqrt{176}$	**10.** $\sqrt{138}$	**11.** $\sqrt{147}$	**12.** $\sqrt{200}$

Use the divide-and-average method twice to approximate each square root.

13. $\sqrt{85}$	**14.** $\sqrt{71}$	**15.** $\sqrt{60.3}$	**16.** $\sqrt{93.5}$
17. $\sqrt{149}$	**18.** $\sqrt{185}$	**19.** $\sqrt{193}$	**20.** $\sqrt{206}$
21. $\sqrt{131.4}$	**22.** $\sqrt{155.1}$	**23.** $\sqrt{175.6}$	**24.** $\sqrt{115.7}$
25. $\sqrt{0.61}$	**26.** $\sqrt{2.314}$	**27.** $\sqrt{0.00462}$	**28.** $\sqrt{0.00932}$

⊞ Using Calculators_____Square Root Key

The key labeled $\sqrt{x}$ on your calculator is the **square root key**. When this key is pressed, the calculator replaces the number in the display with its principal square root. If a square root is irrational, the calculator display will probably show as many decimal places as it can. The result can be rounded to the nearest hundredth or thousandth.

Exercises

1-24. Use a calculator to check your solutions for Written Exercises 1-24 above.

25. Choose any number and enter it on your calculator. Then press the square root key, followed by the x^2 key. What is the result? Why?

26. Choose a negative number and enter it on your calculator. Then press the square root key. What happens? Try some other negative numbers. Can you find any negative numbers that have square roots?

12-4 Simplifying Square Roots

The square root of a positive integer is in *simplest form* if the radicand has no perfect square factor other than 1.

The product property of square roots and prime factorization can be used as shown in these examples to simplify radical expressions in which the radicand is *not* a perfect square.

Examples

1 **Simplify:** $\sqrt{72}$

$$\sqrt{72} = \sqrt{2 \cdot 2 \cdot 2 \cdot 3 \cdot 3} \quad \textit{Prime Factorization}$$
$$= \sqrt{2} \cdot \sqrt{2^2} \cdot \sqrt{3^2} \quad \textit{Product Property}$$
$$= \sqrt{2} \cdot 2 \cdot 3$$
$$= 6\sqrt{2}$$

2 **Simplify:** $\sqrt{150}$

$$\sqrt{150} = \sqrt{2 \cdot 3 \cdot 5 \cdot 5}$$
$$= \sqrt{2} \cdot \sqrt{3} \cdot \sqrt{5^2}$$
$$= \sqrt{2 \cdot 3} \cdot 5$$
$$= 5\sqrt{6}$$

When finding the positive square root of an expression·containing variables, you must be sure that the result is *not* negative. Consider that $5^2 = 25$ and $(-5)^2 = 25$. When you find $\sqrt{25}$, however, you want *only* the principal square root. Therefore, absolute values are used as needed to ensure nonnegative results.

$$\sqrt{x^2} = |x|$$

Examples

3 **Simplify:** $\sqrt{81y^2}$

$$\sqrt{81y^2} = \sqrt{81} \cdot \sqrt{y^2} \quad \textit{Use the product property of square roots.}$$
$$= 9|y| \quad \textit{The absolute value of y ensures a nonnegative result.}$$

4 **Simplify:** $\sqrt{200a^4b^3}$

$$\sqrt{200a^4b^3} = \sqrt{2 \cdot 2 \cdot 2 \cdot 5 \cdot 5 \cdot a \cdot a \cdot a \cdot a \cdot b \cdot b \cdot b}$$
$$= \sqrt{2} \cdot \sqrt{2^2} \cdot \sqrt{5^2} \cdot \sqrt{a^4} \cdot \sqrt{b^2} \cdot \sqrt{b} \quad \textit{Product Property of Square Roots}$$
$$= \sqrt{2} \cdot 2 \cdot 5 \cdot a^2 \cdot b \cdot \sqrt{b}$$
$$= 10a^2b\sqrt{2b} \quad \textit{Note that absolute value is not used because } a^2 \textit{ is always nonnegative}$$
$$\textit{and b is nonnegative in this case. If b were negative then } b^3$$
$$\textit{would be negative and } \sqrt{200a^4b^3} \textit{ would not be defined.}$$

The product property can be used to multiply square roots.

Examples

5 **Simplify:** $\sqrt{10} \cdot \sqrt{20}$

$$\sqrt{10} \cdot \sqrt{20} = \sqrt{10 \cdot 20} \qquad \textit{Notice that } \sqrt{10 \cdot 20} = \sqrt{2} \cdot \sqrt{2^2} \cdot \sqrt{5^2}.$$
$$= \sqrt{10 \cdot 10 \cdot 2}$$
$$= 10\sqrt{2}$$

6 **Simplify:** $\sqrt{7}(\sqrt{7} + \sqrt{5})$

$$\sqrt{7}(\sqrt{7} + \sqrt{5}) = \sqrt{7} \cdot \sqrt{7} + \sqrt{7} \cdot \sqrt{5} \qquad \textit{Use the distributive property.}$$
$$= \sqrt{49} + \sqrt{35} \qquad \textit{Notice that 35 contains no perfect}$$
$$= 7 + \sqrt{35} \qquad \textit{square factor other than 1 and there-}$$
$$\textit{fore cannot be simplified.}$$

Exploratory Exercises

Simplify.

1. $\sqrt{8}$ **2.** $\sqrt{12}$ **3.** $\sqrt{20}$ **4.** $\sqrt{18}$ **5.** $\sqrt{24}$ **6.** $\sqrt{32}$

7. $\sqrt{48}$ **8.** $\sqrt{19}$ **9.** $\sqrt{m^2}$ **10.** $\sqrt{y^6}$ **11.** $\sqrt{x^5}$ **12.** $\sqrt{a^3}$

13. $\sqrt{8a^3}$ **14.** $\sqrt{9a^4}$ **15.** $\sqrt{a^3b^3}$ **16.** $\sqrt{x^4y^4}$ **17.** $\sqrt{4} \cdot \sqrt{9}$ **18.** $\sqrt{8} \cdot \sqrt{3}$

19. $\sqrt{5} \cdot \sqrt{10}$ **20.** $\sqrt{6} \cdot \sqrt{9}$ **21.** $\sqrt{11} \cdot \sqrt{11}$ **22.** $\sqrt{10} \cdot \sqrt{10}$

23. $\sqrt{3}(\sqrt{3} + \sqrt{2})$ **24.** $\sqrt{5}(\sqrt{3} + \sqrt{5})$ **25.** $\sqrt{7}(\sqrt{5} - \sqrt{7})$ **26.** $\sqrt{10}(\sqrt{10} - \sqrt{3})$

Written Exercises

Simplify. Use absolute value symbols when necessary.

1. $\sqrt{27}$ **2.** $\sqrt{75}$ **3.** $\sqrt{45}$ **4.** $\sqrt{58}$

5. $\sqrt{72}$ **6.** $\sqrt{80}$ **7.** $\sqrt{90}$ **8.** $\sqrt{98}$

9. $\sqrt{128}$ **10.** $\sqrt{280}$ **11.** $\sqrt{500}$ **12.** $\sqrt{1000}$

13. $\sqrt{720}$ **14.** $\sqrt{784}$ **15.** $\sqrt{5184}$ **16.** $\sqrt{2916}$

17. $\sqrt{32x^2}$ **18.** $\sqrt{20a^2}$ **19.** $\sqrt{40b^4}$ **20.** $\sqrt{48m^4}$

21. $\sqrt{36a^2b^2}$ **22.** $\sqrt{80a^2b^3}$ **23.** $\sqrt{120a^3b}$ **24.** $\sqrt{44m^4n}$

25. $\sqrt{60x^2y^4}$ **26.** $\sqrt{54a^2b^2}$ **27.** $\sqrt{20m^2n^7}$ **28.** $\sqrt{147x^5y^4}$

29. $\sqrt{320m^4n^6}$ **30.** $\sqrt{88x^{10}y^{10}}$ **31.** $\sqrt{21x^2y}$ **32.** $\sqrt{42xy}$

33. $\sqrt{6} \cdot \sqrt{8}$ **34.** $\sqrt{10} \cdot \sqrt{30}$ **35.** $2\sqrt{5} \cdot \sqrt{5}$ **36.** $4\sqrt{2} \cdot \sqrt{2}$

37. $2\sqrt{3} \cdot 7\sqrt{5}$ **38.** $3\sqrt{7} \cdot 6\sqrt{2}$ **39.** $5\sqrt{10} \cdot 3\sqrt{10}$ **40.** $6\sqrt{8} \cdot 7\sqrt{8}$

41. $4\sqrt{5} \cdot 3\sqrt{15}$ **42.** $7\sqrt{30} \cdot 2\sqrt{6}$ **43.** $\sqrt{3}(\sqrt{3} + \sqrt{6})$ **44.** $\sqrt{7}(\sqrt{14} + \sqrt{7})$

45. $\sqrt{6}(\sqrt{7} - \sqrt{3})$ **46.** $\sqrt{2}(\sqrt{8} - \sqrt{4})$ **47.** $\sqrt{5}(\sqrt{10} - \sqrt{2})$ **48.** $\sqrt{10}(\sqrt{10} - \sqrt{2})$

49. $\sqrt{3}(\sqrt{5} + \sqrt{27})$ **50.** $\sqrt{5}(\sqrt{3} + \sqrt{125})$ **51.** $\sqrt{3}(2\sqrt{12} + 4\sqrt{7})$ **52.** $\sqrt{8}(2\sqrt{3} + 5\sqrt{6})$

53. Find the area of a rectangle whose length is $\sqrt{343}$ cm and whose width is $\sqrt{7}$ cm.

54. Find the area of a triangle whose base is $\sqrt{6}$ in. and whose altitude is $2\sqrt{6}$ in.

Many expressions can be written in several different ways. Consider the expression $\frac{1}{xy}$.

$$\frac{1}{xy} = \frac{1}{x \cdot y} = 1/(xy) = 1 \div (xy)$$

All four of these expressions are equivalent because they name the same number.

Notice the importance of the parentheses in the expressions $1/(xy)$ and $1 \div (xy)$. Without the parentheses, the order of operations dictates that the division would come *before* the multiplication. As a result, $1/xy$ and $1 \div xy$ would *not* be equivalent to $\frac{1}{xy}$.

Sometimes parentheses are *not* important when writing equivalent expressions. For example, both $\sqrt{3}^2$ and $(\sqrt{3})^2$ indicate that $\sqrt{3}$ is to be squared.

But sometimes the placement of the parentheses in an expression is *very* important, as shown in the examples below.

$3\sqrt{5^3}$ is equivalent to $3(\sqrt{5^3})$.

$3\sqrt{5^3}$ is *not* equivalent to $(3\sqrt{5})^3$

$\sqrt{7} \cdot \sqrt{3} + \sqrt{2}$ is equivalent to $(\sqrt{7} \cdot \sqrt{3}) + \sqrt{2}$.

$\sqrt{7} \cdot \sqrt{3} + \sqrt{2}$ is *not* equivalent to $\sqrt{7}(\sqrt{3} + \sqrt{2})$.

Exercises

Decide if the expressions are equivalent. Write *yes* or *no*.

1. $\frac{2}{3a}$ and $\frac{2}{3 \cdot a}$

2. $\frac{4}{a + b}$ and $4/a + b$

3. ab^2 and $(ab)^2$

4. $(7 + \sqrt{2}) \div 8$ and $\frac{7 + \sqrt{2}}{8}$

5. $a + b^2$ and $(a + b)^2$

6. $2 + \sqrt{3} \cdot \sqrt{4}$ and $(2 + \sqrt{3})\sqrt{4}$

Choose the expressions that are equivalent to the first expression. There may be more than one correct answer.

7. $\frac{m + 2n}{4}$ **a.** $(m + 2n)/4$ **b.** $(m + 2n) \div 4$ **c.** $m + (2n/4)$

8. $(2\sqrt{4})^6$ **a.** $2(\sqrt{4})^6$ **b.** $(2 \cdot \sqrt{4})^6$ **c.** $2\sqrt{4}^6$

9. $2(\sqrt{6} + \sqrt{3})$ **a.** $2 \cdot \sqrt{6} + \sqrt{3}$ **b.** $2 \cdot (\sqrt{6} + \sqrt{3})$ **c.** $2\sqrt{6} + \sqrt{3}$

10. $6\sqrt{3} \cdot 4\sqrt{7}$ **a.** $6\sqrt{3}(4\sqrt{7})$ **b.** $(6\sqrt{3})(4\sqrt{7})$ **c.** $(6\sqrt{3} \cdot 4\sqrt{7})$

12-5 Dividing Radical Expressions and Rationalizing Denominators

The quotient property of square roots can be used to simplify expressions and to divide radicals.

Examples

1 **Simplify:** $\dfrac{\sqrt{48}}{\sqrt{3}}$

$\dfrac{\sqrt{48}}{\sqrt{3}} = \sqrt{\dfrac{48}{3}}$ *Quotient Property of Square Roots*

$\phantom{\dfrac{\sqrt{48}}{\sqrt{3}}} = \sqrt{16}$ *Notice that 16 is a perfect square.*

$\phantom{\dfrac{\sqrt{48}}{\sqrt{3}}} = 4$

2 **Simplify:** $\dfrac{\sqrt{32}}{\sqrt{3}}$

$\dfrac{\sqrt{32}}{\sqrt{3}} = \dfrac{\sqrt{32}}{\sqrt{3}} \cdot \dfrac{\sqrt{3}}{\sqrt{3}}$ *Notice that $\dfrac{\sqrt{3}}{\sqrt{3}} = 1$.*

$\phantom{\dfrac{\sqrt{32}}{\sqrt{3}}} = \dfrac{\sqrt{32 \cdot 3}}{\sqrt{3 \cdot 3}}$

$\phantom{\dfrac{\sqrt{32}}{\sqrt{3}}} = \dfrac{\sqrt{96}}{\sqrt{9}}$

$\phantom{\dfrac{\sqrt{32}}{\sqrt{3}}} = \dfrac{\sqrt{2^4} \cdot \sqrt{2} \cdot \sqrt{3}}{3}$ *Now do you see why $\dfrac{\sqrt{3}}{\sqrt{3}}$ was used?*

$\phantom{\dfrac{\sqrt{32}}{\sqrt{3}}} = \dfrac{4\sqrt{6}}{3}$

The method used to simplify $\dfrac{\sqrt{32}}{\sqrt{3}}$ in the above example is called **rationalizing the denominator**. Notice that the denominator becomes a rational number.

Example

3 **Simplify:** $\sqrt{\dfrac{25}{18}}$

$\sqrt{\dfrac{25}{18}} = \dfrac{\sqrt{25}}{\sqrt{18}}$ *Quotient Property of Square Roots*

$\phantom{\sqrt{\dfrac{25}{18}}} = \dfrac{5}{\sqrt{3^2} \cdot \sqrt{2}}$ *Product Property of Square Roots*

$\phantom{\sqrt{\dfrac{25}{18}}} = \dfrac{5}{3\sqrt{2}} \cdot \dfrac{\sqrt{2}}{\sqrt{2}}$ *Rationalize the denominator.*

$\phantom{\sqrt{\dfrac{25}{18}}} = \dfrac{5\sqrt{2}}{6}$

Some quotients may have binomial expressions, such as $8 + \sqrt{2}$, as denominators. Multiplying $8 + \sqrt{2}$ by $8 - \sqrt{2}$ results in a rational number.

$$(8 + \sqrt{2})(8 - \sqrt{2}) = 8^2 - (\sqrt{2})^2 \qquad \textit{Use the pattern}$$
$$= 64 - 2 \qquad \textit{(a - b)(a + b)} = a^2 - b^2$$
$$= 62 \qquad \textit{to simplify.}$$

Binomials of the form $a\sqrt{b} + c\sqrt{d}$ and $a\sqrt{b} - c\sqrt{d}$ are **conjugates** of each other.

Examples

4 **Simplify:** $\dfrac{3}{3 - \sqrt{5}}$

To rationalize the denominator, multiply both numerator and denominator by the conjugate of $3 - \sqrt{5}$, which is $3 + \sqrt{5}$.

$$\frac{3}{3 - \sqrt{5}} = \frac{3}{3 - \sqrt{5}} \cdot \frac{3 + \sqrt{5}}{3 + \sqrt{5}} \qquad \textit{Notice that } \frac{3 + \sqrt{5}}{3 + \sqrt{5}} = 1.$$

$$= \frac{3^2 + 3\sqrt{5}}{3^2 - (\sqrt{5})^2} \qquad \textit{Use the distributive property to}$$
$$\textit{multiply the numerators.}$$

$$= \frac{9 + 3\sqrt{5}}{9 - 5}$$

$$= \frac{9 + 3\sqrt{5}}{4}$$

5 **Simplify:** $\dfrac{2\sqrt{3}}{3\sqrt{6} + 4\sqrt{2}}$

$$\frac{2\sqrt{3}}{3\sqrt{6} + 4\sqrt{2}} = \frac{2\sqrt{3}}{3\sqrt{6} + 4\sqrt{2}} \cdot \frac{3\sqrt{6} - 4\sqrt{2}}{3\sqrt{6} - 4\sqrt{2}} \qquad \textit{The conjugate of } 3\sqrt{6} + 4\sqrt{2} \textit{ is } 3\sqrt{6} - 4\sqrt{2}.$$

$$= \frac{2\sqrt{3} \cdot 3\sqrt{6} - 2\sqrt{3} \cdot 4\sqrt{2}}{(3\sqrt{6})^2 - (4\sqrt{2})^2}$$

$$= \frac{6\sqrt{18} - 8\sqrt{6}}{54 - 32}$$

$$= \frac{18\sqrt{2} - 8\sqrt{6}}{22} \qquad 6\sqrt{18} = 6\sqrt{2 \cdot 3^2} = 18\sqrt{2}$$

$$= \frac{2(9\sqrt{2} - 4\sqrt{6})}{22} \qquad \textit{The GCF of the numerator is 2.}$$

$$= \frac{9\sqrt{2} - 4\sqrt{6}}{11}$$

A radical expression is in simplest form when the following conditions are met.
1. No radicands have perfect square factors other than 1.
2. No radicands contain fractions.
3. No radical appears in the denominator of a fraction.

Exploratory Exercises

Simplify.

1. $(3 - \sqrt{7})(3 + \sqrt{7})$
2. $(\sqrt{6} - 5)(\sqrt{6} + 5)$
3. $(4 + 2\sqrt{2})(4 - 2\sqrt{2})$

State the conjugate of each expression. Then multiply the expression by its conjugate.

4. $3 + \sqrt{2}$
5. $\sqrt{3} + 4$
6. $7 - \sqrt{5}$
7. $6 + \sqrt{8}$
8. $9 - \sqrt{3}$
9. $\sqrt{2} + \sqrt{5}$
10. $\sqrt{3} - \sqrt{7}$
11. $2\sqrt{5} - \sqrt{6}$
12. $2\sqrt{8} + 3\sqrt{5}$

State the fraction that each expression should be multiplied by to rationalize the denominator.

13. $\dfrac{3}{\sqrt{5}}$
14. $\dfrac{7}{\sqrt{11}}$
15. $\dfrac{3\sqrt{2}}{\sqrt{6}}$
16. $\dfrac{2\sqrt{3}}{\sqrt{8}}$

17. $\sqrt{\dfrac{3}{5}}$
18. $\sqrt{\dfrac{8}{7}}$
19. $\dfrac{1}{3 + \sqrt{7}}$
20. $\dfrac{2\sqrt{5}}{4 - \sqrt{3}}$

Written Exercises

Simplify.

1. $\dfrac{\sqrt{42}}{\sqrt{6}}$
2. $\dfrac{\sqrt{20}}{\sqrt{5}}$
3. $\dfrac{\sqrt{10}}{\sqrt{7}}$
4. $\dfrac{\sqrt{7}}{\sqrt{3}}$

5. $\dfrac{\sqrt{6}}{\sqrt{18}}$
6. $\dfrac{\sqrt{5}}{\sqrt{10}}$
7. $\sqrt{\dfrac{3}{7}}$
8. $\sqrt{\dfrac{5}{2}}$

9. $\sqrt{\dfrac{7}{20}}$
10. $\sqrt{\dfrac{11}{32}}$
11. $\sqrt{\dfrac{2}{3}} \cdot \sqrt{\dfrac{5}{2}}$
12. $\sqrt{\dfrac{7}{11}} \cdot \sqrt{\dfrac{10}{7}}$

13. $\sqrt{\dfrac{a}{3}}$
14. $\sqrt{\dfrac{b}{6}}$
15. $\sqrt{\dfrac{a^2}{5}}$
16. $\sqrt{\dfrac{m^4}{11}}$

17. $\sqrt{\dfrac{27}{b^2}}$
18. $\sqrt{\dfrac{54}{r^2}}$
19. $\sqrt{\dfrac{5n^5}{4m^5}}$
20. $\sqrt{\dfrac{11a^3}{10b^3}}$

21. $\dfrac{1}{7 - \sqrt{3}}$
22. $\dfrac{1}{6 + \sqrt{3}}$
23. $\dfrac{11}{\sqrt{2} + 5}$
24. $\dfrac{10}{\sqrt{5} - 9}$

25. $\dfrac{6}{\sqrt{3} + \sqrt{2}}$
26. $\dfrac{12}{\sqrt{6} - \sqrt{5}}$

27. $\dfrac{10a}{2 - \sqrt{a}}$
28. $\dfrac{9b}{6 + \sqrt{b}}$

29. $\dfrac{2\sqrt{5}}{-3 + \sqrt{6}}$
30. $\dfrac{-3\sqrt{5}}{-2 - \sqrt{6}}$

31. $\dfrac{-9\sqrt{2}}{-4 + \sqrt{8}}$
32. $\dfrac{-10\sqrt{6}}{3 + \sqrt{6}}$

33. $\dfrac{2\sqrt{7}}{3\sqrt{5} + 5\sqrt{3}}$
34. $\dfrac{3\sqrt{11}}{7\sqrt{2} - 6\sqrt{5}}$

35. $\dfrac{6\sqrt{5}}{4\sqrt{8} - 2\sqrt{7}}$
36. $\dfrac{4\sqrt{19}}{3\sqrt{7} + 4\sqrt{12}}$

mini-review

1. Given $f(x) = 2x^2 + 6$, find $f(3)$.
2. Determine the slope of the line passing through the points with coordinates $(4, -2)$ and $(-6, 8)$.
3. Solve $25y^2 + 20y = -4$.
4. Solve $(x + 6)(x - 1) = 78$.
5. The sum of two numbers is 132. Their difference is 44. Find the numbers.

12-6 Adding and Subtracting Radical Expressions

Radical expressions in which the radicands are alike can be added or subtracted in the same way that monomials are added or subtracted.

$$3x + 2x = (3 + 2)x = 5x$$
$$3\sqrt{2} + 2\sqrt{2} = (3 + 2)\sqrt{2} = 5\sqrt{2}$$
$$7y - 4y = (7 - 4)y = 3y$$
$$7\sqrt{5} - 4\sqrt{5} = (7 - 4)\sqrt{5} = 3\sqrt{5}$$

Notice that the distributive property was used to simplify each of the radical expressions.

Examples

1 **Simplify:** $3\sqrt{11} + 6\sqrt{11} - 2\sqrt{11}$

$3\sqrt{11} + 6\sqrt{11} - 2\sqrt{11} = (3 + 6 - 2)\sqrt{11}$ *Distributive Property*
$$= 7\sqrt{11}$$

2 **Simplify:** $9\sqrt{7} - 4\sqrt{2} + 3\sqrt{2} - 5\sqrt{7}$

$9\sqrt{7} - 4\sqrt{2} + 3\sqrt{2} - 5\sqrt{7} = 9\sqrt{7} - 5\sqrt{7} - 4\sqrt{2} + 3\sqrt{2}$ *Commutative Property*
$$= (9 - 5)\sqrt{7} + (-4 + 3)\sqrt{2}$$ *Distributive Property*
$$= 4\sqrt{7} - \sqrt{2}$$

If the radical expressions are *not* in simplest form, first simplify. Then, if possible, use the distributive property to further simplify the expression. Some expressions, such as $3\sqrt{5} - 2\sqrt{7}$ and $4\sqrt{2} + \sqrt{17}$, *cannot* be simplified further because the radicands are different and there are no common factors.

Example

3 **Simplify:** $6\sqrt{8} + 11\sqrt{18}$

$6\sqrt{8} + 11\sqrt{18} = 6\sqrt{2^2 \cdot 2} + 11\sqrt{3^2 \cdot 2}$ *Simplify each term.*
$$= 6(2\sqrt{2}) + 11(3\sqrt{2})$$
$$= 12\sqrt{2} + 33\sqrt{2}$$
$$= 45\sqrt{2}$$ *Distributive Property.*

Examples

4 **Simplify:** $7\sqrt{98} + 5\sqrt{32} - 2\sqrt{75}$

$$
\begin{aligned}
7\sqrt{98} + 5\sqrt{32} - 2\sqrt{75} &= 7\sqrt{7^2 \cdot 2} + 5\sqrt{2^4 \cdot 2} - 2\sqrt{5^2 \cdot 3} \\
&= 7(7\sqrt{2}) + 5(4\sqrt{2}) - 2(5\sqrt{3}) \\
&= 49\sqrt{2} + 20\sqrt{2} - 10\sqrt{3} \\
&= 69\sqrt{2} - 10\sqrt{3}
\end{aligned}
$$

5 **Simplify:** $4\sqrt{7} - 5\sqrt{28} + 5\sqrt{\frac{1}{7}}$

$$
\begin{aligned}
4\sqrt{7} - 5\sqrt{28} + 5\sqrt{\frac{1}{7}} &= 4\sqrt{7} - 5\sqrt{2^2 \cdot 7} + 5\left(\frac{\sqrt{1}}{\sqrt{7}} \cdot \frac{\sqrt{7}}{\sqrt{7}}\right) \quad \textit{Rationalize the} \\
&\qquad\qquad\qquad\qquad\qquad\qquad\qquad\qquad \textit{denominator of } 5\sqrt{\frac{1}{7}}. \\
&= 4\sqrt{7} - 5(2\sqrt{7}) + 5\left(\frac{\sqrt{7}}{7}\right) \\
&= 4\sqrt{7} - 10\sqrt{7} + \frac{5\sqrt{7}}{7}
\end{aligned}
$$

$$
\begin{aligned}
4\sqrt{7} - 5\sqrt{28} + 5\sqrt{\frac{1}{7}} &= \frac{28\sqrt{7} - 70\sqrt{7} + 5\sqrt{7}}{7} \quad \textit{The least common} \\
&\qquad\qquad\qquad\qquad\qquad\quad \textit{denominator is 7.} \\
&= -\frac{37\sqrt{7}}{7}
\end{aligned}
$$

Exploratory Exercises

Name the expressions in each group that have the same radicand.

1. $5\sqrt{3},\ 4\sqrt{6},\ 3\sqrt{3}$
2. $5\sqrt{14},\ -3\sqrt{7},\ 4\sqrt{7}$
3. $3\sqrt{12},\ 2\sqrt{6},\ 5\sqrt{12}$
4. $4\sqrt{2},\ 3\sqrt{2},\ 2\sqrt{3}$
5. $-3\sqrt{3},\ 2\sqrt{6},\ 12\sqrt{3}$
6. $3\sqrt{3},\ 2\sqrt{3},\ 3\sqrt{6}$
7. $2\sqrt{10},\ -6\sqrt{10},\ 4\sqrt{2},\ 7\sqrt{10}$
8. $3\sqrt{2},\ 5\sqrt{6},\ 2\sqrt{3},\ 4\sqrt{7}$
9. $2\sqrt{5},\ -\sqrt{10},\ 3\sqrt{5},\ -5\sqrt{5}$

Simplify.

10. $3\sqrt{5} + 2\sqrt{5}$
11. $4\sqrt{3} - 7\sqrt{3}$
12. $4\sqrt{7} + 11\sqrt{7}$
13. $8\sqrt{6} + 3\sqrt{6}$
14. $4\sqrt{x} - 5\sqrt{x}$
15. $5\sqrt{y} + 6\sqrt{y}$
16. $2\sqrt{11} + 3\sqrt{5}$
17. $3\sqrt{15} - 2\sqrt{5}$
18. $10\sqrt{6} - 3\sqrt{6}$
19. $25\sqrt{13} + \sqrt{13}$
20. $15\sqrt{6} - \sqrt{6}$
21. $21\sqrt{19} + 19\sqrt{19}$
22. $18\sqrt{2x} + 3\sqrt{2x}$
23. $2\sqrt{3a} - 7\sqrt{3a}$
24. $3\sqrt{5m} - 5\sqrt{5m}$

Written Exercises

Simplify.

1. $4\sqrt{11} + 7\sqrt{11}$
2. $10\sqrt{21} - 8\sqrt{21}$
3. $3\sqrt{13} - 7\sqrt{13}$
4. $-7\sqrt{7} + 6\sqrt{7}$
5. $5\sqrt{7} + 12\sqrt{7}$
6. $2\sqrt{11} + 4\sqrt{11}$

7. $4\sqrt{3} + 7\sqrt{3} - 2\sqrt{3}$

8. $5\sqrt{2} + 4\sqrt{2} + 7\sqrt{2}$

9. $8\sqrt{7} - 10\sqrt{7} + 3\sqrt{7}$

10. $2\sqrt{11} - 6\sqrt{11} - 3\sqrt{11}$

11. $5\sqrt{5} + 3\sqrt{5} - 18\sqrt{5}$

12. $2\sqrt{10} + 2\sqrt{10} + 2\sqrt{10}$

13. $8\sqrt{3} - 2\sqrt{2} + 3\sqrt{2} + 5\sqrt{3}$

14. $-3\sqrt{5} + 2\sqrt{5} + 5\sqrt{2} + 3\sqrt{2}$

15. $4\sqrt{6} + \sqrt{7} - 6\sqrt{2} + 4\sqrt{7}$

16. $10\sqrt{10} + 4\sqrt{10} - \sqrt{3} + 6\sqrt{10}$

17. $\sqrt{3} + \sqrt{5}$

18. $4\sqrt{6} + 2\sqrt{2}$

19. $2\sqrt{3} + \sqrt{12}$

20. $3\sqrt{8} + 7\sqrt{2}$

21. $3\sqrt{7} - 2\sqrt{28}$

22. $3\sqrt{50} - 4\sqrt{5}$

23. $4\sqrt{20} + 9\sqrt{45}$

24. $3\sqrt{27} + 5\sqrt{48}$

25. $3\sqrt{28} - 8\sqrt{63}$

26. $2\sqrt{50} - 3\sqrt{32}$

27. $\sqrt{18} + \sqrt{108} + \sqrt{50}$

28. $\sqrt{48} - \sqrt{12} + \sqrt{300}$

29. $8\sqrt{72} + 2\sqrt{20} - 3\sqrt{5}$

30. $2\sqrt{20} - 3\sqrt{24} - \sqrt{180}$

31. $2\sqrt{108} - \sqrt{27} + \sqrt{363}$

32. $8\sqrt{50} + 5\sqrt{72} - 2\sqrt{98}$

33. $\sqrt{7} + \sqrt{\dfrac{1}{7}}$

34. $\sqrt{6} + \sqrt{\dfrac{2}{3}}$

35. $\sqrt{3} - \sqrt{\dfrac{1}{3}}$

36. $\sqrt{10} - \sqrt{\dfrac{2}{5}}$

37. $3\sqrt{3} - \sqrt{48} + 3\sqrt{\dfrac{1}{3}}$

38. $14\sqrt{\dfrac{3}{2}} + 9\sqrt{\dfrac{2}{3}} + \sqrt{24}$

39. $3\sqrt{\dfrac{7}{4}} - 10\sqrt{\dfrac{1}{7}} + 3\sqrt{28}$

40. $6\sqrt{\dfrac{3}{5}} - 3\sqrt{60} + 2\sqrt{\dfrac{3}{5}}$

⊞ *Using Calculators* _____ **Verifying Answers**

You can use a calculator to verify answers to exercises such as the ones above.

Example: Use a calculator to verify the answer to Example 5 on page 386.

In Example 5 on page 386, $4\sqrt{7} - 5\sqrt{28} + 5\sqrt{\dfrac{1}{7}}$ is simplified to $\dfrac{-37\sqrt{7}}{7}$.

To verify this answer, first evaluate $4\sqrt{7} - 5\sqrt{28} + 5\sqrt{\dfrac{1}{7}}$.

ENTER: 4 ⊠ 7 ☑ ⊟ 5 ⊠ 28 ☑ ⊞ 5 ⊠ ⎡(1 ÷ 7)⎤ ☑ ⊜

The display shows -13.984686.

Then evaluate $\dfrac{-37\sqrt{7}}{7}$.

ENTER: ⎡(37 ⊠ 7 ☑)⎤ ÷ 7 ⊟ +/−

The display again shows -13.984686.
Therefore, the answer has veen verified.

Exercises

1-10. Use a calculator to verify your answers to Written Exercises 31-40.

The ability to use and compute square roots is often a necessary tool in physics. For example, square roots are used to compute the minimum velocity a spacecraft must have to escape the gravitational force of a planet. The escape velocity, v, can be calculated using the following formula.

$$v = \sqrt{\frac{2GM}{r}}$$

In this formula, G is a gravitational constant, M is the mass of the planet, and r is the radius of the planet.

Example: Compute the escape velocity for earth if its mass is 5.98×10^{24} kg, its radius is 6.37×10^6 m, and $G = 6.67 \times 10^{-11}$ N-m²/kg². The abbreviation N represents newton, a unit of force in the metric system. Using these constants the answers will be in m/s.

$$1\ N = \frac{1\ kg \cdot m}{s^2}$$

$$v = \sqrt{\frac{2GM}{r}} \qquad M = 5.98 \times 10^{24}, r = 6.37 \times 10^6, G = 6.67 \times 10^{-11}$$

$$= \sqrt{\frac{2(6.67 \times 10^{-11})(5.98 \times 10^{24})}{6.37 \times 10^6}}$$

$$= \sqrt{\frac{7.97732 \times 10^{14}}{6.37 \times 10^6}}$$

$$= \sqrt{1.2523265 \times 10^8} \approx 1.12 \times 10^4$$

The escape velocity for earth is approximately 1.12×10^4 m/s.

Exercises

Compute the escape velocity for the indicated planet using the formula above. Use $G = 6.67 \times 10^{-11}$ N-m²/kg².

1. Mars: Mass 6.46×10^{23} kg; radius 3.39×10^6 m

2. Jupiter: Mass 1.90×10^{27} kg; radius 7.15×10^7 m

3. Mercury: Mass 3.35×10^{23} kg; radius 2.44×10^6 m

4. Neptune: Mass 1.03×10^{26} kg; radius 2.25×10^7 m

5. Venus: Mass 4.90×10^{24} kg; radius 6.06×10^6 m

6. Uranus: Mass 8.73×10^{25} kg; radius 2.35×10^7 m

12-7   Radical Equations

Equations containing radicals with variables in the radicand are called **radical equations**. To solve such equations, first isolate the radical on one side of the equation. Then square both sides of the equation to eliminate the radical.

Examples

1 **Solve and check:** $\sqrt{y} = 11$

$$\sqrt{y} = 11$$
$$(\sqrt{y})^2 = (11)^2 \qquad \textit{Square both sides to eliminate the radical.}$$
$$y = 121$$

Check: $\sqrt{y} = 11$
$$\sqrt{121} \overset{?}{=} 11$$
$$11 = 11$$

The solution is 121.

2 **Solve and check:** $\sqrt{3y - 5} - 4 = 0$

$$\sqrt{3y - 5} - 4 = 0$$
$$\sqrt{3y - 5} = 4 \qquad \textit{Isolate the radical by adding 4 to both sides.}$$
$$3y - 5 = 16 \qquad \textit{Square both sides.}$$
$$3y = 21$$
$$y = 7$$

Check: $\sqrt{3y - 5} - 4 = 0$
$$\sqrt{3 \cdot 7 - 5} - 4 \overset{?}{=} 0$$
$$\sqrt{16} - 4 \overset{?}{=} 0$$
$$4 - 4 \overset{?}{=} 0$$
$$0 = 0$$

The solution is 7.

Consider this equation.

$$x = 2 \qquad \textit{The solution is 2.}$$

Now square both sides.

$$x^2 = 4 \qquad \textit{The solutions are 2 and } -2.$$

Notice that squaring both sides of an equation does not necessarily produce results that satisfy the *original* equation. Therefore you must check *all* solutions when solving radical equations.

Example

3 Solve and check: $\sqrt{3x - 14} = 6 - x$

$\sqrt{3x - 14} = 6 - x$

$3x - 14 = (6 - x)^2$ *Square both sides.*

$3x - 14 = 36 - 12x + x^2$ *Recall that $(a - b)^2 = a^2 - 2ab + b^2$.*

$0 = x^2 - 15x + 50$

$0 = (x - 5)(x - 10)$ *Factor.*

$x - 5 = 0$ or $x - 10 = 0$ *Set each factor equal to 0.*

$x = 5$ or $x = 10$

Check: $\sqrt{3x - 14} = 6 - x$

$\sqrt{3 \cdot 5 - 14} \overset{?}{=} 6 - 5$ or $\sqrt{3 \cdot 10 - 14} \overset{?}{=} 6 - 10$

$\sqrt{15 - 14} \overset{?}{=} 1$ $\sqrt{30 - 14} \overset{?}{=} -4$

$\sqrt{1} \overset{?}{=} 1$ $\sqrt{16} \overset{?}{=} -4$

$1 = 1$ $4 \neq -4$

Notice that 10 satisfies $3x - 14 = (6 - x)^2$, but does not satisfy the *original* equation.

Therefore, 5 is the *only* solution of $\sqrt{3x - 14} = 6 - x$.

Exploratory Exercises

State the solution of each equation.

1. $\sqrt{y} = 3$ **2.** $\sqrt{a} = 4$ **3.** $\sqrt{m} = -2$ **4.** $\sqrt{s} = -5$

5. $-\sqrt{r} = -2$ **6.** $-\sqrt{z} = -3$ **7.** $-\sqrt{y} = 4$ **8.** $\sqrt{x - 3} = 6$

Written Exercises

Solve and check.

1. $\sqrt{r} = 5$ **2.** $\sqrt{s} = 9$ **3.** $\sqrt{3x} = 3$ **4.** $\sqrt{2m} = 4$

5. $\sqrt{3m} = -9$ **6.** $\sqrt{4a} = -1$ **7.** $\sqrt{b} - 5 = 0$ **8.** $\sqrt{s} + 3 = 0$

9. $\sqrt{2d} + 1 = 0$ **10.** $4 - \sqrt{3a} = 0$ **11.** $5 + \sqrt{2x} = 8$ **12.** $2 + \sqrt{m} = 13$

13. $\sqrt{4x + 1} = 3$ **14.** $\sqrt{2x + 7} = 5$ **15.** $\sqrt{8s + 1} - 5 = 0$ **16.** $\sqrt{3b - 5} = -4$

17. $\sqrt{\dfrac{x}{4}} = 6$ **18.** $\sqrt{\dfrac{x}{4}} = 10$ **19.** $\sqrt{\dfrac{4a}{3}} - 2 = 0$ **20.** $\sqrt{\dfrac{9s}{2}} - 6 = 0$

21. $\sqrt{\dfrac{5x}{4}} - 8 = 2$ **22.** $\sqrt{\dfrac{k}{7}} - 10 = -3$ **23.** $\sqrt{r} = 3\sqrt{5}$ **24.** $3\sqrt{7} = \sqrt{m}$

25. $5\sqrt{2n^2 - 28} = 20$ **26.** $4\sqrt{3m^2 - 15} = 4$ **27.** $\sqrt{2z^2 - 121} = z$ **28.** $\sqrt{5x^2 - 7} = 2x$

29. $\sqrt{x + 2} = x - 4$ **30.** $\sqrt{1 - 2x} = 1 + x$ **31.** $4 + \sqrt{x - 2} = x$ **32.** $\sqrt{x^2 + 3} = 2x$

33. The square root of the product of 4 and a number is 26. Find the number.

34. The square root of the product of 9 and a number is 27. Find the number.

12-8   The Pythagorean Theorem

On a baseball diamond the distance from one base to the next is 90 feet. How far from home plate is second base? To answer this question, notice that a baseball diamond can be divided into two right triangles.

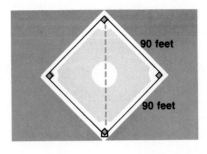

The side opposite the right angle in a right triangle is called the **hypotenuse**. This side is *always* the longest side of a right triangle. The other two sides are called the **legs** of the triangle.

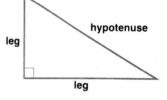

To find the length of the hypotenuse, given the lengths of the legs, you can use a formula proposed by the Greek mathematician Pythagoras.

> **In a right triangle if a and b are the measures of the legs, and c is the measure of the hypotenuse, then $c^2 = a^2 + b^2$.**

The Pythagorean Theorem

If c is the measure of the longest side of a triangle and $c^2 \neq a^2 + b^2$, then the triangle is not a right triangle.

For the baseball diamond, $a = 90$ and $b = 90$. Find the distance from home plate to second base, that is, the length of the hypotenuse.

$$c^2 = a^2 + b^2$$
$$c^2 = 90^2 + 90^2$$
$$c^2 = 8100 + 8100$$
$$c^2 = 2 \cdot 8100$$
$$c = \sqrt{8100 \cdot 2}$$
$$c = 90\sqrt{2} \approx 90(1.414) \qquad \sqrt{2} \approx 1.414$$
$$\approx 127$$

An approximation of $90\sqrt{2}$ is 127. So, the distance from home plate to second base is approximately 127 feet.

The Pythagorean Theorem can be illustrated geometrically as shown below.

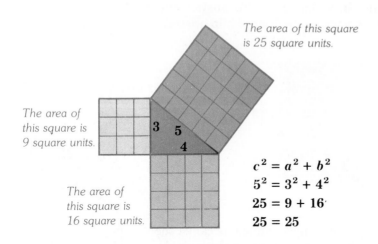

The area of this square is 25 square units.

The area of this square is 9 square units.

The area of this square is 16 square units.

$$c^2 = a^2 + b^2$$
$$5^2 = 3^2 + 4^2$$
$$25 = 9 + 16$$
$$25 = 25$$

The Pythagorean Theorem can be used to find the length of a side of a right triangle when the lengths of the other two sides are known.

Examples

1 **Find the length of the hypotenuse of a right triangle if $a = 15$ and $b = 8$.**

$$c^2 = 15^2 + 8^2$$
$$c^2 = 225 + 64$$
$$c^2 = 289$$
$$c = 17$$

The length of the hypotenuse is 17 units.

2 **Find the length of a leg of a right triangle if $a = 6$ and $c = 14$.**

$$c^2 = a^2 + b^2$$
$$14^2 = 6^2 + b^2$$
$$196 = 36 + b^2$$
$$160 = b^2$$
$$\sqrt{160} = b$$
$$b = 4\sqrt{10} \approx 4(3.162) \qquad \sqrt{10} \approx 3.162$$
$$\approx 12.648$$

The length of the leg is $4\sqrt{10}$ or approximately 12.648 units.

Example

3 The measures of three sides of a triangle are 5, 7, and 9. Determine whether this triangle is a right triangle.

Since the measure of the longest side is 9, let $c = 9$, $a = 5$, and $b = 7$. Then check to see if $c^2 = a^2 + b^2$.

$$c^2 = a^2 + b^2$$
$$9^2 \stackrel{?}{=} 5^2 + 7^2$$
$$81 \stackrel{?}{=} 25 + 49$$
$$81 \neq 74$$

The numbers do not satisfy the Pythagorean Theorem. Therefore, they are *not* the measures of the sides of a right triangle.

Exploratory Exercises

State the value of the variable in each sentence.

1. $3^2 + 4^2 = c^2$ **2.** $6^2 + 8^2 = c^2$ **3.** $5^2 + 12^2 = c^2$ **4.** $a^2 + 12^2 = 13^2$

5. $a^2 + 15^2 = 17^2$ **6.** $a^2 + 24^2 = 25^2$ **7.** $6^2 + b^2 = 10^2$ **8.** $3^2 + b^2 = 5^2$

State whether each sentence is true or false.

9. $3^2 + 4^2 = 5^2$ **10.** $9^2 + 10^2 = 11^2$ **11.** $6^2 + 8^2 = 9^2$ **12.** $5^2 + 12^2 = 13^2$

Written Exercises

In exercises 1-12 below, c is the measure of the hypotenuse of a right triangle. Find each missing measure. Use the table on page 544.

1. $a = 5$, $b = 12$, $c = ?$ **2.** $a = 6$, $b = 3$, $c = ?$ **3.** $a = 4$, $b = \sqrt{11}$, $c = ?$

4. $a = \sqrt{7}$, $b = 9$, $c = ?$ **5.** $b = 12$, $c = 15$, $a = ?$ **6.** $b = 10$, $c = 11$, $a = ?$

7. $b = 30$, $c = 34$, $a = ?$ **8.** $a = 11$, $c = 61$, $b = ?$ **9.** $a = 20$, $c = 29$, $b = ?$

10. $a = \sqrt{5}$, $c = \sqrt{30}$, $b = ?$ **11.** $a = \sqrt{7}$, $b = \sqrt{9}$, $c = ?$ **12.** $a = \sqrt{11}$, $c = \sqrt{47}$, $b = ?$

The measures of three sides of a triangle are given in each of the following. Determine whether each triangle is a right triangle.

13. 9, 16, 20   **14.** 9, 40, 41   **15.** 45, 60, 75   **16.** 11, 12, 16

For each problem, make a drawing. Then use an equation to solve the problem. Use the table on page 544.

17. Find the length of the diagonal of a rectangle whose length is 8 meters and whose width is 5 meters.

18. Justin hikes 7 miles due east and then 3 miles due north. How far is he from the starting point?

19. The diagonal of a rectangular wall measures 14 meters. One side of the wall is 10 meters long. What is the length of the other side?

20. A rope from the top of a mast on a sailboat is attached to a point 2 meters from the base of the mast. The rope is 8 meters long. How high is the mast?

12-9 The Distance Formula

The Pythagorean Theorem can be used to find the distance between any two points in the coordinate plane. For example, find the distance between $(-5, 2)$ and $(4, 5)$.

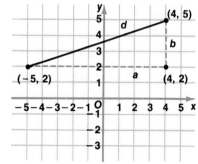

In the diagram at the right, the distance to be found is the length of segment d. Notice that a right triangle can be formed by drawing lines parallel to the axes from $(-5, 2)$ and $(4, 5)$. The coordinates of the point where these lines meet are $(4, 2)$.

The length of side a of the triangle is the difference of the x-coordinates, $4 - (-5)$, or 9 units. The length of side b of the triangle is the difference of the y-coordinates, $5 - 2$, or 3 units.

Now the Pythagorean Theorem can be used to find the length of d, that is, the distance between $(-5, 2)$ and $(4, 5)$.

$$d^2 = 9^2 + 3^2$$
$$d^2 = 81 + 9$$
$$d^2 = 90$$
$$d = \sqrt{90}$$
$$d = 3\sqrt{10}$$

The distance between $(-5, 2)$ and $(4, 5)$ is $3\sqrt{10}$ units. The method for finding the distance between any two points can be generalized as the following formula.

> **The distance between any two points with coordinates (x_1, y_1) and (x_2, y_2) is given by the following formula:**
>
> $$d = \sqrt{(x_2 - x_1)^2 + (y_2 - y_1)^2}$$

The Distance Formula

Example

1 **Find the distance between the points with coordinates $(8, -2)$ and $(5, 3)$.**

$$d = \sqrt{(x_2 - x_1)^2 + (y_2 - y_1)^2} \quad \text{Let } x_2 = 5, \ x_1 = 8, \ y_2 = 3, \text{ and } y_1 = -2.$$
$$d = \sqrt{(5 - 8)^2 + [3 - (-2)]^2}$$
$$d = \sqrt{(-3)^2 + 5^2}$$
$$d = \sqrt{9 + 25}$$
$$d = \sqrt{34} \quad \text{This is approximately 5.831 units.}$$

Example

2 Find y if the distance between the points with coordinates $(5, y)$ and $(7, -3)$ is $\sqrt{85}$ units.

$$d = \sqrt{(x_2 - x_1)^2 + (y_2 - y_1)^2} \qquad \text{Let } x_2 = 7,\ x_1 = 5,\ y_2 = -3,\ \text{and } y_1 = y.$$

$$\sqrt{85} = \sqrt{(7 - 5)^2 + (-3 - y)^2}$$

$$\sqrt{85} = \sqrt{2^2 + (-3 - y)^2}$$

$$\sqrt{85} = \sqrt{4 + 9 + 6y + y^2}$$

$$\sqrt{85} = \sqrt{13 + 6y + y^2}$$

$$85 = 13 + 6y + y^2 \qquad \text{Square both sides.}$$

$$0 = y^2 + 6y - 72$$

$$0 = (y + 12)(y - 6) \qquad \text{Factor.}$$

$$y + 12 = 0 \quad \text{or} \quad y - 6 = 0$$

$$y = -12 \qquad\qquad y = 6$$

The value of y is -12 or 6. *These answers can be checked by substituting -12 and 6 for y in the equation $\sqrt{85} = \sqrt{(7 - 5)^2 + (-3 - y)^2}$.*

Exploratory Exercises

State the values of x_1, x_2, y_1, and y_2 for each pair of points.

1. $(3, 4)$, $(6, 8)$
2. $(5, -1)$, $(11, 7)$
3. $(-4, 2)$, $(4, 17)$
4. $(-2, 8)$, $(3, 20)$
5. $(-3, 5)$, $(2, 7)$
6. $(5, 4)$, $(-3, 8)$
7. $(-8, -4)$, $(-3, 8)$
8. $(2, 7)$, $(10, -4)$
9. $(3, 7)$, $(-2, -5)$
10. $(3, 2)$, $(0, 5)$
11. $(2, 2)$, $(5, -1)$
12. $(-8, -7)$, $(0, 8)$

Written Exercises

Find the distance between each pair of points whose coordinates are given.

1. $(-4, 2)$, $(4, 17)$
2. $(5, -1)$, $(11, 7)$
3. $(-3, 5)$, $(2, 7)$
4. $(5, 4)$, $(-3, 8)$
5. $(-8, -4)$, $(-3, 8)$
6. $(2, 7)$, $(10, -4)$
7. $(7, -9)$, $(4, -3)$
8. $(9, -2)$, $(3, -6)$
9. $(10, 8)$, $(2, -3)$
10. $(11, -2)$, $(-4, 5)$
11. $(-2, 5)$, $\left(-\frac{1}{2}, 3\right)$
12. $(4, 2)$, $\left(6, -\frac{2}{3}\right)$
13. $\left(\frac{2}{3}, -4\right)$, $(3, -2)$
14. $\left(6, -\frac{2}{7}\right)$, $(5, -1)$
15. $\left(\frac{4}{5}, -1\right)$, $\left(2, -\frac{1}{2}\right)$

The coordinates of a pair of points are given in each of the following. Find two possible values for a if the points are the given distance apart.

16. $(4, 7)$, $(a, 3)$; $d = 5$
17. $(3, a)$, $(-4, 2)$; $d = \sqrt{170}$
18. $(8, 1)$, $(5, a)$; $d = 5$
19. $(-3, a)$, $(5, 2)$; $d = 17$
20. $(a, 5)$, $(-7, 3)$; $d = \sqrt{29}$
21. $(5, 9)$, $(a, -3)$; $d = 13$
22. $(a, -4)$, $(2, -3)$; $d = \sqrt{65}$
23. $(-6, -5)$, $(-3, a)$; $d = \sqrt{13}$
24. $(4, -7)$, $(7, a)$; $d = \sqrt{34}$
25. $(-5, a)$, $(4, -2)$; $d = \sqrt{130}$

Use the distance formula to solve each of the following.

26. Show that the points with the coordinates $(0, 0)$, $(7, 0)$, $(7, 4)$, and $(0, 4)$ are the vertices of a rectangle.

27. Show that the point with coordinates $(2, 6)$ is the midpoint of the segment joining the points with coordinates $(-1, 2)$ and $(5, 10)$.

28. Find the distance between $A(\sqrt{8}, \sqrt{3})$ and $B(\sqrt{3}, -\sqrt{8})$.

Write *true* or *false*.

1. The equation $2y = -x + 1$ is in slope-intercept form.

2. The relation $4x + y = 2$ is a function.

3. The ordered pair $(4, -6)$ is a solution to the equation $3y - 2 = x$.

4. The slope of the line with the equation $2y + x = 4$ is $-\frac{1}{2}$.

5. Parallel lines have the same slope.

Excursions in Algebra _____ Equations of Circles

A circle is the set of all points in the coordinate plane that are the same distance from a given point, called the *center*. All points of the circle shown at the right are 4 units from the point with coordinates $(0, 0)$, the center. Choose any point of the circle. The distance from a point (x, y) to the center is 4 units. Now apply the distance formula.

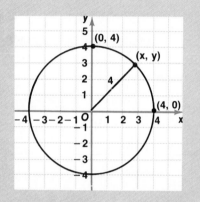

$$d = \sqrt{(x_2 - x_1)^2 + (y_2 - y_1)^2}$$
$$4 = \sqrt{(x - 0)^2 + (y - 0)^2}$$
$$4 = \sqrt{x^2 + y^2}$$
$$16 = x^2 + y^2 \quad \text{\textit{Square both sides.}}$$

Thus, $16 = x^2 + y^2$ is the equation for a circle with center at $(0, 0)$ and radius of 4 units.

> The equation of a circle with center at $(0, 0)$ and a radius of r units is $x^2 + y^2 = r^2$.

Equation of a Circle

Example: Find the equation of a circle with center at $(0, 0)$ and a radius of 7 units.

$$x^2 + y^2 = r^2$$
$$x^2 + y^2 = 7^2 \quad \text{\textit{Substitute 7 for r.}}$$
$$x^2 + y^2 = 49$$

Exercises State the radius of each circle whose equation is given below.

1. $x^2 + y^2 = 100$ 2. $x^2 + y^2 = 81$ 3. $x^2 + y^2 = 8$

4. $x^2 + y^2 = 10$ 5. $x^2 + y^2 = \frac{1}{4}$ 6. $x^2 + y^2 = \frac{4}{9}$

7. $x^2 + y^2 = 256$ 8. $x^2 + y^2 = 576$ 9. $x^2 + y^2 = 0.09$

10. $x^2 + y^2 = 0.16$ 11. $x^2 + y^2 = \frac{100}{121}$ 12. $x^2 + y^2 = \frac{196}{625}$

Computing Square Roots

Recall that one method for computing a square root, called the divide-and-average method, involves first choosing any approximation for the square root and then calculating more accurate approximations.

Another method for computing $\sqrt{N}$ is to substitute any approximation, A, into the expression $\dfrac{A^2 + N}{2A}$. Then repeat this process until successive values of A are close together. This method is demonstrated in the following computer program.

```
10    PRINT "FOR WHAT NUMBER DO YOU WANT
      TO FIND THE SQUARE ROOT?"
20    INPUT N
30    PRINT "CHOOSE ANY APPROXIMATION FOR THE SQUARE ROOT"
40    INPUT A
50    LET L = A
60    PRINT A
70    LET A = (A ↑ 2 + N) / (2 * A)
80    IF ABS (A - L) > .000001 THEN 50     The ABS function finds the absolute value.
90    PRINT "AN APPROXIMATION OF THE SQUARE ROOT OF ";
      N;" IS ";A
100 END
```

Notice that the variable L is used to store the old value of A. Then, in line 60, the next value of A is computed. Finally, in line 70, the values of A and L are compared. If the values are close together (in this case, if their difference is less than .000001), then the program ends. If the difference is not less than .000001, the loop is executed again to obtain a closer approximation.

Exercises

Use the program above to approximate each of the following square roots.

1. $\sqrt{10}$ 2. $\sqrt{19}$ 3. $\sqrt{23}$ 4. $\sqrt{92}$ 5. $\sqrt{198}$

6. $\sqrt{147}$ 7. $\sqrt{323}$ 8. $\sqrt{582}$ 9. $\sqrt{1901}$ 10. $\sqrt{5460}$

11. In the BASIC language, SQR(A) can be used to find an approximation of the square root of A. Write an additional line for the program above to compute and print an approximation using the SQR function. Run the program to compare the two approximations for exercises 1-10.

Vocabulary

Chapter Summary

1. **Definition of Square Root:** If $x^2 = y$ then x is a square root of y. (371)

2. The symbol $\sqrt{}$, called a radical sign, indicates a nonnegative square root. The expression under the radical sign is called the radicand. (371)

3. **Product Property of Square Roots:** For any numbers a and b, if $a \geq 0$ and $b \geq 0$, then $\sqrt{ab} = \sqrt{a} \cdot \sqrt{b}$. (372)

4. **Quotient Property of Square Roots:** For any numbers a and b, if $a \geq 0$ and $b > 0$, then $\sqrt{\dfrac{a}{b}} = \dfrac{\sqrt{a}}{\sqrt{b}}$. (372)

5. The square roots of numbers such as 2, 3, 5, and 7 are irrational numbers. Irrational numbers are numbers that cannot be expressed in the form $\dfrac{a}{b}$, where a and b are integers, $b \neq 0$. (374)

6. Irrational numbers together with the rational numbers form the set of real numbers. Each real number corresponds to exactly one point on the number line. Each point on the number line corresponds to exactly one real number. (375)

7. One method for approximating square roots is the divide-and-average method. (377)

8. Rationalizing the denominator changes the denominator to a rational number. (382)

9. Binomials of the form $a\sqrt{b} + c\sqrt{d}$ and $a\sqrt{b} - c\sqrt{d}$ are called conjugates of each other. They can be used to rationalize some denominators. (383)

10. A radical expression is in simplest form when the following conditions are met.

    1. No radicands have perfect square factors other than 1.
    2. No radicands contain fractions.
    3. No radical appears in the denominator of a fraction. (383)

11. Square roots having like radicands can be added or subtracted. (385)

12. To solve radical equations, first isolate the radical on one side of the equation. Then square both sides of the equation to eliminate the radical. (389)

13. The Pythagorean Theorem: In a right triangle if a and b are the measures of the legs and c is the measure of the hypotenuse, then $a^2 + b^2 = c^2$. (391)

14. The Distance Formula: The distance between any two points with coordinates (x_1, y_1) and (x_2, y_2) is given by the following formula.

$$d = \sqrt{(x_2 - x_1)^2 + (y_2 - y_1)^2} \quad (394).$$

Chapter Review

12-1   **Simplify.**

    1. $\sqrt{121}$ **2.** $-\sqrt{64}$ **3.** $\pm\sqrt{\dfrac{4}{81}}$ **4.** $-\sqrt{\dfrac{100}{225}}$

12-2   **Graph each number on the number line.**

    5. $-\sqrt{5}$ **6.** $\sqrt{15}$

    State whether each decimal represents a rational number or an irrational number.

    7. $0.4\overline{6}$ **8.** $4.2302300230002\ldots$

    Use a table to determine the integers between which the value of the square root lies.

    9. $\sqrt{250}$ **10.** $\sqrt{490}$

12-3   **Approximate each square root. Use the divide-and-average method twice for each exercise.**

    11. $\sqrt{19}$ **12.** $\sqrt{77}$ **13.** $\sqrt{61.7}$

12-4 **Simplify. Use absolute value symbols when necessary.**

14. $\sqrt{18}$ **15.** $\sqrt{108}$ **16.** $\sqrt{720}$ **17.** $\sqrt{2916}$

18. $\sqrt{4b^2}$ **19.** $\sqrt{\dfrac{60}{x^2}}$ **20.** $\sqrt{44a^2b}$ **21.** $\sqrt{6} \cdot \sqrt{8}$

22. $5\sqrt{3} \cdot \sqrt{3}$ **23.** $\sqrt{3}(\sqrt{3} + \sqrt{6})$ **24.** $\sqrt{5}(\sqrt{10} - \sqrt{3})$

12-5 **Simplify.**

25. $\dfrac{\sqrt{35}}{\sqrt{5}}$ **26.** $\dfrac{\sqrt{20}}{\sqrt{7}}$ **27.** $\dfrac{7}{2 - \sqrt{3}}$

28. $\dfrac{9}{3 + \sqrt{2}}$ **29.** $\dfrac{5\sqrt{2}}{7\sqrt{3} + 6\sqrt{5}}$ **30.** $\dfrac{3\sqrt{7}}{4\sqrt{6} - 7\sqrt{7}}$

12-6 **Simplify.**

31. $2\sqrt{13} + 3\sqrt{13}$ **32.** $8\sqrt{15} - 3\sqrt{15}$ **33.** $3\sqrt{7} - 5\sqrt{28}$

34. $4\sqrt{27} + 6\sqrt{48}$ **35.** $\sqrt{8} + \sqrt{\dfrac{1}{8}}$ **36.** $\sqrt{3} - \sqrt{\dfrac{1}{3}}$

12-7 **Solve and check.**

37. $\sqrt{3x} = 6$ **38.** $\sqrt{3x + 5} = 4$ **39.** $\sqrt{7x - 1} - 5 = 0$

40. $\sqrt{w} = 5\sqrt{6}$ **41.** $\sqrt{x + 4} = x - 8$ **42.** $\sqrt{\dfrac{4a}{3}} - 2 = 0$

12-8 **Use the Pythagorean Theorem to find each missing measure.**

43. $a = 6$, $b = 10$, $c = ?$
44. $a = 10$, $c = 15$, $b = ?$
45. $b = 6$, $c = 12$, $a = ?$

46. Find the length of the diagonal of a rectangle whose length is 15 meters and whose width is 8 meters.

12-9 **Find the distance between each pair of points whose coordinates are given.**

47. $(4, 2)$, $(7, -9)$ **48.** $(5, -2)$, $(-8, -3)$

Simplify.

1. $\sqrt{3} \cdot \sqrt{15}$

2. $\sqrt{40}$

3. $\dfrac{5}{\sqrt{2} + \sqrt{3}}$

4. $\sqrt{\dfrac{a^2}{7}}$

5. $\sqrt{54x^4 y}$

6. $(4 + \sqrt{3})(4 - \sqrt{3})$

7. $\dfrac{7}{7 + \sqrt{5}}$

8. $2\sqrt{27} + \sqrt{48} - 3\sqrt{3}$

9. $3\sqrt{50} - 2\sqrt{8}$

10. $\sqrt{\dfrac{3x^2}{4n^3}}$

11. $\sqrt{3xy^3}$

12. $15\sqrt{6} - \sqrt{72}$

13. $\sqrt{\dfrac{32}{9}}$

14. $\sqrt{\dfrac{64x^4}{8x^2}}$

15. $\dfrac{6\sqrt{5}}{2\sqrt{2} + 5\sqrt{3}}$

16. $\sqrt{2}(\sqrt{2} + 4\sqrt{3})$

17. $\sqrt{6} + \sqrt{\dfrac{2}{3}}$

18. $\sqrt{96} \cdot \sqrt{48}$

Solve and check.

19. $\sqrt{t} + 5 = 3$

20. $\sqrt{5x^2 - 9} = 2x$

21. $\sqrt{4x + 1} = 5$

22. $\sqrt{4x - 3} = 6 - x$

Use the Pythagorean Theorem to find the missing measures.

23. Find c if $a = 8$ and $b = 10$.

24. Find b if $a = 2$ and $c = 8$.

25. Find a if $a = b$ and $c = 12$.

Find the distance between each pair of points whose coordinates are given.

26. $(4, 3), (6, -3)$

27. $(-8, 2), (4, -3)$

1. Evaluate $a^2 - 3c - y$ if $a = 3$, $c = \frac{2}{3}$, and $y = -\frac{4}{3}$.

2. Find the sum: $-9.8 + 4.3 + 3.7$

Solve.

3. $b - (-11) = -11$

4. $\frac{3}{4}a - 2 = 7$

5. $0.2(x + 3) = 0.3(x - 0.4)$

6. $7p > -63$

7. $5 - 3k \le k$

Simplify.

8. $(3a^2)(4a^3)(2a)$ 9. $\dfrac{5a^{-2}b}{6a^2b^{-4}}$

10. $(y + 3)(2y - 1)$

Factor, if possible.

11. $y^2 + 2y - 63$

12. $18x^2 + 45xy + 18y^2$

13. Solve: $6x^2 - 17x + 12 = 0$

14. Write the following relation as a set of ordered pairs. Then state the domain and range.

15. Is the relation in Exercise 14 a function?

16. Graph: $y > x + 1$

17. Write an equation in standard form for the line through $(2, -1)$ and $(4, 1)$.

18. Write an equation in slope-intercept form for the line having a slope of $\frac{2}{3}$ and passing through $(5, 1)$.

19. Write an equation for the line that is parallel to the graph of $x + 2y = -1$ and passes through $(1, 4)$. Use slope-intercept form.

20. If the midpoint of line segment AB is $(7, 2)$, find the coordinates of point A if the coordinates of point B are $(2, -5)$.

21. Graph the pair of equations $x + y = 1$ and $-2x + y = 4$. Then state the solution of the system.

22. Use substitution to solve the system of equations $2x - 3y = 5$ and $x - y = 2$.

23. Use elimination to solve the system of equations $x - 2y = 3$ and $2x - 3y = 4$.

Simplify.

24. $\pm\sqrt{196}$

25. $\sqrt{64x^2y^4}$

26. $\dfrac{1}{2 - \sqrt{2}}$

27. $3\sqrt{8} - 4\sqrt{2} + \sqrt{12}$

Solve.

28. $\sqrt{3x - 5} = 5$

Problem Solving

Solve each problem.

29. Find the customer price on a video game tape if there is a 15% discount on the marked price of $27.95.

30. Two cyclists start toward each other from two towns that are 112 miles apart. One cyclist rides at 16 mph and the other at 12 mph. In how many hours will they meet?

31. The square of a number added to 4 times the number equals 45. Find the number.

32. A two-digit number is 5 times the sum of its digits. The units digit is one more than the tens digit. Find the number.

33. An airplane travels 620 miles in 2 hours flying with the wind. Flying against the wind, it takes 4 hours to travel 1160 miles. Find the rate of the wind and the rate of the plane in still air.

The test questions on this page deal with coordinates and geometry. The information at the right may help you with some of the questions.

Directions: Choose the best answer. Write A, B, C, or D.

1. The midpoint of $\overline{AB}$ is M. If the coordinates of A are $(-3, 2)$ and the coordinates of M are $(-1, 5)$, what are the coordinates of B?

   (**A**) $(1, 10)$ (**B**) $(1, 8)$
   (**C**) $(0, 7)$ (**D**) $(-5, 8)$

2.

   S   T

   $-2 \quad -1 \quad 0 \quad 1 \quad 2 \quad 3 \quad 4$

   The length of $\overline{ST}$ is

   (**A**) 5   (**B**) $4\frac{1}{2}$ (**C**) $5\frac{1}{2}$ (**D**) 6

3. What is the area of the shaded triangle in square units?

   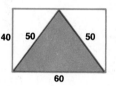

   (**A**) 1600 (**B**) 1200 (**C**) 1500 (**D**) 2400

4. Seven squares of the same size form a rectangle when placed side-by-side. The perimeter of the rectangle is 496. What is the area of each square?

   (**A**) 72 ft^2 (**B**) 324 ft^2
   (**C**) 900 ft^2 (**D**) 961 ft^2

5. What is the total length of fencing needed to enclose a rectangular area 46 feet by 34 feet?

   (**A**) 26 yards 1 foot   (**B**) $26\frac{2}{3}$ yards

   (**C**) 52 yards 2 feet   (**D**) $53\frac{1}{3}$ yards

---

1. The diameter of a circle is twice the length of the radius.

2. The area of a circle with radius r is πr^2.

3. The area of a triangle is the product of $\frac{1}{2}$ the base and the height.

---

6. The number of degrees in the smaller angle formed by the hands of a clock at 12:15 is

   (**A**) 120   (**B**) $82\frac{1}{2}$ (**C**) $92\frac{1}{2}$ (**D**) 90

7. The length of each side of a square is $\frac{3x}{5} + 1$. The perimeter of the square is

   (**A**) $\dfrac{12x + 20}{5}$ (**B**) $\dfrac{12x + 4}{5}$

   (**C**) $\dfrac{3x + 4}{5}$ (**D**) $\dfrac{3x}{5} + 16$

8. If a line passes through point $(0, 2)$ and has a slope of 4, what is the equation of the line?

   (**A**) $x = 2y + 4$ (**B**) $x = 4y + 2$
   (**C**) $y = 4x + 2$ (**D**) $y = 2x + 4$

9. The larger circle has a diameter of b. The area of the shaded ring in square units is

   (**A**) $b^2 - c^2$ (**B**) $\pi b^2 - \pi c^2$

   (**C**) $\frac{1}{4}\pi (b^2 - c^2)$ (**D**) $\frac{1}{2}\pi (b^2 - c^2)$

10. If a circle of radius 10 meters has its radius decreased by 2 meters, by what percent is its area decreased?

    (**A**) 20% (**B**) 40% (**C**) 80% (**D**) 36%

11. What is the value of x if the area of the triangle is $\frac{1}{4}$ the area of the square?

    (**A**) $\sqrt{2}$ (**B**) $2\sqrt{2}$ (**C**) 4   (**D**) 8

CHAPTER 13

Quadratics

Mars Station is the site of a tracking antenna for spacecraft. It is capable of tracking spacecraft to the edge of the solar system.

The reflector of this antenna is 64 meters in diameter, and has a shape whose cross section may be described by a quadratic equation. In this chapter, you will learn about quadratic equations and quadratic functions.

13-1 Graphing Quadratic Functions

An equation such as $y = x^2 - 4x + 1$ describes a type of function known as a **quadratic function**.

> **A quadratic function is a function that can be described by an equation of the form $y = ax^2 + bx + c$, where $a \neq 0$.**

Definition of Quadratic Function

Graphs of quadratic functions have certain common characteristics. For instance, they all have a general shape called a **parabola**.

The table and graph below illustrate some other common characteristics of quadratic functions.

x	$x^2 - 4x + 1$	y
-1	$(-1)^2 - 4(-1) + 1$	6
0	$0^2 - 4(0) + 1$	1
1	$1^2 - 4(1) + 1$	-2
2	$2^2 - 4(2) + 1$	-3
3	$3^2 - 4(3) + 1$	-2
4	$4^2 - 4(4) + 1$	1
5	$5^2 - 4(5) + 1$	6

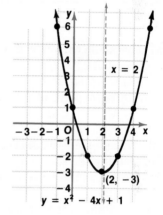

$x = 2$

$(2, -3)$

$y = x^2 - 4x + 1$

Notice the matching values in the y-column.

Notice that -3 does *not* have a matching value in the y-column of the table. Also, -3 is the y-coordinate of the lowest point on the graph of $y = x^2 - 4x + 1$. For the graph of $y = x^2 - 4x + 1$, the *lowest point*, called the **minimum point**, has coordinates $(2, -3)$.

The vertical line containing the minimum point is the **axis of symmetry**. The equation of the axis of symmetry for the graph above is $x = 2$.

If the graph of any quadratic function is folded along the axis of symmetry, the two halves coincide. In other words, the two halves of the parabola are *symmetric*.

Example

1 Graph: $y = -x^2 + 2x + 3$

x	$-x^2 + 2x + 3$	y
-2	$-(-2)^2 + 2(-2) + 3$	-5
-1	$-(-1)^2 + 2(-1) + 3$	0
0	$-0^2 + 2(0) + 3$	3
1	$-(1)^2 + 2(1) + 3$	4
2	$-(2)^2 + 2(2) + 3$	3
3	$-(3)^2 + 2(3) + 3$	0
4	$-(4)^2 + 2(4) + 3$	-5

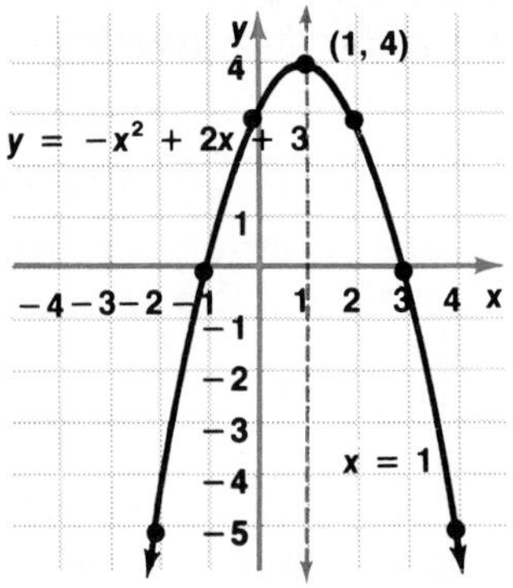

The graph of $y = -x^2 + 2x + 3$ opens *downward*. The equation of the axis of symmetry is $x = 1$. The graph has a *highest point,* or **maximum point**, at $(1, 4)$.

In general, a parabola will open upward and have a minimum point when the coefficient of x^2 is positive. It will open downward and have a maximum point when the coefficient of x^2 is negative. The maximum or minimum point of the graph *always* lies on the axis of symmetry.

Notice that in Example 1 the axis of symmetry is halfway between any two points having the same y-coordinate. Consider the points on the graph whose coordinates are $(-1, 0)$ and $(3, 0)$.

From these coordinates, the equation of the axis of symmetry may be found as shown below.

$$x = \frac{-1 + 3}{2} \quad \text{\textit{Add the x-coordinates and divide by 2.}}$$
$$= 1$$

The equation of the axis of symmetry is $x = 1$.

In general, the equation of the axis of symmetry for the graph of a quadratic function can be found by using the following rule.

> **The equation of the axis of symmetry for $y = ax^2 + bx + c$, where $a \neq 0$, is**
> $$x = -\frac{b}{2a}.$$

Equation of Axis of Symmetry

Example

2

Find the equation of the axis of symmetry and the coordinates of the minimum point for the graph of $y = x^2 - x - 6$. Then use the information to draw the graph.

First, find the equation of the axis of symmetry.

$$x = -\frac{b}{2a}$$
$$= -\frac{-1}{2 \cdot 1} \qquad a = 1,\ b = -1$$
$$= \frac{1}{2}$$

The equation of the axis of symmetry is $x = \frac{1}{2}$.

Next, find the coordinates of the minimum point. The minimum point lies on the axis of symmetry. Here the x-coordinate of the minimum point will be $\frac{1}{2}$. Find the y-coordinate by substituting $\frac{1}{2}$ for x in $y = x^2 - x - 6$.

$$y = x^2 - x - 6$$
$$= \left(\tfrac{1}{2}\right)^2 - \tfrac{1}{2} - 6$$
$$= \tfrac{1}{4} - \tfrac{1}{2} - 6$$
$$= -\tfrac{25}{4}$$

The coordinates of the minimum point are $\left(\frac{1}{2},\ -\frac{25}{4}\right)$.

Then, construct a table. For the values of x, choose some integers greater than $\frac{1}{2}$, and some less than $\frac{1}{2}$. This insures that points on both sides of the axis of symmetry are plotted. Use this information to draw the graph.

x	$x^2 - x - 6$	y
-2	$(-2)^2 - (-2) - 6$	0
-1	$(-1)^2 - (-1) - 6$	-4
0	$0^2 - 0 - 6$	-6
1	$1^2 - 1 - 6$	-6
2	$2^2 - 2 - 6$	-4
3	$3^2 - 3 - 6$	0

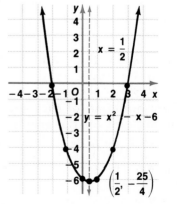

Example

3 Find the coordinates of the maximum point for the graph of $y = -2x^2 - 8x + 9$.

$x = -\dfrac{b}{2a}$ First, find the equation of the axis of symmetry.

$ = -\dfrac{-8}{2(-2)}$ $a = -2,\ b = -8$

$ = -2$ The equation of the axis of symmetry is $x = -2$.

$y = -2(-2)^2 - 8(-2) + 9$ *Since the maximum point lies on*

$ = -8 + 16 + 9$ *the axis of symmetry, substitute*

$ = 17$ *-2 for x in $y = -2x^2 - 8x + 9$.*

The coordinates of the maximum point are $(-2, 17)$.

Exploratory Exercises

State whether the graph of each quadratic function opens upward or downward.

1. $y = x^2 - 1$
    2. $y = -x^2 + 3x$
    3. $y = -x^2 + x + 1$

4. $y = x^2 + x + 3$
    5. $y = -x^2 + 4x + 5$
    6. $y = 2x^2 - 5x + 2$

7. $y = 3x^2 + 9x - 1$
    8. $y = 2x^2 - 8x + 1$
    9. $y = -5x^2 + 3x + 2$

Find the equation of the axis of symmetry for the graph of each quadratic function.

10. $y = x^2 + x + 3$
    11. $y = -x^2 + 4x + 5$
    12. $y = -x^2 + 3x$

13. $y = x^2 + 6x + 8$
    14. $y = 3x^2 + 6x + 16$
    15. $y = 5x^2 + 20x + 37$

16. $y = 8x + 3 + x^2$
    17. $y = \frac{3}{2} + 7x + 5x^2$
    18. $y = -4x^2 + 4x + \frac{5}{2}$

Written Exercises

Find the equation of the axis of symmetry and the coordinates of the maximum or minimum point for the graph of each quadratic function.

1. $y = -x^2 + 5x + 6$
    2. $y = -x^2 + 5x - 14$
    3. $y = x^2 - 4x + 13$

4. $y = x^2 + 2x$
    5. $y = -5x^2 + 15x + 23$
    6. $y = -3x^2 + 4$

7. $y = 3x^2 + 6x - 17$
    8. $y = 3x^2 + 24x + 80$
    9. $y = -2x^2 - 9$

10. $y = -3x^2 - 6x + 5$
    11. $y = 5x^2 + 10x + 6$
    12. $y = 7x^2 + 14x - 9$

13. $y = -7x^2 + 14x + 15$
    14. $y = -4x^2 + 8x + 13$
    15. $y = 3x^2 + 4$

16. $y = 2x^2 + 12x - 17$
    17. $y = -5x^2 + 10x + 37$
    18. $y = 2x^2 - 6x + 19$

Find the equation of the axis of symmetry and the coordinates of the maximum or minimum point for the graph of each quadratic function. Then draw the graph.

19. $y = x^2 - 4x - 5$
    20. $y = -x^2 + 4x + 5$
    21. $y = -x^2 + 6x + 5$

22. $y = x^2 - x - 6$
    23. $y = x^2 - 3$
    24. $y = -x^2 + 7$

25. $y = 2x^2 + 3$
    26. $y = x^2 - 2x - 8$
    27. $y = x^2 - x - 12$

28. $y = \frac{1}{4}x^2 - 4x + 3\frac{3}{4}$
    29. $y = \frac{1}{2}x^2 + 3x + \frac{9}{2}$
    30. $y = -3x^2 - 6x + 4$

Applications in Business

Many times businesses will raise the prices of their goods or services to increase their profit. However, when they raise their prices, they usually lose some customers. In such situations, the price at which the profit would be a maximum needs to be found.

Example

An auditorium has seats for 1,200 people. For the past several days, the auditorium has been filled to capacity for each show. Tickets currently cost $5.00 and the owner wants to increase the ticket prices. He estimates that for each $0.50 increase in price, 100 fewer people will attend. What ticket price will maximize the profit?

Let x = number of $0.50 price increases. Thus $5.00 + 0.50x$ represents the single ticket price and $1200 - 100x$ represents the number of tickets sold.

$$
\begin{aligned}
\text{Income} &= \text{number of tickets sold} \cdot \text{ticket price} \\
&= (1200 - 100x) \cdot (5.00 + 0.50x) \\
&= 6000 + 100x - 50x^2
\end{aligned}
$$

Notice that the result is a quadratic equation. The graph of the related function, $y = -50x^2 + 100x + 6000$, opens downward and thus has a maximum point. Since this is a maximum point, the x-coordinate gives the number of price increases needed to maximize the profit.

Recall that the x-coordinate of the maximum point is given by the equation of the axis of symmetry.

$$x = -\frac{b}{2a}$$

$$= -\frac{100}{2(-50)} \qquad a = -50, b = 100$$

$$= 1$$

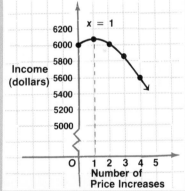

The equation of the axis of symmetry is $x = 1$.

Thus, the profit is maximized when the owner makes one $0.50 price increase. So, the price of one ticket should be $5.50.

Exercises Solve each problem.

1. A grocer sells 50 loaves of bread a day. The cost is $0.65 a loaf. The grocer estimates that for each $0.05 price increase, 2 fewer loaves of bread will be sold. What cost will maximize the profit?

2. A bus company transports 500 people a day between Morse Rd. and High St. A one-way fare is $0.50. The owners estimate that for each $0.10 price increase 50 passengers will be lost. What price will maximize their profit?

13-2 Solving Quadratic Equations by Graphing

Recall that many quadratic equations can be solved by factoring.
For example, solve $x^2 + x - 6 = 0$.

$$x^2 + x - 6 = 0 \qquad \textit{Find the factors of } x^2 + x - 6.$$
$$(x + 3)(x - 2) = 0$$
$$x + 3 = 0 \quad \text{or} \quad x - 2 = 0 \qquad \textit{Zero Product Property}$$
$$x = -3 \qquad\qquad x = 2$$

The solutions of an equation are called the **roots** of the equation.
The roots of $x^2 + x - 6 = 0$ are -3 and 2. Notice that the roots of
$x^2 + x - 6 = 0$ are the x-intercepts of the graph of the related
function, $y = x^2 + x - 6$.

x	$x^2 + x - 6$	y
-3	$(-3)^2 + (-3) - 6$	0
-2	$(-2)^2 + (-2) - 6$	-4
-1	$(-1)^2 + (-1) - 6$	-6
0	$0^2 + 0 - 6$	-6
1	$1^2 + 1 - 6$	-4
2	$2^2 + 2 - 6$	0

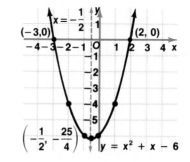

In general, the roots of any quadratic equation of the form
$ax^2 + bx + c = 0$ are the x-intercepts of the graph of the related
function $y = ax^2 + bx + c$.

Many times, only approximations of roots can be found by
graphing. In the following example, the consecutive integers
between which the roots lie are found.

Examples

1 **Locate the roots of $x^2 - 6x + 6 = 0$ by graphing the related function.**

The graph of the related function, $y = x^2 - 6x + 6$, is a parabola that opens upward.

axis of symmetry

$$x = -\frac{b}{2a}$$

$$= -\frac{-6}{2 \cdot 1} \text{ or } 3$$

minimum point

Substitute 3 for x in $y = x^2 - 6x + 6$.

$$y = 3^2 - 6(3) + 6$$

$$= -3$$

The equation of the axis of symmetry is $x = 3$ and the coordinates of the minimum point
are $(3, -3)$.

x	$x^2 - 6x + 6$	y
1	$1^2 - 6(1) + 6$	1
2	$2^2 - 6(2) + 6$	-2
3	$3^2 - 6(3) + 6$	-3
4	$4^2 - 6(4) + 6$	-2
5	$5^2 - 6(5) + 6$	1

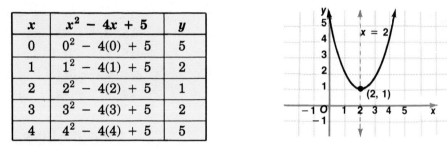

From the graph it can be seen that one root lies between 1 and 2. The other root is between 4 and 5.

2 **Locate the roots of $x^2 - 4x + 5 = 0$ by graphing the related function.**

The graph of the related function $y = x^2 - 4x + 5$ opens upward and has as its axis of symmetry $x = 2$. The coordinates of its minimum point are $(2, 1)$.

x	$x^2 - 4x + 5$	y
0	$0^2 - 4(0) + 5$	5
1	$1^2 - 4(1) + 5$	2
2	$2^2 - 4(2) + 5$	1
3	$3^2 - 4(3) + 5$	2
4	$4^2 - 4(4) + 5$	5

The graph has no x-intercepts since it does not cross the x-axis. Therefore, the equation $x^2 - 4x + 5 = 0$ has no real roots.

Exploratory Exercises

State the roots of each quadratic equation whose related function is graphed below.

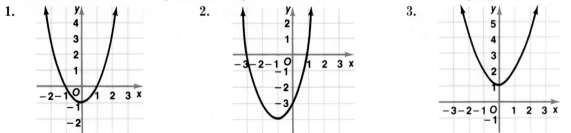

1.

2.

3.

State the roots of each quadratic equation whose related function is graphed below.

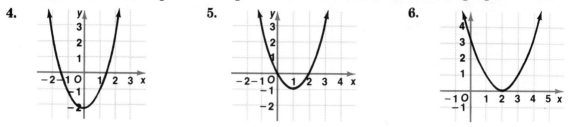

4.

5.

6.

Written Exercises

Locate the roots of each equation by graphing the related function.

1. $x^2 - x - 12 = 0$
2. $x^2 + 7x + 12 = 0$
3. $x^2 - 5x - 6 = 0$
4. $x^2 + 3x - 18 = 0$
5. $x^2 - 4 = 0$
6. $x^2 - 9 = 0$
7. $x^2 - 10x = -21$
8. $x^2 + 4x = 12$
9. $x^2 - 2x + 2 = 0$
10. $x^2 + 6x + 10 = 0$
11. $x^2 - 4x + 1 = 0$
12. $x^2 - 6x + 4 = 0$
13. $x^2 - 8x + 16 = 0$
14. $x^2 + 6x + 9 = 0$
15. $3x^2 + 4x - 1 = 0$
16. $6x^2 - 13x - 15 = 0$
17. $x^2 - 8x + 18 = 0$
18. $x^2 + 2x + 4 = 0$
19. $x^2 - 2x - 1 = 0$
20. $x^2 + 6x + 7 = 0$
21. $x^2 + 5x + 9 = 0$
22. $x^2 - 3x + 7 = 0$
23. $4x^2 - 12x + 3 = 0$
24. $4x^2 + 4x - 35 = 0$

Excursions in Algebra _____ Parabolic Surfaces

Suppose a parabola is rotated about its axis of symmetry. The surface described by this rotation is known as a paraboloid of revolution, or a parabolic surface.

Parabolic surfaces are used in automobile headlamps, radar antennas, solar collectors, and other devices. This is because a parabolic surface can focus incoming energy at a single point, or reflect the energy from a point and send it in one direction.

This point is known as the focus. The focus lies on the axis of symmetry.

The focus for a parabola with equation $y = ax^2 + bx + c$ has the following coordinates.

$$\left(-\frac{b}{2a}, \frac{4ac - b^2 + 1}{4a}\right)$$

Exercises

Find the coordinates of the focus of each parabola whose equation is given.

1. $y = x^2 + 6x + 9$
2. $y = 2x^2 + 4x + 7$
3. $y = \frac{1}{4}x^2 - 2x + 3$

13-3 Completing the Square

An equation like $x^2 - 36 = 0$ can be solved in the following way.

$$x^2 - 36 = 0$$

$$\begin{array}{ll} x^2 = 36 & \text{\textit{Add 36 to both sides.}} \\ \sqrt{x^2} = \sqrt{36} & \text{\textit{Find the square root of both sides.}} \\ |x| = 6 & \text{\textit{Recall that }} |x| = \sqrt{x^2}. \\ x = \pm 6 & x = \pm 6 \text{ \textit{since} } |+6| = |-6| = 6. \end{array}$$

This same method can be used to solve the equation $x^2 - 4x + 4 = 3$.

Example

1 **Solve:** $x^2 - 4x + 4 = 3$

$$\begin{array}{ll} x^2 - 4x + 4 = 3 & \\ (x - 2)^2 = 3 & \text{\textit{Factor }} x^2 - 4x + 4. \\ \sqrt{(x - 2)^2} = \sqrt{3} & \text{\textit{Find the square root of both sides.}} \\ |x - 2| = \sqrt{3} & \\ x - 2 = \pm\sqrt{3} & \text{\textit{Why is this so?}} \\ x = 2 \pm\sqrt{3} & \text{\textit{Add 2 to both sides.}} \end{array}$$

The solution set is $\{2 - \sqrt{3}, 2 + \sqrt{3}\}$.

The quadratic expression must be a perfect square in order to use the above method. If it is not a perfect square, then a method called **completing the square** may be used.

Consider the pattern for squaring a binomial.

$$\begin{aligned} (x + 6)^2 &= x^2 + 2(6)(x) + 6^2 \\ &= x^2 + 12x \quad\;\; + 36 \end{aligned}$$

$$\left(\frac{12}{2}\right) \;\rightarrow\; 6^2 \quad \text{\textit{Notice that 36 is }} 6^2 \text{ \textit{and 6 is one-half of 12.}}$$

To complete the square for an expression of the form $x^2 + bx$, follow the steps listed below.

Step 1 Find one-half of b, the coefficient of x.

Step 2 Square the result of **Step 1**.

Step 3 Add the result of **Step 2** to $x^2 + bx$.

2 **Find the value of c that makes $x^2 + 14x + c$ a perfect square.**

Step 1   Find one-half of 14. $\frac{14}{2} = 7$

Step 2   Square the result of **Step 1.** $7^2 = 49$

Step 3   Add the result of **Step 2** to $x^2 + 14x$. $x^2 + 14x + 49$

Thus, $c = 49$. Notice that $x^2 + 14x + 49$ is equal to $(x + 7)^2$, which is a perfect square.

3 **Solve $x^2 + 6x - 16 = 0$ by completing the square.**

$$x^2 + 6x - 16 = 0 \qquad \textit{Notice that } x^2 + 6x - 16 \textit{ is not a perfect square.}$$
$$x^2 + 6x = 16 \qquad \textit{Add 16 to both sides. Then complete the square.}$$
$$x^2 + 6x + 9 = 16 + 9 \qquad \left(\tfrac{6}{2}\right)^2 = 9, \textit{ so add 9 to both sides of the equation.}$$
$$(x + 3)^2 = 25 \qquad \textit{Factor } x^2 + 6x + 9.$$
$$x + 3 = \pm 5 \qquad \textit{Find the square root of both sides.}$$
$$x = \pm 5 - 3 \qquad \textit{Subtract 3 from both sides.}$$
$$x = 5 - 3 \ \textrm{ or } \qquad x = -5 - 3$$
$$x = 2 \qquad\qquad\quad x = -8$$

The roots of $x^2 + 6x - 16 = 0$ are 2 and -8.   *Check this result.*

Notice that the roots can be used to factor $x^2 + 6x - 16$.
$$x^2 + 6x - 16 = (x - 2)(x + 8)$$

4 **Solve $2x^2 - 9x + 8 = 0$ by completing the square.**

$$2x^2 - 9x + 8 = 0 \qquad \textit{To complete the square, the coefficient of } x^2$$
$$\textit{must be 1. Divide both sides of the equation by 2.}$$
$$x^2 - \tfrac{9}{2}x + 4 = 0$$

$$x^2 - \tfrac{9}{2}x = -4 \qquad \textit{Subtract 4 from both sides. Then complete the square.}$$

$$x^2 - \tfrac{9}{2}x + \tfrac{81}{16} = -4 + \tfrac{81}{16} \qquad \textit{Why was } \tfrac{81}{16} \textit{ added to both sides?}$$

$$\left(x - \tfrac{9}{4}\right)^2 = \tfrac{17}{16}$$

$$x - \tfrac{9}{4} = \pm \frac{\sqrt{17}}{4}$$

$$x = \frac{9 \pm \sqrt{17}}{4}$$

The roots of $2x^2 - 9x + 8 = 0$ are $\dfrac{9 + \sqrt{17}}{4}$ and $\dfrac{9 - \sqrt{17}}{4}$. In decimal form the roots are approximately $\dfrac{9 + 4.123}{4}$, or 3.281, and $\dfrac{9 - 4.123}{4}$, or 1.219.

Exploratory Exercises

State whether each trinomial is a perfect square.

1. $y^2 + 8y + 7$
2. $b^2 + 4b + 3$
3. $m^2 - 10m + 25$
4. $r^2 - 8r + 16$
5. $k^2 + 10k + 9$
6. $z^2 - 18z + 81$
7. $t^2 + 8t + 15$
8. $d^2 + 12d + 27$
9. $h^2 - 13h + \frac{169}{4}$

Find the value of c that makes each trinomial a perfect square.

10. $x^2 + 8x + c$
11. $x^2 + 4x + c$
12. $m^2 - 10m + c$
13. $x^2 - 6x + c$
14. $z^2 + 2z + c$
15. $x^2 + 14x + c$
16. $x^2 - 12x + c$
17. $a^2 + 5a + c$
18. $x^2 + 7x + c$
19. $x^2 - 7x + c$
20. $y^2 + 16y + c$
21. $x^2 - 13x + c$

Written Exercises

Solve by completing the square. Leave irrational roots in simplest radical form.

1. $y^2 + 4y + 3 = 0$
2. $n^2 + 8n + 7 = 0$
3. $t^2 - 4t = 21$
4. $a^2 - 10a - 24 = 0$
5. $a^2 - 6a + 8 = 0$
6. $b^2 - 3b = 10$
7. $z^2 - 4z = 2$
8. $p^2 + 2p - 3 = 0$
9. $y^2 - 8y = 4$
10. $p^2 - p - 6 = 0$
11. $x^2 - 8x = 12$
12. $s^2 + 8s + 15 = 0$
13. $r^2 + 14r - 10 = 5$
14. $y^2 + 7y + 10 = -2$
15. $n^2 + 5n + 6 = 0$
16. $x^2 - 5x + 2 = -2$
17. $n^2 - 11n - 12 = 0$
18. $x^2 - 4x + 1 = 0$
19. $x^2 - 6x + 7 = 0$
20. $b^2 - 6b + 4 = 0$
21. $\frac{1}{2}t^2 - 2t - \frac{3}{2} = 0$
22. $4x^2 - 20x + 25 = 0$
23. $2b^2 - b - 14 = 7$
24. $2d^2 + 3d - 20 = 0$
25. $x^2 - \frac{7}{2}x + \frac{3}{2} = 0$
26. $a^2 - \frac{1}{2}a - \frac{3}{2} = 0$
27. $3y^2 - y - 10 = 0$
28. $0.3x^2 + 0.1x - 0.2 = 0$
29. $0.3n^2 - 0.2n = 0.1$
30. $\frac{1}{2}q^2 - \frac{5}{4}q - 3 = 0$

Challenge

31. $x^2 + 4x + c = 0$
32. $x^2 - bx + 8 = 0$
33. $x^2 + bx + c = 0$
34. $ax^2 + bx + c = 0$
35. $x^2 + xy - 2y^2 = 0$
36. $x^2 + 4bx + b^2 = 0$

Using Calculators _____ Irrational Roots

Solve by completing the square. Then use a calculator to approximate the roots to three decimal places.

1. $x^2 + 2x - 10 = 0$
2. $r^2 + 0.25r - 0.5 = 0$
3. $2m^2 - 5m + 1 = 0$
4. $a^2 - 6a + 6 = 0$
5. $x^2 - 10x = 23$
6. $y^2 - 8y = 13$
7. $2x^2 - 6x - 5 = 0$
8. $4y^2 - 2y = 1$
9. $3x^2 - 7x - 3 = 0$
10. $x^2 - \frac{7}{3}x - \frac{5}{3} = 0$
11. $y^2 - \frac{8}{5}y - \frac{2}{5} = 0$
12. $t^2 - 3t = -\frac{5}{3}$

13-4   The Quadratic Formula

The method of completing the square can be used to develop a general formula for solving any quadratic equation. Begin with the general form of a quadratic equation, $ax^2 + bx + c = 0$, where $a \neq 0$.

$$ax^2 + bx + c = 0$$

$$x^2 + \frac{b}{a}x + \frac{c}{a} = 0$$
Divide by a so the coefficient of x^2 becomes 1.

$$x^2 + \frac{b}{a}x = -\frac{c}{a}$$
Subtract $\frac{c}{a}$ from both sides.

$$x^2 + \frac{b}{a}x + \left(\frac{b}{2a}\right)^2 = -\frac{c}{a} + \left(\frac{b}{2a}\right)^2$$
Complete the square.

$$\left(x + \frac{b}{2a}\right)^2 = -\frac{c}{a} + \frac{b^2}{4a^2}$$
Factor the left side.

$$\left(x + \frac{b}{2a}\right)^2 = \frac{b^2 - 4ac}{4a^2}$$
Simplify the right side.

$$x + \frac{b}{2a} = \pm\sqrt{\frac{b^2 - 4ac}{4a^2}}$$
Find the square root of both sides.

$$x + \frac{b}{2a} = \frac{\pm\sqrt{b^2 - 4ac}}{2a}$$
Simplify the square root on the right side.

$$x = \frac{\pm\sqrt{b^2 - 4ac}}{2a} - \frac{b}{2a}$$
Subtract $\frac{b}{2a}$ from both sides.

$$x = \frac{-b \pm \sqrt{b^2 - 4ac}}{2a}$$
The result is an expression for x.

This result is called the **quadratic formula** and can be used to solve any quadratic equation.

> **The roots of a quadratic equation of the form** $ax^2 + bx + c = 0$, **where** $a \neq 0$, **are given by:**
> $$x = \frac{-b \pm \sqrt{b^2 - 4ac}}{2a}$$

The Quadratic Formula

In order to find a real value for $\sqrt{b^2 - 4ac}$, the value of $b^2 - 4ac$ must be non-negative. If $b^2 - 4ac$ is negative, the equation has no real roots.

1 **Use the quadratic formula to solve $x^2 - 6x - 7 = 0$.**

$$x = \frac{-b \pm \sqrt{b^2 - 4ac}}{2a}$$

$$= \frac{-(-6) \pm \sqrt{(-6)^2 - 4(1)(-7)}}{2(1)} \qquad a = 1,\ b = -6,\ c = -7$$

$$= \frac{6 \pm \sqrt{36 + 28}}{2}$$

$$= \frac{6 \pm \sqrt{64}}{2}$$

$$= \frac{6 \pm 8}{2}$$

$$x = \frac{6 + 8}{2} \quad \text{or} \quad x = \frac{6 - 8}{2} \qquad \textit{Check this result.}$$

$$x = \quad 7 \qquad\qquad x = -1$$

The roots are 7 and -1.

2 **Use the quadratic formula to solve $\frac{4}{3}x^2 - 2x = -\frac{1}{3}$.**

First, change the equation to the general form, $ax^2 + bx + c = 0$.

$$\frac{4}{3}x^2 - 2x = -\frac{1}{3}$$

$$\frac{4}{3}x^2 - 2x + \frac{1}{3} = 0 \qquad \textit{Add } \frac{1}{3} \textit{ to both sides.}$$

$$4x^2 - 6x + 1 = 0 \qquad \textit{Multiply both sides by 3.}$$

$$x = \frac{-b \pm \sqrt{b^2 - 4ac}}{2a}$$

$$= \frac{-(-6) \pm \sqrt{(-6)^2 - 4(4)(1)}}{2(4)} \qquad a = 4,\ b = -6,\ c = 1$$

$$= \frac{6 \pm \sqrt{36 - 16}}{8}$$

$$= \frac{6 \pm \sqrt{20}}{8}$$

$$= \frac{6 \pm \sqrt{4 \cdot 5}}{8}$$

$$= \frac{6 \pm 2\sqrt{5}}{8}$$

$$= \frac{3 \pm \sqrt{5}}{4} \qquad \textit{Check this result.}$$

The roots are $\dfrac{3 + \sqrt{5}}{4}$ and $\dfrac{3 - \sqrt{5}}{4}$.

Exploratory Exercises

State the values of a, b, and c for each quadratic equation.

1. $x^2 + 7x + 6 = 0$
2. $y^2 + 8y + 15 = 0$
3. $m^2 + 4m + 3 = 0$
4. $2t^2 - t = 15$
5. $4x^2 + 8x = -3$
6. $2y^2 + 3 = -7y$
7. $y^2 - 25 = 0$
8. $2y^2 = 98$
9. $2x^2 + 8x = 0$
10. $3n^2 - 18n = 0$
11. $3m^2 + 2 = -5m$
12. $3k^2 + 11k = 4$

State the value of $b^2 - 4ac$ for each quadratic equation.

13. $x^2 + 5x - 6 = 0$
14. $r^2 + 10r + 9 = 0$
15. $y^2 - 7y - 8 = 0$
16. $z^2 - 13z + 36 = 0$
17. $m^2 - 2m = 8$
18. $y^2 - 2y = 35$
19. $y^2 + y = 12$
20. $4n^2 - 20n = 0$
21. $5t^2 = 125$
22. $2x^2 - x = 3$
23. $3x^2 + 14x = 5$
24. $3x^2 + 23x + 14 = 0$

Written Exercises

Use the quadratic formula to solve each equation. Leave irrational roots in simplest radical form.

1. $x^2 + 7x + 6 = 0$
2. $y^2 + 8y + 15 = 0$
3. $m^2 + 4m + 3 = 0$
4. $p^2 + 5p + 4 = 0$
5. $2r^2 + r - 15 = 0$
6. $8t^2 + 10t + 3 = 0$
7. $2t^2 - t = 15$
8. $-4x^2 + 8x = -3$
9. $2y^2 + 3 = -7y$
10. $y^2 - 25 = 0$
11. $2y^2 = 98$
12. $-2x^2 + 8x + 3 = 3$
13. $3n^2 - 18n = 0$
14. $3m^2 + 2 = -5m$
15. $3k^2 + 11k = 4$
16. $-x^2 + 5x - 6 = 0$
17. $r^2 + 10r + 9 = 0$
18. $y^2 - 7y - 8 = 0$
19. $z^2 - 13z + 36 = 0$
20. $m^2 - 2m - 4 = 4$
21. $y^2 - 2y = 35$
22. $y^2 + y = 12$
23. $4n^2 - 20n = 0$
24. $5t^2 = 125$
25. $2x^2 - x = 3$
26. $3x^2 + 14x = 5$
27. $3x^2 + 23x + 10 = -4$
28. $3n^2 - 2n = 1$
29. $y^2 - \frac{3}{5}y + \frac{2}{25} = 0$
30. $3x^2 - \frac{5}{4}x - \frac{1}{2} = 0$
31. $-r^2 - 6r + 3 = 0$
32. $2x^2 - 0.7x - 0.3 = 0$
33. $x^2 - 1.1x - 0.6 = 0$
34. $k^2 - 6k + 1 = 0$
35. $4x^2 - 8x + 3 = 6$
36. $a^2 + 3a + 1 = 0$
37. $4b^2 + 20b + 23 = 0$
38. $4x^2 + 8x - 1 = 0$
39. $-4y^2 + 16y + 13 = 0$
40. $24x^2 - 2x - 15 = 0$
41. $21x^2 + 5x - 6 = 0$
42. $35x^2 - 11x - 6 = 0$

Challenge

Solve each equation by factoring, if possible. Then, solve each equation using the quadratic formula.

43. $y^2 - 2y - 15 = 0$
44. $x^2 - 13x + 42 = 0$
45. $x^2 + 2x - 2 = 0$
46. If a quadratic equation can be factored, what can you say about the value of $b^2 - 4ac$?

mini-review

Factor.

1. $r^2 - 10r - 24$
2. $6p^2 - 16p - 6$

Simplify.

3. $\pm\sqrt{81}$
4. $\sqrt{75} \cdot \sqrt{3}$
5. $\dfrac{\sqrt{2}}{\sqrt{3}}$

Problem Solving

Another strategy for solving problems is to list possibilities. When making a list, use a systematic approach so you do not omit important items. This strategy is often helpful when you need to find the *number* of solutions to a problem. Study the following examples.

Example 1: **Which positive numbers less than 30 are divisible by both 3 and 4?**

List the numbers divisible by 3: 3, 6, 9, 12, 15, 18, 21, 24, 27
List the numbers divisible by 4: 4, 8, 12, 16, 20, 24, 28

Which numbers are in both lists? Since 12 and 24 are in both lists, they are divisible by both 3 and 4.

Example 2: **How many ways can you receive change for a quarter if at least one coin is a dime?**

List the possibilities. List ways which use the fewest number of coins first.

1. dime, dime, nickel   *This is the same as dime, nickel, dime.*
2. dime, dime, 5 pennies
3. dime, nickel, nickel, nickel
4. dime, nickel, nickel, 5 pennies
5. dime, nickel, 10 pennies
6. dime, 15 pennies   *Are there any other solutions?*

Thus, there are 6 ways to receive change for a quarter if at least one coin is a dime.

Exercises

Solve each problem.

1. Which positive numbers less than 50 are divisible by both 8 and 12?

2. Which positive numbers less than 100 are divisible by both 3 and 11?

3. How many ways can you receive change for a half-dollar if you receive at least one dime and one quarter?

4. How many different whole numbers can be written using the digits 3, 6, 6, and 7? Each number must use all four digits.

5. An ice cream shop makes chocolate, butterscotch, or strawberry sundaes. Any sundae can be served with whipped cream, nuts, neither, or both. How many ways can a sundae be served?

6. The president, vice-president, secretary, and treasurer of a club are to be seated in four chairs in the front of a meeting room. How many seating arrangements are possible?

7. In how many ways can you write 45 as the sum of positive consecutive integers?

8. How many positive whole numbers less than 50 can be written as the sum of 2 squares?

13-5 The Discriminant

In the quadratic formula, the expression $b^2 - 4ac$ is called the **discriminant**. The discriminant can give information about the nature of the roots of a quadratic equation.

In particular, the discriminant is used to determine how many real roots there are. Real roots are roots that are real numbers, that is, *either* rational numbers *or* irrational numbers. Recall that the real roots of an equation are represented by the intersection of the x-axis and the graph of the related function.

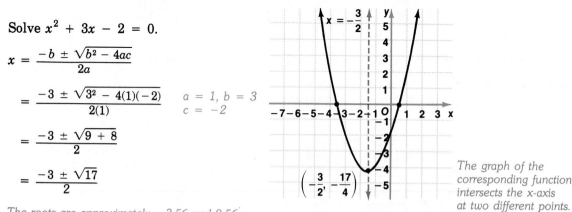

Solve $x^2 + 3x - 2 = 0$.

$$x = \frac{-b \pm \sqrt{b^2 - 4ac}}{2a}$$

$$= \frac{-3 \pm \sqrt{3^2 - 4(1)(-2)}}{2(1)} \qquad a = 1,\ b = 3$$
$$\qquad\qquad\qquad\qquad\qquad\qquad c = -2$$

$$= \frac{-3 \pm \sqrt{9 + 8}}{2}$$

$$= \frac{-3 \pm \sqrt{17}}{2}$$

The roots are approximately -3.56 and 0.56.

The graph of the corresponding function intersects the x-axis at two different points.

Notice that $b^2 - 4ac > 0$ and there are two real roots.

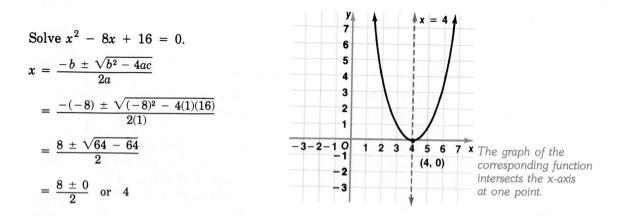

Solve $x^2 - 8x + 16 = 0$.

$$x = \frac{-b \pm \sqrt{b^2 - 4ac}}{2a}$$

$$= \frac{-(-8) \pm \sqrt{(-8)^2 - 4(1)(16)}}{2(1)}$$

$$= \frac{8 \pm \sqrt{64 - 64}}{2}$$

$$= \frac{8 \pm 0}{2} \quad \text{or} \quad 4$$

The graph of the corresponding function intersects the x-axis at one point.

Notice that $b^2 - 4ac = 0$ and there is one real root.

Solve $x^2 + 6x + 10 = 0$.

$$x = \frac{-b \pm \sqrt{b^2 - 4ac}}{2a}$$

$$= \frac{-6 \pm \sqrt{6^2 - 4(1)(10)}}{2(1)}$$

$$= \frac{-6 \pm \sqrt{36 - 40}}{2}$$

$$= \frac{-6 \pm \sqrt{-4}}{2}$$

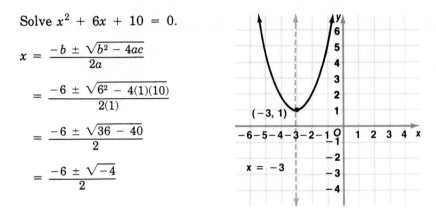

$(-3, 1)$

$x = -3$

The graph of the corresponding function does not intersect the x-axis

Notice that $b^2 - 4ac < 0$ and there are no real roots since *no* real number can be the square root of a negative number.

The relationship between the value of the discriminant and the nature of the roots of an equation can be summarized as follows.

Discriminant	Nature of Roots
$b^2 - 4ac > 0$	two real roots
$b^2 - 4ac = 0$	one real root
$b^2 - 4ac < 0$	no real roots

Nature of Roots of a Quadratic Equation

Examples

1 **State the value of the discriminant of $2x^2 - 10x + 11 = 0$. Then determine the nature of the roots of the equation.**

$$b^2 - 4ac = (-10)^2 - 4(2)(11) \qquad a = 2, b = -10, c = 11$$
$$= 100 - 88$$
$$= 12$$

Since $b^2 - 4ac > 0$, then $2x^2 - 10x + 11 = 0$ has two real roots.

2 **State the value of the discriminant of $4x^2 - 12x + 9 = 0$. Then determine the nature of the roots of the equation.**

$$b^2 - 4ac = (-12)^2 - 4(4)(9) \qquad a = 4, b = -12, c = 9$$
$$= 144 - 144$$
$$= 0$$

Since $b^2 - 4ac = 0$, then $4x^2 - 12x + 9 = 0$ has one real root.

Example

3 State the value of the discriminant of $3x^2 + 4x + 2 = 0$. Then determine the nature of the roots of the equation.

$$b^2 - 4ac = 4^2 - 4(3)(2) \qquad a = 3, b = 4, c = 2$$
$$= 16 - 24$$
$$= -8$$

Since $b^2 - 4ac < 0$, then $3x^2 + 4x + 2 = 0$ has no real roots.

Exploratory Exercises

State the value of the discriminant for each equation. Then determine the nature of the roots of the equation.

1. $x^2 + 3x - 4 = 0$
2. $y^2 + 3y + 1 = 0$
3. $m^2 + 5m - 6 = 0$
4. $r^2 + 3r + 4 = 0$
5. $n^2 + 12n + 5 = 0$
6. $t^2 - 12t + 36 = 0$
7. $s^2 + 8s + 16 = 0$
8. $2k^2 - 7k + 6 = 0$
9. $2p^2 - p - 3 = 0$
10. $2x^2 + 1 = 7x$
11. $h^2 = 6 - h$
12. $b^2 - 10b + 12 = 0$
13. $x^2 - 1.2x = 0$
14. $2z^2 + 7z + 50 = 0$
15. $y^2 - 4y - 8 = 0$
16. $3x^2 + x + 1 = 0$
17. $3x^2 + 7x - 2 = 0$
18. $2x^2 - 2x - 1 = 0$
19. $\frac{4}{3}x^2 + 4x + 3 = 0$
20. $\frac{3}{2}m^2 + m = -\frac{7}{2}$
21. $4a^2 + 10a + 6.25 = 0$

Written Exercises

Determine the nature of the roots of each equation by using the discriminant. Find all real roots. Leave irrational roots in simplest radical form.

1. $x^2 + 5x + 3 = 0$
2. $y^2 - 4y + 1 = 0$
3. $r^2 + 4r - 12 = 0$
4. $z^2 + 8z - 5 = 0$
5. $m^2 + 7m + 6 = 0$
6. $p^2 - 7p + 6 = 0$
7. $k^2 + 6k + 10 = 0$
8. $a^2 + 8a - 12 = 0$
9. $d^2 + 4d + 7 = 0$
10. $2x^2 + 3x + 1 = 0$
11. $2x^2 - 3x + 1 = 0$
12. $3y^2 + y - 1 = 0$
13. $m^2 - 14m + 49 = 0$
14. $3n^2 - n - 5 = 0$
15. $15a^2 + 2a + 16 = 0$
16. $h^2 - 16h + 64 = 0$
17. $y^2 - 4y - 32 = 0$
18. $11z^2 - z - 3 = 0$
19. $3p^2 - 4p - 1 = 0$
20. $9y^2 - 6y + 1 = 0$
21. $3g^2 - 4g + 1 = 0$
22. $2x^2 - x - 2 = 0$
23. $6r^2 - 5r = 7$
24. $-9m + m^2 = -14$
25. $2a^2 + a = 5$
26. $0.3a^2 + 0.8a + 0.4 = 0$
27. $3y^2 - 2y = 1$
28. $3z^2 + 10z + 5 = 0$
29. $2b^2 + 7b + 2 = 0$
30. $7r^2 - 3r - 1 = 0$
31. $8p^2 + 7p + 1 = 0$
32. $3a^2 + 2 = 5a$
33. $0.6v^2 + v = 1.8$
34. $2z^2 + 5 = 8z$
35. $5b^2 = 1 + 6b$
36. $2x^2 - 8x = 7$
37. $x^2 - \frac{5}{3}x = -\frac{2}{3}$
38. $\frac{1}{3}x^2 - 4x + 13\frac{1}{3} = 0$
39. $5c^2 - 7c = 1$

The equation $x^2 = -1$ has *no* solution among the real numbers. This is because the square of a real number is positive.

We define a new number to be a solution to $x^2 = -1$. This number is designated by the letter i and is called the **imaginary unit**. The imaginary unit i is *not* a real number.

$$i^2 = -1$$

Using i as you would any constant, you can rewrite square roots of negative numbers.

$$i^2 = -1 \quad \text{so} \quad \sqrt{-1} = i$$
$$(2i)^2 = 2^2 i^2 \text{ or } -4 \quad \text{so} \quad \sqrt{-4} = 2i$$
$$(i\sqrt{3})^2 = i^2(\sqrt{3})^2 \text{ or } -3 \quad \text{so} \quad \sqrt{-3} = i\sqrt{3}$$

If the value of the discriminant of an equation is less than zero, the roots of the equation are *not* real numbers. However, the roots can be expressed using the imaginary unit.

Consider the equation $x^2 + 6x + 10 = 0$. The discriminant of this equation is a negative number.

$$b^2 - 4ac = 6^2 - 4(1)(10)$$
$$= 36 - 40$$
$$= -4$$

Even though the discriminant is less than zero, the quadratic formula can still be used to find the roots of the equation.

$$x = \frac{-b \pm \sqrt{b^2 - 4ac}}{2a}$$

$$= \frac{-6 \pm \sqrt{-4}}{2}$$

$$= \frac{-6 \pm 2i}{2} \quad \text{or} \quad -3 \pm i$$

The roots of $x^2 + 6x + 10 = 0$ are $-3 + i$ and $-3 - i$. Roots that contain the imaginary unit are known as **imaginary roots**.

Exercises

Find the roots of each equation.

1. $x^2 + x + 1 = 0$
2. $x^2 + 2x + 2 = 0$
3. $x^2 - 4x + 5 = 0$
4. $x^2 + 5x + 7 = 0$
5. $2x^2 - 3x + 4 = 0$
6. $3x^2 + x + 1 = 0$
7. $2z^2 + 2z + 3 = 0$
8. $2x^2 + 3x + 3 = 0$
9. $6y^2 + 8y + 5 = 0$
10. $r^2 - 4r + 10 = 0$
11. $5x^2 - 2x + 8 = 0$
12. $3k^2 + 3k + 2 = 0$

13-6 Solving Quadratic Equations

You have studied a variety of methods for solving quadratic equations. The table summarizes these methods.

Method	Can be Used	Comments
graphing	always	Not always exact; use only when a picture of function is needed.
factoring	sometimes	Use if constant term is 0 or factors are easily determined.
completing the square	always	Useful for equations of form $x^2 + bx + c = 0$ where b is even.
quadratic formula	always	Other methods may be easier, but this method *always* works.

Use the information in this table to help you decide how to solve a quadratic equation.

To solve:	Try:
$x^2 + 9x + 20 = 0$	factoring; quadratic formula
$2m^2 + 7m + 5 = 0$	quadratic formula
$x^2 - 2x - 2 = 0$	factoring; completing the square; quadratic formula
$x^2 + 6x - 315 = 0$	completing the square; quadratic formula
$6n^2 - 5n = 0$	factoring

To solve an equation with fractional or decimal coefficients, it is sometimes easier to first change the coefficients to integers by multiplication.

Example

1 **Solve:** $y^2 - \frac{5}{12}y - \frac{1}{4} = 0$

$y^2 - \frac{5}{12}y - \frac{1}{4} = 0$ *The LCM of 12 and 4 is 12.*

$12\left(y^2 - \frac{5}{12}y - \frac{1}{4}\right) = 12(0)$ *Multiply both sides by 12.*

$12y^2 - 5y - 3 = 0$

$(3y + 1)(4y - 3) = 0$ *Factor or use the*

$3y + 1 = 0$ or $4y - 3 = 0$ *quadratic formula.*

$y = -\frac{1}{3}$ or $y = \frac{3}{4}$ *Check this result.*

The solutions are $-\frac{1}{3}$ and $\frac{3}{4}$.

Example

2 Solve: $x^2 + 0.4x - 3.2 = 0$

$$x^2 + 0.4x - 3.2 = 0$$

$10(x^2 + 0.4x - 3.2) = 10(0)$ *Multiply both sides by 10.*

$$10x^2 + 4x - 32 = 0$$

$x = \dfrac{-4 \pm \sqrt{4^2 - 4(10)(-32)}}{2(10)}$ *Use the quadratic formula or try factoring.*

$= \dfrac{-4 \pm \sqrt{16 + 1,280}}{20}$

$= \dfrac{-4 \pm 36}{20}$

$x = -2$ or $x = 1.6$ *Check this result.*

The solutions are -2 and 1.6.

Exploratory Exercises

State the method that seems easiest for solving each equation.

1. $x^2 - 12x + 27 = 0$ **2.** $y^2 - 19y = -84$ **3.** $2m^2 + 19m + 9 = 0$

4. $a^2 - 12a - 4 = 0$ **5.** $3r^2 - 7r - 5 = 0$ **6.** $z^2 - 2z - 120 = 0$

7. $t^2 - 2t - 15 = 0$ **8.** $y^2 + 4y = 9$ **9.** $2b^2 + 1 = 6b$

10. $m^2 - 12m - 30 = 0$ **11.** $3k^2 - 11k - 7 = 0$ **12.** $3x^2 - 2x - 5 = 0$

State the number that both sides of each equation should be multiplied by before solving.

13. $x^2 - \frac{1}{2}x - \frac{1}{9} = 0$ **14.** $x^2 - \frac{7}{6}x - \frac{1}{2} = 0$ **15.** $3x^2 - \frac{5}{4}x - \frac{1}{2} = 0$

16. $x^2 - 1.3x - 0.3 = 0$ **17.** $2x^2 - 0.7x - 0.3 = 0$ **18.** $0.2x^2 - 0.33x - 0.35 = 0$

Written Exercises

Solve each quadratic equation by an appropriate method.

1. $x^2 - 9x + 20 = 0$ **2.** $y^2 + 10y - 2 = 0$ **3.** $2x^2 + 4x + 1 = 0$

4. $3z^2 - 7z - 3 = 0$ **5.** $x^2 + 3x = -2$ **6.** $r^2 + 13r = -42$

7. $2y^2 - 5y + 2 = 0$ **8.** $3x^2 - 7x - 6 = 0$ **9.** $4x^2 - 7x - 2 = 0$

10. $2k^2 + k - 5 = 0$ **11.** $3h^2 - 5h - 2 = 0$ **12.** $x^2 - 5x - 7 = 0$

13. $r^2 + 4r + 1 = 0$ **14.** $m^2 + 2m + 8 = 0$ **15.** $y^2 - 3y + 3 = 0$

16. $3z^2 = 5z - 1$ **17.** $9b = -5b^2 - 3$ **18.** $a^2 - 15a = -52$

19. $2z^2 + 4z = 5$ **20.** $x^2 = 4x + 2$ **21.** $-2x - 2 = -x^2$

22. $x^2 - x + \frac{3}{16} = 0$ **23.** $2a^2 - 8a + \frac{15}{2} = 0$ **24.** $r^2 + r + \frac{2}{9} = 0$

25. $x^2 - \frac{17}{20}x + \frac{3}{20} = 0$ **26.** $y^2 - \frac{3}{5}y + \frac{2}{25} = 0$ **27.** $x^2 - 1.1x - 0.6 = 0$

28. $2x^2 - 0.7x - 0.6 = 0$ **29.** $5x^2 - 0.5x - 0.3 = 0$ **30.** $0.7a^2 - 2.8a = 7$

13-7 Problem Solving: Quadratic Equations

You can use the methods for solving quadratic equations to solve some types of verbal problems.

Examples

1 A rectangle has a perimeter of 19 centimeters. Its area is 21 square centimeters. Find its dimensions.

Explore
Let l = the measure of the length.
Let w = the measure of the width.

Plan
Use the formula $P = 2l + 2w$.
$19 = 2l + 2w$ *Substitute 19 for P.*
$9.5 = l + w$ *Solve for l.*
$l = 9.5 - w$

Now write an equation using the formula $A = lw$.
$21 = (9.5 - w)w$ *Substitute 21 for A and 9.5 − w for l.*

Solve
$21 = 9.5w - w^2$
$w^2 - 9.5w + 21 = 0$ *Subtract 9.5w − w² from both sides.*
$2w^2 - 19w + 42 = 0$ *Multiply both sides by 2.*
$(2w - 7)(w - 6) = 0$ *Factor.*
$w = 3.5$ or $w = 6$

If $w = 3.5$ then $l = 9.5 - 3.5$ or 6.
If $w = 6$, then $l = 9.5 - 6$ or 3.5.
The dimensions are 3.5 cm and 6 cm.

Examine
The perimeter of a rectangle with dimensions 3.5 cm and 6 cm is 2(3.5) + 2(6) or 19 cm. The area of this rectangle is (3.5)(6) or 21 sq cm.

2 A pan is to be formed by cutting squares measuring 2 cm on a side from a square piece of sheet metal and then folding the sides. If the volume of the pan is to be 392 cm³, what is the original size of the sheet metal?

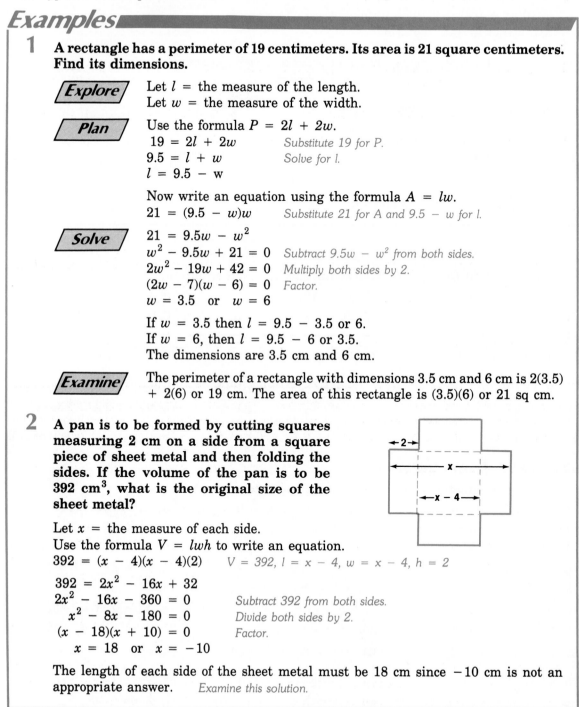

Let x = the measure of each side.
Use the formula $V = lwh$ to write an equation.
$392 = (x - 4)(x - 4)(2)$ *V = 392, l = x − 4, w = x − 4, h = 2*

$392 = 2x^2 - 16x + 32$
$2x^2 - 16x - 360 = 0$ *Subtract 392 from both sides.*
$x^2 - 8x - 180 = 0$ *Divide both sides by 2.*
$(x - 18)(x + 10) = 0$ *Factor.*
$x = 18$ or $x = -10$

The length of each side of the sheet metal must be 18 cm since −10 cm is not an appropriate answer.   *Examine this solution.*

Written Exercises

Find the dimensions of each rectangle described below. Disregard inappropriate solutions.

1. The perimeter is 30 m. The area is 56 m^2.

2. The perimeter is 34 in. The area is 72 in^2.

3. The perimeter is 46 yd. The area is 130 yd^2.

4. The perimeter is 70 cm. The area is 294 cm^2.

5. The length is 2 m more than 3 times the width. The area is 56 m^2.

6. The width is 7 cm less than the length. The area is 78 cm^2.

7. The perimeter is 60 in. The area is 200 in^2.

8. The perimeter is 37 in. The area is 78 in^2.

9. The length is 4 in. more than the width. The area is 45 in^2.

10. The width is 3 ft less than the length. The area is 54 ft^2.

11. The length is $\frac{8}{5}$ times the width. The area is 160 m^2.

12. The width is 0.5 m less than one-half the length. The area is 21 m^2.

Solve each of the following problems. Approximate irrational roots and disregard inappropriate solutions.

13. Find two integers whose sum is 14 and whose product is 48.

14. Find two integers whose sum is 13 and whose product is 42.

15. Find two integers whose difference is 6 and whose product is 135.

16. Find two integers whose sum is 12 and whose squares differ by 24.

17. A rectangular piece of sheet metal is 3 times as long as it is wide. Squares measuring 2 cm on a side are cut from each corner and the sides are folded to form a pan. If the volume of the pan is 512 cm^3, what are the dimensions of the sheet metal.

18. A rectangular piece of sheet metal is twice as long as it is wide. Squares measuring 5 inches on a side are cut from each corner and the sides are folded to form a box. If the volume of the box is 1,760 in.^{3}, what are the dimensions of the sheet metal?

19. A rectangular piece of glass is twice as long as it is wide. If the length and width are both reduced by 1 cm, the area of the glass becomes 10cm^2. What are the original dimensions of the glass?

20. A rectangular piece of sheet metal is 3 in. longer than it is wide. If the length and width are both increased by 2 in. the area increases by 34 in^2. What are the original dimensions of the sheet metal?

21. The perimeter of a rectangle is 8 meters and its area is 3.84 square meters. Find its dimensions.

22. A rectangle has a perimeter of 15.4 cm and an area of 14.4 cm^2. Find the dimensions of the rectangle.

23. The length of a rectangle is $\frac{8}{5}$ times its width. The area is 56 square meters. Find the dimensions of the rectangle.

24. The width of a rectangle is one-half meter less than one-half its length. The area is 21 m^2. Find its dimensions.

25. Dan Kurtz has a rectangular flower garden that measures 15 m by 20 m. He wishes to place a concrete walk of uniform width around the garden. His budget allows him to cover 74 m². How wide can the walk be?

26. A picture has a square frame that is 5 cm wide. The area of the picture is two-thirds of the total area of the picture and the frame. What are the dimensions of the frame?

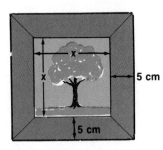

5 cm

5 cm

mini-review

Simplify.

1. $\sqrt{3}(\sqrt{3} - \sqrt{6})$

2. $\dfrac{12}{2 - \sqrt{5}}$

3. $4\sqrt{3} + 5\sqrt{2} - 2\sqrt{18} - 4\sqrt{12}$

4. Solve $\sqrt{3x + 6} = 3$

5. Find the length of the hypotenuse of a right triangle if its legs measure 6 and 12.

Using Calculators ————————————Checking Roots

After finding roots of an equation, verify them by substitution. To see if -4 and 3 are the roots of $2x^2 + 5x - 12 = 0$, replace x with each number and see if the equation holds.

$$2x^2 + 5x - 12 = 0$$

$$2(-4)^2 + 5(-4) - 12 \stackrel{?}{=} 0 \qquad 2(3)^2 + 5(3) - 12 \stackrel{?}{=} 0$$

A calculator may also be used to aid in checking the roots of an equation.

ENTER:	2	×	4	+/−	x²	+	5	×	4	+/−	−	12	=
DISPLAY:	2	2	4	−4	16	32	5	5	4	−4	12	12	0

ENTER:	2	×	3	x²	+	5	×	3	−	12	=
DISPLAY:	2	2	3	9	18	5	5	3	33	12	21

By substitution, it is found that -4 is a root of the equation $2x^2 + 5x - 12 = 0$, but that 3 is not.

Exercises

Use a calculator to determine if the given numbers are roots of each equation.

1. $-6, -5; x^2 + x - 30 = 0$

2. $2, -1; 2x^2 - x - 3 = 0$

3. $0.5, 0.6; 10x^2 - 2x - 3 = 0$

4. $0.5, 1.5; 8x^2 - 16x + 6 = 0$

13-8   The Sum and Product of Roots

An engineer or scientist often must find an equation to describe a certain situation. For example, suppose the roots of a quadratic equation are known to be -3 and 8.

If $x = -3$, then $x + 3 = 0$.   If $x = 8$, then $x - 8 = 0$.

$(x + 3)(x - 8) = 0$ *Why is this so?*

$x^2 - 5x - 24 = 0$

The quadratic equation $x^2 - 5x - 24 = 0$ has roots -3 and 8.

Suppose you find the sum and the product of the roots.

$$\text{sum} = -3 + 8 = 5$$
$$\text{product} = -3 \cdot 8 = -24$$

Now look at the equation.

product of roots   *The product of the roots is the constant term.*

$x^2 - 5x - 24 = 0$

*opposite of sum
of roots*   *The opposite of the sum of the roots is the coefficient of x.*

This *always* works. Suppose the two roots are r_1 and r_2. Then $(x - r_1)(x - r_2) = 0$. Multiplying the binomials results in the equation $x^2 - (r_1 + r_2)x + r_1 r_2 = 0$. Notice that the coefficient of x, $-(r_1 + r_2)$, is the opposite of the sum of the roots. The constant term, $r_1 r_2$, is the product of the roots.

> **To find a quadratic equation of the general form $x^2 + bx + c = 0$ given its roots:**
> 1. **The coefficient of x is the opposite of the sum of the roots.**
> 2. **The constant term is the product of the roots.**

*Finding
Quadratic
Equations*

Example

1 **Find a quadratic equation whose roots are -4 and 7.**

opposite of sum of roots $= -(-4 + 7) = -3$

product of roots $= -4 \cdot 7 = -28$

The opposite of the sum of the roots, -3, is the coefficient of x. The product of the roots, -28, is the constant term.

Thus, a quadratic equation whose roots are -4 and 7 is $x^2 - 3x - 28 = 0$.

Example

2 Find a quadratic equation whose roots are $\frac{4}{3}$ and -2.

opposite of sum of roots $= -\left[\frac{4}{3} + (-2)\right] = \frac{2}{3}$

product of roots $= \frac{4}{3}(-2) = -\frac{8}{3}$

The opposite of the sum of the roots, $\frac{2}{3}$, is the coefficient of x. The product of the roots, $-\frac{8}{3}$, is the constant term. Thus, a quadratic equation is $x^2 + \frac{2}{3}x - \frac{8}{3} = 0$. This equation can also be written as $3x^2 + 2x - 8 = 0$.

By studying Example 2, the following rule may be discovered.

Given the quadratic equation $ax^2 + bx + c = 0$, where $a \neq 0$, the sum of the roots of the equation is $-\frac{b}{a}$ and the product of the roots of the equation is $\frac{c}{a}$.

Sum and Product of Roots

Example

3 Are $\frac{3}{2}$ and $-\frac{4}{3}$ roots of $6x^2 - x - 12 = 0$?

Sum of Roots

$\frac{3}{2} + \left(-\frac{4}{3}\right) = \frac{9}{6} + \left(-\frac{8}{6}\right)$

$= \frac{1}{6}$ *Is this equal to $-\frac{b}{a}$?*

Product of Roots

$\frac{3}{2}\left(-\frac{4}{3}\right) = -2$ *Is this equal to $\frac{c}{a}$?*

Since $\frac{-b}{a} = \frac{1}{6}$ and $\frac{c}{a} = -2$, $\frac{3}{2}$ and $-\frac{4}{3}$ are roots of the equation.

Exploratory Exercises

State the sum and product of the roots of each equation.

1. $x^2 - 5x + 6 = 0$

2. $y^2 - 8y - 20 = 0$

3. $z^2 + 12z - 28 = 0$

4. $3m^2 + 6m - 3 = 0$

5. $4k^2 + 20k - 16 = 0$

6. $4t^2 + 8t + 3 = 0$

7. $4x^2 + 4x = 35$

8. $6a^2 - 13a = 15$

9. $6b^2 - 5b = 21$

State whether the following numbers are roots of the given equation.

10. $-4, 6; x^2 - 2x - 24 = 0$

11. $-6, 3; y^2 + 3y - 18 = 0$

12. $3, 7; a^2 - 10a + 21 = 0$

13. $2, 3; n^2 + 5n - 6 = 0$

14. $-1, 7; b^2 - 8b + 7 = 0$

15. $-2, 4; r^2 + 2r + 8 = 0$

16. $-3, 4; x^2 + x - 12 = 0$

17. $-6, 5; x^2 - x - 30 = 0$

18. $-\frac{1}{3}, \frac{1}{2}; x^2 - \frac{1}{6}x - \frac{1}{6} = 0$

19. $-\frac{1}{4}, \frac{1}{6}; x^2 + \frac{5}{12}x + \frac{1}{24} = 0$

Find a quadratic equation having the given roots.

20. $4, 1$ **21.** $5, 2$ **22.** $-4, 5$ **23.** $3, 8$

24. $0, -5$ **25.** $1, -6$ **26.** $\frac{3}{2}, 6$ **27.** $\frac{1}{2}, \frac{-3}{2}$

28. $\frac{2}{3}, 7$ **29.** $1.4, 2.2$ **30.** $0.3, -0.6$ **31.** $\frac{2}{5}, \frac{-3}{5}$

Written Exercises

State the sum and product of the roots of each equation.

1. $y^2 + 15y + 54 = 0$

2. $a^2 - 5a - 24 = 0$

3. $m^2 - m - 6 = 0$

4. $b^2 + 12b - 28 = 0$

5. $6x^2 + 31x + 35 = 0$

6. $21r^2 + 2r - 8 = 0$

7. $k^2 + 6k - 1 = 0$

8. $4y^2 + 4y + 1 = 0$

9. $7h^2 - 33h - 10 = 0$

10. $n^2 - 10n + 23 = 0$

11. $\frac{1}{2}m^2 - \frac{3}{2}m + 4 = 0$

12. $z^2 + \frac{13}{2}z - \frac{9}{4} = 0$

13. $m^2 - 1.2m + 0.27 = 0$

14. $6k^2 - 0.4k - 0.02 = 0$

15. $2c^2 - \frac{2}{3}c = \frac{1}{6}$

16. $12a^2 - \frac{7}{2}a + \frac{1}{4} = 0$

17. $a^2 + 4a\sqrt{3} + 9 = 0$

18. $2y^2 + y\sqrt{2} - 6 = 0$

Find a quadratic equation having the given roots.

19. $5, 1$ **20.** $4, 7$ **21.** $6, -5$

22. $7, -8$ **23.** $1, -10$ **24.** $8, -3$

25. $5, -9$ **26.** $-2, -17$ **27.** $16, -5$

28. $\frac{5}{2}, 2$ **29.** $\frac{7}{3}, -3$ **30.** $-\frac{3}{4}, 8$

31. $\frac{2}{3}, \frac{-3}{2}$ **32.** $-\frac{4}{5}, \frac{5}{4}$ **33.** $6, -\frac{1}{5}$

34. $\sqrt{2}, -\sqrt{2}$ **35.** $\sqrt{3}, \sqrt{3}$ **36.** $2 + \sqrt{3}, 2 - \sqrt{3}$

37. $5 - \sqrt{2}, 5 + \sqrt{2}$ **38.** $\frac{1 + \sqrt{7}}{2}, \frac{1 - \sqrt{7}}{2}$

39. Find the general form of the quadratic equation with roots q and r.

Using Calculators ————————— Decimal Coefficients

Use the quadratic formula and a calculator to solve the following equations. Approximate the roots to three decimal places.

1. $1.4x^2 + 0.2x - 4.1 = 0$ **2.** $0.2x^2 - 1.3x + 0.6 = 0$

3. $2.1y^2 + 4.6y - 1.3 = 0$ **4.** $3.8m^2 - 2.1m - 1.7 = 0$

5. $0.4r^2 + 5.2r - 2.3 = 0$ **6.** $7.9z^2 - 5.1z + 0.6 = 0$

Graphing Quadratic Functions

The following BASIC program can be used as an aid for graphing quadratic functions.

```
10    PRINT "FOR THE QUADRATIC FUNCTION Y=A*X↑2+B*X+C,
         ENTER A,B, AND C"
20    INPUT A,B,C
30    LET S = -B / (2 * A)       Line 30 determines the axis of symmetry.
40    PRINT "THE EQUATION OF THE AXIS OF SYMMETRY IS X = ";S
50    LET Y = A * S ↑ 2 + B * S + C
60    IF A > 0 THEN PRINT "THE MINIMUM POINT IS (";S;",";Y;")"
70    IF A < 0 THEN PRINT "THE MAXIMUM POINT IS (";S;",";Y;")"
80    IF A = 0 THEN PRINT "A MUST NOT BE ZERO"
90    FOR X = S - 4 TO S + 4
95    LET Y = A * X ↑ 2 + B * X + C
100   PRINT "(";X;",";Y;")"
110   NEXT X
120   END
```

The zeros of a quadratic function are the roots of the related quadratic equation. The program above can be extended to compute the zeros of the function. To do this, delete line 120 and add the lines shown at the right. Notice that the discriminant is used in lines 130 and 140 to check for the number of real zeros. If there are one or two real zeros, the quadratic formula is used to compute the zeros.

```
120   LET D = B ↑ 2 - 4 * A * C
130   IF D > 0 THEN 170
140   IF D = 0 THEN 200
150   PRINT "NO REAL ZEROS"
160   GOTO 220
170   PRINT "THE ZEROS ARE"
180   PRINT ( - B + SQR (D)) /
         (2 * A);" AND ";( - B -
         SQR (D)) / (2 * A)
190   GOTO 220
200   PRINT "THE ZERO IS"
210   PRINT - B / (2 * A)
220   END
```

Exercises

Use the program above to compute the coordinates of several points of the graphs of the following quadratic functions. Also use lines 120-220 above to compute the zeros for each function.

1. $y = x^2 - 2x - 6$ **2.** $y = x^2 + x - 3$ **3.** $y = 2x^2 - 4x + 5$

4. $y = 3x^2 + 6x - 2$ **5.** $y = -x^2 + 4x - 4$ **6.** $y = -2x^2 + 8x - 6$

7. Graph the following equations on one coordinate axis:

$y = 2x^2 + x - 6$, $y = x^2 + x - 6$, and $y = \frac{1}{2}x^2 + x - 6$

8. What effect does the coefficient of x^2 have on the shape of the graph?

Vocabulary

Chapter Summary

1. **Definition of Quadratic Function:** A quadratic function is a function described by an equation of the form $y = ax^2 + bx + c$, where $a \neq 0$. (405)
2. The graph of a quadratic function has a general shape called a parabola. (405)
3. The minimum point is the lowest point on the graph of a parabola that opens upward. The maximum point is the highest point on the graph of a parabola that opens downward. (405–406)
4. If the graph of a parabola is folded along the axis of symmetry, the two halves of the graph coincide. (405)
5. **Equation of Axis of Symmetry:** The equation of the axis of symmetry for the graph of $y = ax^2 + bx + c$, where $a \neq 0$, is given by $x = -\dfrac{b}{2a}$. (406)
6. The roots of a quadratic equation are the x-coordinates of the points where the graph of the corresponding quadratic function crosses the x-axis. (410)
7. To complete the square for $x^2 + bx$, follow these steps.
   Step 1   Find one-half of b, the coefficient of x.
   Step 2   Square the result of **Step 1**.
   Step 3   Add the result of **Step 2** to $x^2 + bx$. (410)
8. **The Quadratic Formula:**   The roots of a quadratic equation of the form $ax^2 + bx + c = 0$, where $a \neq 0$, are given by
$$x = \frac{-b \pm \sqrt{b^2 - 4ac}}{2a} \quad . \quad (416)$$
9. **Nature of Roots of a Quadratic Equation:** The discriminant, $b^2 - 4ac$, gives the following information about the roots of a quadratic equation.
   1. $b^2 - 4ac > 0$, two real roots
   2. $b^2 - 4ac = 0$, one real root
   3. $b^2 - 4ac < 0$, no real roots (421)
10. The table on page 424 summarizes the methods for solving quadratic equations. (424)
11. To find a quadratic equation of the form $x^2 + bx + c = 0$ given its roots:
    1. The coefficient of x is the opposite of the sum of the roots.
    2. The constant term is the product of the roots. (429)
12. **Sum and Product of Roots:** Given the quadratic equation $ax^2 + bx + c = 0$, where $a \neq 0$, the sum of the roots of the equation is $-\dfrac{b}{a}$ and the product of the roots of the equation is $\dfrac{c}{a}$. (430)

Chapter Review

13-1 Find the equation of the axis of symmetry and the coordinates of the **maximum or minimum** point for the graph of each quadratic function.

1. $y = x^2 - 3x - 4$ 2. $y = -x^2 + 6x + 16$ 3. $y = 2x^2 + 9x + 9$

13-2 Locate the roots of each equation by graphing the related function.

4. $x^2 - x - 12 = 0$ 5. $x^2 + 6x + 9 = 0$ 6. $x^2 - 8x + 12 = 0$

13-3 Find the value of c that makes each trinomial a perfect square.

7. $h^2 + 12h + c$ 8. $m^2 + 8m + c$ 9. $r^2 - 5r + c$

Solve by completing the square.

10. $x^2 - 16x + 32 = 0$ 11. $y^2 + 6y + 4 = 0$

12. $x^2 - 7x - 5 = 0$ 13. $4a^2 + 16a + 15 = 0$

13-4 Use the quadratic formula to solve each equation.

14. $x^2 - 8x = 20$ 15. $2x^2 + 7x - 15 = 0$

16. $2m^2 + 3 = 7m$ 17. $9k^2 - 12k - 1 = 0$

18. $3s^2 - 7s - 2 = 0$ 19. $5b^2 + 9b + 3 = 0$

13-5 Use the discriminant to determine the nature of the roots for each equation.

20. $3m^2 - 8m - 40 = 0$ 21. $7x^2 - 6x + 5 = 0$

22. $4p^2 + 4p = 15$ 23. $9k^2 - 13k + 4 = 0$

13-6 State the method that seems easiest for solving each equation. Then use it to solve the equation.

24. $r^2 - 12r = -27$ 25. $m^2 + 10m - 7 = 0$

26. $3a^2 - 11a + 10 = 0$ 27. $9x^2 + 11 = 20x$

28. $2x^2 - \frac{17}{6}x + 1 = 0$ 29. $x^2 - \frac{27}{20}x + \frac{3}{5} = 0$

30. $x^2 - x + 0.21 = 0$ 31. $x^2 - 2.3x + 0.6 = 0$

13-7 Solve each problem.

32. A rectangle has a perimeter of 38 inches. Its area is 84 square inches. Find its dimensions.

33. Find two integers whose sum is 21 and whose product is 90.

13-8 State the sum and product of the roots of each equation.

34. $y^2 + 8y - 14 = 0$ 35. $4a^2 - 6a + 11 = 0$

Write a quadratic equation having the given roots.

36. $1, -8$ 37. $\frac{3}{2}, -4$ 38. $3 + \sqrt{5}, 3 - \sqrt{5}$

Chapter Test

Find the equation of the axis of symmetry and the coordinates of the maximum or minimum point for the graph of each quadratic function.

1. $y = 4x^2 - 8x - 17$

2. $y = -3x^2 + 12x + 34$

Locate the roots of each equation by graphing the related function.

3. $x^2 + x - 2 = 0$

4. $x^2 - 8x + 15 = 0$

Find the value of c that makes each trinomial a perfect square.

5. $x^2 + 14x + c$

6. $x^2 - 21x + c$

Solve by completing the square.

7. $k^2 - 8k - 4 = 0$

8. $m^2 - 6m + 6 = 0$

Use the quadratic formula to solve each equation.

9. $2x^2 - 5x - 12 = 0$

10. $2m^2 - 9m + 8 = 0$

11. $3y^2 - 2y - 5 = 0$

12. $2y^2 + 3y - 20 = 0$

Use the discriminant to determine the nature of the roots for each equation.

13. $3y^2 - y - 10 = 0$

14. $4y^2 + 12y + 9 = 0$

15. $y^2 + \sqrt{3}y - 5 = 0$

16. $x^2 + 2x + 2 = 0$

Solve the following equations.

17. $4x^2 - 5x + 1 = 0$

18. $m^2 + 18m + 75 = 0$

19. $3x^2 + 2x = 5$

20. $2x^2 - 3x = 10$

21. $7x^2 - \frac{23}{3}x + 2 = 0$

22. $x^2 - 4.4x + 4.2 = 0$

Solve each problem.

23. A rectangle has a perimeter of 44 centimeters. Its area is 105 square centimeters. Find its dimensions.

24. Find two integers whose sum is 22 and whose product is 72.

Find a quadratic equation having the given roots.

25. $-2, 5$

26. $6 + \sqrt{3}, 6 - \sqrt{3}$

State the sum and product of the roots of each equation.

27. $m^2 + 15m + 41 = 0$

28. $2x^2 - x - 6 = 0$

CHAPTER 14

Rational Expressions

Many musical instruments are used in a marching band. Even though the instruments are different, the same music scale applies to each instrument. Similarly, the properties and operations you have applied to common fractions can also be applied to rational expressions.

14-1 Simplifying Algebraic Fractions

Algebraic fractions contain variables. The expressions $\frac{5x + 3}{y}$, $\frac{2}{x}$, and $\frac{a - 2}{a^2 + 4}$ are examples of algebraic fractions.

A fraction indicates division. Zero cannot be used as a denominator because division by zero is undefined. Therefore, any value assigned to a variable that results in a denominator of zero must be excluded from the domain of the variable.

For $\frac{5}{x}$, exclude $x = 0$.

For $\frac{3x + 7}{x + 4}$, exclude $x = -4$.

For $\frac{y^2 - 5}{x^2 - 5x + 6}$, exclude $x = 2$ and $x = 3$.   *Factor $x^2 - 5x + 6$ to see why.*

Example

1 **For each fraction state the values of the variable that must be excluded.**

a. $\dfrac{5x}{x + 7}$

Exclude the values for which $x + 7 = 0$.

$x + 7 = 0$

$x = -7$

Therefore, x cannot equal -7.

b. $\dfrac{2a - 3}{a^2 - a - 12}$

Exclude the values for which $a^2 - a - 12 = 0$.

$a^2 - a - 12 = 0$

$(a - 4)(a + 3) = 0$ *Factor $a^2 - a - 12 = 0$.*

$a = 4 \text{ or } a = -3$ *Use the zero product property.*

Therefore, a cannot equal 4 or -3.

Recall that to simplify an algebraic fraction such as $\frac{14a^2bc}{42abc^2}$, first factor the numerator and denominator. Then eliminate common factors.

$$\frac{14a^2bc}{42abc^2} = \frac{2 \cdot 7 \cdot a \cdot a \cdot b \cdot c}{2 \cdot 3 \cdot 7 \cdot a \cdot b \cdot c \cdot c} \qquad a \neq 0, b \neq 0, c \neq 0$$

$$= \frac{\overset{1}{\cancel{2}} \cdot \overset{1}{\cancel{7}} \cdot \overset{1}{\cancel{a}} \cdot a \cdot \overset{1}{\cancel{b}} \cdot \overset{1}{\cancel{c}}}{\underset{1}{\cancel{2}} \cdot 3 \cdot \underset{1}{\cancel{7}} \cdot \underset{1}{\cancel{a}} \cdot \underset{1}{\cancel{b}} \cdot \underset{1}{\cancel{c}} \cdot c} \quad \text{or} \quad \frac{a}{3c} \qquad \textit{The GCF is 14abc.}$$

The same procedure can be used to simplify algebraic fractions having polynomials in the numerator and denominator.

Examples

2 **Simplify** $\dfrac{a^2 - 1}{a^2 + 7a + 6}$. **State the excluded values of a.**

$$\frac{a^2 - 1}{a^2 + 7a + 6} = \frac{(a + 1)(a - 1)}{(a + 6)(a + 1)} \qquad \text{Factor } a^2 - 1.$$
$$\text{Factor } a^2 + 7a + 6.$$

$$= \frac{\overset{1}{\cancel{(a + 1)}}(a - 1)}{(a + 6)\underset{1}{\cancel{(a + 1)}}} \qquad \text{The GCF is } (a + 1).$$

$$= \frac{a - 1}{a + 6}$$

The excluded values of a are any values for which $a^2 + 7a + 6 = 0$.

$$a^2 + 7a + 6 = 0$$
$$(a + 6)(a + 1) = 0$$
$$a = -6 \quad \text{or} \quad a = -1$$

Therefore, a cannot equal -6 or -1.

3 **Simplify** $\dfrac{2x - 2y}{y^2 - x^2}$. **State the excluded values of x and y.**

$$\frac{2x - 2y}{y^2 - x^2} = \frac{2(x - y)}{(y - x)(y + x)} \qquad \text{Use the distributive property.}$$

$$= \frac{2(-1)(y - x)}{(y - x)(y + x)} \qquad \text{Notice that } x - y = -1(y - x).$$

$$= \frac{-2\overset{1}{\cancel{(y - x)}}}{\underset{1}{\cancel{(y - x)}}(y + x)} \qquad \text{Eliminate common factors.}$$

$$= \frac{-2}{y + x} \quad \text{or} \quad -\frac{2}{y + x}$$

The excluded values of x and y are any values for which $y^2 - x^2 = 0$.

$$y^2 - x^2 = 0$$
$$(y - x)(y + x) = 0$$
$$y = x \quad \text{or} \quad y = -x$$

Therefore, y cannot equal x or $-x$.

Exploratory Exercises

Simplify each algebraic fraction. State the excluded values of the variables.

1. $\dfrac{y + 4}{(y - 4)(y + 4)}$

2. $\dfrac{a - 7}{(a + 1)(a - 7)}$

3. $\dfrac{r(r + 3)}{r + 3}$

4. $\dfrac{m(m - 1)}{m - 1}$

5. $\dfrac{2x^3}{2x^2(x^2 - 4)}$

6. $\dfrac{-3z^2}{z(z^2 - 5)}$

7. $\dfrac{(a - 4)(a + 4)}{(a - 2)(a - 4)}$

8. $\dfrac{(c + 6)(c - 2)}{(c - 2)(c - 2)}$

9. $\dfrac{(t + 2)(t - 2)(t + 3)(t - 3)}{(t + 2)(t - 3)}$

10. $\dfrac{(x + 5)(x - 6)}{(x + 5)(x - 5)(x^2 - 6)}$

11. $\dfrac{-1(3w - 2)}{(3w - 2)(w + 4)}$

12. $\dfrac{a(b + 2)(b - 7)}{(b + 1)(b + 2)(b + 3)}$

Written Exercises

Simplify each algebraic fraction. State the excluded values of the variables.

1. $\dfrac{y - 3}{y^2 - 9}$

2. $\dfrac{s + 6}{s^2 - 36}$

3. $\dfrac{a^2 - 25}{a^2 + 3a - 10}$

4. $\dfrac{x^2 - 49}{x^2 - 2x - 35}$

5. $\dfrac{r^3 - r^2}{r - 1}$

6. $\dfrac{z^2 - 3z}{z - 3}$

7. $\dfrac{4n^2 - 8}{4n - 4}$

8. $\dfrac{6y^3 - 12y^2}{12y^2 - 18}$

9. $\dfrac{3m^3}{6m^2 - 3m}$

10. $\dfrac{7a^3b^2}{21a^2b + 49ab^3}$

11. $\dfrac{x + 3}{x^2 + 6x + 9}$

12. $\dfrac{c - 6}{c^2 - 12c + 36}$

13. $\dfrac{g^2 + g - 2}{g^2 - 3g + 2}$

14. $\dfrac{r^2 - r - 20}{r^2 + 9r + 20}$

15. $\dfrac{m^2 - 36}{m^2 + 5m - 6}$

16. $\dfrac{a^2 - 9}{a^2 + 6a - 27}$

17. $\dfrac{2y - 4}{y^2 + 3y - 10}$

18. $\dfrac{4x + 8}{x^2 + 6x + 8}$

19. $\dfrac{k^2 - 1}{k^2 + 2k + 1}$

20. $\dfrac{b^2 - 9}{b^2 + 6b + 9}$

21. $\dfrac{9 - a^2}{a^2 - a - 6}$

22. $\dfrac{25 - x^2}{x^2 + x - 30}$

23. $\dfrac{-x^2 + 6x - 9}{x^2 - 6x + 9}$

24. $\dfrac{a^2 - 2a + 1}{-a^2 + 2a - 1}$

25. $\dfrac{4y^2 + 7y - 2}{8y^2 + 15y - 2}$

26. $\dfrac{4x^2 - 6x - 4}{2x^2 - 8x + 8}$

27. $\dfrac{3m^2 + 9m + 6}{4m^2 + 12m + 8}$

28. $\dfrac{6r^2 + 12r - 48}{5r^2 - 5r - 10}$

29. $\dfrac{2t^2 - t - 21}{28 - 15t + 2t^2}$

30. $\dfrac{3z^2 + 5z - 2}{4 - 13z + 3z^2}$

31. $\dfrac{b^2 + 2b - 8}{b^4 - 20b^2 + 64}$

32. $\dfrac{a^2 + 2a - 3}{a^4 - 10a^2 + 9}$

33. $\dfrac{2x^2 + 7x - 4}{4x^2 - 4x + 1}$

34. $\dfrac{6y^2 + 7y + 2}{6y^2 + 5y + 1}$

35. $\dfrac{x^4 - 1}{x^4 - 5x^2 + 4}$

36. $\dfrac{x^4 - 16}{x^4 - 8x^2 + 16}$

37. $\dfrac{6s^2 + 17s - 14}{3s^2 - 20s + 12}$

38. $\dfrac{8t^2 - 14t - 15}{12t^2 - 19t - 21}$

39. $\dfrac{c^2 - c - 20}{c^3 + 10c^2 + 24c}$

40. $\dfrac{n^2 - 8n + 12}{n^3 - 12n^2 + 36n}$

41. $\dfrac{a^4 - 5a^2 + 4}{a^2 - a - 2}$

42. $\dfrac{y^4 - 13y^2 + 36}{y^2 + 5y + 6}$

43. $\dfrac{12x^3 + 12x^2 - 9x}{12x^3 + 18x^2 - 12x}$

44. $\dfrac{16a^3 - 24a^2 - 160a}{8a^4 - 36a^3 + 16a^2}$

Problem Solving

Sometimes the solution to a problem involves several steps. An important strategy for solving such problems is to identify subgoals. This involves taking steps that will either produce part of the solution, or will make the problem easier to solve. Study the following examples.

Example 1: **Find all whole numbers less than 100 whose digits have a sum of 10.**

Choose a subgoal. Find all pairs of digits that have a sum of 10.

1, 9   2, 8   3, 7   4, 6   5, 5

Then use each pair of digits to write whole numbers. The solutions are 19, 91, 28, 82, 37, 73, 46, 64, and 55.

Example 2: **How many pairs of unit fractions have a sum of $\frac{1}{2}$?**

The unit fractions are $\left\{ \frac{1}{2}, \frac{1}{3}, \frac{1}{4}, \frac{1}{5}, \ldots \right\}$.

Suppose one of the fractions is $\frac{1}{3}$.

Use subtraction to find the other fraction. $\frac{1}{2} - \frac{1}{3} = \frac{1}{6}$

Thus, $\frac{1}{3} + \frac{1}{6} = \frac{1}{2}$. This is one solution to the problem.

Suppose one of the fractions is $\frac{1}{4}$. $\frac{1}{2} - \frac{1}{4} = \frac{1}{4}$

Thus, $\frac{1}{4} + \frac{1}{4} = \frac{1}{2}$. This is a second solution to the problem.

Suppose one of the fractions is $\frac{1}{5}$. $\frac{1}{2} - \frac{1}{5} = \frac{3}{10}$

Notice $\frac{3}{10}$ is *not* a unit fraction. There is no unit fraction which can be added to $\frac{1}{5}$ to get $\frac{1}{2}$.

Are there any other pairs of unit fractions whose sum is $\frac{1}{2}$? Of the two unit fractions, one would have to be greater than $\frac{1}{4}$ and the other would have to be less than $\frac{1}{4}$. Why? But $\frac{1}{3}$ and $\frac{1}{2}$ are the *only* unit fractions greater than $\frac{1}{4}$. Thus, there are only two pairs of unit fractions that have a sum of $\frac{1}{2}$.

Exercises

Solve each problem.

1. How many pairs of unit fractions have a sum of $\frac{1}{6}$.

2. How many whole numbers less than 1000 have digits whose sum is 10?

3. Find all whole numbers between 10 and 1000 that stay the same when the digits are written in reverse order. For example, 686 has this property.

4. Suppose the scoring in football is simplified to 7 points for a touchdown and 3 points for a field goal. What scores are impossible to achieve?

14-2 Multiplying Fractions

To multiply fractions, you multiply the numerators and multiply the denominators.

$$\frac{3}{5} \cdot \frac{4}{7} = \frac{3 \cdot 4}{5 \cdot 7}$$

$$= \frac{12}{35}$$

This method can be generalized as follows.

> **For all rational numbers $\frac{a}{b}$ and $\frac{c}{d}$, where $b \neq 0$ and $d \neq 0$,**
>
> $$\frac{a}{b} \cdot \frac{c}{d} = \frac{ac}{bd}.$$

Multiplying Fractions

The same method can be used to multiply algebraic fractions.

Examples

1 Simplify $\frac{5}{a} \cdot \frac{b}{7}$. State any excluded values.

$$\frac{5}{a} \cdot \frac{b}{7} = \frac{5 \cdot b}{a \cdot 7} \qquad \text{\textit{Multiply the numerators.}}$$
$$\text{\textit{Multiply the denominators.}}$$

$$= \frac{5b}{7a}$$

Since $7a$ cannot equal 0, $a \neq 0$.

2 Simplify $\frac{2a^2d}{3bc} \cdot \frac{9b^2c}{16ad^2}$. State any excluded values.

$$\frac{2a^2d}{3bc} \cdot \frac{9b^2c}{16ad^2} = \frac{18a^2b^2cd}{48abcd^2} \qquad \text{\textit{The GCF is 6abcd.}}$$

$$= \frac{3ab}{8d} \qquad \text{\textit{Change the fraction to simplest form.}}$$

Since bc and ad^2 cannot equal 0, $a \neq 0$, $b \neq 0$, $c \neq 0$, and $d \neq 0$.

From this point on, it will be assumed that all replacements for variables in algebraic fractions that result in denominators equal to zero will be excluded.

You may have used the shortcut shown below for simplifying and finding products at the same time.

$$\frac{3}{4} \cdot \frac{16}{21} = \frac{\overset{1}{\cancel{3}}}{\underset{1}{\cancel{4}}} \cdot \frac{\overset{4}{\cancel{16}}}{\underset{7}{\cancel{21}}} = \frac{4}{7}$$

The same method can be used with algebraic fractions.

3 **Simplify:** $\dfrac{x+5}{3x} \cdot \dfrac{12x^2}{x^2+7x+10}$

$$\dfrac{x+5}{3x} \cdot \dfrac{12x^2}{x^2+7x+10} = \dfrac{x+5}{3 \cdot x} \cdot \dfrac{2 \cdot 2 \cdot 3 \cdot x \cdot x}{(x+5)(x+2)} \qquad x \neq 0,\ x \neq -5,\ \text{or } x \neq -2$$

$$= \dfrac{\overset{1}{\cancel{x+5}}}{\underset{1\ \ 1}{\cancel{3 \cdot \cancel{x}}}} \cdot \dfrac{2 \cdot 2 \cdot \overset{1}{\cancel{3}} \cdot \overset{1}{\cancel{x}} \cdot x}{\underset{1}{\cancel{(x+5)}}(x+2)} \qquad \textit{Eliminate common factors.}$$

$$= \dfrac{4x}{x+2}$$

4 **Simplify:** $\dfrac{4a+8}{a^2-25} \cdot \dfrac{a-5}{5a+10}$

$$\dfrac{4a+8}{a^2-25} \cdot \dfrac{a-5}{5a+10} = \dfrac{4(a+2)}{(a-5)(a+5)} \cdot \dfrac{a-5}{5(a+2)} \qquad a \neq 5,\ a \neq -5,\ \text{or } a \neq -2$$

$$= \dfrac{4\overset{1}{\cancel{(a+2)}}}{\underset{1}{\cancel{(a-5)}}(a+5)} \cdot \dfrac{\overset{1}{\cancel{a-5}}}{5\underset{1}{\cancel{(a+2)}}} \qquad \textit{Eliminate common factors.}$$

$$= \dfrac{4}{5(a+5)}$$

$$= \dfrac{4}{5a+25}$$

5 **Simplify:** $\dfrac{x^2-x-6}{9-x^2} \cdot \dfrac{x^2+7x+12}{x^2+4x+4}$

$$\dfrac{x^2-x-6}{9-x^2} \cdot \dfrac{x^2+7x+12}{x^2+4x+4} = \dfrac{(x-3)(x+2)}{(3-x)(3+x)} \cdot \dfrac{(x+3)(x+4)}{(x+2)(x+2)} \qquad \begin{array}{l} x \neq -3,\ x \neq 3, \\ \text{or } x \neq -2 \end{array}$$

$$= \dfrac{(x-3)(x+2)}{-1(x-3)(x+3)} \cdot \dfrac{(x+3)(x+4)}{(x+2)(x+2)} \qquad \begin{array}{l} \textit{Notice that} \\ \textit{3} - x = -1(x-3). \end{array}$$

$$= \dfrac{\overset{1}{\cancel{(x-3)}}\overset{1}{\cancel{(x+2)}}}{-1\underset{1}{\cancel{(x-3)}}\underset{1}{\cancel{(x+3)}}} \cdot \dfrac{\overset{1}{\cancel{(x+3)}}(x+4)}{\underset{1}{\cancel{(x+2)}}(x+2)} \qquad \begin{array}{l} \textit{Eliminate common} \\ \textit{factors.} \end{array}$$

$$= \dfrac{x+4}{-1(x+2)}$$

$$= -\dfrac{x+4}{x+2}$$

Exploratory Exercises

Find each product.

1. $\frac{1}{3} \cdot \frac{5}{8}$

2. $\frac{3}{4} \cdot \frac{5}{7}$

3. $-\frac{5}{6} \cdot \frac{7}{8}$

4. $\frac{2}{3}\left(-\frac{5}{9}\right)$

5. $-\frac{7}{8}\left(-\frac{5}{9}\right)$

6. $\frac{3}{a} \cdot \frac{b}{4}$

7. $\frac{a}{3} \cdot \frac{a}{5}$

8. $\frac{3a}{5} \cdot \frac{2x}{y}$

9. $\frac{2}{3}\left(\frac{1}{2}\right)$

10. $\frac{4}{5} \cdot \frac{5}{8}$

11. $\left(-\frac{5}{9}\right)\left(\frac{3}{10}\right)$

12. $\left(-\frac{4}{5}\right)\left(-\frac{3}{8}\right)$

13. $\left(-\frac{4}{9}\right)\left(\frac{3}{8}\right)$

14. $\frac{5}{12} \cdot \frac{4}{9}$

15. $\left(\frac{4}{7}\right)\left(\frac{11}{16}\right)$

Written Exercises

Find each product in simplest form.

1. $\frac{2}{9} \cdot \frac{3}{5}$

2. $\frac{4}{9} \cdot \frac{1}{3}$

3. $\frac{16}{75} \cdot \frac{5}{8}$

4. $\frac{32}{7} \cdot \frac{35}{8}$

5. $\left(\frac{1}{4}\right)^2$

6. $\left(\frac{2}{3}\right)^2$

7. $\left(\frac{4}{9}\right)^3$

8. $\left(\frac{8}{5}\right)^3$

9. $\frac{ab}{ac} \cdot \frac{c}{d}$

10. $\frac{a^2b}{b^2c} \cdot \frac{c}{d}$

11. $\frac{6a^2n}{8n^2} \cdot \frac{12n}{9a}$

12. $\frac{10n^3}{6x^3} \cdot \frac{12n^2x^4}{25n^2x^2}$

13. $\frac{8}{m^2}\left(\frac{m^2}{2c}\right)^2$

14. $\left(\frac{2a}{b}\right)^2 \frac{5c}{6a}$

15. $\frac{6m^3n}{10a^2} \cdot \frac{4a^2m}{9n^3}$

16. $\frac{7xy^3}{11z^2} \cdot \frac{44z^3}{21x^2y}$

17. $\frac{y-3}{7} \cdot \frac{14}{y-3}$

18. $\frac{5n-5}{3} \cdot \frac{9}{n-1}$

19. $\frac{3a-3b}{a} \cdot \frac{a^2}{a-b}$

20. $\frac{-(2a+7c)}{6} \cdot \frac{36}{-7c-2a}$

21. $\frac{2a+4b}{5} \cdot \frac{25}{6a+8b}$

22. $\frac{3x+30}{2x} \cdot \frac{4x}{4x+40}$

23. $\frac{3}{x-y} \cdot \frac{(x-y)^2}{6}$

24. $\frac{a^2-b^2}{4} \cdot \frac{16}{a+b}$

25. $\frac{m^2-4}{2} \cdot \frac{4}{m-2}$

26. $\frac{9}{m-3} \cdot \frac{m^2-9}{12}$

27. $\frac{r^2}{r-s} \cdot \frac{r^2-s^2}{s^2}$

28. $\frac{a^2-b^2}{a-b} \cdot \frac{7}{a+b}$

29. $\frac{x^2-16}{9} \cdot \frac{x+4}{x-4}$

30. $\frac{y^2-4}{y^2-1} \cdot \frac{y+1}{y+2}$

31. $\frac{x^2-y^2}{x^2-1} \cdot \frac{x-1}{x-y}$

32. $\frac{r^2+s^2}{r^2-s^2} \cdot \frac{r-s}{r+s}$

33. $\frac{m^2+16}{m^2-16} \cdot \frac{m-4}{m+4}$

34. $\frac{3k+9}{k} \cdot \frac{k^2}{k^2-9}$

35. $\frac{3a-6}{a^2-9} \cdot \frac{a+3}{a^2-2a}$

36. $\frac{y^2-x^2}{y} \cdot \frac{x}{x-y}$

37. $\frac{b+a}{b-a} \cdot \frac{a^2-b^2}{a}$

38. $\frac{3mn^2-3m}{n} \cdot \frac{3m}{n^2-1}$

39. $\frac{x+3}{x+4} \cdot \frac{x}{x^2+7x+12}$

40. $\frac{x}{x^2+8x+15} \cdot \frac{2x+10}{x^2}$

41. $\dfrac{1}{x^2 + x - 12} \cdot \dfrac{x - 3}{x + 5}$

42. $\dfrac{x - 5}{x^2 - 7x + 10} \cdot \dfrac{x - 2}{3}$

43. $\dfrac{b^2 + 20b + 99}{b + 9} \cdot \dfrac{b + 7}{b^2 + 12b + 11}$

44. $\dfrac{z^2 - 15z + 50}{z^2 - 9z + 20} \cdot \dfrac{z^2 - 11z + 24}{z^2 - 18z + 80}$

45. $\dfrac{b^2 + 19b + 84}{b - 3} \cdot \dfrac{b^2 - 9}{b^2 + 15b + 36}$

46. $\dfrac{z^2 + 16z + 39}{z^2 + 9z + 18} \cdot \dfrac{z + 5}{z^2 + 18z + 65}$

47. $\dfrac{y^2 + 3y^3}{y^2 - 4} \cdot \dfrac{2y + y^2}{y + 4y^2 + 3y^3}$

48. $\dfrac{2m^2 - 9m + 9}{3m^2 + 19m - 14} \cdot \dfrac{m^2 + 14m + 49}{9 - 6m + m^2}$

49. $\dfrac{6y^2 - 5y - 6}{3y^2 - 20y - 7} \cdot \dfrac{y^2 - 49}{12y^3 + 23y^2 + 10y}$

50. $\dfrac{3t^3 - 14t^2 + 8t}{2t^2 - 3t - 20} \cdot \dfrac{16t^2 + 34t - 15}{24t^2 - 25t + 6}$

Challenge

Find each product in simplest form.

51. $\dfrac{a}{a^2 + 6a + 9} \cdot \dfrac{a + 3}{a - 5} \cdot \dfrac{a^2 - 25}{5a + 25}$

52. $\dfrac{x^2y}{x^2 + 4xy + 4y^2} \cdot \dfrac{x^2 + 2xy}{xy} \cdot \dfrac{y}{x^4 - 9x^2}$

53. $\dfrac{a^2x - b^2x}{y} \cdot \dfrac{y^2 + y}{a - 2} \cdot \dfrac{4 - 2a}{axy - bxy}$

mini-review

Write *true* or *false*.

1. $(2, -1)$ is a solution to the equation $3x + y = 5$.

2. $(4, 5)$ is a solution to the system of equations $x + y = 9$ and $x - y = 1$.

3. $\dfrac{\sqrt{16}}{\sqrt{5}} = \dfrac{4}{5}$

4. The roots of $x^2 + 3x + 2 = 0$ are -1 and -2.

5. The sum of the roots of $x^2 - 2x - 8 = 0$ is -2.

Excursions in Algebra _____ Does 2 = 1?

Find the fallacy in the following "proof" of "2 = 1."

$$a = b$$
$$a \cdot a = b \cdot a \qquad \text{Multiply both sides by a.}$$
$$a^2 = ab$$
$$a^2 - b^2 = ab - b^2 \qquad \text{Subtract } b^2 \text{ from both sides.}$$
$$(a - b)(a + b) = b(a - b) \qquad \text{Factor.}$$
$$\dfrac{(a - b)(a + b)}{(a - b)} = \dfrac{b(a - b)}{(a - b)} \qquad \text{Divide both sides by } (a - b).$$
$$a + b = b$$
$$b + b = b \qquad \text{Substitute b for a.}$$
$$2b = b$$
$$\dfrac{2b}{b} = \dfrac{b}{b} \qquad \text{Divide both sides by b.}$$
$$2 = 1$$

14-3 Dividing Fractions

Consider the following products. What is the pattern of the factors in each example?

$$\frac{5}{1} \cdot \frac{1}{5} = 1 \qquad \frac{1}{4} \cdot \frac{4}{1} = 1 \qquad \frac{2}{3} \cdot \frac{3}{2} = 1 \qquad \frac{x}{y} \cdot \frac{y}{x} = 1$$

Remember that all replacements for variables that yield a denominator of zero are excluded.

You should recall that two numbers whose product is 1 are called **multiplicative inverses** or **reciprocals**.

To find the quotient of two fractions, you multiply by the reciprocal of the second fraction.

$$\frac{2}{3} \div \frac{3}{4} = \frac{2}{3} \cdot \frac{4}{3} \qquad \textit{The reciprocal of } \frac{3}{4} \textit{ is } \frac{4}{3}.$$

$$= \frac{8}{9}$$

This method can be generalized as follows.

> **For all rational numbers $\frac{a}{b}$ and $\frac{c}{d}$, where $b \neq 0$, $c \neq 0$, and $d \neq 0$,**
>
> $$\frac{a}{b} \div \frac{c}{d} = \frac{a}{b} \cdot \frac{d}{c}.$$

Dividing Fractions

The same method is used to divide algebraic fractions.

Examples

1 Find the quotient in simplest form: $\frac{5}{x} \div \frac{y}{z}$

$$\frac{5}{x} \div \frac{y}{z} = \frac{5}{x} \cdot \frac{z}{y} \qquad \textit{The reciprocal of } \frac{y}{z} \textit{ is } \frac{z}{y}.$$

$$= \frac{5z}{xy}$$

2 Find the quotient in simplest form: $\frac{2x}{x + 1} \div (x - 1)$

$$\frac{2x}{x + 1} \div (x - 1) = \frac{2x}{x + 1} \cdot \frac{1}{x - 1} \qquad \textit{The reciprocal of } (x - 1) \textit{ is } \frac{1}{x - 1}.$$

$$= \frac{2x}{(x + 1)(x - 1)}$$

$$= \frac{2x}{x^2 - 1}$$

3 Find the quotient in simplest form: $\dfrac{x - y}{x^2 - y^2} \div \dfrac{x + y}{x^2 + 2xy + y^2}$

$$\frac{x - y}{x^2 - y^2} \div \frac{x + y}{x^2 + 2xy + y^2} = \frac{x - y}{x^2 - y^2} \cdot \frac{x^2 + 2xy + y^2}{x + y}$$

$$= \frac{x - y}{(x + y)(x - y)} \cdot \frac{(x + y)(x + y)}{x + y}$$

$$= \frac{\overset{1}{\cancel{x - y}}}{\underset{1}{\cancel{(x + y)}}\underset{1}{\cancel{(x - y)}}} \cdot \frac{\overset{1}{\cancel{(x + y)}}\overset{1}{\cancel{(x + y)}}}{\underset{1}{\cancel{x + y}}}$$

$$= 1$$

Exploratory Exercises

State the reciprocal of each of the following.

1. $\dfrac{3}{4}$

2. $\dfrac{-5}{8}$

3. $\dfrac{8}{-3}$

4. $-\dfrac{9}{10}$

5. $\dfrac{m}{2}$

6. $\dfrac{x^2}{4}$

7. $\dfrac{5}{2p}$

8. $\dfrac{-8}{3n}$

9. 6

10. x

11. a^2

12. $\dfrac{1}{3}a$

13. $2bc$

14. $\dfrac{2}{5}m^2$

15. $\dfrac{x + y}{x - y}$

16. $\dfrac{a^2 + b}{a - b}$

17. $\dfrac{3}{5}a^2b^2$

18. $x - 2$

State a multiplication expression for each of the following.

19. $\dfrac{3}{8} \div \dfrac{1}{4}$

20. $\dfrac{1}{7} \div \dfrac{-1}{49}$

21. $\dfrac{1}{3} \div -6$

22. $\dfrac{x}{y} \div \dfrac{y^2}{x}$

23. $\dfrac{2x}{4 - 2a} \div \dfrac{a^2}{b - 2}$

24. $\dfrac{b - a}{a - b} \div (a + b)$

Written Exercises

Find each quotient in simplest form.

1. $\dfrac{5}{6} \div \dfrac{2}{3}$

2. $\dfrac{3}{8} \div \dfrac{-1}{2}$

3. $-\dfrac{5}{6} \div \dfrac{1}{3}$

4. $\dfrac{5}{8} \div 5$

5. $\dfrac{a^2}{b^2} \div \dfrac{b^2}{a^2}$

6. $\dfrac{a}{b} \div \dfrac{b^3}{a^4}$

7. $\dfrac{y^2}{x^2} \div \dfrac{a^2}{x^2}$

8. $\dfrac{a^2}{b} \div \dfrac{a^2}{b^2}$

9. $\dfrac{(-a)^2}{b} \div \dfrac{a}{b}$

10. $\dfrac{p^3}{2q} \div \dfrac{-(p^2)}{4q}$

11. $\dfrac{3m}{m+1} \div (m-2)$

12. $\dfrac{n^2}{n-3} \div (n+4)$

13. $\dfrac{b^2-9}{4b} \div (b-3)$

14. $\dfrac{y^2+8y+16}{y^2} \div (y+4)$

15. $\dfrac{y^2}{x+2} \div \dfrac{y}{x+2}$

16. $\dfrac{2a^3}{a+1} \div \dfrac{a^2}{a+1}$

17. $\dfrac{p^2}{y^2-4} \div \dfrac{p}{2-y}$

18. $\dfrac{q}{y^2-4} \div \dfrac{q^2}{y+2}$

19. $\dfrac{x^2-16}{16-x^2} \div \dfrac{7}{x}$

20. $\dfrac{y}{5} \div \dfrac{y^2-25}{5-y}$

21. $\dfrac{m^2+2m+1}{2} \div \dfrac{m+1}{m-1}$

22. $\dfrac{x^2-4x+4}{3} \div \dfrac{x^2-4}{2x}$

23. $\dfrac{m^2+2mn+n^2}{3m} \div \dfrac{m^2-n^2}{2}$

24. $\dfrac{a^2+2ab+b^2}{2x} \div \dfrac{a+b}{x^2}$

25. $\dfrac{y^2-16}{y^2-64} \div \dfrac{y+4}{y-8}$

26. $\dfrac{k^2-81}{k^2-36} \div \dfrac{k-9}{k+6}$

27. $\dfrac{t^2+8t+16}{w^2-6w+9} \div \dfrac{2t+8}{3w-9}$

28. $\dfrac{k+2}{m^2+4m+4} \div \dfrac{4k+8}{m+4}$

29. $\dfrac{x}{x+2} \div \dfrac{x^2}{x^2+5x+6}$

30. $\dfrac{x^2+x-2}{x^2+5x+6} \div \dfrac{x^2+2x-3}{x^2+7x+12}$

31. $\dfrac{x^2+2x-15}{x^2-x-30} \div \dfrac{x^2-3x-18}{x^2-2x-24}$

32. $\dfrac{2m^2+7m-15}{m+5} \div \dfrac{9m^2-4}{3m+2}$

33. $\dfrac{a^2+3a-10}{a^2+8a+15} \div \dfrac{a^2-6a+8}{12+a-a^2}$

34. $\dfrac{2x^2-x-15}{x^2-2x-3} \div \dfrac{2x^2+3x-5}{1-x^2}$

Challenge

Perform the indicated operations.

35. $\dfrac{x^2+5x+6}{x^2-x-12} \cdot \dfrac{x-4}{x^2+11x+18} \div \dfrac{x+7}{x^2+14x+45}$

36. $\dfrac{2x-3}{2x^2-7x+6} \cdot \dfrac{x^2+3x-10}{5x+1} \div \dfrac{3x^2+14x-5}{3x^2+2x-1}$

37. $\dfrac{x^2+2x-3}{6x^2-5x+1} \cdot \dfrac{2x^2+9x+4}{2x^2+7x+3} \div \dfrac{x^2-5x+4}{6x^2-x-1}$

38. $\dfrac{4x^2-6x-4}{8x^2-2} \div \dfrac{8x^2-8x+2}{4x^2-10x-6} \cdot \dfrac{4x^2-4x+1}{x^2-5x+6}$

39. $\dfrac{x^2-1}{2x^2+14x+12} \div \dfrac{2x^2-3x+1}{8x^2+36x-72} \cdot \dfrac{x^2+3x-4}{x^2+5x-6}$

14-4 Dividing Polynomials

You can use a long division process similar to that used for numbers to divide a polynomial by a polynomial. For example, you can divide $x^2 + 8x + 15$ by $x + 5$ as shown below.

Step 1

To find the first term of the quotient, divide the first term of the dividend (x^2) by the first term of the divisor (x).

$$\begin{array}{r} x \\ x + 5 \overline{)x^2 + 8x + 15} \\ \underline{x^2 + 5x} \\ 3x \end{array}$$

When you divide x^2 by x the result is x.

Multiply $x(x + 5)$.

Subtract.

Step 2

To find the next term of the quotient, divide the first term of the partial dividend ($3x$) by the first term of the divisor (x).

$$\begin{array}{r} x + 3 \\ x + 5 \overline{)x^2 + 8x + 15} \\ \underline{x^2 + 5x} \\ 3x + 15 \\ \underline{3x + 15} \\ 0 \end{array}$$

When you divide $3x$ by x the result is 3.

Multiply $3(x + 5)$.

Subtract.

Therefore, $x^2 + 8x + 15$ divided by $x + 5$ is $x + 3$. Since the remainder is 0, the divisor is a factor of the dividend. This means that $(x + 5)(x + 3) = x^2 + 8x + 15$.

If the divisor is **not** a factor of the dividend, there will be a nonzero remainder. When there is a nonzero remainder the quotient can be expressed as follows:

$$\text{quotient} = \text{partial quotient} + \frac{\text{remainder}}{\text{divisor}}$$

Example

1 **Find the quotient:** $(2x^2 - 11x - 20) \div (2x + 3)$

$$\begin{array}{r} x - 7 \\ 2x + 3 \overline{)2x^2 - 11x - 20} \\ \underline{2x^2 + 3x} \\ -14x - 20 \\ \underline{-14x - 21} \\ 1 \end{array}$$

$\longleftarrow$ *Multiply $x(2x + 3)$.*
$\longleftarrow$ *Subtract, and bring down -20.*
$\longleftarrow$ *Multiply $-7(2x + 3)$.*
$\longleftarrow$ *Subtract. The remainder is 1.*

Therefore, the quotient is $x - 7$ with remainder 1.

Thus, $(2x^2 - 11x - 20) \div (2x + 3) = x - 7 + \dfrac{1}{2x + 3}.$

$\longleftarrow$ *remainder*
$\longleftarrow$ *divisor*

Notice that in an expression such as $s^3 + 9$ there is no s^2 term and no s term. In such situations, the expression can be renamed using 0 as the coefficient of these terms.

$$s^3 + 9 = s^3 + 0s^2 + 0s + 9$$

Example

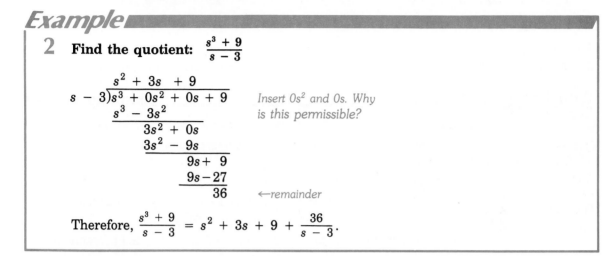

2 **Find the quotient:** $\dfrac{s^3 + 9}{s - 3}$

$$
\begin{array}{r}
s^2 + 3s + 9 \\
s - 3\overline{)s^3 + 0s^2 + 0s + 9} \\
\underline{s^3 - 3s^2} \\
3s^2 + 0s \\
\underline{3s^2 - 9s} \\
9s + 9 \\
\underline{9s - 27} \\
36
\end{array}
$$

Insert $0s^2$ and $0s$. Why is this permissible?

$\leftarrow$*remainder*

Therefore, $\dfrac{s^3 + 9}{s - 3} = s^2 + 3s + 9 + \dfrac{36}{s - 3}$.

Exploratory Exercises

For each of the following, state the first term of the quotient.

1. $\dfrac{a^2 + 3a + 2}{a + 1}$

2. $\dfrac{b^2 + 8b - 20}{b - 2}$

3. $\dfrac{8m^3 + 27}{2m + 3}$

4. $\dfrac{2x^2 + 3x - 2}{2x - 1}$

5. $\dfrac{x^3 + 2x^2 - 5x + 12}{x + 4}$

6. $\dfrac{2x^3 - 5x^2 + 22x + 51}{2x + 3}$

Written Exercises

Find each quotient.

1. $(x^2 + 7x + 12) \div (x + 3)$

2. $(x^2 + 9x + 20) \div (x + 5)$

3. $(a^2 - 2a - 35) \div (a - 7)$

4. $(x^2 + 6x - 16) \div (x - 2)$

5. $(c^2 + 12c + 36) \div (c + 9)$

6. $(y^2 - 2y - 30) \div (y + 7)$

7. $(2r^2 - 3r - 35) \div (2r + 7)$

8. $(3t^2 - 14t - 24) \div (3t + 4)$

9. $\dfrac{10x^2 + 29x + 21}{5x + 7}$

10. $\dfrac{12n^2 + 36n + 15}{6n + 3}$

11. $\dfrac{x^3 - 7x + 6}{x - 2}$

12. $\dfrac{4m^3 + 5m - 21}{2m - 3}$

13. $\dfrac{4t^3 + 17t^2 - 1}{4t + 1}$

14. $\dfrac{2a^3 + 9a^2 + 5a - 12}{a + 3}$

15. $\dfrac{27c^2 - 24c + 8}{9c - 2}$

16. $\dfrac{48b^2 + 8b + 7}{12b - 1}$

17. $\dfrac{6n^3 + 5n^2 + 12}{2n + 3}$

18. $\dfrac{t^3 - 19t + 9}{t - 4}$

19. $\dfrac{3s^3 + 8s^2 + s - 7}{s + 2}$

20. $\dfrac{9d^3 + 5d - 8}{3d - 2}$

21. $\dfrac{20t^3 - 27t^2 + t + 6}{4t - 3}$

22. $\dfrac{6x^3 - 9x^2 - 4x + 6}{2x - 3}$

23. $\dfrac{56x^3 + 32x^2 - 63x - 36}{7x + 4}$

Find each quotient.

24. $\dfrac{2x^4 + 3x^3 - 6x^2 + 7x - 6}{x^2 + 2x - 3}$

25. $\dfrac{6x^4 + 11x^3 - 15x^2 + 16x - 6}{2x^2 + 5x - 3}$

26. Find the value of k if $(x + 2)$ is a factor of $x^3 + 7x^2 + 7x + k$.

27. Find the value of k if $(2m - 5)$ is a factor of $2m^3 - 5m^2 + 8m + k$.

28. When $x^3 - 7x^2 + 4x + k$ is divided by $(x - 2)$, the remainder is 15. Find k.

Using Calculators ———————————— Finding Factors

Is $(x - 2)$ a factor of $x^3 + 3x^2 - 6x - 8$? One way to determine this is to divide $x^3 + 3x^2 - 6x - 8$ by $(x - 2)$ using the long division process. If the remainder is 0, then $(x - 2)$ is a factor of $x^3 + 3x^2 - 6x - 8$.

Another method can be used to determine whether $(x - 2)$ is a factor. If $(x - 2)$ is a factor, then when $x^3 + 3x^2 - 6x - 8 = 0$, $x - 2 = 0$ and $x = 2$. Substitute 2 for x and evaluate $x^3 + 3x^2 - 6x - 8$. If the result is 0, then $(x - 2)$ is a factor.

You can use your calculator to evaluate $x^3 + 3x^2 - 6x - 8$ when $x = 2$. First rename $x^3 + 3x^2 - 6x - 8$ as a **nested polynomial**.

$$x^3 + 3x^2 - 6x - 8 = [x^2 + 3x - 6]x - 8 \qquad \textit{Write the polynomial in descending order.}$$
$$\textit{Factor x out of the first three terms.}$$
$$= [(x + 3)x - 6]x - 8 \qquad \textit{Within the brackets, factor x out of the first two terms.}$$

The nested polynomial $[(x + 3)x - 6]x - 8$ is equivalent to $x^3 + 3x^2 - 6x - 8$. Notice that in the nested polynomial no exponent is greater than 1. Since you do *not* have to raise x to a power, the evaluation process is simplified.

Example: Evaluate $[(x + 3)x - 6]x - 8$ when $x = 2$.

ENTER: 2 STO + 3 = × RCL − 6 = × RCL − 8 =
DISPLAY: 2 2   2 3 5   5 2 10 6 4   4 2 8 8 0

Since the result is 0, $(x - 2)$ is a factor of $x^3 + 3x^2 - 6x - 8$.

Example: Rename $x^4 + 2x^3 + 3x^2 + 4x - 5$ as a nested polynomial.

$$x^4 + 2x^3 + 3x^2 + 4x - 5 = [x^3 + 2x^2 + 3x + 4]x - 5 \qquad \textit{Factor x out of the first 4 terms.}$$
$$= [(x^2 + 2x + 3)x + 4]x - 5 \quad \textit{Continue this process until no}$$
$$= [[(x + 2)x + 3]x + 4]x - 5 \quad \textit{exponent is greater than 1.}$$

Exercises

Rename each of the following as a nested polynomial. Then use your calculator to determine whether the given binomial is a factor.

1. $x^3 + 2x^2 - 22x + 21$; $(x - 3)$ **2.** $x^3 - 6x^2 + 14x - 12$; $(x - 2)$

3. $x^3 - 8x^2 + 13x - 16$; $(x - 8)$ **4.** $x^4 + 3x^3 + 2x^2 - x + 6$; $(x - 2)$

14-5 Adding and Subtracting Fractions with Like Denominators

To add or subtract fractions with *like* denominators, you simply add or subtract the numerators. Then write this sum or difference over the common denominator.

$$\frac{3}{7} + \frac{2}{7} = \frac{5}{7} \qquad \frac{7}{9} - \frac{2}{9} = \frac{5}{9}$$

Sometimes the result needs to be changed to simplest form.

$$\frac{3}{8} + \frac{1}{8} = \frac{4}{8} \quad \text{\textit{The GCF of}} \qquad \frac{9}{16} - \frac{3}{16} = \frac{6}{16} \quad \text{\textit{The GCF of}}$$
$$\qquad\qquad\qquad \text{\textit{4 and 8 is 4.}} \qquad\qquad\qquad\qquad \text{\textit{6 and 16 is 2.}}$$
$$= \frac{1}{2} \qquad\qquad\qquad\qquad\qquad = \frac{3}{8}$$

These methods can be generalized as follows.

For all rational numbers $\frac{a}{c}$ and $\frac{b}{c}$, where $c \neq 0$,

$$\frac{a}{c} + \frac{b}{c} = \frac{a + b}{c} \text{ and } \frac{a}{c} - \frac{b}{c} = \frac{a - b}{c}.$$

Adding or Subtracting Fractions with Like Denominators

These methods can be used to add or subtract algebraic fractions.

Examples

1 **Add and simplify:** $\dfrac{3}{x + 2} + \dfrac{1}{x + 2}.$

$$\frac{3}{x + 2} + \frac{1}{x + 2} = \frac{3 + 1}{x + 2} \qquad \text{\textit{Since the denominators are both $x + 2$,}}$$
$$\text{\textit{add the numerators.}}$$
$$= \frac{4}{x + 2}$$

2 **Subtract and simplify:** $\dfrac{3a + 2}{a - 7} - \dfrac{a - 3}{a - 7}.$

$$\frac{3a + 2}{a - 7} - \frac{a - 3}{a - 7} = \frac{(3a + 2) - (a - 3)}{a - 7} \qquad \text{\textit{The parentheses indicate that}}$$
$$\text{\textit{the quantity $(a - 3)$ is sub-}}$$
$$\text{\textit{tracted from the quantity}}$$
$$= \frac{3a + 2 - a + 3}{a - 7} \qquad \text{\textit{$(3a + 2)$. Remember to change the}}$$
$$\text{\textit{signs of the second polynomial.}}$$
$$= \frac{2a + 5}{a - 7}$$

Example

3 **Subtract and simplify:** $\dfrac{8n + 3}{3n + 4} - \dfrac{2n - 5}{3n + 4}$

$$\frac{8n + 3}{3n + 4} - \frac{2n - 5}{3n + 4} = \frac{(8n + 3) - (2n - 5)}{3n + 4}$$

$$= \frac{8n + 3 - 2n + 5}{3n + 4} \qquad \textit{Why?}$$

$$= \frac{6n + 8}{3n + 4}$$

$$= \frac{2\overset{1}{\cancel{(3n + 4)}}}{\underset{1}{\cancel{(3n + 4)}}} \quad \textit{Factor and simplify.}$$

$$= 2$$

Sometimes the denominators are additive inverses.

Example

4 **Subtract and simplify:** $\dfrac{x}{x - 2} - \dfrac{x + 1}{2 - x}$

$$\frac{x}{x - 2} - \frac{x + 1}{2 - x} = \frac{x}{x - 2} - \frac{x + 1}{-(x - 2)} \qquad \textit{Notice that } 2 - x = -(x - 2).$$

$$= \frac{x}{x - 2} - \left(-\frac{x + 1}{x - 2}\right)$$

$$= \frac{x}{x - 2} + \frac{x + 1}{x - 2}$$

$$= \frac{2x + 1}{x - 2}$$

Exploratory Exercises

Find each sum or difference in simplest form.

1. $\dfrac{5}{8} + \dfrac{2}{8}$

2. $\dfrac{9}{16} + \dfrac{5}{16}$

3. $\dfrac{4}{a} + \dfrac{3}{a}$

4. $\dfrac{6}{b} + \dfrac{7}{b}$

5. $\dfrac{b}{x} + \dfrac{2}{x}$

6. $\dfrac{5}{2z} + \dfrac{-7}{2z}$

7. $\dfrac{-4k}{t} + \dfrac{6k}{t}$

8. $\dfrac{2n}{m^2} + \dfrac{3n}{m^2}$

9. $\dfrac{3}{11} - \dfrac{2}{11}$

10. $\dfrac{14}{16} - \dfrac{15}{16}$

11. $\dfrac{a}{5} - \dfrac{b}{5}$

12. $\dfrac{7}{a} - \dfrac{4}{a}$

13. $\dfrac{4}{x} - \dfrac{6}{x}$

14. $\dfrac{7}{a} - \dfrac{c}{a}$

15. $\dfrac{8k}{5m} - \dfrac{3k}{5m}$

16. $\dfrac{r}{y^2} - \dfrac{s}{y^2}$

Written Exercises

Find each sum or difference in simplest form.

1. $\dfrac{y}{2} + \dfrac{y}{2}$

2. $\dfrac{a}{12} + \dfrac{2a}{12}$

3. $\dfrac{8}{x} + \dfrac{2}{x}$

4. $\dfrac{3}{a} + \dfrac{6}{a}$

5. $\dfrac{2y}{b} - \dfrac{y}{b}$

6. $\dfrac{3}{x} - \dfrac{7}{x}$

7. $\dfrac{12a}{7} - \dfrac{3a}{7}$

8. $\dfrac{y}{14} - \dfrac{3y}{14}$

9. $\dfrac{y}{2} + \dfrac{y-6}{2}$

10. $\dfrac{m+4}{5} + \dfrac{m-1}{5}$

11. $\dfrac{a+2}{6} - \dfrac{a+3}{6}$

12. $\dfrac{b+3}{7} - \dfrac{b+1}{7}$

13. $\dfrac{x}{x-1} + \dfrac{1}{x-1}$

14. $\dfrac{x}{x+1} + \dfrac{1}{x+1}$

15. $\dfrac{8}{y-2} - \dfrac{6}{y-2}$

16. $\dfrac{y}{b+6} - \dfrac{2y}{b+6}$

17. $\dfrac{2n}{2n-5} + \dfrac{5}{5-2n}$

18. $\dfrac{x+y}{y-2} + \dfrac{x-y}{2-y}$

19. $\dfrac{y}{a+1} - \dfrac{y}{a+1}$

20. $\dfrac{y}{y-1} - \dfrac{1}{y-1}$

21. $\dfrac{a+b}{x-3} + \dfrac{a+b}{3-x}$

22. $\dfrac{a+b}{x-3} - \dfrac{a+b}{3-x}$

23. $\dfrac{r^2}{r-s} + \dfrac{s^2}{r-s}$

24. $\dfrac{x^2}{x-y} - \dfrac{y^2}{x-y}$

25. $\dfrac{m^2}{m+n} + \dfrac{2mn+n^2}{m+n}$

26. $\dfrac{x^2}{x-y} - \dfrac{2xy+y^2}{x-y}$

27. $\dfrac{12n}{3n+2} + \dfrac{8}{3n+2}$

28. $\dfrac{6x}{x+y} + \dfrac{6y}{x+y}$

29. $\dfrac{12n}{3n-2} - \dfrac{8}{3n-2}$

30. $\dfrac{a}{2a-2b} - \dfrac{b}{2a-2b}$

31. $\dfrac{a^2}{a-b} + \dfrac{-(b^2)}{a-b}$

32. $\dfrac{a^2}{a^2-b^2} + \dfrac{-(b^2)}{a^2-b^2}$

33. $\dfrac{r^2}{r-3} + \dfrac{9}{3-r}$

34. $\dfrac{m^2}{4+m} - \dfrac{16}{m+4}$

35. $\dfrac{x^2}{x^2-1} + \dfrac{2x+1}{x^2-1}$

36. $\dfrac{2x+1}{(x+1)^2} + \dfrac{x^2}{(x+1)^2}$

37. $\dfrac{x-1}{(x+1)^2} - \dfrac{x-1}{(x+1)^2}$

38. $\dfrac{25}{k+5} - \dfrac{k^2}{k+5}$

39. $\dfrac{x}{x^2+2x+1} + \dfrac{1}{x^2+2x+1}$

40. $\dfrac{x}{x^2-6x+9} - \dfrac{3}{x^2-6x+9}$

41. $\dfrac{3m}{m^2+2m+1} + \dfrac{3}{m^2+2m+1}$

42. $\dfrac{8y}{4y^2+12y+9} + \dfrac{12}{4y^2+12y+9}$

43. $\dfrac{2}{t^2-t-2} - \dfrac{t}{t^2-t-2}$

44. $\dfrac{4}{3r^2-r-4} - \dfrac{3r}{3r^2-r-4}$

45. $\dfrac{b^2+2b}{b^2+b-6} + \dfrac{3b+6}{b^2+b-6}$

mini-review

Simplify.

1. $\dfrac{2}{3-\sqrt{3}}$

2. $\sqrt{5} - \sqrt{\dfrac{1}{5}}$

Solve.

3. $y^2 - 4y - 2 = 0$

4. $3m^2 - 5m = 6$

5. $a^2 + \dfrac{1}{2}a - \dfrac{3}{2} = 0$

14-6 Adding and Subtracting Fractions with Unlike Denominators

When you add or subtract fractions with unlike denominators, you must first name the fractions so that the denominators are alike. Any common denominator could be used. However, the computation is easier if the **least common denominator** (LCD) is used. Recall that the least common denominator is the **least common multiple** (LCM) of the denominators. Consider the following example.

$$\frac{1}{6} + \frac{3}{8}$$ *To add these fractions, first find the LCM of 6 and 8.*

The set of multiples of 6 and 8 can be found by multiplying 6 and 8 by each positive integer.

The multiples of 6 are: $1 \cdot 6, 2 \cdot 6, 3 \cdot 6, 4 \cdot 6, 5 \cdot 6, 6 \cdot 6, \ldots$
　　　　　　　　　　　　6,　12,　18,　24,　30,　36, . . .

The multiples of 8 are: $1 \cdot 8, 2 \cdot 8, 3 \cdot 8, 4 \cdot 8, 5 \cdot 8, 6 \cdot 8, \ldots$
　　　　　　　　　　　　8,　16,　24,　32,　40,　48, . . .

The least number that is common to both sets of multiples is 24. Thus, 24 is the LCM of 6 and 8.

Prime factorization can also be used to find the LCM. First, find the prime factorization of each number.

$$6 = 2 \cdot 3$$
$$8 = 2 \cdot 2 \cdot 2$$

Then, to find the LCM, use each prime factor the greatest number of times it appears in either of the factorizations. Notice that the greatest number of times 2 appears as a factor is three times. The greatest number of times 3 appears is once. Therefore, the LCM of 6 and 8 is $2 \cdot 2 \cdot 2 \cdot 3$, or 24.

Thus, the LCD of $\frac{1}{6}$ and $\frac{3}{8}$ is 24. Rename $\frac{1}{6}$ and $\frac{3}{8}$ so that they have denominators of 24.

$$\frac{1}{6} + \frac{3}{8} = \frac{1}{6} \cdot \frac{4}{4} + \frac{3}{8} \cdot \frac{3}{3}$$ *Notice that $\frac{4}{4} = 1$ and $\frac{3}{3} = 1$.*
Also, $6 \cdot 4 = 24$ and $8 \cdot 3 = 24$.

$$= \frac{4}{24} + \frac{9}{24}$$

$$= \frac{13}{24}$$

Similarly to add or subtract algebraic fractions with different denominators, find the LCM of the denominators.

Examples

1 **Find the LCM of $12x^2y$ and $15x^2y^2$.**

$12x^2y = 2 \cdot 2 \cdot 3 \cdot x \cdot x \cdot y$ *Factor each expression.*

$15x^2y^2 = 3 \cdot 5 \cdot x \cdot x \cdot y \cdot y$

$\text{LCM} = 2 \cdot 2 \cdot 3 \cdot 5 \cdot x \cdot x \cdot y \cdot y$ *Use each factor the greatest number of times it appears in*
$\quad\quad = 60x^2y^2$ *either factorization.*

2 **Find the LCM of $x^2 + x - 2$ and $x^2 + 5x - 6$.**

$x^2 + x - 2 = (x - 1)(x + 2)$
$x^2 + 5x - 6 = (x + 6)(x - 1)$
$\quad\quad\quad \text{LCM} = (x - 1)(x + 2)(x + 6)$

After finding the LCM, rename the fractions so that the denominators are alike. Then, add or subtract the numerators.

Examples

3 **Add and simplify:** $\dfrac{6}{5x} + \dfrac{7}{10x^2}$

$5x = 5 \cdot x$ *Use each factor the greatest*
$10x^2 = 2 \cdot 5 \cdot x \cdot x$ *number of times it appears.*

The LCD for $\dfrac{6}{5x}$ and $\dfrac{7}{10x^2}$ is $2 \cdot 5 \cdot x \cdot x$ or $10x^2$. Since the denominator of $\dfrac{7}{10x^2}$ is already $10x^2$, only $\dfrac{6}{5x}$ needs to be renamed.

$\dfrac{6}{5x} + \dfrac{7}{10x^2} = \dfrac{6}{5x} \cdot \dfrac{2x}{2x} + \dfrac{7}{10x^2}$ *Why do you multiply $\dfrac{6}{5x}$ by $\dfrac{2x}{2x}$?*

$\quad\quad\quad\quad\quad = \dfrac{12x}{10x^2} + \dfrac{7}{10x^2}$

$\quad\quad\quad\quad\quad = \dfrac{12x + 7}{10x^2}$

4 **Subtract and simplify:** $\dfrac{a}{a^2 - 4} - \dfrac{a}{a + 2}$

Since $a^2 - 4 = (a - 2)(a + 2)$ and $a + 2 = (a + 2)$, the LCD for $\dfrac{a}{a^2 - 4}$ and $\dfrac{4}{a + 2}$ is $(a - 2)(a + 2)$ or $a^2 - 4$.

$\dfrac{a}{a^2 - 4} - \dfrac{4}{a + 2} = \dfrac{a}{(a - 2)(a + 2)} - \dfrac{4}{(a + 2)} \cdot \dfrac{(a - 2)}{(a - 2)}$

$\quad\quad\quad\quad\quad\quad = \dfrac{a - 4(a - 2)}{(a - 2)(a + 2)}$ $a - 4(a - 2) = a - 4a + 8$

$\quad\quad\quad\quad\quad\quad = \dfrac{-3a + 8}{a^2 - 4}$

Example

5 **Add and simplify:** $\dfrac{x+4}{(2-x)(x+3)} + \dfrac{x-5}{(x-2)^2}$.

Multiply the first fraction by $\dfrac{-1}{-1}$ to change $(2-x)$ to $(x-2)$.

$$\frac{x+4}{(2-x)(x+3)} + \frac{x-5}{(x-2)^2} = \frac{-1}{-1} \cdot \frac{(x+4)}{(2-x)(x+3)} + \frac{x-5}{(x-2)^2}$$

$$= \frac{-(x+4)}{(x-2)(x+3)} + \frac{x-5}{(x-2)^2}$$

The LCD for $(x-2)(x+3)$ and $(x-2)^2$ is $(x+3)(x-2)(x-2)$.   *Why?*

$$\frac{-(x+4)}{(x-2)(x+3)} + \frac{x-5}{(x-2)^2} = \frac{-(x+4)}{(x-2)(x+3)} \cdot \frac{(x-2)}{(x-2)} + \frac{(x-5)}{(x-2)^2} \cdot \frac{(x+3)}{(x+3)}$$

$$= \frac{-x^2 - 2x + 8 + x^2 - 2x - 15}{(x+3)(x-2)(x-2)}$$

$$= \frac{-4x - 7}{(x+3)(x-2)^2}$$

Exploratory Exercises

State the LCD for each pair of fractions.

1. $\dfrac{3}{8}, \dfrac{5}{12}$

2. $\dfrac{6}{a}, \dfrac{7}{13}$

3. $\dfrac{6}{11a}, \dfrac{2}{5}$

4. $\dfrac{2}{a^2}, \dfrac{5}{7}$

5. $\dfrac{2}{a}, \dfrac{3}{b}$

6. $\dfrac{4}{a^2}, \dfrac{5}{a}$

7. $\dfrac{6}{b^3}, \dfrac{7}{ab}$

8. $\dfrac{4}{b^4}, \dfrac{5}{b^5}$

9. $\dfrac{3}{20a^2}, \dfrac{1}{24ab^3}$

10. $\dfrac{7}{60x^2y^2}, \dfrac{6}{35xz^3}$

11. $\dfrac{1}{12an^2}, \dfrac{3}{40a^4}$

12. $\dfrac{11}{56x^3y}, \dfrac{10}{49ax^2}$

13. $\dfrac{7}{a+5}, \dfrac{a}{a-3}$

14. $\dfrac{m}{m+n}, \dfrac{6}{n}$

15. $\dfrac{x+5}{3x-6}, \dfrac{x-3}{x-2}$

Written Exercises

Find each sum or difference in simplest form.

1. $\dfrac{3}{4} + \dfrac{1}{8}$

2. $\dfrac{5}{7} + \dfrac{3}{14}$

3. $\dfrac{3}{4} + \dfrac{2}{9}$

4. $\dfrac{2}{3} + \dfrac{-7}{8}$

5. $\dfrac{-1}{4} - \dfrac{1}{8}$

6. $\dfrac{7}{10} - \dfrac{3}{20}$

7. $\dfrac{6}{7} - \dfrac{2}{11}$

8. $\dfrac{-3}{12} - \dfrac{-5}{18}$

9. $\dfrac{8}{11} + \dfrac{y}{4}$

10. $\dfrac{t}{3} + \dfrac{2t}{7}$

11. $\dfrac{x}{7} - \dfrac{4}{5}$

12. $\dfrac{2n}{5} - \dfrac{3m}{4}$

13. $\dfrac{5}{2a} + \dfrac{-3}{6a}$

14. $\dfrac{6}{5} + \dfrac{a}{5b}$

15. $\dfrac{7}{3a} - \dfrac{3}{6a^2}$

16. $\dfrac{7}{a} - \dfrac{x+1}{2a}$

17. $\dfrac{5b}{7x} + \dfrac{3a}{21x^2}$

18. $\dfrac{5}{xy} + \dfrac{6}{yz}$

19. $\dfrac{3z}{7w^2} - \dfrac{2z}{w}$

20. $\dfrac{6}{x} - \dfrac{5}{x^2}$

21. $\dfrac{2}{t} + \dfrac{t+3}{s}$

22. $\dfrac{7}{a} - \dfrac{x-1}{b}$

23. $\dfrac{a}{a+b} + \dfrac{6}{b}$

24. $\dfrac{m}{m-n} - \dfrac{5}{m}$

25. $\dfrac{4a}{2a+6} + \dfrac{3}{a+3}$

26. $\dfrac{5}{3x-9} + \dfrac{3}{x-3}$

27. $\dfrac{2x}{x^2-5x} - \dfrac{-3x}{x-5}$

28. $\dfrac{-3}{a-5} + \dfrac{-6}{a^2-5a}$

29. $\dfrac{b+8}{b^2-64} + \dfrac{1}{b-8}$

30. $\dfrac{2y}{y^2-25} + \dfrac{y+5}{y-5}$

31. $\dfrac{m-n}{m+n} - \dfrac{1}{m^2-n^2}$

32. $\dfrac{3a+2}{3a-6} - \dfrac{a+2}{a^2-4}$

33. $\dfrac{a^2}{a^2-b^2} + \dfrac{a}{(a-b)^2}$

34. $\dfrac{x^2}{4x^2-9} + \dfrac{x}{(2x+3)^2}$

35. $\dfrac{x}{x^2+2x+1} + \dfrac{1}{x+1}$

36. $\dfrac{y}{y^2-2y+1} - \dfrac{1}{y-1}$

37. $\dfrac{x^2-1}{x+1} + \dfrac{x^2+1}{x-1}$

38. $\dfrac{a}{a-b} + \dfrac{b}{2b+3a}$

39. $\dfrac{k}{2k+1} - \dfrac{2}{k+2}$

40. $\dfrac{m-1}{m+1} + \dfrac{4}{2m+5}$

41. $\dfrac{-18}{y^2-9} + \dfrac{7}{3-y}$

42. $\dfrac{-3}{5-a} + \dfrac{5}{a^2-25}$

43. $\dfrac{a-1}{4ab} + \dfrac{a^2-a}{16b^2}$

44. $\dfrac{x-1}{3xy} - \dfrac{x^2-x}{9y^2}$

45. $\dfrac{6}{a^2-2ab+b^2} - \dfrac{6}{a-b}$

46. $\dfrac{x^2+4x-5}{x^2-2x-3} + \dfrac{2}{x+1}$

47. $\dfrac{3}{m-2} + \dfrac{2}{2-m}$

48. $\dfrac{4}{5-p} - \dfrac{3}{p-5}$

49. $\dfrac{m-n}{m^2+2mn+n^2} - \dfrac{m+n}{m-n}$

50. $\dfrac{a-2}{a^2+4a+4} + \dfrac{a+2}{a-2}$

51. $\dfrac{3m}{m^2+3m+2} - \dfrac{3m-6}{m^2+4m+4}$

52. $\dfrac{4a}{6a^2-a-2} - \dfrac{5a+1}{2-3a}$

53. $\dfrac{2x+1}{(x-1)^2} + \dfrac{x-2}{(1-x)(x+4)}$

54. $\dfrac{a+3}{3a^2-10a-8} + \dfrac{2a}{a^2-8a+16}$

55. $\dfrac{a+2}{a^2-9} - \dfrac{2a}{6a^2-17a-3}$

Using Calculators ——— Evaluating Sums and Differences

Exercises

Use a calculator to evaluate each sum or difference for the values given.

1. $\dfrac{3}{x-2} + \dfrac{4}{x^2-4}$; $x = 2.1$

2. $\dfrac{5y}{4-w^2} - \dfrac{3y}{w}$; $y = 0.2,\ w = -0.1$

3. $\dfrac{m^2-1}{m+1} + \dfrac{m^2+1}{m-1}$; $m = 0.5$

4. $\dfrac{r-s}{r^2+4rs+4} - \dfrac{r+2s}{r-s}$; $r = -0.2,\ s = -0.1$

To take good pictures, photographers must make sure the correct amount of light enters the camera. The light enters the camera through an adjustable opening. The sizes of the opening are called *f*-stops. The *f*-stops are determined by dividing the focal length of the lens by the diameter of the opening. For example, suppose a camera lens has a focal length of 50 mm. The diameter of the opening is 6.25 mm.

$$f\text{-stop} = \frac{\text{focal length}}{\text{diameter of opening}}$$
$$= \frac{50 \text{ mm}}{6.25 \text{ mm}}$$
$$= 8 \qquad \text{The } f\text{-stop is 8.}$$

The dial that shows *f*-stops has the numbers 1.4, 2, 2.8, 4, 5.6, 8, 11, and 16. Each *f*-stop lets twice as much light into the camera as the next *f*-stop. For example, *f*/4 lets in *twice* as much light as *f*/5.6.

Another dial marked 1, 2, 4, 8, 15, 30, 60, 125, 250, 500, and 1000 shows the shutter speed. The shutter speed, in seconds, is the multiplicative inverse of the number on the dial. For example, a shutter speed marked 30 means light enters the camera for $\frac{1}{30}$ of a second. Each shutter speed lets light into the camera for twice as long as the next setting.

Suppose you want to photograph a parked sports car on a sunny day. The setting *f*/11 at $\frac{1}{60}$ would allow the correct amount of light into the camera. For a moving car, you need a faster shutter speed, such as $\frac{1}{125}$. At $\frac{1}{125}$, only half the amount of light is allowed into the camera. For proper exposure, the *f*-stop must be increased to *f*/8.

Exercises

A lens has a focal length of 200 mm. Find the *f*-stop for each opening whose diameter is given.

1. 50 mm **2.** 25 mm **3.** 12.5 mm **4.** 36 mm

For each exposure combination, state two others that give the same exposure.

5. *f*/8 at $\frac{1}{60}$ **6.** *f*/5.6 at $\frac{1}{60}$ **7.** *f*/2.8 at $\frac{1}{125}$ **8.** *f*/4 at $\frac{1}{30}$

14-7 Mixed Expressions and Complex Fractions

Algebraic expressions such as $a + \dfrac{b}{c}$, and $5 + \dfrac{x - y}{x + 3}$ are called **mixed expressions.** Changing mixed expressions to algebraic fractions is similar to changing mixed numerals to improper fractions.

Mixed expressions contain monomials <u>and</u> algebraic fractions.

Mixed Numeral to Improper Fraction	Mixed Expression to Algebraic Fraction
$3\dfrac{2}{5} = \dfrac{3(5) + 2}{5}$	$a + \dfrac{a^2 + b}{a - b} = \dfrac{a(a - b) + (a^2 + b)}{a - b}$
$\quad = \dfrac{15 + 2}{5}$	$\quad = \dfrac{a^2 - ab + a^2 + b}{a - b}$
$\quad = \dfrac{17}{5}$	$\quad = \dfrac{2a^2 - ab + b}{a - b}$

Example

1 Add and simplify: $8 + \dfrac{x^2 - y^2}{x^2 + y^2}$.

Notice that $8 + \dfrac{x^2 - y^2}{x^2 + y^2}$ is a mixed expression. Therefore, use the method shown above to find the sum.

$$8 + \frac{x^2 - y^2}{x^2 + y^2} = \frac{8(x^2 + y^2) + (x^2 - y^2)}{x^2 + y^2}$$

$$= \frac{8x^2 + 8y^2 + x^2 - y^2}{x^2 + y^2}$$

$$= \frac{9x^2 + 7y^2}{x^2 + y^2}$$

If a fraction has one or more fractions in the numerator *or* denominator, it is called a **complex fraction**. Some complex fractions are shown below.

$$\frac{3\frac{1}{2}}{5\frac{2}{3}} \qquad \frac{8}{\frac{a}{b}} \qquad \frac{\frac{a + b}{a}}{\frac{a - b}{b}} \qquad \frac{\frac{1}{x} - \frac{1}{y}}{\frac{1}{x} + \frac{1}{y}}$$

Consider the complex fraction $\dfrac{\frac{3}{5}}{\frac{7}{8}}$.

To simplify this fraction, rewrite it as $\dfrac{3}{5} \div \dfrac{7}{8}$ and proceed as follows.

$$\frac{3}{5} \div \frac{7}{8} = \frac{3}{5} \cdot \frac{8}{7} \text{ or } \frac{24}{35}$$

Recall that to find the quotient, you multiply by $\dfrac{8}{7}$, the reciprocal of $\dfrac{7}{8}$.

Similarly, to simplify $\dfrac{\frac{a}{b}}{\frac{c}{d}}$, rewrite it as $\dfrac{a}{b} \div \dfrac{c}{d}$ and proceed as follows.

$$\frac{a}{b} \div \frac{c}{d} = \frac{a}{b} \cdot \frac{d}{c} \text{ or } \frac{ad}{bc}$$

The reciprocal of $\dfrac{c}{d}$ is $\dfrac{d}{c}$.

Any complex fraction $\dfrac{\frac{a}{b}}{\frac{c}{d}}$, where $b \neq 0, c \neq 0,$ and $d \neq 0,$ may be expressed as $\dfrac{ad}{bc}.$

Simplifying
Complex
Fractions

Example

2   Simplify: $\dfrac{\frac{1}{x} + \frac{1}{y}}{\frac{1}{x} - \frac{1}{y}}$

$$\frac{\frac{1}{x} + \frac{1}{y}}{\frac{1}{x} - \frac{1}{y}} = \frac{\frac{y}{xy} + \frac{x}{xy}}{\frac{y}{xy} - \frac{x}{xy}}$$

The LCD of the numerator and the denominator is xy.

$$= \frac{\frac{y + x}{xy}}{\frac{y - x}{xy}}$$

Add to simplify the numerator.

Subtract to simplify the denominator.

$$= \frac{(y + x)}{xy} \cdot \frac{xy}{(y - x)}$$

The reciprocal of $\dfrac{(y - x)}{xy}$ is $\dfrac{xy}{(y - x)}$.

$$= \frac{(y + x)}{\cancel{xy}_1} \cdot \frac{\cancel{xy}^1}{(y - x)}$$

Eliminate common factors.

$$= \frac{y + x}{y - x}$$

3 Simplify: $\dfrac{x + 4 - \dfrac{1}{x + 4}}{x + 11 + \dfrac{48}{x - 3}}$

$\dfrac{x + 4 - \dfrac{1}{x + 4}}{x + 11 + \dfrac{48}{x - 3}}$

$= \dfrac{\dfrac{(x + 4)(x + 4) - 1}{x + 4}}{\dfrac{(x + 11)(x - 3) + 48}{x - 3}}$

$= \dfrac{\dfrac{x^2 + 8x + 16 - 1}{x + 4}}{\dfrac{x^2 + 8x - 33 + 48}{x - 3}}$

$= \dfrac{\dfrac{x^2 + 8x + 15}{x + 4}}{\dfrac{x^2 + 8x + 15}{x - 3}}$

$= \dfrac{x^2 + 8x + 15}{x + 4} \cdot \dfrac{x - 3}{\overset{1}{\cancel{x^2 + 8x + 15}}}$

$= \dfrac{x - 3}{x + 4}$

4 Simplify: $\dfrac{x - \dfrac{x + 4}{x + 1}}{x - 2}$

$\dfrac{x - \dfrac{x + 4}{x + 1}}{x - 2}$

$= \dfrac{\dfrac{x(x + 1) - (x + 4)}{x + 1}}{x - 2}$

$= \dfrac{\dfrac{x^2 + x - x - 4}{x + 1}}{x - 2}$

$= \dfrac{\dfrac{x^2 - 4}{x + 1}}{\dfrac{x - 2}{1}}$

$= \dfrac{x^2 - 4}{x + 1} \cdot \dfrac{1}{x - 2}$

$= \dfrac{(x + 2)\overset{1}{\cancel{(x - 2)}}}{(x + 1)\underset{1}{\cancel{(x - 2)}}}$

$= \dfrac{x + 2}{x + 1}$

Exploratory Exercises

Add and simplify.

1. $4 + \dfrac{2}{x}$

2. $8 + \dfrac{5}{3y}$

3. $x + \dfrac{x}{y}$

4. $z + \dfrac{2z}{w}$

5. $2m + \dfrac{4 + m}{m}$

6. $3a + \dfrac{a + 1}{2a}$

7. $b^2 + \dfrac{2}{b - 2}$

8. $3r^2 + \dfrac{4}{2r + 1}$

Written Exercises

Simplify.

1. $\dfrac{3\frac{1}{2}}{4\frac{3}{4}}$

2. $\dfrac{\dfrac{x^2}{y}}{\dfrac{y}{x^3}}$

3. $\dfrac{\dfrac{x + 4}{y - 2}}{\dfrac{x^2}{y^3}}$

4. $\dfrac{\dfrac{x^3}{y^2}}{\dfrac{x + y}{x - y}}$

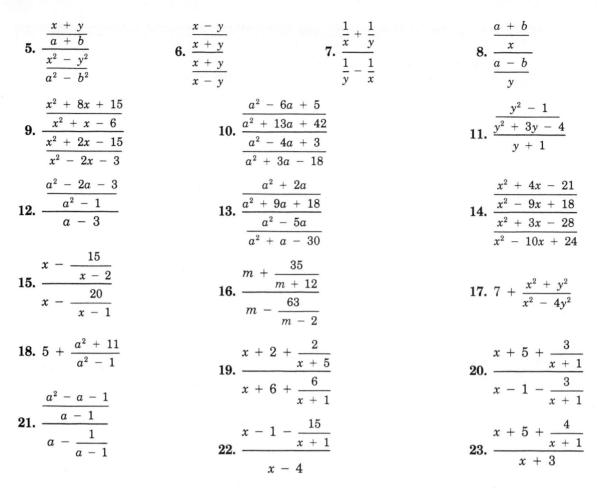

5. $\dfrac{\dfrac{x+y}{a+b}}{\dfrac{x^2-y^2}{a^2-b^2}}$

6. $\dfrac{\dfrac{x-y}{x+y}}{\dfrac{x+y}{x-y}}$

7. $\dfrac{\dfrac{1}{x}+\dfrac{1}{y}}{\dfrac{1}{y}-\dfrac{1}{x}}$

8. $\dfrac{\dfrac{a+b}{x}}{\dfrac{a-b}{y}}$

9. $\dfrac{\dfrac{x^2+8x+15}{x^2+x-6}}{\dfrac{x^2+2x-15}{x^2-2x-3}}$

10. $\dfrac{\dfrac{a^2-6a+5}{a^2+13a+42}}{\dfrac{a^2-4a+3}{a^2+3a-18}}$

11. $\dfrac{\dfrac{y^2-1}{y^2+3y-4}}{y+1}$

12. $\dfrac{\dfrac{a^2-2a-3}{a^2-1}}{a-3}$

13. $\dfrac{\dfrac{a^2+2a}{a^2+9a+18}}{\dfrac{a^2-5a}{a^2+a-30}}$

14. $\dfrac{\dfrac{x^2+4x-21}{x^2-9x+18}}{\dfrac{x^2+3x-28}{x^2-10x+24}}$

15. $\dfrac{x-\dfrac{15}{x-2}}{x-\dfrac{20}{x-1}}$

16. $\dfrac{m+\dfrac{35}{m+12}}{m-\dfrac{63}{m-2}}$

17. $7+\dfrac{x^2+y^2}{x^2-4y^2}$

18. $5+\dfrac{a^2+11}{a^2-1}$

19. $\dfrac{x+2+\dfrac{2}{x+5}}{x+6+\dfrac{6}{x+1}}$

20. $\dfrac{x+5+\dfrac{3}{x+1}}{x-1-\dfrac{3}{x+1}}$

21. $\dfrac{\dfrac{a^2-a-1}{a-1}}{a-\dfrac{1}{a-1}}$

22. $\dfrac{x-1-\dfrac{15}{x+1}}{x-4}$

23. $\dfrac{x+5+\dfrac{4}{x+1}}{x+3}$

Using Computers

Adding Fractions

You do not have to write special programs to tell a computer how to add integers and decimals. However, this is not the case with addition of fractions. The following program tells the computer how to add two fractions. The program uses the definition $\dfrac{a}{b} + \dfrac{c}{d} = \dfrac{ad+bc}{bd}$.

```
10    PRINT "ENTER THE NUMERATOR AND THE
       DENOMINATOR OF THE FIRST FRACTION."
20    PRINT "ENTER THE NUMERATOR AND THE
       DENOMINATOR OF THE SECOND FRACTION."
30    INPUT A,B,C,D
40    LET N = A * D + B * C
50    LET X = B * D
60    PRINT "THE SUM IS ";N;"/";X
70    END
```

However, the sum given by this program may not always be in simplest form. The following lines can be added to the program so that the sum is given in simplest form.

```
60   IF N < X THEN 90
70   LET Y = X
80   GOTO 100
90   LET Y = N
100  FOR I = Y TO 1 STEP - 1
110  IF INT (N / I) < > N / I THEN 130
120  IF INT (X / I) = X / I THEN 140
130  NEXT I
140  LET N = N / I
150  LET X = X / I
160  PRINT "THE SUM IS ";N;"/";X
170  END
```

Exercises

Use the program to find the following sums in simplest form.

1. $\frac{2}{3} + \frac{4}{9}$ **2.** $\frac{8}{11} + \frac{1}{22}$ **3.** $\frac{4}{6} + \frac{1}{4}$ **4.** $\frac{7}{16} + \frac{9}{10}$ **5.** $\frac{5}{12} + \frac{7}{18}$

6. Write a program similar to the one above to subtract two fractions.

Vocabulary

algebraic fractions (437)
multiplicative inverse (445)
reciprocal (445)
least common denominator (454)

least common multiple (454)
mixed expression (459)
complex fraction (459)

Chapter Summary

1. Algebraic fractions contain variables. (437)
2. Zero cannot be used as a denominator because division by zero is undefined. (437)
3. To simplify an algebraic fraction, first factor the numerator and denominator. Then eliminate common fractors. (437)
4. Multiplying Fractions: For all rational numbers $\frac{a}{b}$ and $\frac{c}{d}$, where $b \neq 0$ and

   $d \neq 0$, $\frac{a}{b} \cdot \frac{c}{d} = \frac{ac}{bd}$. (441)

5. Dividing Fractions: For all rational numbers $\frac{a}{b}$ and $\frac{c}{d}$, where $b \neq 0, c \neq 0$,

   and $d \neq 0$, $\frac{a}{b} \div \frac{c}{d} = \frac{a}{b} \cdot \frac{d}{c}$. (445)

6. Adding or Subtracting Fractions with Like Denominators: For all rational

numbers $\frac{a}{c}$ and $\frac{b}{c}$, where $c \neq 0$,

$$\frac{a}{c} + \frac{b}{c} = \frac{a + b}{c} \text{ and } \frac{a}{c} - \frac{b}{c} = \frac{a - b}{c}. \quad (451)$$

7. To add or subtract fractions that have unlike denominators, rename the fractions by using the least common denominator. (454)

8. Simplifying Complex Fractions: Any complex fraction $\dfrac{\frac{a}{b}}{\frac{c}{d}}$, where $b \neq 0, c \neq 0,$

and $d \neq 0$, may be expressed as $\frac{ad}{bc}$. (460)

Chapter Review

14-1 Simplify each algebraic fraction. State the excluded values of the variables.

1. $\dfrac{3x^2y}{12xy^3z}$

2. $\dfrac{x + y}{x^2 + 3xy + 2y^2}$

3. $\dfrac{x^2 - 9}{x^2 - 6x + 9}$

4. $\dfrac{x^2 + 10x + 21}{x^3 + x^2 - 42x}$

14-2 Find each product in simplest form.

5. $\dfrac{7}{9} \cdot \dfrac{a^2}{b}$

6. $\dfrac{5x^2y}{8ab} \cdot \dfrac{12a^2b}{25x}$

7. $\dfrac{2x + 5}{x^2 - 7x + 12} \cdot \dfrac{3x^2 - 10x - 8}{6x^2 + 19x + 10}$

8. $\dfrac{x^2 + x - 12}{x + 2} \cdot \dfrac{x + 4}{x^2 - x - 6}$

14-3 Find each quotient in simplest form.

9. $\dfrac{7x^2y}{10a^3} \div \dfrac{14x^3}{25a^2b}$

10. $\dfrac{2x^2 + x - 15}{x^2 + x - 6} \div \dfrac{x + 3}{2x^2 - 9x + 10}$

11. $\dfrac{7a^2b}{x^2 + x - 30} \div \dfrac{3a}{x^2 + 15x + 54}$

12. $\dfrac{m^2 + 4m - 21}{m^2 + 8m + 15} \div \dfrac{m^2 - 9}{m^2 + 12m + 35}$

14-4 Find each quotient.

13. $x + 3\overline{)x^3 + 7x^2 + 10x - 6}$

14. $2a - 5\overline{)6a^3 - 19a^2 + 2a + 15}$

15. $m - 4\overline{)m^3 - 13m^2 + 33m - 28}$

14-5 Find each sum or difference in simplest form.

16. $\dfrac{x}{x^2 - 1} + \dfrac{1}{x^2 - 1}$

17. $\dfrac{7}{x^2} + \dfrac{a}{x^2}$

18. $\dfrac{2x}{x - 3} - \dfrac{6}{x - 3}$

19. $\dfrac{2}{x - y} + \dfrac{x}{y - x}$

14-6 Find each sum or difference in simplest form.

20. $\dfrac{5a}{3x} - \dfrac{2}{4x^2y}$

21. $\dfrac{x}{x + 3} - \dfrac{5}{x - 2}$

22. $\dfrac{2x + 3}{x^2 - 4} + \dfrac{6}{x + 2}$

23. $\dfrac{3x}{x^2 + 3x - 10} + \dfrac{7}{x^2 - 5x + 6}$

14-7 Simplify.

24. $\dfrac{\dfrac{x^2}{y^3}}{\dfrac{3x}{9y^2}}$

25. $\dfrac{\dfrac{x-3}{x+5}}{\dfrac{x+5}{x}}$

26. $\dfrac{\dfrac{a^2-13a+40}{a^2-4a-32}}{\dfrac{a-5}{a+7}}$

27. $\dfrac{x-\dfrac{35}{x+2}}{x+\dfrac{42}{x+13}}$

Chapter Test

Simplify.

1. $\dfrac{\dfrac{5}{9}}{\dfrac{2}{3}}$

2. $\dfrac{21x^2y}{28ax}$

3. $\dfrac{x^2+7x-18}{x^2+12x+27}$

4. $\dfrac{x^2-x-56}{x^2+x-42}$

5. $\dfrac{7x^2-28}{5x^3-20x}$

6. $\dfrac{2x^2-5x-3}{x^2+2x-15}$

Perform the indicated operations and simplify.

7. $\dfrac{3x}{x+3}+\dfrac{5x}{x+3}$

8. $\dfrac{2x}{x-7}-\dfrac{14}{x-7}$

9. $\dfrac{2x}{x+7}+\dfrac{4}{x+4}$

10. $\dfrac{2a+1}{2a-3}+\dfrac{a-3}{3a+2}$

11. $\dfrac{x+5}{x+2}+6$

12. $\dfrac{x-2}{x-8}+x+5$

13. $\dfrac{3x+2}{4x+1}+\dfrac{7}{x}$

14. $\dfrac{3x-8}{x+4}+\dfrac{9}{x+1}$

15. $\dfrac{x^2+4x-32}{x+5}\cdot\dfrac{x-3}{x^2-7x+12}$

16. $\dfrac{3x^2+2x-8}{x^2-4}\div\dfrac{6x^2+13x-28}{2x^2-3x-35}$

17. $\dfrac{4x^2+11x+6}{x^2-x-6}\div\dfrac{x^2+8x+16}{x^2+x-12}$

18. $\dfrac{3x^2+5x-28}{x^2-3x-28}\cdot\dfrac{x^2-8x+7}{3x-7}$

19. $\dfrac{x-\dfrac{24}{x+5}}{x-\dfrac{72}{x-1}}$

20. $\dfrac{\dfrac{x+5}{x-2}}{\dfrac{x^2}{x-3}}$

21. $\dfrac{\dfrac{x^2-x-6}{x^2+2x-15}}{\dfrac{x^2-2x-8}{x^2+x-20}}$

22. $\dfrac{\dfrac{2}{3m}+\dfrac{3}{m^2}}{\dfrac{2}{5m}+\dfrac{5}{m}}$

1. State the property shown by $(a + b)(b - a) = (b + a)(b - a)$.

2. Find the difference: $-\frac{4}{5} - \left(-\frac{3}{8}\right)$

3. Solve: $5(a + 21) = -2(-7a - 4)$

4. Graph the solution set of the inequality $y \geq 5$ on a number line.

5. Simplify: $(4a^2b^4)^3$

6. Solve: $24 - (3c + 1) = 4(c - 2) + 2c$

Factor, if possible.

7. $9x^2 - 16y^4$

8. $12a^2 + 53an + 30n^2$

9. Solve: $(x + 5)(x - 4) = 0$

10. Solve the equation $3x - 10y = -5$ if the domain is $\{-3, -1, 0, 4, 6\}$.

11. Write an equation for the relationship between the variables in the following chart.

a	1	2	3	4
b	-5	-4	-3	-2

12. Determine the slope of the line passing through $(8, -1)$ and $(0, 0)$.

13. Find the slope and y-intercept for the graph of $-3x + 4y = 16$. Then write the equation in slope-intercept form.

14. Graph $x - 5y = 5$ using the x- and y-intercepts.

15. Graph the system $-x - 2y = -8$ and $-3x - 6y = 6$. Then state whether the system has one solution, no solutions, or an infinite number of solutions. If the system has one solution, state it.

16. Use elimination to solve the system of equations $2x = 5 - 2y$ and $2x - 2y = 3$.

17. Solve the system $y \leq x - 1$ and $y \geq -x + 2$ by graphing.

18. State the integers between which the value of $\sqrt{5894}$ lies.

19. Approximate $\sqrt{85}$. Use the divide-and-average method twice.

20. Use the Pythagorean Theorem to find the measure of the hypotenuse of a right triangle if the measures of the legs are 7 and 8.

21. Find the equation of the axis of symmetry and the coordinates of the maximum or minimum point for the graph of $y = x^2 + 2x + 1$. Then use the information to draw the graph.

22. Use the quadratic formula to solve $n^2 - 2n = 56$.

23. Find a quadratic equation having the roots 3 and -4.

Simplify.

24. $\dfrac{x^2 - 9}{x^2 - 6x + 9}$

25. $\dfrac{x - y}{x + y} \cdot \dfrac{x^2 - y^2}{x + y}$

26. $\dfrac{2a}{a^2 - b - 2b^2} + \dfrac{2b}{a + b}$

Problem Solving

Solve each problem.

27. Reggie is 10 years older than Lois. Five years ago, Reggie was three times as old as Lois. How old is Lois now?

28. A certain triangle has two congruent sides. The third side is 7 in. shorter than either of the equal sides. If the perimeter is 31 in., what is the length of the third side?

29. The sum of the squares of two consecutive even positive integers is 164. Find the integers.

30. A rectangle is 2 cm longer than it is wide. If the length and width are both increased by 3 cm, the area becomes 288 cm². Find the original dimensions of the rectangle.

The test questions on this page deal with averages and rational expressions. The information at the right may help you with some of the questions.

Directions: Choose the best answer. Write A, B, C, or D.

1. $\dfrac{68 + 68 + 68 + 68}{4} =$

   (A) 17   **(B)** 68   **(C)** 136   **(D)** 272

2. Carrie's bowling scores for four games are $b + 2$, $b + 3$, $b - 2$, and $b - 1$. What must her score be on her fifth game to average $b + 2$?

   (A) $b + 8$ **(B)** b
   (C) $b - 2$ **(D)** $b + 5$

3. Which of the following *cannot* be the average of 10, 7, 13, 2, and x, if $x > 4$?

   (A) 7   **(B)** 9   **(C)** 13   **(D)** 258

4. The average of eight integers can be

   (A) 127.6   **(B)** 130.8
   (C) 131.3   **(D)** 135.5

5. The sum of six integers is what percent of the average of six integers?

   (A) 0.001% **(B)** 2% **(C)** 10% **(D)** 600%

6. What is the average of $70 - c$, $70 + 2c$, and $45 - c$?

   (A) 75   **(B)** $61\frac{2}{3} + \frac{2}{3}c$ **(C)** $61\frac{2}{3}$ **(D)** 75

7. What is the average of $2b - 4$, $b + 5$, and $3b + 8$?

   (A) $b + 3$ **(B)** $2b$
   (C) $6b + 9$ **(D)** $2b + 3$

8. If $\frac{x}{2}, \frac{x}{5}$, and $\frac{x}{7}$ are whole numbers, x could be

   (A) 20   **(B)** 35   **(C)** 50   **(D)** 70

---

1. To find the average of a group of numbers, first add the numbers. Then divide by the quantity of numbers added.

2. The average of a group of numbers cannot be greater than the greatest number in the group, nor less than the least number.

3. Most questions involving rational expressions can be solved by writing the expression in a different form.

---

9. If $abc = 4$ and $b = c$, then $a =$

   (A) c^2 **(B)** $\dfrac{1}{4c}$ **(C)** $\dfrac{4}{c^2}$ **(D)** $\dfrac{1}{c^2}$

10. If $\dfrac{1}{b - d} = 4$, then $d =$

   (A) $b - \frac{1}{4}$ **(B)** $4b - 1$

   (C) $\dfrac{b + 1}{4}$ **(D)** $b + 4$

11. If $\dfrac{2a}{5b} = 6$, then $\dfrac{2a - 5b}{5b} =$

   (A) 6   **(B)** $\frac{2}{5}$ **(C)** 15   **(D)** 5

12. If $3\frac{1}{5}c = 2\frac{1}{2}b$ and $c \neq 0$, then $\dfrac{b}{c} =$

   (A) $\frac{25}{32}$ **(B)** $\frac{32}{25}$ **(C)** $\frac{7}{8}$ **(D)** $\frac{11}{10}$

13. If the product of a number and b is increased by y, the result is t. Find the number in terms of b, y, and t.

   (A) $\dfrac{t - y}{b}$ **(B)** $\dfrac{y - t}{b}$

   (C) $\dfrac{b + y}{t}$ **(D)** $t - by$

14. Mark can type 60 words per minute and there is an average of 360 words per page. At this rate, how many *hours* would it take him to type k pages?

   (A) $\dfrac{k}{6}$ **(B)** $\dfrac{k}{60}$ **(C)** $\dfrac{k}{10}$ **(D)** $\dfrac{10}{k}$

CHAPTER 15

Applications of Rational Expressions

The construction of a hot air balloon requires an understanding of the property of gases. The volume of the balloon varies inversely with the applied pressure. That is, the volume decreases as the pressure increases. As a balloon rises, changes in air pressure occur. How does a balloonist compensate for changing air pressure?

Rational expressions are used to solve problems involving variations. In this chapter, you will learn more about using rational expressions.

15-1   Solving Fractional Equations

   Recall that you can solve equations containing fractions by using the least common denominator of all the fractions in the equation. The fractions are eliminated by multiplying both sides of the equation by the common denominator. This method can also be used with equations containing rational expressions.

Examples

1   **Solve:** $\dfrac{x-4}{4} + \dfrac{x}{3} = 6$

$$\dfrac{x-4}{4} + \dfrac{x}{3} = 6$$ *The LCD of the fractions is 12.*

$$12\left(\dfrac{x-4}{4} + \dfrac{x}{3}\right) = 6 \cdot 12$$ *Multiply both sides of the equation by 12.*

$$3(x-4) + 4(x) = 72$$ *The fractions are eliminated.*

$$3x - 12 + 4x = 72$$

$$7x = 84$$

$$x = 12$$

Check: $\dfrac{x-4}{4} + \dfrac{x}{3} = 6$

$$\dfrac{12-4}{4} + \dfrac{12}{3} \overset{?}{=} 6$$

$$2 + 4 \overset{?}{=} 6$$

$$6 = 6$$

The solution is 12.

2   **Solve:** $\dfrac{3}{2x} - \dfrac{2x}{x+1} = -2$

$$\dfrac{3}{2x} - \dfrac{2x}{x+1} = -2$$ *Note that $x \neq -1$, $x \neq 0$.*
The LCD of the rational expressions is $2x(x+1)$.

$$2x(x+1)\left(\dfrac{3}{2x} - \dfrac{2x}{x+1}\right) = 2x(x+1)(-2)$$ *Multiply both sides of the equation by $2x(x+1)$.*

$$3(x+1) - 2x(2x) = -4x^2 - 4x$$

$$3x + 3 - 4x^2 = -4x^2 - 4x$$

$$7x = -3$$

$$x = -\dfrac{3}{7}$$ *Check this result.*

The solution is $-\dfrac{3}{7}$.

Examples

3 Solve: $x - \dfrac{2}{x-3} = \dfrac{x-1}{3-x}$

$$x - \frac{2}{x-3} = \frac{x-1}{3-x}$$

$x \neq 3$
Note that $3 - x = -(x - 3)$.

$$x - \frac{2}{x-3} = -\frac{x-1}{(x-3)}$$

The LCD is $(x - 3)$.

$$(x-3)\left(x - \frac{2}{x-3}\right) = -\left(\frac{x-1}{x-3}\right)(x-3)$$

Multiply both sides of the equation by $(x - 3)$.

$$x(x-3) - 2 = -(x-1)$$
$$x^2 - 3x - 2 = -x + 1$$
$$x^2 - 2x - 3 = 0$$
$$(x-3)(x+1) = 0$$

Factor.

$$x - 3 = 0 \quad \text{or} \quad x + 1 = 0$$

Zero Product Property.

$$x = 3 \quad \text{or} \quad x = -1$$

Since x cannot equal 3, the only solution is -1.

4 Solve: $\dfrac{2m}{m-1} + \dfrac{m-5}{m^2-1} = 1$

$$\frac{2m}{m-1} + \frac{m-5}{m^2-1} = 1$$

What values for m are excluded?

$$\frac{2m}{m-1} + \frac{m-5}{(m+1)(m-1)} = 1$$

Factor $m^2 - 1$.
The LCD is $(m + 1)(m - 1)$.

$$(m+1)(m-1)\left(\frac{2m}{m-1} + \frac{m-5}{(m+1)(m-1)}\right) = (m+1)(m-1)\cdot 1$$

$$2m(m+1) + (m-5) = m^2 - 1$$
$$2m^2 + 2m + m - 5 = m^2 - 1$$
$$m^2 + 3m - 4 = 0$$
$$(m+4)(m-1) = 0$$

Factor.

$$m + 4 = 0 \quad \text{or} \quad m - 1 = 0$$

Zero Product Property

$$m = -4 \quad \text{or} \quad m = 1$$

The solution is -4. Why is 1 not a solution?

Exploratory Exercises

State the LCD for each pair of fractions.

1. $\dfrac{m}{2}, \dfrac{m}{3}$

2. $\dfrac{x}{5}, \dfrac{2x}{3}$

3. $\dfrac{3b}{4}, \dfrac{5b}{8}$

4. $\dfrac{1}{x}, \dfrac{5x}{x+1}$

5. $\dfrac{r}{r^2-1}, \dfrac{5}{r-1}$

6. $\dfrac{m}{2m^2+3m-35}, \dfrac{8}{2m-7}$

State the LCD for each set of fractions.

7. $\dfrac{6}{x}, \dfrac{7}{x-1}, \dfrac{1}{4}$

8. $\dfrac{5}{k-1}, \dfrac{7}{k}, \dfrac{1}{k+1}$

9. $\dfrac{5k}{k+5}, \dfrac{k^2}{k+3}, \dfrac{1}{k+3}$

10. $\dfrac{7}{h+1}, \dfrac{1}{2}, \dfrac{2h+5}{h-1}$

11. $\dfrac{3x}{x^2-1}, \dfrac{1}{x+1}, \dfrac{1}{x-1}$

12. $\dfrac{2x+1}{4x^2-1}, \dfrac{1}{3}, \dfrac{1}{2x+1}$

Written Exercises

Solve each equation.

1. $\dfrac{2a-3}{6} = \dfrac{2a}{3} + \dfrac{1}{2}$

2. $\dfrac{3x}{5} + \dfrac{3}{2} = \dfrac{7x}{10}$

3. $\dfrac{3a}{2} + \dfrac{5}{4} = \dfrac{5a}{2}$

4. $\dfrac{2b-3}{7} - \dfrac{b}{2} = \dfrac{b+3}{14}$

5. $\dfrac{x+1}{x} + \dfrac{x+4}{x} = 6$

6. $\dfrac{18}{b} = \dfrac{3}{b} + 3$

7. $\dfrac{3}{5x} + \dfrac{7}{2x} = 1$

8. $\dfrac{11}{2x} - \dfrac{2}{3x} = \dfrac{1}{6}$

9. $\dfrac{5x}{x+1} + \dfrac{1}{x} = 5$

10. $\dfrac{5k}{k+2} + \dfrac{2}{k} = 5$

11. $\dfrac{2}{3r} - \dfrac{3r}{r-2} = -3$

12. $\dfrac{3n}{n+2} - \dfrac{5}{7} = 4$

13. $\dfrac{m}{m+1} + \dfrac{5}{m-1} = 1$

14. $\dfrac{r-1}{r+1} - \dfrac{2r}{r-1} = -1$

15. $\dfrac{4x}{2x+3} - \dfrac{2x}{2x-3} = 1$

16. $\dfrac{4x}{3x-2} + \dfrac{2x}{3x+2} = 2$

17. $\dfrac{c}{c-4} - \dfrac{6}{4-c} = c$

18. $\dfrac{5}{z-3} - \dfrac{z}{3-z} = z$

19. $\dfrac{5}{5-p} - \dfrac{p^2}{5-p} = -2$

20. $\dfrac{r^2}{r-7} + \dfrac{50}{7-r} = 14$

21. $\dfrac{14}{b-6} = \dfrac{1}{2} + \dfrac{6}{b-8}$

22. $\dfrac{2a-3}{a-3} - 2 = \dfrac{12}{a+3}$

23. $\dfrac{r}{3r+6} - \dfrac{r}{5r+10} = \dfrac{2}{5}$

24. $\dfrac{x-2}{x} - \dfrac{x-3}{x-6} = \dfrac{1}{x}$

25. $\dfrac{2b-5}{b-2} - 2 = \dfrac{3}{b+2}$

26. $\dfrac{z+3}{z-1} + \dfrac{z+1}{z-3} = 2$

27. $\dfrac{7}{k-3} - \dfrac{1}{2} = \dfrac{3}{k-4}$

28. $\dfrac{x+2}{x-2} - \dfrac{2}{x+2} = \dfrac{-7}{3}$

29. $\dfrac{3w}{w^2-5w+4} = \dfrac{2}{w-4} + \dfrac{3}{w-1}$

30. $\dfrac{3k}{k^2-5k+6} = \dfrac{2}{k-3} + \dfrac{3}{k-2}$

31. $\dfrac{7}{x^2-5x} + \dfrac{5}{3-x} = \dfrac{4}{x}$

32. $\dfrac{9}{b^2-7b+12} = \dfrac{5}{b-3} + \dfrac{2}{b-4}$

33. $\dfrac{6}{z+2} + \dfrac{3}{z^2-4} = \dfrac{2z-7}{z-2}$

34. $\dfrac{m+3}{m+5} + \dfrac{2}{m-9} = \dfrac{-20}{m^2-4m-45}$

35. $\dfrac{4}{k^2-8k+12} = \dfrac{k}{k-2} + \dfrac{1}{k-6}$

36. $\dfrac{h^2-7h-8}{3h^2+2h-8} + \dfrac{1}{h+2} = 0$

15-2 Problem Solving: Work and Uniform Motion

Katina Marsh can wash and wax cars at the rate of 1 every 3 hours. Working at this rate, in 1 hour she can complete $\frac{1}{3}$ of the job. In 2 hours she can complete $\frac{1}{3} \cdot 2$ or $\frac{2}{3}$ of the job. In t hours, she can complete $\frac{1}{3} \cdot t$ or $\frac{t}{3}$ of the job.

This and many other similar examples suggest the following formula.

$$(\text{rate of working}) \cdot (\text{time}) = (\text{work done})$$
$$r \quad \cdot \quad t \quad = \quad w$$

Suppose Toshio Meko washes and waxes 1 car in 4 hours. If Katina and Toshio work together, how long will it take them to wash and wax one car? This problem can be solved as follows.

Example

1 Solve the problem above to find how long it will take Katina and Toshio to wash and wax one car.

Explore Let t = time in hours for Katina and Toshio to wash and wax one car.

In t hours, Katina can do $\frac{1}{3} \cdot t$

Plan or $\frac{t}{3}$ of the job.

In t hours, Toshio can do $\frac{1}{4} \cdot t$

or $\frac{t}{4}$ of the job.

	r	$\cdot$ t	$=$ w
Katina	$\frac{1}{3}$	t	$\frac{t}{3}$
Toshio	$\frac{1}{4}$	t	$\frac{t}{4}$

$\frac{t}{3} + \frac{t}{4} = 1$ *Together they complete 1 job.*

Solve $4t + 3t = 12$ *Multiply both sides of the equation by the LCD, 12.*

$7t = 12$

$t = \frac{12}{7}$

Katina and Toshio can do the job in $\frac{12}{7}$, or $1\frac{5}{7}$ hours.

This is about 1 hour and 43 minutes.

Examine Replace t by $\frac{12}{7}$. $\dfrac{\frac{12}{7}}{3} + \dfrac{\frac{12}{7}}{4} = \frac{4}{7} + \frac{3}{7} = \frac{7}{7}$ or 1

Recall that uniform motion problems can be solved by using a formula similar to the one used to solve work problems.

$$(\text{rate}) \cdot (\text{time}) = (\text{distance})$$
$$r \quad \cdot \quad t \quad = \quad d$$

Example

2 While on a fishing trip, Sally and her brother rented a boat. The top speed of the boat in still water was 3 miles per hour. At this rate a 9-mile trip downstream with the current took the same amount of time as a 3-mile trip upstream against the current. What was the rate of the current?

Explore Let c = the rate of the current.

The rate of the boat when traveling downstream, or *with the current*, is 3 mph *plus* the rate of the current. That is, $3 + c$. The rate when traveling upstream, or *against the current*, is 3 mph *minus* the rate of the current. That is, $3 - c$.

Plan

	r	$\cdot$	t	$= d$
downstream	$3 + c$		$\dfrac{9}{3 + c}$	9
upstream	$3 - c$		$\dfrac{3}{3 - c}$	3

Solving $rt = d$ for t, $t = \dfrac{d}{r}$.

Solve

$$\frac{9}{3 + c} = \frac{3}{3 - c}$$ *time downstream = time upstream*

$$9(3 - c) = 3(3 + c)$$ *Multiply both sides of the equation by the LCD, $(3 + c)(3 - c)$.*

$$27 - 9c = 9 + 3c$$

$$-12c = -18$$

$$c = \frac{3}{2}$$

The rate of the current is $\frac{3}{2}$ or $1\frac{1}{2}$ miles per hour. *Examine this solution.*

Exploratory Exercises

Answer each question.

1. Luisa can paint her house in 8 days. What part of it will she paint: **a.** in 1 day?   **b.** in 3 days?   **c.** in x days?

2. Drew can build a garage in n days. What part of it will he build: **a.** in 1 day?   **b.** in 4 days?   **c.** in x days?

3. Gabe can do a job alone in 8 days. Stephen can do the same job alone in 10 days. What part of the job can Gabe do: **a.** in 1 day?   **b.** in x days?   What part of the job can Stephen do: **c.** in 1 day?   **d.** in x days?   What part of the job can they do together: **e.** in 1 day?   **f.** in x days?

4. Pat can do a job alone in 4 days. Yoki can do the same job alone in 12 days. What part of the job can Pat do: **a.** in 1 day?   **b.** in x days?   What part of the job can Yoki do: **c.** in 1 day?   **d.** in x days?   What part of the job can they do together: **e.** in 1 day?   **f.** in x days?

5. The top flying speed of an open cockpit biplane is 120 mph. At this speed, a 420-mile trip flying with the wind takes the same amount of time as a 300-mile trip flying against the wind. What is the speed of the wind?

a. Let s = the speed of the wind. Copy and fill in each entry in the chart at the right.

b. Write an equation to solve this problem.

	r	$\cdot$ t	$=$ d
with the wind			
against the wind			

Written Exercises

Solve each problem. Use $rt = w$ or $rt = d$ and a chart.

1. Jane can wash the windows of a building in 4 hours. Jim can do the same job in 6 hours. If they work together, how long will it take them to wash the windows?

2. Mark can clean the garage in 6 hours. Rosetta can do the same job in 8 hours. If they work together, how long will it take them to clean the garage?

3. Helena can do a job in 5 days. Jefferson can do the same job in 8 days. If they work together, how long will it take them to complete the job?

4. Frank can do a job in 10 hours. Keith can do the same job in 15 hours. If they work together, how long will it take them to complete the job?

5. A swimming pool can be filled by one pipe in 12 hours and by another pipe in 4 hours. How long will it take to fill the pool if the water flows through both pipes?

6. A swimming pool can be filled by one pipe in 10 hours. The drain pipe can empty the pool in 15 hours. If both pipes are open, how long will it take to fill the pool?

7. John and Denise together can mow a lawn in 12 minutes. It takes John 20 minutes to do the job alone. How long would it take Denise to do the job alone?

8. Cindy and Erica together can do a job in $3\frac{3}{5}$ hours. Cindy can do the job alone in 6 hours. How many hours will it take Erica to do the job alone?

9. A long distance cyclist pedaling at a steady rate travels 30 miles with the wind. He can travel only 18 miles against the wind in the same amount of time. If the rate of the wind is 3 mph, what is the cyclist's rate without the wind?

10. A tugboat pushing a barge up the Ohio River takes 1 hour longer to travel 36 miles up the river than to travel the same distance down the river. If the rate of the current is 3 mph, find the speed of the tugboat and barge in still water.

11. An airplane can fly at a rate of 600 mph in calm air. It can fly 2520 miles with the wind in the same time it can fly 2280 miles against the wind. Find the speed of the wind.

12. A motorboat takes $\frac{2}{3}$ as much time to travel 10 miles downstream as it does to travel the same distance upstream. If the rate of the current is 5 mph, find the speed of the motorboat in still water.

Problem Solving

Another problem-solving strategy is to use subgoals. Study the following example.

Example: **Three workers can make three lamps in three days. How many lamps can seven workers working at the same rate make in twenty-one days?**

To solve this problem, first find out how many lamps each worker can make in three days. To do this, divide 3 lamps by 3 workers.

$$3 \div 3 = 1$$

So, each worker can make 1 lamp in 3 days. Use this information to find how many lamps each worker can make in 21 days. To do this, divide 21 by 3 since each worker takes 3 days to make a lamp.

$$21 \div 3 = 7$$

So, each worker can make 7 lamps in 21 days. Now determine how many lamps 7 workers can make by multiplying 7, the number of lamps each worker can make, by 7, the number of workers.

$$7 \times 7 = 49$$

Thus, 7 workers can make 49 lamps in 21 days.

Exercises

Solve each problem.

1. Five farmers can plow five fields in five hours. How many fields can eight farmers plow in fifteen hours?

2. Four people can pick eight baskets of apples in two hours. How many baskets of apples can 12 people pick in $\frac{1}{2}$ hour?

3. A flower shop has 112 orders for corsages. Three designers can make 12 corsages in 2 hours. How many designers are needed to complete the orders in 8 hours?

4. A pipe 250 cm long needs to be cut into pieces 25 cm long. How many minutes will it take to cut the pipe if each cut takes two minutes?

15-3 Using Formulas

Expressions and equations involving rational expressions often contain more than one variable. Sometimes it is useful to solve the equations or formulas for one of the variables. This is often true with formulas. Study the following example.

Example

1 Solve for n: $S = \frac{n}{2}(A + t)$

$$S = \frac{n}{2}(A + t)$$

$$2S = 2\left[\frac{n}{2}(A + t)\right]$$

$$2S = n(A + t)$$

$$\frac{2S}{A + t} = n$$

The formula below applies to camera and lens systems. In the formula, f is the focal length of the lens, a is the distance from the object to the lens, and b is the distance from the image to the lens.

$$\frac{1}{f} = \frac{1}{a} + \frac{1}{b}$$

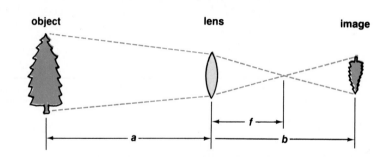

object   lens   image

Example

2 Solve for f: $\frac{1}{f} = \frac{1}{a} + \frac{1}{b}$

$$\frac{1}{f} = \frac{1}{a} + \frac{1}{b}$$

$$abf\left(\frac{1}{f}\right) = abf\left(\frac{1}{a} + \frac{1}{b}\right) \qquad \text{The LCD is } abf.$$

$$ab = bf + af$$
$$ab = (b + a)f \qquad \text{Factor } bf + af.$$

$$\frac{ab}{b + a} = f$$

$$f = \frac{ab}{b + a} \qquad \text{Symmetric Property of Equality.}$$

Exploratory Exercises

Answer each question.

1. In Example 1, what steps would you take to solve for A?

2. In Example 1, what steps would you take to solve for t?

3. In Example 2, what steps would you take to solve for a?

4. In Example 2, what steps would you take to solve for b?

Written Exercises

Solve each motion formula for the variable indicated.

1. $a = \frac{v}{t}$, for t

2. $v = r + at$, for a

3. $s = vt + \frac{1}{2}at^2$, for v

4. $s = vt + \frac{1}{2}at^2$, for a

5. $F = G\left(\frac{Mm}{d^2}\right)$, for M

6. $F = G\left(\frac{Mm}{d^2}\right)$, for d

7. $f = \frac{W}{g} \cdot \frac{V^2}{R}$, for V

8. $f = \frac{W}{g} \cdot \frac{V^2}{R}$, for R

Solve each business formula for the variable indicated.

9. $A = P + Prt$, for P

10. $Prt = I$, for r

11. $I = \left(\frac{100 - P}{P}\right)\frac{365}{R}$, for P

12. $I = \frac{365d}{360 - dr}$, for d

13. $a = \frac{r}{2y} - 0.25$, for y

14. $c = \frac{P - 100}{P}$, for P

Solve each electronics formula for the variable indicated.

15. $H = (0.24)I^2Rt$, for R

16. $P = \frac{E^2}{R}$, for E

17. $\frac{1}{R_T} = \frac{1}{R_1} + \frac{1}{R_2}$, for R_1

18. $I = \frac{E}{r + R}$, for R

19. $I = \frac{nE}{nr + R}$, for n

20. $I = \frac{E}{\frac{r}{n} + R}$, for r

Solve each mathematical formula for the variable indicated.

21. $y = mx + b$, for m

22. $A = \frac{1}{2}h(a + b)$, for h

23. $m = \frac{y_2 - y_1}{x_2 - x_1}$, for y_2

24. $m = \frac{y_2 - y_1}{x_2 - x_1}$, for x_1

25. $\frac{P}{D} = Q + \frac{R}{D}$, for R

26. $\frac{P}{D} = Q + \frac{R}{D}$, for D

Solve each equation for n.

27. $\frac{1}{2}n + b = n$

28. $\frac{n}{x} = \frac{y}{r}$

29. $\frac{n}{a} + \frac{b}{c} = d$

30. $\frac{a}{c} = n + bn$

31. $\frac{n}{a + b} = c - n$

32. $\frac{1}{n} = \frac{1}{a} + \frac{1}{b}$

33. $\frac{n + 2}{b} = \frac{n + b}{c}$

34. $r = \frac{16M}{a(n + 1)}$

35. $\frac{a}{n} = \frac{n}{b}$

36. $\frac{a}{n} + \frac{a}{b} = \frac{b}{n}$

37. $\frac{r}{n} - \frac{2}{k} = \frac{k}{n}$

38. $\frac{1}{2n} = \frac{n}{2x}$

15-4 Direct Variation

Diego delivers newspapers. He is paid 3¢ for each newspaper he delivers. The following table relates the number of newspapers Diego delivers (x) and his income (y).

x	20	50	100	120	150
y	$0.60	$1.50	$3.00	$3.60	$4.50

Diego's income depends *directly* on the number of newspapers he delivers. The relationship between newspapers delivered and income is shown by the equation $y = 0.03x$. Such an equation is called a **direct variation**. We say that *y varies directly as x.*

> **A direct variation is described by an equation of the form $y = kx$, where k is not zero.**

Definition of Direct Variation

In a direct variation, k is called the **constant of variation**. To find the constant of variation, divide both sides of $y = kx$ by x.

$$\frac{y}{x} = k \quad \text{or} \quad k = \frac{y}{x}$$

Example

1 The weight of an object on the moon varies directly as its weight on the earth. A certain astronaut weighs 168 pounds on earth and 28 pounds on the moon. Kristina weighs 108 pounds on earth. What would she weigh on the moon?

Let x = weight on the moon.
Let y = weight on the earth.
Then $y = kx$. Find the value of k.

$k = \dfrac{y}{x}$

$k = \dfrac{168}{28}$ *Substitute the astronaut's weights for x and y.*

$k = 6$ *The constant of variation is 6.*

Next find Kristina's weight on the moon. Find x when y is 108.

$y = kx$
$108 = 6x$ *Substitute 108 for y and 6 for k.*
$18 = x$

Thus, Kristina would weigh 18 pounds on the moon.

Recall that an equation of the form $y = mx + b$ is a linear equation. Notice that the equation for direct variation, $y = kx$, is also a linear equation, where $m = k$ and $b = 0$.

Direct variations are also related to proportions. From the table on Diego's newspapers and income, many true proportions can be formed. Two proportions are shown below.

$$\text{number of papers} \rightarrow \frac{20}{60} = \frac{50}{150} \leftarrow \text{income} \qquad \text{number of papers} \rightarrow \frac{20}{50} = \frac{60}{150} \leftarrow \text{income}$$

Two general forms for proportions such as these can be derived from the equation $y = kx$. Let (x_1, y_1) be a solution for $y = kx$. Let a second solution be (x_2, y_2). Then $y_1 = kx_1$ and $y_2 = kx_2$. A proportion can be written using x_1, x_2, y_1, and y_2. Study the following.

$y_1 = kx_1$ — *This equation describes a direct variation.*

$\dfrac{y_1}{y_2} = \dfrac{kx_1}{kx_2}$ — *Use the division property of equality. Since y_2 and kx_2 are equivalent, you can divide the left side by y_2 and the right side by kx_2.*

$\dfrac{y_1}{y_2} = \dfrac{x_1}{x_2}$ — *Simplify.*

Study how another proportion can be formed from this proportion.

$\dfrac{y_1}{y_2} = \dfrac{x_1}{x_2}$

$x_2 y_1 = x_1 y_2$ — *Find the cross products.*

$\dfrac{x_2 y_1}{y_1 y_2} = \dfrac{x_1 y_2}{y_1 y_2}$ — *Divide both sides by $y_1 y_2$.*

$\dfrac{x_2}{y_2} = \dfrac{x_1}{y_1}$ — *Simplify.*

You can use proportions to solve problems involving **direct variation.**

Be consistent when using proportions: compare x's and y's; or compare the first two elements and the second two elements.

Example

2 **If y varies directly as x and $y = 27$ when $x = 6$, find x when $y = 45$.**

Use the following proportion to solve the problem.

$\dfrac{y_1}{y_2} = \dfrac{x_1}{x_2}$

Since y is 27 when x is 6, let $y_1 = 27$ and $x_1 = 6$. Let $y_2 = 45$ and solve for x_2.

$\dfrac{27}{45} = \dfrac{6}{x_2}$ — *Substitute.*

$27x_2 = 6(45)$ — *Find the cross products.*

$27x_2 = 270$

$x_2 = 10$ — Thus, $x = 10$ when $y = 45$.

Exploratory Exercises

State which of the following are direct variations. For each direct variation, state the constant of variation.

1. $y = 3x$

2. $ab = 8$

3. $5x^2 = 6y$

4. $-3a = b$

5. $d = 7t$

6. $r = \frac{1}{3}m$

7. $\frac{1}{6}y = \frac{5}{3}$

8. $z = \frac{3}{p}$

Written Exercises

Solve each problem. Assume that y varies directly as x.

1. If $y = 12$ when $x = 3$, find y when $x = 7$.

2. If $y = -8$ when $x = 2$, find y when $x = 10$.

3. If $y = 3$ when $x = 15$, find y when $x = -25$.

4. If $y = -7$ when $x = -14$, find y when $x = 20$.

5. If $y = -6$ when $x = 9$, find x when $y = -4$.

6. If $y = -8$ when $x = -3$, find x when $y = 6$.

7. If $y = 12$ when $x = 15$, find x when $y = 21$.

8. If $y = 17$ when $x = 22$, find x when $y = 13$.

9. If $y = 1.7$ when $x = 2.6$, find x when $y = 3.4$.

10-18. For exercises 1-9, find the constant of variation. Then write an equation of the form $y = kx$ for each variation.

Solve each problem.

19. If 6 pounds of sugar cost $2.00, how much will 40 pounds cost?

20. If 2 m of copper wire weigh 0.3 kg, how much will 75 m weigh?

21. Ken's wages vary directly as the time he works. If his wages for 4 days are $110, how much will they be for 17 days?

22. Deidre's wages vary directly as the time she works. If her wages for six days are $121, what are her wages for 20 days?

23. A car uses 5 gallons of gasoline to travel 143 miles. How much gasoline will the car use to travel 200 miles?

24. A car uses 9 liters of gasoline to travel 88 km. How much gasoline will the car use to travel 215 km?

25. Charles' Law says that the volume of a gas is directly proportional to its temperature. If the volume of a gas is 2.5 cubic feet at 150° (absolute temperature), what is the volume of the same gas when the temperature is 200° (absolute temperature)?

26. In an electrical transformer, voltage is directly proportional to the number of turns on the coil. If 110 volts comes from 55 turns, what would be the voltage produced by 66 turns?

Using Calculators——————————————Variations

Use a calculator to help solve each problem. Assume that y varies directly as x.

1. If $y = 5.8$ when $x = 6.5$, find x when $y = 8.7$.

2. If $y = 4.6$ when $x = 2.4$, find y when $x = 6.3$.

15-5 Inverse Variation

Anne Marie plans to drive on a trip of 600 miles. Her time, in hours, for the trip will be determined by her average rate in miles per hour. The following table shows the time (t) for various rates (r).

r	30	40	45	50	60
t	20	15	$13\frac{1}{3}$	12	10

The formula $d = rt$ is used to find values for t.

Notice that as the rate *increases*, the time to make the trip *decreases*. As the rate *decreases*, the time *increases*. We say that the *rate varies inversely as the time*.

> **An inverse variation is described by an equation of the form $xy = k$, where k is not zero.**

Definition of Inverse Variation

Sometimes an inverse variation is written in the form $y = \frac{k}{x}$. We say that *y varies inversely as x.*

Example

1 **If y varies inversely as x and $y = 6$ when $x = 18$, find x when $y = -3$.**

First find the value of k.

$$xy = k$$
$$18(6) = k \qquad \text{Substitute 18 for x and 6 for y.}$$
$$108 = k \qquad \text{The constant of variation is 108.}$$

Then find x when $y = -3$.

$$xy = k$$
$$x(-3) = 108 \qquad \text{Substitute } -3 \text{ for y and 108 for k.}$$
$$x = -36$$

Thus, $x = -36$ when $y = -3$.

Consider again the table of rates and times for Anne Marie's trip. There are many ways to form true mathematical statements from the data. Compare the following mathematical statements.

$$50 \cdot 12 = 60 \cdot 10 \qquad \frac{50}{60} = \frac{10}{12}$$

Two general forms for mathematical statements such as these can be derived from the equation $xy = k$.

Let (x_1, y_1) be a solution of an inverse variation, $xy = k$. Let (x_2, y_2) be a second solution. Then $x_1 y_1 = k$ and $x_2 y_2 = k$. Study the following.

$x_1 y_1 = k$

$\boxed{x_1 y_1 = x_2 y_2}$ *You can substitute x_2y_2 for k because $x_2y_2 = k$.*

The equation $x_1 y_1 = x_2 y_2$ is called the *product rule for inverse variations*. Study how it can be used to form a proportion.

$x_1y_1 = x_2y_2$

$\dfrac{x_1\,y_1}{x_2\,y_1} = \dfrac{x_2\,y_2}{x_2\,y_1}$ *Divide both sides by x_2y_1.*

$\boxed{\dfrac{x_1}{x_2} = \dfrac{y_2}{y_1}}$ *Notice that this proportion is different from the proportions for direct variation on page 479.*

The product rule or the proportion above can be used to solve problems involving inverse variation.

Example

2   If y varies inversely as x and $y = 3$ when $x = 12$, find x when $y = 4$.

Let $x_1 = 12$, $y_1 = 3$, *and* $y_2 = 4$. Solve for x_2.

a. Use the product rule.

$x_1 y_1 = x_2 y_2$

$12 \cdot 3 = x_2 \cdot 4$

$\dfrac{36}{4} = x_2$

$9 = x_2$

b. Use the proportion.

$\dfrac{x_1}{x_2} = \dfrac{y_2}{y_1}$

$\dfrac{12}{x_2} = \dfrac{4}{3}$

$36 = 4 \cdot x_2$

$9 = x_2$

Thus, $x = 9$ when $y = 4$.

Exploratory Exercises

State which of the following are inverse variations. For each inverse variation, state the constant of variation.

1. $ab = 6$

2. $c = 3.14\,d$

3. $\dfrac{50}{y} = x$

4. $\dfrac{1}{5}a = d$

5. $\dfrac{-13}{a} = b$

6. $14 = ab$

7. $xy = 1$

8. $y = \dfrac{1}{x}$

9. $bh = 40$

10. $a = \dfrac{7}{b}$

11. $d = 4t^2$

12. $s = 3t$

Written Exercises

Solve each problem. Assume that y varies inversely as x.

1. If $y = 24$ when $x = 8$,
   find y when $x = 4$.

2. If $y = -6$ when $x = -2$,
   find y when $x = 5$.

3. If $y = \frac{1}{3}$ when $x = 5$,
   find y when $x = \frac{1}{4}$.

4. If $y = 7$ when $x = \frac{2}{3}$,
   find y when $x = 7$.

5. If $y = -8$ when $x = 2$,
   find x when $y = 7$.

6. If $y = 99$ when $x = 11$,
   find x when $y = 11$.

7. If $x = 2.8$ when $y = 5.6$,
   find y when $x = 3.5$.

8. If $x = 2.7$ when $y = 8.1$,
   find y when $x = 3.6$.

9. If $x = 1.2$ when $y = 1.8$,
   find x when $y = 1.5$.

10. If $x = 6.9$ when $y = 4.3$,
    find x when $y = 6.45$.

11-20. For exercises 1-10, find the constant of variation, k. Write an equation of the form $xy = k$ for each variation.

Solve each problem.

21. Susan drove 3 hours at a rate of 50 mph. How long would the same distance take Susan if she drove at 45 mph?

22. Gary drove 4 hours at a rate of 80 km/h. How long would the same distance take Gary if he drove at 75 km/h?

Boyle's law states that the volume of a gas (V) varies inversely with applied pressure (P). This is shown by the formula $P_1V_1 = P_2V_2$. Use this formula to solve each problem.

23. Pressure acting on 60 m³ of a gas is raised from 1 atmosphere to 2 atmospheres. What new volume does the gas occupy?

24. Pressure acting on 8.0 m³ of a gas is 20 atmospheres. The pressure is reduced until the volume is 20 m³. What is the new pressure acting on the gas?

25. A helium-filled balloon has a volume of 16 m³ at sea level. The pressure at sea level is 1 atmosphere. The balloon rises to a point in the atmosphere where the pressure is 0.75 atmosphere. What is its volume?

26. A helium-filled balloon has a volume of 2 m³ at sea level. The pressure at sea level is 1 atmosphere. The balloon rises to a point in the atmosphere where its volume is 6 m³. What is the pressure at this height?

Suppose the area of a triangle remains constant, while the lengths of the base and the altitude vary. The altitude is 6 inches when the base is 10 inches. Use this information to solve each problem.

27. Find the altitude when the base is 15 inches.

28. Find the base when the altitude is 12 inches.

In sound and harmonics, the frequency of a vibrating string is inversely proportional to its length. Use this information to solve each problem.

29. A violin string 10 inches long vibrates at a frequency of 512 cycles per second. Find the frequency of an 8-inch string.

30. A piano string 36 inches long vibrates at a frequency of 480 cycles per second. Find the frequency of the string if it were shortened to 24 inches.

15-6   Lever Problems

Laura and Jason are on a seesaw. They want the seesaw to balance. Laura weighs 132 pounds and Jason weighs 108 pounds. Which person should sit closer to the fulcrum (the pivot point)?

If you have observed people on a seesaw, you may have noticed that the heavier person must sit closer to the fulcrum to balance the seesaw. This is an example of an inverse variation. A seesaw is a type of lever. All lever problems involve inverse variation.

For all lever problems in this section, assume that the lever is weightless.

Suppose weights w_1 and w_2 are placed on a lever at a distance d_1 and d_2, respectively, from the fulcrum. The lever is balanced when $w_1 d_1 = w_2 d_2$.

Property of Levers

The property of levers is illustrated at the right.

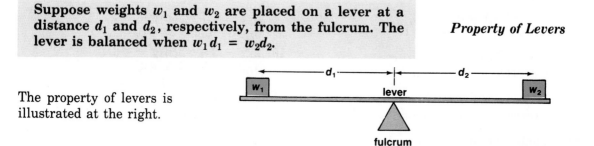

Examples

1   **The fulcrum of a 16-ft seesaw is placed in the middle. Jason, who weighs 108 pounds, is seated 8 feet from the fulcrum. How far from the fulcrum should Laura sit if she weighs 132 pounds?**

Use the property of levers, $w_1 d_1 = w_2 d_2$.

Let $w_1 = 108$, $d_1 = 8$, and $w_2 = 132$. Solve for d_2.

$$w_1 d_1 = w_2 d_2$$
$$108 \cdot 8 = 132 \cdot d_2$$
$$864 = 132 d_2$$
$$6\frac{6}{11} = d_2$$

Laura should sit $6\frac{6}{11}$ feet from the fulcrum.

2   **An 8-ounce weight is placed at one end of a yardstick. A 10-ounce weight is placed at the other end. Where should the fulcrum be placed to have the yardstick balanced?**

Let d = distance from fulcrum to 8-ounce weight, in inches.
Then $36 - d$ = distance from fulcrum to 10-ounce weight, in inches.

$$8d = 10(36 - d)$$
$$8d = 360 - 10d$$
$$18d = 360$$
$$d = 20$$

The fulcrum should be placed 20 inches from the 8-ounce weight.

Examples

3 Dean Cadwell wants to lift a large rock with the use of a long crowbar. The short end of the crowbar is 6 inches from the fulcrum and the long end is 5 feet from the fulcrum. What is the maximum weight that Dean can lift using this method if he weighs 165 pounds?

The distances from the fulcrum must be expressed with the same unit of measure.

$$5 \text{ feet} = 60 \text{ inches}$$

Dean's weight should be at the long end of the crowbar, so let $w_1 = 165$, $d_1 = 60$, and $d_2 = 6$.

$$w_1 d_1 = w_2 d_2$$
$$165 \cdot 60 = w_2 \cdot 6$$
$$9900 = 6w_2$$
$$1650 = w_2$$

Dean can lift 1650 pounds with the crowbar.

4 Patti and Cathy are seated on the same side of a seesaw. Patti is 6 feet from the fulcrum and weighs 115 pounds. Cathy is 8 feet from the fulcrum and weighs 120 pounds. Jack is seated on the other side of the seesaw, 10 feet from the fulcrum. If the seesaw is balanced, how much does Jack weigh?

Draw a diagram.

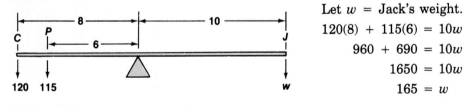

Let w = Jack's weight.
$$120(8) + 115(6) = 10w$$
$$960 + 690 = 10w$$
$$1650 = 10w$$
$$165 = w$$

Thus, Jack weighs 165 pounds.

Exploratory Exercises

For each of the following, suppose the two people are on a seesaw. For the seesaw to balance, which person must sit closer to the fulcrum?

1. Jorge, 168 pounds
   Emilio, 220 pounds

2. Shawn, 114 pounds
   Shannon, 97 pounds

3. Juanita, 49 pounds
   Lucia, 49 pounds

4. Ryna, 52 kg
   Helen, 55 kg

5. Jack, 50 kg
   Betty, 58 kg

6. Jimmy, 72 pounds
   Jeff, 68 pounds

Written Exercises

Solve each problem.

1. Mary Jo weighs 120 pounds and Doug weighs 160 pounds. They are seated at opposite ends of a seesaw. Doug and Mary Jo are 14 feet apart, and the seesaw is balanced. How far is Mary Jo from the fulcrum?

2. Grant, who weighs 150 pounds, is seated 8 feet from the fulcrum of a seesaw. Mariel is seated 10 feet from the fulcrum. If the seesaw is balanced, how much does Mariel weigh?

3. Weights of 100 pounds and 115 pounds are placed on a lever. The two weights are 15 feet apart, and the lever is balanced. How far from the fulcrum is the 100-pound weight?

4. A lever has a 140-pound weight on one end and a 160-pound weight on the other end. The lever is balanced, and the 140-pound weight is exactly one foot farther from the fulcrum than the 160-pound weight. How far from the fulcrum is the 160-pound weight?

5. Amy, who weighs 108 pounds, is seated 5 feet from the fulcrum of a seesaw. Barbara is seated on the same side of the seesaw, two feet farther from the fulcrum than Amy. Barbara weighs 96 pounds. The seesaw is balanced when Sue, who weighs 101 pounds, sits on the other side. How far is Sue from the fulcrum?

6. Christy, who weighs 112 pounds, is seated 6 feet from the fulcrum of a seesaw. Sooyun, who weighs 124 pounds, is seated on the same side of the seesaw, 8 feet from the fulcrum. The other side of the seesaw is 9 feet long. Is it possible for Seiju, who weighs 180 pounds, to balance the seesaw?

7. John Kofmehl is using a crowbar to move a boxcar in a railyard. The total length of the bar is 6 feet, and the fulcrum is 4 inches from one end. If John weighs 180 pounds, how much force can he exert against the wheel?

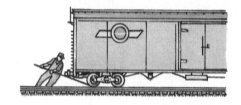

8. To move a log, Norma Barone places a rock 2 feet from the log to use as a fulcrum. She then uses a 12-foot plank as a lever. If Norma weighs 140 pounds, will she be able to lift the log that weighs 600 pounds?

mini-review

Write *True* or *false*.

1. $(3a^2b)^3 = 9a^5b^3$

2. $(2m^2n + mn^2) - (m^2n - 2mn^2) = m^2n - mn^2$

3. $x^3 + 2x^2 + x + 2 = (x^2 + 1)(x + 2)$

4. $\dfrac{6x^2 - x - 12}{2x + 3} = 3x - 4$

5. $\dfrac{y}{y - 1} - \dfrac{y + 1}{y + 2} = \dfrac{1}{(y - 1)(y + 2)}$

Legend has it that while watching an apple fall from a tree, Sir Isaac Newton recognized that the apple fell because an unbalanced force acted on it. This force was gravity. Newton wondered if this special force was peculiar to the earth. Did other bodies also have it? Perhaps every body exerts a gravitational force on every other body.

Newton assumed that the gravitational force between any two bodies acts in the same way as the force between a planet and the sun. From this assumption, he wrote the **law of universal gravitation**. This law states that *every body in the universe attracts every other body in the universe with a force that varies directly with the product of the masses and inversely with the square of the distance between the centers of the two masses.* This law is written as follows.

$$F = G\frac{m_1 m_2}{r^2}$$

In the equation, m_1 and m_2 are the masses of the two bodies in kilograms, r is the distance in meters between the centers of the masses, and G is a universal constant. The value of G is $6.67 \times 10^{-11}\,N \cdot m^2/kg^2$. Using these units, the force, F, will be in newtons (N).

Example: Two freight cars, each of mass 3.0×10^5 kg, are located on adjacent tracks. Their centers are 9.0 m apart. What gravitational force exists between them?

$$F = G\frac{m_1 m_2}{r^2}$$

$$= (6.67 \times 10^{-11})\frac{(3.0 \times 10^5)(3.0 \times 10^5)}{(9.0)^2}$$

$$= (6.67 \times 10^{-11})\frac{(9.0 \times 10^{10})}{81}$$

$$= 0.074 \qquad \text{The force between them is } 0.074\ N.$$

Exercises

Solve each problem. Assume the distance, r, is the distance between the centers of the two masses.

1. Two people are standing 2.0 m apart. One has a mass of 80 kg. The other has a mass of 60 kg. What is the gravitational force between them?

2. Two ships are docked next to each other. Their centers of gravity are 40 m apart. One ship weighs 9.8×10^7 N. The other ship weighs 1.96×10^8 N. What gravitational force exists between them?

15-7   Rational Expressions in Science

Many scientific formulas, such as the ones for electrical resistance, contain rational expressions.

Current electricity can be described as the flow of electrons through a conductor, such as a copper wire. Electricity flows more freely through some conductors than others. The force opposing the flow is called *resistance.* The unit of resistance commonly used is the *ohm.*

Resistances can occur one after another, in *series.* They can also occur in branches of the conductor going in the same direction, in *parallel.* Study the diagrams below. Formulas for the total resistance, R_T, are given under the diagrams.

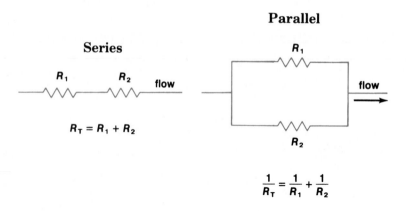

$$\frac{1}{R_T} = \frac{1}{R_1} + \frac{1}{R_2}$$

Example

1   Assume that $R_1 = 4$ ohms and $R_2 = 3$ ohms. Compute the total resistance of the conductor when the resistances are in series.

$R_T = R_1 + R_2$

$R_T = 4 + 3$

$R_T = 7$

Thus, the total resistance is 7 ohms.

Example

2 Assume that $R_1 = 5$ ohms and $R_2 = 6$ ohms. Compute the total resistance of the conductor when the resistances are in parallel.

$$\frac{1}{R_T} = \frac{1}{R_1} + \frac{1}{R_2}$$

$$\frac{1}{R_T} = \frac{1}{5} + \frac{1}{6}$$

$$\frac{1}{R_T} = \frac{11}{30}$$

$30 \cdot 1 = R_T \cdot 11$ *Find the cross products.*

$$\frac{30}{11} = R_T$$

Thus, the total resistance is $\frac{30}{11}$, or $2\frac{8}{11}$ ohms.

A *circuit*, or path for the flow of electrons, often has some resistances connected in series and others in parallel.

Example

3 A parallel circuit has one branch in series as shown at the right. Given that the total resistance is $2\frac{1}{4}$ ohms, $R_1 = 3$ ohms, and $R_2 = 4$ ohms, find R_3.

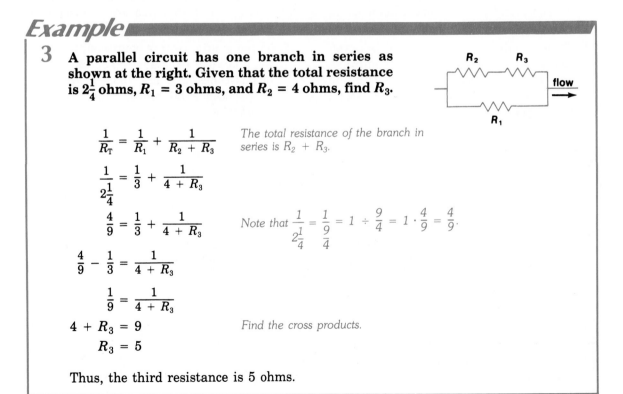

$$\frac{1}{R_T} = \frac{1}{R_1} + \frac{1}{R_2 + R_3}$$ *The total resistance of the branch in series is $R_2 + R_3$.*

$$\frac{1}{2\frac{1}{4}} = \frac{1}{3} + \frac{1}{4 + R_3}$$

$$\frac{4}{9} = \frac{1}{3} + \frac{1}{4 + R_3}$$ *Note that $\dfrac{1}{2\frac{1}{4}} = \dfrac{1}{\frac{9}{4}} = 1 \div \dfrac{9}{4} = 1 \cdot \dfrac{4}{9} = \dfrac{4}{9}$.*

$$\frac{4}{9} - \frac{1}{3} = \frac{1}{4 + R_3}$$

$$\frac{1}{9} = \frac{1}{4 + R_3}$$

$4 + R_3 = 9$ *Find the cross products.*

$R_3 = 5$

Thus, the third resistance is 5 ohms.

Written Exercises

Problems 1-6 relate to the diagram below. Solve each problem.

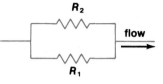

1. Find the total resistance, R_T, given that $R_1 = 8$ ohms and $R_2 = 6$ ohms.

2. Find the total resistance, R_T, given that $R_1 = 4.5$ ohms and $R_2 = 3.5$ ohms.

3. Find R_1, given that total resistance is $2\frac{2}{9}$ ohms and $R_2 = 5$ ohms.

4. Find R_1, given that total resistance is $3\frac{3}{7}$ ohms and $R_2 = 8$ ohms.

5. Find R_1 and R_2, given that total resistance is $2\frac{2}{3}$ ohms and R_1 is two times as great as R_2.

6. Find R_1 and R_2, given that total resistance is $2\frac{1}{4}$ ohms and R_1 is three times as great as R_2.

Solve each problem.

7. Resistances of 3 ohms, 6 ohms, and 9 ohms are connected in series. What is the total resistance?

8. Eight lights on a Christmas tree are connected in series. Each has a resistance of 12 ohms. What is the total resistance?

9. Three coils with resistances of 3 ohms, 4 ohms, and 6 ohms are connected in parallel. What is the total resistance?

10. Three coils with resistances of 4 ohms, 6 ohms, and 15 ohms are connected in parallel. What is the total resistance?

11. Three appliances are connected in parallel: a lamp of resistance 120 ohms, a toaster of resistance 20 ohms, and an iron of resistance 12 ohms. Find the total resistance.

12. Three appliances are connected in parallel: a lamp of resistance 60 ohms, an iron of resistance 20 ohms, and a heating coil of resistance 80 ohms. Find the total resistance.

Problems 13-15 relate to the diagram below. Solve each problem.

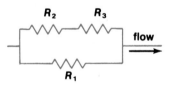

13. Find the total resistance, given that $R_1 = 5$ ohms, $R_2 = 4$ ohms, and $R_3 = 3$ ohms.

14. Find R_1, given that the total resistance is $2\frac{10}{13}$ ohms, $R_2 = 3$ ohms, and $R_3 = 6$ ohms.

15. Find R_2, given that the total resistance is $3\frac{1}{2}$ ohms, $R_1 = 5$ ohms, and $R_3 = 4$ ohms.

Challenge

Solve each problem.

16. Write an expression for the total resistance for the diagram at the right.

17. Find the total resistance, given that $R_1 = 5$ ohms, $R_2 = 4$ ohms, and $R_3 = 6$ ohms.

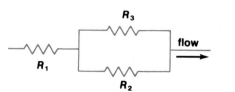

15-8 Other Variations

Consider the formula for the area of a triangle, $A = \frac{1}{2}bh$. Notice that the area depends directly on *both* the base and the height. We say that the area *varies jointly* as the base and the height. Such a variation is known as a **joint variation**.

> **A joint variation is described by an equation of the form $z = kxy$, where k is not zero.**

Definition of Joint Variation

A joint variation can also be expressed as a proportion. One such proportion that can be derived from the equation $z = kxy$ is shown below.

$$\frac{z_1}{x_1 y_1} = \frac{z_2}{x_2 y_2}$$

Example

1 Assume z varies jointly as x and y, and $z = 42$ when $x = 18$ and $y = 7$. Find z when $x = \frac{3}{4}$ and $y = 8$.

Use the proportion $\frac{z_1}{x_1 y_1} = \frac{z_2}{x_2 y_2}$ to solve the problem. Let $z_1 = 42$, $x_1 = 18$, $y_1 = 7$, $x_2 = \frac{3}{4}$, and $y_2 = 8$.

$\dfrac{42}{18 \cdot 7} = \dfrac{z_2}{\frac{3}{4} \cdot 8}$ *Substitute.*

$\dfrac{42}{126} = \dfrac{z_2}{6}$ *Find the cross products.*

$252 = 126z_2$

$2 = z_2$

Thus, $z = 2$ when $x = \frac{3}{4}$ and $y = 8$.

Consider the formula for the area of a circle, $A = \pi r^2$. Notice that the area depends directly on the *square* of the radius. We say that the area varies directly as the square of the radius. Such a variation is known as a **quadratic direct variation**.

A quadratic direct variation is described by an equation of the form $y = kx^2$, where k is not zero.

A quadratic direct variation can also be expressed as a proportion of the form $\dfrac{y_1}{x_1^2} = \dfrac{y_2}{x_2^2}$.

Example

2 **If y varies directly as x^2 and $y = 10$ when $x = 2$, find y when $x = 5$.**

Use the proportion $\dfrac{y_1}{x_1^2} = \dfrac{y_2}{x_2^2}$ to solve the problem. Let $y_1 = 10$, $x_1 = 2$, and $x_2 = 5$.

$\dfrac{10}{2^2} = \dfrac{y_2}{5^2}$ *Substitute.*

$250 = 4y_2$ *Find the cross products.*

$62\frac{1}{2} = y_2$

Thus, $y = 62\frac{1}{2}$ when $x = 5$.

When a slide projector illuminates a screen, the brightness of the picture depends on the intensity of the bulb used in the projector. However, as the screen is moved farther away from the projector, the same amount of light must cover a larger area on the screen. As a result, the picture becomes less bright. The brightness of the picture varies directly as the intensity of the bulb and inversely as the square of the distance from the bulb. Such a variation is known as a **combined variation**.

A combined variation is described by an equation of the form $z = \dfrac{kx}{y}$, where k is not zero.

A combined variation can also be expressed as a proportion of the form $\dfrac{z_1 y_1}{x_1} = \dfrac{z_2 y_2}{x_2}$.

Example

3

If z varies directly as x and inversely as the square of y, and $z = 1.8$ when $x = 100$ and $y = 0.4$, find z when $x = 150$ and $y = 0.3$.

Use the proportion $\dfrac{z_1(y_1)^2}{x_1} = \dfrac{z_2(y_2)^2}{x_2}$ to solve the problem.

Let $z_1 = 1.8$, $x_1 = 100$, $y_1 = 0.4$, $x_2 = 150$, and $y_2 = 0.3$.

$$\dfrac{1.8(0.4)^2}{100} = \dfrac{z_2(0.3)^2}{150} \qquad \textit{Substitute.}$$

$$\dfrac{0.288}{100} = \dfrac{0.09z_2}{150} \qquad \textit{Find the cross products.}$$

$$43.2 = 9z_2$$

$$4.8 = z_2$$

Thus, $z = 4.8$ when $x = 150$ and $y = 0.3$.

Exploratory Exercises

State whether each of the following is joint variation, a quadratic direct variation, or a combined variation.

1. $a = 4bc$
2. $0.2x = yz$
3. $r = \dfrac{4s}{t}$
4. $q = \dfrac{2}{3}mn$
5. $w = 8z^2$
6. $\dfrac{2}{3}a^2 = b$
7. $xy = \dfrac{8}{9}w$
8. $\dfrac{0.46c}{d} = a$

Written Exercises

Solve each problem. Assume that z varies jointly as x and y.

1. If $z = 4$ when $x = 2$ and $y = 4$, find z when $x = 1$ and $y = 4$.
2. If $z = -6$ when $x = -1$ and $y = -2$, find x when $z = -3$ and $y = 2$.
3. If $z = 3$ when $x = 15$ and $y = 10$, find y when $x = -25$ and $z = 5$.
4. If $z = 18$ when $x = 22$ and $y = 12$, find y when $x = 10$ and $z = -3$.

Solve each problem. Assume that y varies directly as the square of x.

5. If $y = 2$ when $x = 2$, find y when $x = 4$.
6. If $y = -8$ when $x = -4$, find y when $x = 6$.
7. If $y = 0.1$ when $x = 0.3$, find x when $y = 0.009$.
8. If $y = -2$ when $x = -3$, find x when $y = -4$.

Solve each problem. Assume that z varies directly as x and inversely as y.

9. If $z = 4$ when $x = 1$ and $y = 2$, find z when $x = 10$ and $y = 20$.
10. If $z = -5$ when $x = -12$ and $y = -2$, find x when $z = -4$ and $y = -1$.
11. If $z = 14$ when $x = -2$ and $y = 14$, find y when $z = -15$ and $x = 6$.
12. If $z = 0.6$ when $x = 2$ and $y = 0.4$, find z when $x = 9$ and $y = 0.1$.

The power (P) of an electrical circuit varies directly as the square of the voltage (V) and inversely as the resistance (R). Use this information to solve each problem.

13. If $P = 8$ when $V = 12$ and $R = 6$, find R when $P = 6$ and $V = 15$.
14. If $P = 2$ when $V = 8$ and $R = 4$, find R when $P = 5$ and $V = 10$.

Variations

A computer can be used to solve problems involving variations. The following program is for problems involving combined variations. It uses the proportion $\frac{z_1 y_1}{x_1} = \frac{z_2 y_2}{x_2}$.

```
10    PRINT "ENTER VALUES FOR Z1,Y1,X1,Z2,Y2,AND X2."
20    PRINT "(ENTER 999999 FOR THE VARIABLE WHOSE VALUE
        IS UNKNOWN)"
30    INPUT Z1,Y1,X1,Z2,Y2,X2
40    IF Z2 = 999999 THEN 90
50    IF Y2 = 999999 THEN 120
60    LET X2 = (Z2 * Y2 * X1) / (Z1 * Y1)      Line 60 is executed when X2 = 999999.
70    PRINT "X = ";X2;" WHEN Z = ";Z2;" AND Y = ";Y2
80    GOTO 140
90    LET Z2 = (Z1 * Y1 * X2) / (Y2 * X1)
100   PRINT "Z = ";Z2;" WHEN X = ";X2;" AND Y = ";Y2
110   GOTO 140
120   LET Y2 = (Z1 * Y1 * X2) / (Z2 * X1)
130   PRINT "Y = ";Y2;" WHEN X = ";X2;" AND Z = ";Z2
140   END
```

Notice that the number 999999 is not used in any computations in the program. This number tells the computer which formula to use to solve the problem. For example, in line 40, if $z_2 = 999999$ then the computer goes to line 90. In line 90, the proportion $\frac{z_1 y_1}{x_1} = \frac{z_2 y_2}{x_2}$ has been solved for z_2, the variable whose value is unknown.

Exercises

1. Use the program above to verify your answers to Written Exercises 9-12 on page 493.

2. Write a program similar to the one above to solve problems involving joint variations. Use the program to verify your answers to Written Exercises 1-4 on page 493.

3. Write a program similar to the one above to solve problems involving quadratic direct variations. Use the program to verify your answers to Written Exercises 5-8 on page 493.

Vocabulary

direct variation (478)
constant of variation (478)
inverse variation (481)
property of levers (484)

joint variation (491)
quadratic direct variation (491)
combined variation (492)

Chapter Summary

1. Equations containing rational expressions can be solved by first multiplying every term by the least common denominator. (469)
2. The formula $rt = w$ is used to solve work problems. (472)
3. Definition of Direct Variation: A direct variation is described by an equation of the form $y = kx$, where k is not zero. (478)
4. Direct variation can be expressed in terms of two proportions. Let (x_1, y_1) and (x_2, y_2) be solutions of a direct variation. Then $\dfrac{x_1}{y_1} = \dfrac{x_2}{y_2}$ and $\dfrac{x_1}{x_2} = \dfrac{y_1}{y_2}$. The cross product can also be used: $x_1 y_2 = x_2 y_1$. (479)
5. Definition of Inverse Variation: An inverse variation is described by an equation of the form $xy = k$, where k is not zero. (481)
6. Inverse variation can be expressed in terms of a proportion. Let (x_1, y_1) and (x_2, y_2) be solutions of an inverse variation. Then $\dfrac{x_1}{x_2} = \dfrac{y_2}{y_1}$. The product rule for inverse variation is: $x_1 y_1 = x_2 y_2$. (482)
7. Property of Levers: Suppose weights w_1 and w_2 are placed on a lever at distances d_1 and d_2, respectively, from the fulcrum. The lever is balanced when $w_1 d_1 = w_2 d_2$. (484)
8. Definition of Joint Variation: A joint variation is described by an equation of the form $z = kxy$, where k is not zero. (492)
9. Definition of Quadratic Direct Variation: A quadratic direct variation is described by an equation of the form $y = kx^2$, where k is not zero. (492)
10. Definition of Combined Variation: A combined variation is described by an equation of the form $z = \dfrac{kx}{y}$, where k is not zero. (492)

Chapter Review

15-1 **Solve each equation.**

1. $\dfrac{4x}{3} + \dfrac{7}{2} = \dfrac{7x}{12}$

2. $\dfrac{y + 2}{y} - \dfrac{y - 3}{y} = \dfrac{3}{4}$

3. $\dfrac{3}{x} + \dfrac{1}{x - 5} = \dfrac{1}{2x}$

4. $\dfrac{1}{h + 1} + \dfrac{2}{3} = \dfrac{2h + 5}{h - 1}$

5. $\dfrac{3x + 2}{x^2 + 7x + 6} = \dfrac{1}{x + 6} + \dfrac{4}{x + 1}$

6. $\dfrac{3m - 2}{2m^2 - 5m - 3} - \dfrac{2}{2m + 1} = \dfrac{4}{m - 3}$

15-2 **Solve each problem.**

7. Bill can paint the outside of a house in 40 hours. Roberta can do the job in 48 hours. If they work together, how long will it take them to complete the job?

8. An airplane can fly at a rate of 525 mph in calm air. It can fly 1605 miles with the wind in the same amount of time it can fly 1545 miles against the wind. Find the speed of the wind.

15-3 **Solve each formula for the variable indicated.**

9. $\dfrac{1}{f} = \dfrac{1}{a} + \dfrac{1}{b}$, for a

10. $S = \dfrac{a}{1 - r}$, for r

15-4 **Solve each problem.**

11. If y varies directly as x and $y = 9$ when $x = 3$, find y when $x = 4$.

12. If y varies directly as x and $y = 12.5$ when $x = 5$, find y when $x = 6$.

13. Bill uses 16 gallons of gasoline every 3 days while driving to work. How much gasoline will he use in 14 days of driving?

15-5 **Solve each problem.**

14. If y varies inversely as x and $y = 2$ when $x = 5$, find y when $x = 20$.

15. If y varies inversely as x and $y = 6.9$ when $x = 1.7$, find y when $x = 5.1$.

16. If the volume of a gas is inversely proportional to applied pressure, and the volume is 80 m^3 at 2 atmospheres of pressure, what will be the volume at $\frac{1}{4}$ atmosphere of pressure?

15-6 **Solve each problem.**

17. A meter stick rests on a fulcrum at the 50 centimeter mark. A 10-gram weight is placed on the meter stick 25 cm from the fulcrum. Where should a 5-gram weight be placed in order to balance the stick?

18. A fulcrum is placed 1 foot from the end of an 8-foot lever. Will a 200-pound man on the other end of the lever be able to lift a 1500-pound stone?

15-7 **Solve each problem.**

19. Assume that $R_1 = 4$ ohms and $R_2 = 6$ ohms. What is the total resistance of the conductor if R_1 and R_2 are: **a.** connected in series? **b.** connected in parallel?

20. A parallel circuit has one branch in series. The total resistance is expressed by the formula: $\dfrac{1}{R_T} = \dfrac{1}{R_1} + \dfrac{1}{R_2 + R_3}$. Find R_1 if $R_T = 3$ ohms, $R_2 = 3$ ohms, and $R_3 = 9$ ohms.

15-8 **Solve each problem.**

21. If z varies jointly as x and y, and $z = 12$ when $x = 4$ and $y = 6$, find z when $x = 3$ and $y = 2$.

22. If y varies directly as x^2 and $y = 30$ when $x = 5$, find y when $x = 10$.

23. If z varies directly as x and inversely as y, and $z = 0.3$ when $x = 10$ and $y = 0.2$, find z when $x = 20$ and $y = 0.6$.

Chapter Test

Solve each equation.

1. $\dfrac{y + 3}{6} = \dfrac{y + 2}{12} - \dfrac{2}{5}$

2. $\dfrac{x + 1}{x} + \dfrac{6}{x} = x + 7$

3. $\dfrac{4m}{m - 3} + \dfrac{6}{3 - m} = m$

4. $\dfrac{-2b - 9}{b^2 + 7b + 12} = \dfrac{b}{b + 3} + \dfrac{2}{b + 4}$

5. $\dfrac{1}{y - 4} - \dfrac{2}{y - 8} = \dfrac{-1}{y + 6}$

6. $\dfrac{m + 3}{m - 1} + \dfrac{m + 1}{m - 3} = \dfrac{22}{3}$

Solve each formula for the variable indicated.

7. $F = G\left(\dfrac{Mm}{d^2}\right)$, for G

8. $\dfrac{1}{R_T} = \dfrac{1}{R_1} + \dfrac{1}{R_2}$, for R_2

Solve each problem.

9. Willie can do a job in 6 days. Myra can do the same job in $4\frac{1}{2}$ days. If they work together how long will it take to complete the job?

10. The top speed of a boat in still water is 5 mph. At this speed, a 21-mile trip downstream took the same amount of time as a 9-mile trip upstream. Find the rate of the current.

11. If y varies directly as x and $y = 7$ when $x = 3$, find y when $x = 5$.

12. If y varies inversely as x and $y = 4$ when $x = 9$, find y when $x = 5$.

13. Pressure varies inversely with volume of a confined gas. If the volume of a gas is 400 cm^3 at a pressure of 4 atmospheres, what is the pressure when the volume is 300 cm^3?

14. Jimmie and Anne Marie are on a seesaw. Jimmie weighs 60 pounds and is seated 8 feet from the center. How far from the center should Anne Marie sit if she weighs 75 pounds?

15. Given the formula $\dfrac{1}{R_T} = \dfrac{1}{R_1} + \dfrac{1}{R_2}$ for the resistance of a circuit, determine the resistance R_1 if $R_T = 1.2$ ohms and $R_2 = 4$ ohms.

16. If z varies directly as x and inversely as y, and $z = -6$ when $x = -1$ and $y = 2$, find z when $x = 4$ and $y = -3$.

CHAPTER 16

Trigonometry

In playing pool, similar triangles are used when banking a shot. Pool is one of many games that involve triangles. Trigonometry is a branch of mathematics that involves triangles.

16-1 Angles

A protractor can be used to measure angles as shown below.

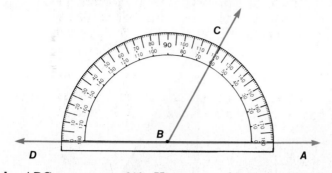

Angle *ABC* measures 60°. However, where ray *BC* cuts the protractor, there are two readings—60° and 120°. The 120° is the measure of angle *DBC*. What is the sum of the measures of angles *ABC* and *DBC*?

| Two angles are **supplementary** if the sum of their measures is 180°. | *Supplementary Angles* |

Example

1

The measure of an angle is three times its supplement. Find the measure of each angle.

$x + 3x = 180$ *Let x be the measure of the lesser angle*
$4x = 180$ *and 3x the measure of the greater angle.*
$x = 45$

The measures are 45° and 3 · 45°, or 135°.

| Two angles are **complementary** if the sum of their measures is 90°. | *Complementary Angles* |

Example

2

An angle is 16° greater than its complement. Find the measure of each angle.

$x + (x + 16) = 90$ *Let x be the measure of the lesser angle*
$2x + 16 = 90$ *and x + 16 the measure of the greater angle.*
$2x = 74$
$x = 37$

The measures are 37° and 37° + 16°, or 53°.

What is the sum of the measures of the three angles of a triangle?
Use a protractor to measure the angles of each triangle below. Then
find the sum of the angle measures of each triangle.

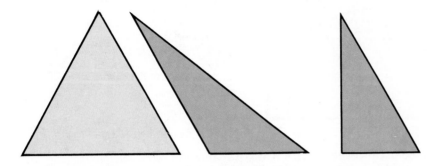

What did you discover? In each case, your sum should be
approximately 180°.

| The sum of the measures of the angles in any triangle is 180°. | *Sum of the Angles of a Triangle* |

Examples

3 **What are the measures of the angles of an equilateral triangle?**

In an equilateral triangle, the sides are congruent and the angles have equal measures.

$x + x + x = 180$ *Let x be the measure of each angle.*

$\quad\quad 3x = 180$

$\quad\quad\ \ x = 60$

Each angle measures 60°.

4 **What are the measures of the angles of an isosceles right triangle?**

An isosceles right triangle contains a right angle and two congruent angles.

$x + x + 90 = 180$ *What does x represent?*

$\ \ 2x + 90 = 180$ *How do you know one angle is 90°?*

$\quad\quad 2x = 90$

$\quad\quad\ \ x = 45$

The measures are 45°, 45°, and 90°.

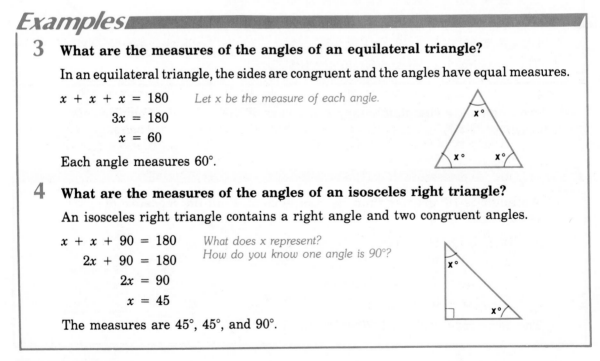

Exploratory Exercises

Find the complement of each angle whose measure is listed below.

1. 85°
2. 42°
3. 13°
4. 45°
5. 55°
6. $x°$
7. $(2x + 40)°$
8. $(x - 7)°$

Find the supplement of each angle whose measure is listed below.

9. 130°
10. 65°
11. 127°
12. 87°
13. 90°
14. $y°$
15. $(3x + 5)°$
16. $(x - 20)°$

Written Exercises

Find both the complement and the supplement for each angle whose measure is listed below.

1. 42°
2. 87°
3. 125°
4. 160°
5. 90°
6. 68°
7. 21°
8. 174°
9. 99°
10. $x°$
11. $3y°$
12. $(x + 30)°$
13. $(x - 38)°$
14. $5x°$
15. $(90 - x)°$
16. $(180 - y)°$

In each of the following, the measures of two angles of a triangle are given. Find the measure of the third angle.

17. 16°, 42°
18. 40°, 70°
19. 50°, 45°
20. 90°, 30°
21. 89°, 90°
22. $x°$, $y°$
23. $x°$, $(x + 20)°$
24. $y°$, $(y - 10)°$

Solve each of the following.

25. One of the congruent angles of an isosceles triangle measures 37°. Find the measures of the other angles.

26. The measures of the angles of a certain triangle are consecutive even integers. Find their measures.

27. An angle measures 38° less than its complement. Find the measures of the two angles.

28. One angle of a triangle measures 53°. Another angle has measure 37°. What is the measure of the third angle?

29. One angle of a triangle measures 10° more than the second. The measure of the third angle is twice the sum of the first two angles. Find the measure of each angle.

30. One of two complementary angles measures 30° more than 3 times the other. Find the measure of each of the angles.

31. Find the measure of an angle that measures 10° more than its complement.

32. Find the measure of an angle that is 30° less than its supplement.

33. Find the measure of an angle that is one-half the measure of its complement.

34. Find the measure of an angle that is one-half the measure of its supplement.

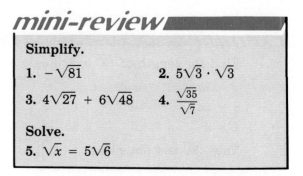

mini-review

Simplify.

1. $-\sqrt{81}$
2. $5\sqrt{3} \cdot \sqrt{3}$
3. $4\sqrt{27} + 6\sqrt{48}$
4. $\dfrac{\sqrt{35}}{\sqrt{7}}$

Solve.

5. $\sqrt{x} = 5\sqrt{6}$

16-2   30° – 60° Right Triangles

Suppose the measure of one acute angle of a right triangle is 30°. The measure of the other acute angle is 90° – 30° or 60°. Such triangles are called **30° – 60° right triangles**.

Examine the equilateral triangle shown at the right. What is the measure of angle B?

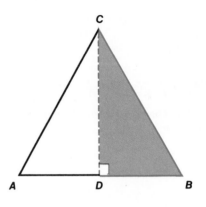

Line segment CD (denoted $\overline{CD}$) can be drawn perpendicular to $\overline{AB}$. What kind of right triangle is triangle CDB?

$\overline{CD}$ bisects $\overline{AB}$. Since the measure of $\overline{DB}$ is one-half the measure of $\overline{AB}$, it is also one-half the measure of the hypotenuse, $\overline{BC}$.

In any 30° – 60° right triangle, the measure of the side opposite the 30° angle is one-half the measure of the hypotenuse.

30° – 60° Right Triangles

In calculations, lower case letters are used to designate the measures of the sides of a triangle. For example, the measure of the side opposite angle R is r.

Example

1 Find the length of $\overline{BC}$ in triangle ABC.

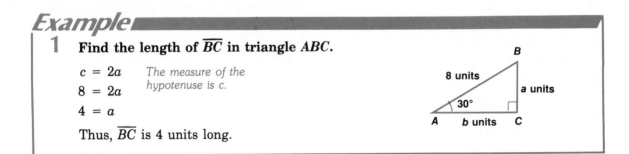

$c = 2a$ *The measure of the hypotenuse is c.*
$8 = 2a$
$4 = a$

Thus, $\overline{BC}$ is 4 units long.

Example

2 **Find the length of $\overline{PQ}$ in triangle PQR.**

$r = 2q$ *The measure of the side*
$= 2 \cdot 6$ *opposite the 30° angle*
             is q.
$= 12$

Thus, $\overline{PQ}$ is 12 units long.

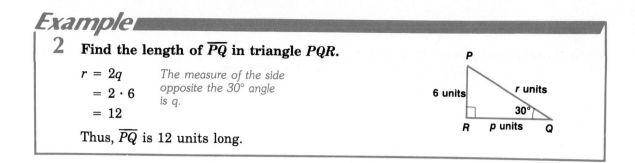

Suppose a represents the measure of the side opposite the 30° angle. The Pythagorean Theorem is used to find the length of the side opposite the 60° angle in a 30° − 60° right triangle.

$a^2 + b^2 = c^2$ *Pythagorean Theorem*

$a^2 + b^2 = (2a)^2$ *The measure of the hypotenuse is*
                       twice the measure of the side
$a^2 + b^2 = 4a^2$ *opposite the 30° angle.*

$b^2 = 4a^2 - a^2$

$b^2 = 3a^2$

$b = a\sqrt{3}$ *How is this obtained?*

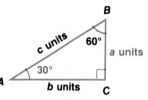

In a 30° − 60° right triangle, if a is the measure of the side opposite the 30° angle, then $a\sqrt{3}$ is the measure of the side opposite the 60° angle.

This relationship should be memorized.

Examples

3 **Find the length of $\overline{AC}$ in triangle ABC.**

$b = a\sqrt{3}$ *The measure of the side opposite*
$= 5\sqrt{3}$ *the 30° angle is a.*

$\approx 5 \cdot 1.732$

≈ 8.660

Thus, $\overline{AC}$ is approximately 8.660 units long.

4 **Find the length of $\overline{XY}$ and $\overline{XZ}$ in triangle XYZ.**

$x = z\sqrt{3}$

$8\sqrt{3} = z\sqrt{3}$

$8 = z$

Since $y = 2z$, it is clear that $y = 2 \cdot 8$, or 16.

Thus, $\overline{XY}$ is 8 units long and $\overline{XZ}$ is 16 units long.

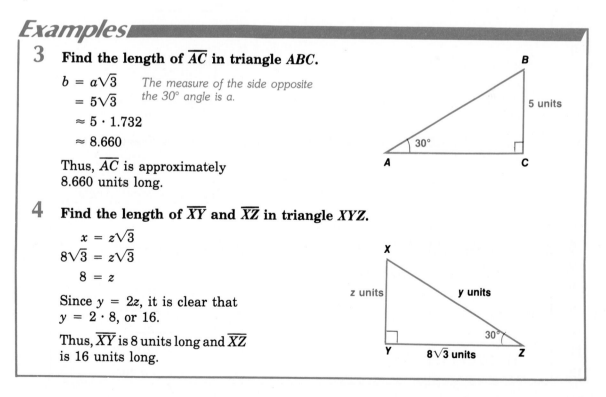

Exploratory Exercises

Each of the following is the length of the hypotenuse of a 30°–60° right triangle. For each triangle, find the length of the side opposite the 30° angle.

1. 8 m
2. 16 cm
3. 13 mm
4. 9 mi
5. $4\frac{1}{2}$ in.
6. $3\frac{3}{8}$ in.
7. 16.36 m
8. 4.63 cm

Each of the following is the length of the side opposite the 30° angle in a 30°–60° right triangle. Find the length of the hypotenuse in each triangle.

9. 7 m
10. 6.2 cm
11. 4.35 mm
12. $4\frac{1}{2}$ mi
13. $6\frac{3}{8}$ in.
14. 13 m
15. 3.86 cm
16. $7\frac{3}{4}$ in.

Each of the following is the length of the side opposite the 60° angle in a 30°–60° right triangle. Find the length of the other two sides in each triangle.

17. $4\sqrt{3}$ ft
18. $2\sqrt{3}$ cm
19. $8\sqrt{3}$ m
20. $\sqrt{3}$ mi
21. $7\sqrt{3}$ yd
22. $9\sqrt{3}$ mm

Written Exercises

Find the length of the third side in each triangle. (Use $\sqrt{3} \approx 1.732$.)

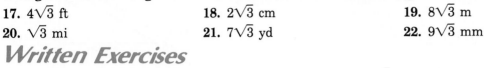

1.   2.

3.   4.

Find the missing lengths for each of the 30°–60° right triangles described below. (Use $\sqrt{3} \approx 1.732$.)

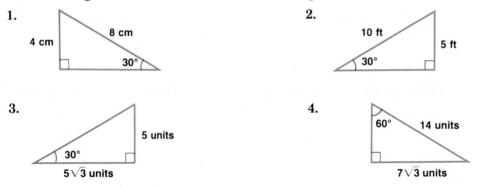

	Hypotenuse	Side Opposite 30° Angle	Side Opposite 60° Angle
5.	6 m	_____	_____
6.	4.75 mm	_____	_____
7.	$3\frac{1}{2}$ in.	_____	_____
8.	_____	8 cm	_____
9.	_____	6.5 m	
10.	_____	$3\frac{1}{4}$ in.	_____
11.	_____	_____	$\sqrt{12}$ m
12.	_____	_____	$3.5\sqrt{3}$ cm

16-3　Similar Triangles

Are the triangles below the same size? Do they have the same shape?

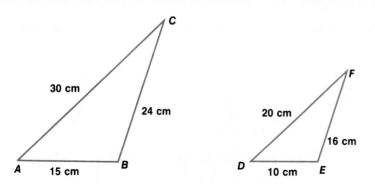

Measure the angles of triangle ABC. Compare these with the measures of triangle DEF. What do you discover?

Triangles that have three congruent angles are called **similar triangles**. The two triangles above are similar triangles. Similar triangles have the same shape, but not necessarily the same size.

If two triangles are similar, the congruent angles are called **corresponding angles**. Also, the sides opposite congruent angles are called **corresponding sides**.

Let's compare the measures of the corresponding sides. Throughout the remainder of this chapter, AB will mean the measure of $\overline{AB}$, BC will mean the measure of $\overline{BC}$, and so on.

$$\frac{AB}{DE} = \frac{15}{10} \qquad \frac{BC}{EF} = \frac{24}{16} \qquad \frac{AC}{DF} = \frac{30}{20}$$

$$= \frac{3}{2} \qquad\qquad = \frac{3}{2} \qquad\qquad = \frac{3}{2}$$

What do you discover?

> **If two triangles are similar, the measures of their corresponding angles are equal and the measures of their corresponding sides are proportional.**

Similar Triangles

This means that for the triangles above you can write the following proportions.

$$\frac{AB}{DE} = \frac{BC}{EF} \qquad \frac{AB}{DE} = \frac{AC}{DF} \qquad \frac{BC}{EF} = \frac{AC}{DF}$$

Proportions can be used to find the missing measures of similar triangles.

Example

1 **If a tree 6 feet tall casts a shadow 4 feet long, how high is a flagpole that casts a shadow 18 feet long?**

Triangle JKL is similar to triangle PQR.

$$\frac{JK}{PQ} = \frac{KL}{QR}$$

$$\frac{6}{x} = \frac{4}{18}$$

$4x = 6 \cdot 18$ *Cross multiply.*

$4x = 108$

$x = 27$

The flagpole is 27 feet high.

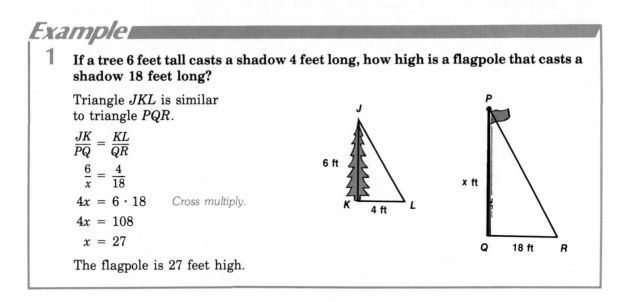

Tell how you could use the method shown above to find the height of a building.

Example

2 **Find the distance, UV, across the pond shown below.**

Triangle STU is similar to triangle WVU.

$$\frac{TU}{VU} = \frac{ST}{WV}$$

$$\frac{70}{x} = \frac{50}{75}$$

$50x = 70 \cdot 75$

$50x = 5250$

$x = 105$

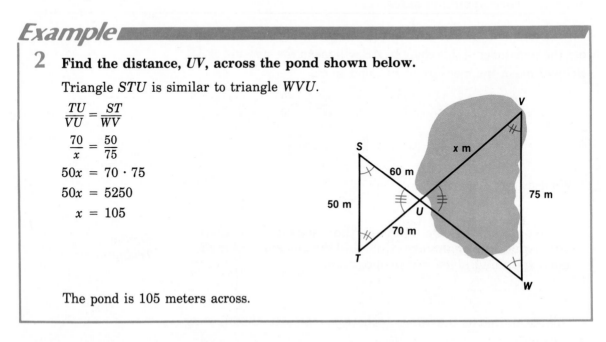

The pond is 105 meters across.

Can you name some other instances where you can use similar triangles as above to find distances?

Exploratory Exercises

For each pair of similar triangles, list the corresponding angles and the corresponding sides.

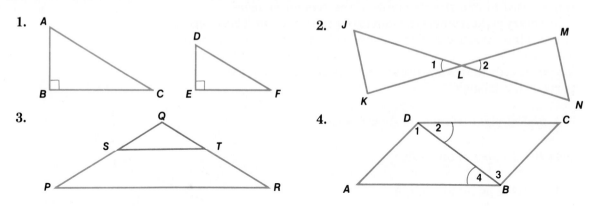

1.

2.

3.

4.

Written Exercises

Triangles _ABC_ and _DEF_ are similar. For each set of measures, find the measure of the missing sides.

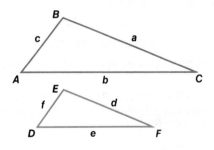

1. $a = 5, d = 7, f = 6, e = 5$
2. $c = 11, f = 6, d = 5, e = 4$
3. $b = 4.5, d = 2.1, e = 3.4, f = 3.2$
4. $a = 16, c = 12, b = 13, e = 7$
5. $a = 17, b = 15, c = 10, f = 6$
6. $c = 18, f = 12, d = 18, e = 16$
7. $a = 4\frac{1}{4}, b = 5\frac{1}{2}, e = 2\frac{3}{4}, f = 1\frac{3}{4}$
8. $c = 7\frac{1}{2}, f = 5, a = 10\frac{1}{2}, b = 15$

Use similar triangles to solve each of the following.

9. In building a roof, a 5-foot support is to be placed at point _B_ as shown on the diagram. Find the length of the support that is to be placed at point _A_.

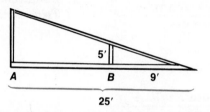

10. Triangle _ABC_ is similar to triangle _EDC_. Find the distance across the lake from point _A_ to point _B_.

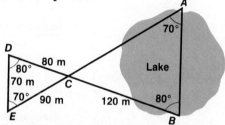

11. A triangle has sides of 9, 15, and 18 cm. The longest side of a similar triangle is 22 cm in length. Find the length of the shortest side of that triangle.

12. A fence post one meter high casts a shadow 170 cm long. Find the height of a flagpole whose shadow is 8000 cm in length.

16-4 Trigonometric Ratios

For similar triangles, ratios of the measures of corresponding sides can be written. If enough of these measures are known, these ratios can be used to find the measures of the remaining sides.

For every right triangle, certain ratios can be set up. These ratios, called **trigonometric ratios**, involve not only the measures of the sides but the measures of the acute angles as well. Again, if enough is known, these ratios can be used to find the measures of the remaining parts of the triangle.

A typical right triangle is shown below.

Side BC is *opposite* angle A.

Side AC is *adjacent* to angle A.

Side AB is the *hypotenuse* and is opposite the right angle C.

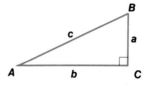

Notice that in this triangle
   a denotes the measure of the side opposite angle A.
   b denotes the measure of the side opposite angle B.
   c denotes the measure of the side opposite angle C.

Three common trigonometric ratios are defined as follows.

$$\text{sine of angle } A = \frac{\text{measure of side opposite angle } A}{\text{measure of hypotenuse}}$$

$$\sin A = \frac{a}{c}$$

$$\text{cosine of angle } A = \frac{\text{measure of side adjacent to angle } A}{\text{measure of hypotenuse}}$$

$$\cos A = \frac{b}{c}$$

$$\text{tangent of angle } A = \frac{\text{measure of side opposite angle } A}{\text{measure of side adjacent to angle } A}$$

$$\tan A = \frac{a}{b}$$

Definition of Trigonometric Ratios

Example

1

Find the sine of angle D in the $30°-60°$ right triangle below.

$\sin D = \dfrac{EF}{DE}$

Since side EF is opposite the $30°$ angle, its measure is one-half the measure of hypotenuse DE.

Therefore, $\sin D = \frac{1}{2}$ or $\sin 30° = \frac{1}{2}$.

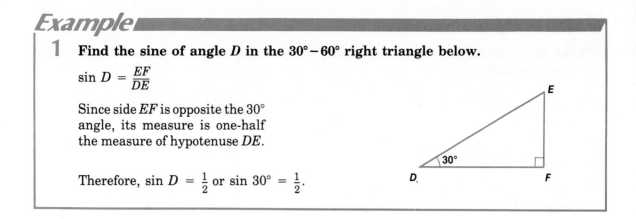

Are all $30°-60°$ right triangles the same size?

Regardless of the size, the measure of the side opposite the $30°$ angle is one-half the measure of the hypotenuse. Therefore, we see that a trigonometric ratio like sine $30°$ will always be the same regardless of the triangle's size.

Example

2

For triangle ABC, express $\sin A$, $\cos A$, $\tan A$, $\sin B$, $\cos B$, and $\tan B$ to 3 decimal places.

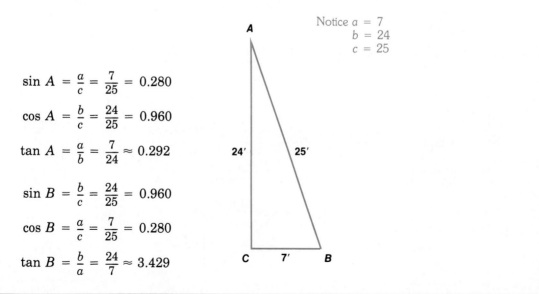

Notice $a = 7$
$b = 24$
$c = 25$

$\sin A = \dfrac{a}{c} = \dfrac{7}{25} = 0.280$

$\cos A = \dfrac{b}{c} = \dfrac{24}{25} = 0.960$

$\tan A = \dfrac{a}{b} = \dfrac{7}{24} \approx 0.292$

$\sin B = \dfrac{b}{c} = \dfrac{24}{25} = 0.960$

$\cos B = \dfrac{a}{c} = \dfrac{7}{25} = 0.280$

$\tan B = \dfrac{b}{a} = \dfrac{24}{7} \approx 3.429$

Exploratory Exercises

For the three triangles below, express each of the following trigonometric ratios as a fraction in simplest form.

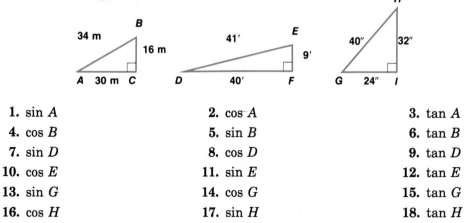

1. sin A	2. cos A	3. tan A
4. cos B	5. sin B	6. tan B
7. sin D	8. cos D	9. tan D
10. cos E	11. sin E	12. tan E
13. sin G	14. cos G	15. tan G
16. cos H	17. sin H	18. tan H

19. Are angles A and B complementary angles? Is sin A = cos B?

20. Are angles D and E complementary angles? Is cos D = sin E?

21. Based on your answers for problems 19-20, what is the relationship of the sine and cosine of complementary angles?

Written Exercises

Express the sine, cosine, and tangent of each acute angle below to 3 decimal places.

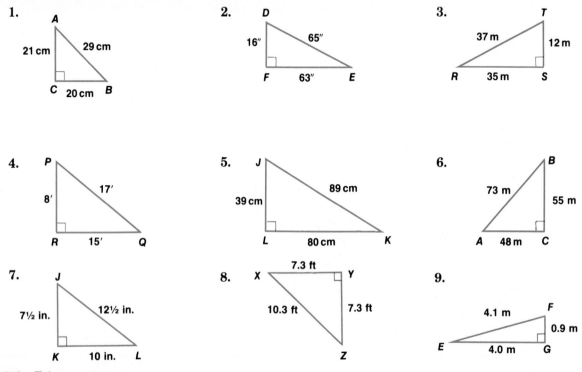

Reading Algebra

As shown below, letters from the English alphabet can be used to convey mathematical concepts.

$$x^2 + 7 = 0 \qquad A = \tfrac{1}{2}bh \qquad \overline{AB} \qquad \sin A$$

In higher mathematics, letters from the Greek alphabet are often used in the same way. The table below shows upper case and lower case letters of the Greek alphabet.

GREEK ALPHABET

Greek Letter		Greek Name	English Equivalent	Greek Letter		Greek Name	English Equivalent
A	α	Alpha	a	N	ν	Nu	n
B	β	Beta	b	Ξ	ξ	Xi	x
Γ	γ	Gamma	g	O	o	Omicron	ŏ
Δ	δ	Delta	d	Π	π	Pi	p
E	ε	Epsilon	ĕ	P	ρ	Rho	r
Z	ζ	Zeta	z	Σ	σ	Sigma	s
H	η	Eta	ē	T	τ	Tau	t
Θ	θ	Theta	th	Y	υ	Upsilon	u
I	ι	Iota	i	Φ	φ	Phi	ph
K	κ	Kappa	k	X	χ	Chi	ch
Λ	λ	Lambda	l	Ψ	ψ	Psi	ps
M	μ	Mu	m	Ω	ω	Omega	ō

The most commonly used Greek letter in mathematics is π. This letter is used to represent the ratio of the circumference of a circle to its diameter. An approximate value for π is 3.14.

Other Greek letters are commonly used in higher mathematics. For example, Δ is commonly used to represent the difference between two measures, θ is often used to represent the measure of an angle, and Σ stands for the sum of a set of numbers.

Exercises

How would you say each of the following?

1. $\sin \theta$

2. $\cos \phi$

3. $\tan \psi$

4. Δx

5. $r = 0.7\,\Omega$

6. $\alpha - \lambda$

7. $\sin(\alpha + \beta)$

8. $|x - y| < \gamma$

16-5　Using Tables

If you know the measures of the sides of a right triangle, you can calculate the sine, cosine, and tangent of any of its angles.

Tables such as those on page 545 list approximations of these ratios in decimal form.

Examples

1　**Find tan 28°.**

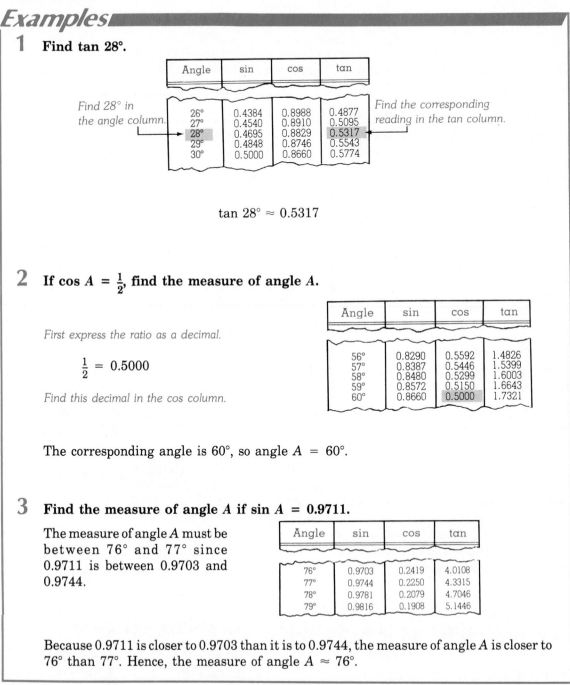

Find 28° in the angle column.

Angle	sin	cos	tan
26°	0.4384	0.8988	0.4877
27°	0.4540	0.8910	0.5095
28°	0.4695	0.8829	0.5317
29°	0.4848	0.8746	0.5543
30°	0.5000	0.8660	0.5774

Find the corresponding reading in the tan column.

tan 28° ≈ 0.5317

2　**If cos A = $\frac{1}{2}$, find the measure of angle A.**

First express the ratio as a decimal.

$$\frac{1}{2} = 0.5000$$

Find this decimal in the cos column.

Angle	sin	cos	tan
56°	0.8290	0.5592	1.4826
57°	0.8387	0.5446	1.5399
58°	0.8480	0.5299	1.6003
59°	0.8572	0.5150	1.6643
60°	0.8660	0.5000	1.7321

The corresponding angle is 60°, so angle A = 60°.

3　**Find the measure of angle A if sin A = 0.9711.**

The measure of angle A must be between 76° and 77° since 0.9711 is between 0.9703 and 0.9744.

Angle	sin	cos	tan
76°	0.9703	0.2419	4.0108
77°	0.9744	0.2250	4.3315
78°	0.9781	0.2079	4.7046
79°	0.9816	0.1908	5.1446

Because 0.9711 is closer to 0.9703 than it is to 0.9744, the measure of angle A is closer to 76° than 77°. Hence, the measure of angle A ≈ 76°.

Exploratory Exercises

Use the table on page 545 to answer the following.

1. At what angle is the sine at its maximum (greatest value)? At its minimum (least value)?
2. At what angle is the cosine at its minimum? At its maximum?
3. For what angle are the sine and cosine equal?
4. What is the tangent of the angle at which the sine and cosine are equal?
5. What are the minimum and maximum values of the tangent?

Written Exercises

Use the table on page 545 to find a value for each of the following ratios.

1. cos 25°	2. tan 31°	3. sin 89°	4. tan 14°
5. cos 76°	6. sin 22°	7. cos 83°	8. tan 24°
9. sin 68°	10. tan 9°	11. sin 27°	12. cos 18°
13. cos 42°	14. tan 50°	15. sin 45°	16. cos 30°
17. sin 30°	18. tan 30°	19. sin 60°	20. cos 60°

Use the table to find the measure of each angle to the nearest degree.

21. sin A = 0.4384	22. cos B = 0.4848	23. tan D = 1.3250
24. cos $\angle 1$ = 0.9781	25. tan $\angle ABC$ = 5.1446	26. sin A = 0.9620
27. cos B = 0.3900	28. tan $\angle 2$ = 1.7321	29. sin D = 0.2756
30. cos A = 0.3746	31. cos B = 0.7660	32. sin $\angle DEF$ = 0.9848
33. tan C = 57.2900	34. sin X = 0.0520	35. cos Z = 0.9986
36. tan A = 0.0524	37. sin B = 0.5000	38. cos B = 0.8660

Find values for each of the following.

39. sin 30° − cos 60°	40. tan 45° + sin 0°	41. sin 90° + cos 0°
42. tan 0° + sin 90°	43. sin 0° − cos 60°	44. sin 90° − tan 0°
45. sin 30° − cos 30°	46. cos 60° − sin 30°	47. tan 45° − tan 45°

Using Calculators ——————————Trigonometric Functions

You can use a calculator to find the value for cos 25° as follows.

ENTER: 25 | COS |

The display shows 0.963078. Thus, rounded to ten-thousandths, cos 25° = 0.9631.
You can also find the measure of the angle for sin A = 0.4384 as follows.

ENTER: 0.4384 | INV | | SIN |

The display shows 26.001839. Thus, to the nearest degree, angle $A \approx 26°$.

Exercises

Use a calculator to check your answers for Written Exercises 1-38 above.

16-6 Solving Right Triangles

To solve a triangle means to find all the missing measures of the triangle. The trigonometric ratios can be used to solve a triangle. The ratio used depends upon what measures are given and what measures are missing. Sometimes, more than one ratio can be used.

Example

1 **Find the measures of angles *A* and *C* below.**

Suppose you use the sine ratio.

$$\sin A = \frac{4}{5}$$
$$= 0.8000$$

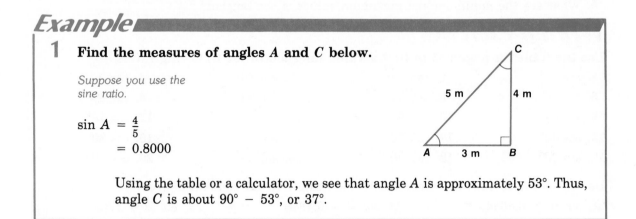

Using the table or a calculator, we see that angle *A* is approximately 53°. Thus, angle *C* is about 90° − 53°, or 37°.

How would you use the cosine ratio to find the measure of angle *A*? Tell how you could use the tangent ratio to find the measure of angle *A*.

Example

2 **Find the length of $\overline{DE}$ in triangle *DEF*.**

In this case, use the cosine ratio.

$$\cos 40° = \frac{x}{7.6}$$
$$0.7660 \approx \frac{x}{7.6}$$
$$(0.7660)7.6 \approx x$$
$$5.8 \approx x$$

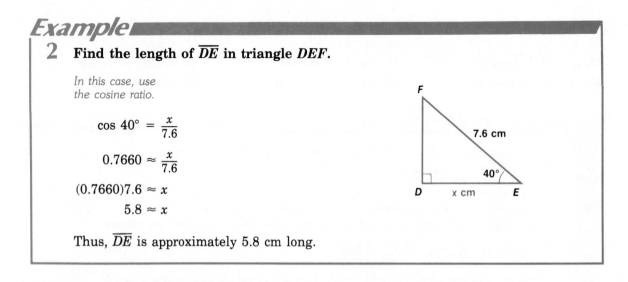

Thus, $\overline{DE}$ is approximately 5.8 cm long.

Try using $\sin 50° = \frac{x}{7.6}$ to solve for the measure of $\overline{DE}$. Did you get the same result as in Example 2?

Examples

3 Find the length of $\overline{JK}$ in triangle *JKL*.

In this case, use the tangent ratio.

$$\tan 48° = \frac{5.8}{x}$$

$$1.1106 \approx \frac{5.8}{x}$$

$$1.1106x \approx 5.8$$

$$x \approx 5.2$$

Thus, $\overline{JK}$ is about 5.2 mm long.

4 Find the missing measures in the triangle below.

Angle $R = 90° - 36°$, or $54°$

$$\sin 36° = \frac{x}{18}$$

$$0.5878 \approx \frac{x}{18}$$

$$10.6 \approx x$$

Thus, $\overline{QR}$ is about 10.6 inches long.

$$\cos 36° = \frac{y}{18}$$

$$0.8090 \approx \frac{y}{18}$$

$$14.56 \approx y$$

Thus, $\overline{PQ}$ is about 14.56 inches long.

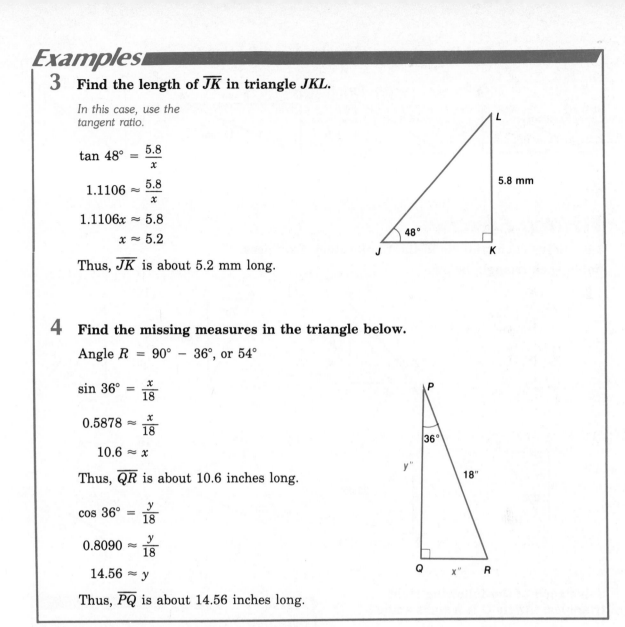

Exploratory Exercises

State which trigonometric ratios you would use to find the missing measures in each of the following.

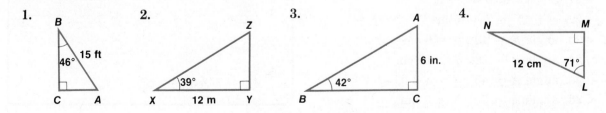

1.

2.

3.

4.

How would you find the measures of angles _A_ and _B_ below?

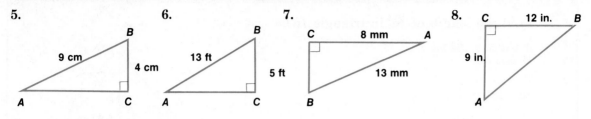

5.   6.   7.   8.

Written Exercises

1-8.   Solve each triangle in the Exploratory Exercises.
Solve each triangle below.

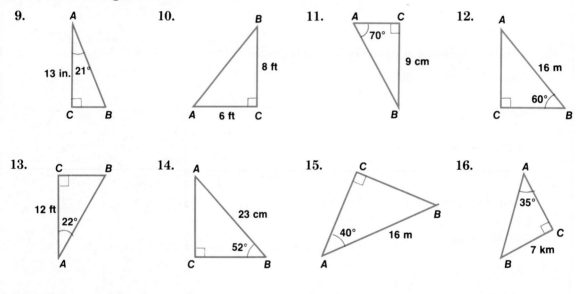

9.   10.   11.   12.

13.   14.   15.   16.

Solve each of the following right
triangles. (Angle _C_ is a right angle.)

17. angle $A = 31°$, $a = 6$ m

18. $a = 6$ in., $c = 10$ in.

19. angle $B = 42°$, $c = 10$ in.

20. $b = 5$ ft, $a = 4$ ft

21. $c = 14$ ft, $b = 11$ ft

22. $c = 11$ m, $b = 6$ m

23. angle $B = 40°$, $b = 6$ cm

24. angle $B = 28°$, $a = 16$ cm

25. angle $A = 45°$, $c = \sqrt{2}$ ft

26. angle $A = 75°$, $b = 3$ km

mini-review

Multiply or divide.

1. $\dfrac{2a + 8}{a^2 - 25} \cdot \dfrac{a - 5}{5a + 10}$ 2. $\dfrac{y^2}{x^2} \div \dfrac{a^2}{x^3}$

Add or subtract.

3. $\dfrac{2x}{x - 7} - \dfrac{14}{x - 7}$ 4. $\dfrac{2}{x - y} + \dfrac{y}{y - x}$

Solve.

5. $\dfrac{3}{x} + \dfrac{1}{x - 5} = \dfrac{1}{2x}$

16-7   Problem Solving: Using Trigonometry

In order to use the trigonometric ratios to solve problems, it is helpful to understand the meaning of angles of **elevation** and **depression**.

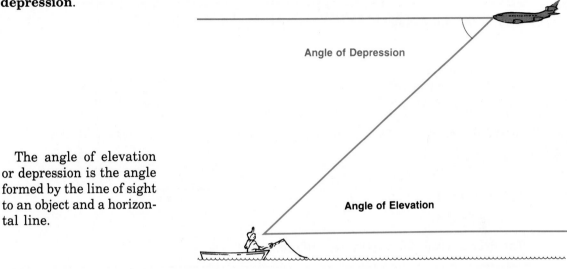

Angle of Depression

Angle of Elevation

The angle of elevation or depression is the angle formed by the line of sight to an object and a horizontal line.

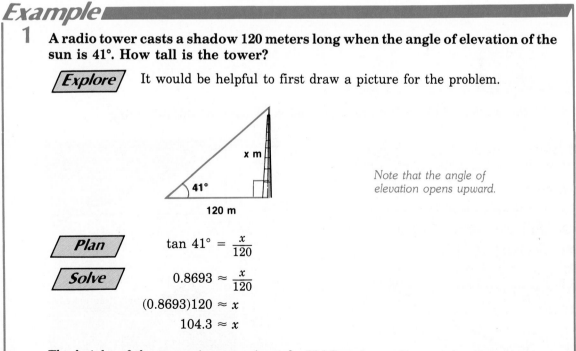

Example

1   **A radio tower casts a shadow 120 meters long when the angle of elevation of the sun is 41°. How tall is the tower?**

Explore   It would be helpful to first draw a picture for the problem.

x m

41°

120 m

Note that the angle of elevation opens upward.

Plan $\tan 41° = \dfrac{x}{120}$

Solve $0.8693 \approx \dfrac{x}{120}$

$(0.8693)120 \approx x$

$104.3 \approx x$

The height of the tower is approximately 104.3 meters.   *Examine the solution.*

2 From the top of an observation tower 50 meters high, a forest ranger spotted a deer at an angle of depression of 28°. How far was the deer from the base of the tower?

First make a drawing.

Notice that the angle of depression opens downward.

$$\tan 62° = \frac{x}{50}$$

$$1.8807 \approx \frac{x}{50}$$

$$(1.8807)50 \approx x$$

$$94 \approx x$$

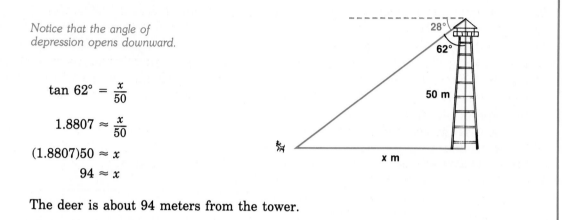

The deer is about 94 meters from the tower.

Exploratory Exercises

Name the angles of elevation and depression in each of the following.

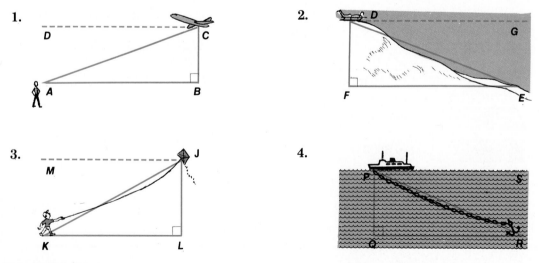

1.

2.

3.

4.

Written Exercises

Use trigonometric ratios and the table on page 545 to solve each problem.

1. A road rises 38 feet vertically over a horizontal distance of 540 feet. What is the angle of elevation of the road?

2. At a point 200 feet from the base of a flagpole, the angle of elevation is 62°. Find the height of the flagpole and the distance from the point to the top.

3. A chimney casts a shadow 75 feet long when the angle of elevation of the sun is 41°. How tall is the chimney?

4. A train in the mountains rises 8 feet for every 200 feet it moves along the track. Find the angle of elevation of the tracks.

5. At a point 210 feet from the base of a building, the angle of elevation to the top of the building is 55°. How tall is the building?

6. How far will a submarine travel when going to a depth of 300 feet if its course has an angle of depression of 25°?

7. How long of a guy wire will be needed for a TV tower if the wire is fastened to the tower 40 feet above the ground and forms an angle of 52° with the tower?

8. A roof is constructed as shown in the diagram below. Find the pitch (angle of elevation) of the roof.

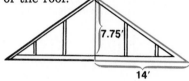

9. Find the area of a right triangle in which one acute angle is 25° and the leg opposite that angle is 40 cm in length.

10. From the top of a 70-meter lighthouse, an airplane was observed that was directly over a ship. The angle of elevation of the plane was 18°, while the angle of depression of the ship was 25°. Find the distance from the ship to the foot of the lighthouse and the height of the plane.

11. A camera has a field of vision of 50° as shown below. The camera is being used to photograph a ship that is 1300 feet long. How far from the ship must the camera be held to photograph the entire ship?

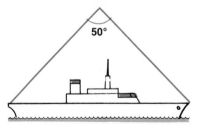

12. An airplane, at an altitude of 2000 feet, is directly over a power plant. The navigator finds the angle of depression of the airport to be 19°. How far is the plane from the airport? How far is it from the power plant to the airport?

Challenge

Solve the following triangles.

13.

14.

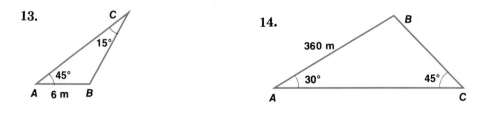

Glenn Hatfield is a licensed surveyor. In addition to measuring land, he uses his surveying instruments to check building construction. Glenn frequently uses trigonometry in his work.

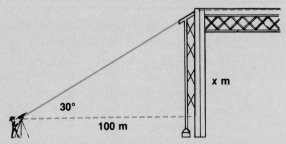

As shown above, Glenn has used his instrument to measure the angle of elevation and find the height from the top of the instrument to the top of the bridge.

$$\tan 30° = \frac{x}{100}$$

$$0.5774 \approx \frac{x}{100}$$

$$57.74 \approx x$$

If the instrument height is 1.54 m, what is the height of the bridge?

Use trigonometry to find the heights of various objects for the following measurements.

	Angle of Elevation	Distance from Instrument	Instrument Height
1.	35°	100 m	1.45 m
2.	26°	62.56 m	1.73 m
3.	11°	131.37 m	1.68 m
4.	3°	895 m	1.54 m

Trigonometric Functions

Trigonometric functions are used in many applications of mathematics. A computer can calculate values of trigonometric functions very rapidly. However, the values are found for angle measures in *radians*, not for angle measures in degrees. For an angle whose measure is D degrees, the measure in radians, R, is $D \cdot \pi/180$.

Trigonometric functions usually available in BASIC include SIN (sine), COS (cosine), and TAN (tangent). The following program uses the SIN function to print a table of sines.

```
 5  PRINT "ANGLE" , "SINE"
10  FOR D = 0 TO 360 STEP 30
20  LET R = D * 3.1416 / 180
25  LET R1 = INT ( SIN (R) * 1000 + .5)/1000
30  PRINT D,R1
40  NEXT D
50  END
```

ANGLE	SINE
0	0
30	.5
60	.866
90	1
120	.866
150	.5
180	0
210	-.5
240	-.866
270	-1
300	-.866
330	-.5
360	0

The sine function generates ordered pairs. To graph the sine function, use the horizontal axis for the degree values. Use the vertical axis for the sine. After plotting the points, complete the graph by connecting the plotted points with a smooth continuous curve as shown.

Exercises

1. Modify the program to print a table of cosines and then graph the cosine function.

State whether the value of each of the following is positive or negative.

2. sin 30°   **3.** cos 150°   **4.** sin 330°   **5.** cos 60°

State which is greater.

6. cos 30° or cos 90°   **7.** sin 0° or sin 90°

Find the values of x for which each of the following is true.

8. cos x = 1   **9.** sin x = 1   **10.** sin x = 0   **11.** cos x = -1

12. How are the graphs of the sine function and cosine function related?

Vocabulary

supplementary angles (499)
complementary angles (499)
30° − 60° right triangles (502)
similar triangles (505)
corresponding angles (505)
corresponding sides (505)
trigonometric ratios (508)

sine (508)
cosine (508)
tangent (508)
solving triangles (514)
angle of elevation (5107)
angle of depression (517)

Chapter Summary

1. Two angles are supplementary if the sum of their measures is 180°. (499)
2. Two angles are complementary if the sum of their measures is 90°. (499)
3. The sum of the measures of the angles in any triangle is 180°. (500)
4. In any 30° − 60° right triangle, the measure of the side opposite the 30° angle is one half the measure of the hypotenuse. (502)
5. In a 30° − 60° right triangle, if a is the measure of the side opposite the 30° angle, then $a\sqrt{3}$ is the measure of the side opposite the 60° angle. (503)
6. Two triangles are similar if the measures of their corresponding angles are equal. (505)
7. If two triangles are similar, the measures of their corresponding sides are proportional. (505)
8. Sine of an angle:

$$\sin A = \frac{\text{measure of side opposite angle } A}{\text{measure of hypotenuse}} \quad (508)$$

9. Cosine of an angle:

$$\cos A = \frac{\text{measure of side adjacent to angle } A}{\text{measure of hypotenuse}} \quad (508)$$

10. Tangent of an angle:

$$\tan A = \frac{\text{measure of side opposite angle } A}{\text{measure of side adjacent to angle } A} \quad (508)$$

11. The trigonometric ratios can be used to find the missing measures of a triangle. (514)

Chapter Review

16-1 Find the complement of each angle whose measure is listed below.

  1. 66° **2.** 42° **3.** $y°$

Find the supplement of each angle whose measure is listed below.

  4. 62° **5.** 148° **6.** $m°$

In each of the following, the measures of two angles of a triangle are given. Find the measure of each third angle.

  7. 16°, 72° **8.** 42°, 121° **9.** $y°$, $x°$

16-2 Find the missing measures of each of the 30° − 60° right triangles described below. (Use $\sqrt{3} \approx 1.732$.)

	Hypotenuse	Side Opposite 30° Angle	Side Opposite 60° Angle
10.	8 cm	————	————
11.	4.25 cm	————	————
12.	————	6.2 m	————
13.	————	$3\frac{1}{2}$ in.	
14.	————	————	$2\sqrt{3}$ in.
15.	————	————	$4.5 \sqrt{3}$ m

16-3 Triangles *ABC* and *DEF* are similar.

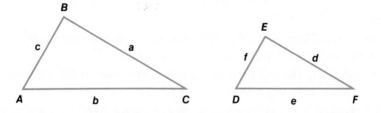

For each set of measures, find the measures of the missing sides.

  16. $a = 5$, $d = 11$, $f = 6$, $e = 14$ **17.** $c = 16$, $b = 12$, $a = 10$, $f = 9$
  18. $a = 8$, $c = 10$, $b = 6$, $f = 12$

16-4 Use the triangle below. Express each of the following ratios as a fraction.

  19. $\sin A$ **20.** $\cos B$
  21. $\cos A$ **22.** $\sin B$
  23. $\tan A$ **24.** $\tan B$

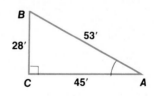

State each of the following correct to 3 decimal places.

25. sin A

26. cos A

27. tan B

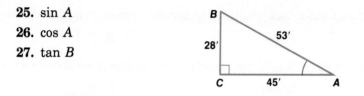

16-5 Use the table of trigonometric ratios on page 545 or a calculator to find a value for each of the following.

28. cos 61°   29. sin 42°   30. tan 13°

31. sin 84°   32. cos 17°   33. tan 66°

16-6 Using the triangles below, find each of the following.

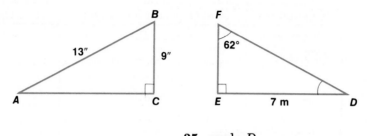

34. angle A 35. angle D

36. angle B 37. side EF

38. side AC 39. side FD

16-7 Solve each problem.

40. A cliff is 250 feet above the ocean. From the cliff, the angle of depression of a boat in the water is 10°. How far is the boat from the base of the cliff?

41. A weather balloon is directly above a tree. The angle of elevation is 60° when you are 100 meters from the tree. How high is the balloon?

42. The diagonal of a rectangle is 16 cm long and makes an angle of 50° with a side of the rectangle. Find the length and width of the rectangle.

Find the complement and supplement of each angle whose measure is listed below.

1. 28°

2. 69°

3. $(y + 20)°$

In each of the following, the measures of two angles of a triangle are given. Find the measure of the third angle.

4. 16°, 47°

5. 89°, 66°

6. 45°, 120°

Find the missing measures of each of the 30° − 60° right triangles described below. (Use $\sqrt{3} \approx 1.732$.)

	Hypotenuse	Side Opposite 30° Angle	Side Opposite 60° Angle
7.	17 in.	_____	_____
8.	_____	8 ft	_____
9.	_____	_____	$9\sqrt{3}$ m

Triangles *ABC* and *JKL* are similar. For each set of measures, find the missing side measures.

10. $c = 20,\ l = 15,\ k = 16,\ j = 12$

11. $c = 12,\ b = 13,\ a = 6,\ l = 10$

12. $k = 5,\ c = 6.5,\ b = 7.5,\ a = 4.5$

13. $l = 1\frac{1}{2},\ c = 4\frac{1}{2},\ k = 2\frac{1}{4},\ a = 3$

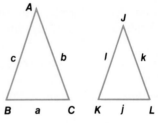

Solve each of the following right triangles. (Angle *C* is a right angle.)

14. angle $A = 56°,\ a = 17$

15. $a = 12,\ b = 16$

16. angle $B = 42°,\ c = 10$

17. $b = 21,\ c = 29$

Solve each problem.

18. A 6-foot pole casts a 4-foot shadow. How tall is a tree which casts a 50-foot shadow?

19. A kite is flying at the end of a 300-foot string. Assuming the string is straight and forms an angle of 58° with the ground, how high is the kite?

20. A plane is 1000 feet above the ground. The angle of depression of the landing strip is 20°. How far is the plane from the landing strip?

1. State the property shown by $4379 \cdot 0 = 0$
2. Solve: $63 = 11 - x$
3. 40% of what number is 30?
4. Solve: $\frac{1}{2}a + 3 \geq -\frac{1}{3}(a + 6)$
5. Simplify: $\frac{-18x^6y^2}{24x^4y^6}$

Factor, if possible.

6. $5x^2 + 25xy - 30xy^2$
7. $m^2 + 14m + 35$

8. Solve: $3y^2 - 13y = -14$
9. Graph: $2x + 5y = 8$

10. Given $f(x) = x^2 - 2x - 4$, find $f\left(\frac{1}{2}\right)$.

11. Write an equation in standard form for the line passing through $(1, 3)$ and having a slope of -2.

12. Write an equation for the line that is perpendicular to the graph of $5x - 9y = 4$ and passes through $(2, 1)$. Use slope-intercept form.

13. Use substitution to solve the system of equations $\frac{1}{2}x - y = 6$ and $4x + 2y = 8$.

14. Solve: $\sqrt{4x^2 + 4x + 1} = 7$
15. Find the distance between $(3, -6)$ and $(-7, -4)$.
16. Solve $r^2 - 6r + 4 = 0$ by completing the square.
17. Determine the number of real roots for $6x^2 + x = 1$ by using the discriminant. Find all real roots.
18. Solve: $8k = k^2 + 1$

Find each quotient.

19. $\frac{2m^2 + 5m - 3}{m^2 - 9} \div \frac{4m^2 - 1}{2m^2 - 5m - 3}$
20. $(3t^3 - 11t^2 - 31t + 7) \div (3t + 1)$

21. Simplify: $2 + \frac{a^2 + 1}{a - 1}$
22. Solve: $\frac{4}{t - 2} - \frac{2t - 3}{t^2 - 4} = \frac{5}{t - 2}$
23. If y varies directly as x and $y = 14$ when $x = 3$, find x when $y = 28$.
24. If y varies inversely as x and $y = 2$ when $x = 15$, find x when $y = 3$.
25. Find the complement and the supplement of an angle whose measure is $32°$.
26. The length of the side opposite the $60°$ angle in a $30°-60°$ right triangle has a length of $5\sqrt{3}$ cm. Find the length of the other two sides.

Problem Solving

Solve each problem.

27. Find four consecutive integers such that the sum of the first and third is 26.
28. Tom and Carroll live 70 miles apart. At noon, they begin bicycling towards each other. If Tom rides 4 mph faster than Carroll and they meet at 2:30 P.M., how fast does each travel?
29. The length of a rectangle is 3 times its width. The area of the rectangle is 243 square meters. Find the length and width.
30. The product of the digits of a two-digit number is 18. The units digit is 3 more than the tens digit. Find the number.
31. Carlos can do a job in 5 days. Cameron can do the same job in 3 days. If they work together, how long will it take them to complete the job?
32. A helicopter flying at an altitude of 3000 feet is directly over a car. How far is the car from the helicopter's landing spot if the angle of depression of the landing spot is $20°$?

The questions on this page involve comparing two quantities, one in Column A and one in Column B. In certain questions, information related to one or both quantities is centered above them. All variables used stand for real numbers.

Directions:
Write A if the quantity in Column A is greater.
Write B if the quantity in Column B is greater.
Write C if the quantities are equal.
Write D if there is not enough information to determine the relationship.

Column A	Column B
1. $(0.64)^2$	$\sqrt{64}$
2. $\dfrac{1}{\sqrt{2}}$	$\dfrac{1}{2}\sqrt{2}$
3. 9^2	$\sqrt{900}$

$$x^2 = 25$$
$$y^2 = 36$$

4. x	y

$$x > 1$$

5. $\dfrac{x^3 + x^2}{x}$	$\dfrac{x^3 + x^2}{x^2}$

6. a given chord in a given circle	the radius of the same circle

7.

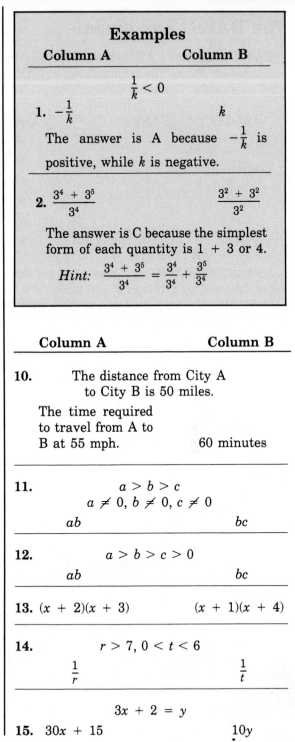

BC	FD
8. $\dfrac{3}{4} + \dfrac{3}{7}$	$\dfrac{19}{21} - \dfrac{3}{7}$
9. $(5 + 7)^2$	$5^2 + 7^2$

Examples

Column A	Column B

$$\frac{1}{k} < 0$$

1. $-\dfrac{1}{k}$ $\qquad\qquad$ k

The answer is A because $-\dfrac{1}{k}$ is positive, while k is negative.

2. $\dfrac{3^4 + 3^5}{3^4}$ $\qquad\qquad$ $\dfrac{3^2 + 3^2}{3^2}$

The answer is C because the simplest form of each quantity is $1 + 3$ or 4.

$Hint:$ $\dfrac{3^4 + 3^5}{3^4} = \dfrac{3^4}{3^4} + \dfrac{3^5}{3^4}$

Column A	Column B

10. The distance from City A to City B is 50 miles.	
The time required to travel from A to B at 55 mph.	60 minutes

$$a > b > c$$
$$a \neq 0,\ b \neq 0,\ c \neq 0$$

11. ab	bc

$$a > b > c > 0$$

12. ab	bc

13. $(x + 2)(x + 3)$	$(x + 1)(x + 4)$

$$r > 7,\ 0 < t < 6$$

14. $\dfrac{1}{r}$	$\dfrac{1}{t}$

$$3x + 2 = y$$

15. $30x + 15$	$10y$

Appendix: BASIC

The BASIC Language

BASIC (Beginner's All-Purpose Symbolic Instruction Code) is a computer language. The symbols used in BASIC are similar to those used in algebra. Compare the symbols in the following lists.

Algebra	BASIC	Algebra	BASIC
$+$	$+$	$>$	$>$
$-$	$-$	$\geq$	$> =$
$\times$ or $\cdot$	$*$	$<$	$<$
$\div$	$/$	$\leq$	$< =$
$=$	$=$	$\neq$	$< >$
4^3	$4{\uparrow}3$ or $4 \wedge 3$	x	X

A variable in BASIC is represented by a capital letter or a capital letter followed by a numeral. Examples are A, B, X, N1, and M2.

In BASIC, the multiplication symbol may never be omitted. To write A times B, write A $*$ B, not AB as in algebra.

Examples of algebraic and BASIC expressions are shown below.

Algebra	BASIC
$6 + 3$	$6 + 3$
$a - 4$	A $-$ 4
$7t, 7 \times t,$ or $7 \cdot t$	$7 * $ T
$24 \div x$ or $\dfrac{24}{x}$	$24 / $ X
$S \geq n^2$	S $> = $ N${\uparrow}$2
$y = 8\frac{1}{2}$	Y $= 8.5$
$y_2 \neq x_1 + 4$	Y2 $< >$ X1 $+ 4$

BASIC uses parentheses as they are used in algebra for grouping. Also, the same order of operations is used as in algebra.

> 1. **Do all operations in parentheses, from the innermost parentheses outward.**
> 2. **Evaluate all powers from left to right.**
> 3. **Then do all multiplications and divisions from left to right.**
> 4. **Then do all additions and subtractions from left to right.**

Order of Operations in BASIC

1 **Evaluate:** $4 * 5 + 9 + 8$

$$
\begin{aligned}
4 * 5 + 9 + 8 &= 20 + 9 + 8 \qquad \textit{First, multiply.}\\
&= 29 + 8 \qquad\quad\;\; \textit{Then, add from left to right.}\\
&= 37
\end{aligned}
$$

2 **Evaluate:** $3 + 9 - 2 * (6 - 1)\uparrow 2 / 10$

$$
\begin{aligned}
3 + 9 - 2 * (6 - 1)\uparrow 2 / 10 &= 3 + 9 - 2 * (5)\uparrow 2 / 10 \qquad \textit{Do all operations in parentheses.}\\
&= 3 + 9 - 2 * 25 / 10 \qquad\quad \textit{Evaluate powers.}\\
&= 3 + 9 - 50 / 10 \qquad\qquad\;\; \textit{Do all multiplications and divisions}\\
&= 3 + 9 - 5 \qquad\qquad\qquad\; \textit{from left to right. Then, do all}\\
&= 12 - 5 \qquad\qquad\qquad\qquad \textit{additions and subtractions from}\\
&= 7 \qquad\qquad\qquad\qquad\qquad\; \textit{left to right.}
\end{aligned}
$$

A **computer program** is a series of statements that gives directions to the computer. The purpose of a program is to get information into the computer (**input**), do the calculations, and then get the results out of the computer (**output**).

A sample program is shown below.

$$
\left.\begin{array}{ll}
10 & \text{PRINT } 11.2 + 9.3\\
20 & \text{END}
\end{array}\right\}\text{statements}
$$

line numbers ⟶

In a computer program, each statement has a **line number**. Numbering by tens permits statements to be inserted later. The computer follows the instructions in numerical order. A program must end with an END statement.

One way to get information into the computer is to use an INPUT statement. When the computer executes an INPUT statement it prints a question mark and waits until the user types in a number.

The programmer chooses the line numbers, integers from 1 to 9999, usually.

3 **Write a program to compute the sum of two numbers.**

10	INPUT A	*Type a number and press RETURN*
20	INPUT B	*Type a number and press RETURN*
30	PRINT A + B	*The computer adds the two numbers and prints the sum.*
40	END	

The program may also be written this way.

10	INPUT A, B	*Type a number, a comma, and a number.*
20	PRINT A + B	
30	END	

Another way to get information into the computer is to use a READ statement and a DATA statement. Each READ statement needs a DATA statement. The DATA statement may appear anywhere in the program but is usually placed after the READ statement. To modify the program in example 3 to include READ and DATA statements, we would replace lines 10 and 20 with

          10   READ A, B
          20   DATA 22, 37

After the program is entered, the command RUN is entered into the computer. This command instructs the computer to execute, or run, the program.

Commands, such as RUN, do not have line numbers.

If the program in example 3 is entered into the computer followed by RUN, the value of A + B is computed and printed.

Written Exercises

Change each algebraic expression to a BASIC expression.

1. $a + b + c$
2. $6m - 7n + 8$
3. $a + b \cdot 9$
4. $4(y + 3)$
5. $38 \div y$
6. $3x^2 + 4x + 9$
7. $a + \dfrac{5}{3 + a}$
8. $\dfrac{a}{b} + n$
9. $\dfrac{5x + 3}{2x - 1}$

Evaluate each of the following expressions.

10. $4 + 15 - 3$
11. $3 * 9 * 4 - 2$
12. $3 \uparrow 2 + 5$
13. $(3 + 4) \uparrow (2 + 1)$
14. $2 * ((4 + 9) * 3)$
15. $8 * (4 * (-6 + 9)/2)/16$

Copy each of the following BASIC expressions. Put numerals under each operation sign to show the order of operations.

Sample:	(6+ A)/3 + X↑3
	1 3 4 2

16. $(X - Y)/Z\uparrow 3 + X * Y - Z$
17. $4 * (A + B)\uparrow 2 + D/E$
18. $(M2 - M1)/(N2 - N1) + C$
19. $A + B/C - 5 * M + 6$

Evaluate each BASIC expression. Let A = 1, B = 2, C = 3, X = 12, Y = 0, Z = 0.5, A1 = 0.25, and A2 = 6.

20. $B * C$
21. $C * X$
22. $X - B * C$
23. $A1 * X + A2$
24. $A * C - Y * Z$
25. $(B * B) * C\uparrow 2$
26. $B * X/A2$
27. $B * C * (X - Y)$
28. $(X - 2 * C) * (2 * C - B)$
29. $(X - 2 * C)/B$
30. $X * A1 * Z$
31. $4 * (B * C\uparrow 2 - X * Z)/B$

Write a program to do each of the following using either an INPUT statement or READ and DATA statements.

32. Find the sum of 31, 64, and 82.
33. Find the product of 31, 64, and 82.
34. Find the quotient of 382 and 94.
35. Find the difference of 382 and 94.
36. Find the perimeter of a rectangle with a width of 3.9 cm and a length of 8.2 cm.

Assignment Statements

In BASIC, the equals sign, =, is used in a slightly different way than in algebra. In algebra, both sides of an equation may have many terms and variables. In BASIC the left side of an equation may have only a variable. This is shown by the examples below.

Algebra	BASIC
$x + 16 = 7$	X = 7 − 16
$4x + 7y = 5x + 16$	X = 7 * Y − 16
$y − 4 = 3(x − 2)^2$	Y = 3 * (X − 2)↑2 + 4

The LET statement is used to assign values to variables. The general form of a LET statement is shown below.

line number LET *variable* = *expression*

In a LET statement, the equals sign tells the computer to assign the value of the expression on the right to the variable on the left. The LET statement is another way to provide a program with data.

10	LET X = 6	*In this program 6 is assigned to X, 12 to Y,*
20	LET Y = 12	*and 20 to Z. The value of X + Y + Z is*
30	LET Z = 20	*computed and assigned to W. The output is*
40	LET W = X + Y + Z	*38, the value of W.*
50	PRINT W	
60	END	

READ-DATA statements also assign values to variables.

10	READ R	*Lines 10 and 20 assign 0.05 to R.*
20	DATA 0.05	
30	LET I = 1000 * R * 10	
40	PRINT R, I	*A comma in a PRINT statement causes the*
50	END	*output to be printed in columns.*

Sometimes a programmer wishes to repeat the same operation in a program. This can be done using a GO TO statement.

The general form of the GO TO statement follows.

Line number GO TO *line number*

Study the use of the GO TO statement in the following program.

10	READ R	*The computer assigns the first value in line 20 to R.*
20	DATA 0.05, 0.055, 0.06, 0.065	
30	I = 1000 * R * 10	
40	PRINT R, I	
50	GO TO 10	*Line 50 instructs the computer to return to line 10. Then the second value in line 20 is assigned to R.*
60	END	

The process of returning to line 10 is continued until all the values in line 20 are used. Then the computer prints an error message such as OUT OF DATA.

Example

1 **Write and run a program which finds the areas of four rectangles with dimensions 8 cm and 5 cm, 7 cm and 2 cm, 9 cm and 6.2 cm, and 4.5 cm and 3 cm.**

10	READ L, W	*Use A = lw, the formula for the area of a rectangle.*
20	LET A = L * W	
30	PRINT A,	
40	GO TO 10	
50	DATA 8, 5, 7, 2, 9, 6.2, 4.5, 3	
60	END	
RUN		*The result of assigning 8 to L and 5 to W is 40. The results from the other values are 14, 55.8, and 13.5.*
40	14	55.8
13.5		
OUT OF DATA IN 10		

Compare the two programs below. Notice that the program on the right uses READ-DATA statements in place of LET statements. What advantage do you see in using READ-DATA statements rather than LET statements?

10 LET A = 3	10 READ A, B, C, D, X
11 LET B = 4	15 DATA 3, 4, 5, 6, 2
12 LET C = 5	20 LET Y = (A + B + C)/(D * X)
13 LET D = 6	30 PRINT Y
14 LET X = 2	40 END
20 LET Y = (A + B + C)/(D * X)	
30 PRINT Y	
40 END	

Written Exercises

Find the value of X in each statement. Let A = 3, B = 4, and M1 = 16.

1. 190 LET X = 6 * A
2. 25 LET X = A * B + 5
3. 20 LET X = B + M1 * B
4. 30 LET X = M1 / B
5. 20 LET X = A↑4
6. 40 LET X = M1 − B + 3 * A

Each algebraic expression below is followed by a BASIC expression. Rewrite each BASIC expression so that it matches the algebraic expression.

7. $\dfrac{a + 2}{y + 3}$ A + 2 / Y + 3

8. $\dfrac{(3 + x)^2}{2r}$ (3 + X)↑2 / 2 * R

9. $\dfrac{3a}{y + 2}$ 3A / (Y + 2)

10. $3a^2 + y$ 3 * A↑(2 + Y)

Correct the error in each BASIC expression or statement below.

11. 7Y + 16
12. (3 + 2/5
13. 4 * Y↑3 + 5Y
14. 30 LET Y = 2A
15. 60 LET 4 * A = B + 3 + C
16. 90 LET A + B = C

For each of the following, write a program to find the value of X.

17. A = 2, B = 4, C = −1,
    X = A + B * (C − 1)

18. A = 5, B = 2, C = 10,
    X = A / B + C↑2 − A

Write the output for each program below.

19. 10 LET A = 4
    20 LET B = 5
    30 PRINT A * B
    40 END

20. 10 READ P, R, T
    20 DATA 300, 0.06, 5
    30 LET I = P * R * T
    40 PRINT P, R, T, I
    50 END

21. 10 READ R
    20 LET P = 3.14159
    30 LET C = 2 * P * R
    40 DATA 2, 4, 7, 9
    50 PRINT C
    60 GO TO 10
    70 END

22. 10 READ A, B, C
    20 LET S = A + B + C
    30 LET A1 = S / B
    40 PRINT A, B, C, A1
    50 DATA 4, 5, 6
    60 END

Write a program to solve each of the following.

23. Find the area of a triangle with a base of 15 units and an altitude of 8 units.

24. Find the volume of a sphere with a radius of 14 cm if $V = \frac{4}{3}\pi r^3$.

25. Find the total surface area of a box with a length of 17 cm, a width of 9 cm, and a height of 4.5 cm. Use $A = 2lw + 2lh + 2hw$.

IF-THEN Statements

The IF-THEN statement is used to compare two numbers. It instructs the computer what to do based on the results of the comparison. The general form of the IF-THEN statement is as follows.

line number IF *sentence* THEN *line number*

The sentence uses one of the following symbols.

Symbol	Meaning	Example
=	is equal to	X = 3
>	is greater than	A > B
<	is less than	10 < 21
> =	is greater than or equal to	A > = 16
< =	is less than or equal to	R < = 10
< >	is not equal to	6 < > 10

The IF-THEN statement is used to compare two numbers. If the sentence containing the two numbers is true, then the computer goes to the line whose number follows THEN. If the sentence is false, then the computer simply goes to the next line of the program.

Study the use of IF-THEN statements in the programs below.

```
10   LET X = 5
20   IF X > 10 THEN 40
30   PRINT X
40   END
```

Line 10 instructs the computer to assign the value 5 to X.
In line 20, the sentence X > 10 is false, and the computer goes to line 30.
The output for this program is 5, the value of X.

```
10   LET X = 15
20   IF X > 10 THEN 40
30   GO TO 50
40   PRINT X
50   END
```

Since X = 15, the sentence in line 20 is true, and the computer goes to line 40. What line would the computer go to if the sentence in line 20 were X < 10?

Suppose you wish to find the areas of ten different squares with sides of 1 unit, 2 units, 3 units, and so on up to 10 units. You can use a LET statement to assign the variables. Consider the following.

```
10   LET S = 1
20   LET S = S + 1
```

In algebra, the statement S = S + 1 is nonsense. But in BASIC, it means that S should be assigned a new value equal to 1 more than its previous value.

The program continues as follows.

```
10  LET S = 1
12  LET A = S↑2        Use A = s², the formula for the area of a square.
14  PRINT A
20  LET S = S + 1      In line 20, the value of S is increased by 1.
30  GO TO 12           Line 30 repeats the program for each new value of S.
40  END
```

As the program is written now, it will continue indefinitely. A line is needed to stop the program when S is greater than 10. An IF-THEN statement can be used to do this.

25 IF S > 10 THEN 40

Study the use of the IF-THEN statement in the program below.

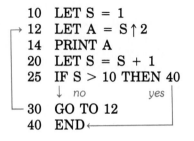

```
10  LET S = 1
12  LET A = S↑2
14  PRINT A
20  LET S = S + 1
25  IF S > 10 THEN 40
      ↓ no          yes
30  GO TO 12
40  END
```

If S is less than or equal to 10, the computer is sent back to line 12. If S is greater than 10, the program ends.

Example

1

Write a program that tells whether each of the following numbers is positive or negative: −3, 6, −11.

```
10  READ N
20  DATA −3, 6, −11, 1000
30  IF N = 1000 THEN 90
40  IF N > 0 THEN 70
50  PRINT N; " IS NEGATIVE"
60  GO TO 10
70  PRINT N; " IS POSITIVE"
80  GO TO 10
90  END
RUN
−3 IS NEGATIVE
6 IS POSITIVE
−11 IS NEGATIVE
```

Line 30 stops the program when 1000 is read in the DATA line.

Line 40 asks. "Is N positive?" If yes, the computer goes to line 70. If no, the computer goes to the next statement, line 50.

The computer prints characters enclosed in quotation marks. A semicolon causes output to be printed close together.

No OUT OF DATA line is printed.

Written Exercises

In each of the following, state the line number the computer goes to after line 10. Let A = 10, B = 6, and X = 20.

1. 10 IF A < 20 THEN 75
   20 PRINT A

2. 10 IF A > = 20 THEN 80
   20 PRINT 3 * A

3. 10 IF A <> B THEN 60
   20 PRINT "HELLO"

4. 10 IF A + X < B THEN 40
   20 PRINT A + X

5. 10 IF X↑3 > A * B THEN 60
   20 X = X + 2

6. 10 IF A − X = B − 16 THEN 40
   20 PRINT A, B, X

For problems 7-10, tell whether the values of X, Y, or both X and Y will be printed. Give the values to be printed. Use the program below.

7. X = 12, Y = 12

8. X = 14, Y = 19

9. X = 9, Y = 10

10. X = 21, Y = 5

```
10  IF X > Y THEN 40
20  LET X = X + 3
30  LET Y = Y + 2
40  IF X > = Y THEN 60
50  PRINT X
60  PRINT Y
70  END
```

Write a BASIC program, using an IF-THEN statement, to solve each of the following problems.

11. Print the integers from 10 to 1 in descending order.

12. Print the squares of the integers from 20 to 40 inclusive.

13. Print the cubes of the odd integers from 7 to 21 inclusive.

14. Read a real number. Print the number, its additive inverse, and its multiplicative inverse if it exists.

Compound statements may be used in IF-THEN statements as shown in the programs in problems 15 and 16. Write the output for each program.

15.
```
10  READ A, B
20  DATA 3, 4, 2, 4
30  IF A = 3 AND B = 4 THEN 60
40  PRINT "HOW ARE YOU?"
50  GO TO 80
60  PRINT "HELLO"
70  GO TO 10
80  END
```

16.
```
10  READ A, B
20  DATA 3, 5, 5, 6
30  IF A = 3 OR B = 4 THEN 60
40  PRINT "HOW ARE YOU?"
50  GO TO 80
60  PRINT "HELLO"
70  GO TO 10
80  END
```

FOR-NEXT Statements

FOR-NEXT statements can increase the efficiency of a program.
Compare the following programs.

```
10   LET S = 1
12   LET A = S↑2
14   PRINT A
20   LET S = S + 1
25   IF S > 10 THEN 40
30   GO TO 12
40   END
```

```
100   FOR S = 1 TO 10 STEP 1
120   LET A = S↑2
140   PRINT A
300   NEXT S
400   END
```

In a single line in the program at the right, line 100, the value of
S is stated at 1 and is increased in steps of 1 until it reaches 10.

100 FOR S = 1	TO 10	STEP 1
LET S = 1	If S > 10 THEN 40	S = S + 1

Line 100 in the program at the right above accomplishes the same thing as lines 10, 20, and 25 do in the program on the left above.

When the computer reads line 100 the first time, S is assigned the
value 1. When line 300, NEXT S, is encountered, the computer
returns to line 100 and increases the value of S by 1. This process
continues until the value of S is greater than 10. The computer then
goes to the line following NEXT S.

The general form for FOR-NEXT statements is shown below.

line number FOR *variable* = *number* TO *number* STEP *number*

line number NEXT *variable*

A FOR statement must always be paired with a NEXT statement.
The number following STEP may be positive or negative.

Example

1 Write a program to print the integers from 1 to 10. Use **FOR-NEXT** statements.

```
10   FOR I = 1 TO 10      STEP is not needed when increasing by 1.
20   PRINT I
30   NEXT I
40   END
```

2 **Write a program that prints the even integers from 2 to 100.**

```
10   FOR I = 2 TO 100 STEP 2
20   PRINT I
30   NEXT I
40   END
```

3 **Write a program that prints a table of the integers from 1 to 3 and their squares.**

```
10   PRINT "NUMBER", "SQUARE"      Line 10 prints headings for a table.
20   FOR I = 1 TO 3
30   PRINT I, I↑2
40   NEXT I
50   END
```

NUMBER	SQUARE	
1	1	*This is how the table appears.*
2	4	
3	9	

FOR-NEXT statements, like GO TO statements and IF-THEN statements, can be used in programs to create loops so that parts of the programs are repeated. There are only two ways these loops can appear.

Nested Loops
```
┌─ FOR X
│ ┌─ FOR Y
│ └─ NEXT Y
└─ NEXT X
```
The loops do not cross.

Independent Loops
```
┌─ FOR X
└─ NEXT X
┌─ FOR Y
└─ NEXT Y
```
The loops do not cross. They are not nested.

Not Acceptable
```
┌─ FOR X
├─ FOR Y
└─ NEXT X
└─ NEXT Y
```
These loops cross.

The program below generates all ordered pairs with first element from set A and second element from set B where A = {1, 2, 3, 4} and B = {6, 7, 8}.

```
10   FOR A = 1 TO 4        Note that the loop for B is nested
20   FOR B = 6 TO 8        within the loop for A.
30   PRINT A; ","; B,
40   NEXT B
50   NEXT A
60   END
```

The output for the program on the preceding page follows.

```
1, 6    1, 7    1, 8    2, 6    2, 7    2, 8
3, 6    3, 7    3, 8    4, 6    4, 7    4, 8
```

Notice that A equals the same value while B goes through the loop.

Written Exercises

Find the error or errors in each of the following.

1.
```
10   IF I = 1 TO 5
20   LET Y = 3 * I + 4
30   PRINT I, Y
40   NEXT I
50   END
```

2.
```
10   FOR I = 1 TO 10 STEP 2
20   LET Y = 3 * I + 10
30   PRINT I, Y
40   NEXT Y
50   END
```

3.
```
 5   LET S = 0
10   READ M, N
20   FOR J = M + N STEP 3
30   LET S = S + J
40   NEXT J
50   PRINT S
60   END
```

4.
```
10   FOR X = 1 TO 5
20   FOR Y = 2 TO 10
30   PRINT X * Y
40   NEXT X
50   NEXT Y
60   END
```

Write a program using FOR-NEXT statements, to do each of the following.

5. Print the odd numbers from 1 to 25.

6. Find the sum of any five numbers. Use READ-DATA statements.

7. Print a table of squares and cubes from 1 to 25.

8. The formula for converting Fahrenheit to Celsius temperature is $C = \frac{5}{9}(F - 32)$. Generate Celsius temperatures for all even Fahrenheit values from 0 to 100.

9. Use the formula in problem 8 to generate Fahrenheit values for all integer Celsius values from -20 to 40.

10. Print an addition table showing all addition facts from $1 + 1 = 2$ to $4 + 4 = 8$.

11. Print a multiplication table showing all multiplication facts from $1 \cdot 1 = 1$ to $10 \cdot 10 = 100$.

12. Print a table of all positive integers and their squares such that none of the squares is greater than 1,000.

13. Find the pairs of integers that satisfy the equation $x^2 + y^2 = 100$.

14. Find the pairs of integers that satisfy the equation $x^2 \cdot y^2 = 400$.

Special Features of BASIC

When the results of computations exceed 6 significant digits, the computer will use E notation. This is the computer equivalent to scientific notation. The E means "times 10 to the given power."

Result of computation	E Notation	Meaning
15,000,000	1.5E + 07	1.5×10^7
37,867,275	3.7867275E + 07	3.7867275×10^7
0.003629	3.629E − 03	3.629×10^{-3}

Sometimes it is necessary to save the values of variables for use later in a program. Consider the following program in which values of variables are *not* saved.

```
10   READ N
20   DATA 3, 4, 7, 11, −2, 14
30   PRINT N
40   GO TO 10
50   END
```
Each time the computer executes line 10, the previous value of N is erased.

The use of subscripted variables allows you to save values for future use. A subscripted variable is written as a letter A to Z followed by a numeral in parentheses.

```
10   DIM A(15)
20   FOR I = 1 TO 15
30   READ A(I)
35   PRINT A(I)
40   NEXT I
50   DATA 15, 14, 13, 12, 11, 10, 9, 8, 7, 6, 5, 4, 3, 2, 1
60   END
```
A(I) is a subscripted variable where I represents an integer from 1 to 15.

Line 10 uses a DIMENSION statement that tells the computer to reserve 15 spaces for the values of the subscripted variables A(I). The number of spaces reserved must be greater than or equal to the number of spaces needed. Line 30 reads and stores numbers from the data line in subscripted variables. For example, 15 is stored in position A(1), 13 is stored in position A(3), 11 is stored in position A(5), and so on. Line 35 will cause the computer to print all stored values in subscripted variables A(I).

BASIC contains useful internal functions. These are functions that are built into the computer to perform special operations. Some of them are shown below. Examples of their use follow.

ABS(X)   This function finds the absolute value of X.
SQR(X)   This function finds the square root of X.
INT(X)   This function finds the greatest integer
          less than or equal to X.

Examples

1   **Write a program to read a number and print it and its absolute value.**

```
10   READ N
20   DATA 6, −3, 0, 4, 0.31, −9, 10000
30   IF N = 10000 THEN 60
40   PRINT N, ABS(N)
50   GO TO 10
60   END
```
The programmer does not need the absolute value of 10000. 10000 is a flag that signals the end of the data.

2   **Write a program to print the square and square root of the first 10 positive integers.**

```
 5   PRINT "N", "N SQUARED", "SQRT of N"
10   FOR N = 1 TO 10
20   PRINT N,N↑2, SQR(N)
30   NEXT N
40   END
```

Some examples of the greatest integer function are given as follows.

$$INT(5.72) = 5 \qquad INT(-8.9) = -9$$
$$INT(-13) = -13 \qquad INT(44.99) = 44$$

Suppose you wish to determine if 2 is a factor of 7. If $INT(7/2) = 7/2$, then $7/2$ must be an integer. Of course, you know that $7/2 = 3.5$ and $INT(7/2) = 3$. Therefore, 2 is *not* a factor of 7.

In general, if $INT(N/X) = N/X$, then X is a factor of N. Example 3 illustrates this principle.

Example

3 **Write a program to find all the factors of 48.**

```
10  FOR I = 1 TO 48
20  IF INT(48/I) = 48/I THEN 40
30  GO TO 50
40  PRINT I
50  NEXT I
60  END
```

Written Exercises

Write each of the following using scientific notation. Then write each in E notation.

1. 8,200,000

2. 0.00000005108

3. 27,372,800,000

Write the value of each expression in decimal notation.

4. 8.091E + 08

5. 2.2771E − 04

6. 1.461E + 11

Write the output of each of the following PRINT statements. Let A = −5.1, B = 9, C = 5.1, and D = 1.

7. PRINT ABS(A)

8. PRINT ABS(A * D)

9. PRINT SQR(B) − SQR(D)

10. PRINT INT(C)

11. PRINT INT(ABS(A))

12. PRINT ABS(INT(A))

Write a program to solve each of the following. Use BASIC functions.

13. Store 15 given numbers in a subscripted variable. Print the 3rd, 7th, and 14th numbers.

14. Store 20 given numbers in a subscripted variable. Print the numbers in reverse order.

15. Read a given number and test if it is negative. If it is, then print its absolute value.

16. Subtract two given numbers and print the absolute value of their difference.

17. Test each of the following to see if it is negative: 7, −3, 0, −9, 42, 36. If not, print the number and its square root.

18. Print the square roots of all integers from 93 to 121 inclusive.

19. Find the greatest integer less than or equal to each of these numbers: 3.7, 0, 6, 0.31, −2.56, −4.01.

20. Use the greatest integer function to determine if nine given numbers are even or odd.

21. Use the greatest integer function to round a given decimal to the nearest tenth.

22. Find all integers between 1 and 100 that are multiples of 6.

Symbols

$=$	is equal to	π	pi
$\neq$	is not equal to	$\{\ \}$	set
$>$	is greater than	$\%$	percent
$<$	is less than	$\circ$	degrees
$\geq$	is greater than or equal to	$a{:}b$	ratio of a to b
$\leq$	is less than or equal to	$f(x)$	f of x, the value of f at x
$\approx$	is approximately equal to	(a, b)	ordered pair a, b
$\cdot$	times	$\overline{AB}$	line segment AB
$-$	negative	AB	measure of $\overline{AB}$
$+$	positive	$\sqrt{}$	principal square root
$\pm$	positive or negative	$\cos A$	cosine of A
$-a$	opposite or additive inverse of a	$\sin A$	sine of A
$\|a\|$	absolute value of a	$\tan A$	tangent of A
$a \stackrel{?}{=} b$	Does a equal b?		

Metric System

mm	millimeter	h	hour
cm	centimeter	min	minute
m	meter	s	second
km	kilometer	km/h	kilometer per hour
g	gram	m/s	meters per second
kg	kilogram	°C	degrees Celsius
mL	milliliter		
L	liter		

SQUARES AND APPROXIMATE SQUARE ROOTS

n	n^2	$\sqrt{n}$	n	n^2	$\sqrt{n}$
1	1	1.000	51	2601	7.141
2	4	1.414	52	2704	7.211
3	9	1.732	53	2809	7.280
4	16	2.000	54	2916	7.348
5	25	2.236	55	3025	7.416
6	36	2.449	56	3136	7.483
7	49	2.646	57	3249	7.550
8	64	2.828	58	3364	7.616
9	81	3.000	59	3481	7.681
10	100	3.162	60	3600	7.746
11	121	3.317	61	3721	7.810
12	144	3.464	62	3844	7.874
13	169	3.606	63	3969	7.937
14	196	3.742	64	4096	8.000
15	225	3.873	65	4225	8.062
16	256	4.000	66	4356	8.124
17	289	4.123	67	4489	8.185
18	324	4.243	68	4624	8.246
19	361	4.359	69	4761	8.307
20	400	4.472	70	4900	8.367
21	441	4.583	71	5041	8.426
22	484	4.690	72	5184	8.485
23	529	4.796	73	5329	8.544
24	576	4.899	74	5476	8.602
25	625	5.000	75	5625	8.660
26	676	5.099	76	5776	8.718
27	729	5.196	77	5929	8.775
28	784	5.292	78	6084	8.832
29	841	5.385	79	6241	8.888
30	900	5.477	80	6400	8.944
31	961	5.568	81	6561	9.000
32	1024	5.657	82	6724	9.055
33	1089	5.745	83	6889	9.110
34	1156	5.831	84	7056	9.165
35	1225	5.916	85	7225	9.220
36	1296	6.000	86	7396	9.274
37	1369	6.083	87	7569	9.327
38	1444	6.164	88	7744	9.381
39	1521	6.245	89	7921	9.434
40	1600	6.325	90	8100	9.487
41	1681	6.403	91	8281	9.539
42	1764	6.481	92	8464	9.592
43	1849	6.557	93	8649	9.644
44	1936	6.633	94	8836	9.695
45	2025	6.708	95	9025	9.747
46	2116	6.782	96	9216	9.798
47	2209	6.856	97	9409	9.849
48	2304	6.928	98	9604	9.899
49	2401	7.000	99	9801	9.950
50	2500	7.071	100	10000	10.000

TRIGONOMETRIC RATIOS

Angle	sin	cos	tan	Angle	sin	cos	tan
0°	0.0000	1.0000	0.0000	45°	0.7071	0.7071	1.0000
1°	0.0175	0.9998	0.0175	46°	0.7193	0.6947	1.0355
2°	0.0349	0.9994	0.0349	47°	0.7314	0.6820	1.0724
3°	0.0523	0.9986	0.0524	48°	0.7431	0.6691	1.1106
4°	0.0698	0.9976	0.0699	49°	0.7547	0.6561	1.1504
5°	0.0872	0.9962	0.0875	50°	0.7660	0.6428	1.1918
6°	0.1045	0.9945	0.1051	51°	0.7771	0.6293	1.2349
7°	0.1219	0.9925	0.1228	52°	0.7880	0.6157	1.2799
8°	0.1392	0.9903	0.1405	53°	0.7986	0.6018	1.3270
9°	0.1564	0.9877	0.1584	54°	0.8090	0.5878	1.3764
10°	0.1736	0.9848	0.1763	55°	0.8192	0.5736	1.4281
11°	0.1908	0.9816	0.1944	56°	0.8290	0.5592	1.4826
12°	0.2079	0.9781	0.2126	57°	0.8387	0.5446	1.5399
13°	0.2250	0.9744	0.2309	58°	0.8480	0.5299	1.6003
14°	0.2419	0.9703	0.2493	59°	0.8572	0.5150	1.6643
15°	0.2588	0.9659	0.2679	60°	0.8660	0.5000	1.7321
16°	0.2756	0.9613	0.2867	61°	0.8746	0.4848	1.8040
17°	0.2924	0.9563	0.3057	62°	0.8829	0.4695	1.8807
18°	0.3090	0.9511	0.3249	63°	0.8910	0.4540	1.9626
19°	0.3256	0.9455	0.3443	64°	0.8988	0.4384	2.0503
20°	0.3420	0.9397	0.3640	65°	0.9063	0.4226	2.1445
21°	0.3584	0.9336	0.3839	66°	0.9135	0.4067	2.2460
22°	0.3746	0.9272	0.4040	67°	0.9205	0.3907	2.3559
23°	0.3907	0.9205	0.4245	68°	0.9272	0.3746	2.4751
24°	0.4067	0.9135	0.4452	69°	0.9336	0.3584	2.6051
25°	0.4226	0.9063	0.4663	70°	0.9397	0.3420	2.7475
26°	0.4384	0.8988	0.4877	71°	0.9455	0.3256	2.9042
27°	0.4540	0.8910	0.5095	72°	0.9511	0.3090	3.0777
28°	0.4695	0.8829	0.5317	73°	0.9563	0.2924	3.2709
29°	0.4848	0.8746	0.5543	74°	0.9613	0.2756	3.4874
30°	0.5000	0.8660	0.5774	75°	0.9659	0.2588	3.7321
31°	0.5150	0.8572	0.6009	76°	0.9703	0.2419	4.0108
32°	0.5299	0.8480	0.6249	77°	0.9744	0.2250	4.3315
33°	0.5446	0.8387	0.6494	78°	0.9781	0.2079	4.7046
34°	0.5592	0.8290	0.6745	79°	0.9816	0.1908	5.1446
35°	0.5736	0.8192	0.7002	80°	0.9848	0.1736	5.6713
36°	0.5878	0.8090	0.7265	81°	0.9877	0.1564	6.3138
37°	0.6018	0.7986	0.7536	82°	0.9903	0.1392	7.1154
38°	0.6157	0.7880	0.7813	83°	0.9925	0.1219	8.1443
39°	0.6293	0.7771	0.8098	84°	0.9945	0.1045	9.5144
40°	0.6428	0.7660	0.8391	85°	0.9962	0.0872	11.4301
41°	0.6561	0.7547	0.8693	86°	0.9976	0.0698	14.3007
42°	0.6691	0.7431	0.9004	87°	0.9986	0.0523	19.0811
43°	0.6820	0.7314	0.9325	88°	0.9994	0.0349	28.6363
44°	0.6947	0.7193	0.9657	89°	0.9998	0.0175	57.2900
45°	0.7071	0.7071	1.0000	90°	1.0000	0.0000	∞

Algebraic Skills Review

Integer Equations: Addition and Subtraction

Solve each equation.

1. $-5 + (-8) = x$
2. $-7 + 4 = y$
3. $-4 + 8 = t$
4. $9 + (-2) = a$
5. $6 + 6 = b$
6. $3 + (-8) = m$
7. $-7 + (-9) = v$
8. $-5 + 5 = z$
9. $-19 + 43 = c$
10. $51 + (-26) = w$
11. $-37 + (-48) = d$
12. $-93 + 44 = e$
13. $67 + (-82) = n$
14. $28 + 46 = f$
15. $29 + (-37) = s$
16. $-94 + (-58) = g$
17. $-18 + 63 = p$
18. $28 + (-52) = j$
19. $77 + 57 = r$
20. $47 + (-29) = x$
21. $-18 + 26 = a$
22. $-65 + (-75) = k$
23. $21 + (-47) = h$
24. $-15 + 52 = q$
25. $y = -13 + (-98)$
26. $u = -5 + 82$
27. $s = -47 + 26 + (-18)$
28. $a = -71 + (-85) + (-16)$
29. $41 + 57 + (-32) = m$
30. $82 + (-14) + (-35) = c$

31. $-4 - (-2) = t$
32. $5 - (-6) = p$
33. $-9 - 3 = x$
34. $5 - (-5) = k$
35. $-3 - (-8) = m$
36. $3 - 9 = w$
37. $-6 - 8 = w$
38. $0 - 6 = v$
39. $j = -10 - (-4)$
40. $-23 - 45 = a$
41. $28 - (-14) = z$
42. $-53 - (-61) = f$
43. $c = -16 - 47$
44. $90 - 43 = g$
45. $71 - (-47) = q$
46. $-99 - (-26) = s$
47. $38 - (-19) = t$
48. $-20 - (-92) = j$
49. $18 - 47 = y$
50. $h = -15 - (-81)$
51. $-42 - 63 = b$
52. $-84 - 47 = r$
53. $42 - (-47) = d$
54. $y = -19 - (-63)$
55. $16 - (-84) = n$
56. $42 - (-26) = k$
57. $-52 - (-33) = x$
58. $-35 - 86 = a$
59. $v = -8 - (-47)$
60. $33 - 51 = t$

61. $-2 + g = 7$
62. $9 + s = -5$
63. $-7 + k = -2$
64. $-4 + y = -9$
65. $m + 6 = 2$
66. $t + (-4) = 10$
67. $h - (-2) = 6$
68. $v - 7 = -4$
69. $a - (-6) = -5$
70. $r - (-3) = -8$
71. $j - (-8) = 5$
72. $x - 8 = -9$
73. $-2 - x = -8$
74. $14 = -48 + b$
75. $c + (-26) = 45$
76. $z - (-57) = -39$
77. $d + (-44) = -61$
78. $n - 38 = -19$
79. $-77 = w + 23$
80. $e - (-26) = 41$
81. $p - 47 = 22$
82. $-63 - f = -82$
83. $87 = t + (-14)$
84. $q + (-53) = 27$

Integer Equations: Multiplication and Division

Solve each equation.

1. $x = (-8)(-4)$
2. $(-3)5 = t$
3. $(-7)(-2) = a$
4. $(-9)8 = b$
5. $6(-5) = v$
6. $k = 8(6)$
7. $14(-26) = s$
8. $(-46)(-25) = g$
9. $(-71)(-20) = y$
10. $(-42)66 = h$
11. $(-97)47 = w$
12. $53(-32) = c$
13. $19(-46) = x$
14. $(-82)0 = e$
15. $72(43) = m$
16. $(-18)(-18) = d$
17. $24(-29) = u$
18. $f = (-39)45$
19. $(-76)(-34) = s$
20. $(-81)(-18) = q$
21. $(-65)28 = t$
22. $71(-38) = p$
23. $j = 49(-92)$
24. $36(24) = a$
25. $(-42)78 = z$
26. $(-54)(-77) = r$
27. $n = (-6)(-127)(-4)$
28. $(13)(-12)(95) = w$
29. $(-1)(45)(-45) = v$
30. $(-3)(61)(99) = y$

31. $72 \div (-8) = g$
32. $-64 \div 8 = b$
33. $-45 \div (-9) = y$
34. $56 \div (-7) = z$
35. $42 \div 6 = e$
36. $-24 \div (-6) = m$
37. $992 \div (-32) = a$
38. $-4428 \div 54 = k$
39. $x = -600 \div (-24)$
40. $1472 \div (-64) = p$
41. $-564 \div (-47) = h$
42. $-504 \div 14 = j$
43. $-2201 \div 71 = r$
44. $1512 \div (-28) = n$
45. $765 \div (-85) = q$
46. $-1591 \div (-37) = f$
47. $s = -1080 \div 36$
48. $3432 \div (-52) = v$
49. $2730 \div 78 = k$
50. $-3936 \div 96 = c$
51. $-1476 \div 41 = z$
52. $1496 \div (-22) = a$
53. $2646 \div (-63) = t$
54. $w = -4730 \div (-55)$
55. $-1092 \div (-26) = x$
56. $-2700 \div (-75) = e$
57. $1127 \div 49 = y$
58. $d = 1900 \div (-38)$
59. $-845 \div 13 = w$
60. $-1596 \div (-42) = a$

61. $-5p = 35$
62. $7g = -49$
63. $-3x = -24$
64. $a \div (-6) = -2$
65. $m \div (-8) = 8$
66. $q \div 9 = -3$
67. $41j = 1476$
68. $62y = -2356$
69. $b \div (-21) = 13$
70. $-33n = -1815$
71. $k \div 46 = -41$
72. $w \div 17 = 24$
73. $c \div (-59) = -7$
74. $-56h = 1792$
75. $-42z = 1512$
76. $j \div (-27) = 27$
77. $89s = -712$
78. $-18v = -1044$
79. $d \div (-34) = -43$
80. $f \div 14 = -63$
81. $45t = 810$
82. $-74w = 1554$
83. $-49e = -2058$
84. $r \div (-16) = -77$
85. $x \div (-26) = 47$
86. $-23 = t \div 44$
87. $-962 = -37g$
88. $-3040 = 95k$
89. $84 = x \div 97$
90. $-108 = m \div (-12)$

Fraction Equations: Addition and Subtraction

Solve each equation and express answers in simplest form.

1. $\frac{3}{11} + \frac{6}{11} = x$

2. $\frac{4}{7} + \frac{5}{7} = a$

3. $\frac{5}{9} - \frac{2}{9} = t$

4. $\frac{17}{18} - \frac{5}{18} = w$

5. $\frac{1}{3} + \frac{2}{9} = b$

6. $\frac{1}{2} - \frac{1}{3} = v$

7. $\frac{3}{4} - \frac{9}{16} = s$

8. $\frac{2}{3} + \frac{8}{15} = r$

9. $\frac{5}{6} - \frac{3}{4} = d$

10. $\frac{4}{9} + \frac{1}{6} = c$

11. $m = \frac{7}{9} + \frac{3}{8}$

12. $\frac{11}{12} - \frac{7}{10} = j$

13. $\frac{5}{6} - \frac{5}{12} = p$

14. $4\frac{2}{3} + 1\frac{8}{15} = k$

15. $5\frac{1}{2} - 2\frac{1}{3} = w$

16. $8\frac{1}{12} - 5\frac{5}{12} = e$

17. $7 - 1\frac{4}{9} = h$

18. $n = \frac{3}{16} + \frac{7}{12}$

19. $4\frac{1}{2} - 2\frac{2}{3} = q$

20. $7\frac{1}{12} - 4\frac{5}{8} = x$

21. $11\frac{5}{6} + 9\frac{7}{15} = f$

22. $y = 9\frac{2}{7} - 5\frac{5}{6}$

23. $\frac{1}{4} + \frac{5}{6} + \frac{7}{12} = c$

24. $\frac{5}{6} + \frac{2}{9} + \frac{3}{4} = z$

25. $-\frac{2}{13} + \left(-\frac{3}{13}\right) = t$

26. $-\frac{11}{18} + \frac{17}{18} = f$

27. $-\frac{9}{10} - \frac{7}{10} = n$

28. $-\frac{7}{11} - \left(-\frac{3}{11}\right) = a$

29. $\frac{1}{12} - \left(-\frac{7}{12}\right) = w$

30. $\frac{17}{21} + \left(-\frac{10}{21}\right) = g$

31. $\frac{1}{4} + \left(-\frac{2}{3}\right) = p$

32. $b = -\frac{1}{6} - \frac{8}{9}$

33. $\frac{1}{3} - \frac{5}{6} = m$

34. $-\frac{1}{2} + \left(-\frac{3}{5}\right) = a$

35. $\frac{3}{7} + \left(-5\right) = s$

36. $-\frac{5}{9} - 2 = k$

37. $t = 1\frac{1}{2} - \left(-\frac{3}{4}\right)$

38. $-\frac{3}{8} + \frac{4}{7} = c$

39. $\frac{3}{5} - \left(-3\frac{1}{4}\right) = v$

40. $-8\frac{7}{8} - \left(-4\frac{5}{12}\right) = r$

41. $-3\frac{1}{6} + 5\frac{1}{15} = d$

42. $-1\frac{8}{9} + \left(-5\frac{7}{12}\right) = h$

43. $7\frac{5}{6} + \left(-8\frac{7}{8}\right) = j$

44. $-3\frac{1}{2} - 4\frac{5}{9} = e$

45. $q = \frac{11}{16} - 12$

46. $-5\frac{11}{20} + 4\frac{7}{12} = z$

47. $-1\frac{1}{12} - \left(-\frac{2}{3}\right) = w$

48. $-4\frac{16}{21} + \left(-7\frac{5}{9}\right) = y$

49. $\frac{3}{13} + p = \frac{10}{13}$

50. $e + \frac{4}{15} = \frac{13}{15}$

51. $\frac{2}{5} + n = \frac{2}{3}$

52. $j - \frac{5}{18} = \frac{17}{18}$

53. $r - \frac{1}{4} = \frac{5}{16}$

54. $b - \frac{1}{2} = \frac{2}{5}$

55. $s + \frac{2}{7} = 2$

56. $\frac{7}{10} - a = \frac{1}{2}$

57. $1\frac{5}{6} + x = 2\frac{1}{4}$

58. $4\frac{1}{4} = w + 2\frac{1}{3}$

59. $d - 1\frac{5}{7} = 6\frac{1}{4}$

60. $h - \frac{3}{4} = 2\frac{5}{8}$

61. $t - \frac{2}{3} = 1\frac{5}{8}$

62. $g + \frac{5}{6} = \frac{4}{9}$

63. $q - \frac{7}{10} = -\frac{11}{15}$

64. $-\frac{3}{7} + c = \frac{1}{2}$

65. $-\frac{3}{4} = v + \left(-\frac{1}{8}\right)$

66. $f - \left(-\frac{1}{8}\right) = \frac{3}{10}$

67. $m - \left(-1\frac{3}{8}\right) = -2\frac{1}{2}$

68. $-6\frac{5}{6} + y = 7\frac{7}{15}$

69. $7\frac{1}{6} - z = -5\frac{2}{3}$

70. $-2\frac{1}{3} + w = -5\frac{5}{6}$

71. $-6\frac{1}{7} + k = -\frac{4}{21}$

72. $-4\frac{5}{12} = t - \left(-10\frac{1}{36}\right)$

Fraction Equations: Multiplication and Division

Solve each equation and express answers in simplest form.

1. $\frac{1}{7}\left(\frac{1}{3}\right) = x$

2. $\frac{2}{3}\left(\frac{1}{5}\right) = v$

3. $\frac{5}{6}\left(\frac{3}{10}\right) = y$

4. $2 \div \frac{1}{3} = j$

5. $\frac{5}{6} \div \frac{1}{6} = f$

6. $\frac{1}{4} \div \frac{5}{8} = c$

7. $\frac{2}{3}(9) = b$

8. $\frac{5}{18}\left(\frac{3}{10}\right) = r$

9. $\frac{8}{15} \div \frac{1}{10} = k$

10. $g = \frac{1}{2} \div 8$

11. $\frac{3}{14} \div \frac{2}{7} = y$

12. $\frac{7}{12}\left(\frac{4}{5}\right) = w$

13. $\frac{6}{13} \div \frac{5}{7} = z$

14. $\frac{24}{25}\left(\frac{15}{32}\right) = a$

15. $\frac{7}{10}\left(\frac{5}{28}\right) = w$

16. $2\frac{2}{3}\left(\frac{4}{5}\right) = n$

17. $t = \frac{7}{8}\left(4\frac{1}{4}\right)$

18. $1\frac{3}{4} \div \frac{7}{12} = e$

19. $1 \div 2\frac{3}{5} = d$

20. $2\frac{1}{10}\left(4\frac{2}{7}\right) = q$

21. $1\frac{3}{5} \div 11\frac{1}{5} = s$

22. $3\frac{1}{8}\left(2\frac{4}{5}\right)\left(\frac{5}{7}\right) = p$

23. $3\frac{2}{3}\left(\frac{1}{8}\right)\left(1\frac{1}{11}\right) = h$

24. $m = 3\frac{1}{21} \div 1\frac{21}{35}$

25. $\frac{1}{5}\left(-\frac{1}{8}\right) = p$

26. $-\frac{2}{9}\left(\frac{1}{3}\right) = w$

27. $-\frac{5}{8}\left(-\frac{4}{5}\right) = c$

28. $-3 \div \frac{1}{2} = y$

29. $-\frac{7}{9} \div \left(-\frac{1}{9}\right) = r$

30. $\frac{2}{3} \div \left(-\frac{4}{9}\right) = t$

31. $-\frac{2}{5}(-10) = m$

32. $\frac{2}{3} \div \left(-\frac{7}{9}\right) = h$

33. $-\frac{9}{15}\left(\frac{5}{9}\right) = s$

34. $-\frac{9}{14} \div \left(-\frac{3}{7}\right) = a$

35. $\frac{7}{16} \div \left(-\frac{7}{11}\right) = z$

36. $j = -\frac{4}{5}(30)$

37. $-7 \div 4 = q$

38. $-4\frac{9}{10}\left(-1\frac{5}{21}\right) = b$

39. $-5\frac{3}{5} \div 4\frac{1}{5} = g$

40. $-5\frac{3}{5} \div \left(-4\frac{1}{5}\right) = e$

41. $v = 6\frac{1}{4}\left(-1\frac{7}{15}\right)$

42. $3\frac{1}{3}\left(-4\frac{1}{2}\right) = w$

43. $-2\left(1\frac{5}{18}\right) = k$

44. $4\frac{2}{5} \div \left(-\frac{11}{15}\right) = p$

45. $-2\frac{5}{8} \div 7\frac{1}{2} = x$

46. $5 \div (-11) = n$

47. $d = -2\frac{3}{10}\left(-\frac{5}{12}\right)$

48. $-9\frac{1}{3}\left(-3\frac{3}{4}\right) = f$

49. $\frac{1}{3}a = 5$

50. $\frac{4}{7}k = 4$

51. $\frac{2}{5}x = \frac{4}{7}$

52. $w \div 5 = 3$

53. $w \div \frac{1}{4} = \frac{3}{8}$

54. $c \div \frac{3}{10} = \frac{1}{2}$

55. $\frac{7}{11}t = \frac{4}{5}$

56. $h \div \frac{1}{8} = \frac{4}{11}$

57. $z \div 6 = \frac{5}{12}$

58. $1\frac{1}{2}d = \frac{6}{7}$

59. $\frac{10}{33} = b \div 4\frac{2}{5}$

60. $2\frac{1}{6}j = 5\frac{1}{5}$

61. $s \div 2\frac{1}{6} = 2\frac{2}{5}$

62. $1\frac{3}{24}g = 3\frac{1}{8}$

63. $3 = 1\frac{7}{11}q$

64. $n \div \frac{2}{3} = -\frac{4}{9}$

65. $-1\frac{3}{4}p = -\frac{5}{8}$

66. $v \div \left(-\frac{7}{11}\right) = 1\frac{2}{7}$

67. $-1\frac{3}{5} = e \div \left(-3\frac{1}{5}\right)$

68. $-\frac{5}{9}r = 7\frac{1}{2}$

69. $3\frac{4}{7}x = -3\frac{3}{4}$

70. $a \div 3\frac{2}{7} = -8\frac{3}{4}$

71. $-2\frac{4}{7}m = -3\frac{3}{8}$

72. $f \div \left(-3\frac{1}{8}\right) = -3\frac{2}{5}$

Decimal Equations: Addition and Subtraction

Solve each equation.

1. $0.53 + 0.26 = x$

2. $14.756 + 0.185 = k$

3. $0.711 - 0.158 = z$

4. $12.01 - 0.83 = s$

5. $0.4 + 0.86 = n$

6. $1.4 - 0.12 = a$

7. $57.5 + 7.94 = m$

8. $10.04 - 0.18 = f$

9. $5 - 1.63 = r$

10. $5.92 + 7.3 = b$

11. $12 + 9.6 = y$

12. $28.05 - 9.95 = c$

13. $0.2 + 6.51 + 2.03 = y$

14. $4.4 + 30.6 + 11.2 = z$

15. $0.007 + 3 + 10.02 = h$

16. $w = 20.13 - 12.5$

17. $2.3 - 0.846 = t$

18. $11 - 1.1 = p$

19. $6.2 + 5.54 + 13.66 = g$

20. $a = 412 - 0.007$

21. $101.12 + 9.099 = s$

22. $66.4 - 5.288 = d$

23. $84.083 - 17 = m$

24. $q = 0.046 + 5.8 + 11.37$

25. $8 - 3.49 = n$

26. $8.77 + 0.3 + 52.9 = x$

27. $14.7 - 5.8364 = e$

28. $66.68421 - 18.465 = v$

29. $y = 0.0013 + 2.881$

30. $127.11 + 48 + 0.143 = u$

31. $-0.47 + 0.62 = h$

32. $-4.5 + (-12.8) = x$

33. $-1.7 + 0.24 = p$

34. $-6.831 - (-2.648) = c$

35. $-4.23 - 2.47 = b$

36. $2.64 - (-5.9) = k$

37. $10 + (-0.43) = r$

38. $6.7 - (-0.64) = v$

39. $-6.71 - (-8) = e$

40. $14.14 + (-1.4) = a$

41. $1.2 - 6.73 = j$

42. $-9.7 + (-0.86) = d$

43. $-7 - 4.63 = w$

44. $-0.17 - (-14.6) = g$

45. $m = 1.8 + (-14.14)$

46. $5.003 + (-0.47) = f$

47. $0.88 - 42 = s$

48. $-6.2 + (-27.47) = j$

49. $n = -1.4962 + 2.118$

50. $2.4 - (-1.736) = q$

51. $4.16 + (-5.909) = t$

52. $17 + (-0.45) = w$

53. $10 - 13.463 = a$

54. $f = -82.007 - 3.218$

55. $-11.264 + (-8.2) = z$

56. $-56 + 2.783 = s$

57. $-0.682 - (-0.81) = y$

58. $r = -23 + 4.093$

59. $2.08 - (-0.094) = t$

60. $-51.34 + (-5.1346) = x$

61. $2.2 + a = 11.4$

62. $h + 1.83 = 8.42$

63. $c + 5.4 = -11.33$

64. $m - 0.41 = 0.85$

65. $p - 1.1 = 14.9$

66. $r - 0.76 = -3.2$

67. $t + (-6.47) = -22.3$

68. $-6.11 + b = 14.321$

69. $k - (-4) = 7.9$

70. $k - 99.7 = -46.88$

71. $w + (-17.8) = -5.63$

72. $-5 = y - 22.7$

73. $13.475 + d = 4.09$

74. $-5 - q = 1.19$

75. $-3.214 + f = -16.04$

76. $-88.9 = s - 6.21$

77. $2 + e = 1.008$

78. $n + (-4.361) = 59.78$

79. $4.8 - j = -5.834$

80. $w - 0.73 = -1.8$

81. $-8 = g - (-4.821)$

82. $-2.315 + x = -15$

83. $m + (-1.4) = 0.07$

84. $v - 5.234 = -1.051$

85. $7.1 = v - (-0.62)$

86. $s + 6.4 = -0.11$

87. $t - (-46.1) = -3.673$

88. $k + (-1.604) = -0.45$

89. $81.6 + p = -6.73$

90. $-0.1448 - z = -2.6$

Decimal Equations: Multiplication and Division

Solve each equation.

1. $46(0.5) = e$

2. $108(0.9) = b$

3. $g = 6.47(39)$

4. $0.04(197) = f$

5. $r = 67(5.892)$

6. $2.8(4.27) = d$

7. $0.061(5.5) = m$

8. $0.62(0.13) = c$

9. $4.007(1.95) = q$

10. $6.25 \div 5 = w$

11. $t = 91.8 \div 27$

12. $7.31 \div 43 = h$

13. $5.91 \div 0.3 = a$

14. $167.5 \div 2.5 = k$

15. $4.7208 \div 0.84 = v$

16. $p = 278.1 \div 6.18$

17. $30,176 \div 9.43 = n$

18. $0.1001 \div 0.77 = j$

19. $2.11(0.059) = w$

20. $s = 0.4484 \div 1.18$

21. $0.0062(84.7) = x$

22. $0.03912 \div 1.63 = z$

23. $230.4 \div 0.072 = m$

24. $w = 59.8(100.23)$

25. $v = 432 \div 9.6$

26. $0.008(0.0045) = x$

27. $1.21(0.47)(9.3) = s$

28. $0.0418 \div 0.19 = x$

29. $0.032(13)(2.6) = t$

30. $0.0001926 \div 0.00321 = y$

31. $-5(0.2) = x$

32. $-1.7(-44) = f$

33. $72(1.01) = c$

34. $627(-0.14) = a$

35. $-2.3(7.81) = n$

36. $r = -1.02(-4.4)$

37. $57.6 \div (-12) = b$

38. $160.8 \div 24 = h$

39. $-16.38 \div (-0.7) = t$

40. $m = -15.54 \div 2.1$

41. $-0.405 \div (-0.27) = a$

42. $-598 \div 0.13 = p$

43. $0.45(-0.0016) = k$

44. $y = -0.002052 \div 0.054$

45. $6.7284 \div 1.08 = d$

46. $-0.0066(-91.8) = w$

47. $455 \div (-1.82) = q$

48. $-0.905(0.208) = g$

49. $-2.4827 \div (-6.71) = e$

50. $0.153 \div (-0.017) = z$

51. $j = -462.1(0.0094)$

52. $56.1(2.3) = y$

53. $0.07553 \div 0.0083 = v$

54. $-1.7(-0.121) = s$

55. $t = -0.6612 \div (-0.114)$

56. $-0.026(45.1) = x$

57. $59(-0.00042) = w$

58. $7.93(-5.036) = c$

59. $9.2397 \div 1.9 = t$

60. $-0.000101 \div 0.001 = m$

61. $7c = 4.2$

62. $37p = 81.4$

63. $57k = 0.1824$

64. $1.5m = 9.9$

65. $1.296 = 0.48d$

66. $0.0022b = 0.1958$

67. $t \div 110 = 2.8$

68. $x \div 71 = 0.33$

69. $r \div 0.85 = 10$

70. $h \div 1.98 = 6.7$

71. $a \div 0.002 = 0.109$

72. $n \div 40.6 = 0.021$

73. $100.8x = 9374.4$

74. $2.61 = f \div 9.5$

75. $1.7118 = 0.317e$

76. $0.0603g = 0.0043416$

77. $w \div 0.0412 = 60$

78. $q \div 1.07 = 0.088$

79. $5j = -32.15$

80. $-1.2v = 112.8$

81. $-0.013s = -0.00923$

82. $w \div (-2) = -2.48$

83. $z \div 2.8 = -6.2$

84. $a \div (-0.53) = -0.034$

85. $k \div (-0.013) = -0.7$

86. $-4.63t = -125.473$

87. $7.9y = 1583.16$

88. $6.05p = -1573$

89. $g \div 9.9 = 12$

90. $x \div (-0.063) = 0.015$

Forms of Real Numbers

Write each fraction in simplest form.

1. $\frac{13}{26}$
2. $\frac{9}{12}$
3. $-\frac{36}{42}$
4. $\frac{5}{60}$

5. $-\frac{24}{32}$
6. $-\frac{10}{35}$
7. $\frac{54}{63}$
8. $-\frac{45}{60}$

9. $\frac{48}{84}$
10. $-\frac{28}{42}$
11. $-\frac{72}{96}$
12. $\frac{75}{105}$

13. $-\frac{16}{100}$
14. $\frac{24}{60}$
15. $\frac{15}{27}$
16. $-\frac{99}{111}$

17. $\frac{126}{700}$
18. $-\frac{198}{462}$
19. $-\frac{84}{1080}$
20. $-\frac{525}{1155}$

Change each fraction to a decimal.

21. $\frac{1}{4}$
22. $-\frac{3}{10}$
23. $\frac{1}{50}$
24. $\frac{2}{3}$

25. $-\frac{1}{9}$
26. $-\frac{16}{25}$
27. $-\frac{9}{20}$
28. $\frac{1}{11}$

29. $\frac{5}{9}$
30. $-\frac{5}{8}$
31. $\frac{43}{100}$
32. $-\frac{5}{6}$

33. $-\frac{7}{11}$
34. $\frac{3}{7}$
35. $\frac{4}{5}$
36. $-\frac{7}{12}$

37. $-\frac{15}{16}$
38. $-\frac{8}{15}$
39. $\frac{1}{6}$
40. $-\frac{11}{32}$

41. $\frac{9}{11}$
42. $\frac{11}{16}$
43. $-\frac{11}{15}$
44. $\frac{124}{125}$

Change each mixed numeral to a decimal.

45. $-5\frac{1}{2}$
46. $14\frac{17}{100}$
47. $6\frac{3}{25}$
48. $-7\frac{1}{3}$

49. $4\frac{3}{25}$
50. $-20\frac{2}{9}$
51. $12\frac{3}{4}$
52. $-10\frac{5}{6}$

53. $-1\frac{4}{9}$
54. $-9\frac{16}{50}$
55. $-2\frac{2}{11}$
56. $13\frac{13}{40}$

57. $3\frac{5}{12}$
58. $-8\frac{5}{7}$
59. $2\frac{3}{5}$
60. $11\frac{1}{12}$

61. $-44\frac{3}{8}$
62. $19\frac{8}{15}$
63. $-67\frac{7}{10}$
64. $5\frac{3}{16}$

65. $78\frac{2}{9}$
66. $-108\frac{1}{20}$
67. $-51\frac{6}{7}$
68. $8\frac{1}{15}$

Change each decimal to a fraction in simplest form.

69. 0.3
70. 0.14
71. 0.013
72. -1.25

73. 4.2
74. -20.05
75. $0.\bar{3}$
76. -14.50

77. $-12.\bar{7}$
78. 6.125
79. -8.6
80. $-8.\bar{6}$

81. 23.15
82. -0.37
83. -33.85
84. 1.16

85. -2.27
86. 16.75
87. -5.375
88. 4.26

89. 7.1875
90. -9.45
91. $5.2\bar{6}$
92. -0.324

Percents

Write each decimal as a percent.

1. 0.71   **2.** 0.4   **3.** 0.835   **4.** 1.05

5. 0.009   **6.** 0.27   **7.** 2.5   **8.** 0.706

Write each fraction as a percent.

9. $\frac{31}{100}$ **10.** $\frac{1}{2}$ **11.** $\frac{4}{5}$ **12.** $\frac{3}{10}$

13. $\frac{1}{8}$ **14.** $\frac{5}{4}$ **15.** $\frac{2}{3}$ **16.** $\frac{4}{11}$

Write each percent as a decimal.

17. 14%   **18.** 10%   **19.** 450%   **20.** 6%

21. 27.5%   **22.** 4.2%   **23.** 190.5%   **24.** 0.3%

Write each percent as a fraction in simplest form.

25. 17%   **26.** 40%   **27.** 8%   **28.** 75%

29. 0.9%   **30.** 2.5%   **31.** 45.6%   **32.** 1.05%

Solve each of the following.

33. 10% of 70 is __.   **34.** 20% of 35 is __.   **35.** 4% of 250 is __.

36. 255% of 160 is __.   **37.** 115% of 24 is __.   **38.** 130% of 60 is __.

39. __ is 3.7% of 300.   **40.** __ is 22.5% of 260.   **41.** __ is 52.6% of 150.

42. 5 is __% of 20.   **43.** 3 is __% of 10.   **44.** 17 is __% of 68.

45. __% of 500 is 55.   **46.** __% of 96 is 12.   **47.** __% of 81 is 27.

48. 40% of __ is 12.   **49.** 10% of __ is 16.   **50.** 65% of __ is 26.

51. 25 is $33\frac{1}{3}$% of __.   **52.** 54 is 108% of __.   **53.** 1.28 is 16% of __.

54. 6.3% of 400 is __.   **55.** __% of 40 is 25.   **56.** 68% of __ is 85.

57. 44% of __ is 37.4.   **58.** 53% of 62 is __.   **59.** __% of 16 is 56.

60. __ is 235% of 270.   **61.** __ is 5.8% of 45.   **62.** 28 is __% of 21.

63. 2.5% of __ is 1.   **64.** __% of 20 is 26.2.   **65.** 420% of __ is 336.

66. __% of 45 is 30.   **67.** $87\frac{1}{2}$% of __ is 14.   **68.** $66\frac{2}{3}$% of 81 is __.

69. __ is 12.4% of 15.   **70.** 135 is 675% of __.   **71.** 45 is __% of 36.

72. 14.5% of 18 is __.   **73.** 180.5% of 200 is __.   **74.** 98.1 is __% of 90.

75. __% of 85 is 102.   **76.** 3% of __ is 18.   **77.** 44% of __ is 37.4.

78. __% of 170 is 153.   **79.** 738 is 72% of __.   **80.** $266\frac{2}{3}$% of 561 is __.

Evaluating Expressions

Evaluate each expression if $a = 3$, $b = 5$, $c = 12$, and $d = 9$.

1. $8 + c$
2. $d - 4$
3. $b \cdot d$
4. $c \div a$

5. $a + c + d$
6. $c - d$
7. $a \cdot b \cdot c$
8. $d - a$

9. $a \cdot c$
10. $\dfrac{d}{a}$
11. $\dfrac{13 + c}{b}$
12. $\dfrac{a + d}{4}$

Evaluate each expression if $e = 2$, $f = 5$, $g = 6$, and $h = 10$.

13. $8g$
14. fh
15. g^2
16. e^5

17. $7f^2$
18. $g^2 h^3$
19. $\dfrac{h^4}{f^2}$
20. $3e^2 g$

21. $8g^2 f^2$
22. $e^4 f^2 h^3$
23. $20e^3 f^3 g$
24. $\dfrac{3e^2 f^3}{g}$

Evaluate each expression if $x = 3$, $j = 4$, $k = 9$, and $m = 20$.

25. $k^2 - 4k + 6$
26. $(m + j) \div 3$
27. $x^3 j^2 - 4m$

28. $(xj + k) \div x$
29. $5j^2 \div m + k^2$
30. $j^3 + mk + 4x^4$

31. $(j^3 + m)k - 4x$
32. $(xj)^2 + km^2$
33. $k^3 + m \div j - 5j^2$

34. $(5 + j)^2 \div k + m^2$
35. $(m - k)^3 \div (2j + 3)$
36. $(x^4 + k)\, m^2 - kx$

Evaluate each expression if $n = -1$, $p = 6$, $q = -8$, $r = 15$, and $s = -24$.

37. $pr + 2q$
38. $pn^4 + s$
39. $r^2 - q + 5s$

40. $pq^2 \div ns$
41. $(p + 2q)n - r$
42. $(p + q)^5 n^5 + s$

43. $pr^2 + ns - 6q$
44. $p(r^2 + ns) - 6q$
45. $(q + r + s)p + n$

46. $\dfrac{4(p^2 + q^2)}{2q} - s$
47. $(p + n)^3 + \left(\dfrac{s}{p}\right)q$
48. $[(r + s)q]\, p$

The formula for the total surface area of a rectangular solid is $T = 2lw + 2wh + 2lh$ where T is the total surface area of the solid, l is its length, w is its width, and h is its height. Find the total surface area of each rectangular solid.

49. $l = 8$, $w = 5$, $h = 14$.
50. $l = 4$, $w = 2.5$, $h = 3$
51. $l = 7$, $w = 7$, $h = 16$

52. $l = 14$, $w = 17$, $h = 11$
53. $l = 21$, $w = 18$, $h = 6$
54. $l = 3.7$, $w = 1.2$, $h = 3.5$

The formula to change Fahrenheit degrees to Celsius degrees is $C = \frac{5}{9}(F - 32)$ where C is the temperature in Celsius degrees and F is the temperature in Fahrenheit degrees. Change each temperature in Fahrenheit degrees to Celsius degrees.

55. $86°$ F
56. $5°$ F
57. $-13°$ F
58. $41°$ F

59. $-40°$ F
60. $23°$ F
61. $-58°$ F
62. $374°$ F

Inequalities

Replace each ▨ with >, <, or = to make each sentence true.

1. 9 ▨ 12 **2.** 14 ▨ 7 **3.** −3 ▨ 0 **4.** −7 ▨ −3

5. −5 ▨ 3 **6.** 7 + 8 ▨ 15 **7.** −8 + 5 ▨ −6 **8.** −24 ÷ (−8) ▨ −3

9. −3 − (−9) ▨ −12 **10.** −9 ▨ −3 + (−4) **11.** −6 · 3 ▨ −18 **12.** 10 ▨ 36 ÷ 4

13. 8 ▨ −40 ÷ 5 **14.** 5 − (−4) ▨ 9 **15.** 27 ▨ 4 · 7 **16.** 4 − 7 ▨ 3

Solve each inequality.

17. $x + 4 < 10$ **18.** $a + 7 \geq 15$ **19.** $g + 5 > -8$

20. $c + 9 \leq 3$ **21.** $z - 4 > 20$ **22.** $h - (-7) > -2$

23. $m - 14 \leq -9$ **24.** $d - (-3) < 13$ **25.** $\frac{g}{-8} < 4$

26. $\frac{w}{3} > -12$ **27.** $\frac{p}{5} < 8$ **28.** $\frac{t}{-4} \geq -10$

29. $7b \geq -49$ **30.** $-5j < -60$ **31.** $-8f < 48$

32. $-2 + 9n \leq 10n$ **33.** $-5e + 9 > 24$ **34.** $3y - 4 > -37$

35. $7s - 12 < 13$ **36.** $-6v - 3 \geq -33$ **37.** $-2k + 12 < 30$

38. $-2x + 1 < 16 - x$ **39.** $15t - 4 > 11t - 16$ **40.** $13 - y \leq 29 + 2y$

41. $5q + 7 \leq 3(q + 1)$ **42.** $2(w + 4) \geq 7(w - 1)$ **43.** $-4t - 5 > 2t + 13$

44. $9m + 7 < 2(4m - 1)$ **45.** $3\left(a + \frac{2}{3}\right) \geq a - 1$ **46.** $3(3y + 1) < 13y - 8$

47. $2 + x < -5$ or $2 + x > 5$ **48.** $-4 + t > -5$ or $-4 + t < 7$

49. $3 \leq 2g + 7$ and $2g + 7 \leq 15$ **50.** $7 - 3s < 13$ and $7s < 3s + 12$

51. $2x + 1 < -3$ or $3x - 2 > 4$ **52.** $2v - 2 \leq 3v$ and $4v - 1 \geq 3v$

53. $3b - 4 \leq 7b + 12$ and $8b - 7 \leq 25$ **54.** $-9 < 2z + 7 < 10$

55. $5m - 8 \geq 10 - m$ or $5m + 11 < -9$ **56.** $12c - 4 \leq 5c + 10$ or $-4c - 1 \leq c + 24$

57. $2h - 2 \leq 3h \leq 4h - 1$ **58.** $3p + 6 < 8 - p$ and $5p + 8 \geq p + 6$

59. $4a + 3 < 3 - 5a$ or $a - 1 \geq -a$ **60.** $d - 4 < 5d + 14 < 3d + 26$

61. $2r + 8 > 16 - 2r$ and $7r + 21 < r - 9$ **62.** $-4j + 3 < j + 22$ and $j - 3 < 2j - 15$

63. $3n \neq 9$ and $6n - 5 \leq 2n + 7$ **64.** $7e \neq -21$ and $5e + 8 \geq e + 6$

65. $2(q - 4) \leq 3(q + 2)$ or $q - 8 \leq 4 - q$ **66.** $\frac{1}{2}w + 5 \geq w + 2 \geq \frac{1}{2}w + 9$

67. $|g + 6| > 8$ **68.** $|t - 5| \leq 3$ **69.** $|a + 5| \geq 0$ **70.** $|y - 9| < 19$

71. $|2m - 5| > 13$ **72.** $|14 - w| \geq 20$ **73.** $|3p + 5| \leq 23$ **74.** $|6b - 12| \leq 36$

75. $|25 - 3x| < 5$ **76.** $|7 + 8x| > 39$ **77.** $|4c + 5| \geq 25$ **78.** $|4 - 5s| > 46$

79. $|8 - 2h| \leq 25$ **80.** $|-8 - 10q| \geq 17$ **81.** $|7r - 5| < 3$ **82.** $|-3n - 12| < 15$

Polynomials: Addition and Subtraction

Find each sum.

1. $(3x - 4y) + (8x + 6y)$

2. $(12b + 2a) + (7b - 13a)$

3. $(7m - 8n) + (4m - 5n)$

4. $(5x^2 + 3x) + (4x^2 + 2x)$

5. $(-6s - 11t) + (5s - 6t)$

6. $(-14g - h) + (-8g + 5h)$

7. $(4p - 7q) + (5q - 8p)$

8. $(5y^2 - 7y) + (7y - 3y^2)$

9. $(9b^3 - 3b^2) + (12b^2 + 4b)$

10. $(2r + 8s) + (-3s - 9t)$

11. $(2a^2 + 4a + 5) + (2a^2 - 10a + 6)$

12. $(7x - 2y - 5z) + (x + 7y - 8z)$

13. $(-3m + 9mn - 5n) + (14m - 2n - 5mn)$

14. $(5x + 8y + 3z) + (-6z + 6y)$

15. $(6 - 4g - 9h) + (12g - 4h - 6j)$

16. $(x^2 - 4x + 8) + (12 + 7x - 4x^2)$

17. $(-7t^2 + 4ts - 6s^2) + (3s^2 - 12ts - 5t^2)$

18. $(7g + 8h - 9) + (-g - 3h - 6k)$

19. $(8a^2 - 4ab - 3b^2 + a - 4b) + (3a^2 + 6ab - 9b^2 + 7a + 9b)$

20. $(-3v + 14w - 12x - 13y + 6z - 8) + (16 - 6v + 2x - 5y - 2z)$

21. $(3y^2 - 7y + 6) + (3 - 2y^2 - 5y) + (y^2 - 8y - 12)$

22. $(4a^2 - 10b^2 + 7c^2) + (2c^2 - 5a^2 + 2b) + (7b^2 - 7c^2 + 7a)$

23. $(5x^2 + 3) + (4 - 7x - 9x^2) + (2x - 3x^2 - 5) + (2x - 6)$

24. $(9p - 13p^2) + (7p^2 + 5q^2) + (-6p - 12q) + (3q - 8q^2)$

Find each difference.

25. $(5g + 3h) - (2g + 7h)$

26. $(2e - 5f) - (7e - f)$

27. $(-3m + 8n) - (6m - 4n)$

28. $(6a^2 - 9a) - (4a^2 + 2a)$

29. $(-11k + 6) - (-6k - 8)$

30. $(9y^2 - 4y) - (-6y^2 - 8y)$

31. $(-r - 3s) - (2s - 5r)$

32. $(13c^2 - 4c) - (5c - 12c^2)$

33. $(g^3 - 2g^2) - (5g^2 - 7)$

34. $(7a + 4b) - (7b - 6c)$

35. $(z^2 + 6z - 8) - (4z^2 - 7z - 5)$

36. $(6v - 12w - 2x) - (2v + 8w - 10x)$

37. $(6a^2 - 7ab - 4b^2) - (6b^2 + 2a^2 + 5ab)$

38. $(3r - 7t) - (2t + 2s + 9r)$

39. $(7ax^2 + 2ax - 4a) - (5ax - 2ax^2 + 8a)$

40. $(h^3 + 4h^2 - 7h) - (3h^2 - 7h - 8)$

41. $(4d + 3e - 8f) - (-3d + 10e - 5f + 6)$

42. $(-3z^2 + 4x^2 - 8y^2) - (7x^2 - 14z^2 - 12)$

43. $(2b^2 + 7b - 2) - (2b^2 + 3b - 16)$

44. $(15j^4k^2 - 7j^2k + 8) - (8j^2k + 11)$

45. $(9x^2 - 11xy - 3y^2) - (12y^2 + x^2 - 16xy)$

46. $(17z^4 - 5z^2 + 3z) - (4z^4 + 2z^3 + 3z)$

47. $(-4p - 7q - 3t) - (-8t - 5q - 8p)$

48. $(-14h + 16j - 7k) - (-3j + 5h - 6k - 3)$

49. $(14a + 9b - 2x - 11y + 4z) - (8a + 8b + 6x - 5y - 7z)$

50. $(7m^2 - 3mn + 4n^2 - 2m - 8n) - (4m^2 + 3m - 4n^2 - 13n + 4mn)$

Polynomials: Multiplication and Division

Find each product.

1. $t^3 \cdot t^6$

2. $g^5 \cdot g^9$

3. $(3x^2y)(-5x^3y^8)$

4. $(7p^4q^7r^2)(4p^5r^7)$

5. $(2a^2b)(-b^2c^3)(-8ab^2c^4)$

6. $(e^4f^6g)^5$

7. $(-2m^6n^2)^6$

8. $(-3h^2k^3)^3(5hj^6k^8)^2$

9. $(v^4w)^6(-1v^3w^2)^8$

10. $5y(y^2 - 3y + 6)$

11. $-ab(3b^2 + 4ab - 6a^2)$

12. $4st^2(-4s^2t^3 + 7s^5 - 3st^3)$

13. $(d + 2)(d + 3)$

14. $(z + 7)(z - 4)$

15. $(m - 5)(m - 8)$

16. $(2x - 5)(x + 6)$

17. $(7a - 4)(2a - 5)$

18. $(t + 7)^2$

19. $(q - 4h)^2$

20. $(w - 12)(w + 12)$

21. $(2b + 4d)(2b - 4d)$

22. $(4x + y)(2x - 3y)$

23. $(7v + 3)(v + 4)$

24. $(4e + 3)(4e + 3)$

25. $(7s - 8)(3s - 2)$

26. $(5b - 6)(5b + 6)$

27. $(4g + 3h)(2g - 5h)$

28. $(5c - 2d)^2$

29. $(10x + 11y)(10x - 11y)$

30. $(12r - 4s)(5r + 8s)$

Divide.

31. $\dfrac{24x^5}{8x^2}$

32. $\dfrac{s^7t^4}{s^5}$

33. $\dfrac{-9h^2k^4}{18h^5j^3k^4}$

34. $\dfrac{3m^7n^2p^4}{9m^2np^3}$

35. $\dfrac{9a^2b^7c^3}{12a^5b^4c}$

36. $\dfrac{-15xy^5z^7}{-10x^4y^6z^4}$

37. $\dfrac{-5w^4v^2 - 3w^3v}{w^3}$

38. $\dfrac{8g^4h^4 + 4g^3h^3}{2gh^2}$

39. $\dfrac{x^2 - 2x - 15}{x - 3}$

40. $\dfrac{q^2 - 10q + 24}{q - 4}$

41. $\dfrac{2j^2 + 10j + 12}{j + 3}$

42. $\dfrac{12d^2 + d - 6}{3d - 2}$

43. $\dfrac{4s^3 + 4s^2 - 9s - 18}{2s + 3}$

44. $\dfrac{z^3 - 27}{z - 3}$

45. $\dfrac{6n^3 + 7n^2 - 29n + 12}{3n - 4}$

46. $\dfrac{3e^2 + 3e - 80}{e - 5}$

47. $\dfrac{-6k^2 + 3k + 12}{2k + 3}$

48. $\dfrac{t^3 + 3t}{t - 1}$

49. $\dfrac{4g^3 - 4g - 20}{2g - 4}$

50. $\dfrac{9a^3 - 3a^2 + 7a + 2}{3a + 1}$

51. $\dfrac{8c^3 - 2c^2 + 2c - 4}{2c - 2}$

52. $\dfrac{8y^3 - 1}{2y + 1}$

53. $\dfrac{12m^3 + m^2 - 20}{4m - 5}$

54. $\dfrac{5b^3 - 2b^2 + 7b + 4}{5b + 3}$

Factoring

Find the prime factorization of each integer. Write each negative integer as the product of -1 and its prime factors.

1. 35
2. 12
3. 72
4. 64
5. -75
6. 70
7. 85
8. -92
9. -117
10. -114
11. 243
12. -360
13. 405
14. 605
15. -5292
16. 5076

Factor.

17. $10g + 35h$
18. $t^3s^2 - t^2$
19. $15a^2b - 24a^5b^2$
20. $18c^4d - 30c^3e$
21. $36m^4n^2p + 12m^5n^3p^2$
22. $6g^5h^3 - 12g^4h^6k - 18g^6h^5$
23. $p^2 - q^2$
24. $144x^2 - 49y^2$
25. $75r^2 - 48$
26. $64v^2 - 100w^4$
27. $g^2 + 4g + 4$
28. $t^2 - 22t + 121$
29. $9n^2 - 36nm + 36m^2$
30. $2a^2b^2 + 4ab^2c^2 + 2b^2c^4$
31. $g^2 - 14g + 48$
32. $z^2 + 15z + 36$
33. $12 - 13b + b^2$
34. $x^2 + 17xy + 16y^2$
35. $g^2 - 4g - 32$
36. $h^2 + 12h - 28$
37. $s^2 - 13st - 30t^2$
38. $3a^2 + 11a + 10$
39. $6y^2 + 2y - 20$
40. $12j^2 - 34j - 20$
41. $24a^2 - 57ax + 18x^2$
42. $2sx - 4tx + 2sy - 4ty$
43. $8ac - 2ad + 4bc - bd$
44. $2e^2g + 2fg + 4e^2h + 4fh$
45. $5x^3 - 2x^2y - 5xy^2 + 2y^3$
46. $4p^2 + 12pr + 9r^2$
47. $169 - 16t^2$
48. $b^2 - 11b - 42$
49. $30g^2h - 15g^3$
50. $3b^2 - 13bd + 4d^2$
51. $a^2x - 2a^2y - 5x + 10y$
52. $s^2 + 30s + 225$
53. $18v^2 + 42v + 12$
54. $4k^2 + 2k - 12$
55. $5z^3 - 8z^2 - 21z$
56. $5g^2 - 20h^2$
57. $30x^2 - 125x + 70$
58. $a^2b^2 - b^2 + a^2 - 1$
59. $8t^4 + 56t^3 + 98t^2$
60. $3p^3q^2 + 27pq^2$
61. $a^2c^2 + b^2c^2 - 4a^2d^2 - 4b^2d^2$
62. $36m^3n - 90m^2n^2 + 36mn^2$
63. $4x^2z^2 + 7xyz^2 - 36y^2z^2$
64. $4g^2j^2 - 25h^2j^2 - 4g^2 + 25h^2$

Algebraic Fractions

Simplify.

1. $\dfrac{48a^2b^5c}{32a^7b^2c^3}$

2. $\dfrac{-28x^3y^4z^5}{42xyz^2}$

3. $\dfrac{k+3}{4k^2+7k-15}$

4. $\dfrac{t^2-s^2}{5t^2-2st-3s^2}$

5. $\dfrac{6g^2-19g+15}{12g^2-6g-18}$

6. $\dfrac{2d^2+4d-6}{d^4-10d^2+9}$

Find each product or quotient in simplest form.

7. $\dfrac{5m^2n}{12a^2}\cdot\dfrac{18an}{30m^4}$

8. $\dfrac{25g^7h}{28t^3}\cdot\dfrac{42s^2t^3}{5g^5h^2}$

9. $\dfrac{6a+4b}{36}\cdot\dfrac{45}{3a+2b}$

10. $\dfrac{x^2y}{18z}\div\dfrac{2yz}{3x^2}$

11. $\dfrac{p^2}{14qr^3}\div\dfrac{2r^2p}{7q}$

12. $\dfrac{3d}{2d^2-3d}\div\dfrac{9}{2d-3}$

13. $\dfrac{t^2-2t-15}{t-5}\cdot\dfrac{t+5}{t+3}$

14. $\dfrac{5e-f}{5e+f}\div(25e^2-f^2)$

15. $\dfrac{8}{6c^2+17c+10}\div\dfrac{6}{c+2}$

16. $\dfrac{3v^2-27}{15v}\cdot\dfrac{v^2}{v+3}$

17. $\dfrac{3k^2-10k+3}{5}\div\dfrac{3k-1}{15k}$

18. $\dfrac{3g^2+15g}{4}\cdot\dfrac{g^2}{g+5}$

19. $\dfrac{x^2-2x-15}{2x^2-7x-15}\cdot\dfrac{4x^2-4x-15}{2x^2+x-15}$

20. $\dfrac{a^2-16}{3a^2-13a+4}\div\dfrac{3a^2+11a-4}{a^3}$

Find each sum or difference in simplest form.

21. $\dfrac{j+4}{3}+\dfrac{j-7}{3}$

22. $\dfrac{15n}{5n+3}+\dfrac{9}{5n+3}$

23. $\dfrac{2a-3}{b}-\dfrac{a-5}{b}$

24. $\dfrac{25}{5-g}-\dfrac{g^2}{5-g}$

25. $\dfrac{s}{t^2}-\dfrac{r}{3t}$

26. $\dfrac{7}{ab}+\dfrac{4}{bc}$

27. $\dfrac{2}{2p+3}+\dfrac{p}{3p+2}$

28. $\dfrac{x}{x+y}-\dfrac{5}{y}$

29. $\dfrac{c}{c^2-4c}-\dfrac{5c}{c-4}$

30. $\dfrac{t+10}{t^2-100}+\dfrac{1}{t-10}$

31. $\dfrac{1}{g^2-6gh+9h^2}-\dfrac{3}{g-3h}$

32. $\dfrac{x}{x+2}+\dfrac{x^2+3x}{x^2+5x+6}$

33. $\dfrac{3d}{d^2-3d-10}+\dfrac{d+1}{d^2-8d+15}$

34. $\dfrac{k+2}{k^2-8k+16}-\dfrac{k+3}{k^2+k-20}$

Solving Equations

Solve each equation.

1. $2x - 5 = 3$
2. $4t + 5 = 37$
3. $7a + 6 = -36$
4. $47 = -8g + 7$
5. $-3c - 9 = -24$
6. $5k - 7 = -52$
7. $5s + 4s = -72$
8. $6(y - 5) = 18$
9. $-21 = 7(p - 10)$
10. $2m + 5 - 6m = 25$
11. $3z - 1 = 23 - 3z$
12. $5b + 12 = 3b - 6$
13. $\frac{e}{5} + 6 = -2$
14. $\frac{d}{4} - 8 = -5$
15. $\frac{p + 10}{3} = 4$
16. $\frac{h - 7}{6} = 1$
17. $\frac{5f + 1}{8} = -3$
18. $\frac{4n - 8}{-2} = 12$
19. $\frac{2a}{7} + 9 = 3$
20. $\frac{-3t - 4}{2} = 8$
21. $\frac{6v - 9}{3} = v$

22. $|s - 4| = 7$
23. $|5g + 8| = 33$
24. $|16 - 3b| = 22$

25. $t(t - 4) = 0$
26. $4p(p + 7) = 0$
27. $7m(2m - 12) = 0$
28. $(x - 5)(x + 8) = 0$
29. $(3s + 6)(2s - 7) = 0$
30. $(4g + 5)(2g + 10) = 0$
31. $h^2 + 4h = 0$
32. $3b^2 - 3b = 0$
33. $m^2 - 16 = 0$
34. $w^2 + w - 30 = 0$
35. $2c^2 - 14c + 24 = 0$
36. $6p^2 + 10p - 24 = 0$
37. $5n^2 = 15n$
38. $4x^2 + 20x + 25 = 0$
39. $3y^2 = 75$

40. $\frac{a}{3} - \frac{a}{4} = 3$
41. $\frac{k}{6} + \frac{2k}{3} = -\frac{5}{2}$
42. $\frac{r + 3}{r} + \frac{r - 12}{r} = 5$

43. $\frac{2y}{y - 4} - \frac{3}{5} = 3$
44. $\frac{2t}{t + 3} + \frac{3}{t} = 2$
45. $\frac{2g}{2g + 1} - \frac{1}{2g - 1} = 1$

46. $\frac{8n^2}{2n^2 - 5n - 3} = 4$
47. $5 - \frac{5x}{x - 4} = \frac{2}{x^2 - 4x}$
48. $\frac{2}{e + 1} - \frac{3}{e + 2} = 0$

49. $\frac{1}{2d - 1} - \frac{12d}{6d^2 + d - 2} = \frac{-4}{3d + 2}$
50. $\frac{4z}{2z + 1} - \frac{6 - z}{2z^2 - 5z - 3} = 2$

51. $\frac{b + 1}{b - 2} - \frac{3b}{3b + 2} = \frac{20}{3b^2 - 4b - 4}$
52. $\frac{2s}{9s^2 - 3s - 2} + \frac{2}{3s + 1} = \frac{4}{3s - 2}$

53. $\frac{m}{20} = \frac{9}{15}$
54. $\frac{12}{21} = \frac{20}{f}$

55. $\frac{4}{9} = \frac{16}{t + 8}$
56. $\frac{4}{14} = \frac{2h - 1}{21}$

57. $\frac{2 + c}{c - 5} = \frac{8}{9}$
58. $\frac{2y + 4}{y - 3} = \frac{2}{3}$

Radicals

Simplify.

1. $\sqrt{25}$

2. $-\sqrt{64}$

3. $\pm\sqrt{576}$

4. $\sqrt{900}$

5. $\pm\sqrt{0.01}$

6. $\sqrt{1.44}$

7. $-\sqrt{0.0016}$

8. $\sqrt{4.84}$

9. $\sqrt{\dfrac{36}{121}}$

10. $-\sqrt{\dfrac{16}{36}}$

11. $\sqrt{\dfrac{81}{49}}$

12. $\pm\sqrt{\dfrac{64}{100}}$

13. $\sqrt{75}$

14. $\sqrt{20}$

15. $\sqrt{162}$

16. $\sqrt{700}$

17. $\sqrt{4x^4y^3}$

18. $\sqrt{12ts^3}$

19. $\sqrt{175m^4n^6}$

20. $\sqrt{99a^3b^7}$

21. $\sqrt{\dfrac{54}{g^2}}$

22. $\sqrt{\dfrac{32c^5}{9d^2}}$

23. $\sqrt{\dfrac{27p^4}{3p^2}}$

24. $\sqrt{\dfrac{243y^7}{3y^4}}$

25. $\sqrt{7}\,\sqrt{3}$

26. $\sqrt{3}\,\sqrt{15}$

27. $6\sqrt{2}\,\sqrt{3}$

28. $5\sqrt{6}\cdot 2\sqrt{3}$

29. $\sqrt{5}(\sqrt{3}+\sqrt{10})$

30. $\sqrt{2}(\sqrt{6}+\sqrt{32})$

31. $\sqrt{5}\,\sqrt{t}$

32. $\sqrt{18}\,\sqrt{g^3}$

33. $\sqrt{12k}\,\sqrt{3k^5}$

34. $\sqrt{15m^2}\,\sqrt{6n^3}$

35. $\dfrac{\sqrt{3}}{\sqrt{5}}$

36. $\sqrt{\dfrac{2}{7}}$

37. $\dfrac{3\sqrt{6}}{\sqrt{2}}$

38. $\sqrt{\dfrac{x}{8}}$

39. $\sqrt{\dfrac{t^2}{3}}$

40. $\sqrt{\dfrac{20}{a}}$

41. $(5+\sqrt{3})(5-\sqrt{3})$

42. $(\sqrt{17}+\sqrt{11})(\sqrt{17}-\sqrt{11})$

43. $(2\sqrt{5}+\sqrt{7})(2\sqrt{5}-\sqrt{7})$

44. $\dfrac{1}{3+\sqrt{5}}$

45. $\dfrac{2}{\sqrt{3}-5}$

46. $\dfrac{12}{\sqrt{8}-\sqrt{6}}$

47. $\dfrac{10}{\sqrt{13}+\sqrt{7}}$

48. $\dfrac{14}{3\sqrt{2}+\sqrt{5}}$

49. $\dfrac{\sqrt{3}}{\sqrt{3}-5}$

50. $\dfrac{\sqrt{6}}{7-2\sqrt{3}}$

51. $\dfrac{5\sqrt{10}}{3\sqrt{3}+2\sqrt{5}}$

52. $6\sqrt{13}+7\sqrt{13}$

53. $9\sqrt{15}-4\sqrt{15}$

54. $2\sqrt{11}-8\sqrt{11}$

55. $2\sqrt{12}+5\sqrt{3}$

56. $2\sqrt{27}-4\sqrt{12}$

57. $4\sqrt{8}-3\sqrt{5}$

58. $8\sqrt{32}+4\sqrt{50}$

59. $6\sqrt{20}+\sqrt{45}$

60. $2\sqrt{63}+8\sqrt{45}-6\sqrt{28}$

61. $10\sqrt{\dfrac{1}{5}}-\sqrt{45}-12\sqrt{\dfrac{5}{9}}$

62. $3\sqrt{\dfrac{1}{3}}-9\sqrt{\dfrac{1}{12}}+\sqrt{243}$

Solve and check.

63. $\sqrt{t}=10$

64. $\sqrt{3g}=6$

65. $\sqrt{y}-2=0$

66. $5+\sqrt{a}=9$

67. $\sqrt{2k}-4=8$

68. $\sqrt{5y+4}=7$

69. $\sqrt{10x^2-5}=3x$

70. $\sqrt{2a^2-144}=a$

71. $\sqrt{b^2+16}+2b=5b$

72. $\sqrt{m+2}+m=4$

73. $\sqrt{3-2c}+3=2c$

Use the quadratic formula to solve each equation.

74. $s^2+8s+7=0$

75. $d^2-14d+24=0$

76. $3h^2=27$

77. $n^2-3n+1=0$

78. $2z^2+5z-1=0$

79. $3w^2-8w+2=0$

80. $3f^2+2f=6$

81. $2r^2-r-3=0$

82. $x^2-9x=5$

Equations in Two Variables

Write an equation in slope-intercept form for each given slope and *y*-intercept.

1. $m = 2, b = 5$
2. $m = -4, b = 1$
3. $m = \frac{1}{2}, b = -3$
4. $m = -1, b = -6$

5. $m = \frac{3}{2}, b = 1$
6. $m = 5, b = \frac{1}{4}$
7. $m = \frac{2}{5}, b = -4$
8. $m = -\frac{3}{4}, b = \frac{1}{2}$

Write each equation in slope-intercept form.

9. $-3x + y = 2$
10. $6x + y = -5$
11. $2x - y = -3$
12. $-x - y = 4$

13. $2x + 5y = 10$
14. $x - 4y = -2$
15. $-9x + 3y = -18$
16. $4x + 7y = 3$

Write each equation in standard form.

17. $y = 3x + 6$
18. $y = -4x + 1$
19. $y = \frac{2}{3}x - 7$
20. $y = \frac{1}{4}x + \frac{1}{2}$

21. $y = -\frac{5}{3}x - \frac{1}{3}$
22. $y = 2x - \frac{1}{2}$
23. $\frac{5}{6}y = \frac{1}{4}x + \frac{2}{3}$
24. $\frac{1}{5}x = \frac{7}{10}y - \frac{3}{4}$

Write the equation of the line with each *x*-intercept and *y*-intercept. Use slope-intercept form.

25. *x*-intercept $= 2$; *y*-intercept $= -1$
26. *x*-intercept $= -3$; *y*-intercept $= -2$

27. *x*-intercept $= 1$; *y*-intercept $= 5$
28. *x*-intercept $= -\frac{1}{2}$; *y*-intercept $= 3$

Write the equation of the line that passes through each pair of points. Use slope-intercept form.

29. $(1, 3), (2, 7)$
30. $(4, 8), (2, 4)$
31. $(-2, 3), (3, 1)$
32. $(0, 0), (-2, -3)$

33. $(5, 1), (3, -2)$
34. $(2, -1), (5, -4)$
35. $(8, 6), (10, 3)$
36. $(-4, -1), (-1, -7)$

Solve each system of equations.

37. $y = 3x$
    $4x + 2y = 30$

38. $a = -2b$
    $3a + 5b = 21$

39. $n = m + 4$
    $3m + 2n = 19$

40. $h = k - 7$
    $2h - 5k = -2$

41. $s + 2t = 6$
    $3s - 2t = 2$

42. $c + 2d = 10$
    $-c + d = 2$

43. $3v + 5w = -16$
    $3v - 2w = -2$

44. $e - 5f = 12$
    $3e - 5f = 6$

45. $-3p + 2q = 10$
    $-2p - q = -5$

46. $2a + 5b = 13$
    $4a - 3b = -13$

47. $5s + 3t = 4$
    $-4s + 5t = -18$

48. $2g - 7h = 9$
    $-3g + 4h = 6$

49. $2c - 6d = -16$
    $5c + 7d = -18$

50. $6m - 3n = -9$
    $-8m + 2n = 4$

51. $3x - 5y = 8$
    $4x - 7y = 10$

52. $9a - 3b = 5$
    $a + b = 1$

Find the equation of the axis of symmetry and the maximum or minimum point for the graph of each quadratic function.

53. $y = -x^2 + 2x - 3$
54. $y = x^2 - 4x - 4$
55. $y = 3x^2 + 6x + 3$

56. $y = 2x^2 + 12x$
57. $y = x^2 - 6x + 5$
58. $y = 4x^2 - 1$

59. $y = -2x^2 - 2x + 4$
60. $y = \frac{1}{2}x^2 + 4x + \frac{1}{4}$
61. $y = 6x^2 - 12x - 4$

Glossary

abscissa (271) The first component of an ordered pair; the x-coordinate.

absolute value (44) The absolute value of a number is the number of units that it is from zero on the number line.

addend (44) In an addition expression of the form $a + b = c$, the addends are a and b.

additive identity (12) The number 0 is the additive identity since the sum of any number and 0 is equal to the number.

additive inverse (53) Two numbers are additive inverses if their sum is zero. The additive inverse, or opposite, of a is $-a$.

algebraic fractions (437) Fractions that contain variables are algebraic fractions.

area of a polygon (195) The measurement of the region bounded by the polygon.

associative property for addition (18) For any numbers a, b, and c,
$$(a + b) + c = a + (b + c).$$

associative property for multiplication (18) For any numbers a, b, and c,
$$(ab)c = a(bc).$$

axis of symmetry (405) A straight line with respect to which a figure is symmetric.

base (3) In an expression of the form x^n, the base is x.

binomial (175) A polynomial with exactly two terms.

boundary (291) A line that separates a graph into half-planes.

coefficient (16) *See* numerical coefficient.

combined variation (492) A combined variation is described by an equation of the form $zy = kx$, where k is not 0.

commutative property for addition (18) For any numbers a and b,
$$a + b = b + a.$$

commutative property for multiplication (18) For any numbers a and b, $ab = ba$.

comparison property (111) For any two numbers a and b, exactly one of the following sentences is true.
$$a < b \qquad a = b \qquad a > b$$

complementary angles (499) Two angles are complementary if the sum of their measures is 90°.

completeness property for points in the plane (272) When plotting points, the following is true.
1. Exactly one point in the plane is located by a given ordered pair of numbers.
2. Exactly one ordered pair of numbers locates a given point in the plane.

complex fraction (459) If a fraction has one or more fractions in the numerator or denominator, it is called a complex fraction.

composite number (211) Any positive integer, except 1, that is not prime.

compound sentence (128) Two sentences connected by *and* or *or*.

conjugates (383) Two binomials of the form $a\sqrt{b} + c\sqrt{d}$ and $a\sqrt{b} - c\sqrt{d}$.

consecutive even integers (93) Numbers given when beginning with an even integer and counting by two's.

consecutive integers (93) Integers in counting order.

consecutive odd integers (93) Numbers given when beginning with an odd integer and counting by two's.

consistent (319) A system of equations is consistent and independent if it has one ordered pair as its solution. A system of equations is consistent and dependent if it has infinitely many ordered pairs as its solution.

constant (145) A monomial that does not contain variables.

coordinate (39) The coordinate of a point is the number that corresponds to it on the number line.

coordinate plane (271) The number plane formed by two perpendicular number lines that intersect at their zero points.

cosine (508) In a right triangle, the cosine of angle $A =$

$$\frac{\text{measure of side adjacent to angle } A}{\text{measure of hypotenuse}}$$

degree (175) The degree of a monomial is the sum of the exponents of its variables. The degree of a nonzero constant is 0. The degree of a polynomial is the greatest of the degrees of its terms.

direct variation (478) A direct variation is described by an equation of the form $y = kx$, where k is not zero.

discriminant (420) In the quadratic formula, the expression $b^2 - 4ac$ is called the discriminant.

distance formula (394) The distance between any two points (x_1, y_1) and (x_2, y_2) is given by the formula
$$d = \sqrt{(x_2 - x_1)^2 + (y_2 - y_1)^2}.$$

distributive property (15) For any numbers a, b, and c:
1. $a(b + c) = ab + ac$ and $(b + c)a = ba + ca$.
2. $a(b - c) = ab - ac$ and $(b - c)a = ba - ca$.

dividend (3) In the division expression $a \div b = c$, the dividend is a.

divisor (3) In the division expression $a \div b = c$, the divisor is b.

domain (274) The domain of a relation is the set of all first components from each ordered pair.

element (11) One of the members of a set.

elimination method (345) A method for solving systems of equations in which the equations are added or subtracted to eliminate one of the variables. Multiplication of one or both equations may occur before the equations are added or subtracted.

empty set (11) A set with no elements.

equals sign (9) The equals sign between two expressions indicates that if the sentence is true, the expressions name the same number.

equation (9) A mathematical sentence that contains the equals sign.

equivalent equations (57) Equations that have the same solution.

evaluate (6) To find the value of an expression when the values of the variables are known.

exponent (4) A number used to tell how many times a number is used as a factor. In an expression of the form x^n, the exponent is n.

expression (3) An expression consists of one or more numbers and variables with the operations of addition, subtraction, multiplication, and division.

extremes (97) *See* proportion.

factor (3) In a multiplication expression, the numbers multiplied are called factors.

FOIL method for multiplying binomials (185) To multiply two binomials, find the sum of the products of
    F the first terms,
    O the outer terms,
    I the inner terms, and
    L the last terms.

formula (22) An equation that states a rule for the relationship between certain quantities.

function (286) A function is a relation in which each element of the domain is paired with exactly one element of the range.

greatest common factor (GCF) (212) The GCF of two or more integers is the greatest factor that is common to each of the integers.

grouping symbols (7) Symbols used to clarify or change the order of operations in an expression. Parentheses, brackets, and the fraction bar are grouping symbols.

half-plane (291) The region of a graph on one side of a boundary.

hypotenuse (391) The side opposite the right angle in a right triangle.

identity (88) An equation that is true for every value of the variable.

inconsistent (319) A system of equations is inconsistent if it has no solution.

inequality (111) Any sentence containing $<, >, \neq, \leq,$ or $\geq$.

integers (Z) (39) The set of numbers $\{\ldots, -3, -2, -1, 0, 1, 2, 3, \ldots\}$.

intersection (118) The intersection of two sets consists of all the points that belong to both of the sets.

inverse operations (80) Operations that undo each other, such as addition and subtraction.

inverse variation (481) An inverse variation is described by an equation of the form $xy = k$, where k is not zero.

irrational numbers (I) (374) Numbers that cannot be expressed in the form $\frac{a}{b}$, where a and b are integers, $b \neq 0$.

isosceles triangle (500) A triangle that has two congruent sides.

joint variation (491) A joint variation is described by an equation of the form $z = kxy$, where k is not zero.

least common denominator (LCD) (454) The least common multiple of the denominators of two or more fractions.

least common multiple (LCM) (454) The LCM of two or more integers is the least positive integer that is divisible by each of the integers.

legs (391) The adjacent sides of the right angle of a right triangle.

like terms (16) Terms that contain the same variables, with corresponding variables raised to the same power.

linear equation (283) A linear equation is an equation that may be written in the form $Ax + By = C$, where $A, B,$ and C are any numbers and A and B are not both 0.

maximum point (406) The highest point on the graph of a curve such as a parabola which opens down.

means (97) *See* proportion.

midpoint (327) The midpoint of a line segment is the point that is halfway between the endpoints of the segment.

minimum point (405) The lowest point on the graph of a curve such as a parabola which opens up.

monomial (145) A number, a variable, or a product of numbers and variables.

multiplicative identity (12) The number 1 is the multiplicative identity since the product of any number and 1 is equal to the number.

multiplicative inverse (79) Two numbers are multiplicative inverses if their product is 1. The multiplicative inverse, or reciprocal, of a is $\frac{1}{a}$.

multiplicative property of zero (12) For any number a, $a \cdot 0 = 0$.

natural numbers (N) (374) The set of numbers $\{1, 2, 3, \ldots\}$.

negative number (39) A number that is graphed on the negative side of the number line.

numerical coefficient (16) The numerical part of a term.

open sentence (9) A sentence containing a symbol(s) to be replaced in order to determine if the sentence is true or false.

opposite (53) The opposite of a number is its additive inverse.

order of operations (6)
1. Evaluate all powers.
2. Then do all multiplications and divisions from left to right.
3. Then do all additions and subtractions from left to right.

ordered pair (271) In mathematics, pairs of numbers used to locate points in the plane.

ordinate (271) The second component of an ordered pair; the y-coordinate.

origin (271) The point of intersection of the two axes of the coordinate plane.

parabola (405) The general shape of the graph of a quadratic function.

parallel lines (324) Lines that have the same slope are parallel. All vertical lines are parallel.

percent of decrease (159) The ratio of an amount of decrease to the previous amount, expressed as a percent.

percent of increase (159) The ratio of an amount of increase to the previous amount, expressed as a percent.

percent proportion (102)
$$\frac{\text{Percentage}}{\text{Base}} = \text{Rate or } \frac{P}{B} = \frac{r}{100}.$$

perimeter (195) The perimeter of a polygon is the sum of the lengths of its sides.

perpendicular lines (325) Two lines are perpendicular if the product of their slopes is -1. In a plane, vertical lines are perpendicular to horizontal lines.

polynomial (175) An expression that can be written as a sum of monomials.

point-slope form (309) For a given point (x,y) on a nonvertical line, the point-slope form of a linear equation is $y - y_1 = m(x - x_1)$.

power (4) An expression in the form x^n. The base is x and the exponent is n.

prime factorization (211) The expression of a composite number as the product of its prime factors.

prime number (211) An integer, greater than 1, whose only positive factors are 1 and itself.

prime polynomial (226) A polynomial that cannot be written as a product of two or more polynomials.

principal square root (371) The nonnegative square root of the expression.

product (3) The result of multiplication.

product property of square roots (372) For any numbers a and b, where $a \geq 0$ and $b \geq 0$, $\sqrt{ab} = \sqrt{a} \cdot \sqrt{b}$.

proportion (97) An equation of the form $\frac{a}{b} = \frac{c}{d}$ which states that two ratios are equal. The first and fourth terms (a and d) are called the extremes. The second and third terms (b and c) are called the means.

Pythagorean Theorem (391) In a right triangle if a and b are the measures of the legs, and c is the measure of the hypotenuse, then $c^2 = a^2 + b^2$.

quadrant (271) One of the four regions into which two perpendicular number lines separate the plane.

quadratic formula (416) The solutions of a quadratic equation of the form $ax^2 + bx + c = 0$, where $a \neq 0$, are given by
$$x = \frac{-b \pm \sqrt{b^2 - 4ac}}{2a}.$$

quadratic function (405) A quadratic function is a function described by an equation of the form $y = ax^2 + bx + c$, where $a \neq 0$.

quotient property of square roots (372) For any numbers a and b, where $a \geq 0$ and $b > 0$,
$$\sqrt{\frac{a}{b}} = \frac{\sqrt{a}}{\sqrt{b}}.$$

radical expression (371)   An expression of the form $\sqrt{a}$.

radical equations (389)   Equations containing radicals with variables in the radicand.

radical sign (371)   The symbol $\sqrt{\ }$ indicating the principal or nonnegative square root.

radicand (371)   The expression under the radical sign.

range (274)   The range of a relation is the set of all second components from each ordered pair.

ratio (97)   A comparison of two numbers by division. The ratio of a to b is $\frac{a}{b}$.

rational numbers (Q) (47)   Numbers that can be expressed in the form $\frac{a}{b}$, where a and b are integers, $b \neq 0$.

real numbers (R) (375)   Irrational numbers together with rational numbers form the set of real numbers.

reciprocal (79)   The reciprocal of a number is its multiplicative inverse.

reflexive property of equality (12)   For any number a, $a = a$.

relation (274)   A set of ordered pairs.

repeating decimal (374)   A decimal numeral in which a digit or a group of digits repeat is called a repeating decimal.

replacement set (11)   The set of numbers that a variable may represent.

right triangle (391)   A triangle that has a 90° angle.

root of an equation (410)   A solution of the equation.

scientific notation (153)   A number is expressed in scientific notation when it is in the form $a \times 10^{n}$, where $1 \leq a < 10$ and n is an integer.

set (11)   A collection of objects or numbers.

similar triangles (505)   If two triangles are similar, the measures of their corresponding angles are equal and the measures of their corresponding sides are proportional.

simplest form of an expression (16)   An expression in simplest form has no like terms and no parentheses.

sine (508)   In a right triangle, the sine of angle A =
$$\frac{\text{measure of side opposite angle } A}{\text{measure of hypotenuse}}.$$

slope (305)   The slope of a line is the ratio of the change in y to the corresponding change in x.
$$\text{slope} = \frac{\text{change in } y}{\text{change in } x}$$

slope-intercept form (312)   The slope-intercept form of the equation of a line is $y = mx + b$. The slope of the line is m, and the y-intercept is b.

solution (9)   A replacement for the variable in an open sentence which results in a true sentence.

solution set (113)   The set of all replacements for the variable in an open sentence which make the sentence true.

solve (9)   To solve an open sentence means to find all the solutions.

square root (371)   If $x^{2} = y$, then x is a square root of y.

standard form of linear equation (310)   A linear equation in standard form is $Ax + By = C$ where $A, B,$ and C are integers, and A and B are not both zero.

subset (11)   A set that is made from the elements of another set.

substitution method (342)   A method for solving systems of equations. One variable is expressed in terms of the other variable in one equation. Then the expression is substituted into the other equation.

substitution property of equality (13) For any numbers a and b, if $a = b$ then a may be replaced by b.

supplementary angles (499) Two angles are supplementary if the sum of their measures is 180°.

symmetric property of equality (12) For any numbers a and b, if $a = b$ then $b = a$.

system of equations (337) A set of equations with the same variables.

tangent (508) In a right triangle the tangent of angle $A =$

$$\frac{\text{measure of side opposite angle } A}{\text{measure of side adjacent to angle } A}.$$

term (15) A number, a variable, or a *product* or *quotient* of numbers and variables. The terms of an expression are separated by the symbols $+$ and $-$.

terminating decimal (374) A specific type of repeating decimal in which only a zero repeats.

transitive property of equality (12) For any numbers $a, b,$ and c, if $a = b$ and $b = c$, then $a = c$.

trigonometric ratios (508) Ratios in a right triangle that involve the measures of the sides and the measures of the angles.

trinomial (175) A polynomial having exactly three terms.

union (129) The union of two sets consists of all the points that belong to at least one of the sets.

uniform motion (201) When an object moves at a constant speed, or rate, it is said to be in uniform motion.

variable (3) In a mathematical sentence, a variable is a symbol used to represent an unspecified number.

vertical line test (287) If any vertical line drawn on the graph of a relation passes through no more than one point of its graph, then the relation is a function.

whole numbers (W) (374) The set of numbers $\{0, 1, 2, 3, \ldots\}$.

x-axis (271) The horizontal number line which helps to form the coordinate plane.

x-coordinate (271) The first component of an ordered pair.

x-intercept (312) The value of x when y is 0.

y-axis (271) The vertical number line which helps to form the coordinate plane.

y-coordinate (271) The second component of an ordered pair.

y-intercept (312) The value of y when x is 0.

zero product property (245) For all numbers a and b, if $ab = 0$, then $a = 0$ or $b = 0$.

Selected Answers

CHAPTER 1   THE LANGUAGE OF ALGEBRA

1-1   Page 5

Exploratory   **1.** $7x$ **3.** $a + 19$ **5.** b^3 **7.** $2 \div k$
or $\frac{2}{k}$ **9.** 25^2 **11.** $n - 4$ **13.** x squared or x to the
second power   **15.** 5 cubed or 5 to the third power
17. n to the first power   ***Written***   **1.** 5^3 **3.** $7a^4$
5. $\frac{1}{2}a^2b^3$ **7.** 5^3x^2y **9.** $x + 17$ **11.** x^3 **13.** $2x^2$
15. $8x - 17$ **17.** $94 + 2x$ **19.** $\frac{3}{4}x^2$ **21.** $x^3 + 7$
23. 16   **25.** 125   **27.** 1024

1-2   Page 7

Exploratory   **1.** Multiply 2 and 4. Then add 3.
3. Divide 8 by 4. Then multiply by 2.   **5.** Multiply 6
and 2. Then subtract from 12.   **7.** Subtract 3 from 9.
Then square the result.   **9.** Square 9. Square 3. Then
subtract.   **11.** Square 3. Then multiply by 7.
13. Subtract 3 from 5. Square the result. Then
multiply by 4.   **15.** Add 8 and 6. Divide by 2. Then
add 2.   ***Written***   **1.** 2   **3.** 48   **5.** 48   **7.** 14   **9.** 6
11. 8   **13.** 316   **15.** 1   **17.** $\frac{11}{13}$ **19.** $\frac{26}{3}$ or $8\frac{2}{3}$
21. 15   **23.** 1.32   **25.** 31   **27.** 75   **29.** 3   **31.** 2
33. 13.2   **35.** 3.04   **37.** 413   **39.** $\frac{11}{18}$ **41.** 1920
43. $2(a + b); 7$ **45.** $b^2 + c; \frac{1}{4}$

1-3   Page 10

Exploratory   **1.** false   **3.** false   **5.** false   **7.** true
9. false   **11.** true   **13.** true   **15.** false   **19.** 2
21. Foster, Rath, or Winters   ***Written***   **1.** 11
3. 11.97   **5.** 9   **7.** 1.45   **9.** 5   **11.** 2   **13.** 11.05
15. 6   **17.** $\frac{7}{13}$ **19.** $\frac{7}{8}$ **21.** $\frac{7}{4}$ **23.** $5\frac{5}{6}$

1-4   Page 13

Exploratory   **1.** reflexive   **3.** symmetric
5. transitive   **7.** substitution   **9.** 7   **11.** 1
Written   **1.** symmetric   **3.** transitive
5. multiplicative identity   **7.** reflexive
9. multiplicative property of zero   **11.** reflexive
13. substitution   **15.** symmetric   **17.** multiplicative
property of zero   **19.** multiplicative identity

1-5   Page 17

Exploratory   **1.** 5   **3.** 0.2   **5.** $\frac{1}{5}$ **7.** 0.5   **9.** $6bc$ and bc
11. $4xy$ and $5xy$ **13.** $\frac{m^2n}{2}$ and $5m^2n$ **15.** v^3 and $4v^3$
17. $2cd^2$ and $3d^2c$ **19.** $3a + 3c$ **21.** $28 - 8a$
23. $x(c + d)$ **25.** $r(3 - k)$ ***Written***   **1.** $10a$

3. $18a$ **5.** am **7.** $38mn$ **9.** $22x^2$ **11.** $41a$
13. $22y^2 + 3$ **15.** $16a + 17b + 6$ **17.** $12a + 5b$
19. $2a + 3b$ **21.** $8x - 3y$ **23.** $30a + 6b$
25. $2a^2b + 6ab^2$ **27.** $14x + 14$ **29.** $x^2 + \frac{3}{4}x$
31. $0.98k^2 + 8.5k$ **33.** $\frac{5}{4}n + 3n^2$

1-6   Page 19

Exploratory   **1.** associative property for addition
3. distributive property   **5.** commutative property for
multiplication   **7.** associative property for
multiplication   **9.** commutative property for addition
11. no, no, no   **13. a.** commutative property for
addition   **b.** associative property for addition
c. distributive property   **d.** substitution property of
equality   ***Written***   **1.** commutative property for
addition   **3.** associative property for addition
5. commutative property for multiplication
7. additive identity property   **9.** commutative
property for addition   **11.** distributive property
13. multiplicative identity property   **15.** $12a + 6b$
17. $5x + 10y$ **19.** $\frac{5}{3}x^2 + 5x$ **21.** $3a + 13b + 2c$
23. $5 + 9ac + 14b$ **25.** $15x + 10y$ **27.** $\frac{3}{4} + \frac{5}{3}x + \frac{4}{3}y$
29. $3.1x + 1.54$ **31.** $12 + 30x + 45y$

1-7   Page 23

Exploratory   **1.** $A = s^2$ **3.** $p = 4s$
Written   **1.** 236 square units   **3.** 499 square units
5. 503.68 square units   **7.** 129 square units
9. 384 square units   **11.** $\frac{25}{64}$ square units   **13.** 63.2
square units   **15.** 21 square units   **17.** 3740 square
units   **19.** 8 square units   **21.** 191 square units
23. $2x + y^2 = z$ **25.** $x + a^2 = n$ **27.** $r = (a - b)^3$
29. $(abc)^2 = k$ **31.** $y = 2m + n^2$ **33.** $z = 29 - xy$
35. 150 miles   **37.** 3300 meters

1-8   Page 25

Written   **1. a.** \$1 bills   **b.** 7   **c.** \$267   **d.** none
e. \$157   **f.** end of day   **g.** $5n$ **3. a.** doesn't say
b. 7¢   **c.** \$7.18   **d.** more   **e.** $(n - 7)$¢ or $(359 - n)$¢
5. a. nickels   **b.** pennies   **c.** 3   **d.** 2   **e.** doesn't say
f. dimes   **7. a.** $\frac{3}{4}$ **b.** $\frac{1}{3}$ **c.** $\frac{n}{4}$ **d.** yes   **9. a.** no
b. $x - 8$ **c.** juniors   **d.** juniors   **11. a.** 48   **b.** 72
c. no

1-9   Page 30

Exploratory   **1.** $49 - n$ **3.** $w + 4$ **5.** $2t + 8$
7. \$1.59 ÷ 3   **9.** \$5.65n ***Written***   **1.** Let $n =$ the

number; $n + 24 = 89$ **3.** Let n = the number; $n - 19 = 83$ **5.** Let a = Tyrone's age; $2a + 17 = 53$ **7.** Let n = Melissa's age now; $(n + 4) + (n + 3 + 4) = 59$ **9.** Let x = Bob's height (in inches); $x + (x + 5) = 137$ **11.** Let x = Bob's age now; $(x - 5) + (x + 27 - 5) = 45$ **13.** Let n = the total; $(134) + (134 - 17) = n$ **15.** Let n = the number of pounds lost each week; $145 - 6n = 125$

CHAPTER REVIEW   Page 36

1. a^4 **3.** $2x - 17$ **5.** $8x$ **7.** 320 **9.** 4 **11.** 0.45 **13.** 4 **15.** 2 **17.** 2.2 **19.** additive identity property **21.** multiplicative property of zero **23.** reflexive **25.** $11x$ **27.** $8b + 6$ **29.** commutative property for addition **31.** associative property for addition **33.** $14a + 9b$ **35.** $18 - d^2 = f$ **37.** less **39.** Let x = Carol's weight; $x + (x + 8) = 182$

CHAPTER 2 ADDING AND SUBTRACTING RATIONAL NUMBERS

2-1   Page 40

Exploratory **1.** 3 **3.** -10 **5.** 6 **7.** -7 **9.** -9 **11.** -2 **13.** $\{-3, 1, 2\}$ **15.** $\{-3, -2, -1\}$ **17.** $\{\ldots, -4, -3, -2, -1, 0, 1\}$ **19.** -3 **21.** $+650$ **23.** $+12$ **25.** -450 **27.** $+37$ *Written* **1.** $\{-1, 0, 1, 2\}$ **3.** $\{-5, -3, -1\}$ **5.** $\{-3, -2, -1, 0\}$ **7.** $\{-6, -4, -2, 0, 2\}$ **23.** 9, 1, -7 **25.** $-5, -13, -21$ **27.** $-2, -10, -18$

2-2   Page 43

Exploratory **1.** $-3 + 5 = 2$ **3.** $4 + (-5) = -1$ **5.** $-1 + (-4) = -5$ **7.** $-4 + 3 = -1$ **9.** $4 + (-6) = -2$ **11.** In $4 + (-6)$, the parentheses show the sign of the number. In $4 + (5 - 3)$ the parentheses mean to evaluate $5 - 3$ first.   *Written* **1.** 13 **3.** -16 **5.** -5 **7.** -5 **9.** 0 **11.** 4 **13.** -5 **15.** 5 **17.** 9 **19.** -3 **21.** 0 **23.** 12 **25.** -17 **27.** -26 **29.** $-12°C$ **31.** 25th floor

2-3   Page 45

Exploratory **1.** 8 **3.** 6 **5.** 17 **7.** 21 **9.** 0 **11.** $-$ **13.** $+$ **15.** $+$ **17.** $-$ **19.** $+$ **21.** $+$ **23.** n **25.** n *Written* **1.** 16 **3.** -19 **5.** 13 **7.** 26 **9.** 21 **11.** -8 **13.** -29 **15.** 4 **17.** -9 **19.** 16 **21.** 90 **23.** -54 **25.** 8 **27.** 9 **29.** -15 **31.** -22 **33.** 0 **35.** -18 **37.** 6 **39.** 2 **41.** 5 **43.** 3 **45.** -2 **47.** -30 **49.** 613 **51.** -539 **53.** -203 **55.** 500 **57.** 343 **59.** 587 **61.** 74 **63.** 672 **65.** -1074

2-4   Page 48

Exploratory **1.** $\frac{3}{4}$ **3.** 1.76 **5.** $\frac{3}{11}$ **7.** 1.82 **9.** $\frac{3}{82}$ **11.** $+$ **13.** $-$ **15.** $-$ **17.** $+$ **19.** $-$ **21.** $+$ *Written* **1.** -2 **3.** $-\frac{1}{11}$ **5.** $-\frac{1}{6}$ **7.** 0.88 **9.** -5.6 **11.** -14.7 **13.** $\frac{1}{6}$ **15.** $-\frac{1}{6}$ **17.** $-\frac{21}{8}$ **19.** 0.622 **21.** -0.665 **23.** -0.3005 **25.** $\frac{7}{30}$ **27.** $\frac{29}{60}$ **29.** $\frac{3}{20}$

2-5   Page 52

Exploratory **1.** 0 **3.** -0.1 **5.** 1 **7.** $4m$ **9.** $4r$ **11.** $3b - 4y$ *Written* **1.** -26 **3.** 6 **5.** 80 **7.** $-5a$ **9.** $30b$ **11.** $-38z$ **13.** $-\frac{19}{12}$ **15.** $\frac{5}{14}$ **17.** $\frac{7}{48}$ **19.** -14 **21.** -12 **23.** -8.7 **25.** -7.54 **27.** -17.4 **29.** $-97a + 48k$ **31.** $89mp - 24ps$ **33.** $3a$ **35.** $24w$ **37.** $2.2k$ **39.** $-0.73x$ **41.** -6 **43.** $-\$4.66$ (decrease)

2-6   Page 55

Exploratory **1.** -6 **3.** -5 **5.** 13 **7.** a **9.** 0 **11.** -3.7 **13.** $-\frac{3}{7}$ **15.** $\frac{8}{17}$ **17.** -7 **19.** 13 **21.** 7 **23.** 16 **25.** -56 **27.** -7.1 **29.** $\frac{3}{4}$ **31.** $8 + (-13)$ **33.** $-17 + (-8)$ **35.** $-1.7 + 1.5$ **37.** $9y + (-3y)$ *Written* **1.** 8 **3.** 15 **5.** -18 **7.** 40 **9.** 52 **11.** -11 **13.** $\frac{4}{5}$ **15.** $\frac{1}{4}$ **17.** -21 **19.** 11.5 **21.** -28.9 **23.** -153.8 **25.** -17 **27.** -1.4 **29.** $7m$ **31.** $-22p$ **33.** $33b$ **35.** $-35z$ **37.** -2 **39.** 58 **41.** 8.9 **43.** -16.7 **45.** -5.5 **47.** 8 **49.** $-\frac{5}{8}$ **51.** $-\frac{52}{21}$ **53.** $-\frac{67}{34}$

2-7   Page 59

Exploratory **1.** -21 **3.** 5 **5.** 10 **7.** 16 **9.** 5 **11.** -3 *Written* **1.** -3 **3.** -19 **5.** -32 **7.** -19 **9.** -19 **11.** -16 **13.** 15 **15.** 52 **17.** 28 **19.** -10 **21.** 8 **23.** -6 **25.** -3.6 **27.** -0.8 **29.** -1.3 **31.** $-\frac{17}{16}$ **33.** 2 **35.** $-\frac{52}{45}$

2-8   Page 61

Exploratory **1.** $m - 8$ **3.** $y + 11$ **5.** $b - 17$ **7.** $n + 23$ **9.** $z - 31$ **11.** $p + 47$ *Written* **1.** -17 **3.** -25 **5.** -12 **7.** 20 **9.** -14 **11.** -15 **13.** -3 **15.** -19 **17.** -2 **19.** -12 **21.** 9 **23.** -24 **25.** -36 **27.** -9 **29.** -21 **31.** -9 **33.** 21 **35.** -20 **37.** -2.8 **39.** -8.4 **41.** 2.32 **43.** $\frac{15}{14}$ **45.** $\frac{31}{20}$ **47.** $-\frac{23}{42}$

2-9   Page 64

Exploratory **1. a.** How far downstream was she from her starting point? **b.** 110 km **c.** 320 km **d.** Use a positive number for the distance upstream and a negative number for the distance downstream.

e. Let d = distance from starting point; $110 + (-320) = d$ **3. a.** $35\frac{3}{8}$ in.   **b.** $10\frac{1}{8}$ and $12\frac{3}{16}$ **d.** third side   **e.** The perimeter is equal to the sum of the lengths of the three sides.   **f.** Let x = the measure of the third side; $10\frac{1}{8} + 12\frac{3}{16} + x = 35\frac{3}{8}$ **5.** Let f = floor; $1 + 14 + (-9) = f$ **7.** Let n = number; $n - 13 = -5$ **9.** Let r = runs; $41 - 17 = r$ **Written**   **1.** -210 (210 km downstream)   **3.** $13\frac{1}{16}$ **5.** 6   **7.** 8   **9.** 24   **11.** 63   **13.** $-19°$ **15.** 153 seconds   **17.** $54.44   **19.** 77   **21.** -38 **23.** -43 m (43 m below sea level)   **25.** -74 m (74 m below sea level)   **27.** -85 m (85 m below cave entrance)   **29.** $35\frac{5}{8}$

CHAPTER REVIEW   Page 69

1. $\{-3, 1, 2, 5\}$ **3.** $\{3, 4, 5, \ldots\}$ **9.** -1 **11.** -6 **13.** 8   **15.** -4 **17.** -53 **19.** -1 **21.** 2.7   **23.** 3.649   **25.** 66   **27.** $-23b$ **29.** $\frac{23}{12}$ **31.** -3.9 **33.** $-51pq + 53k$ **35.** -22 **37.** 4   **39.** 12.37   **41.** $-6x$ **43.** 17   **45.** -6.7 **47.** $-\frac{11}{14}$ **49.** -8 **51.** -24 **53.** 38   **55.** 53   **57.** -13 **59.** 19   **61.** Let n = the number; $n + (-16) = 39$; 55   **63.** Let c = change in temperature; $15 - (-2) = c$; The temperature rose $17°$ F.

CHAPTER 3   MULTIPLYING AND DIVIDING RATIONAL NUMBERS

3-1   Page 77

Exploratory   **1.** negative   **3.** positive   **5.** positive   **7.** negative   **9.** negative   **11.** negative   **13.** positive   **15.** negative   **17.** Both a and b are positive or both are negative.   **19.** a can be either positive or negative.   **21.** positive   **Written**   **1.** -6 **3.** 56   **5.** 30   **7.** -110 **9.** $-\frac{1}{6}$ **11.** $-\frac{1}{2}$ **13.** 24   **15.** $-\frac{6}{5}$ **17.** 60   **19.** $-\frac{12}{35}$ **21.** $-\frac{7}{2}$ **23.** 3   **25.** $-\frac{1}{5}$ **27.** 0   **29.** -26 **31.** -10 **33.** 14   **35.** -5 **37.** $\frac{4}{3}$ or $1\frac{1}{3}$ **39.** $-\frac{5}{8}$ **41.** $7t$ **43.** $-21x$ **45.** $2x$ **47.** $5a - 3b$ **49.** $\frac{1}{6}a - \frac{1}{6}b$

3-2   Page 80

Exploratory   **1.** $\frac{1}{3}$ **3.** none   **5.** $-\frac{1}{14}$ **7.** $\frac{3}{2}$ **9.** $-\frac{11}{3}$ **11.** $\frac{7}{10}$ **13.** $-\frac{5}{3}$ **15.** $\frac{4}{13}$ **17.** $-\frac{7}{17}$ **Written**   **1.** 6   **3.** -5 **5.** 14   **7.** -5 **9.** 6   **11.** 4   **13.** -19 **15.** -4 **17.** $6a$ **19.** $-7a$ **21.** 7   **23.** -5 **25.** $-\frac{5}{48}$ **27.** $-\frac{7}{80}$ **29.** $\frac{1}{12}$ **31.** $-\frac{35}{2}$ **33.** $\frac{21}{2}$ **35.** $\frac{27}{2}$ **37.** $a + 3$ **39.** $-a - 5$ **41.** $-10a - 15b$ **43.** $-10a + 5b$

3-3   Page 83

Exploratory   **1.** 3   **3.** $\frac{4}{3}$ **5.** $\frac{9}{4}$ **7.** $-\frac{1}{8}$ **9.** 9   **11.** 4   **13.** 4   **15.** -7 **17.** -8 **19.** -6 **Written**   **1.** 7   **3.** -7 **5.** -7 **7.** 17   **9.** $\frac{40}{9}$ **11.** $-\frac{11}{3}$ **13.** $\frac{14}{3}$ **15.** $\frac{81}{11}$ **17.** -14 **19.** 48   **21.** 70   **23.** -275 **25.** -90 **27.** -1885 **29.** -9 **31.** -25 **33.** 35   **35.** $-\frac{81}{4}$ **37.** $\frac{250}{3}$ **39.** $-\frac{336}{11}$ **41.** $\frac{14}{9}$ **43.** 6   **45.** -8

3-4   Page 85

Exploratory   **1.** Add 7 to both sides. Then divide both sides by 3.   **3.** Subtract 5. Then divide by 2.   **5.** Multiply by 5. Then subtract 2.   **7.** Subtract 2. Then multiply by $\frac{11}{3}$.   **Written**   **1.** 3   **3.** 5   **5.** $\frac{6}{5}$ **7.** -9 **9.** $-\frac{25}{3}$ **11.** 4   **13.** -153 **15.** -69 **17.** -81 **19.** -32 **21.** 25   **23.** -104 **25.** 11   **27.** $\frac{65}{7}$ **29.** 28   **31.** 8   **33.** 8   **35.** 16   **37.** -12 **39.** -3

3-5   Page 89

Exploratory   **1.** Add 1 to both sides. Subtract $3x$ from both sides.   **3.** Add 3 to both sides. Add $5y$ to both sides. Divide both sides by 9.   **5.** Multiply $x + 1$ by 3. Subtract 3 from both sides. Divide both sides by 3.   **7.** Multiply $2x - 3$ by 6. Add 18 to both sides. Then divide both sides by 12.   **Written**   **1.** 10   **3.** $-\frac{1}{2}$ **5.** no solutions   **7.** identity   **9.** 2   **11.** 4   **13.** identity   **15.** $\frac{13}{5}$ **17.** no solutions   **19.** -11 **21.** -2 **23.** no solutions   **25.** 2   **27.** identity   **29.** 15   **31.** 10   **33.** -30 **35.** 10   **37.** -9 **39.** 4.2   **41.** $\frac{45}{26}$ **43.** $\frac{1}{3}$ **45.** $\frac{3}{5}$ **47.** no solutions   **49.** $\frac{5}{3}$

3-6   Page 91

Exploratory   **1.** $12, 9x - 84 = 96 + 8x$ **3.** $2, 8t - 14 = 5t - 6$ **5.** $10, 52z = 30 + 17z$ **Written**   **1.** 16   **3.** $\frac{11}{6}$ **5.** 49   **7.** 44   **9.** $\frac{8}{5}$ **11.** 18   **13.** $\frac{3}{8}$ **15.** -2 **17.** 9.6   **19.** $\frac{21}{2}$ **21.** -1 **23.** $2d - r$ **25.** $ef - d$ **27.** $\frac{3z + 2y}{e}$ **29.** $\frac{c - d}{2}$ **31.** $\frac{b}{a} - 1$ **33.** $\frac{5}{3}(b - a)$

3-7   Page 94

Exploratory   **1.** 2, 3, 4   **3.** $-4, -2, 0$ **5.** 13, 15, 17, 19   **7.** $x + (x + 1) = 17$ **9.** $x + (x + 2) = -36$ **11.** $3x + 4 = -11$ **Written**   **1.** 28, 29, 30   **3.** 31, 32, 33, 34   **5.** no solutions   **7.** 31, 33   **9.** 31, 33, 35   **11.** 21   **13.** 46   **15.** 38   **17.** 260 m   **19.** 8th, 9th, 10th, 11th   **21.** $64   **23.** 16   **25.** 140   **27.** 30, 32, 34, 36   **29.** 17, 19   **31.** 21, 22   **33.** 50 m, 60 m   **35.** 9 m, 7 m

Exploratory 1. $\frac{3}{11}$ 3. $\frac{21}{16}$ 5. $\frac{2}{1}$ 7. $\frac{24}{7}$ 9. $\frac{4}{1}$

Written 1. 6 3. 5 5. $\frac{28}{3}$ 7. 6 9. 5 11. $\frac{8}{5}$
13. 20 15. 33 gallons 17. 267.9 km 19. 27

Exploratory 1. 31% 3. 30% 5. 80% 7. $37\frac{1}{2}$%
9. 175% 11. 40% 13. 70% 15. $12\frac{1}{2}$% 17. 300%
19. 32 21. 68 23. 25%   *Written* 1. 24 3. 60
5. 65% 7. 30.375 9. 140 11. 25% 13. $242.80
15. $62\frac{1}{2}$% 17. $6540 19. $560 21. 160% 23. 40
25. $5 27. 540 29. 40 31. 480 33. 30% 35. $65

CHAPTER REVIEW   Page 106

1. -99 3. $-\frac{3}{7}$ 5. $-5a - 12b$ 7. $-9b$ 9. 18
11. 8 13. -16 15. 10 17. -18 19. 69 21. 7
23. 3 25. -6 27. $\emptyset$ 29. $cd - y$ 31. $\frac{4a + 9b}{5}$
33. 25, 27, 29 35. 50 37. 22 39. 60% 41. 17%
43. 48 45. $87\frac{1}{2}$%

CHAPTER 4 INEQUALITIES

Exploratory 1. false 3. true 5. true 7. true
9. false 11. true 13. false 15. {all numbers
greater than 3} 17. {all numbers less than 6}
19. {all numbers greater than or equal to -4}
21. yes 23. no 25. yes   *Written* 1. $x > 3$
3. $x \neq -3$ 5. $x \geq 0$ 7. $x < -3$ 9. $x \geq -7$
11. $<$ 13. $=$ 15. $<$ 17. $>$ 19. $=$ 21. $<$
23. $<$ 25. $>$ 27. $<$ 29. $<$ 31. $<$

Exploratory 1. -7 3. 13 5. $-3y$ 7. $-5z$
9. -3 11. 7   *Written* 1. $a < 8$ 3. $r \geq 32$
5. $b < 8$ 7. $m > -19$ 9. $y \leq -8$ 11. $n > 11$
13. $n > 34$ 15. $n \leq -9$ 17. $n < -11$ 19. $s > -15$ 21. $t \leq 34.6$ 23. $m > 6.38$ 25. $r > 1$
27. $x < \frac{5}{6}$ 29. $-6 > f$ 31. $n > 6$ 33. $14 > x$
35. $-4 \leq a$ 37. $r < -6.6$ 39. $z > 168.93$ 41. $y \geq -\frac{1}{12}$ 43. $r < \frac{29}{12}$

Exploratory 1. 3, no 3. -8, yes 5. $\frac{1}{3}$, no 7. $-\frac{1}{4}$,
yes 9. 6, no 11. -11, yes 13. $\frac{3}{4}$, no 15. $-\frac{3}{5}$,
yes   *Written* 1. $p < 6$ 3. $s < -7$ 5. $r \leq -\frac{35}{2}$
7. $s > \frac{17}{4}$ 9. $h < 450$ 11. $b \leq -128$ 13. $r < -0.7$ 15. $y > \frac{10}{3}$ 17. $s \leq -6$ 19. $k < -\frac{8}{7}$

21. $m > 0.7$ 23. $t \leq -1.4$ 25. $z < 0.08$ 27. $x > -\frac{4}{5}$ 29. $w \geq \frac{13}{12}$ 31. $a < -9$

Exploratory 1. Add 1 to both sides. Then divide both
sides by 3. 3. Add 7 to both sides. Then divide both
sides by 4. 5. Subtract 32 from both sides. Then
divide both sides by 14. 7. Add 12 to both sides.
Then divide both sides by 11. 9. Subtract 7 from
both sides. Then multiply both sides by 4. 11. Add 5
to both sides. Then multiply both sides by -4 and
reverse the direction of the inequality. 13. Subtract
13 from both sides. Then divide both sides by -2 and
reverse the direction of the inequality. 15. Subtract
k from both sides. Subtract 7 from both sides.
Written 1. $r > 8$ 3. $p < -\frac{3}{2}$ 5. $y \geq -1$ 7. $x > 80$
9. $x < -5$ 11. $n < \frac{21}{5}$ 13. $y \leq 0$ 15. $c < 2$
17. $x < 40$ 19. $x > -\frac{1}{2}$ 21. $x \geq -31$ 23. $y < 4$

Exploratory 1. $\frac{4}{5}$ 3. $\frac{10}{11}$ 5. $\frac{6}{5}$ 7. $-\frac{1}{4}$ 9. $-\frac{9}{7}$
11. $-\frac{15}{13}$ 13. $\frac{0.2}{2}$ 15. $\frac{0.8}{3}$ 17. $\frac{459}{10}$
Written 1. $<$ 3. $>$ 5. $<$ 7. $>$ 9. $<$ 11. $=$
13. $<$ 15. $<$ 17. $\frac{79}{21}$ and $\frac{97}{28}$; second item
19. $\frac{91}{184}$ and $\frac{189}{340}$; first item 21. $\frac{179}{2.1}$ and $\frac{169}{1.9}$; first
item 23. $\frac{93}{27}, \frac{79}{20}$; first item 25. $\frac{149}{100}, \frac{98}{75}$; second item
27. Dudley's Market 29. 26-ounce pie

Exploratory 1. false 3. true 5. false 7. true
9. true 11. true   *Written* 1. $0 \leq m < 9$
3. $\frac{3}{4} < p \leq \frac{11}{9}$ 5. $-\frac{4}{5} < z < \frac{2}{3}$ 7. $-\frac{13}{7} < m < -\frac{6}{5}$
9. $-4.9 \leq a \leq -2.4$ 27. {all numbers} 29. $m < -1$ 31. $q < -2$ or $q > -1$ 33. $x \geq -5$ and
$x < 1$ 35. $x > -1$ and $x < 3$ 37. $x > -4$ and $x < 1$
39. $x < \frac{3}{2}$ 41. $x \leq -3$ or $x \geq 1$ 43. $x < -3$ or
$x > 3$ 45. $x \geq -3$ and $x < 5$

Exploratory 1. $x = 4$ or $x = -4$ 3. $y > 3$ or
$y < -3$ 5. $y < \frac{5}{2}$ and $y > -\frac{5}{2}$ 7. $x + 2 > 3$ or
$x + 2 < -3$ 9. $x + 2 < 3$ and $x + 2 > -3$
11. $2x - 5 \geq 3$ or $2x - 5 \leq -3$ 13. $7 - x = 4$ or
$7 - x = -4$ 15. $3x + 1 > 6$ or $3x + 1 < -6$
Written 1. $y > 3$ or $y < -5$ 3. $y < 5$ and $y > -3$
5. $y \geq 1$ and $y \leq 3$ 7. {all numbers} 9. $y \geq 8$ or
$y \leq 2$ 11. {1} 13. $x \leq \frac{5}{2}$ and $x \geq \frac{9}{2}$ 15. $x \leq$

−10 or $x \geq 8$ **17.** $y \leq \frac{1}{2}$ or $y \geq \frac{9}{2}$ **19.** $\left\{\frac{4}{3}\right\}$

21. $t < \frac{4}{3}$ and $t > -1$ **23.** $\{2, -2\}$ **25.** $|x| = 1$

27. $|x| < 3$ **29.** $|x| \geq 2$

4-8   Page 137

Written   **1.** The number is greater than or equal to 5
3. 7 and 9; 5 and 7; 3 and 5; 1 and 3   **5.** He must
deliver 70 or more   **7.** 145 kg or greater   **9.** His
sales were greater than $150,000 and less than
$250,000   **11.** $12.10 or less   **13.** 3, 4, or 5
15. Her score must be 9.7 or greater.   **17.** His score
must be greater than 9.4.   **19.** 38, 40

CHAPTER REVIEW   Page 140

1. false   **3.** true   **5.** >   **7.** <   **13.** $y \geq 6$ **15.** $n <$
-11 **17.** $y < -\frac{1}{6}$ **19.** $h \geq -104$ **21.** $a \leq -4$
23. $r < -24$ **25.** $t < -1.4$ **27.** $k > \frac{1}{5}$ **29.** $z >$
$-\frac{7}{10}$ **31.** $r > 1.8$ **33.** $y \leq -\frac{19}{3}$ **35.** $z < -10$
37. <   **39.** second item   **41.** $-3 \leq x \leq 17$
47. $m \leq 6$ and $m \geq -4$ **49.** The number is greater
than $\frac{7}{8}$ and less than $\frac{17}{8}$.

CHAPTER 5   POWERS

5-1   Page 146

Exploratory   **7.** x^8 **9.** a^8 **11.** m^4 **13.** $12a^5$
15. $-20x^5y$ **17.** y^5z^4 *Written*   **1.** a^7 **3.** m^6
5. t^6 **7.** a^{13} **9.** a^3b^5 **11.** m^4n^3 **13.** $6a^3b^6$
15. $-6x^8y^3$ **17.** $12x^6y^3$ **19.** $-6x^9y$ **21.** $6x^4y^4z^4$
23. $-35a^5b^2c$ **25.** $6a^3m^3n$ **27.** $a^2b^2c^2$ **29.** $9ab^2$
31. $3a^3b^2$ **33.** $\frac{1}{8}a^2b^2c$ **35.** abc

5-2   Page 149

Exploratory   **1.** m^8 **3.** $9y^2$ **5.** x^4y^4 **7.** $-a^3b^6$
9. x^4y^{10} **11.** $\frac{8}{27}a^6$ *Written*   **1.** 5^9 **3.** $(-5)^6$ or 5^6
5. x^{12} **7.** y^{18} **9.** $125c^3$ **11.** $-343z^3$ **13.** $\frac{1}{4}c^2$
15. $0.16d^2$ **17.** a^3b^6 **19.** $4a^4b^2$ **21.** $4a^6b^9$
23. $-125x^9y^3$ **25.** $\frac{1}{8}x^3y^6$ **27.** $0.008a^6$ **29.** $0.01x^4$
31. 10^5 **33.** $-48x^3y^2$ **35.** $-24a^3b$ **37.** $64x^6y^9$
39. $16a^8b^{12}$ **41.** x^4y^4 **43.** $16a^{14}b^6$ **45.** $152a^6$
47. $-30x^9y^3$ **49.** $101a^6 + 15{,}625a^6b^6$

5-3   Page 152

Exploratory   **1.** 1   **3.** $\frac{1}{y^3}$ **5.** $\frac{1}{s^4}$ **7.** $\frac{1}{c^7}$ **9.** $\frac{x^3}{2y^6}$
11. $\frac{1}{d^2e}$ **13.** k^5 **15.** $\frac{1}{x}$ **17.** $\frac{5}{n^3}$ **19.** $\frac{b^7}{a^2}$ **21.** x
23. $\frac{b^3}{a^4}$ *Written*   **1.** n^3 **3.** $\frac{1}{x}$ **5.** a^2 **7.** $\frac{1}{k^6}$ **9.** an

11. $\frac{a}{n^2}$ **13.** b^3c^3 **15.** $-\frac{1}{y^3}$ **17.** $3b$ **19.** $\frac{b^3}{5}$
21. y^3 **23.** ab^2 **25.** $\frac{w^2}{t^5}$ **27.** $-\frac{5y^5}{x^9}$ **29.** $-\frac{4b^3}{c^2}$
31. $-2ab^4c^5$ **33.** $\frac{9yz^5}{x^3}$ **35.** $\frac{7x^3}{4z^{10}}$ **37.** a^9b **39.** $\frac{5}{rs}$
41. $\frac{m^3n^2}{2k}$ **43.** $\frac{2z^5}{3y^3}$

5-4   Page 155

Exploratory   **1.** 5000; 5.79×10^7 **3.** 12,760;
1.4959×10^8 **5.** 142,700; 7.7812×10^8
Written   **1.** 4.293×10^3 **3.** 2.4×10^5 **5.** $3.19 \times$
10^{-4} **7.** 9.2×10^{-8} **9.** 3.2×10^6 **11.** 7.6×10^6
13. 3×10^2; 300   **15.** 6×10^2; 600   **17.** 5.5×10^{-9};
0.0000000055   **19.** 6×10^{-3}; 0.006   **21.** 6.51×10^3;
6510   **23.** 7.8×10^8; 780,000,000   **25.** 2.1×10^{-1};
0.21   **27.** 4×10^8; 400,000,000

5-5   Page 157

Exploratory   **1. a.** $n - 5$ **b.** $n + 11$ **c.** $n - x$
3. a. $n + 14$ **b.** $n + 3$ **c.** 7   **d.** $2n + 9$ **e.** 11
f. $6n + 7$ **5. a.** $2m$ **b.** $\frac{m}{3}$ **c.** $m - 5$ **d.** $m + 8$
Written   **1.** Abe, 21; Mindy, 18   **3.** 2   **5.** 25
7. 11   **9.** 1   **11.** 30   **13.** not enough information
15. 19

5-6   Page 161

Exploratory   **1.** 10   **3.** 8   **5.** 45   **7.** 36   **9.** 40
Written   **1.** 10   **3.** 28   **5.** $3.00   **7. a.** D   **b.** $6
c. 6%   **9. a.** $28   **b.** $172   **11. a.** $48   **b.** 25%
13. 39   **15.** $54\frac{6}{11}$%   **17.** 20%   **19.** $27   **21.** $303.60
23. $78.81   **25.** $41.18   **27.** $88.50   **29.** $17.45
31. 4%   **33.** 100

5-7   Page 166

Exploratory   **1.** $60x + 75(16 - x) = 1095$ **3.** $6x +$
$36 = 4.20(12 + x)$ *Written*   **1.** 1 L   **3.** 250 mL
5. 12   **7.** 5 pounds   **9.** 110 at 95¢ and 154 at $1.25
11. 6 nickels, 12 quarters, 9 dimes

CHAPTER REVIEW   Page 170

1. b^9 **3.** a^4b^3 **5.** $-12a^3b^4$ **7.** $49a^2$ **9.** $\frac{1}{9}b^4$
11. $576x^5y^2$ **13.** y^4 **15.** $3b^3$ **17.** $\frac{a}{6b^2c^2}$
19. 2.4×10^5 **21.** 6×10^{11} **23.** 6×10^{-7}
25. Jim, 27; Joe, 37   **27.** 18   **29.** $22.11
31. 11 dimes, 21 nickels

CHAPTER 6   POLYNOMIALS

6-1   Page 176

Exploratory   **1.** trinomial   **3.** monomial   **5.** not
polynomial   **7.** not polynomial   **9.** binomial

11. trinomial 13. monomial 15. not polynomial
17. 0 19. 2 21. 4 23. 7 25. 5 27. 5 29. 0
31. 4 33. 4 35. 29 37. 7 39. 6
Written 1. 2 3. 3 5. 5 7. 4 9. 4 11. 7
13. 14 15. 7 17. 2 19. $3 + 2x^2 + x^4$ 21. $a^3 + 5ax + 2x^2$ 23. $11b^2x + 17bx^2 - x^3$ 25. $x^2 + 4x - 7$ 27. $-3x^3 + 5x^2 + 2x + 7$ 29. $b^3x^2 + \frac{2}{3}bx + 5b$ 31. $x + a$ 33. $4x^3y - x^2y^3 + 3xy^4 + y^4$
35. $4x^4 + \frac{1}{3}s^2x^3 - \frac{2}{5}s^4x^2 + \frac{1}{4}x$ 37. $2.4tx^5 + 5.1x^3 - 0.3tx^2 + 1.7t^3x$

6-2 **Page 180**

Exploratory 1. -29 3. $-3x - 2y$ 5. $-7a + 6b$
7. $8m - 7n$ 9. $-x^2 - 3x - 7$ 11. $-2y^2 + 7y - 12$ 13. $10r^2 - 4rs + 6s$ 15. $x^3 + x + 1$
17. $3ab^2 - 5a^2b + b^3$ 19. $10n + 9p$ 21. $7a + b$
23. $8x + 3y$ 25. $12n - 2r$ 27. $-6s$
Written 1. $7x + 14y$ 3. $7m + 5n$ 5. $7x - 4y$
7. $3a - 11m$ 9. $13m + 3n$ 11. $13x - 2y$ 13. $3n^2 + 13n + 11$ 15. $-2 - 6a$ 17. $x^2 + \frac{4}{3}x + \frac{1}{4}$
19. $7ax^2 + 3a^2x - 5ax + 2x$ 21. $-3x^2y + 6xy^2 - 2y^2$ 23. $-2mn^2 + 3mn - n - 3n^3$ 25. $9a - 3b - 4c + 16d$ 27. $7ax^2 - 5a^2x - 7a^3 + 4$ 29. $x^2y^2 - 5xy - 10$ 31. $6m^2n^2 + 8mn - 28$ 33. $6m^2n^2 + 10mn - 23$ 35. $-3y^2$ 37. $2x + 6y$

6-3 **Page 183**

Exploratory 1. $-60a^3$ 3. $10x - 6$ 5. $35a^2 + 56a$
7. $15a^2b - 9ab$ 9. $-24a^4 - 56a^3$ 11. $9x^2y^2 + 6x^2y$ *Written* 1. $15a + 35$ 3. $-24x - 15$
5. $4x^2 + 3x$ 7. $15b^2 + 24b$ 9. $-10x^2 - 22x$
11. $2.2a^2 + 7.7a$ 13. $21a^3 - 14a^2$ 15. $15s^3t + 6s^2t^2$ 17. $35x^3y - 7xy^3$ 19. $10a^4 - 14a^3 + 4a$
21. $35x^4y - 21x^3y^2 + 7x^2y^2$ 23. $40y^4 + 35y^3 - 15y^2$ 25. $-28x^3 + 16x^2 - 12x$ 27. $15x^4y - 35x^3y^2 + 5x^2y^3$ 29. $36m^4n + 4m^3n - 20m^2n^2$
31. $-32x^2y^2 - 56x^2y + 112xy^3$ 33. $-3x^3 - \frac{1}{3}x^2 + \frac{5}{3}x$ 35. $-16m^3n + 6m^2n^2 - 2mn^3$ 37. $-\frac{1}{4}ab^4 + \frac{1}{3}ab^3 - \frac{3}{4}ab^2$ 39. $7a^4 + 21a^3 - a + 25$
41. $-3m^3 + 41m^2 - 14m - 16$ 43. $21a^3 - 6a^2 - 46a + 28$ 45. $50.6t^2 + 21t - 102$ 47. $6m^3 + 21m^2 - \frac{33}{2}m$

6-4 **Page 187**

Exploratory 1. $8x$ 3. $11a$ 5. $22x$ 7. $13x$ 9. $-b$
11. $14m$ *Written* 1. $a^2 + 10a + 21$ 3. $m^2 - 16m + 55$ 5. $x^2 + 7x - 44$ 7. $2x^2 + 17x + 8$
9. $8a^2 + 2a - 3$ 11. $40a^2 + 47a + 12$ 13. $10a^2 + 11ab - 6b^2$ 15. $14y^2 - 23y + 3$ 17. $20r^2 -$

$13rs - 21s^2$ 19. $20x^2 - 2x - \frac{2}{9}$ 21. $12x^2 + \frac{3}{2}x - \frac{3}{8}$ 23. $\frac{3}{16}y^2 + \frac{1}{12}xy - \frac{2}{9}x^2$ 25. $6a^2 + 3.7a + 0.56$
27. $0.63x^2 + 3.9xy + 6y^2$ 29. $0.24a^2 - 0.63a - 1.32$
31. $m^3 + 14m^2 + 47m - 14$ 33. $5a^3 - 13a^2 + 49a + 22$ 35. $12s^3 + 47s^2 + 4s - 45$ 37. $30x^3 - 37x^2y + 55xy^2 - 18y^3$ 39. $0.15n^3 + 3.07n^2 - 24.35n + 12$ 41. $0.63t^3 - 0.40t^2 + 1.41t + 0.34$
43. $\frac{4}{9}x^3 - \frac{5}{6}x^2y + \frac{13}{24}xy^2 - \frac{1}{8}y^3$ 45. $\frac{1}{12}a^3 + \frac{5}{12}a^2 + \frac{1}{12}a - \frac{5}{6}$ 47. $a^4 - a^3 - 8a^2 - 29a - 35$ 49. $20x^4 - 9x^3 + 73x^2 - 39x + 99$ 51. $-24a^3 - 34a^2 + 19a + 15$ 53. $5x^6 - 25x^5 + 13x^4 + 10x^3 - 5x^2 - 5x + 3$ 55. $\frac{1}{4}a^6 + 2a^3 - 9a^2 + 4$ 57. $0.6x^5 + 9x^4 - 6.06x^3 - 1.5x^2 - 8.4x + 6$

6-5 **Page 191**

Exploratory 1. $a^2 + 4ab + 4b^2$ 3. $4x^2 + 4xy + y^2$ 5. $9m^4 + 12m^2n + 4n^2$ 7. $a^4 + 2a^2b + b^2$
9. $9a^2 - 48ab + 64b^2$ 11. $25a^2 - 30ab + 9b^2$
13. $9x^2 - 6xy + y^2$ 15. $4x^4 - 12x^2y^3 + 9y^6$
Written 1. $16x^2 + 8xy + y^2$ 3. $4a^2 - 4ab + b^2$
5. $36m^2 + 24mn + 4n^2$ 7. $16x^2 - 72xy + 81y^2$
9. $25a^2 - 120ab + 144b^2$ 11. $25x^2 + 60xy + 36y^2$
13. $\frac{1}{4}a^2 + ab + b^2$ 15. $\frac{16}{9}x^2 - \frac{16}{3}xy + 4y^2$
17. $0.49x^2 - 1.54x + 1.21$ 19. $1.21x^2 + 2.2xy + y^2$
21. $a^4 - 6a^2b^3 + 9b^6$ 23. $9x^2 - 25$ 25. $10.24x^4 - 8.96x^2y + 1.96y^2$ 27. $\frac{1}{9}a^2 - \frac{9}{4}b^2$ 29. $49a^4 - 14a^2b + b^2$ 31. $9a^4 + 6a^2b + b^2$ 33. $36a^6 - 12a^5 + a^4$ 35. $\frac{1}{16}a^4 - \frac{1}{6}a^2b^3 + \frac{1}{9}b^6$ 37. $1.69x^4 + 5.46x^2y^3 + 4.41y^6$ 39. $x^{6n} - 2x^{3n}y^{2n} + y^{4n}$
41. $x^{4n} - y^{2n}$ 43. $x^{6n} + 2x^{3n}y^{5n} + y^{10n}$

6-6 **Page 194**

Exploratory 1. $7x - 11$ 3. $8y - 42$ 5. $-36y + 34$ 7. $10q + 48$ 9. $2x - 79$ *Written* 1. $-\frac{1}{5}$
3. $-\frac{13}{9}$ 5. $\frac{15}{7}$ 7. $-\frac{7}{2}$ 9. 8 11. $\frac{21}{2}$ 13. -3
15. -83 17. 2 19. $\frac{58}{33}$ 21. $\frac{23}{4}$ 23. $\frac{1}{3}$ 25. 2
27. 0 29. $-\frac{3}{2}$ 31. 17

6-7 **Page 196**

Exploratory 1. a. $n + 5$ b. $2t + 5$ c. $2n + 8$
d. $t + 4$ *Written* 1. 18 ft × 40 ft 3. 11 in. × 11 in. 5. 8 cm, 16 cm, 13 cm 7. 60 yd × 80 yd

6-8 **Page 199**

Exploratory 1. $480 3. $3\frac{1}{2}$ yr 5. 12% 7. $2400

9. $15\frac{1}{2}\%$ **Written 1.** \$6400 at 8% and \$3600 at

12% **3.** \$3800 **5.** \$3000 **7.** $14\frac{1}{2}\%$

6-9   Page 202

Exploratory **1. a.** 160 km **b.** 480 km **c.** 80 h km

3. a. 40 mph **b.** $\frac{240}{t}$ mph **5. a.** 8 hr **b.** 4 hr

Written **1.** $3\frac{1}{2}$ **3.** 44 mph **5.** $2\frac{1}{2}$ **7.** 11:30 A.M.

9. 240 km **11.** 450 mph and 530 mph **13.** 320 mph

CHAPTER REVIEW   Page 206

1. $3x^4 + x^2 - x - 5$ **3.** $-3x^3 + x^2 - 5x + 5$

5. $x^2 - 8x + 7$ **7.** $7x^3y + 28x^2y^2 - 56xy^3$ **9.** $x^3 +$

$56x^2 - 30x + 3$ **11.** $4x^2 + 13x - 12$ **13.** $\frac{3}{8}a^3 -$

$\frac{1}{4}a^2 + 4$ **15.** $25x^2 - 9y^2$ **17.** $64x^2 - 80x + 25$

19. 4 **21.** 18 in. **23.** \$5240 **25.** 2 hours later

CHAPTER 7   FACTORING

7-1   Page 212

Exploratory **1.** yes **3.** no **5.** yes **7.** composite;
$3 \cdot 13$ **9.** composite; $7 \cdot 13$ **11.** 4 **13.** 9 **15.** 11
17. 10 **19.** 36 *Written* **1.** $3 \cdot 7$ **3.** $2^2 \cdot 3 \cdot 5$
5. $3 \cdot 13$ **7.** $2 \cdot 17$ **9.** $2^4 \cdot 7$ **11.** $2^4 \cdot 19$
13. $2^2 \cdot 3 \cdot 5^2$ **15.** $2^2 \cdot 5 \cdot 7 \cdot 11$ **17.** $-1 \cdot 2 \cdot 13$
19. $-1 \cdot 2 \cdot 2 \cdot 5 \cdot 5 \cdot 5$ **21.** $2 \cdot 7 \cdot 7 \cdot a \cdot a \cdot b$
23. $2 \cdot 2 \cdot 7 \cdot 7 \cdot b \cdot b$ **25.** $-1 \cdot 2 \cdot 3 \cdot 17 \cdot x \cdot x \cdot x \cdot y$
27. 5 **29.** 29 **31.** 126 **33.** 19 **35.** $17a$ **37.** $2x$
39. 5 **41.** 6 **43.** 2 **45.** $4a$ **47.** $4a$ **49.** mn
51. 1 **53.** $2ab$ **55.** $4a$

7-2   Page 215

Exploratory **1.** 3 **3.** y **5.** 1 **7.** $3y$ **9.** $4x$
11. $7a$ **13.** xy **15.** 1 *Written* **1.** $4(4x + y)$
3. $12x(y + x)$ **5.** $11x(1 + 4xy)$ **7.** $5ab^2(5a + 6b)$
9. $2xy(7 - 9y)$ **11.** $12ab(3ab - 1)$ **13.** $2xy(7y + 1)$
15. $x(x^4y - 1)$ **17.** $a(17 - 41a^2b)$ **19.** $3(x^2y +$
$3y^2 + 2)$ **21.** $2ab(a^2b - 8ab^2 + 4)$ **23.** $x(24xy^2 +$
$12y + 1)$ **25.** $4x(3a + 5b + 8c)$ **27.** $x^3(a + 5b +$
$9c)$ **29.** $3x(2x - 3y + 8xy^2)$ **31.** $6x(4ab + 2ax +$
$x^2)$ **33.** $\frac{1}{2}x\left(x - \frac{1}{2}a\right)$ **35.** $\frac{1}{5}y\left(4x^2 + 3y\right)$

7-3   Page 218

Exploratory **1.** yes **3.** yes **5.** no **7.** no **9.** no
11. yes *Written* **1.** $(a - 3)(a + 3)$ **3.** $(2x - 3y)$
$(2x + 3y)$ **5.** $(a - 2b)(a + 2b)$ **7.** $(4a - 3b)(4a + 3b)$
9. $(4a - 5)(4a + 5)$ **11.** $6(x^2 + 2)$ **13.** $2(z - 7)$
$(z + 7)$ **15.** $2(2x - 3)(2x + 3)$ **17.** $(5y - 7z^2)$
$(5y + 7z^2)$ **19.** $17(1 - 2a)(1 + 2a)$ **21.** $(5ax - 1)$
$(5ax + 1)$ **23.** $12(a - 1)(a + 1)$ **25.** $9(2x - 3y^2)$
$(2x + 3y^2)$ **27.** $9(3 - x)(3 + x)$ **29.** $(2y - 3)(2y + 3)$

31. $(x - y)(x + y)(x^2 + y^2)$ **33.** $(x - 1)(x + 1)(x^2 + 1)$

35. $\frac{1}{2}(3x - 7y)(3x + 7y)$ **37.** $(x - 1)(x + 1)$

$(x^2 + 1)(x^4 + 1)$ **39.** $(x - y - y)(x - y + y)$ or $(x - 2y)x$
41. $[a - (b - c)][a + (b - c)]$ or
$(a - b + c)(a + b - c)$ **43.** $(x - 2)(x + 2)(x^2 + 4)$
45. $2(7x^3 - 8y^4)(7x^3 + 8y^4)$

7-4   Page 222

Exploratory **1.** yes, $(a + 2)^2$ **3.** no **5.** no **7.** no
9. yes, $(2x - 1)^2$ **11.** yes, $(3b - 1)^2$
Written **1.** $(a + 6)^2$ **3.** $(x + 8)^2$ **5.** $(2a + 1)^2$
7. $(1 - 5a)^2$ **9.** not factorable **11.** $(5x + 2)^2$
13. $(11y + 1)^2$ **15.** $(5b - 3)^2$ **17.** not factorable
19. $(m + 8n)^2$ **21.** $(3x + 4y)^2$ **23.** $9(4p + 1)^2$
25. $(8x - 5)^2$ **27.** $3(x + 6)^2$ **29.** $6(x^2 + 3x + 4)$
31. $(2x + z^2)^2$ **33.** $\left(\frac{1}{2}a + 3\right)^2$ **35.** $(m^2 + 6n^2)^2$
37. $\left(3a + \frac{4}{5}\right)^2$ **39.** 42 or -42 **41.** 4 **43.** y^2 **45.** $4y^2$

7-5   Page 226

Exploratory **1.** 1, 14 **3.** -2, -6 **5.** 9, -4
7. 3, -10 **9.** 3, 15 **11.** 3, -20 **13.** 10 **15.** 7
17. $+8$ **19.** $+7m$ *Written* **1.** $(y + 3)(y + 9)$
3. $(c + 3)(c - 1)$ **5.** $(y - 3)(y - 5)$
7. $(m - 5)(m + 4)$ **9.** prime **11.** $(z - 13)(z + 3)$
13. $(r - 12)(r + 2)$ **15.** $(y + 10)(y - 2)$
17. $(p + 2)(p + 8)$ **19.** $(b - 4)(b - 7)$
21. $(15 + m)(1 + m)$ **23.** $(y + 4)(y + 7)$
25. $(a - 20)(a + 2)$ **27.** $(x - 6)(x + 3)$
29. prime **31.** $(m - 11)(m + 5)$ **33.** $(11 - j)(6 - j)$
35. $(21 - a)(2 - a)$ **37.** $(c - 4d)(c + 2d)$
39. $(a + 3b)(a - b)$ **41.** $(a + b - 6)(a + b + 1)$
43. 7, -7, 11, -11 **45.** 12, -12 **47.** 8, -8
49. 4, -4 **51.** 10, -10, 22, -22 **53.** 13, 5, -5, -13

7-6   Page 229

Exploratory **1.** $(k - m)(r + s)$ **3.** $(4b + y)(x - y)$
5. $(7rp - 4q)(r - 3p)$ **7.** $(8m + 1)(x + y)$
9. $(5mp - 3bc)(2m + 3p)$ **11.** $(4m - 3p)(y - 5)$
13. $(7x + 3m - 4p)(a + b)$
15. $(a + b - c)(8r - 3y)$ *Written* **1.** $x + y$
3. $a + 3b$ **5.** $a - 4c$ **7.** $4m - 3p$ or $3p - 4m$
9. $6x + 7y$ **11.** $3a + 2b^2$ **13.** $(2x + b)(a + 3c)$
15. $(y + 4)(a + p)$ **17.** $(m + x)(2y + 7)$ **19.** $(a - c)$
$(y - b)$ **21.** $(a + 1)(a - 2b)$ **23.** $(4x + 3y)(a + b)$
25. $(m^2 + p^2)(3 - 5p)$ **27.** $(a - 3b^2)(5a - 4b)$
29. $3(2a - c)(a - b)$ **31.** $a(x + ax - 1 - 2a)$
33. $(7m + 2n)(p + q)(p - q)$ **35.** $(x + 1)(x - 1)(x + 2)$
37. $(a^2 + b^2)(a - b)$ **39.** $(7m - 5y)(a + b)(a - b)$
41. $(m - 2)(a + 2)(a + 3)$
43. $(2x + 3y)(a - 4)(a - 3)$

Exploratory 1. 2, 9   3. 3, 8   5. −2, − 6
7. −5, −4   9. − 4, 10   11. −15, 2   13. −4, 15
Written 1. $(3y + 5)(y + 1)$ 3. $(3x + 2)(x + 2)$
5. $(4m − 3)(2m − 1)$ 7. $(2h − 3)(h + 1)$
9. $(3k − 2)(k + 3)$ 11. $(3p − 2)(2p + 1)$
13. $(2a + 7)(a − 2)$ 15. $(3t − 2)(2t + 3)$
17. $(2y − 3)(y − 1)$ 19. $(2q + 3)(q − 6)$
21. $(3m + 2)(2m + 5)$ 23. $(3x − 11)(2x + 1)$ 25. prime
27. $(4p − 3)(2p − 3)$ 29. $(5p − 2)(3p + 4)$
31. $(2y − 3)(3y − 5)$ 33. $(2s + 5)(3s − 4)$
35. $(9x + 5)(2x + 5)$ 37. $(9c − 2)(2c + 5)$
39. $(2r − 3)(9r + 4)$ 41. $(4m − n)(2m − 3n)$
43. $(4x − 5y)(4x + y)$ 45. $(4p − q)(5p + 4q)$
47. $(3k + 5m)(3k + 5m)$ 49. $(5s + 8t)(4s − 3t)$
51. $(4x − 3q)(2x − 9q)$ 53. $(2c + 5d)(7c + 3d)$

7-8   **Page 237**

Exploratory 1. $3(x^2 + 5)$ 3. $a(5x + 6y)$
5. $6a(2x^2 + 3y^2)$ 7. $5x^2(1 − 2y)$ 9. $3ab(a + 2 + 3b)$
11. $(a + 3b)(a − 3b)$ *Written* 1. $2(a + 6)(a − 6)$
3. $m(m + 3)^2$ 5. $4a(a + 3)(a − 3)$ 7. $(m^2 + p)$
$(m^2 − p)$ 9. $(2k + 1)(k + 1)$ 11. $6(y + 2x)(y − 2x)$
13. $3(y + 8)(y − 1)$ 15. $2(5y + 1)(2y + 3)$
17. $2(b^2 + 3b + 1)$ 19. $(m + 4n)^2$
21. $3(2p − 7)(p + 5)$ 23. $a(3x + 7)(x + 3)$
25. $3a(3a − 2)(a + 8)$ 27. $3(x − 5y)(x + 2y)$
29. $m(mn + 7)(mn − 7)$ 31. $3(x + 11y)(x − 3y)$
33. $4(x^2 + 9)(x + 3)(x − 3)$ 35. $(3y + 1)(3y − 1)(y^2 + 1)$
37. $6r(5r − 2s)(2r − s)$ 39. $(y^2 + z^2)(x + 1)(x − 1)$
41. $0.7(y + 3)(y − 3)$ 43. $\frac{1}{3}(b + 3)^2$ 45. $\frac{1}{4}(r + 4)(r + 2)$
47. $0.7(y + 2)(y + 3)$

CHAPTER REVIEW   Page 240
1. $2 \cdot 3 \cdot 7$ 3. $2 \cdot 2 \cdot 2 \cdot 2 \cdot 5$ or $2^4 \cdot 5$
5. $11 \cdot 11 \cdot a \cdot a \cdot a \cdot a \cdot b \cdot b \cdot b \cdot b$ 7. 5   9. $2ab$
11. $6(x^2y + 2xy + 1)$ 13. $2a(12b + 9c + 16a)$
15. $\frac{1}{4}(3x + y)$ 17. $(5 + 3y)(5 − 3y)$
19. $2(y + 8)(y − 8)$ 21. $(x^2 + 1)(x + 1)(x − 1)$
23. $(4x − 1)^2$ 25. $2(4x − 5)^2$ 27. $\left(y − \frac{3}{4}\right)^2$
29. $(b − 3)(b − 5)$ 31. $(b − 1)(b + 6)$
33. $(a − 7)(a + 4)$ 35. $(s + 13)(s − 3)$
37. $(m − 7n)(m + 6n)$ 39. $(r − 13s)(r + 5s)$
41. $(m − 1)(4m − 3p)$ 43. $(m + 7)(b + r)$
45. $(4k − p)(4k − 7p)$ 47. $(4m + 3)(m + 2)$
49. $(2r + 5)(r − 4)$ 51. $(2m − 1)(2m − 3)$
53. $(3x − 4)(x + 5)$ 55. $3(x + 2)(x − 2)$
57. $a(3y + 4)(4y + 5)$ 59. $(x + 7)(x − 7)(m + b)$

8-1   **Page 246**

Exploratory 1. $x = 0$ or $x + 3 = 0$ 3. $3r = 0$ or
$r − 4 = 0$ 5. $3t = 0$ or $4t − 32 = 0$ 7. $x − 6 = 0$
or $x + 4 = 0$ 9. $a + 3 = 0$ or $3a − 12 = 0$
11. $2y + 8 = 0$ or $3y + 24 = 0$ 13. $x − 3 = 0$
15. $3x + 2 = 0$ or $x − 7 = 0$ 17. $4x − 7 = 0$ or
$3x + 5 = 0$ 19. $2x + 3 = 0$ or $x + 7 = 0$
Written 1. $\{0, −3\}$ 3. $\{0, 4\}$ 5. $\{0, 8\}$
7. $\{6, −4\}$ 9. $\{−3, 4\}$ 11. $\{−4, −8\}$ 13. $\{3\}$
15. $\left\{−\frac{2}{3}, 7\right\}$ 17. $\left\{\frac{7}{4}, −\frac{5}{3}\right\}$ 19. $\left\{−\frac{3}{2}, −7\right\}$
21. Sue is 16 years old.   23. The number is − 2.

8-2   **Page 249**

Exploratory 1. GCF   3. Perfect Square Trinomial
5. Trinomial with two binomial factors   7. GCF
9. Difference of Squares   11. Trinomial with two
binomial factors   *Written* 1. $x^2(x − 5)$
3. $(3x − 2y)^2$ 5. $(7z − 3)(5z + 4)$ 7. $2(2x − 9)^2$
9. $(1 + 7k)(1 − 7k)$ 11. $(x − 2)(x − 3)$
13. $2x(3x + 5y)$ 15. $(2a + 3b)(2a − 3b)$
17. $(x + 6)^2$ 19. $(4y − 3)(3y + 7)$
21. $(x + 5)(x + 3)(x − 3)$ 23. $m^2(m + n)(m − n)$
25. $5a^2(2c + 3)^2$ 27. $3x^2y(5x − 2y^2 + z)$
29. $8x(x + 2y^2)(x − 2y^2)$ 31. $(x + 2)(x^2 + 8)$
33. $12(x + 2y)(x − 3y)$ 35. $[(x + y) + (a − b)]$
$[(x + y) − (a − b)]$ 37. $2(3x − 2y)(x + y)$
39. $\left(\frac{m}{2} + \frac{3}{5}\right)\left(\frac{m}{2} − \frac{3}{5}\right)$ 41. $(2x − 7y)(3a + 5b)$
43. prime   45. $[(x + 3) + y][(x + 3) − y]$

8-3   **Page 252**

Exploratory 1. $n(n − 3) = 0$ 3. $8c(c + 4) = 0$
5. $3x\left(x − \frac{1}{4}\right) = 0$ 7. $7y(y − 2) = 0$
9. $13y(2y − 1) = 0$ 11. $(y + 4)(y − 4) = 0$
13. $(y − 8)(y − 8) = 0$ 15. $(y − 5)(y − 5) = 0$
Written 1. $\{0, 6\}$ 3. $\{0, −2\}$ 5. $\{9, −9\}$
7. $\{0, − 9\}$ 9. $\{0, − 8\}$ 11. $\{6, − 6\}$ 13. $\{0, − 5\}$
15. $\left\{\frac{2}{3}, −\frac{2}{3}\right\}$ 17. $\{3, − 3\}$ 19. $\{2, −2\}$ 21. $\{−5\}$
23. $\left\{−\frac{2}{9}\right\}$ 25. $\left\{\frac{4}{9}, −\frac{4}{9}\right\}$ 27. $\left\{0, \frac{1}{6}\right\}$ 29. 2 meters
31. 5   33. 10 or − 10   35. 25 or −25

8-4   **Page 255**

Exploratory 1. $\{−7, 3\}$ 3. $\{8, 2\}$ 5. $\left\{−\frac{3}{2}, −1\right\}$
7. $\left\{\frac{4}{3}, \frac{1}{2}\right\}$ 9. $\{5, −3\}$ 11. $\left\{0, −\frac{7}{2}, −\frac{4}{3}\right\}$
Written 1. $\{−4, −9\}$ 3. $\{−7, 3\}$ 5. $\{−9, 7\}$

7. $\{-7, 7\}$ **9.** $\{0, 12\}$ **11.** $\{8, -3\}$ **13.** $\left\{\frac{3}{2}, -5\right\}$

15. $\left\{-\frac{1}{3}, -\frac{5}{2}\right\}$ **17.** $\left\{\frac{3}{2}, -8\right\}$ **19.** $\{0, 9, -9\}$

21. $\{0, 2, 4\}$ **23.** $\left\{0, \frac{1}{5}, -7\right\}$ **25.** $\left\{0, -\frac{5}{2}, 3\right\}$

27. $\{-4, 12\}$ **29.** $\left\{\frac{10}{3}, 30\right\}$ **31.** $\{-4, -5\}$

33. $\left\{\frac{2}{3}, -4\right\}$ **35.** $\{-2, -1, 2\}$ **37.** $\left\{\frac{1}{3}, -\frac{1}{3}, 2\right\}$

39. $\{2, -2\}$ **41.** $\{(x, y) \,|\, x = 3 \text{ or } y = -4\}$

43. $\left\{(r, s) \,|\, r = -2 \text{ or } s = \frac{4}{3}\right\}$

8-5   **Page 257**

Exploratory   **1.** Let x = smaller integer; $x(x + 1) = 110$ **3.** Let x = smaller integer; $x(x + 2) = 168$
5. Let x = one integer; $x(15 - x) = 44$ **7.** Let x = smaller integer; $x^2 + (x + 1)^2 = 181$ **9.** Let x = smaller integer; $(x + 1)^2 - x^2 = 17$ or $x^2 - (x + 1)^2 = 17$ *Written*   **1.** 10, 11; $-10, -11$
3. 12, 14; $-12, -14$ **5.** 4, 11   **7.** 9, 10; $-9, -10$
9. 8, 9; $-8, -9$ **11.** 10, 12; $-10, -12$ **13.** 13, 15
15. 13, 14   **17.** 3, 8   **19.** 8, 11; $-8, -11$ **21.** 9, 11
23. 4, 9   **25.** 5, 6; $-8, -7$ **27.** 6, 8; $-12, -10$
29. 13, 15, 17   **31.** Colleen is 48; Jim is 49

8-6   **Page 261**

Exploratory   **1.** Let x = width; $x(x + 3) = 108$
3. Let x = length; $x(x - 9) = 90$ **5.** Let x = side of smaller square; $(x + 7)^2 = x^2 + 231$
7. Let x = side of smaller square; $(2x)^2 = x^2 + 363$
Written   **1.** length, 12 ft; width, 9 ft   **3.** length, 15 ft; width, 6 ft   **5.** 13 in., 20 in.   **7.** 11 in.

9. 5m $\times$ 8m   **11.** 6″ $\times$ 9″   **13.** $2\frac{1}{2}$ ft   **15.** 176 ft/s
17. 156 ft   **19.** 12 s   **21.** 20 s, 125 s   **23.** $\frac{1}{2}$s, 102 s

8-7   **Page 264**

Exploratory   **1.** $24; \frac{1}{3}$ **3.** $6y; \frac{7}{3x}$ **5.** $2a; \frac{19a}{21b}$

7. $3x^2y^2; \frac{-y^3}{6x^3}$ **9.** $x; \frac{y + 1}{y - 2}$ **11.** $m + 5; \frac{1}{2}$

Written   **1.** $\frac{1}{y + 4}$ **3.** $\frac{1}{a - b}$ **5.** $\frac{c - 2}{c + 2}$ **7.** a

9. $\frac{1}{x^2 - 4}$ **11.** $\frac{x^2 + 3}{x + 3}$ **13.** $\frac{-2}{1 - 2y}$ **15.** $\frac{-4a}{a^2 + 6ab + 9b}$

17. $\frac{1}{x + y}$ **19.** $\frac{1}{x + 4}$ **21.** $\frac{m - 4}{m + 4}$ **23.** $\frac{y - 3}{y + 3}$

25. $x + 5$ **27.** $\frac{6x}{x + 4}$ **29.** $\frac{2k + 5}{2k - 5}$ **31.** $\frac{1}{2 - 5x}$

33. $\frac{5}{3}$ **35.** $\frac{m - 4}{m - 3}$ **37.** $\frac{p - 2}{p + 6}$ **39.** $\frac{2x - 3}{3x - 2}$

41. $y + 3$ **43.** $\frac{2x + 8}{x - 11}$ **45.** $\frac{1}{x}$

CHAPTER REVIEW   **Page 266**

1. $\{0, -11\}$ **3.** $\{0, 5\}$ **5.** $\left\{\frac{2}{3}, -\frac{7}{4}\right\}$ **7.** $\{6\}$

9. $m(2m - 3)(3m + 5)$ **11.** $(8m - 3n)(3a + 5b)$
13. $(7m + 5n)^2$ **15.** $8(a^2 + 4b^2)$ **17.** $\{0, -7\}$
19. $\{0, 3\}$ **21.** $\left\{-\frac{2}{5}\right\}$ **23.** $\{-5, -8\}$ **25.** $\left\{\frac{3}{2}, -8\right\}$
27. $\left\{\frac{4}{3}, \frac{1}{2}\right\}$ **29.** 11, 13; $-11, -13$ **31.** 8″ $\times$ 10″
33. $\frac{x}{4y^2z}$ **35.** $\frac{x + 3}{x - 3}$

CHAPTER 9   FUNCTIONS AND GRAPHS

9-1   **Page 273**

Exploratory   **1.** (1, 4)   **3.** $(-3, 3)$ **5.** $(-1, -2)$
7. (4, 0)   **9.** (1, 1)   **11.** $(-1, -1)$ **13.** $(-2, 2)$
15. $(-3, -4)$ **17.** (2, 2)   **19.** $3, -1$ **21.** I   **23.** II
25. none   **27.** IV   **29.** IV   **31.** II   **33.** II   **35.** III
37. IV   **39.** none   **41.** I   **43.** III

9-2   **Page 275**

Exploratory   **1.** $D = \{0, 1, 2\}, R = \{2, -2, 4\}$
3. $D = \{-3, -2, -1, 0\}, R = \{1, 0, 2\}$
5. $D = \{7, -2, 4, 5, -9\}, R = \{5, -3, 0, -7, 2\}$
7. $D = \{-3, -2, 3, 0\}, R = \{0, -5, 6, 7, -17\}$
9. $D = \{3.1, 4.7, 2.4, -9\}, R = \{-1, 3.9, -3.6,$

12.12$\}$ **11.** $D = \left\{\frac{1}{2}, 1\frac{1}{2}, -3, -5\frac{1}{4}\right\},$

$R = \left\{\frac{1}{4}, -\frac{2}{3}, \frac{2}{5}, -7\frac{2}{7}\right\}$ **13.** $\{(1, 5), (2, 7),$

$(3, 9), (4, 11)\}, D = \{1, 2, 3, 4\},$
$R = \{5, 7, 9, 11\}$ **15.** $\{(-4, 1), (-2, 3), (0, 1) (2, 3)$
$(4, 1)\}, D = \{-4, -2, 0, 2, 4\} R = \{1, 3\}$
Written   **1.** $\{(1, 5), (2, 3), (3, -2), (4, 9)\}$ **3.** $\{1, 7),$
$(-2, 7), (3, 7)\}$ **5.** $\{(4, 2), (-3, 2), (8, 2), (8, 9),$
$(7, 5)\}$ **7.** $\{(1, 3), (2, 4), (3, 5), (4, 6), (5, 7)\}$
9. $\{(8, 1), (7, 3), (6, 5), (2, -2)\}$ **11.** $\{(1, 3), (2, 5),$
$(1, -7), (2, 9)\}$ **13.** $\{(-2, 2), (-1, 1), (0, 1), (1, 1),$
$(1, -1), (2, -1), (3, 1)\}; D = \{-2, -1, 0, 1, 2, 3\},$
$R = \{2, 1, -1\}$ **15.** $\{(-3, 0), (-2, 2), (-1, 3),$
$(0, 1), (1, -1), (1, -2), (1, -3), (3, -2)\};$
$D = \{-3, -2, -1, 0, 1, 3\}, R = \{-3, -2, -1, 0,$
$1, 2, 3\}$ **17.** $\{(-3, 3), (-1, 2), (1, 1), (1, 3), (2, 0),$
$(2, -1), (3, -1)\}, D = \{-3, -1, 1, 2, 3\},$
$R = \{-1, 0, 1, 2, 3\}$

9-3   **Page 281**

Exploratory   **1.** $\{(-4, -12), (-2, -6), (0, 0), (1, 3),$

$(2, 6), (3, 9)\}$ **3.** $\left\{(-4, -1), \left(-2, \frac{1}{3}\right), \left(0, \frac{5}{3}\right), \left(1, \frac{7}{3}\right),$

$\left(3, \frac{11}{3}\right)\right\}$ *Written*   **1.** $y = 5 - x$ **3.** $b = 3 + 5a$

5. $y = 3 - 4x$ **7.** $b = \frac{7 - 4a}{3}$ **9.** $y = \frac{6x - 2}{3}$

11. $q = \frac{4p - 7}{-2}$ **13.** a, c   **15.** a, d   **17.** a, c
19. $\{(-2, -3), (-1, -1), (0, 1), (2, 5), (5, 11)\}$

21. $\{(-2, 9), (-1, 8), (0, 7), (2, 5), (5, 2)\}$

23. $\{(-2, 11), (-1, 9), (0, 7), (2, 3), (5, -3)\}$

25. $\left\{\left(-2, \frac{17}{3}\right), (-1, 5), \left(0, \frac{13}{3}\right), (2, 3), (5, 1)\right\}$

27. $\left\{\left(-2, -\frac{11}{2}\right), (-1, -4), \left(0, -\frac{5}{2}\right), \left(2, \frac{1}{2}\right), (5, 5)\right\}$

29. $\left(-2, \frac{9}{2}\right), \left(-1, \frac{13}{4}\right), (0, 2), \left(2, -\frac{1}{2}\right), \left(5, -\frac{17}{4}\right)\}$

31. $\left\{(-2, 5), \left(-1, \frac{31}{6}\right), \left(0, \frac{16}{3}\right), \left(2, \frac{17}{3}\right), \left(5, \frac{37}{6}\right)\right\}$

33. $\left\{\left(-2, \frac{23}{5}\right), \left(-1, \frac{17}{5}\right), \left(0, \frac{11}{5}\right), \left(2, -\frac{1}{5}\right), \left(5, -\frac{19}{5}\right)\right\}$

35. $\left\{\left(-2, \frac{2}{5}\right), (-1, 1), \left(0, \frac{8}{5}\right), \left(2, \frac{14}{5}\right), \left(5, \frac{23}{5}\right)\right\}$

9-4   Page 285

Exploratory **1.** yes **3.** no **5.** yes **7.** no **9.** no
11. no **13.** no **15.** yes **17.** yes   *Written* **1.** no
3. no **5.** yes **7.** no **9.** yes **11.** no

9-5   Page 289

Exploratory **1.** no **3.** yes **5.** yes **7.** yes **9.** no
11. no **13.** no **15.** yes **17.** 3 **19.** -13 **21.** 0
Written **1.** yes **3.** no **5.** no **7.** yes **9.** yes
11. yes **13.** no **15.** yes **17.** yes **19.** yes **21.** 1

23. 20 **25.** $-3\frac{1}{2}$ **27.** $\frac{3}{4}$ **29.** $6a - 5$ **31.** 30

33. 11.5 **35.** $3a + 4$

9-6   Page 293

Exploratory **1.** a **3.** a, b, c **5.** a, c **7.** b

9-7   Page 295

Exploratory **1.** 11, 13, 15 **3.** 0, -3, -6 **5.** 55, 62,
69 **7.** 28, 39, 52 **9.** 25, 36, 49 **11.** 34, 55, 89
Written **1.** 13, 15, 17 **3.** $-13, -16,$ **5.** 16, 21, 31
7. $\frac{1}{9} \frac{1}{27}, \frac{1}{81}$ **9.** 1, 0, 1 **11.** $-5, -7, -9$ **13.** $y =$
$4x$; 20, 24 **15.** $n = 2m + 1$; 1, 3, 5, 7
17. $b = 4a + 3$; 19, 27, 35 **19.** $y = -x + 15$; 11, 9, 8
21. $b = -5a + 3$; $-2, -7, -17, -32$

CHAPTER REVIEW   Page 299

1. IV **3.** I **9.** $D = \{3, 2, 5\}, R = \{5, 6, 7\}$
11. $D = \{-3, 4\}, R = \{5, 6\}$ **13.** $\{(-1, 4), (3, 4),$
$(4, 6), (0, -4)\}; D = \{-1, 3, 4, 0\}, R = \{4, 6, -4\}$
15. $\{(3, 6), (3, -3), (4, 8), (5, 8), (5, 11), (5, 3)\};$
$D = \{3, 4, 5\}, R = \{6, -3, 8, 11, 3\}$ **17.** $\{(-2, -1),$
$(-1, -1), (0, 1), (1, 2), (3, 2)\}; D = \{-2, -1, 0, 1, 3\},$
$R = \{-1, 1, 2\}$ **19.** $y = 7 - 3x$ **21.** c
23. $\{(-4, -11), (-2, -3), (0, 5), (2, 13), (4, 21)\}$

25. $\left\{\left(-4, \frac{21}{2}\right), \left(-2, \frac{15}{2}\right), \left(0, \frac{9}{2}\right), \left(2, \frac{3}{2}\right), \left(4, -\frac{3}{2}\right)\right\}$

27. no **29.** yes **35.** no **37.** yes **39.** 3 **41.** 1
43. 3 **49.** $y = 3x + 5$

CHAPTER 10   LINES AND SLOPES

10-1   Page 307

Exploratory **1.** 3 **3.** -1 **5.** $\frac{2}{1} = 2$ **7.** $\frac{-1}{1} = -1$
9. $\frac{-4}{3} = -\frac{4}{3}$ **11.** 1 **13.** $\frac{7}{3}$ **15.** $\frac{2}{3}$
Written **1.** 3 **3.** $\frac{4}{3}$ **5.** undefined **7.** $\frac{1}{3}$ **13.** 2
15. $-\frac{3}{2}$ **17.** $\frac{2}{5}$ **19.** $\frac{3}{2}$ **21.** $\frac{1}{2}$ **23.** 0 **25.** $\frac{1}{2}$
27. $-\frac{2}{3}$ **29.** 9 **31.** 2 **33.** -23 **35.** 6

10-2   Page 311

Exploratory **1.** 3, (5, 2) **3.** $-2, (-1, -5)$

5. $-\frac{3}{2}, (-5, -6)$ **7.** 2, $\left(3, -\frac{3}{2}\right)$ **9.** $-\frac{3}{5}, \left(-6, -\frac{3}{8}\right)$

11. 0, (0, -2) **13.** $2x - y = -6$ **15.** $2x - 3y = -1$
17. $5x - 3y = -37$ *Written* **1.** $2x + 3y = 22$
3. $2x - 3y = 15$ **5.** $2x - y = 11$ **7.** $3x - 2y =$
-20 **9.** $y = 7$ **11.** $x = 1$ **13.** $x + y = 9$ **15.** $5x$
$+ y = 31$ **17.** $x + 4y = -4$ **19.** $x + 2y = -4$
21. $4x + 7y = -18$ **23.** $x = 5$ **25.** $4x + 10y = 13$
27. $2x + 3y = 6$ **29.** $2y = 1$ **31.** $x = -2$
33. $x = -2$

10-3   Page 314

Exploratory **1.** 5, 3, **3.** 3, -7 **5.** $\frac{1}{3}, 0$ **7.** $\frac{3}{5}, -\frac{1}{4}$
9. $\frac{3}{5}, \frac{1}{4}$ **11.** $\frac{1}{4}, \frac{3}{4}$ **13.** 6, 5 **15.** $\frac{3}{2}, \frac{7}{2}$ **17.** $\frac{1}{2}, \frac{7}{4}$
19. $x = c$ (c is any number)   *Written* **1.** $y = 3x + 1$
3. $y = -3x + 5$ **5.** $y = 4x - 2$ **7.** $y = \frac{1}{2}x + 5$
9. $y = -\frac{5}{4}x + 3$ **11.** 3, 5 **13.** 3, 6 **15.** 14, -4
17. $-\frac{11}{2}, -\frac{11}{5}$ **19.** $\frac{1}{2}, \frac{3}{2}$ **21.** $-1, -\frac{8}{3}$ **23.** $y =$
$-\frac{3}{4}x + 3$; $m = -\frac{3}{4}$, $b = 3$ **25.** $y = 3x - 9$; $m = 3$,
$b = -9$ **27.** $y = -\frac{7}{4}x + 2$; $m = -\frac{7}{4}$, $b = 2$
29. $y = \frac{7}{3}x - \frac{10}{3}$; $m = \frac{7}{3}$, $b = -\frac{10}{3}$ **31.** $y = 12x - 24$;
$m = 12, b = -24$ **33.** $y = -4x + 12$; $m = -4$;
$b = 12$ **35.** $y = -\frac{5}{2}x + 4$; $m = -\frac{5}{2}$, $b = 4$
37. $y = \frac{1}{2}x + \frac{3}{2}$; $m = \frac{1}{2}$, $b = \frac{3}{2}$ **39.** $y = \frac{3}{5}x - \frac{18}{5}$;
$m = \frac{3}{5}, b = -\frac{18}{5}$

10-4   Page 318

Exploratory **1.** 2, 8 **3.** 2, $\frac{3}{2}$ **5.** 4, -8 **7.** $\frac{10}{7}, 5$
9. $\frac{2}{5}, -4$ **11.** $\frac{1}{3}, -1$ **13.** $\frac{5}{2}, \frac{5}{3}$ **15.** 0, 0 **17.** (1, 3),
(2, 5) **19.** (1, -3), (2, -10) **21.** (7, 3), (9, 4)
23. $(-2, 14), (-1, 22)$

Exploratory **1.** -5 **3.** 9 **5.** -5 **7.** $-\frac{1}{3}$ **9.** $\frac{1}{3}$

11. $2, -2, y = 2x - 2$ **13.** $-4, 4, y = -4x + 4$

15. $-\frac{2}{3}, 2, y = -\frac{2}{3}x + 2$ *Written* **1.** $y = 3x - 17$

3. $y = \frac{2}{3}x + \frac{2}{3}$ **5.** $y = -5x + 29$ **7.** $y = \frac{3}{4}x - \frac{5}{2}$

9. $y = \frac{1}{4}x + 8$ **11.** $y = \frac{1}{2}x - \frac{1}{2}$ **13.** $y = x - 3$

15. $y = -x + 1$ **17.** $y = -\frac{4}{5}x - \frac{1}{5}$ **19.** $y = \frac{1}{6}x + \frac{37}{6}$

21. $y = \frac{1}{5}x + 6$

Exploratory **1.** $5, -\frac{1}{5}$ **3.** $2, -\frac{1}{2}$ **5.** $\frac{2}{3}, -\frac{3}{2}$

7. undefined, 0 **9.** $\frac{5}{3}, -\frac{3}{5}$ **11.** $4, -\frac{1}{4}$ **13.** $\frac{2}{3}, -\frac{3}{2}$

15. $-1, 1$ *Written* **1.** $y = -\frac{3}{5}x - 1$ **3.** $y = \frac{3}{4}x$

5. $y = \frac{5}{2}x - 4$ **7.** $y = \frac{3}{4}x + \frac{1}{2}$ **9.** $y = x - 9$

11. $y = \frac{8}{3}x + 4$ **13.** $y = \frac{1}{3}x + 2$

15. $y = -\frac{3}{2}x - \frac{9}{2}$ **17.** $y = \frac{9}{5}x$

Exploratory **1.** 6 **3.** 14 **5.** 5 **7.** $1\frac{1}{2}$ **9.** $2\frac{1}{2}$

11. $(5, 3)$ **13.** $(9, -8)$ **15.** $(1, 6)$ **17.** $\left(-1, -1\frac{1}{2}\right)$

19. $\left(5\frac{1}{2}, -5\frac{1}{2}\right)$ **21.** $(4x, 2y)$ *Written* **1.** $(10, 3)$

3. $(10, 3)$ **5.** $(8, 2)$ **7.** $(6, -2)$ **9.** $(1, -3)$

11. $\left(10, -1\frac{1}{2}\right)$ **13.** $\left(8\frac{1}{2}, 2\frac{1}{2}\right)$ **15.** $(3, 3)$

17. $\left(\frac{1}{2}, 5\frac{1}{2}\right)$,   **19.** $\left(\frac{3}{4}, \frac{1}{2}\right)$,   **21.** $\left(4\frac{5}{12}, 1\frac{7}{8}\right)$

23. $B(19, 9)$ **25.** $P(-1, 6)$ **27.** $A(13, 11)$

29. $B(6, -7)$ **31.** $P(-2, -3)$ **33.** $B(9, -18)$

35. $(-2, -7)$ **37.** $\left(\frac{1}{2}, 2\right)$ **39.** $\left(4\frac{1}{2}, -\frac{1}{2}\right)$ **41.** $(4, 1)$

43. $\left(-1\frac{1}{2}, 1\right)$

CHAPTER REVIEW   Page 332

1. 0 **3.** undefined   **5.** $y - 1 = -\frac{4}{11}(x - 8)$;

$4x + 11y = 43$ **7.** $y - 5 = \frac{5}{2}x; 5x - 2y = -10$

9. $\frac{3}{2}, -\frac{7}{2}$ **11.** $-8, 4$ **13.** $(5, 0)(0, 2)$

19. $y = 4x - 26$ **21.** $y = -\frac{5}{2}x + 7$ **23.** $y = 4x - 9$

25. $y = -\frac{7}{2}x - 14$ **27.** $(6, 1)$

CHAPTER 11   SYSTEMS OF OPEN SENTENCES

Exploratory **1.** $(6, 3)$ **3.** $(1, 3)$ **5.** $(0, 0)$ **7.** $(6, 3)$

9. $(3, -3)$ **11.** a, c, d **13.** a, d *Written* **1.** $(3, 1)$

3. $(5, 3)$ **5.** $(2, 2)$ **7.** $(2, 3)$ **9.** $(0, 0)$

11. $(-1, 2)$ **13.** $(-1, -5)$ **15.** $(-3, 1)$ **17.** $(3, 4)$

19. $(-2, -3)$ **21.** $(0.75, 0.5)$ **23.** $(4, -7)$

Exploratory **1.** $m = -1, b = 4; m = -\frac{2}{3}, b = 3$;

one   **3.** $m = -1, b = 6; m = -1, b = 1$; none

5. $m = -\frac{1}{2}, b = \frac{5}{2}; m = -\frac{1}{2}, b = \frac{5}{2}$; infinitely many

7. $m = -3, b = 0; m = \frac{1}{6}, b = -\frac{19}{3}$; one   **9.** $m = \frac{3}{7}$,

$b = \frac{6}{7}; m = -\frac{1}{2}, b = \frac{11}{2}$; one   **11.** $m = \frac{3}{8}, b = -\frac{1}{2}$;

$m = \frac{3}{8}, b = -\frac{21}{8}$; none   *Written* **1.** $(2, 0)$

3. none   **5.** $(2, 3)$ **7.** none   **9.** infinitely many

11. $(7, -3)$ **13.** none   **15.** infinitely many

17. $(0, -4)$

Exploratory **1.** $x = y + 1, y = x - 1$ **3.** $x = -\frac{3}{2}y$

$+ 3, y = -\frac{2}{3}x + 2$ **5.** $x = 6y - 14, y = \frac{1}{6}x + \frac{7}{3}$

7. $x = -y - 5, y = -x - 5$ **9.** $x = \frac{3}{4}y + 15, y = $

$\frac{4}{3}x - 20$ **11.** $x = -\frac{0.8}{0.75}y - \frac{6}{0.75}, y = -\frac{0.75}{0.8}x - \frac{6}{0.8}$

Written **1.** $\left(\frac{8}{5}, \frac{16}{5}\right)$ **3.** $\left(3, \frac{3}{2}\right)$ **5.** infinitely many

7. none   **9.** $(0, 0)$ **11.** $(-9, -7)$ **13.** $(4, 2)$

15. $(4, 3)$ **17.** $(1, 1)$

Exploratory **1.** yes   **3.** no   **5.** yes   **7.** no   **9.** yes

Written **1.** $(8, -1)$ **3.** $\left(\frac{11}{2}, -\frac{1}{2}\right)$ **5.** $(3, 4)$

7. $(1, 2)$ **9.** $(2, 1.5)$ **11.** $\left(3, \frac{19}{3}\right)$ **13.** $\frac{14}{9}, -\frac{16}{3}$

15. $(0, 25)$ **17.** $12, 36$ **19.** $38, 63$ **21.** 55 m, 45 m

23. $14, 23$ **25.** 18 men, 25 women

Exploratory **1.** To eliminate x, multiply the first equation by 3 and subtract. To eliminate y, multiply the second equation by 2 and subtract.   **3.** To eliminate x, multiply the first equation by 4 and subtract. To eliminate y, multiply the second equation by 4 and add.   **5.** To eliminate x, multiply the second equation by 4 and subtract. To eliminate y, multiply the first equation by 2 and add.   **7.** To eliminate x, multiply the second equation by 8 and subtract. To eliminate y, multiply the second equation by 3 and subtract.   **9.** To eliminate x, multiply the second equation by 2 and subtract. To eliminate y, simply subtract. **11.** To eliminate x, multiply the second equation by 1.2 and subtract. To eliminate y, multiply the first equation by 2 and add. *Written* **1.** $\left(\frac{11}{2}, -\frac{1}{2}\right)$

3. $\left(\frac{5}{2}, 5\right)$ **5.** (1, 1) **7.** $\left(-1, \frac{9}{2}\right)$ **9.** $\left(\frac{20}{9}, \frac{5}{3}\right)$
11. (5, 1) **13.** (8, −2) **15.** (−9, −2) **17.** (6, 2)
19. (3, 3) **21.** (10, 25) **23.** (4, 16) **25.** (0, 0)
27. (0, −2) **29.** 14, 34 **31.** 6, 2 **33.** 28 m, 112 m
35. Layla is 30; Diana is 10. **37.** 13 cm, 7 cm

39. 19, 5 **41.** 16, 36

11-6   Page 353

Exploratory **1.** yes **3.** yes **5.** B **7.** C
Written **21.** $x \le 2, y \ge 2$ **23.** $y \ge -x, y < -x + 3$

25. $y < -\frac{1}{2}x + 2, y \ge 0$

11-7   Page 357

Written **1.** 24 **3.** 82 **5.** 16 **7.** 48 **9.** 51 **11.** 35
13. 94 **15.** 72 **17.** 603 **19.** 370 **21.** 39
23. 40, 51, 62, 73, 84, 95 **25.** $\frac{21}{12}, \frac{42}{24}, \frac{63}{36}, \frac{84}{48}$

11-8   Page 360

Written **1.** The rate of the boat is 4 mph. The rate of the current is 1 mph. **3.** 7 lb., 3 lb. **5.** 20 at 20¢, 10 at 35¢ **7.** The rate of the wind is 50 mph. The rate of the plane is 550 mph. **9.** $1000 at 10%, $3000 at 12% **11.** 280 miles **13.** 42 mph and 48 mph **15.** 4 mph **17.** 1 mph

CHAPTER REVIEW   Page 365

1. (1, 1) **3.** (6, 5) **5.** none **7.** one **9.** (3, −5)
11. (4, −2) **13.** $\left(\frac{1}{2}, \frac{1}{2}\right)$ **15.** (2, 0) **17.** (2, −1)
19. (5, 1) **21.** (−9, −7) **23.** (2, −1) **25.** (−4, 6)
29. 16 cm, 9 cm **31.** 35 **33.** 5 mph

CHAPTER 12   RADICALS

12-1   Page 373

Exploratory **1.** 100 **3.** 49 **5.** .009 **7.** $\frac{1}{4}$ **9.** $\frac{49}{64}$
11. 11 **13.** −9 **15.** $\frac{2}{3}$ **17.** $\pm\frac{7}{11}$ **19.** 0.04

Written **1.** 7 **3.** 4 **5.** $\frac{5}{6}$ **7.** $\frac{3}{7}$ **9.** 0.03 **11.** 0.06
13. 6 **15.** −10 **17.** ±5 **19.** 0.6 **21.** 23
23. 26 **25.** −21 **27.** ±32 **29.** 27 **31.** 42
33. $-\frac{17}{10}$ **35.** 3 **37.** $\frac{16}{19}$ **39.** $\pm\frac{31}{27}$ **41.** $\frac{8}{9}$ **43.** $\frac{3}{4}$

12-2   Page 376

Exploratory **1.** Z, Q **3.** N, W, Z, Q **5.** Q **7.** N, W, Z, Q **9.** I **11.** Q **13.** 1.414 **15.** 4.472

17. 256 **19.** 5.568 **21.** 9.434 **23.** 4,356
Written **7.** I **9.** Q **11.** Q **13.** I **15.** Q, 82
17. I, $61 < \sqrt{3,800} < 62$ **19.** I, $29 < \sqrt{888} < 30$
21. Q, 95 **23.** I, $84 < \sqrt{7,166} < 85$ **25.** Q, 38

12-3   Page 378

Exploratory **1.** 16 **3.** 49 **5.** 64 **7.** 49 **9.** 9
11. 81 **13.** 4 **15.** 6 **17.** 5 *Written* **1.** 8 **3.** 6
5. 10 **7.** 12 **9.** 13 **11.** 12 **13.** 9.219
15. 7.765 **17.** 12.206557 **19.** 13.892444
21. 11.462986 **23.** 13.251415 **25.** 0.781
27. 0.06797

12-4   Page 380

Exploratory **1.** $2\sqrt{2}$ **3.** $2\sqrt{5}$ **5.** $2\sqrt{6}$ **7.** $4\sqrt{3}$
9. $|m|$ **11.** $x^2\sqrt{x}$ **13.** $2a\sqrt{2a}$ **15.** $ab\sqrt{ab}$ **17.** 6
19. $5\sqrt{2}$ **21.** 11 **23.** $3 + \sqrt{6}$ **25.** $\sqrt{35} - 7$
Written **1.** $3\sqrt{3}$ **3.** $3\sqrt{5}$ **5.** $6\sqrt{2}$ **7.** $3\sqrt{10}$
9. $8\sqrt{2}$ **11.** $10\sqrt{5}$ **13.** $12\sqrt{5}$ **15.** 72 **17.** $4|x|\sqrt{2}$
19. $2b^2\sqrt{10}$ **21.** $6|ab|$ **23.** $2|a|\sqrt{30ab}$
25. $2|x|y^2\sqrt{15}$ **27.** $2|m|n^3\sqrt{5n}$ **29.** $8m^2|n^3|\sqrt{5}$
31. $|x|\sqrt{21y}$ **33.** $4\sqrt{3}$ **35.** 10 **37.** $14\sqrt{15}$
39. 150 **41.** $60\sqrt{3}$ **43.** $3 + 3\sqrt{2}$ **45.** $\sqrt{42} - 3\sqrt{2}$
47. $5\sqrt{2} - \sqrt{10}$ **49.** $\sqrt{15} + 9$ **51.** $12 + 4\sqrt{21}$
53. 49 cm^2

12-5   Page 384

Exploratory **1.** 2 **3.** 8 **5.** $\sqrt{3} - 4; -13$
7. $6 - \sqrt{8}; 28$ **9.** $\sqrt{2} - \sqrt{5}; -3$ **11.** $2\sqrt{5} + \sqrt{6};$
14 **13.** $\frac{\sqrt{5}}{\sqrt{5}}$ **15.** $\frac{\sqrt{6}}{\sqrt{6}}$ **17.** $\frac{\sqrt{5}}{\sqrt{5}}$ **19.** $\frac{3 - \sqrt{7}}{3 - \sqrt{7}}$
Written **1.** $\sqrt{7}$ **3.** $\frac{\sqrt{70}}{7}$ **5.** $\frac{\sqrt{3}}{3}$ **7.** $\frac{\sqrt{21}}{7}$ **9.** $\frac{\sqrt{35}}{10}$
11. $\frac{\sqrt{15}}{3}$ **13.** $\frac{\sqrt{3a}}{3}$ **15.** $\frac{|a|\sqrt{5}}{5}$ **17.** $\frac{3\sqrt{3}}{|b|}$
19. $\frac{n^2\sqrt{5mn}}{2|m^3|}$ **21.** $\frac{7 + \sqrt{3}}{46}$ **23.** $\frac{55 - 11\sqrt{2}}{23}$ **25.** $6\sqrt{3}$
$- 6\sqrt{2}$ **27.** $\frac{20a + 10a\sqrt{a}}{4 - a}$ **29.** $\frac{-6\sqrt{5} - 2\sqrt{30}}{3}$
31. $\frac{9\sqrt{2} + 9}{2}$ **33.** $\frac{5\sqrt{21} - 3\sqrt{35}}{15}$ **35.** $\frac{12\sqrt{10} + 3\sqrt{35}}{25}$

12-6   Page 386

Exploratory **1.** $5\sqrt{3}, 3\sqrt{3}$ **3.** $3\sqrt{12}, 5\sqrt{12}$
5. $-3\sqrt{3}, 12\sqrt{3}$ **7.** $2\sqrt{10}, -6\sqrt{10}, 7\sqrt{10}$ **9.** $2\sqrt{5},$
$3\sqrt{5}, -5\sqrt{5}$ **11.** $-3\sqrt{3}$ **13.** $11\sqrt{6}$ **15.** $11\sqrt{y}$
17. $3\sqrt{15} - 2\sqrt{5}$ **19.** $26\sqrt{13}$ **21.** $40\sqrt{19}$
23. $-5\sqrt{3a}$ *Written* **1.** $11\sqrt{11}$ **3.** $-4\sqrt{13}$
5. $17\sqrt{7}$ **7.** $9\sqrt{3}$ **9.** $\sqrt{7}$ **11.** $-10\sqrt{5}$ **13.** $\sqrt{2} +$
$13\sqrt{3}$ **15.** $4\sqrt{6} + 5\sqrt{7} - 6\sqrt{2}$ **17.** $\sqrt{3} + \sqrt{5}$
19. $4\sqrt{3}$ **21.** $-\sqrt{7}$ **23.** $35\sqrt{5}$ **25.** $-18\sqrt{7}$
27. $8\sqrt{2} + 6\sqrt{3}$ **29.** $48\sqrt{2} + \sqrt{5}$ **31.** $20\sqrt{3}$
33. $\frac{8\sqrt{7}}{7}$ **35.** $\frac{2\sqrt{3}}{3}$ **37.** 0 **39.** $\frac{85\sqrt{7}}{14}$

12-7   Page 390

Exploratory **1.** 9 **3.** none **5.** 4 **7.** none
Written **1.** 25 **3.** 3 **5.** none **7.** 25 **9.** none
11. $\frac{9}{2}$ **13.** 2 **15.** 3 **17.** 144 **19.** 3 **21.** 80
23. 45 **25.** $\pm\sqrt{22}$ **27.** 11 **29.** 7 **31.** 6
33. 169

12-8   Page 393

Exploratory **1.** 5 **3.** 13 **5.** 8 **7.** 8 **9.** True
11. False   *Written* **1.** 13 **3.** $3\sqrt{3}$ **5.** 9 **7.** 16
9. 21 **11.** 4 **13.** no **15.** yes **17.** $\sqrt{89}\ m$
19. $4\sqrt{6}\ m$

12-9   Page 395

Exploratory **1.** $x_1 = 3, x_2 = 6, y_1 = 4, y_2 = 8$
3. $x_1 = -4, x_2 = 4, y_1 = 2, y_2 = 17$ **5.** $x_1 = -3, x_2 = 2, y_1 = 5, y_2 = 7$ **7.** $x_1 = -8, x_2 = -3, y_1 = -4, y_2 = 8$ **9.** $x_1 = 3, x_2 = -2, y_1 = 7, y_2 = -5$
Written **1.** 17 **3.** $\sqrt{29}$ **5.** 13 **7.** $3\sqrt{5}$
9. $\sqrt{185}$ **11.** $\frac{5}{2}$ **13.** $\frac{\sqrt{85}}{3}$ **15.** $\frac{13}{10}$ **17.** 13, -9
19. 17, -13 **21.** 10, 0 **23.** $-7, -3$ **25.** $-9, 5$

CHAPTER REVIEW   Page 399
1. 11 **3.** $\pm\frac{2}{9}$ **7.** Q **9.** $15 < \sqrt{250} < 16$
11. 4.359 **13.** 7.855 **15.** $6\sqrt{3}$ **17.** 54 **19.** $\frac{2\sqrt{15}}{|x|}$
21. $4\sqrt{3}$ **23.** $3 + 3\sqrt{2}$ **25.** $\sqrt{7}$ **27.** $14 + 7\sqrt{3}$
29. $\frac{30\sqrt{10} - 35\sqrt{6}}{33}$ **31.** $5\sqrt{13}$ **33.** $-7\sqrt{7}$ **35.** $\frac{9\sqrt{2}}{4}$
37. $x = 12$ **39.** $x = \frac{26}{7}$ **41.** $x = 12$ **43.** $c = 2\sqrt{34}$ **45.** $a = 6\sqrt{3}$ **47.** $\sqrt{130}$

CHAPTER 13   QUADRATICS

13-1   Page 408

Exploratory **1.** upward **3.** downward **5.** downward
7. upward **9.** downward **11.** $x = 2$ **13.** $x = -3$;
15. $x = -2$; **17.** $x = -\frac{7}{10}$; *Written* **1.** $x = \frac{5}{2}$; $\left(\frac{5}{2}, \frac{49}{4}\right)$ **3.** $x = 2$; $(2, 9)$ **5.** $x = \frac{3}{2}$; $\left(\frac{3}{2}, \frac{137}{4}\right)$
7. $x = -1$; $(-1, -20)$ **9.** $x = 0$; $(0, -9)$
11. $x = -1$; $(-1, 1)$ **13.** $x = 1$; $(1, 22)$ **15.** $x = 0$; $(0, 4)$ **17.** $x = 1$; $(1, 42)$ **19.** $x = 2$; $(2, -9)$
21. $x = 3$; $(3, 14)$ **23.** $x = 0$; $(0, -3)$ **25.** $x = 0$; $(0, 3)$ **27.** $x = \frac{1}{2}$; $\left(\frac{1}{2}, -\frac{49}{4}\right)$ **29.** $x = -3$; $(-3, 0)$

13-2   Page 411

Exploratory **1.** 1, -1 **3.** no real roots **5.** 0, 2
Written **1.** $-3, 4$ **3.** 6, -1 **5.** $-2, 2$ **7.** 3, 7
9. no real roots

11. between 0 and 1, between 3 and 4 **13.** 4
15. between -1 and -2, between 0 and 1 **17.** no
real roots **19.** between 0 and -1, between 2 and 3
21. no real roots **23.** between 0 and 1, between 2
and 3

13-3   Page 415

Exploratory **1.** no **3.** yes **5.** no **7.** no **9.** yes
11. 4 **13.** 9 **15.** 49 **17.** $\frac{25}{4}$ **19.** $\frac{49}{4}$ **21.** $\frac{169}{4}$
Written **1.** $-1, -3$ **3.** 7, -3 **5.** 4, 2 **7.** $2 \pm \sqrt{6}$
9. $4 \pm 2\sqrt{5}$ **11.** $4 \pm 2\sqrt{7}$ **13.** 1, -15
15. $-2, -3$ **17.** 12, -1 **19.** $3 \pm \sqrt{2}$ **21.** $2 \pm \sqrt{7}$
23. $\frac{7}{2}, -3$ **25.** 3, $\frac{1}{2}$ **27.** $-\frac{5}{3}, 2$ **29.** 1, $-\frac{1}{3}$

13-4   Page 418

Exploratory **1.** $a = 1, b = 7, c = 6$ **3.** $a = 1, b = 4, c = 3$ **5.** $a = 4, b = 8, c = 3$ **7.** $a = 1, b = 0, c = -25$ **9.** $a = 2, b = 8, c = 0$ **11.** $a = 3, b = 5, c = 2$ **13.** 49 **15.** 81 **17.** 36 **19.** 49
21. 2,500 **23.** 256   *Written* **1.** -6 **3.** $-1, -3$
5. $\frac{5}{2}, -3$ **7.** 3, $-\frac{5}{2}$ **9.** $-\frac{1}{2}, -3$ **11.** 7, -7
13. 6, 0 **15.** $\frac{1}{3}, -4$ **17.** $-1, -9$ **19.** 9, 4
21. 7, -5 **23.** 5, 0 **25.** $\frac{3}{2}, -1$ **27.** $-\frac{2}{3}, -7$
29. $\frac{2}{5}, \frac{1}{5}$ **31.** $-3 \pm 2\sqrt{3}$ **33.** 1.5, -0.4 **35.** $\frac{2 \pm \sqrt{7}}{2}$
37. $\frac{-5 \pm \sqrt{2}}{2}$ **39.** $\frac{4 \pm \sqrt{29}}{2}$ **41.** $-\frac{2}{3}, \frac{3}{7}$

13-5   Page 422

Exploratory **1.** 25; 2 **3.** 49; 2 **5.** 124; 2 **7.** 0; 1
9. 25; 2 **11.** 25; 2 **13.** 1.44; 2 **15.** 48; 2 **17.** 73; 2
19. 0; 1 **21.** 0; 1   *Written* **1.** $\frac{-5 \pm \sqrt{13}}{2}$ **3.** 2, -6
5. $-1, -6$ **7.** no real roots **9.** no real roots
11. 1, $\frac{1}{2}$ **13.** 7 **15.** no real roots **17.** 8, -4
19. $\frac{2 \pm \sqrt{7}}{3}$ **21.** 1, $\frac{1}{3}$ **23.** $\frac{5 \pm \sqrt{193}}{12}$ **25.** $\frac{-1 \pm \sqrt{41}}{4}$
27. 1, $-\frac{1}{3}$ **29.** $\frac{-7 \pm \sqrt{33}}{4}$ **31.** $\frac{-7 \pm \sqrt{17}}{16}$
33. $\frac{-5 \pm \sqrt{133}}{6}$ **35.** $\frac{3 \pm \sqrt{14}}{5}$ **37.** 1, $\frac{2}{3}$ **39.** $\frac{7 \pm \sqrt{69}}{10}$

13-6   Page 425

Exploratory **1.** factoring **3.** formula or factoring
5. formula **7.** factoring **9.** formula **11.** formula **13.** 18
15. 4 **17.** 10   *Written* **1.** 4, 5 **3.** $\frac{-2 \pm \sqrt{2}}{2}$
5. $-2, -1$ **7.** $\frac{1}{2}, 2$ **9.** $-\frac{1}{4}, 2$ **11.** $-\frac{1}{3}, 2$ **13.** $-2 \pm \sqrt{3}$ **15.** no real roots **17.** $\frac{-9 \pm \sqrt{21}}{10}$
19. $\frac{-2 \pm \sqrt{14}}{2}$ **21.** $1 \pm \sqrt{3}$ **23.** $\frac{3}{2}, \frac{5}{2}$ **25.** $\frac{1}{4}, \frac{3}{5}$

27. $-\dfrac{2}{5}, \dfrac{3}{2}$ 29. $-\dfrac{1}{5}, \dfrac{3}{10}$

13-7   Page 427

Written 1. 7 m, 8 m   3. 10 yd, 13 yd   5. 4 m, 14 m   7. 10 in., 20 in.   9. 5 in., 9 in.   11. 10 m, 16 m   13. 6, 8   15. $-15, -9$ or 9, 15   17. 12 cm, 36 cm   19. 3 cm, 6 cm   21. 1.6 m, 2.4 m   23. 5.92 m, 9.47 m   25. 1 m

13-8   Page 430

Exploratory 1. 5; 6   3. $-12; -28$ 5. $-5; -4$ 7. $-1; -\dfrac{35}{4}$ 9. $\dfrac{5}{6}; -\dfrac{21}{6}$ 11. yes   13. no   15. no   17. no   19. no   21. $x^2 - 7x + 10 = 0$ 23. $x^2 - 11x + 24 = 0$ 25. $x^2 + 5x - 6 = 0$ 27. $4x^2 + 4x - 3 = 0$ 29. $x^2 - 3.6x + 3.08 = 0$ 31. $25x^2 + 5x - 6 = 0$ *Written* 1. $-15; 54$

3. 1; -6 5. $-\dfrac{31}{6}; \dfrac{35}{6}$ 7. $-6; -1$ 9. $\dfrac{33}{7}; -\dfrac{10}{7}$

11. 3; 8   13. 1.2; 0.27   15. $\dfrac{1}{3}; -\dfrac{1}{12}$ 17. $-4\sqrt{3}; 9$ 19. $x^2 - 6x + 5 = 0$ 21. $x^2 - x - 30 = 0$ 23. $x^2 + 9x - 10 = 0$ 25. $x^2 + 4x - 45 = 0$ 27. $x^2 - 11x - 80 = 0$ 29. $3x^2 + 2x - 21 = 0$ 31. $6x^2 + 5x - 6 = 0$ 33. $5x^2 - 29x - 6 = 0$ 35. $x^2 - 2x\sqrt{3} + 3 = 0$ 37. $x^2 - 10x + 23 = 0$ 39. $x^2 - (q + r)x + qr = 0$

CHAPTER REVIEW   Page 434

1. $x = \dfrac{3}{2}; \left(\dfrac{3}{2}, -\dfrac{25}{4}\right)$ 3. $x = -\dfrac{9}{4}; \left(-\dfrac{9}{4}, -\dfrac{9}{8}\right)$ 5. -3
7. 36   9. $\dfrac{25}{4}$ 11. $-3 \pm \sqrt{5}$ 13. $-\dfrac{3}{2}, -\dfrac{5}{2}$
15. $-5, \dfrac{3}{2}$ 17. $\dfrac{2 \pm \sqrt{5}}{3}$ 19. $\dfrac{9 \pm \sqrt{21}}{10}$ 21. no real roots   23. 2   25. formula; $-5 \pm 4\sqrt{2}$
27. formula; 1, $\dfrac{11}{9}$ 29. formula; no real roots
31. factoring; $\dfrac{3}{10}, 2$ 33. 6, 15   35. $\dfrac{3}{2}, \dfrac{11}{4}$
37. $2x^2 + 5x - 12 = 0$

CHAPTER 14   RATIONAL EXPRESSIONS

14-1   Page 439

Exploratory 1. $\dfrac{1}{y - 4}; y \neq -4, 4$ 3. $r; r \neq -3$
5. $\dfrac{x}{x^2 - 4}; x \neq 0, 2, -2$ 7. $\dfrac{a + 4}{a - 2}; a \neq 2, 4$
9. $(t - 2)(t + 3); t \neq -2, 3$ 11. $\dfrac{-1}{w + 4}; w \neq \dfrac{2}{3}, -4$
Written 1. $\dfrac{1}{y + 3}; y \neq -3, 3$ 3. $\dfrac{a - 5}{a - 2}; a \neq -5, 2$
5. $r^2; r \neq 1$ 7. $\dfrac{n^2 - 2}{n - 1}; n \neq 1$ 9. $\dfrac{m^2}{2m - 1}; m \neq 0,$

$\dfrac{1}{2}$ 11. $\dfrac{1}{x + 3}; x \neq -3$ 13. $\dfrac{g + 2}{g - 2}; g \neq 1, 2$
15. $\dfrac{m - 6}{m - 1}; m \neq -6, 1$ 17. $\dfrac{2}{y + 5}; y \neq -5, 2$
19. $\dfrac{k - 1}{k + 1}; k \neq -1$ 21. $-\dfrac{a + 3}{a + 2}; a \neq -2, 3$
23. $-1; x \neq 3$ 25. $\dfrac{4y - 1}{8y - 1}; y \neq -2, \dfrac{1}{8}$ 27. $\dfrac{3}{4}$;
$m \neq -2, -1$ 29. $\dfrac{t + 3}{t - 4}; t \neq \dfrac{7}{2}, 4$ 31. $\dfrac{1}{(b - 4)(b + 2)}$;
$b \neq \pm 4, \pm 2$ 33. $\dfrac{x + 4}{2x - 1}; x \neq \dfrac{1}{2}$ 35. $\dfrac{x^2 + 1}{(x - 2)(x + 2)}$,
$x \neq \pm 2$ 37. $\dfrac{2s + 7}{s - 6}; s \neq \dfrac{2}{3}, 6$ 39. $\dfrac{c - 5}{c(c + 6)}; c \neq -6,$
$-4, 0$ 41. $(a + 2)(a - 1); a \neq -1, 2$ 43. $\dfrac{2x + 3}{2(x + 2)}$;
$x \neq -2, 0, \dfrac{1}{2}$

14-2   Page 443

Exploratory 1. $\dfrac{5}{24}$ 3. $-\dfrac{35}{48}$ 5. $\dfrac{35}{72}$ 7. $\dfrac{a^2}{15}$ 9. $\dfrac{1}{3}$
11. $-\dfrac{1}{6}$ 13. $-\dfrac{1}{6}$ 15. $\dfrac{11}{28}$

Written   1. $\dfrac{2}{15}$ 3. $\dfrac{2}{15}$ 5. $\dfrac{1}{16}$

7. $\dfrac{64}{729}$ 9. $\dfrac{b}{d}$ 11. a 13. $\dfrac{2m^2}{c^2}$

15. $\dfrac{4m^4}{15n^2}$ 17. 2   19. $3a$ 21. $\dfrac{5a + 10b}{3a + 4b}$

23. $\dfrac{x - y}{2}$ 25. $2m + 4$

27. $\dfrac{r^3 + r^2s}{s^2}$ 29. $\dfrac{x^2 + 8x + 16}{9}$

31. $\dfrac{x + y}{x + 1}$ 33. $\dfrac{m^2 + 16}{m^2 + 8m + 16}$

35. $\dfrac{3}{a^2 - 3a}$ 37. $\dfrac{a^2 + 2ab + b^2}{-a}$

39. $\dfrac{x}{x^2 + 8x + 16}$ 41. $\dfrac{1}{x^2 + 9x + 20}$

43. $\dfrac{b + 7}{b + 1}$ 45. $b + 7$

47. $\dfrac{y^2}{y^2 - y - 2}$ 49. $\dfrac{2y^2 + 11y - 21}{12y^3 + 19y^2 + 5y}$

14-3   Page 446

Exploratory 1. $\dfrac{4}{3}$ 3. $-\dfrac{3}{8}$ 5. $\dfrac{2}{m}$ 7. $\dfrac{2p}{5}$ 9. $\dfrac{1}{6}$
11. $\dfrac{1}{a^2}$ 13. $\dfrac{1}{2bc}$ 15. $\dfrac{x - y}{x + y}$ 17. $\dfrac{5}{3a^2b^2}$ 19. $\dfrac{3}{8} \cdot \dfrac{4}{1}$
21. $\dfrac{1}{3} \cdot \left(-\dfrac{1}{6}\right)$ 23. $\dfrac{2x}{4 - 2a} \cdot \dfrac{b - 2}{a^2}$ *Written* 1. $\dfrac{5}{4}$
3. $-\dfrac{5}{2}$ 5. $\dfrac{a^4}{b^4}$ 7. $\dfrac{y^2}{a^2}$ 9. a 11. $\dfrac{3m}{m^2 - m - 2}$
13. $\dfrac{b + 3}{4b}$ 15. y 17. $-\dfrac{p}{y + 2}$ 19. $-\dfrac{x}{7}$ 21. $\dfrac{m^2 - 1}{2}$
23. $\dfrac{2m + 2n}{3m^2 - 3mn}$ 25. $\dfrac{y - 4}{y + 8}$ 27. $\dfrac{3t + 12}{2w - 6}$ 29. $\dfrac{x + 3}{x}$

31. $\dfrac{x^2 + x - 12}{x^2 - 3x - 18}$ **33.** -1

Exploratory   **1.** a **3.** $4m^2$ **5.** x^2
Written   **1.** $x + 4$ **3.** $a + 5$ **5.** $c + 3$ R9

7. $r - 5$ **9.** $2x + 3$ **11.** $x^2 + 2x - 3$

13. $t^2 + 4t - 1$ **15.** $3c - 2 + \dfrac{4}{9c - 2}$ **17.** $3n^2 - 2n$

$+ 3 + \dfrac{3}{2n + 3}$ **19.** $3s^2 + 2s - 3 - \dfrac{1}{s + 2}$

21. $5t^2 - 3t - 2$ **23.** $8x^2 - 9$

Exploratory   **1.** $\dfrac{7}{8}$ **3.** $\dfrac{7}{a}$ **5.** $\dfrac{b + 2}{x}$ **7.** $\dfrac{2k}{t}$ **9.** $\dfrac{1}{11}$

11. $\dfrac{a - b}{5}$ **13.** $-\dfrac{2}{x}$ **15.** $\dfrac{k}{m}$ *Written*   **1.** y **3.** $\dfrac{10}{x}$

5. $\dfrac{y}{b}$ **7.** $\dfrac{9a}{7}$ **9.** $y - 3$ **11.** $-\dfrac{1}{6}$ **13.** $\dfrac{x + 1}{x - 1}$

15. $\dfrac{2}{y - 2}$ **17.** 1 **19.** 0 **21.** 0 **23.** $\dfrac{r^2 + s^2}{r - s}$

25. $m + n$ **27.** 4 **29.** 4 **31.** $a + b$ **33.** $r + 3$

35. $\dfrac{x + 1}{x - 1}$ **37.** 0 **39.** $\dfrac{1}{x + 1}$ **41.** $\dfrac{3}{m + 1}$

43. $-\dfrac{1}{t + 1}$ **45.** $\dfrac{b + 2}{b - 2}$

Exploratory   **1.** 24 **3.** $55a$ **5.** ab **7.** ab^3

9. $120a^2b^3$ **11.** $120a^4n^2$ **13.** $(a + 5)(a - 3)$

15. $3(x - 2)$ *Written*   **1.** $\dfrac{7}{8}$ **3.** $\dfrac{35}{36}$ **5.** $-\dfrac{3}{8}$ **7.** $\dfrac{52}{77}$

9. $\dfrac{32 + 11y}{44}$ **11.** $\dfrac{5x - 28}{35}$

13. $\dfrac{2}{a}$ **15.** $\dfrac{14a - 3}{6a^2}$ **17.** $\dfrac{5bx + a}{7x^2}$ **19.** $\dfrac{3z - 14wz}{7w^2}$

21. $\dfrac{2s + t^2 + 3t}{st}$ **23.** $\dfrac{ab + 6a + 6b}{b(a + b)}$ **25.** $\dfrac{2a + 3}{a + 3}$

27. $\dfrac{3x + 2}{x - 5}$ **29.** $\dfrac{2}{b - 8}$ **31.** $\dfrac{m^2 - 2mn + n^2 - 1}{m^2 - n^2}$

33. $\dfrac{a^3 - a^2b + a^2 + ab}{(a + b)(a - b)^2}$ **35.** $\dfrac{2x + 1}{(x + 1)^2}$ **37.** $\dfrac{2(x^3 + 1)}{x^2 - 1}$

or $\dfrac{2(x^2 - x + 1)}{x - 1}$ **39.** $\dfrac{k^2 - 2k - 2}{(2k + 1)(k + 2)}$

41. $\dfrac{-7y - 39}{y^2 - 9}$ **43.** $\dfrac{4ab - 4b + a^3 - a^2}{16ab^2}$ or

$\dfrac{(4b + a^2)(a - 1)}{16ab^2}$ **45.** $\dfrac{6 - 6a + 6b}{a^2 - 2ab + b^2}$ or $\dfrac{6(1 - a + b)}{(a - b)^2}$

47. $\dfrac{1}{m - 2}$

49. $\dfrac{-m^3 + m^2 - 3m^2n - 3mn^2 - 2nm + n^2 - n^3}{(m + n)^2(m - n)}$

51. $\dfrac{9m + 6}{(m + 2)^2(m + 1)}$ **53.** $\dfrac{x^2 + 12x + 2}{(x - 1)^2(x + 4)}$

55. $\dfrac{4a^2 + 7a + 2}{(6a + 1)(a + 3)(a - 3)}$

Exploratory   **1.** $\dfrac{4x + 2}{x}$ **3.** $\dfrac{xy + x}{y}$ **5.** $\dfrac{2m^2 + m + 4}{m}$

7. $\dfrac{b^3 - 2b^2 - 2}{b - 2}$ *Written*   **1.** $\dfrac{14}{19}$ **3.** $\dfrac{y^3(x + 4)}{x^2(y - 2)}$

5. $\dfrac{a - b}{x - y}$ **7.** $\dfrac{x + y}{x - y}$ **9.** $\dfrac{x + 1}{x - 2}$ **11.** $\dfrac{1}{y + 4}$ **13.** $\dfrac{a + 2}{a + 3}$

15. $\dfrac{(x + 3)(x - 1)}{(x - 2)(x + 4)}$ **17.** $\dfrac{8x^2 - 27y^2}{(x - 2y)(x + 2y)}$ **19.** $\dfrac{x + 1}{x + 5}$

21. 1 **23.** $\dfrac{x + 3}{x + 1}$

CHAPTER REVIEW   **Page 464**

1. $\dfrac{y}{4y^2z}$ **3.** $\dfrac{x + 3}{x - 3}$ **5.** $\dfrac{7a^2}{9b}$ **7.** $\dfrac{1}{x - 3}$ **9.** $\dfrac{5by}{4ax}$

11. $\dfrac{7ab(x + 9)}{3(x - 5)}$ **13.** $x^2 + 4x - 2$ **15.** $m^2 - 9m - $

$3 - \dfrac{40}{m - 4}$ **17.** $\dfrac{7 + a}{x^2}$ **19.** $\dfrac{2 - x}{x - y}$ **21.** $\dfrac{x^2 - 7x - 15}{(x + 3)(x - 2)}$

23. $\dfrac{3x^2 - 2x + 35}{(x + 5)(x - 2)(x - 3)}$ **25.** $\dfrac{x(x - 3)}{(x + 5)^2}$

27. $\dfrac{(x - 5)(x + 13)}{(x + 2)(x + 6)}$

**CHAPTER 15   APPLICATIONS OF RATIONAL
EXPRESSIONS**

Exploratory   **1.** 6 **3.** 8 **5.** $r^2 - 1$ **7.** $4x(x - 1)$ or

$4x^2 - 4x$ **9.** $(k + 5)(k + 3)$ or $k^2 + 8k + 15$

11. $(x + 1)(x - 1)$ or $x^2 - 1$ *Written*   **1.** -3

3. $\dfrac{5}{4}$ **5.** $\dfrac{5}{4}$ **7.** $\dfrac{41}{10}$ **9.** $\dfrac{1}{4}$ **11.** $-\dfrac{1}{4}$ **13.** $-\dfrac{3}{2}$ **15.** $\dfrac{1}{2}$

17. $6, -1$ **19.** $-5, 3$ **21.** $20, 10$ **23.** -3 **25.** 1

27. $5, 10$ **29.** 7 **31.** $\dfrac{27}{7}$ **33.** $-\dfrac{1}{2}, 5$ **35.** -1

Exploratory   **1. a.** $\dfrac{1}{8}$ **b.** $\dfrac{3}{8}$ **c.** $\dfrac{x}{8}$ **3. a.** $\dfrac{1}{8}$ **b.** $\dfrac{x}{8}$ **c.** $\dfrac{1}{10}$

d. $\dfrac{x}{10}$ **e.** $\dfrac{9}{40}$ **f.** $\dfrac{9x}{40}$ **5. a.** $r = 120 + s$; $t = \dfrac{420}{120 + s}$;

$d = 420$; against the wind, $r = 120 - s$; $t = \dfrac{300}{120 - s}$;

$d = 300$ **b.** $\dfrac{420}{120 + s} = \dfrac{300}{120 - s}$ *Written*   **1.** $2\dfrac{2}{5}$ hours

3. $3\dfrac{1}{13}$ days   **5.** 3 hours   **7.** 30 minutes   **9.** 12 mph

11. 30 mph

Exploratory   **1.** Multiply by 2, divide by n, then subtract t.   **3.** Multiply by abf, subtract af, then divide by $b - f$ *Written*   **1.** $t = \dfrac{v}{a}$

3. $v = \dfrac{2s - at^2}{2t}$ **5.** $M = \dfrac{Fd^2}{Gm}$ **7.** $V = \pm\sqrt{\dfrac{fgR}{W}}$

9. $P = \dfrac{A}{1 + rt}$ **11.** $P = \dfrac{36{,}500}{IR + 365}$ **13.** $y = \dfrac{r}{2a + 0.5}$

15. $R = \dfrac{H}{0.24I^2t}$ **17.** $R_1 = \dfrac{R_TR_2}{R_2 - R_T}$ **19.** $n = \dfrac{IR}{E - Ir}$

21. $m = \dfrac{y - b}{x}$ **23.** $y_2 - mx_2 - mx_1 + y_1$

25. $R = P - DQ$ **27.** $n = 2b$ **29.** $n = \dfrac{acd - ab}{c}$

31. $n = \dfrac{ac + bc}{a + b + 1}$ **33.** $n = \dfrac{b^2 - 2c}{c - b}$ **35.** $n = \pm\sqrt{ab}$

37. $n = \dfrac{rk - k^2}{2}$

15-4   Page 480

Exploratory **1.** yes, 3   **3.** no   **5.** yes, 7   **7.** no

Written **1.** 28   **3.** -5 **5.** 6   **7.** $26\frac{1}{4}$ **9.** 5.2

11. -4, $y = -4x$ **13.** $\frac{1}{2}$, $y = \frac{1}{2}x$ **15.** $\frac{8}{3}$, $y = \frac{8}{3}x$

17. $\frac{17}{22}$, $y = \frac{17}{22}x$ **19.** $13.33   **21.** $467.50

22. $6\frac{142}{143}$ or about 7 gallons   **25.** $3\frac{1}{3}$ ft^3

15-5   Page 482

Exploratory **1.** yes, 6   **3.** yes, 50   **5.** yes, -13
7. yes, 1   **9.** yes, 40   **11.** no   *Written* **1.** 48

3. $6\frac{2}{3}$ **5.** $-2\frac{2}{7}$ **7.** 4.48   **9.** 1.44   **11.** 192; $xy = 192$

13. $\frac{5}{3}$; $xy = \frac{5}{3}$ **15.** -16; $xy = -16$ **17.** 15.68;

$xy = 15.68$ **19.** 2.16; $xy = 2.16$ **21.** $3\frac{1}{3}$ hours

23. 30 m^3 **25.** $21\frac{1}{3}$ m^3 **27.** 4 in.   **29.** 640 cycles

per second

15-6   Page 485

Exploratory **1.** Emilio   **3.** They must both sit the
same distance away.   **5.** Betty   *Written* **1.** 8 ft

3. 8.02 ft **5.** 12 ft   **7.** 3060 pounds

15-7   Page 490

Written **1.** $3\frac{3}{7}$ ohms   **3.** 4 ohms   **5.** 8 ohms, 4 ohms

7. 18 ohms   **9.** $1\frac{1}{3}$ ohms   **11.** $7\frac{1}{17}$ ohms

13. $2\frac{11}{12}$ ohms   **15.** $7\frac{2}{3}$ ohms

15-8   Page 493

Exploratory **1.** joint   **3.** combined   **5.** quadratic
direct   **7.** joint   *Written* **1.** 2   **3.** -10 **5.** 8
7. ± 0.09 **9.** 4   **11.** 39.2   **13.** 12.5

CHAPTER REVIEW   Page 496

1. $-\dfrac{14}{3}$ **3.** $\dfrac{25}{7}$ **5.** $-\dfrac{23}{2}$ **7.** $21\dfrac{9}{11}$ hours

9. $a = \dfrac{bf}{b - f}$ **11.** 12   **13.** $74\frac{2}{3}$ gallons   **15.** 2.3

17. On the other end of the meter stick, 50 cm from
the fulcrum.   **19. a.** 10 ohms **b.** $2\frac{2}{5}$ ohms   **21.** 3
23. 0.2

CHAPTER 16   TRIGONOMETRY

16-1   Page 501

Exploratory **1.** 5°   **3.** 77°   **5.** 35°   **7.** $(50 - 2x)°$
9. 50°   **11.** 53°   **13.** 90°   **15.** $(175 - 3x)°$
Written **1.** 48°; 138°   **3.** none; 55°   **5.** 0°; 90°
7. 69°; 159°   **9.** none; 81°   **11.** $(90 - 3y)°$; $(180 -$
$3y)°$ **13.** $(128 - x)°$; $(218 - x)°$ **15.** $x°$; $(90 + x)°$
17. 122°   **19.** 85°   **21.** 1°   **23.** $(160 - 2x)°$ **25.** 37°;
106°   **27.** 26°; 64°   **29.** 25°; 35°; 120°   **31.** 50°
33. 30°

16-2   Page 504

Exploratory **1.** 4 m   **3.** 6.5 mm   **5.** $2\frac{1}{4}$ in.   **7.** 8.18
m   **9.** 14 m   **11.** 8.70 mm   **13.** $12\frac{3}{4}$ in.   **15.** 7.72 cm
17. 4 ft; 8 ft   **19.** 8 m; 16 m   **21.** 7 yd; 14 yd
Written **1.** $4\sqrt{3}$ cm   **3.** 10 units   **5.** 3 m; $3\sqrt{3}$ m
7. $1\frac{3}{4}$ in; $\frac{7}{4}\sqrt{3}$ in.   **9.** 13 m; $6.5\sqrt{3}$ m   **11.** 4 m, 2 m

16-3   Page 507

Exploratory **1.** $\angle A$ and $\angle D$; $\angle B$ and $\angle E$;
$\angle C$ and $\angle F$; AB and DE; BC and EF; AC and DF
3. $\angle Q$ and $\angle Q$; $\angle S$ and $\angle P$; $\angle T$ and $\angle R$; QS and QP;
QT and QR; ST and PR *Written* **1.** $b = \dfrac{25}{7}$,
$c = \dfrac{30}{7}$ **3.** $a \approx 2.8$, $c \approx 4.2$ **5.** $d = 10.2$, $e = 9$
7. $c = \dfrac{7}{2}$, $d = \dfrac{17}{8}$ **9.** $\dfrac{125}{9}$ ft   **11.** 11 cm

16-4   Page 510

Exploratory **1.** $\frac{8}{17}$ **3.** $\frac{8}{15}$ **5.** $\frac{15}{17}$ **7.** $\frac{9}{41}$ **9.** $\frac{9}{40}$
11. $\frac{40}{41}$ **13.** $\frac{4}{5}$ **15.** $\frac{4}{3}$ **17.** $\frac{3}{5}$ **19.** yes; yes   **21.** The
sine of an angle is equal to the cosine of its
complement.   *Written* **1.** $\sin A = 0.690$. $\cos A =$
0.724, $\tan A = 0.952$; $\sin B = 0.724$, $\cos B = 0.690$,
$\tan B = 1.050$ **3.** $\sin R = 0.324$, $\cos R = 0.946$,
$\tan R = 0.343$; $\sin T = 0.946$, $\cos T = 0.324$,
$\tan T = 2.917$ **5.** $\sin J = 0.899$, $\cos J = 0.438$,
$\tan J = 2.051$, $\sin K = 0.438$, $\cos K = 0.899$,
$\tan K = 0.488$ **7.** $\sin J = 0.800$, $\cos J = 0.600$,
$\tan J = 1.333$, $\sin L = 0.600$, $\cos L = 0.800$,
$\tan L = 0.750$ **9.** $\sin E = 0.220$, $\cos E = 0.976$,
$\tan E = 0.225$, $\sin F = 0.976$, $\cos F = 0.220$,
$\tan F = 4.444$

16-5   Page 513

Exploratory **1.** 90°; 0°   **3.** 45°   **5.** No maximum or

minimum value. **Written** **1.** 0.9063 **3.** 0.9998
5. 0.2419 **7.** 0.1219 **9.** 0.9272 **11.** 0.4540
13. 0.7431 **15.** 0.7071 **17.** 0.5000 **19.** 0.8660
21. 26° **23.** 53° **25.** 79° **27.** 67° **29.** 16°
31. 40° **33.** 89° **35.** 3° **37.** 30° **39.** 0 **41.** 2
43. −0.5000 **45.** 0.3660 **47.** 0

16-6   Page 515

Exploratory **1.** cos 46; sin 46° **3.** sin 42°; tan 42°
5. $\sin A = \frac{4}{9}$; $\cos B = \frac{4}{9}$ **7.** $\cos A = \frac{8}{13}$; $\sin B = \frac{8}{13}$
Written **1.** $A = 44°$, $AC = 10.8$ ft, $BC = 10.4$ ft
3. $A = 48°$, $AB = 9.0$ in, $BC = 6.7$ in. **5.** $A = 26°$,
$B = 64°$, $AC = 8.1$ cm **7.** $A = 52°$, $B = 38°$, $BC =$
10.2 mm **9.** $B = 69°$, $AB = 13.9$ in., $BC = 5$ in.
11. $B = 20°$, $AB = 9.6$ cm, $AC = 3.3$ cm **13.** $B =$
68°, $AB = 12.9$ ft, $BC = 4.8$ ft **15.** $B = 50°$, $AC =$
12.3 m, $BC = 10.3$ m **17.** $B = 59°$, $AB = 11.6$ m,

$AC = 10m$ **19.** $A = 48°$, $AC = 6.7$ in., $BC = 7.4$ in.
21. $A = 38°$, $B = 52°$, $BC = 8.7$ ft **23.** $A = 50°$,
$AB = 9.3$ cm, $AC = 7.2$ cm **25.** $B = 45°$,
$AC = 1$ ft, $BC = 1$ ft

16-7   Page 518

Exploratory **1.** $\angle CAB$; $\angle DCA$ **3.** $\angle JKL$; $\angle MJK$
Written **1.** 4° **3.** 65 ft **5.** 300 ft **7.** 65 ft
9. 1716 cm **11.** 1394 ft

CHAPTER REVIEW   Page 523

1. 24° **3.** $(90 − y)°$ **5.** 32° **7.** 92°
9. $(180 − x − y)°$ **11.** 2.125 cm, 3.681 cm
13. 7 in., 6.062 in. **15.** 9 m, 4.5 m **17.** $d = \frac{45}{8}$,
$e = \frac{27}{4}$ **19.** $\frac{28}{53}$ **21.** $\frac{45}{53}$ **23.** $\frac{28}{45}$ **25.** 0.528
27. 1.607 **29.** 0.6691 **31.** 0.9945 **33.** 2.2460
35. 28° **37.** 3.7 m **39.** 7.9 m **41.** 173.2 m

Index

of ordered pairs, 272
of sine function, 521
of systems of equations,
337-340
of number lines, 39-40, 68,
113, 128-133
parabolas, 405-411, 433
quadrants, 272, 298
reading, 282
relations, 274-275, 283-284
systems of inequalities,
352-353
Greatest common factors of
integers, 212, 239
of monomials, 212
Greek letters, 511
Grouping symbols, 6-7, 35
brackets, 7, 35
fraction bars, 3, 7
in inequalities, 122-123
in solving equations, 88
parentheses, 7, 21, 35

H

Half-plane, 291-292, 299
boundaries, 291, 299
closed, 291, 299
open, 291, 299
Hamilton, Sir William Rowan,
20
Hexadecimal numbers, 28
History
Hamilton, 20
Newton, 487
Noether, 184
Pythagoras, 391
radical sign, 373
Rudolff, 373
Hypotenuse, 391

I

Identities, 88, 106
additive, 12, 19, 35
multiplicative, 12, 19, 35
IF-THEN statements, 138,
534-535, 538
Imaginary unit, 423
Inconsistent equations, 340
Independent equations, 340
Inequalities, 111-139
absolute values, 132-133,
139
addition property for, 116,
139
comparing rational
numbers, 124-125, 139

compound sentences,
128-133, 139
division property for, 120,
139
graphs of, 113, 128-133,
291-292, 299
in two variables, 291-292,
299
multiplication property for,
119, 139
problem solving, 136
solving, 116-123, 251
solving using factoring, 251
subtraction property for,
116, 139
symbols of, 112, 139
systems of, 352-353, 365
tolerance interval, 135
using calculators, 134
with grouping symbols,
122-123
Input, 529
Integers, 39-45, 68, 374
adding, 42-45, 68, 265
consecutive even, 93
consecutive odd, 93
even, 265
factoring, 211-212
greatest, 541-542
greatest common factors,
212, 239
problems, 256-257
Interest
compound, 204, 250
principal, 198
rate, 198
simple, 198
using calculators, 199
INT function, 541-542
Inverses
additive, 53-54, 68, 179
multiplicative, 79, 105, 445
Inverse variations, 481-482,
495
product rule for, 482, 495
proportions, 482, 495
Irrational numbers, 374-376,
398
Isosceles right triangles, 500

J

Joint variations, 491, 495
proportions, 491, 495

K

Kilograms, 100, 220

L

Law of universal gravity, 487
Least common denominators,
454-456, 464, 469-470
Least common multiples,
454-455
Legs, 391
Length, 14
LET statements, 531-532
Lever problems, 484-485
Like terms, 15-16, 35
Linear equations, 283-284, 298
direct variations, 478-479
graphs of, 283-284, 316-317
point-slope form, 309, 331
slope-intercept form,
312-313, 317, 331
standard form, 310, 317, 331
writing, 320-322
Lines
horizontal, 311, 316
parallel, 324, 331, 340, 343,
364
perpendicular, 325-326, 331
point-slope form, 309, 331
slope-intercept form,
312-313, 317, 331
slope of, 305-315, 317,
320-321, 324-326, 331
standard form, 310, 317, 331
vertical, 306, 311, 316
Line segments, 327-328, 331
Liters, 100
Loops, 297
independent, 538
nested, 538

M

Magic squares, 56
Mappings, 274-275
Mass, 100, 220
Maximum points, 406, 409,
433
Means, 97, 106
Means-extremes property of
proportions, 97-98, 106
Meters, 14
Metric system
capacity in, 100